The Abiding Word

The Abiding Word

VOLUME TWO

An Anthology
of Doctrinal Essays

EDITED BY
THEODORE LAETSCH

CONCORDIA PUBLISHING HOUSE • SAINT LOUIS

CONCORDIA CLASSICS

Copyright © 1947, 1975
Published by Concordia Publishing House
3558 S. Jefferson Avenue, St. Louis, MO 63118-3968
Manufactured in the United States of America

All rights reserved. No part of this publication may be reproduced, stored in a retrieval system, or transmitted, in any form or by any means, electronic, mechanical, photocopying, recording, or otherwise, without the prior written permission of Concordia Publishing House.

Concordia Classics 2000

3   4   5   6   7   8   9   10   11   25   24   23   22   21   20   19   18   17

Preface

THE *Abiding Word* is the title chosen for two volumes published by our Concordia Publishing House under the auspices of the Centennial Committee appointed by instruction of the General Convention of 1941 by the venerable President of Synod, Dr. J. W. Behnken: Dr. Theo. Hoyer, chairman; Rev. H. W. Romoser, secretary; Dr. L. Fuerbringer; Dr. H. B. Hemmeter, Dr. E. T. Lams; Teacher A. H. Kramer; Mr. G. A. Fleischer. A close study of the doctrinal essays presented in this second volume, which, like those of Volume I, are based on the writings of the fathers and founders of our Synod, has confirmed the conviction of the editor that the title of these volumes is well chosen. In the first place, the title implies that these volumes do not intend to bring any new doctrine, an unheard-of wisdom, but present the doctrines of God's Word as they have been taught in our midst during the past century, the theology of the Word. In the second place, on that very account it is the abiding Word, for God Himself declares that the Word of our God shall stand forever (Is. 40:8), that it liveth and abideth forever (1 Pet. 1:23).

With the sincere prayer that the God of Truth would keep our Church ever faithful to His abiding Word and that to this end He would grant His gracious blessing to the labor spent upon these essays and their publication, we send this volume onward on its journey.

THE EDITOR

Contents

ESSAY		PAGE
	PREFACE	V
I	HOLY SCRIPTURE THE WORD OF GOD *Walter W. F. Albrecht*	1
II	BIBLE INTERPRETATION *Victor E. Mennicke*	35
III	THE NATURE AND ATTRIBUTES OF GOD *R. R. Caemmerer*	59
IV	THE PROVIDENCE OF GOD *Paul F. Bente*	78
V	OFFICE, OR WORK, OF CHRIST *Oswald C. J. Hoffmann*	112
VI	SIN *Th. F. A. Nickel*	145
VII	TEMPTATION *R. R. Caemmerer*	171
VIII	THE GRACE OF GOD *Theo. Hoyer*	200
IX	THE DOCTRINE OF JUSTIFICATION *Wm. Arndt*	235
X	REPENTANCE *Karl H. Ehlers*	258
XI	SANCTIFICATION *Roger L. Sommer*	275
XII	SYNERGISM *Ewald M. Plass*	299

XIII	THE MEANS OF GRACE *Edwin E. Pieplow*	322
XIV	THE GOSPEL *Siegbert W. Becker*	347
XV	THE SACRAMENTS *Arthur E. Neitzel*	367
XVI	HOLY BAPTISM *J. T. Mueller*	394
XVII	THE LORD'S SUPPER *F. R. Zucker*	423
XVIII	THE LUTHERAN CONGREGATION *Geo. H. Perlich*	447
XIX	THE OFFICE OF THE PUBLIC MINISTRY *E. E. Foelber*	474
XX	DOCTRINE, TRUE AND FALSE *W. A. Baepler*	493
XXI	CHURCH FELLOWSHIP *Arnold H. Grumm*	517
XXII	CHURCH DISCIPLINE *Edgar J. Otto*	538
XXIII	CHURCH AND STATE *Theo. Hoyer*	562
XXIV	LUTHER'S CATECHISM *Louis H. Koehler*	608
XXV	CHRISTIAN TRAINING OF YOUTH *H. E. Plehn*	630
XXVI	THE LUTHERAN PAROCHIAL SCHOOL *Arthur C. Repp*	658
XXVII	ADIAPHORA *Lorenz Wunderlich*	686
XXVIII	THE PAPACY *Theo. Hoyer*	709
	BIBLIOGRAPHY	767
	TOPICAL INDEX	777

The Abiding Word

Holy Scripture the Word of God

INTRODUCTION

IF the Bible is not God's Word, Christianity is a sect among sects, a man-made religion like all the rest. If the Bible is not God's Word, not a single doctrine we teach has a sure foundation, we are adrift on the sea of doubt and despair.

Systematic efforts to disprove the divine inspiration of Scripture and to get rid of the Bible as the only source and standard of religious truth are increasing in boldness and strength, and practically every church body is infested with men who deny the authority of Holy Writ either in part or entirely.

Our Savior Jesus Christ says: "I am the *Truth*" (John 14:6). "The *words* that I speak unto you, they are spirit, and they are life" (John 6:63). He is the Word *incarnate*, as John calls Him. And the Scriptures are, in a way, an incarnation of God.

"Choose you this day whom *ye* will serve!" (Josh. 24:15.) With this thought let us approach our subject, *Holy Scripture the Word of God*.

I. THE HUMAN SIDE OF THE SCRIPTURES

Our old Lutheran theologians have been attacked as totally ignoring or even denying the human side of Scripture. It is true, they do not dwell at length on what we call the human side of Scripture. But why? When human writers speak in a human language to human addressees of human interests, can there be any danger that the human side of Scripture, correctly understood, will be overlooked?

Let me remind you of *a few of the human things* about the Bible that need no stressing because everyone who takes up this Book and reads it sees them. We find the Holy Scriptures to be sixty-six different books written in two distinct periods by more than thirty different people of all sorts and cultures and addressed to nations, congregations, and individuals. See Wm. Dallmann, *Why Do I Believe the Bible Is God's Word?*, p. 6.

In many cases the *author* is definitely known. Thus Christ names *Moses* as the author of the Pentateuch (John 5:46-47); *Isaiah* as the author of the book bearing his name (Matt. 15:7); *David* as the author of Ps. 110 (Luke 20:42). *Paul* frequently refers in his epistles to himself as the speaker or writer (Rom. 1:1; Eph. 1:1; etc.). In like manner Peter (I Pet. 1:1). See *Proceedings*, Synodical Conference, 1886, 47. Regarding a number of books whose authors are not mentioned there has been general agreement in the Church from the time the books appeared as to who are the authors, for example, the Gospels according to SS. Matthew, Mark, Luke, and John. In the case of some books neither Scripture nor history reveals the author, for example, Joshua, Judges, Ruth, Hebrews, etc. But in the case of every book we intuitively feel that a *human being* is speaking to his readers, narrating some event or the history of longer periods, instructing the addressees in doctrine, or expressing his sentiments.

The writing itself was done in some cases by the author, in others by the secretary to whom the author dictated.

In studying the individual books we find that there is *planning* and *order* in their arrangement. Weigh the words Luke 1:1-4. Luke made up his own mind to write an account of the life of Christ. So he prepared himself, he studied the sources, he interviewed eyewitnesses of the things he wanted to write about, he accurately traced everything from the first, for he wanted to give Theophilus an orderly, correct, and inerrant account of these things. In gathering their material we find some of the holy writers going also to *uninspired books* and quoting from them. See Kretzmann, *The Foundations Must Stand*, p. 37. Even heathen poets are quoted (Tit. 1:12) when they express the thought in mind in a particularly fortunate manner.

When their material was gathered, the writers weighed it, studied it to get the correct meaning of it, revolved in their mind for some time the matter which they intended to write, and then gave thought to the composition and arrangement of it. Then they wrote what they saw fit to write and in the manner which they regarded as best. "The *mind* of the holy authors moved freely, according to its natural bent; freely it expressed itself in the sacred writings." Stoeckhardt, *Lehre und Wehre*, 1886, 283; quoted in Engelder, *Scripture Cannot Be Broken*, p. 308.

An examination of their writings will also show that just as freely they express their *feelings*. Serenity and deep emotion, delight and anger, joy and sorrow, grief and indignation, commendation and criticism, admonition and warning, pleading and commanding, suavity and severity, blessing and curse, are to be found in these pages.

With what freedom they wrote is evident, too, from the fact that they inserted at their will remarks about *personal matters* and affairs of their own (II Tim. 4:13) or gave advice to some particular friend (I Tim. 5:23) or permitted their secretary to add his personal greetings. Thus Rom. 16:22: "I, Tertius, who wrote this epistle, salute you in the Lord."

Also the *memory* of the writers came into play. Frequently the writers call attention to it that they were *eyewitnesses* of the events they are recording. Thus the First Epistle of St. John begins with the words: "That which was from the beginning, which we have heard, which we have seen with our eyes, which we have looked upon and our hands have handled, of the Word of life, . . . declare we unto you, . . . and these things write we unto you." How they used their memory is also evident from St. Paul's remark in I Cor. 1: "I thank God that I baptized none of you but Crispus and Gaius, lest any should say that I had baptized in mine own name" (vv. 14-15). Then, going on, he corrects himself, since he suddenly recalls the Baptism of another family and says: "And I baptized also the household of Stephanas; besides, I know not whether I baptized any other" (v. 16).

Each one of the holy writers also used his own definite *style* and diction. By style we mean the distinctive manner of the individual writer, characteristic of him in the use of certain words and expressions, in the formation of his sentences, and in the connection of his sentences. There is no abstract human style of writing. But there are as many concrete styles of writing as there are human writers. Moses' diction differs from that found in other historical books. Each of the Prophets had his own style. Paul uses a lofty and sustained eloquence, John very simple sentences, and his usual conjunction is "and"; Peter's language again is poetical. See P. E. Kretzmann, *The Foundations Must Stand*, p. 5.

In the case of most of the books of Holy Scripture we can also establish a definite *purpose* which the human writers had in mind in writing their books. Thus the principal purpose of the first book of the Bible, Genesis, is to tell us of the fall of man into sin and of the salvation promised by God in the coming of a divine-human Savior, the Seed of Woman, the Seed of Abraham. It records, too, the fearful judgment of God over all mankind in the Flood, showing what the rejection of this salvation will mean to man.

It is evident, then, that the writers of Scripture were not deprived of *intelligence* and *consciousness* when they wrote. Their normal intellectual activity was not temporarily arrested or neutralized. They were not "completely possessed." They were not sleeping or dreaming in producing their book. They did not speak "with the mantic frenzy of sibyls and soothsayers." They did not first have their memory, next their natural intellect, and, third, their will power put out of commission; they were not thus put into a hypnotic state. *Theological Quarterly*, 1913, pp. 2, 17. They were not impassive machines controlled by a person distinct from them. They were not "in a passive state of receptivity like a stenographer who takes dictation." *Lutheran Church Quarterly*, 1936, p. 244 f. How could a stenographer dare to insert in a letter dictated by his employer such statements as I Tim. 5:23: "Drink no longer water (only), but use a little wine for thy stomach's sake and thine often infirmities," or II Tim. 4:13: "The cloak that I left at Troas with Carpus, when thou comest, bring with thee, and the books, but especially the parchments"?

It is not true, therefore, when theologians both in Europe and America accuse our old Lutheran theologians and us of a "dictation theory" which "crowds out the human mind" of the writers. "There is a theory of verbal inspiration," one of them says, "that must be refuted. It is that theory of inspiration that degrades the authors of the Biblical books to dead writing machines who without any inner participation wrote down word for word what was dictated to them by the Spirit. We meet this doctrine in the Lutheran Church occasionally during the sixteenth century, more frequently in the seventeenth century, although it can hardly be called the earmark of the presentation of all orthodox dogmaticians; later it is limited to popular writers, and today it is found only in some fundamental camps." M. Reu, *In the Interest of Lutheran Union,* p. 68. The man in the sixteenth century whom Dr. Reu accuses of this dictation theory is Justus Menius, who defined the doctrine of inspiration beautifully in the confession he wrote for the Duchy of Saxony and which that duchy accepted in March, 1549. Of this confession of Menius Dr. Reu says: "Here we for the first time have a purely mechanical conception of inspiration, and that in a Lutheran confession written by a man who was an adherent of the Gospel since 1522 . . . and always had Luther's confidence." *Luther and the Scriptures,* p. 126 f.

The man in the seventeenth century who is above all others accused of teaching the "dictation theory" is Quenstedt, one of the most outstanding dogmaticians of the Lutheran Church. But Quenstedt says: "Not as though these divine penmen wrote ignorantly and unwillingly, beyond the reach of, and contrary to, their own will; for they wrote cheerfully, willingly, and intelligently . . . but (they are called penmen) because they wrote nothing of their own accord, but everything at the dictation of the Holy Ghost." J. T. Mueller, *Christian Dogmatics,* 103 f. "The inspired authors were not dead or mechanical, but living instruments, endowed with intelligence and will and employing a definite style and using their own particular mode of expression." Pieper, *What Is Christianity?* p. 242; see Engelder, *Scripture Cannot Be Broken,* p. 306.

Hence the products of these writers, that is, the individual books they wrote, are truly *their* works, *their* books.

On the other hand, there are some things about these books making up the Holy Scriptures which strike an observant reader and make him realize that the fact that these books are the products of men is far from being the whole truth. In *The Lutheran Teacher* (Feb. 13, 1938, Norwegian Lutheran Church) we read: "The holy writers were not mere machines. . . . They knew what they were writing, though it might be true that *they did not at all times realize to the full the deep significance of all they said.*" This is Biblical. I Pet. 1:10-11: "Of which salvation the Prophets have *inquired* and *searched* diligently," etc. The *Theological Quarterly* pictures what this passage says in these words: "The messages which these men (the Prophets) bore to their people had aroused their intensest interest. They knew, and were conscious of, the wonderful character of their utterance; but they had no misgivings as to their genuineness. The Spirit had employed them as bearers of marvelous news, but they were wide-awake and sympathetic messengers. They began to *study* the very prophecies which they had uttered. . . . They thoroughly *investigated* and *explored* what they had uttered. They knew that they had spoken of the Messiah, and particularly of His suffering and glory. But in the details which they had predicted of the Passion of the Christ there were matters that they did not exactly understand. They could not see what special event the Spirit pointed to, or when the event would take place. David (Ps. 22) had no such view of the Christ hanging on the tree with parched lips and distended limbs, the soldiers beneath Him casting lots for His garments, as we have who have read the Gospels. He heard the cry of distress from the Cross, but he could not picture to himself that scene of awful grandeur when the earth was wrapped in the gloom of an unnatural eclipse, as we can to whom Matthew and Luke have depicted Golgotha. Isaiah (7:14; 9:6) and Micah (5:2) had no view of the Christ Child in the manger, Zechariah (11:12-13) no view of the despairing traitor hurling the blood money into the sanctuary and then passing out into the eternal night, or of the jubilant procession (9:9) that met the Lord at Bethany and brought Him into the city as Zion's King. But they studied these matters just because they were aware that something remarkable had been stated by them." *Theological Quarterly*, 1913, p. 13 f.

Furthermore, one can discern a wonderful *unity* in this book, the Bible. The plan according to which this collection of sixty-six books is built up surpasses the ingenuity of any man or the planning of any body of men. There could be no collusion. The writers are scattered over sixteen centuries. "Many writers in many ages, in many lands, wrote many books, of many kinds, of many sizes; but when put together, they fit perfectly and form the dark and lost world's beacon." Dallmann, *Why Do I Believe the Bible Is God's Word?* pp. 9, 10. Still complete *harmony* pervades all that was written by these holy writers in the course of sixteen hundred years. Compare *Proceedings*, Synodical Conference, 1886, 42. Even where at first sight there seems to be a conflict, for example, between Paul and James, closer scrutiny reveals that instead of standing face to face and attacking each other, they stand back to back, beating off common foes. And this progress throughout the Book, filling in line after line until the picture is complete, this doctrinal harmony with never a collision, never a break, could not become apparent until the work was done, the structure finished. Can this be called the work and plan of men? These were dimensions beyond the reach of mere mortals.

Scripture is *one organic whole.* "When you come to the last chapters of Revelation, you find yourself mysteriously touching the first chapters of Genesis; and lo! as you survey the whole track of your thought, you find you have been following the perimeter of a golden ring; the extremities actually bend around, touch, and blend. You read in the first chapter of Genesis of the first creation; in the last of the Revelation, of the new creation, the new heaven and the new earth; there, of the river that watered the Garden; here, of the pure river of the water of life; there, of the Tree of Life in the first Eden; here of the Tree of Life which is in the midst of the Paradise of God; there, of the God who came down to walk with and talk with man; here, we read that the Tabernacle of God is with men; there we read of the curse that came by sin, here we read: 'And there shall be no more curse.'" *The Fundamentals,* VII, 68 f.

This leads us to another observation. We ask: Is anything in the Scriptures the *independent* product of men? Is there any book of the Bible that is the uninfluenced output of human mind? Is there any statement or thought of any of the holy writers that sprang solely from their fallible intellect? "Some modern critics distinguish between fundamental, or Christocentric, doctrines on the one hand, and the non-fundamental doctrines on the other, according to the latter only a secondary position in any form of inspiration. Others prefer to distinguish between doctrinal and non-doctrinal matters, insisting that all information on secular history, geography, geology, astronomy, and similar subjects contained in the Bible is subject to error, the writers of the Bible presenting views such as were current in their days, many of which, as the critics assert, have been found to be erroneous." Kretzmann, *The Foundations Must Stand,* p. 59. This view of Scripture we firmly refuse to endorse, for "all the criticism of more than 3,000 years has failed to point out one important or irreconcilable contradiction in the testimony and the teachings of those who are farthest separated — there is no collision, yet there could be no collusion!" *The Fundamentals,* VII, p. 56.

II. HOLY SCRIPTURE IS, IN CONTRAST TO ALL OTHER BOOKS IN THE WORLD, THE VERY WORD OF GOD BY INSPIRATION OF THE HOLY GHOST

Men who pretend to be confessional Lutherans call "all Scripture" the Word of God only in a restricted sense. The Bible *is* not really *God's* Word, but the Bible *contains* God's Word. The Bible is a human book in which God's Word lies buried for him who can find it and sort it out. God indeed assisted the writers with a special degree of illumination, but original conception and independent action dare not be denied the human authors. They are ready to call Scripture a *"memorial* of the sacred history," the history of God's dealings with men, a *"description"* of God's self-disclosure toward men and the reaction of men towards this revelation, a *"record"* of God's Word and the Prophets' own reflections, a *"report"* on the divine revelation, which divine revelation consisted simply in the particular occurrence related by the writer. The doctrine propounded by the Prophets and the Apostles is simply *their* abstraction from what occurred, *their* reflection on the historical event which God somehow shaped. In abstracting the doctrinal content of what the writers regarded as divine action God indeed guided them toward a greater, far distant goal, namely, the *"organic whole,"* the harmonious union of all these writings to form the canon, the standard for the Church. But due to the fact that Scripture after all is only a human representation of divine revelations experienced by the writers, their account cannot be inerrant, but must today be cleansed of many errors which have been discovered.

What does *Scripture* say of itself? The Bible calls itself *"the Book,"* that is, the Book of all books. (Ps. 40:7-8; Heb. 10:4-10.) In numerous passages of the New Testament the Bible is called *"the Scriptures"* or *"the Scripture."* (Matt. 21:42; Mark 15:28; John 10:35.) The Bible calls itself *"the Book of the Lord."* (Is. 34:16.) It calls itself *"the Law of the Lord."* (Jer. 8:8-9; Ps. 1:2; Neh. 8: 8, 18; John 10:34.) Again, the Bible calls itself *"the Holy Scriptures."* (Rom. 1:2; II Tim. 3:15.) The Revised Version has rendered the words "the sacred writings." All that is written in the Bible the Bible claims to be holy. The Bible furthermore calls itself *"the Oracles of God."* (Rom. 3:1-2.) David speaks of the Bible as *"Thy*

Word." (Ps. 119:38, 105.) Compare Iowa District, 1891, 13 ff.; Kretzmann, *The Foundations Must Stand*, p. 37 f.

The *Law*, that is, the first part of the Old Testament, lays claim to being the Word of God. Ex. 24:3, 7 we are told that "Moses *wrote* all the words of the Lord" and that this book was then called *"the Book of the Covenant."* This writing Moses had done at the express command of God, for "the Lord said unto Moses: *Write thou these words*, for after the tenor of these words I have made a covenant with thee and with Israel" (Ex. 34:27).

Likewise the *prophetic* books of the Old Testament claim to bring the very Word of God. (Is. 1:2; 8:1, 5, 11; Jer. 1:1; Dan. 12:4.)

Of *the Psalms* David declares II Sam. 23:1-3: "Now these be the last words of David. David, the son of Jesse, said, . . . and the sweet Psalmist of Israel said: The Spirit of the Lord spake by me, and His Word was in my tongue." Compare *Lehre und Wehre*, 1886, 205 ff.; Kretzmann, *The Foundations Must Stand*, p. 38.

What the Old Testament asserts regarding itself is *confirmed by the New Testament. Christ* bears testimony to the divine origin of the *three main divisions* of the Old Testament, the Law of Moses, the Prophets, and the Psalms. He does not name all the writers of the Old Testament, but "the Law is ascribed to Moses; David's name is connected with the Psalms; the prophecies of Isaiah are attributed to Isaiah, and the prophecies of Daniel to Daniel." He nowhere corrects the common opinion of His day as to the identity of the authors. And this was no accommodation to error, for God does not condescend to error. Christ quotes the various commandments of the *Law* as God's commandments. "*God* commanded, saying: Honor thy father and thy mother." (Matt. 15:4. See also Matt. 5:21, 27, 31, 33, 43; 19:18-19; Mark 7:10; 10:19.) He calls the *Pentateuch* "the commandments of God" and distinguishes from it "the tradition of men." (Mark 7:7 ff.) Time and again Christ refers to *Moses* as the giver of the Law. "Did not Moses give you the Law?" (John 7:19. See also Matt. 8:4; 19:8; Luke 16:31; Mark 7:10; Luke 24:27, 44; John 5:45-47; 7:22-23.) But what Moses wrote, God spoke. "As touching the resurrection of the dead, have ye not read that which was *spoken* unto you *by God*, saying: I am the God of Abraham and the God of Isaac and the God of Jacob?" (Matt. 22:32.)

Christ also quotes the *Prophets*. Mark 7:6 He quotes from Is. 29: "Well hath Esaias prophesied concerning you hypocrites, as it is written: This people honoreth Me with their lips, but their heart is far from Me." (See also Luke 4:16-21.) Moreover, Christ says: "Think not that I am come to destroy the Law or the Prophets; I am not come to destroy, but to fulfill. For verily I say unto you: Till heaven and earth pass, one jot or one tittle shall in no wise pass from the Law till all be fulfilled" (Matt. 5:17-18). The Law must be fulfilled, the Prophets must be fulfilled, and Christ is the one who will do it. Not the smallest letter or hook of a letter will remain unfulfilled, because they are God's Word. Not even angels dare interfere, for "how then should the Scriptures be fulfilled, that thus it must be?" (Matt. 26:54.)

Likewise Christ gives His stamp of approval to the *Psalms*. Ps. 41 prophesied the treachery of Judas in these words: "He that eateth bread with Me hath lifted up his heel against Me"; and the defection of the son of perdition takes place "that the Scriptures may be fulfilled" (John 17:12.) Matt. 22:42 Jesus asks the Pharisees: "What think ye of Christ? Whose son is He?" They answered Him: "The Son of David." And now Jesus quotes Psalm 110, saying: "How, then, doth David *in Spirit* call Him Lord, saying: The Lord said unto my Lord: Sit Thou on My right hand," etc. In the Psalms the Spirit of God is talking. This testimony of Christ to the entire canon of the Old Testament Christ Himself then sums up in the words: "All things must be fulfilled which were written in the *Law of Moses* and in the *Prophets* and in the *Psalms* concerning Me" (Luke 24:44).

And as Christ over and over affirms that Scripture is the voice of God, so also the *Apostles* and *Evangelists* bear witness to the divine origin of the Holy Writ. They frequently emphasize that the Scriptures *must be fulfilled*. (Matt. 2:17, 23; John 19:24; James 2:23; Rom. 4:17.) Recall "the many things which were *foretold* by the Prophets to be literally *fulfilled* in history. This holds with regard to scores of individual cases concerning the fate of the various peoples and nations, Edom, and Moab, and Ammon, and the Philistines, and the Syrians, and the Assyrians, and the Babylonians, and the many others whom the Bible enumerates. It holds in particular with regard to the prophecies concerning the salvation through Jesus Christ, many of which were so literally fulfilled that one seems to be dealing with the account of eyewitnesses, as in Is. 53." Kretzmann, *The Foundations* etc., p. 33 f. "If all things written in the Scriptures must be fulfilled, the Scriptures cannot be the word of man, but must be the Word of Him who holds all things in heaven and earth in the hollow of His hand, who guides all events, without whom nothing in heaven and earth can occur, who is all-powerful and all-knowing, in short, is the great majestic God Himself." F. Pieper, *Christliche Dogmatik*, I, 259.

We find *personal* properties stated of the Bible. "Scripture *saith*" is an expression often met with in Holy Writ, for example, Rom. 4:3; Gal. 4:30. The Scriptures speak as a *person* speaks. For Scripture is simply God speaking. For that reason we find the subject "God" substituted for "the Scriptures." "The *Scripture* saith unto Pharaoh: Even for this same purpose have *I [God]* raised thee up, that I might show My power in thee" (Rom. 9:17). Another personal attribute, namely, *"foreseeing,"* is ascribed to Scripture Gal. 3:8. Scripture here is dealt with as a rational, thinking being, even as an omniscient person. For it is the living God who in the thought of the writer is identified with Scripture.

Often, however, it is said expressly that God is speaking through the Prophet, through Scripture. "Now all this was done that it might be fulfilled which was spoken of the *Lord* by the Prophet." (Matt. 1:22. See also Matt. 2:15; Rom. 1:2; 9:25; Heb. 1:1; 8:8.)

The moderns call the statement *"God* is the *true Author"* of the Bible" a "dogmatic statement" and disdainfully reject it. Thus they deny what Scripture solemnly affirms.

As Author particularly the *Holy Ghost* is mentioned. "Wherefore, as the *Holy Ghost* saith: Today if ye will hear His voice, harden not your hearts." (Heb. 3:8. See also Heb. 10:15; Acts 1:16; 28:25; Mark 12:36; I Cor. 2:13; I Thess. 1:5; Heb. 9:8; II Pet. 1:21.) Compare Kretzmann, *The Foundations*, etc., pp. 41—45.

As the Old Testament, so also the *New Testament* is the very Word of God. Christ demanded the same acceptance for *His* Word as Moses' Word found with the Jews. (John 5:46.) The Apostles likewise place *their* Word on a level with the Scriptures of the Prophets. They emphasize the commission they received from Christ and stress their full agreement with the Prophets. I Pet. 1: 10-12 Peter first states that the Prophets of the Old Testament prophesied by "the Spirit of Christ, which was in them," of the grace that should come in the New Testament era. Then, however, he adds of the Apostles of the New Testament: "Which are now (in the New Testament era) reported unto you by them that have preached the Gospel unto you *with the Holy Ghost* sent down from heaven." They, the Apostles, preached the identical Gospel which the Prophets proclaimed, and, like the Prophets, they spoke by the Spirit of Christ, which was in them. And in his Second Epistle (3:2) he reminds the Christians "of the words which were spoken before by the holy Prophets, and of the commandment of us, the Apostles of the Lord and Savior." Old and New Testament are co-ordinated in the well-known passage: "Now therefore ye are no more strangers and foreigners, but fellow citizens with the saints and of the household of God; and are built upon the foundation of the Apostles and Prophets, Jesus Christ Himself being the chief Cornerstone" (Eph. 2:19-20).

Some grant that the Apostles *preached* with the Holy Ghost sent down from heaven, but deny it of their *writings*. The Apostles themselves, however, expressly declare that they *wrote* the identical things they preached. St. John says: "That which we have seen and heard *declare* we unto you, . . . and these things *write* we unto you (I John 1:3-4). St. Paul says: "Therefore, brethren, stand fast and hold the traditions which ye have been taught, whether by *word* or our *epistle*" (II Thess. 2:15).

The Apostles were fully *conscious* of writing not their own, but Christ's Word. They had four special promises from the mouth of Christ regarding the Comforter, the Holy Ghost, who would teach them all things, testify through them, guide them into all truth, fill them with power, and make them witnesses to all the world. (John 14:26; 15:26-27; 16:13-14; Acts 1:8.) Paul, therefore, demands of the "prophets" and of the "men with the Spirit" in Corinth subjection to *his* Word because "the things that I write unto you are the commandments of the Lord" (I Cor. 14:37). II Cor. 13:3 he reminds them of the fact that Christ is speaking in him. Emphatic is his statement: "Which things also *we speak,* not in the words which man's wisdom teacheth, but *which the Holy Ghost teacheth*. . . . For who hath known the mind of the Lord that he may instruct Him? But we have the mind of Christ" (I Cor. 2:13, 16). Only a man conscious of being filled with power from on high could dare to write: "If any man obey not our word by this epistle, note that man" (II Thess. 3:14). Gal. 1:8, 11-12 St. Paul writes: "Though we or an angel from heaven preach any other Gospel unto you than that which we have preached unto you, let him be accursed. ... But I certify you, brethren, that the Gospel which was preached of me is not after men. For I neither received it of man, neither was I taught it, but by the revelation of Jesus Christ." Here we must either believe that Paul's word actually is Christ's Word or that Paul in great conceit had become unbalanced. But so sure is Paul of his ground that he again speaks in a very sharp manner in I Tim. 6:3-4: "If any man teach otherwise and consent not to the wholesome words, even *the words of our Lord Jesus Christ,* and to the doctrine which is according to godliness, he is proud (bloated), knowing nothing." And *Peter* we heard say that he and the other Apostles "have preached the Gospel unto you with the Holy Ghost sent down from heaven" (I Pet. 1:12). Also *John* asserts that his writings carry in themselves the conviction of God's wisdom and power, are able to kindle faith in Christ. He says: "These things have I *written* unto you that believe on the name of the Son of God that ye may know that ye have eternal life and that ye may *believe* on the name of the Son of God" (I John 5:13). A parallel thought he expresses in his Gospel. (John 20:30-31.) And in the Apocalypse he repeats again and again: "He that hath an ear, let him hear what the *Spirit* saith unto the churches" (Rev. 2:11). For his instructions from the Lord read: "What thou seest *write in a book,* and send it unto the seven churches which are in Asia" (Rev. 1:11). And to add the testimony of *Jude,* he says (v. 17): "But, beloved, remember ye the words which were spoken before of the Apostles of our Lord Jesus Christ."

So abundantly the Scriptures themselves testify that both the Old and the New Testament are *God's* Word. Hence Scripture and God's Word are really one and the same thing.

The Holy Ghost is the real Author of the Scriptures *by inspiration,* by breathing them into the writers. Ps. 45:2 David says literally: "Moved is my heart with a good word; speaking am I my works (productions) to a King; my tongue is the pen of a fast (skillful) writer." Here "the chief features of inspiration are briefly set forth: the impulse to write, the consciousness of being inspired in his writing, and the fact that he was the instrument of One greater than himself in setting down his words." Kretzmann, *The Founda-*

tions, etc., p. 24. II Sam. 23:2 f. reads literally: "The Spirit of Jehovah has spoken into me, and His speech is upon my tongue. Spoken has the God of Israel." David was not an unconscious, merely mechanical tool of the Holy Ghost. David's tongue was speaking, his mind was composing his Psalms in praise of God. But the impulse to say these things and the wording he gave to them came from the Holy Spirit, so that in David's words God was speaking. I Cor. 2:12 f. according to the Revised Standard Version reads: "Now we have not received the spirit of the world, but the Spirit which is from God, that we might understand the gifts bestowed on us by God. And we impart this in words not taught by human wisdom, but taught by the Spirit, interpreting spiritual truths in spiritual language." What God's Spirit had revealed to him of the mystery of God otherwise hidden from the eyes of the world, the Apostle taught in a manner not employing words of human wisdom, but only words proposed by the wisdom of the Spirit. I Pet. 1:10-11 it is said that the Spirit of Christ which was in the Prophets testified beforehand the sufferings and glory of Christ. Another passage is II Pet. 1:21, which reads according to the Revised Standard Version: "Because no prophecy ever came by the impulse of men, but moved by the Holy Spirit, holy men of God spoke." The Holy Spirit moved, impelled, carried the writers along as does the wind the sailing vessel. A text that has always been regarded as the bulwark of the doctrine of inspiration is II Tim. 3: 15-17, which, literally rendered, reads: "And that from babehood thou knowest the Sacred Writings, which have the power to make thee wise unto salvation through faith which is in Christ Jesus. All Scripture (is) God-breathed and is valuable for teaching, for reproof, for correction (setting straight again), for training in righteousness, that perfect may be a man of God, to every good work fully prepared." "Scripture inspired by God, God-breathed, is the expression coined by the Spirit of God. And the matter concerns writings, the production of the Holy Spirit intended for future generations, for men of all times. God wanted to present His eternal thoughts, the wholesome and saving truth, to the world in inspired writings, in a form fashioned by Himself, in a form and appearance which would adequately reproduce the divine content. . . . Scripture is inspired by *God*. God breathed the Scripture, had it proceed out of Himself like breath, breathed it into the men who wrote it, transmitted it to their minds. This God-breathing is the characteristic, the specific activity of the Spirit of God. God, the Spirit of God, breathed at, breathed into the Prophets and Apostles, what they were to write. The Holy Scripture consists of words. . . . If we do not accept verbal inspiration, then it is senseless, nonsensical, to speak of an inspiration of the Bible. The inspiration of the Bible as such is verbal inspiration and plenary inspiration." Stoeckhardt, *Lehre und Wehre*, 1892, 289 ff.; quoted in Kretzmann, *The Foundations*, etc., p. 29. I John 1:3-4 the Apostle John writes (Revised Standard Version): "That which we have seen and heard we proclaim also to you so that you may have fellowship with us; and our fellowship is with the Father and with His Son Jesus Christ. And we are writing this that our (your) joy may be complete." This text teaches that the power of inspiration was not confined to the spoken message, rather is inherent also in the written Word of the Apostles. Other pertinent passages are Ex. 24:4, 7; Is. 8:20; 34:16; 59:21; Jer. 1:9; I Cor. 14:37; II Cor. 13:10; Rom. 15:18; I Pet. 1:25; II Pet. 3:2.

The Scriptures, then, teach *verbal* inspiration, inspiration of *words*. Some who call themselves Lutheran tell us that inspiration does not extend to the letter, the words of the Bible. "Dr. H. E. Jacobs assured us that, 'if the verbal theory of inspiration means that every word and letter is inspired,' he will have none of it. . . . The editor of *The Lutheran* (June 21, 1928) is saying: 'For every essential issue there is divine truth at hand; that its verbal expression is of human origin can be frankly recognized.' . . . J. A. W. Haas: 'Men were never saved by a Bible that was mechanically perfect in its verbality.' . . . G. T. Ladd: 'Inspiration is not "verbal" in the technical sense of the term; that is, it does not consist in, or involve, the selection and dictation, by the Holy Ghost Himself, of all the words employed by the writers.'" Engelder, *Scripture Cannot Be Broken*, p. 321 f. Instead of verbal inspiration it is inspiration of *things* or inspiration of *persons*, a "dynamic inspiration," we are told. "Dr. Drach has defined it for us as 'the inspiration of the *contents*, not the dictation of words.' J. De Witt: 'Verbal accuracy is not needed. . . . It is the thought that is inspired.'" "C. E. Lindburg: 'The orthodox *dynamic* theory . . . sets forth the divine activity but also places proper emphasis on the human side. . . . The holy writers were not merely mechanical instruments, such as pens or amanuenses (secretaries); there was an *auto-activity* analogous to the new life that succeeds the new birth, when the regenerated soul co-operates with the Holy Ghost.'" Engelder, *Scripture Cannot Be Broken*, pp. 322, 325.

But as certainly as II Tim. 3:16 says that what is breathed by God is "Scripture," written matter, so certainly inspiration is *verbal* inspiration, inspiration of words. And when according to II Pet. 1:21 holy men of God *spoke* as they were moved by the Holy Ghost, this refers to the *written* words of Scripture, as the verse preceding shows, where the speaking of the holy men of God is defined more exactly as "the prophecy *of the Scripture*."

Moreover, if we observe how Christ and the Apostles used the Scriptures, we note that they insist upon the *words* of Scripture. When Christ says John 10:35 that the Scripture cannot be broken, He bases His argument that He cannot be committing blasphemy when He calls Himself the "Son of God" on the fact that in Ps. 82 the one word "gods" is used even of mere men, namely, of earthly judges. In His temptation in the wilderness Christ appeals to the *words* of Scripture by His threefold "It is *written*," and the devil does not counter with the inspiration of *things* or the inspiration of *persons*. The *words* are all-important, they are the thing faith is to cling to, Christ says John 8:31-32: "If ye continue in My *Word*, then are ye My disciples indeed; and ye shall know the truth, and the truth shall make you free." Everything depends so entirely on the *words* that St. Paul says of all teachers who teach otherwise and consent not (agree not) to wholesome *words*, even the *words* of our Lord Jesus Christ, they are proud (bloated), knowing nothing. (I Tim. 6:3 f.)

In short, inspiration which is not verbal inspiration is no inspiration at all. If we could not maintain that the very words of Scripture are *God's* words, Scripture would be of no value to us, for we would forever remain in doubt whether the human authors had also chosen the right words for the exalted, divine matters they are speaking of. But now that Scripture, that is, the *words* written in our Bible, is divinely inspired, our faith rests on a foundation firmer than heaven and earth. And we guard against departing even in one point from what is written, for we know that it is *God* speaking.

The texts adduced above also make it apparent that inspiration does not consist in a mere divine *guidance* and *preservation from error*, but in the divine furnishing or the divine *giving* of the words of which Scripture consists. II Tim. 3:16 does not say of Scripture: All Scripture is given under God's guidance and direction, but: "All Scripture is God-breathed." Guided and directed by God and inspired by God are two entirely different concepts.

In the Lutheran Church Geo. Calixt of Helmstedt, in agreement with Cardinal Bellarmine and other Jesuits and the Arminian Grotius, taught that in regard to facts already familiar to the holy writers, or at any rate of less importance, the Holy Ghost merely guided and protected the writers against error. Calixt's doctrine was justly rejected by the Lutheran Church of the seventeenth century as contrary to Scripture. Mere preservation from error would have made the Scriptures an errorless *human* word, but never the life-giving, majestic Word of God, throbbing with divine power. Only God's breathing into the writers the very words they wrote makes Scripture *God's* Word, makes it more than a human report about God's Word.

Similarly, the *illumination* theory holds that inspiration is simply a greater measure of spiritual illumination than ordinary Christians are given in conversion, an intensification and elevating of the religious perceptions of the writers of Holy Writ, enabling them to understand better and picture more correctly the will and intention of God. Dr. Stoeckhardt writes: "The thought of the modern at bottom is that the holy men of God took all they wrote from their own recollection, knowledge, and experience, merely that during the writing the Holy Ghost directed and illumined them. To call *such* an operation of the Spirit inspiration is a grave deception." *Proceedings*, Mittlerer, 1894, p. 21.

"*All* Scripture is given by inspiration of God." These words also exclude the idea that inspiration pertains only to a *part* of Scripture, the chief matters, the doctrinal content, or the things not known to the writers. Dr. R. N. Melhorn in *The Lutheran* of July 16, 1941, declares: "Inspiration, while beyond human understanding of its nature, can be defined as that action of God whereby certain chosen servants of Him were protected from error in recording *revelation*." Accordingly, what is revelation in the Scriptures is inspired. The Baltimore Declaration of the United Lutheran Church says: "We accept the Scriptures as the infallible truth of God in all matters that pertain to His revelation and our salvation." Jos. Stump: "Thus the Bible is the inspired and inerrant record of all that God has supernaturally revealed to men concerning Himself and *the way of salvation.*" "According to H. E. Jacobs 'the Holy Scriptures are the infallible and inerrant record of God's revelation of His *saving grace to men.*'" H. C. Alleman: "What is infallible in the Bible? The good news, or the *Gospel of God* which God revealed in the prophets and fulfilled in Christ." Quotations from Engelder, *Scripture Cannot Be Broken,* p. 276. These are a few quotations from Lutherans here in America. Dr. Engelder calls this teaching *"the stop-and-go theory"* or *"the inspiration-in-spots theory,"* p. 294.

What is *our* doctrine? Dr. Stoeckhardt says: "Certainly, all of Scripture in all its separate parts is God's Word, is spoken by the Holy Ghost. Everything written in the Pentateuch belongs under the heading 'Law of God.' The books of the Prophets from beginning to end are 'prophecy.' Here everything belongs into the column: 'Thus saith the Lord.' Christ the Lord and the Apostles appeal to the Scriptures without limitation, to the entire Scriptures of the Old Testament. Everything reported in the Gospels is 'the Gospel of Christ,' 'the Gospel of God.' Every epistle of the Apostles from the greeting at its beginning to the farewell blessing is apostolic witness. Every book in Scripture is a unit made up of all the separate parts it contains. It is at bottom a most unreasonable idea, this modern distinction between essentials and non-essentials, which recognizes the former as God's Word, but finds the latter fallible. That is a 'mechanical' construction. On this theory the Holy Ghost sometimes, when unimportant matters were being recorded, rested and slept, as Homer sometimes nodded, and the human pen just kept on writing and, no longer guided by the Holy Spirit, often wrote down nonsense (*hat vielfach gefaselt*)." *Lehre und Wehre,* 1886, 256 f.; quoted in Engelder, *Scripture Cannot Be Broken,* p. 294 f. Dr. F. Pieper says: "In considering the question how far in Scripture the inspiration extends, we underline the word 'all.' '*All* Scripture is given by inspiration of God.'" *Proceedings,* Oregon and Washington, 1921, p. 21 f. Dr. Walther says: "When you assert that the divine content of the Bible is mixed with human elements and false statements, you make not only this part of the Bible, but the entire Bible unreliable and untrustworthy." *Lehre und Wehre,* 1911, 156.

Theologians today object: The Bible is *not a textbook of science.* J. Stump: "It must be borne in mind that the Bible is a religious book, and not a textbook of science. The holy writers were inspired with a supernatural knowledge of God and His will; and on these subjects their words were final and infallible. On scientific matters they neither knew, nor professed to know, more than other men of their day." Cp. Engelder, *Scripture Cannot Be Broken*, p. 175 f. This is by no means a clever objection. Self-evidently it is not the chief purpose of the Bible to teach science, history, etc. Scripture is given to make us wise unto salvation through faith which is in Christ Jesus. (II Tim. 3:15 f.) But by sending His Son into the flesh to live and die for the salvation of men and by giving us the glad news of this salvation in written form God has entered upon, taken part in the *history* of mankind. And when God then casually states some scientific or historical or astronomical fact in His Word, such remarks also are inspired and infallible because they are a part of Scripture.

Paul boldly asserted before the tribunal of Felix that he believed "*all things*" which are written in the Law and in the Prophets" (Acts 24:14). And so do we believe that the Bible *as a whole*, as an entity or unit, and *in its every word* is the product of God Himself.

If, however, every book and every part of every book in the Bible is inspired, if every word in every book is spoken of God, the Holy Scriptures must be *infallible* and *inerrant* in *all* their statements and in their *every* word. This is the purport of Christ's testimony of Scripture John 10:35, when He remarks regarding the single word "gods" (Ps. 82:6): "The Scripture cannot be broken."

Finally, it is also self-evident that the *impulse* and *command* to write is implied in the concept "inspiration." If all Scripture is God-breathed (II Tim. 3:16), if holy men of God wrote as they were moved, carried along by the Holy Spirit (II Pet. 1:21), if Paul is writing the commandments of the Lord (I Cor. 14:37), if the Church's one foundation is the Scriptures of the Apostles and Prophets (Eph. 2:20), then it is more than stupidity, it is impudence, to deny a divine *command* to write while acknowledging a divine inspiration. The Romanists, in the interest of the supreme authority of the *Pope*, deny the command to write. Their aim is to lower the value and necessity of Holy Scripture and exalt the value and necessity of the so-called "unwritten Word of God," administered, controlled, and *manufactured* by the Pope under the trade name "tradition" (the Pope's *Gaukelsack*, magician's bag, as Luther called it). This has resulted in statements such as these by Roman theologians: That the Christian doctrine is preserved purer by tradition than by the Holy Scriptures; that the Church could very well exist without the Scriptures, but not without tradition; that the Church would have been served better had there never been a Bible.

Similarly liberal *Protestants* today assert that the Apostles wrote their epistles induced by a "chance happening." They, too, want to rid themselves of the rule of Scripture as the only source and standard of doctrine and life, only that they want to substitute their own ego for the Pope. Christ expressly says that He will teach Christendom to the end of time through the Word of His Apostles. (John 17:20.) The Apostles also well realized that their doctrine was to remain the standard for the Church to the Last Day. Paul warns Timothy: "In the latter times *some shall depart* from the faith, giving heed to seducing spirits and doctrines of devils" (I Tim. 4:1), and admonishes him: "I give thee charge in the sight of God, who quickeneth all things, and before Christ Jesus, who before Pontius Pilate witnessed a good confession: that thou *keep* this commandment without spot, unrebukable, *until the appearing of our Lord Jesus Christ*" (I Tim. 6:13 f.). "God forbid," says Luther, "that there should be one jot or one tittle in all of Paul which the whole Church Universal is not bound to follow and keep." Holman Ed., II, 184.

But now the question becomes urgent: Just what is the *relation of the Holy Ghost to the writers* of Scripture?

Modern theologians have pronounced the relation of the Holy Ghost to the writers of Holy Writ an *unsolvable* problem. They want the relation left indefinite, because they do not want to acknowledge the authority of the Bible. Dr. R. F. Grau says: "The boundaries of the divine and human in the Scriptures cannot at all be determined mechanically and quantitatively," that is, it cannot be determined what in Scripture is to be attributed to the Holy Ghost and what to the human spirit of its human writers. *Hastings Encyclopedia*, VII, 346: "There is in reality no clear dividing line between what is and what is not worthy of a place in Scripture. See J. L. Neve, *Churches and Sects of Christendom*, p. 199 f. But a Bible in which the boundaries between divine truth and human error remain forever uncertain, would not be the Book of which David says: "The testimony of the Lord is sure, making wise the simple." (Ps. 19:7. — See also Ps. 119:105.)

The Bible itself defines the relation of the Holy Ghost to the writers of the Scriptures very exactly. As Peter says of Silvanus, his scribe: "By Silvanus . . . I have written briefly" (I Pet. 5:12), so Scripture says of the relation of the Holy Spirit to the writers of the Bible: "Which was spoken *of the Lord by* (R. V.: *through*) *the Prophet*" (Matt. 1:22). "Men and brethren, this Scripture must needs have been fulfilled, which *the Holy Ghost by the mouth of David* spake concerning Judas" (Acts 1:16). Compare also Matt. 2:5, 17; 8:17; 12:17; 13:35; 24:15; 27:9; Luke 18:31; Acts 2:16; 4:25; 28:25; Rom. 1:2; in all these passages the Greek has the preposition "through," which the English versions render with "by" or "through." Hence we confess in the Nicene Creed: "I believe in the Holy Ghost, . . . who spake *by* the Prophets." Compare *Proceedings*, Synodical Conference, 1886, p. 48 ff.

God, then, employed the holy writers as His *mouthpieces*, His *organs*, His *pens*, so that in spite of all freedom in writing they wrote not *their* word, but *God's* Word. God spoke in them, through them. To express this relationship between the Holy Ghost and the human writers the Church Fathers and our old Lutheran theologians call the holy writers "secretaries, notaries, hands, pens of the Holy Ghost." These terms are generally derided by newer theologians. But they agree fully with Scripture, if only the *point of comparison*, namely, the mere instrumentality, is kept in view. The expressions are simply to bring out the fact that the holy writers did not write their own, but the Word of God. We say with Dr. Stoeckhardt: "The Christian minister of the right sort, who simply repeats what he hears Scripture saying, will instruct his congregation on the question: Given by inspiration of God — what does that mean? about as follows: That does not mean that God dictated the Bible to men after the fashion of the teacher who dictates something to little boys and girls or that God called out these words and the holy writers wrote them out thoughtlessly. But it does mean that God really inspired all the words of Scripture, infused them into the minds of the holy writers, gave them into their heart and pen, spoke and pronounced to them inwardly what they should write and did write. Just look at the text! It is written: 'All Scripture is given by inspiration of God.' Any child can understand these words, and we must understand them to mean what they say." Quoted in Engelder, *Scripture Cannot Be Broken*, p. 315 f.

The neo-theologians say that calling the holy writers clerks, secretaries, hands, pens, of the Holy Ghost degrades them to lifeless machines, dead typewriters, impassive dictaphones, "who without inner participation wrote down word for word what was dictated to them by the Spirit." But not even those among our orthodox theologians who used the expression "dictation," a term the use of which is warranted by Scripture (see Rev. 2:1, 8, 12, 18; 3:1, 7, 14; 10:4), taught that the intellect and will of the holy writers were put out of commission while they wrote the words of the Holy Spirit.

The Holy Spirit used the *mind* of the writers, and in a supernatural and extraordinary manner He *illuminated* it, conveyed to it the truths to be written. As one writer describes it: "When Isaiah saw the throne of glory and heard the Tersanctus, when the Man of Sorrows, stricken, smitten of God and afflicted, entered into his prophetic vision and he beheld Him being led out as a lamb to the slaughter, being placed in the tomb, and afterwards gathering about Him many who were made righteous because He had borne their sin, we are compelled to say that, if the Prophet at all saw, understood, and was able to speak of these things, it must have been by just such an illumination as Quenstedt has assumed. . . . Or when Paul speaks of the 'working of the mystery of iniquity,' and follows it to its blasphemous consummation in the 'man of sin,' or when he declares that the survivors at the second coming of Christ shall be 'changed as in the twinkling of an eye,' that 'the trumpet shall sound' for the rising of the dead, and the believers shall be 'caught up in the air' to be with the Lord, is there any more reasonable explanation for such knowledge and such language than by saying, God conveyed both to Paul?" *Theological Quarterly*, 1913, 11 f.

And just so the Holy Spirit used the *will* of the holy writers in the composition of the Scriptures. Quenstedt says, the writers participated in this work not only according to their *natural* will, according to which man is induced to action by God in the natural domain, also not only according to their *regenerate* will, according to which all Christians are impelled to good works by God, but according to the *extraordinary* impulse, according to which they in their *special* calling and office, namely, as Prophets and Apostles, were impelled by the Holy Ghost to *reduce to writing* God's own Word. The holy writers, therefore, did not write without and contrary to their will, without consciousness and unwillingly, but they wrote uncoerced, willingly, and knowingly.

As, however, it was their mind that received and reproduced the truths conveyed to them, and their will to record and fix these truths in writing, so the Holy Spirit also used their *own definite style* and their own peculiar mode of expression. Quenstedt says: "For, according as the sacred writers were accustomed to a sublime or homely style of speaking and writing, the Holy Spirit would adapt Himself and condescend to the natural qualities of men, and thus express the same matter in a magnificent style by some and in a humbler style by others. However, it is owing solely to the divine instinct and to inspiration that they employed just such or such phrases, and no others, just such or such terms, and no others, nor terms of equal force. For the Holy Spirit accommodated Himself to the natural capacity and quality of the sacred writers, in order that the divine mysteries might be written down according to the accustomed manner of speech. Accordingly, the Holy Spirit inspired to the penmen such words as they would have employed, had they been left to draw upon their own resources." *Theological Quarterly,* 1913, 80; see also p. 77 f.; 85 f. For a comprehensive *definition* of inspiration see Kretzmann, *The Foundations,* etc., p. 63 f.

Inspiration, then, is a *miraculous,* a supernatural process. Men cannot comprehend it. "The Bible is itself a miracle, of miraculous origin, the result of a direct, immediate, unique operation of God." Engelder, *Scripture Cannot Be Broken,* p. 135. In vain do men appeal to the laws of psychology. God is not bound to our psychological wisdom. "Am I, then, a 'mechanical instrument' when with deep devotion and with enthusiasm I repeat after Christ, word for word, the prayer which He taught His disciples?" Bettex says, *The Fundamentals,* IV, 77. And Dr. Stoeckhardt says: "Verbal inspiration presents an incomprehensible mystery, which the human mind cannot elucidate. . . . We may perhaps find an *analogy* in the miracle of *conversion.* The conversion of the sinner is entirely the work of the Holy Spirit; not the least part of it is effected by man's own powers. Still conversion is not effected by way of coercion;

it does not change man mechanically; but it is a mysterious, inscrutable working of God on the will, the mind of man, which so influenced his will and mind that he now wills, and gladly wills, what is God's will and thinks that which is godly." Engelder, *Scripture Cannot Be Broken*, p. 313. The *saints in heaven* furnish another *analogy*. They are incapable of thinking any but God's thoughts and cannot but speak God's words. Have they on that account lost their personal freedom? Cp. *Proceedings*, Synodical Conference, 1886, 52 f.

III. THE OBJECTIONS ADVANCED AGAINST THE VERBAL INSPIRATION OF HOLY SCRIPTURE ARE BASELESS AND MOST DEPLORABLE

Whoever denies that the Scriptures of the Apostles and Prophets are the very Word of God destroys the very *foundation* of the Christian Church, for it is built on the foundation of the Apostles and Prophets, Jesus Christ Himself being the Chief Cornerstone (Eph. 2:20). In addition, the judgment pronounced Matt. 11:25 ("I thank Thee, O Father, Lord of heaven and earth, because *Thou hast hid* these things from the *wise and prudent* and hast revealed them unto babes") strikes these enemies of the doctrine of inspiration. "None of us," says Dr. F. Pieper, "even though he were doctor in all four learned professions, can deny the inspiration of Holy Scripture without suffering an impairment of his natural mental powers. This fact also becomes evident from the nature of the arguments advanced against the inspiration of Holy Writ." *Christliche Dogmatik*, I, 280; compare Engelder, *Scripture Cannot Be Broken*, p. 78 ff.

It is alleged that, if we accept the Bible as inspired word for word by God, the *style* of speaking ought to be identical throughout Scripture. But Chas. Hodge is right when he says: "When God ordains praise out of the mouth of babes, they must speak as babes, or the whole power and beauty of the tribute will be lost." *Systematic Theology*, I, 157. Inspiration actually *demands* the *variety* of style found in the Scriptures. The Holy Ghost makes use of His instruments as He finds them. In the case of each writer He uses that man's vocabulary and from it picks and hands him the word which he should use in writing his account. Thus while each writer uses his own words and expressions, his own style, he is prevented from making a wrong choice of words and thus perverting the truth. Compare Hoenecke, *Ev.-Luth. Dogmatik*, I, 344.

Another objection to verbal inspiration is taken from the *human knowledge* and *research* the writers made use of. The argument is: If God the Holy Spirit breathed into the writers everything they were to write, why do they stress their historical research, the information gained from others, and their own experience of these matters? They are contradicting themselves. It is true, the holy writers did follow the ordinary human manner of preparing and composing a treatise, as we stated above. But as the Holy Ghost made use of their way of speaking, their education, their gift of writing history or poetry, their personal affections, so He also made use of their study, their research, their personal experiences, and information they gleaned from others. This is *really another proof* that all Scripture is given by inspiration of God and not a valid objection. Matthew and John report long speeches of Jesus many years after Jesus had uttered them. They did not have such superhuman memories that they could recall these speeches word for word. But while they at their writing were using their mind and memory, the Holy Ghost flashed on their mind and revived in their memory what Christ had taught or done. This alone explains why, in relating the deeds and miracles of Christ, they relate the minutest details. Or go back to the first day of Pentecost. Of Christ's resurrection the Apostles knew before Pentecost from their own experience. They had seen and spoken with and handled or felt the resurrected Savior. But on Pentecost they spoke, as of the other great deeds of God, so also of the resurrection of the Lord, "as the *Spirit* gave them utterance" (Acts 2:4). Compare Kretzmann, *The Foundations*, etc., p. 66; Hoenecke, *Dogmatik*, I, 342.

Another contention, based on the *variant readings* found in the papyri or codices unearthed in the last 200 years, is that the Bible as we have it can have little or no divine authority, since the autographs, the originals, of the books have long ceased to exist and the copies manifestly are faulty. It is said to be impossible, therefore, to determine exactly what God originally had spoken, and that, therefore, verbal inspiration is a dead issue. Critical scholars, we are told, "have found 10,000 diversities in the preserved manuscripts of the Old Testament and 150,000 in the New Testament, a total of 160,000 in the Bible." — Here note, first of all, that we have never asserted that the 760 or more manuscripts of parts or all of the two Testaments which have been found are infallible. The variants in the copies and the inspiration of the originals are two distinct and separate questions. Note, secondly, "if the original manuscripts of the holy writers were inerrant, then it was at least *possible* for scribes to transmit an inerrant message to posterity. If the original writings were (and not merely contained) the Word of God, then the copies transmit to us the Word of God in the degree in which they are faithful to the original. If the original manuscripts were not, but merely contained, the Word of God, accuracy of transcription did not avail to render that divine which was not divine. Yes, a great deal depends on the nature of the original." *Concordia Theological Monthly*, X, 105. Much depends on whether the original text was verbally inspired and therefore absolutely pure.

Do the variants in the copies found really invalidate the Bible? Is it no longer the Word of God? Dr. W. H. T. Dau answers: "If in a copy of the Bible that should fall into the hands of Pastor Montelius one leaf were missing, the *Bible* would not on that account be defective. If in the translation which we have something should have been rendered incorrectly, the *Bible* would not on that account be faulty. If the manuscripts that have been preserved till our time should in some cases be undecipherable, or some mistake of the copyist should be found in it, the *Bible* would not on that account be erroneous." *Theological Monthly*, 1923, p. 75.

A printer once printed a Bible in which the Seventh Commandment read: "Thou shalt steal." Is it now forever uncertain what God said on Sinai and engraved on two tablets? Every sensible person will correct misprints and, where the sense is altered, compare other copies made by a different typist or printer to get the original wording. This is the work of the so-called textual critics. They have worked long and arduously, in fact, for two centuries, to restore the original purity of the text. And they do not talk of the Bible text as unreliable. They speak of an *established, authentic, accepted* text. They regard the arbitrary assertions of men who speak of a badly corrupted text as a reflection on their labor, often unrecognized. Prof. Moses Stuart, one of the ablest scholars of modern times, says: "Out of some 800,000 various readings of the Bible that have been collected, about 795,000 are of about as much importance as the question in English orthography is whether the words 'honor' or 'Savior' should be spelled with a 'u' or without it." *Proceedings,* Southeastern, 1939, 27.

That leaves us 5,000 variants. Even of these only a few affect the sense of the text, as the text critics tell us. L. Gaussen says: "It is reckoned that of the 7,959 verses of the New Testament there hardly exist ten or twelve in which the corrections that have been introduced by the new readings of Griesbach and Scholz, as a result of their immense researches, have any weight at all. Further, in most instances they consist but in the difference of a single word, and sometimes even of a single letter." Quoted in Engelder, *Scripture Cannot Be Broken,* p. 186. And now mark well! These few variants which do affect the sense, *in no case affect any Scriptural doctrine*. In short, "the text of the Bible is in such a condition that in every instance where we need a plain, direct, clear statement of doctrine or important fact, the text is there — clear and uncorrupted." Engelder, *Scripture Cannot Be Broken,* p. 186 f.

But not only the text critics assure us that in the Bible of today we have the very words which the Holy Ghost moved the holy writers to write down. More important, this we are *promised* and guaranteed by our Savior. John 8:31-32 Christ says: "If ye continue in My Word, then are ye My disciples indeed; and ye shall know the truth, and the truth shall make you free." But if Christ admonishes us to *continue* in His Word, He therewith *guarantees* that we shall have a good text, perfectly good and reliable. When our Lord prays John 17:20 "for them also which shall believe on Me through *their* Word," namely, the Word of the Apostles, He thereby guarantees that the Church will remain in possession of the Word of the Apostles, a reliable text. When He tells us Matt. 28:20 to make disciples of all men, "teaching them to observe *all* things *whatsoever* I have commanded you," He gives us His warranty that in our Bible we shall still *have* all things commanded by Him. And so, when Paul tells us that the Church is built on the foundation of the Apostles and Prophets (Eph. 2:20), we must still have those "Apostles and Prophets," the Scriptures of the Old and New Testaments. Therefore Dr. Pieper is right when he says: "What the Church lacks in our day is not a reliable text of the Bible, but the faith in the sufficiently reliable text." *Christliche Dogmatik*, I, 410.

Perhaps the chief objection brought against verbal inspiration is the alleged *contradictions* in the Scriptures. Dr. Engelder calls it the *Panzerdivision*, the tank corps of the moderns. Dr. Hoenecke of the Wisconsin Synod says: "The Bible contains contradictions — this has ever been considered the weightiest and most serviceable objection against Verbal Inspiration. They say there are contradictions and there could be no contradictions if the Holy Ghost were the real Author of the sacred books and had dictated every single word; the infallible Holy Ghost cannot contradict Himself, can He?" *Ev.-Luth. Dogmatik*, I, p. 367; quoted in Engelder, *Scripture Cannot Be Broken*, p. 19.

There are *seeming* contradictions in Scripture. Volck of Dorpat holds that Paul's statement I Cor. 10:8, that there "fell in one day *three and twenty* thousand," plainly contradicts Num. 25:9: "And those that died in the plague were *twenty and four* thousand." Others point to Gen. 7:4, 17, that the *Flood* lasted forty days, while v. 24 speaks of 150 days; that in Exodus it is stated both that Moses wrote the words of the Law and that the Lord wrote them; that the Ten Commandments in Ex. 20 do not agree with the Ten Commandments in Deut. 5; that King Saul is said not to have recognized the youth who fought Goliath though David had already been Saul's favorite harpist; that there are two accounts of the creation not agreeing with each other; two contradictory accounts of David's census taking; that Matthew speaks of two blind men at Jericho, Luke of one; that Stephen when "full of the Holy Ghost" twice contradicted the Old Testament; that the accounts of the institution of the Lord's Supper do not agree, etc., etc. (If you are troubled by such seeming contradictions, buy the two books by Dr. W. Arndt, *Does the Bible Contradict Itself?* and *Bible Difficulties*.)

Let us note, "a real contradiction, precluding any solution as unthinkable and impossible, has not yet been discovered." *Lehre und Wehre*, 1898, p. 107; quoted in Engelder, *Scripture Cannot Be Broken*, p. 153. And as to the *seeming* contradictions the only sensible and Christian attitude is to hold that if a possible way of harmonizing them can be shown, they plainly are no contradictions. With a little good will and close attention to the wording of the text such passages can usually be shown to agree with each other. And that is all any fair-minded person will ask.

If we should meet with a case, however, where we can find no way of harmonizing two statements, we leave the matter in suspense, since we as Christians trust in the infallibility of Scripture on the authority and clear testimony of the Son of God, who in John 10:35 says specifically of the *words* of Scripture: "The Scripture cannot be broken." "We bide the time when the problem will be solved, and die in good cheer, even if that time has not come," as one Christian put it, *Lehre und Wehre*, 1891, 357. "Many a passage of the Bible which for centuries was regarded as containing unsolvable contradictions has finally found its solution." Hoenecke, *Ev.-Luth. Dogmatik*, I, p. 368. A Christian doubting the inspiration and infallibility of Scripture is a contradiction in himself. Said the professor of science to the Christian: "The Bible? Why, I didn't suppose that any intelligent person today believed the Bible!" "Oh, yes," answered Margaret Bottome with assurance, "I believe it all. You see, *I know the Author*." *Lutheran Annual*, 1941, p. 25. The Christian knows his Lord and Savior Jesus Christ. Because he believes Christ when He says: "For God so loved the world that He gave His only-begotten Son" (John 3:16), he also believes Christ when He says: "The Scripture cannot be broken" (John 10:35). A Christian accepts the admirable advice of Dr. C. F. Deems: "Believe your beliefs and doubt your doubts. Do not make the common mistake of the skeptics, doubting your beliefs and believing your doubts." Quoted in Engelder, *Scripture Cannot Be Broken*, page 39.

A further contention of the liberals is that the Old Testament is *misquoted* in the New Testament. It is true, though the Apostles and Evangelists introduce their quotations by the words "as it is written" or "as the Scripture saith," still the quotation is often not given in the exact words of the Old Testament. The liberal theologians assume that in quoting one must give the *exact words* of the author. But in literature the rule has always been that one is quoting correctly if one gives the true sense of the text, unless one indicates that the quotation is verbatim. And of the quotations in the New Testament it is true that the original sense of the Old

Testament passage is always preserved. This is self-evident for all who believe that the Apostles and Evangelists wrote as they were moved by the Holy Ghost. And investigation substantiates it.

When a pastor, however, quotes Scripture with a "Thus saith the Lord," we expect him to bring the *exact words* of the passage. What, then, may be the reason why this is not always done in the New Testament? The reason is not a lapse of memory or plain ignorance on the part of the writers. The correct reason Dr. Pieper states in the words: "There is only *one* explanation for this treatment, often so bold, of the wording of the Old Testament Scripture texts in the New Testament. The explanation is given in passages such as I Pet. 1:10-12, where it is expressly stated that the same Spirit of Christ who spoke through the Old Testament Prophets also spoke through the Apostles and Evangelists. Part of the testimony of the Spirit is, of course, also the citation and explanation of the Old Testament Scripture passages. Thus in quoting the Old Testament the Holy Ghost in a manner quotes *Himself.*" *Christliche Dogmatik,* I, p. 150. But when an author quotes himself, he may quote "as he pleases and give a different turn to an expression here and there as a changed condition of affairs renders it necessary or desirable," as J. M. Gray writes in *Fundamentals,* III, p. 33. But the modern critics deny this privilege to God. "Strange hallucination this! . . . As if God could not alter or add to, modify or use a part of, give fresh application to, or light on, His own earlier Word!" M'Intosh therefore exclaims. These liberals "operate on the principle that, when we cannot account for a certain statement of the writer, the writer must have made a mistake." Engelder, *Scripture Cannot Be Broken,* pp. 94, 96. A little more modesty would befit these critics. If they would use what reason they have left, they would see that these inaccurate quotations in the New Testament are a *strong proof for inspiration.* If the writers had not been inspired, would they not have quoted verbatim, would they not have carefully avoided exposing themselves to the very criticism now leveled against them? "There is but one explanation: The *Holy Ghost* is speaking through the Apostles and in them does according to His pleasure with His Word." Pieper, *Christliche Dogmatik,* I, 152.

A further contention of the gainsayers is that the *trivialities* related in Scripture disprove its verbal inspiration, since it does not comport with the dignity of the Holy Ghost to write such things. Usually they refer to II Tim. 4:13 and I Tim. 5:23. In the former passage Paul says: "The cloak [winter overcoat] that I left at Troas with Carpus, when thou comest, bring with thee, and the books [papyri], but especially the parchments [codices]," perhaps his own copy of the Old Testament written on vellum. I Tim. 5:23 he says: "Drink no longer water [R. V.: only], but use a little wine for thy stomach's sake and thine often infirmities." In addition, the critics mention the insignificant affairs of daily life as recounted in the lives of the *patriarchs*. But is it really an insignificant thing to learn that God loves men with all their petty affairs? And that, when we come to Him with our troubles in prayer, we can have the sure confidence that He will give ear to our petitions and help us? Our gracious God takes a personal interest in us and shares our troubles. Luther says: "How now? Has God nothing else to do than to count the tears and wanderings of David (Ps. 56:8)? . . . Friend, what can be meaner and of less account on the body of man than a hair or nail? But they are all counted, and the Father in heaven is concerned about them. . . . Therefore this is of great, immense comfort to the believer. . . . This is what the Holy Ghost would teach us when He condescends to write about the saints and their petty affairs. . . . It shows that God loves these small affairs." St. Louis, II:469 ff.; quoted in Engelder, *Scripture Cannot Be Broken*, p. 252 f.

And what *weighty lessons* these seemingly trivial passages contain! In Paul's concern to have his cloak brought, old teachers find an indication of the Apostle's *poverty*, which, however, did not depress or discourage him in performing his duty as an Apostle of Jesus Christ. In this incidental manner we are taught to expect privations and suffering as messengers of the Gospel. Moreover, Paul's desire for the parchments reveals his *zeal* in the performance of his office. Can we draw no inspiration from the example of the Apostle who, imprisoned and facing trial and death, was concerned with his studies and the needs of the Church? The passage also shows that Paul was *no fanatic*. He does not expect God to perform a miracle in order that he get his cloak and books, perhaps send an angel to bring them. He knows that God has directed us to the *natural means* appointed by Him as long as such means are available, and therefore asks Timothy to bring along his cloak and books.

The same thing is evident from his advice to Timothy regarding his stomach trouble. Why did Paul not try the *faith cure* on Timothy? Because he was not a fanatic. Besides praying for help, Timothy is directed to the *natural remedies* given us by God. This teaches us that we are to use medical help. Also that it is the Christian duty of the pastor to *take care of his health* in order that his usefulness in the Church be not impaired, as this of course is the duty of all Christians. Other lessons of value might be and have been learned from these seeming trivialities. It is ever true, *All* that is written was written for our learning. (Rom. 15:4.)

IV. GOD'S GRACIOUS PURPOSE AND AIM IN GIVING US A VERBALLY INSPIRED SCRIPTURE

The Holy Scriptures are given us by God to serve us as the only source and norm of all *doctrine* in the Church. "All Scripture . . . is profitable for doctrine" (II Tim. 3:16). Paul here directs Timothy to the Holy Scriptures which he has known from a child. He is to cling to the doctrine of Scripture and faithfully keep that. Then he is and will remain secure against error. The Scriptures, because they are given by inspiration of God, are profitable for doctrine, offer us the true doctrine, the whole truth, all that we need for our everlasting salvation.

When Christ wanted to prove to the Jews that He is the promised Messiah, He directed them into the Scriptures: "Search the Scriptures!" (John 5:39.) "They are they which testify of Me." From the Scriptures every one can become sure who Christ is, that this Jesus is truly the Christ, the Son of the living God. Likewise, St. Paul I Cor. 15 reminds the Christians that Christ died for our sins "according to the Scriptures," that Christ was buried, and rose again the third day "according to the Scriptures." By the Scriptures Paul mightily convinced the Jews that Jesus was the Christ (Acts 18:28), and before Festus and Agrippa he solemnly asserted that he said "none other things than those which the Prophets and Moses did say should come" (Acts 26:22). Scripture was the norm of the apostolic teaching and is to be the norm and source of all teaching in the Christian Church. Only if we continue in Christ's Word can we be sure of knowing and of preaching the truth, just because Scripture, every word of it, is the infallible Word of the God of truth.

For that very reason Scripture alone is able to make us wise unto salvation. In Scripture alone is revealed the Gospel, the Word of Reconciliation. The Gospel tells us that God justifies the ungodly (Rom. 4:5). The Gospel preaches "peace to you which were afar off and to them that were nigh" (Eph. 2:17). We would know nothing of God's plan of salvation had He not revealed it to us in His Word of truth.

This Word of God not only brings God's forgiveness to us and offers it to us, it also *induces us to accept* the proffered forgiveness, it calls forth saving faith in our heart, for it is the Word of the omnipotent God, who alone can bring us out of spiritual death to spiritual life. (II Cor. 4:6; Eph. 2:1-9.) Being the Word of the almighty God, the Gospel also *strengthens* and *sustains* our faith and works sanctification in us. (Acts 20:32; II Tim. 3:16.) Thus Scripture makes us wise unto *salvation*. (II Tim. 3:15; John 5:39; James 1:21.) The Scriptures are written that we may believe that Jesus is the Christ, the Son of God; and that, believing, we may have life through His name. (John 20:31.) Whoever seeks eternal life elsewhere than in Scripture will not find it, but go to his doom.

The denial of verbal inspiration will, therefore, have very sad consequences for us and our children. We lose the *knowledge of the divine truth,* for if any man teach otherwise and consent not to the wholesome words of our Lord Jesus Christ, he is bloated, ignorant, and spiritually sick abed. (I Tim. 6:3-4.) We lose the Christian *faith,* which comes by hearing the Word of God. (Rom. 10:17; James 1:18; I Pet. 1:23.) We lose Christian *prayer,* since that presupposes the continuing in Christ's Word. (John 15:7.) We lose the *victory over death*. (John 8:51.) We lose the one effective *means of doing mission work,* namely, teaching men to observe all things whatsoever *Christ* has commanded His Church. (Matt. 28:19.) We lose the true *Christian unity* of the Church, consisting in faith in the Word of Christ. (Eph. 4:5.) We lose the true *communion* with God. (I John 1:3.) Outside of Scripture God is dwelling in the light which no man can approach unto. In Scripture God reveals Himself. Whoever does not commune with God solely through His Word, is communing with his own phantasies and dreams. We lose, in short, the Christian *religion,* the "wisdom that is from *above*," "which God ordained before the world unto our glory," which "now is made manifest, and by the Scriptures of the Prophets according to the commandment of the everlasting God made known to all nations for the obedience of faith" (James 3:17; I Cor. 2:7-9; Rom. 16:25-26), and for it substitute a "wisdom of this world," a "wisdom which descendeth not from above, but is earthly, sensual, devilish," by making men the judges as to what in Scripture can be accepted as truth.

If, however, we *adhere* to the doctrine of the verbal inspiration of Holy Writ, if we insist on it that anything taught us must come from this Book, and reject as false doctrine whatever does not come from this Book, if we diligently read this Book to feed our souls and the souls of our children with the Bread of Life, if we have our pastors instruct us in the things contained in this Book and thus grow to spiritual manhood, if we stand up for the Bible in the unbelieving world around us and help in every way to interest the ignorant in this Book in which there is eternal life for them: then we can rest assured that the God of our fathers is still with us, will continue to bless us, and will not fail to fulfill the promise of His Word: "Ye are kept by the power of God through faith unto salvation" (I Pet. 1:5). To Him be glory and thanksgiving for His holy Word, the infallible rock of our salvation!

Bible Interpretation

The Lutheran Church is properly known as the Church of the open Bible. Our members are encouraged to read the Bible. The message of the Bible is readily understood. It needs no special interpretation. The Bible interprets itself. We have no council or other human authority to whose interpretation we must bow. On the other hand, we dare not follow our private interpretation. We are held only to the Bible. The Bible itself has laid down certain rules for its own interpretation. These rules our Lutheran Church accepts and by God's grace follows. Fundamental to all the specific rules, according to *Synodal Bericht, Noerdlicher Distrikt,* 1867, p. 7, is the general axiom

I

The principles of Bible interpretation rest upon the Bible itself.

Our rules for Bible interpretation are lifted from Scripture itself. Christians are warned not to believe every spirit but to try the spirits whether they be of God. (I John 4:1.) This warning is much in place, because proponents of false doctrines quite generally like to operate with the Bible and would have us believe that their teachings are found in the Bible. To safeguard us against their aberrations the Lord charges us to try the spirits whether they be of God, whether their teaching is really God's Word or merely the idea of man couched in Biblical language.

To guide us in the correct use of the Bible, the Lord Himself has laid down certain rules in Scripture which must be followed if we are to interpret the Scripture correctly. These God-given rules are to be presented in our doctrinal discussion.

These rules for Bible interpretation are clearly enunciated in Scripture, and we merely lift them from Scripture. Though the work of gathering is comparatively simple, the understanding of these rules and following them is extremely important. Whenever we would explain any portion of Scripture we must carefully abide by these God-given rules, and if we are to deal with any teaching which is brought to us by others, we must again follow these rules in examining that doctrine, to be sure it teaches what God's Word says.

These rules are to be carefully distinguished from those not based on Scripture. Since the proper rules for Bible interpretation are stated in the Bible, they are from God Himself, and as such of an entirely different nature from those not based on Scripture. Many types of man-made principles of interpretation sprang up in the course of time. In the early Eastern Church the attempt was made to superimpose a system of philosophy on the Bible. Others attempted to interpret the Bible in the light of tradition. From Alexandria sprang the allegorizing method. (Klotsche, *History of Christian Doctrine*, pp. 25, 30, 40, 45.) Later the Pope in Rome usurped the right of Bible interpretation and claimed it as a prerogative for himself. The founders of the Reformed churches made reason the norm of interpretation. At the present time the "general sense of Scripture" or the "totality of Scripture" (*das Schriftganze*) is used as a basis for interpretation. (Richardson, *Preface to Bible Study*, pp. 5, 23.) Over against all these human systems of Bible interpretation the Bible presents the principles established by God. All systems of Bible interpretation not based on Scripture have the serious defect that they would elevate themselves over the Bible, and thereby usurp the place of the Bible. The Lord wants the Bible to be free, untrammeled by all human restraint. Luther rightly remarks that the Bible, which is the source of all liberty, dare not itself be bound. (Luther, St. Louis XV:792.)

It must be clearly understood that our Church never evolved a set of rules for Bible interpretation. Those which the Lord established are all-sufficient and of such a perfect nature that all human attempts lead only to confusion. But while the Church does not possess the duty, nor even the privilege, of decreeing rules for Bible interpretation, the Church and all its members are charged most definitely to learn from Scripture how to recognize and use the Biblical rules for proper interpretation of the Scripture. We are to observe most carefully how the Prophets and Apostles, and especially Jesus Himself, explained and interpreted the Bible.

The observance of these principles removes all doubt; it presents to us a firm foundation for our faith. (Fuerbringer, L., *Theologische Hermeneutik* [St. Louis, 1912], p. 22. *Canons and Decrees of the Council of Trent*, Sess. IV, p. 19. Luther, St. Louis, IX:1361 ff.; XVIII:1294. Formula of Concord, Thorough Declaration, par. 9—10. *Triglot*, pp. 853 and 855.)

Some of these Biblical rules are self-evident according to the light of human reason, but this is not why we accept them. Certain rules are innate to our human nature, and a person cannot disregard them without becoming unreasonable. Such rules are that 2 plus 2 equal 4, that it is impossible for something to be and not to be at the same time, that every action has its motivating cause. Similarly there are some fundamental rules of interpretation; every writing must be understood according to the common usage of human language, and the purpose and context of every passage must be observed, the writer is the best interpreter of his own words. Now, the Scripture itself substantiates these rules. Accordingly we accept them as Scriptural rules for Bible interpretation.

It is important for us to realize that our Bible interpretation rests on principles of Scripture itself. Only thus can we base our faith and trust upon the Word of God. Were we to accept principles because they are self-evident according to the light of human reason, we should always have a weak link in our religion. There could be no certainty nor confidence, no faith to stand up in the face of doubt.

The charge that the Biblical principles of interpretation are *contrary* to human reason is untrue. It has been argued that taking the doctrine of the Trinity in its literal meaning is illogical, for 3 cannot equal 1, and 1 is not 3. The charge is incorrect, for Scripture does not say that 3 times 1 equals 1; but rather that God is one Being, and that in this one Being there are three Persons. While it is true that Scripture is not contrary to human reason, it is also true that in matters of faith it transcends reason.

Human reason is frequently not used correctly. Through sin, man's mental faculties are perverted so that the light which should be his by nature has been darkened and through ignorance becomes an unsafe aid.

Where, however, the light of human reason is properly used, it is confirmed by the rules established by God Himself in the Bible.

By employing these God-revealed principles of Bible interpretation, which we are to consider in detail, we obtain the true and correct meaning of a given Scripture passage.

The first and foremost purpose of Bible interpretation is to give glory to God (I Cor. 10:31). If even our eating and drinking is to be done to the glory of God, then certainly our work dealing with the Bible and its interpretation. A further purpose of Bible interpretation is to instruct man relative to this life and that which is to come. "Whatsoever things were written aforetime were written for our learning, that we through patience and comfort of the Scripture might have hope" (Rom. 15:4).

If all Scripture is profitable for doctrine, for reproof, for correction, for instruction in righteousness, then our interpretation of Scripture must certainly further those purposes. Conversely we can say that any Bible interpretation which detracts from the glory of God and does not serve the advancement of Christian faith and life is incorrect and without any authority. To be worthy of recognition, Bible interpretation must glorify and extol the divine goodness, wisdom, righteousness, truth, and power and confirm the basis of our faith and increase our zeal in godliness. (Gerhard, Jn., *Loci Theologici*, ed. of Ed. Preuss, Berlin, 1863, p. 237. Cf. *Lehre und Wehre*, 1871, p. 261 ff.)

II

The first and foremost principle of Bible Interpretation is that the Scripture interprets itself. (*Synodal Bericht, Noerdlicher Distrikt*, 1876, pp. 9-20.)

Christ and the Apostles explain Scripture by Scripture. (Formula of Concord, Thorough Declaration, VII, par. 50, *Triglot*, p. 88.) When Christ answered Satan at the time of the great temptation, He proved the correct meaning of Ps. 91:11-12: "For He shall give His angels charge over thee to keep thee in all thy ways; they shall bear thee up in their hands lest thou dash thy foot against a stone," by appealing to the words of Deut. 6:16: "Ye shall not tempt the Lord your God." In his great Pentecost sermon (Acts 2:29) Peter showed from the context and attending circumstances that the words of Ps. 16:10 do not apply to David but to Christ. In the same manner the Christian Church still lets Scripture interpret itself.

Since the Holy Spirit speaks only through the Scripture, the intent of the Holy Spirit is not to be separated from the words of Scripture. In Bible interpretation we are bound to the very words of Scripture. With these words we are to busy ourselves; with them our task ends. Accordingly all true Bible interpretation resolves itself into merely finding out what the Holy Spirit tells us in the words of Scripture. Our interpretation must be prefaced with the words "It is written." The realization that the Holy Spirit speaks to us in Scripture and only in Scripture (Smalcald Articles, Part III, Art. 8, par. 3, 10, *Triglot,* pp. 495, 497) will also give us the proper approach to Bible interpretation. We shall recognize the sacredness of our task and confine ourselves to understanding the words of the text.

No human being has the right to inject his own views into the Scripture. The Bible explicitly says: "No prophecy of the Scripture is of any private interpretation" (II Pet. 1:20). Private interpretation is responsible for the deplorable confusion in the visible Church of today. The Bible is not to be regarded as the happy hunting grounds which people can approach with their own preconceived notions and seek to substantiate them with remarks plucked at random out of the Scripture. The attempt to inject private views into Scripture is adulterating the pure Word of God. It is plain forgery and no interpretation.

To be certain that the interpretation is correct, we must accept that interpretation which the Holy Ghost gives us, for *the Holy Ghost is the only safe and true interpreter of the Scripture.* He has inspired the Scripture. Accordingly He is the only one whose interpretation is infallible. At times He gives the interpretation in direct words. In John 2:19 Jesus told the unbelieving Jews: "Destroy this temple and in three days I will raise it up," and immediately in verse 21 the Holy Spirit gives this interpretation: "But He spake of the temple of His body." In Rev. 5:8 mention is made of "golden vials full of odors, which are the prayers of saints." Here the Holy Spirit at once offers the correct interpretation. In other instances He offers the interpretation in the context, the parallel passages, and through similar helps. In every instance, however, "The Holy Spirit is the best interpreter of His words" (Kromayer, *Theologia Positiva,* II, p. 15).

The interpreter of Scripture is merely to set forth the meaning of the Holy Ghost. No one has the right to set himself up as a dictator whose interpretations must be accepted because of his position. There is no one person or class of persons whose sole right is to interpret Scripture; nor is it permissible for anyone to interpret the Bible according to his own notion. Members of the clergy as well as the laity must remember that interpreters are but to follow in the footsteps of the Holy Spirit. Scripture can be interpreted only by Scripture.

The Church accepts the meaning given by the Holy Spirit and is certain in its faith. Christ made this promise, saying (John 8: 31-32): "If ye continue in My Word, then are ye My disciples indeed; and ye shall know the truth, and the truth shall make you free." He also keeps this promise. Where Christians accept Scripture as interpreted by Scripture, they are not wavering, or uncertain, in their faith, but can say with Dr. Luther: "You yourself must be so certain of this word of grace that if all people should speak otherwise, yes, if all angels should say no, you could nevertheless stand alone and say, 'And yet I know that this word is correct.'" (Luther, VIII:1003.) In matters of faith it is not sufficient to say that a passage might have a certain meaning. We must be so certain that we can say, It *must* be understood this way and not otherwise. (Luther, XVIII:1680; XIX:1307.) No teaching of Scripture can therefore be called an open question, something which the Church must first decide. The Church must merely recognize the teaching of the Holy Spirit as correct. Speaking about the grief which comes to Christians who do not have a positive and certain understanding of Scripture, the Augsburg Confession states: "There are many good men to whom this doubt is more bitter than death." (Augsburg Confession, Article VI, par. 31, *Triglot*, p. 291.)

Since the Holy Spirit gives His message only through Scripture, **neither tradition nor the authority of the Church Fathers can be a rule of interpretation.** The Lord has nowhere directed us to the Church Fathers, but only to the Scriptures. Tradition adds; the private views of Church Fathers substitute. But the Lord says (Deut. 4:2): "Ye shall not add to the Word which I command you, neither shall ye diminish ought from it." Basing interpretation on the views of the Church Fathers would also add to confusion since they present utterly divergent views. (*Lehre und Wehre*, 1871, p. 263.)

Nor may human reason be admitted as a norm of interpretation. The doctrines of the Scriptures are a stumbling block unto the Jews and foolishness unto the Greeks. (I Cor. 1:23.) These things God hid from the wise and prudent and revealed them unto babes. (Matt. 11:25.) Reason has its proper auxiliary use in Bible interpretation. (*Lehre und Wehre*, 1867, p. 108.) By its use we perceive intellectually what the words of the Bible say. We, furthermore, understand what the Bible tells us about the realm of nature. But reason has no authoritative place in Bible interpretation. Reason cannot fathom, much less explain, the deep things of God; not even the so-called "enlightened" reason of believers can be a norm of interpretation. How could reason shed light upon Scripture, since it is Scripture that must illumine reason? Holy Scripture, accordingly, describes the believers as "bringing into captivity every thought to the obedience of Christ" (II Cor. 10:5). (F. Pieper, *Christliche Dogmatik*, Vol. I, p. 386. Formula of Concord, Thorough Declaration, Comprehensive Summary, 3; *Triglot*, p. 851.)

Also the so-called *"inner light" dare not be used as a rule in interpreting Scripture.* Ever since Adam and Eve fell into sin people have been tempted to depart from the outward Word of God to spiritualizing and self-conceit. (Smalcald Articles, *Triglot*, p. 495, par. 5.) Those who boast that they have the Spirit without and before the Word, or who claim to interpret Scripture by their "inner light," which they say they have received over and above the Bible, are either deceiving themselves, or else are conscious mouthpieces of the devil. (*Popular Symbolics*, p. 381.)

An interpreter of the Bible must prove the correctness of his interpretation solely by and from Scripture, for true Bible interpretation is nothing else than Scripture itself. In his polemical writings Luther called attention to the fact that when the Church Fathers properly interpreted a passage, they did not do so with their own words or meaning, but interpreted and illuminated Scripture with Scripture. And then he remarks that the books of the Church Fathers must be read with discretion, that we should not believe *them*, but rather see whether they present clear Scripture. (Luther, XVIII:1293 ff.) This advice still holds good.

III

All Scripture must be interpreted according to the analogy of faith.

The expression "analogy of faith" is based on Rom. 12:6, where it is translated "proportion of faith." "Faith" is taken as designating the articles of faith. The analogy, or rule, of faith is defined by Gerhard as follows: "By rule of faith we mean the plain passages of Scripture in which the articles of faith are set forth in plain and express terms." (Gerhard, *Loci*, De Interpr. Scr., par. 75.) Our Confessions are in complete agreement with this principle. The Apology says: "Besides, examples ought to be interpreted according to the rule, *i. e.*, according to certain and clear passages of Scripture, not contrary to the rule, that is, contrary to the Scriptures." (*Triglot*, p. 441, par. 60.) And the Formula of Concord confesses: "First (then, we receive and embrace with our whole heart) the Prophetic and Apostolic Scriptures of the Old and New Testaments as the pure, clear fountain of Israel, which is the only true standard by which all teachers and doctrines are to be judged." (*Triglot*, p. 851, par. 3.)

This principle is clearly laid down in the Bible. Writing to Timothy, Paul says: "Hold fast the form of sound words which thou hast heard of me, in faith and love which is in Christ Jesus" (II Tim. 1:13). And again he commands him to nourish the brethren on the words of faith and good doctrine (I Tim. 4:6). And in I Tim. 6:3 we read: "If any man teach otherwise and consent not to wholesome words, even the words of our Lord Jesus Christ, and to the doctrine which is according to godliness." The Apostle Peter admonishes: "If any man speak, let him speak as the oracles of God; if any man minister, let him do it as of the ability which God giveth, that God in all things may be glorified through Jesus Christ, to whom be praise and dominion forever and ever" (I Pet. 4:11). The Savior Himself operated on this principle. When the Pharisees (Matt. 19:3 ff.) raised the question of an arbitrary divorce and, to substantiate their error, appealed to an exceptional case mentioned in Deut. 24:1, Jesus refuted this error and based His interpretation on the clear central doctrine of marriage as stated in Gen. 2:24. (*Lehre und Wehre*, 1871, p. 263; 1903, p. 321; 1904, p. 405; *Theological Quarterly*, Vol. 12, p. 193.)

Bible Interpretation 43

This analogy of faith, therefore, is not something external, outside of and above Scripture. The expression has been much misused. Oral tradition and decrees of Popes have been advanced as the analogy of faith. To the present day the Roman Catholic Church would have the Bible interpreted in the light of oral tradition and be recognized as supreme authority over Scripture, namely, "holy mother church, whose it is to judge the true sense and interpretation of the holy Scripture." (*Canons and Decrees, Trent*, Sess. IV, p. 19.)

The principle of Ulrich Zwingli, the Swiss leader at the time of the Reformation, was in effect that the analogy of faith meant the Scripture as interpreted by reason. (Klotsche, *The History of Christian Doctrine*, p. 191.) Philosophers have understood it to mean the code of moral law. (*Lehre und Wehre*, 1907, p. 12.) None of these principles, however, can serve as a basis of interpretation, since they are something extraneous to Scripture.

Over against more modern assertions (Richardson, Allen, *Preface to Bible Study*, pp. 5, 23 ff.; Smith, Roy, *How Your Bible Grew Up*, p. 21, par. 74) we maintain that the analogy of faith is not a human aspect and impression of the Biblical content as a whole (see p. 13, par. 6). Since the days of the philosopher Schleiermacher (Pieper, F., *Christliche Dogmatik*, Vol. I, p. 438) it has become a popular practice among the theologians to claim that by reading the Scripture they had absorbed a Biblical aspect and impression and that now they must interpret the Bible according to this human point of view. This attempt is not an analogy of faith but rather an analogy of human pride and self-conceit. It is bound to create endless confusion, for the impressions will not be the same, and the so-called pious attitude will vary with each individual.

Minds are disturbed and faith becomes uncertain through such an unreliable basis of interpretation. "As the Apostle testifies (Rom. 15:4): 'For whatsoever things were written aforetime were written for our learning, that we through patience and comfort of the Scripture might have hope.' But when this consolation and hope are weakened or entirely removed by Scripture, it is certain that it is understood and explained contrary to the will and meaning of the Holy Ghost." (*Formula of Concord, Triglot*, p. 1093.) Accordingly we reject the theory that human aspects and impressions of the Biblical content and teaching as a whole be allowed as a basis of Biblical interpretation. Since all Scripture is given for the purpose of engendering hope, every interpretation which destroys our Christian hope must be false. (Illustrations listed in *It All Happened Once Before*, by R. L. Smith, pp. 16, 17, 20.)

Viewing this matter from the negative side, we affirm that no passage can have a meaning which is not in agreement with the clear chief doctrines of Scripture, or the analogy of faith. To illustrate this point, we refer to the chiliastic interpretation of certain passages of Scripture. Rev. 20 is said to teach a mundane rule of Christ, a twofold physical resurrection, and that the Day of Judgment may be known in advance. That this attempted interpretation is false is evident from the fact that it is opposed to the clear doctrine of Christ's kingdom, Christ's return to Judgment, and the resurrection of the dead. When the attempt was made in the Lutheran Church of America some sixty years ago to teach that God had chosen certain people to salvation because of their "lesser guilt" or their "better attitude," these interpretations were rejected because they opposed the clear teaching of Scripture, the Scriptural analogy of faith. (*Lehre und Wehre*, 1907, p. 72 ff.)

Great care must be exercised in interpreting a passage according to the analogy of faith so that we do not attempt to interpret one dark passage by another which is just as dark. Dr. Luther found occasion to speak some very emphatic words on this subject. Debating with Carlstadt on the doctrine of the Lord's Supper, he wrote: "If every passage of Scripture must be interpreted by another passage of Scripture, where will you put an end to this comparison? By employing this method no passage of Scripture would be certain and clear, and this comparing would be unlimited. . . . The rule that one passage must be interpreted by another is without doubt specific: a doubtful and dark passage must be interpreted by one that is clear and definite." (Luther, XX:327.)

In this connection the question has been asked, How can we be sure that a certain passage of Scripture is clear? We answer: *The perspicuity of a passage of Scripture is its own proof.* Should we be standing out in the bright sunlight with someone and he insist that we prove to him that the sun is shining, we can only come to the conclusion that either he is joking or else devoid of his senses. The same applies to the clear passages of Scripture. As the sun proves itself a light, so the clear passages of Scripture prove themselves clear. It would be nothing short of the sophistry and mockery of agnosticism to demand that the clearness of a passage of Scripture be proved by others still more clear. (*Lehre und Wehre*, 1907, p. 72.) The perspicuity of Scripture is of such a nature that we not only *can* understand the correct meaning, but *must* understand it as long as our heart and mind is directed exclusively to the Word. The correct meaning forces itself upon us. At the time of the Reformation the Swiss theologians realized just as well as Luther that, according to the words of the institution of the Lord's Supper, Christ's body and blood are truly present in the Holy Communion, but declared this doctrine to be impossible and useless. The words were clear even to them, but they refused to believe them. (*Lehre und Wehre*, 1907, p. 73.) By their very pleading not to consider these words of institution until they had established their teaching on the Lord's Supper from other passages of Scripture, they proved that the words were so clear they could not oppose them.

Our discussion of the analogy of faith would be incomplete if we should fail to show that *humble faith and complete submission to the Word of God is essential to accepting the analogy of faith in the interpretation of Scripture*. Only those who renounce all claims of their own wisdom and in devout humility plead with God to give them grace to accept His doctrine in all simplicity will be able to interpret the Bible according to the analogy of faith. We further observe that the clear passages of Scripture are the very means a Christian uses to suppress his self-conceit and to humble himself under the Word. (Luther, XII:1175.)

Our own wisdom and cleverness will not prevent us from perverting the Scripture. We need more than the knowledge of language and grammar to keep us from error in Bible interpretation. Whoever is proud of his human erudition and philosophical acumen is unfit to interpret the Bible. The plain, simple doctrines of Scripture must be upheld. In answer to the objection that some of these doctrines do not seem to agree Luther wrote: "Of course, they do not agree; that is why you lose it if you consider it without the Word. This knowledge is too high. My mind cannot grasp it. Yours even less." (XII:1605.) "We shall let the Scripture be its own interpreter, and the worry how these matters agree we shall leave to Him in whose hands our salvation rests securely." (*Lehre und Wehre*, 1907, p. 534.) Only by despairing of our own sagacity and ability and contritely pleading with God to direct our heart and mind to His Word will we be able to remain faithful to the Scripture (analogy of faith) and reject our own thoughts. To keep us from interpreting the Bible according to the analogy of our own wisdom, Dr. Luther gives the sound advice "Kneel down in your own room and in true humility and sincerity pray that He would give you His Holy Spirit through His dear Son to enlighten you, lead you, and give you understanding." (XIV:434 f.)

IV

Scripture is a Light, and as such it alone can cast light upon those passages which to us seem dark. (Synodal Bericht, Noerdlicher Distrikt, 1867, pp. 24—32.)

When Scripture says (Ps. 119:105): "Thy Word is a lamp unto my feet, and a light unto my path," it rejects the idea that the Bible is a dark, obscure book, unintelligible without outside help. (Luther, XVIII:1293.) Being a light, the Bible casts light not only on those things that are outside, but especially upon itself.

A. The New Testament casts light upon the Old Testament. Accordingly *the Old Testament must be interpreted in the light of the New Testament.* The ever-recurring statement "Now, all this was done that it might be fulfilled which was spoken of the Lord by the Prophet, saying . . ." (Matt. 1:22) emphasizes the truth that the New Testament interprets the Old Testament. If, however, the New Testament interprets the Old Testament, then these doctrines must be contained even in the Old Testament. The Old Testament in itself is a light unto salvation. When Adam and Eve heard God say (Gen. 3:15): "I will put enmity between thee and the woman and between thy seed and her Seed; It shall bruise thy head, and thou shalt bruise His heel," they had the fundamental facts of the Christian religion: that God does not countenance sin, that a Savior would be born who would crush Satan and the power of sin, a Redeemer who Himself must suffer in the act. These facts Adam had and believed.

In rebuking the Jews that sought to kill Him, Jesus said: "Search the Scriptures, for in them ye think ye have eternal life; and they are they which testify of Me." Luther says: "The entire Old Testament contains nothing else than Christ just as He is presented in the Gospel. Accordingly we see how the Apostles quote their proof from Scripture." (XI:133.) At times the Old Testament speaks as clearly as if the fulfillment had taken place, e. g., Is. 9:1-9. (Luther, XIII:2590.) At other times we find the Prophets "searching what or what manner of time the Spirit of Christ, which was in them, did signify" (I Pet. 1:11). Passages which to them seemed and to us seem dark the New Testament interprets. Luther confessed: "I would not have been able to perceive that this prophecy of the Prophet Joel must be understood as referring to Jesus of Nazareth. . . . But the Holy Ghost revealed it to the Apostles that they understood the Scripture." (XIII:2073.) We read that Christ on the way to Emmaus interpreted the Old Testament with the New Testament. "Beginning at Moses and all the Prophets, He expounded unto them in all the Scriptures the things concerning Himself." The same method is still to be employed. We must read the Old Testament in the light of the New.

B. *Those passages of Scripture which to us seem difficult must be interpreted by means of those that are clear.*

The Bible contains many passages which are so clear that they need no further interpretation (*Lehre und Wehre*, 1907, p. 14), and any attempt to interpret them would only tend to make them doubtful and uncertain. The Scripture is very explicit. It says that there is one God (Deut. 6:4; etc.) and that there are three persons (Matt. 28:19; etc.), that Christ is true God and man (Gal. 4:4; Heb. 2:14), and that there is a sin against the Holy Ghost, which will not be forgiven (Matt. 12:31; Mark 3:28, 29). There is nothing dark or obscure in these words. "But how this is possible Scripture does not tell us, nor is it necessary for us to know." (Luther, XVIII:1293, 1683; XX:327, 780—782.)

"These clear passages of Scripture contain everything that pertains to faith and life." (Augustine, *De Doctrina Christiana*, Book 2, par. 9.) A careful examination of Scripture will show that those passages of Scripture which to us seem dark either do not touch upon specific doctrines, but refer to problems of chronology, geography, archaeology, etc., or where they do present doctrines, these are taught clearly and expressly in other passages of the Bible. (Pieper, *Christliche Dogmatik*, Vol. I, p. 391.) For this very reason Luther gives the advice: "If a passage of Scripture is dark, don't harbor any doubts. It certainly contains the same doctrine which is taught clearly in other places." (Luther, V:338.) And then he adds this bit of advice: "Whoever cannot understand the darker portions, let him be satisfied with those that are clear." These clear passages of Scripture may be compared to the sun, from which all planets receive their light.

As a darker passage of Scripture we may quote Luke 14:26: "If any man come unto Me and hate not his father and mother and wife and children and brethren and sisters, yea, and his own life also, he cannot be My disciple." The Ten Commandments, however, insist that we love father and mother and wife, etc. Now the solution. In Matt. 10:37 Christ says: He that loveth father or mother more than Me is not worthy of Me." When the Lord says, "Hate father and mother, He tells us that whoever loves them more than Christ cannot be His disciple; for parents are to be loved less than Christ. He uses the word "hate" because it easily looks like hating them, and unbelievers think that we are hating them when we love them less than Christ. Thus the passage which formerly was dark to us has become clear.

C. *Passages of Scripture in which a doctrine is merely touched upon must be interpreted by those passages where a doctrine is expressly taught.* Each article of faith is expressed clearly and distinctly at least once in the Bible. Thus we find the doctrine of the Lord's Supper clearly and expressly taught in Matt. 26, Mark 14, Luke 22, I Cor. 10 and 11. These are the passages from which the doctrine of the Lord's Supper is to be learned, and other passages must be interpreted in their light. (Gerhard, *Loci*, De Interpret. S. S., par. 212.)

When the Savior was discussing the doctrine regarding holy matrimony, He based His argument on the passage in Genesis which deals with the institution of marriage (Gen. 2:24). These words contain no figurative expression and are basic for all else that the Bible says on marriage.

In proving his doctrine of justification, Paul adduces such passages as deal expressly with his teaching. In Gal. 3:8 he wrote: "And the Scripture, foreseeing that God would justify the heathen through faith, preached before the Gospel unto Abraham, saying, In thee shall all nations be blessed." Quoting from Gen. 15:6,

Paul wrote (Gal. 3:16): "Even as Abraham believed God, and is was counted to him for righteousness."

While the method of basing a teaching on specific prooftexts finds little favor today (Richardson, A., *A Preface to Bible Study*, p. 5), it is the method approved by Scripture, and it at the same time is the only certain guarantee against false teaching. One cause of false teaching is that someone takes a dark passage of the Bible and interprets it according to his own preconceived notion and then either ignores the clear passages which refute his doctrine, or changes their meaning.

D. *In the interpretation of Scripture both the purpose and the context must be observed.* (*Lehre und Wehre*, 1871, p. 265.) While it is true that specific words and sentences of the Bible are the material to be interpreted, care must be taken to consider the words preceding and following the passage. We must not take the words out of their connection. The interpretation must agree with the scope of each passage, with its detail, and the order of presentation. "Whoever does not pay attention to that which precedes and follows in Holy Scripture, perverts the words of the living God, said the Hebrews" (Gerhard, *Loci*, Vol. I, p. 239, par. 536). Since the early days of the Christian Church interpreters have agreed that "the words of the Gospel are correctly understood when they agree with the preceding; for that which precedes must agree with that which follows where the truth is expressed." (Augustine, *De Civitate Dei*, Book 17, chap. 15.)

No interpretation dare contradict the preceding context nor that which follows. To illustrate this axiom, we refer to Gen. 6:2, which reads: "The sons of God saw the daughters of men, that they were fair, and they took them wives of all which they chose." Now the question: Does "sons of God" refer to men or angels? The answer is apparent from the context, which does not speak about angels, but about the propagation of the human race. Also in other passages the expression "sons of God" is used to designate human beings. Inasmuch as nothing compels us to interpret "sons of God" as angels and all evidence refers to human beings, we equate "sons of God" with men. The apparition in I Samuel 28 was an evil spirit and not the spirit of Samuel, because the words spoken are out of harmony with Samuel's faith. The argument of Julian Apostate that the Christian principle not to avenge evil invalidates civil authority is exposed as untrue because the Bible in the passages forbidding revenge is speaking of the conduct of Christians as individuals and not of the government.

E. The foremost help in Bible interpretation is the knowledge that *the central thought of Scripture is to present Christ as Savior of the world.* (*Lehre und Wehre,* 1882, p. 57 ff.)

Scripture makes much of the fact that Christ is the center of all Biblical knowledge. Philip introduced the Savior by saying: "We have found Him of whom Moses in the Law and the Prophets did write, Jesus of Nazareth" (John 1:45). Preaching in the home of Cornelius, Peter said of Jesus: "To Him give all the Prophets witness (Acts 10:43). Speaking about his own message, Paul wrote: "I determined not to know anything among you save Jesus Christ, and Him crucified" (I Cor. 2:2). And Jesus emphasizes the necessity of the centrality of His person and work in Scripture by saying: "Had ye believed Moses, ye would have believed Me; for he wrote of Me. But if ye believed not his writings, how shall ye believe My words?" (John 5:46, 47.)

Luther continually reminded his readers: "All Prophets preached of the Christ who was to come." (XII:335.) "That alone is the true Gospel which presents Christ to us and teaches what good things we should expect from Him. . . . In the Gospel nothing else should count than only this person Jesus Christ. Whoever knows that may thank God." (XI:1835 f.) "Thus the entire Holy Scriptures, and especially the Prophets and Psalms, say that He [Jesus] was sent to take upon Himself the woe of the entire human race." (XI:1,526 f.)

Taking those passages which clearly tell us of Christ and letting these illumine the rest of the Scripture, we are certain to see and believe all that the Bible tells us about our life on earth and the gaining of life everlasting.

V

In the interpretation of Scripture the common usage of human language must be observed. (*Synodal Bericht, Noerdlicher Distrikt,* 1867, pp. 32—36.)

A. *The Holy Spirit gave the Scripture in human language.* In the Book of Deuteronomy, chap. 30:11-14, Moses taught this truth and gave a practical application. He was answering the charge of such people as said: "You demand obedience to the Word of the

Bible Interpretation

Lord; but who knows whether we grasp it, since it is a heavenly Word?" Moses' reply was: "The Word is very nigh unto thee." You need not go up into heaven or cross the uncharted deep to discover the meaning of the Lord. He speaks to you in your own language as you use it in your own home or on the street.

B. Since the Holy Spirit gave the Scriptures in human language, it necessarily follows that *the grammatical usage of language must be observed in interpreting words and sentences.* Our Lutheran Church has always been very determined on this point. Taking those to task who perverted the common usage of language, the Apology to the Augsburg Confession says: "Our adversaries, by a wonderful metamorphosis, transform passages of Scripture to whatever meaning they please. They produce from the Scripture black and white, as they please, contrary to the natural knowledge of the clear words. Here (Prov. 27:23) *to know* signifies with them to hear confessions, *the state*, not the outward life, but the secrets of conscience, and the *flocks* signify men. [*Stable* we think means a school within which there are such doctors and orators. But it has happened aright to those who thus despise the Holy Scriptures and all fine arts that they make gross mistakes in grammar.]" (*Triglot*, p. 283, par. 9.)

Attention must be called to the fact that before Scripture can be understood theologically, it must be understood grammatically. Christian doctrine is based on the correct grammatical meaning of the words, *i. e.*, on the common usage of human language. The importance of this practice is shown by the fact that Luther's insistence on the correct grammatical understanding of the Bible re-established purity of doctrine in the Church.

In the Epistle to the Galatians the Apostle Paul stresses the importance of interpreting the Bible according to the common usage of human language. He writes (chap. 3:16): "He saith not, And to seeds, as of many; but as of one, And to thy Seed, which is Christ." By the simple application of the rules of human language the Apostle establishes a very important point of interpretation.

Where this common usage of human language is not observed, false doctrine is the inevitable consequence. The followers of Swedenborg claimed that the Bible was nothing but a series of parables which only God could explain. (Swedenborg, E., *The*

True Christian Religion, p. 326 ff.) At the present time some of the worst offenders are the Christian Scientists, who brazenly impose their false and blasphemous ideas upon the clear words of Scripture.

To observe the common usage of human language in Bible interpretation, we must remember that "the sense of Scripture can be found only in the *words* of Scripture" (*Theological Quarterly*, 2, p. 23). "We should stay with the clear, bare words of Scripture and its natural style and peculiarity, as is customary according to the rules of grammar, the common usage of language, the natural way of speaking; just as God gave language to mankind." (Luther, XVIII:1820.) Whoever would interpret the Bible must be sure that he has the words of Scripture and that he knows their true meaning. The fact is that if we are to understand the Bible, we must learn its language, so that we may be sure that we are understanding what the Biblical writers meant by the words they used. It is essential to learn the precise meaning and relation of the words used by the holy writers. In Bible interpretation we are dealing with words — primarily with their basic meaning, but at the same time we must be careful that we do not attach meanings to them which we have learned from extra-Biblical sources. We call attention to such words as "sin," "forgiveness," "righteousness," and "faith." The form of the word and its combination with other words dare not be overlooked, and thus the entire field of philology is essential in Bible interpretation.

For the sake of exactness and thoroughness *teachers in the Church should base their interpretation of the Scripture on the original text.*

The original text of the Bible is Hebrew, with brief sections of Aramaic, in the Old Testament, and Greek in the New Testament. Scholars operate with these languages because the *original text contains many shades of meaning which cannot be reproduced in a translation.* If it could truthfully be said about Luther's writings, "It is not easy to make the great, rugged, impetuous German speak our language acceptably" (F. V. N. Painter, *Luther on Education*, p. IV), this holds all the more true in translating the Bible. The New Testament word which is translated "sin" (*hamartanoo*) means just that. If, however, we know that its original connotation is "missing the mark," a world of pictures is opened to us. The word "stumbling block (*skandalon*) is very correctly so translated, but the picture is unfolded much richer when we realize that the Greek word refers to a stumbling block connected with a snare, which, if touched, will not merely cause you to stumble, but at the same time spring a trap and cause the death-dealing noose to choke you. To unfold such rich pictures, theologians use the original languages of the Bible.

There is another reason why the theologian should know the original language of the Bible. *By using the original text the teacher in the Church is better equipped to disprove false interpretations.* Leaders in the Church are not only to feed the flock of Christ but at the same time also to warn and caution against false doctrine. It is their business not only to interpret the Bible correctly but also to disprove the false interpretations of errorists. These false interpreters can most easily and effectively be exposed by referring to the original text. Luther remarked: "I might have been pious and preached the Gospel in obscurity; but I could not have disturbed the Pope, his adherents, and all the reign of Antichrist. . . . I should have failed in my work if the language had not come to my aid and made me strong and immovable in the Scriptures." (Painter, p. 193.) Illustrating his remarks by a reference to the Waldenses, who despised the use of the original text of the Bible, he wrote: "I have also been able to accomplish somewhat, while they have remained without influence." Speaking upon the basis of personal experience, Luther pleads with the theologians of all times: "In the same measure that the Gospel is dear to us, should we zealously cherish the languages" (Painter, p. 185).

A thorough understanding of the original languages of the Bible equips the theologian to guard against misinterpretation of Bible translations. The Biblical languages are at times, in a derogatory sense, called dead languages, but we are thankful that they are "dead," for, being dead, they are static, and the meaning of their words does not grow or change. In our modern languages the meaning of words continually changes. The translation of I Thess. 4:15 is: "We . . . shall not prevent them which are asleep." Three hundred years ago, when our English translation was made, "prevent" meant precede, get ahead of. That is what the original text says. Today the word "prevent" has an entirely different meaning. By a knowledge of the original text the theologian avoids misinterpretations which might otherwise occur.

While the competent use of the original languages is of great importance to the theologian, we must guard against the idea that the theologians thereby discover new doctrines. *No new doctrines are found by the use of the original text.* Regardless of whether the Bible is studied in Hebrew or Greek, in English or German, in Chinese or Swahili, the truths remain the same. "Baptism doth also now save us" (I Pet. 3:21), "God is Love" (I John 4:16), present no other doctrine in English than in Greek. Doctrines do not change with language. Nor is it possible to find new doctrines in one language which are not contained in another.

Also those who have merely a correct translation of the Bible can be certain that they have the correct doctrines of the Bible. The saving truths of Scripture are expressed in such clear and unmistakable terms that also a preacher who is not able to read the Bible in its original text can immediately recognize them. The same holds true of everyone who carefully reads his Bible in translation. We should be very grateful for these translations. Up to the days of Luther and Tyndale the Bible had been published throughout the Middle Ages chiefly in those same languages in which Pilate had put his superscription on the Cross of Jesus. Then, of course, it was difficult for most laymen to know whether they had the correct doctrine; but now, with the Bible or at least parts of it translated into about 1,100 languages, we all can read "in our tongues the wonderful works of God" and be certain of the correctness of our doctrine.

VI

Each passage of Scripture has only one Spirit-intended meaning. (*Synodal Bericht, Noerdlicher Distrikt*, 1867, pp. 36—49.)

Every passage of the Bible is to be understood only in that sense which the Holy Spirit intended to convey when He inspired it. Only this sense is the true, the real, the actual sense. "No sentence or form of words can have more than one true sense, and this is the only one we have to inquire for. This is the very basis of all interpretation. Interpretation without it has no meaning. Every man or body of persons making use of words does so in order to convey a certain meaning, and to find this precise meaning is the object of all interpretation. To have two meanings in view is equivalent to having no meaning. The interpretation of two meanings implies absurdity." (Quoted from Lieber, *Legal and Political Hermeneutics*, 3d ed., p. 74 f., in *Theological Quarterly*, 1902, p. 110.)

Only a deceiver intentionally writes so that his words have more than one meaning, and only a deceiver imputes more than one meaning to a passage of Scripture. It is generally agreed that the Bible directs us to heaven, but directions which are ambiguous are no directions at all. Since the Holy Spirit does not speak to deceive but to teach and instruct us, we must all agree that each passage has but one actual, one intended, sense and that this is the only meaning it has.

During the Middle Ages it was customary to interpret the Bible in a fourfold sense. This attempt caused confusion and uncertainty in doctrine. To guard against such misuse Luther warns: "The Holy Spirit is the most simple Writer — in heaven and earth; accordingly His words cannot have more than a single meaning." "We should not say that Scripture, or God's Word, has more than one sense." (IV:1305; V:1169; XVIII:1307.)

The so-called "spiritual, or allegorical, or typical, meaning" is not another meaning besides the real sense, but it is the true meaning as recorded by the Holy Spirit. To illustrate this point, we may refer to the statement in Gal. 4:22 that "Abraham had two sons, the one by a bondmaid, the other by a freewoman." When the Holy Ghost caused Moses to write the story about Hagar, He intended to use this story as an allegory later. This is evident from Gal. 4:24, where the Apostle, speaking by the same Holy Spirit, calls this story an allegory. Only in the New Testament does the Holy Ghost open up to us the full sense of this story, His own intended sense. Thus the passage has a "spiritual meaning," but this is and remains nothing else than the originally intended sense.

The "spiritual interpretation" by the Holy Spirit is to be carefully distinguished from that attempted by human interpreters. Peter declares the flood of Noah to be a type of Baptism (I Pet. 3: 20-21). This interpretation is correct, for it is given by the Holy Spirit Himself. But when human interpreters would continue the picture and say that the ark represents the Church, the door stands for the Word of God through which the people enter the Church, this interpretation may be according to the analogy of faith; yet it cannot be proved, and no one should build his faith upon such interpretations or demand Scriptural authority for it. "Whatever interpretations would present an article of faith must be so well grounded and so certain that you must be ready to die for it," Luther fittingly remarks (III:152). Only when the Holy Spirit Himself has interpreted a passage as an allegory, may such interpretations be used as proof. If human interpreters could interpret allegorically, they could prove anything from anything. (III:1389.)

Yet *the real, the actual sense is not always to be found in the literal, but frequently in the figurative meaning of the words.* Scripture speaks of God's arm (Ps. 77:15, *et al.*), His hand (Heb. 1:10), His ear (Dan. 9:18). How absurd to insist that these words are to be taken in their proper sense! To understand the opening words of the Lord's Prayer in this sense would mean that God were locked up in heaven. To guard against such absurdity, we must carefully note that the real sense of a passage is at times found in the figurative meaning of the words. When Christ says, "I am the Vine" (John 15:1), these words do not mean that He is a woody growth. To understand these words in their literal sense would make only nonsense. Again, when Christ says of the false prophets, "By their fruits ye shall know them" (Matt. 7:20), it is evident that He is not speaking of fruits like apples or pears but of their doctrine. Or when Jesus speaks of Herod as a fox (Luke 13:32), He uses this word in a figurative meaning. He says Herod is a sly and cunning person who possesses these characteristics of a fox. In instances like those cited, only the figurative meaning gives us the true sense of the text.

It is not human fancy but God's Word that determines whether a passage is to be understood in the literal or the figurative sense. Therefore we dare not depart from the literal sense of any word or sentence unless Scripture itself compels us to do so. Such compelling reasons are: circumstances of the text itself, parallel passages, and the analogy of faith.

If human interpreters were free to determine whether a passage is to be understood in the literal or the figurative sense, we could never have any certainty of the meaning of the text and its language. "For if everyone be allowed, according to his own lust, to invent conclusions and tropes in the Scriptures, what will the whole Scripture together be but a reed shaken with the wind, or a kind of Vertumnus? Then, in truth, nothing could to a certainty be determined on or proved concerning any one article of faith, which you might not subject to cavillation by means of some trope. But every trope which is not absolutely required by Scripture itself ought to be avoided as the most deadly poison." (Luther, XVIII: 1820; XX:1317.)

The danger of permitting interpreters to depart from the literal sense of a Scripture passage according to their own inclination is pointed out by Luther in his reply to Erasmus: "All heresies and errors have not arisen from the simplicity of the words in the Scriptures, . . . but from men not attending to the simplicity of the words and hatching tropes and conclusions out of their own brain." (XVIII:1820.)

There need be no confusion as to when a word is to be taken in a figurative sense. Scripture itself clearly indicates in what sense a word is to be understood. If a passage contains a figurative expression, the same teaching will be stated clearly, in direct words, somewhere else in Scripture.

Unless the circumstances of the text itself, or some parallel passage, or an article of faith force us to understand a passage of Scripture in a figurative meaning, we must understand it in its literal sense. (Luther, III:20, par. 9; XX:249.)

All proof passages must be taken in their literal sense. Stressing this axiom of interpretation, our Lutheran Confessions say very pointedly: "Now, surely there is no interpreter of the words of Jesus Christ as faithful and sure as the Lord Christ Himself, who understands best His words and His heart and opinion, and who is the wisest and most knowing for expounding them; and here, as in the making of His last will and testament and of His everabiding covenant and union, as elsewhere in [presenting and confirming] all articles of faith, and in the institution of all other signs of the covenant and of grace or sacraments, as [for example] circumcision, the various offerings in the Old Testament and Holy Baptism, He uses not allegorical, but entirely proper, simple, indubitable, and clear words." (Formula of Concord, Thorough Declaration, VII, par. 50, *Triglot*, p. 989.)

Where Scripture teaches doctrines of faith, it does not employ figurative language. The old exegete Lyra compares the basing of doctrine on figurative language to removing a house from its foundations, so that it crashes. Luther would not even let an angel from heaven base any doctrine on a figurative explanation of Scripture. The great dogmatician of the Lutheran Church John Gerhard says: "In articles of faith we dare not depart from the proper, exact, literal meaning of the words." (*Loci*, ed. Eduard Preuss, I, p. 239.) Accordingly "the Evangelical Lutheran Church takes the articles of faith from the texts constituting the seat of doctrine" (*Walther and the Church*, p. 125), and these are stated in clear and unmistakable words.

Proof that a passage must be understood in a figurative sense must be both apparent and sufficient. "There is a great difference whether I say, This *may* be the meaning, or whether I say, This and nothing else *must* be the meaning. By the former conscience cannot be bound; on the latter it rests securely," says Luther, XX:576. By taking clear passages of Scripture and interpreting them in a figurative sense much modern unbelief has arisen. Chiliasm, old and new, has been propagated on the principle that certain passages of Scripture may be interpreted allegorically. Such argumentation has no place in the Christian Church. If a passage is to be interpreted figuratively, the proof must be obvious and sufficient. A Christian is to accept only such doctrines as are so certain that he is willing to live and die for them. Each passage of Scripture has of necessity only one intended meaning.

One more thought should be stressed regarding Bible interpretation. It should not be a mere pastime or academic exercise. The linguist, the philosopher, the jurist, will all find the work of interpreting the Scripture fascinating, but its real objective is far greater. The chief purpose of the laymen as well as the theologians in searching the Scripture should be to find therein eternal life. Every Christian should busy himself with Bible interpretation, *i. e.*, aim to read the Bible with understanding, for his own blessing and salvation. "Especially should the theological exegete endeavor to serve his hearers or readers by opening to them the Scriptures and thereby making their hearts burn within them, chiefly by expounding unto them in all the Scriptures the things concerning Christ" and in sound Scriptural theology present unto them "the abundance of gold, silver, and precious stones which he has lifted from the inexhaustible mines of Scripture." (*Theological Quarterly*, 1898, pp. 30—32.)

The Nature and Attributes of God

INTRODUCTION

CHRISTIANS worship God. That means that they regard God the most important fact in their lives, and that they seek to understand Him always more perfectly. We shall study God, and we know that He Himself wants us to do so (Jer. 31:34). We seek to know God not merely in order to satisfy our curiosity or to pride ourselves in knowledge which others do not have. But we need to know God. We need not merely to know facts about Him and His character, but we need an insight into His designs toward us, His will for us. Such knowledge of God gives us not merely items to be stored up in the memory, but the supply of the very life of God which alone makes us blessed (John 17:3). We propose to review the doctrines concerning God which have been taught in our Church for one hundred years. In so doing, may we meet the goal of the Apostle (Col. 1:9-10).

I

Man is unable to know God perfectly, because he is a being created by God and because his natural knowledge of God has been vitiated by sin. But God has revealed Himself sufficiently that man may regain life in Him.

To the non-Christian world our study of the nature and attributes of God seems hopeless and presumptuous. Human science is confined to observation, to proof on the basis of evidence which can be provided and renewed by experiment. Christian and non-Christian alike, however, agree that God cannot be perceived by human senses (John 1:18; 5:37; I Tim. 6:16). The people of God are in the peculiar position that they are surrounded by men who cannot understand God, and yet they themselves are led to know Him (Is. 45:14-19). Zophar asked Job: "Canst thou by searching find out God?" (Job 11:7). And the Scriptures echo the inscrutability of God (Eccl. 8:17; Is. 40:28; Rom. 11:33-34).

Since God is so hidden from human eyes, should we not first inquire whether God exists at all? Before we ask how God is, should we not first make sure that He is? The Christian takes that existence for granted (Heb. 11:6). To deny that God exists strikes the believer as the thought of a fool (Ps. 14:1). Christian thinkers have long pointed out that even without the special revelation of God mankind can know that God exists and that He has certain properties. St. Paul attests to this fact (Rom. 1:20-21, 25). Also pagan thinkers have reasoned, by observing the richness, order, and designs of nature, that a powerful and planning intellect was behind it all, ready to sustain mankind and make it happy; the Apostle uses that thought (Acts 14:15-17). Mankind reveals a universal bent to morality, a uniform awareness of differences between right and wrong; and the inner dispositions of conscience and reverence tend to exalt God as the Lawgiver and Judge (Rom. 2:14-15; Acts 17:22-30).

The natural knowledge of God has, however, sharp limitations. The Christian believes that it was implanted in man at creation. God made man in His image (Gen. 1:27). In the new birth through the Spirit that image is renewed "in knowledge after the image of Him that created him" (Col. 3:10). Man was made to be aware of God, to understand His will and plan for man, to respond to His desires, and to desire to serve Him in purity. Still that knowledge was short of understanding the Creator, who, as we shall see, made man subject to limitations which could not confine Him.

Man's knowledge of God has been sharply curtailed, however, by another fact. That is sin, man's turning away from God. The temptation to which the first human pair succumbed was the devil's lure to be as great as God; and in holy irony God said of fallen man: "Behold, the man is become as one of Us, to know good and evil" (Gen. 3:22). The result throughout all humanity is that the knowledge of the true God is lost (Rom. 3:11, 18). Man's weakened understanding is rendered still more incapable of comprehending God by the fact that man is, in his hereditary sin, riddled with selfishness, fear, hostility toward God (cf. F. Pieper, *Christliche Dogmatik*, I, p. 656).

The Nature and Attributes of God

The perversion and debasement of man's natural knowledge of God shows itself most abundantly in idolatry. God warned His people against it on Sinai (Ex. 20:4). And the Apostle voices the same warning in the close of the Apostolic age (I John 5:21). The makers and worshipers of idols revealed a dreadful folly serving idols (Deut. 4:28; cf. Ps. 115) and deserving God's indictment (Is. 45:20). Idolatry, in the view of Scripture, is a device by which the sinner seeks to gain a better conscience and to cover up his sin (Ps. 53:4). It is important to realize that perhaps a majority of the inhabitants of the earth still take recourse to worship of images in order to cover their sense of sin.

Not only worshipers of idols, however, are tainted with the defacement by sin of the knowledge of God. Throughout the ages man, even the instructed child of God, tends to turn away from God, to disregard His clear marks in nature and history, and to erect barriers of sin for the clear insight into God's love (Jer. 5:22-25). Religion itself is debased to become an instrument for human selfishness and a mere anesthetic for the sense of sin, a dulling of the recognition of God (Jer. 5:30-31).

A dreadful vicious circle results in the life of sinful man, as far as the knowledge of God is concerned. As the meaning and understanding of God fades in his mind, he senses less and less dependence upon God, less and less thankfulness for His care; but as dependence and thanksgiving wane, the distance between God and man increases, and the knowledge of God becomes still more vague. Hence the destruction of the knowledge of God in man's heart is accompanied with pride (I John 2:16; Is. 5:18-19; Rom. 1:20-21).

This process climaxes in the complete repudiation of God. This may take a practical form in that the human being finds it unnecessary to reckon with God as a factor in his living; he becomes completely materialistic, self-sufficient, animal (Eph. 2:12; cf. Ps. 9:17: "the nations that forget God"). Or godlessness may climax, as it has in our own age, in the more theoretical rejection of God as Creator of the world. Masquerading under the guise of a scientific theory and penetrating every domain of thought, evolutionary materialism is a powerful agency for perverting what remains of man's knowledge of the nature of God and for relaxing his dependence upon a supreme being and his sense of responsibility toward this Being; it attacks the spiritual and moral life on every front simultaneously (II Pet. 3:3-7). We are now at the peak of a trend toward secularism and materialism in which the natural knowledge of God in civilized man is at its lowest ebb and in which the concern of even the Christian for the understanding of God is, because of the fashions of the world round about him, piecemeal and weakened. A true knowledge of God, as far as it is possible for man, is impossible where man has systematically erased the fear and reverence of God, the responsibility and concern toward God, out of his life.

Conversely, however, the Lord will not leave him uninstructed who will know Him and seek Him (Ps. 25:12; Mal. 3:14-17). God made man to know Him, that is, to understand His will and to trust Him as his Father. Even though that knowledge has been defaced by man's own doing, God seeks to restore it (Col. 3:10). God has witnessed that He is alive and good, through the supply of nature (Acts 14:17). That witness, however, is easily perverted by the willful godlessness and pride of man; and it is insufficient to do more than to make man aware of his need for God (Acts 17:27). Hence God has a greater revelation of Himself to give. That revelation gives not merely facts from which we may deduce some of the characteristics of God. But it tells us that God wishes us to belong to Him, to return to Him even though we had strayed from Him and incurred His wrath through sin. It gives us not merely information about God, but it gives us the life of God which had perished in man because of sin. It does not change us into gods, it does not provide information which a creature cannot apprehend; but it changes us into the sons of God, it gives us a new mind by which we can understand that God is our Father, even though He is holy and sinless. That mighty knowledge of God is life eternal. It comes to us in a triple exercise of God's power and glory: through Jesus Christ, through the Word of God, through the Spirit of God (I John 5:9-11).

"No man hath seen God at any time; the only-begotten Son, which is in the bosom of the Father, He hath declared Him" (John 1:18)—thus John the Baptist described the manner in which God tells man about Himself, namely, through Jesus Christ. John the Evangelist describes Jesus Christ as the Word of God (John 1:

The Nature and Attributes of God 63

1, 2, 4, 12, 14; I John 5:20). Much of God remains inscrutable to the senses of His creatures. But through Christ Jesus we Christians have been placed into a situation in which we know God as our Father, and are certain of knowing Him even more fully in the life to come (I John 3:1-2). In Jesus Christ we have a demonstration of those characteristics of God, those facts about God of which we are in greatest need (John 14:6 ff.). In Jesus Christ we have the Atonement, the power by which sin and Satan are defeated, and the life of God is again restored to us, and hence the knowledge of God (II Pet. 1:2-4; 3:18; Heb. 1:1-3).

This Christ speaks to us in His Word; in fact, all we know about Christ we know through His self-revelation laid down for us in the Scriptures of the Old and New Testaments. The Old Testament Scriptures make us wise unto salvation through faith which is in Christ Jesus and are profitable for doctrine (II Tim. 3:15-16). Their writers through the Spirit of God testified of Christ not only to themselves, but also to the writers of the New Testament, who then preached that Gospel by that same Spirit (I Pet. 1:11-12); these gave us their more sure word of prophecy, whereunto we do well that we take heed (II Pet. 1:19). The writers of the Scriptures give us a richly detailed but closely woven pattern of description of the nature and characteristics of God. The natural knowledge of God gives us deductions about God from the outside, from His works; the knowledge of God revealed in His Word gives us an insight into God's very nature, "what He has in mind for man, how man may be saved" (Luther, St. Louis, XII: 629 ff., quoted in Pieper, *Christliche Dogmatik*, I, 453). "God cannot be treated with, God cannot be apprehended, except through the Word. Accordingly, justification occurs through the Word, just as Paul says Rom. 1:16, etc.," (Apology of Augsburg Confession, *Triglot*, 139). (John 5:39; Is. 2:3.)

In this Holy Scripture the Holy Spirit, the Spirit of the Father and the Son, gives witness to God. Therefore Paul says that it is through the Spirit that we know God (I Cor. 2:11-16). The Spirit taught the writers of the sacred record what they were to give us of the revelation of God. He impelled them to minister the revelation of God to men (Col. 1:25 f.). He works in the hearts of men with His Word, leading them not merely to learn facts about God, but to trust in Him as their Father, with a faith which is the mark of a newborn soul (I Pet. 1:22-25; I John 5:5-6; John 16:13).

The purpose of the knowledge of God is as great as the God who gives this knowledge. It is not for the sake of the theological pride or hairsplitting; not for the sake of dreary repeating of words as religious exercises. But the knowledge of God is our life and salvation (cf. Pieper, *Christliche Dogmatik*, I, 453). For that purpose may we study it, grow in it, rejoice in it.

II

The true God is one God, all-powerful, unlimited by time or space.

The Word of God describes God in human language. That is its purpose: to impart a picture of God's nature and characteristics. Several dangers arise in this process, however, because of the limited capactiy of human understanding. The one is to envision God simply as a collection of individual characteristics. The other is to imagine the characteristics of God as enlarged versions of our own (cf. Pieper, *Christliche Dogmatik*, I, 539). The Word of God itself wrestles with the human mind to overcome these limitations. It reminds us that we know God here only in part (I Cor. 13:9) and that we can understand Him even to that degree only through the help of the Holy Spirit (I Cor. 2:12; Ps. 145:3; Ps. 147:5). When we discuss the individual attributes of God, accordingly, let us endeavor to use these materials of Scripture only as illuminations and highlights of one great Fact and Being behind and greater than all of them; and let us be aware of the poverty of our own language and imagination as we, the works of His hand, endeavor to grasp Him in our own language. Theologians have sought to classify the attributes of God in various ways. They have spoken of quiescent, abstract, static qualities of God, in which we think of Him unrelated to the world; and of active, concrete, dynamic qualities, in which He comes to grips with man. The disadvantage with this classification is that everything that the Word of God tells us about God concerns itself with His relation to man. Another classification distinguishes between negative characteristics of God, which we can describe only by saying that they are the opposite of our own shortcomings, and positive characteristics, which have their imperfect counterpart in our own personality and life. Here,

The Nature and Attributes of God 65

too, we have to realize that everything about God is on a completely higher level than man, in a different world of thought (Pieper, *Christliche Dogmatik*, I, 533).

"Hear, O Israel, the Lord, our God, is one Lord; and thou shalt love the Lord, thy God, with all thine heart and with all thy soul and with all thy might" (Deut. 6:4-5; cf. Mark 12:29-30). That keynote of the Old Testament revelation of God expresses two great facts: that God is one, whole in Himself, complete, and perfect; and that He is the only God, different from every false god and false understanding of God, the one object of the worship of man. The purpose of God's revelation of Himself is to make clear that He is the only true God (John 17:3; Ps. 86:9-11; Is. 42:8; 43:10-11; 44:6, 8; cf. 45:5; Deut. 4:32-35; I Cor. 8:3-7; Acts 14:15). That God reveals Himself to man as Father, Son, and Holy Ghost does not destroy the fact that He is One God, as we shall ponder in our fourth proposition.

In contrast to every other thing that men call god, in contrast to every weakened understanding of what God really is, the true God is the living God (Ps. 42:2; 84:2; Jer. 23:36; Dan. 6:26; John 5:26; Acts 14:15; I Thess. 1:9-10; I Tim. 4:10). He is not a dead, static principle; He is not a counterfeit product of human wishes; He is not an idol with the function merely of removing fear from the mind; but He is alive, the Giver of life and Source of all life (Deut. 32:39-40).

God is the Creator of all things. He made not only the things; but He made their whole setting in time and space. That means that His creatures are unable to comprehend the mode of His existence. They are subject to the limitations of physical existence; yet God is not physical, but a spirit; He is not limited, but is almighty; He does not begin or end, but He is eternal; He is not confined in space, but dwells in an existence that has nothing to do with space (Ps. 115:1-3).

God is eternal (Gen. 21:33; Deut. 33:26-27; Job 26:26; Is. 57:15; I Tim. 1:17). For the human being, time is marked by a series of moments, their memory going back into the past, their sequence continuing out into the future. But before there were any moments, God was. (Ps. 90:2; Is. 43:13.) Beyond all the change of circumstance and life, beyond all the years, God will continue (Ps. 9:7;

Lam. 5:19). This means more than that God lives in unending time. Eternity is more than an endless series of moments and years; eternity is an endless now, it is the mode of living peculiar to God, unthinkable to His creatures this side of the grave (Pieper, *Christliche Dogmatik*, I, 548; Stoeckhardt, Nebraska District, 1888, p. 29; Ps. 90:4; II Pet. 3:8-9; Ps. 102:24-27). As we shall see, this fact is closely bound up with all of the revelations of God's will and grace to man. His planning of the world and of man's salvation, His revealing of Himself in prophecy, His management of human history, and His preparation for judgment, all are to be thought of in the setting of eternity. The ages of human achievement are nothing before God (Ps. 90:9-10). The eternal God is the one Source of eternal life (Is. 41:4; 40:28-31). The eternal God is busy through Christ Jesus to impart that eternal life to mankind, a life which is not simply unending time or a life beyond the grave, but a sharing of the very life of God (Rom. 16:25-27).

God has revealed these unique facts about Himself, namely, that He lives, that He gives life, that He is One, and that He is on a plane of existence totally beyond human nature and experience, in a most persistent and pervasive manner in His Word. To Moses He revealed and explained the Name by which He should be known to His people; that Name describes His being (Ex. 3:13-15; Luther, XX: 2057; Pieper, *Christliche Dogmatik*, I, 463).

God is also the Creator of space; and that means the He is unlimited by space. Again we find it hard to express this fact in words or to imagine it adequately. We speak of God's omnipresence (Deut. 4:39; I Kings 8:27; Ps. 139:7-12; Jer. 23:23-24; Acts 17:27-28). Our problem in this connection is to overcome the thought of space. Irresistibly we think of God distributed in particles throughout the universe. But He does not expand or become compressed; He is great enough to comprehend the universe, He dwells completely in the crannies of the atom. (Luther, XX: 960 f., quoted in Pieper, *Christliche Dogmatik*, I, 545 f.) God pervades all space; but He is greater than space; and He pervades it not as a material substance, but with His indefinable and infinite presence and person. We shall point out that God's infinite presence means one thing to the sinner, another to the child of God, for whom He is Father (Eph. 4:6; Is. 43:1-2).

The Nature and Attributes of God

God's Word describes Him as all-powerful and all-knowing. Frequently it describes His knowledge as an ability and skill to carry out His purposes (Job 26:6, 13 f.; 42:2; Ps. 115:3; cf. 135:6; 147:5; Heb. 4:13; Gen. 18:14; Luke 1:37; 18:27; Zech. 8:6). But God's omnipotence means more than that He has the ability to do all things. It means that He actually does work all things, just as He knows all things and is exactly present with all things (Stoeckhardt, *Nebraska*, p. 40; Heb. 1:3; Rom. 1:20). Countless passages of Scripture extol the power and wisdom of God in creation (e. g., Ps. 19; 97; 104; Acts 14:17; Rom. 1:20; Job 33:4; Acts 17; Job 40). Others describe the power and wisdom of God at work in protecting His people and proclaiming His salvation (Ps. 98; Eph. 1:22-23), in converting sinners to salvation (Eph. 1:19) and preserving them in it (I Pet. 1:5), in equipping them with the vitality for Christian living (Eph. 3:16, 20), and in resurrecting them to everlasting life (Phil. 3:21).

Men have found it difficult to hold to the doctrine of an eternal, almighty, and all-knowing God, since it seems to imply God's activity in evil (Job 34:21-22; Ps. 147:5-6; Is. 43:13). We shall point out in the next section that God cannot be charged with evil; He is utterly hostile to sin. When God knows evil in advance, therefore, it cannot mean that He wills that this evil should happen, but only that He recognizes that it will happen because of the impulse of sin. (Cf. Pieper, *Christliche Dogmatik*, I, 552, and Formula of Concord and Epitome, *Triglot*, 871, 41 f.) This does not solve the problem for the human mind, but it serves to set the proper limitations upon human judgment. The fact remains that God knows all (Ps. 139:1-6). The wisdom and power of God are not to be regarded independently of God's purposes and designs. But the Word of God unveils the activity of God only in regard to God's concern with men (Is. 40:13-23; 45:6-12).

God does more than know all things. He is endowed not merely with perfect knowledge. But His knowing is for a purpose. His knowledge is also wisdom (Rom. 11:33). He is impelled by desires and plans to carry out results of His insight into men and mankind (Job 28:20-28). Hence the wisdom and power of God combine to produce what we call the providence of God; that means not merely His knowledge of all things, but His direction and concern for man in them (Pieper, *Christliche Dogmatik*, I, 587—600). From the tiniest aspect of man's existence (e. g., Matt. 10:30) to the most stupendous, God is aware of man and actively concerned for man.

Thus the Word of God directs our thinking about God away from any human speculation. It bids us forsake any concept of a multitude of divine powers operating in various domains of life. It repudiates any idea of God as simply congealing or emanating in the forms of the physical life and universe. But it also reminds us of our own limitations in conceiving of God at all. Our thoughts are bound to time and space; but God is not bound. Above all, the Word of God counteracts any idea, natural to our own scientific age, that God is simply the figure of speech and summary for the great intangible forces in the universe by which it maintains its equilibrium in space and time. The explorers of cosmic space or atomic forces stand aghast at the revelation of unbelievably great energies latent in all matter; it is easy for them to take another step and identify God with energy, just as philosophers thousands of years ago identified God with substance. This is a final and climactic hint that the Word of God has to give us about God: He is not impersonal or detached from life or mechanical in the exercise of His power. But He is personal. True, we cannot think of Him in terms of human personality. (Is. 55:8-9; John 4:24.) But God is actuated by thoughts and plans nevertheless, by judgments and desires; He "worketh all things after the counsel of His own will" (Eph. 1:11). That means that we do not have to do with a blind fate, or a sum of physical laws. But we are confronted, in God, with a perfect Intelligence, a mighty Heart. To explore that Mind and Will, that is to know God; and in that Mind and Will lies our salvation and our peace.

III

The true God personally concerns Himself with man, with holiness and justice, and with love and mercy.

God wills. He has plans and designs. Many things about God remain forever hidden to our minds; but much of His counsel God has revealed to us. As we scan that revelation, the nature of God unfolds before us. We find ourselves face to face with a personal

The Nature and Attributes of God

Being. He is higher and greater than man (Rom. 11:36). But He is interested in man, concerned about man, occupying Himself with man with every quality and attribute of His nature, with every device of His providence (Ps. 33:4 ff.; Is. 14:24, 27; 25:1; 46:9-11).

What are the characteristics of this concern, this will of God for man? To describe them, we list them one after another; actually they are all continuing qualities of the same God at the same time.

God is holy. By that word the Scriptures often imply simply God's total exaltation over everything human, God's total majesty (Ex. 15:11; Ps. 71:19, 22; 77:13-14; 99:9). More exactly, however, the word applies to God's contrast to everything impure. He is completely beyond sin, against sin, above sin; He is righteous (Ps. 92:15; 97:2; 119:137; 145:17; Is. 6:3, 5; Rev. 15:4).

But there is more to God's holiness than that He is holy. God reveals Himself to man as desiring man to be the way He is. God's holiness is not simply a code to which He conforms; it is His very nature and will (Luther, XII: 811 ff. on Ex. 9, 16, in Pieper, *Christliche Dogmatik*, I, 562). God wants man to be the way He is. This emerges from His very creation of man in His own image (Gen. 1:26-27; Eph. 4:24; Col. 3:10). It follows from His commands to men and from His Law, the schedule of interests and desires which are in keeping with His will (Lev. 11:45; 19:2; 20:7; Deut. 4: 1, 6). To be the way God is remains the great aim and goal for the Christian's living (Luke 1:75; II Cor. 7:1; Heb. 12:14; Matt. 5: 48; I Pet. 1:15-16; Ps. 15).

The holiness of God moves Him to survey man with the scrutiny of judgment and justice. He cannot overlook disregard of Him; He cannot be aloof to sin (Deut. 32:3-6; Prov. 16:5, 7). Sin moves God to wrath. The human language with which this concept is clothed should not limit it in our minds to any petty peevishness or anger. But it is altogether a part of God's holiness, of His repugnance and abomination of sin. He is life; hence in His eyes sin can mean only death (Ps. 5:5-6; 45:7; Is. 59:2; Ezek. 18:4; Rom. 5:12). The wrath of God for sin is not a fact locked up in His mind; but God expresses it, makes it clear through His judgments upon sin and reminders of its unholiness this side of the grave, and through the final Judgment, the everlasting rejection of the sinner. The holy God can do no otherwise (Rom. 2:2 ff.; II Cor. 5:10; I Pet. 1:17; Zeph. 3:8; II Thess. 1:6-9).

The holiness and justice of God comprise only one facet of His character. There is another side, expressed by the Word of God in many different terms and concepts, which can be summed up in the word love. To the uninstructed human mind the austere justice and spotless holiness of God seem at opposite poles from God's love, grace, goodness, mercy, patience. This is due to the handicaps of the finite mind and the perversions of sin. For all of these qualities of God are reflections of one and the same perfect will of God. God does not fluctuate between hot and cold emotions. To the human eye He may seem to "repent" and change; but in His own nature He remains consistent and complete (I Sam. 15:29).

God is Love (I John 4:8, 16). Love is a characteristic of God's will. It is not simply an emotion or a sentiment. But it denotes the fact that the person exists for the sake of others rather than himself. God is not merely loving; but He is Love. That means that His entire nature is bound up in the process, turned in the direction, of serving and being for others. The Law of God, which is the revelation and description of His will, can be summarized in the concept of love (Rom. 13:8, 10). The Word of God reveals that nature of God as reaching out and putting itself at the disposal of mankind; in so doing, it heaps synonyms, and it strains for adequate expressions (Ps. 36:5 ff.; Ps. 136, every verse describing the care of God for His people; Ps. 145:1-6 describes the might of God, 7 ff. the love of God; Ex. 34:5-7). One word frequently used to describe this complex of God's characteristics is goodness. With that word the believer seeks to express his conviction that God's love is pure and that all of God's actions, even when they seem painful to the individual, are in the great plan of love for man (Ps. 34:8; Rom. 2:4; 11:22; Ps. 107).

God describes His care for men, whether believer or unbeliever, in the physical realm. That care is not always a supply of comfort; but it is always calculated to achieve goals higher than the preserving of the body (Matt. 5:45; Luke 6:35; Luke 13:1 ff.).

God reveals His love to the human being. That being has cut himself off from God by sin and is born a sinner; he is undeserving. Hence God's love for man is the mercy of God to those who deserved judgment and condemnation; it is the pity of God for those in bitter need, unable to help themselves (Ps. 108:4; Lam. 3:

The Nature and Attributes of God 71

22; Micah 7:18-19; Rom. 9:22; II Pet. 3:9; Ps. 86:15; 111:4; 112:4; Is. 63:9; James 5:11).

Hence the most remarkable feature in the love of God for man is that it exists in God at one and the selfsame moment and toward the same person for whom God has wrath. His love is a love for sinners (Eph. 2:4-5; John 3:17; John 6:40; Tit. 3:4-5; Ps. 103:1-13). It must be at once apparent that this readiness of God to love man, even in the face of his sin, does not happen blindly. But it is due to God's plan of redemption and reconciliation through Christ, the major fact in the revelation of God's love to man. This fact forms the bulk of the consideration of our fourth proposition. But already here we may emphasize this fact: God's love is not contrary to His holiness or His justice. His love is not the forgetting or the condoning of sin; it marks no miscarriage of divine justice. God's love succeeds in giving life only to that sinner who accepts Christ as his Savior by faith; and that sinner's sin is not forgotten, but is imputed to Christ (John 3:36; Ps. 32:1, 2, 10; v. 5; II Cor. 5:19).

God's love for the sinner is not an abstract transaction. God is involved in it with all of His regard for His Son; and He is engaged in a pursuit of the sinner, a seeking and a winning, carried on with a truly divine patience (Ex. 34:6-7; Ezek. 36:22 ff.; Rom. 2:4; Luke 18:7; Matt. 23:37; Is. 1:18; cf. Is. 55:1; Rev. 3:20; Micah 6:3; Rom. 10:21, quoting Is. 65:1; II Pet. 3:9).

God seeks the sinner, gives potency to the means of grace, and directs all of His providence to the end that the believing sinner may become righteous in His sight with the righteousness of His own Son. So God is both loving and just (Rom. 3:23-26; Micah 7:18-19; Ps. 111:7-10; John 17:25-26; I John 1:9).

God's loving design and will toward His people reaches beyond their imputed righteousness. He plans for them a life which participates in the service of love to God and to men, which enjoys the blessedness of communing with God in prayer and trusting in Him for every need, which clings to Him throughout this present world and out into the life to come. These precious privileges and blessings of the Christian are in the design of God; He has planned them for His children; they are the gift of His love (I John 2:4-6; cf. John 13:15; I John 4:16; I Thess. 3:12;

I Cor. 15:10; I Pet. 4:11; James 1:18-20; Ps. 34:22; Is. 26:3; I Pet. 1: 3; Ps. 31:23-24).

The marvel of God's character and a final mark of its perfection in contrast to every human trait is that He is true and faithful. He remains consistent to His own agreements and promises; He remains true to His own holiness and love (Num. 24:19; Tit. 1:2; Heb. 6:17; Deut. 7:9; I Kings 8:56; Ps. 36:5; Ps. 89:1; I Cor. 1: 9; 13:10).

Thus God reveals Himself as the God interested in His people. To them who do not know Him, He may be an enigma or a blind fate or a consuming fire. But to those who know Him He appears to be, more and more, a Father (Is. 64:8). But God will not let this thought of ours, this insight of Him, degenerate into mere wishful thinking; nor will He permit us ever to be satisfied with the picture of an indulgent God, strong in physical powers, but weak in truth and purity. So it is that God has revealed Himself not only in phrases of His holy men, in verbal reminders of His will and love. But He has communicated Himself to men. That remains the subject of our fourth proposition.

IV

The One God reveals Himself to man as Father, Son, and Holy Ghost.

We have seen that the Word of God describes His nature by listing certain qualities of His being, such as infinity and eternity; or of His will, such as holiness and love. However, God has revealed Himself more amply still. In the Word of God we see Him at work as Father, Son, and Holy Ghost. Since the third century this doctrine has been called the Trinity, to denote that one God reveals Himself toward man as three persons. At once we must assert that also this revelation of God lies beyond the capacity of the human mind. It is, however, a cardinal item in the description of the Word of God concerning the nature of God. Let us understand why we discuss it. We study this truth because, as the Word of God describes it, it shows us not merely how God is, but it teaches us to realize that the eternal Triune God from eternity concerned Himself with the salvation of sinful mankind and what He has done and still does to restore man, dead in trespasses and sin, to life; that He not merely wills that we belong to Him and live in Him, but that He actually comes to us and imparts Himself to us. The doctrine of the Holy Trinity is the doctrine of God's love in action (Pieper, *Christliche Dogmatik*, I, 492; Luther, XII: 628 ff., quoted in Pieper, I, 455-457).

The God of Israel is one God. The doctrine of the Trinity does not violate this fact. God is not divided in His essence between three beings. The Savior said that He and the Father constitute one Being (John 10:30; cf. John 14:9; 1:1-2; Col. 1:19; 2:9; I Tim. 3:16). The Spirit of God and God are synonymous terms and are spoken of as one (Acts 5:3-4; I Cor. 3:16; II Cor. 3:17; Ps. 139:7-8). When we speak of "persons" in the Trinity, therefore, we are not talking about three divine natures or about a split in the being of God. The one God has one nature; and that one nature is completely at work in each person.

The most superhuman, supra-rational elements in God's revelation of Himself concern the difference between the three persons of the Trinity. What is there that the Father does and the Son does not do? What is there that the Father and the Son do that the Spirit does not do? That Father "hath life in Himself" (John 5:26). But He gives this life to the Son (John 5:26; Ps. 2:7; I John 4:9; cf. John 3:16, 18; 1:18). The Father and the Son together send the Spirit (John 14:26; 15:26; Gal. 4:6; Rom. 8:9; II Cor. 3:17). One act, furthermore, distinguishes the Son from Father and Spirit: He became man. But in all of these acts in which the persons of the Godhead are distinguished from each other, the revelation of God speaks, although in human language, of processes which are totally beyond the understanding of man. It is not the business of the Christian to try to find explanations for these processes. Rather are they given us so that we can discern the great God at work for the imparting of the divine life to man. How the three persons of the Trinity can be linked in one Godhead we do not know. But that they work together in a magnificent plan of care for man, that is the crucial fact in the revelation of God. While God's revelation of Himself does not become more understandable because of its loving purpose, still it does become dearer to us for that reason, and it becomes the very message and tool for life (Matt. 28: 19; John 14:15-17).

God's revelation of Himself as Father, Son, and Holy Ghost is not merely a listing of descriptions of His characteristics. But it is a story, the account of God's dealing with man. God makes Himself as clear as He can to our understanding, not simply by saying who He is, but telling us what He intends to do for us and what He does.

God made man. We have seen that the creation is essential in our understanding of God's power, majesty, wisdom. Here it is important to understand God's purpose. His purpose was to create a setting for man, and this man should be in God's image. Father, Son, and Spirit co-operated in the act of creation (John 1:3; Eph. 3:9; cf. I Cor. 8:6; Col. 1:16; Heb. 1:2; Prov. 8:27; Gen. 1:2; Job 33:4). The image of God was no physical counterpart of God in man; but it means the very life of God at work in man. To that end God breathed His own breath, His Spirit, into man, and man became a living soul (Gen. 2:7). This life of God in man was complete; but God made clear to man that if he would sever himself from God and go against the will and life of God, in that day he would die, not simply the death of the stopping of physical respiration, but the death of voiding the life of God (Gen. 2:17).

Man sinned, and died. As the story of God and man unrolls, we now see God coming forward with a plan for the re-establishing of His life in man. Actually, God had that plan before He ever made the world; the plan unfolds in time, but was conceived in eternity (I Pet. 1:20; Eph. 1:7-10; "the determinate counsel and foreknowledge of God," Acts 2:23).

To understand this plan of restoring life and salvation to man, we have to understand the problem of death and sin. Sin, we heard, works the wrath of God; God, the Holy One, can have nothing to do with the sinner and is separated from Him in death. God cannot simply dismiss His wrath and condone the sin. God's will is that man should be the way God is; man's sin is that he has taken his life and has used it to his own interests instead of the purposes and plan of God. Hence, man's sin has caused a debt; his every moment and breath only increases that debt; the whole human race is thus in debt to God, and therefore under the wrath of God (Rom. 3:19; Gal. 3:10). Furthermore, man's state of death renders him unable to do anything to remedy it, to make any

The Nature and Attributes of God 75

payment to God in atonement; for man is wholly unrighteous and ungodly in his life and thought (Ps. 51:7; John 3:6; Gal. 5:19-21).

God's plan for the restoring of life and salvation to man was prompted by His love; and He did not merely love man abstractly, but in a most real and powerful way. God gave His Son to redeem the world (I Pet. 1:18-21; cf. John 3:16; Luke 2:30). The Son of God moved among the people of God also during the years of the Old Testament. As the Angel of the Lord He is identified in many places with God Himself, carrying out specific and important representations of God toward man (Gen. 22:11-18; Ex. 3: 1-15; Gen. 16:7-14; 18:19; 21:17-19; 31:11-13; 28:11-22; 33:25-30 and Hos. 12:5; 48:15 f.; Ex. 13:21; 41:19; 23:20; 33:14; Josh. 5:13; 6:2; Judges 6:11-24; 13:3-25; Is. 63:8-9; Zech. 3:1; Mal. 3:1; in Daniel, Michael; cf. Pieper, *Christliche Dogmatik*, I, 477 ff.; E. Pardieck, Western District, 1909, p. 14 ff.). The most important of His assignments is that He should come to carry out the covenant of God's peace with His people (Mal. 3:1). The name "Jehovah" is given not only to the Father, but also to the Son (Ex. 3:2, 4, 7, 15). The Old Testament is rich particularly in prophecy concerning the work of the Son of God that He should redeem His people from their sins (e. g. Is. 9:6-9; Is. 53; Ps. 22; 40; Dan. 7:13-14; Micah 5: 1; Gen. 3:15; Is. 7:14; Deut. 18:15; Ps. 110:4; Is. 11:2; Ps. 16; 68). This prophecy is not merely remarkable; but it is an insight into the eternal God at work in time with the carrying out of His plan for man. It was also the tool which the Father employed in the Old Testament era for restoring life to His people. He revealed His love and promise to the first human pair, to Abraham, to the patriarchs, and to the Prophets in ever more detailed fashion. He held before His people the spectacle of their sins, He reproved and chastened them; but He also reminded them of His forgiving love and revealed Himself as their Redeemer (Ps. 130:7-8; Is. 41:14; 43:14; 44:24; 47:4; 59:20; Jer. 50:34; Jer. 31:3).

Then, in the fullness of the time, Christ came in the flesh. The redemption of the world could not take place in the counsels of the Trinity, but it had to reach into mankind itself; the Redeemer had to be man to lift man's burden and to sustain man's penalty (John 1:14; Gal. 4:4-5; Is. 7:14; Phil. 2:5-8). Christ Jesus took that burden upon Himself. He took the burden of others, for He Himself remained sinless and spotless throughout the process of the redemption (John 8:46; Heb. 4:15; 7:26; cf. 9:14; I Pet. 2:22; cf. Is. 53:9). Hence, when Christ paid the penalty of man's redemption, He gave the most remarkable revelation that we have of the love of God (John 15:9; I John 3:16; Luther, XI: 151, Stoeckhardt, Nebraska, p. 56 f.). For in atoning for the sins of mankind He literally became a sacrifice in the place and stead of man. All the consequence and penalty of man's sin, all the wrath and condemnation that God has for man's sin struck Christ; and God forsook Him in the agony of the separation from God that is the lot of the sinner (II Cor. 5:21; Ps. 22: 1 ff.; Matt. 27:46; Mark 15:34; II Cor. 5:19). Thus the wrath of God for man is removed; the love of God has found a way to free spiritually dead and evil man from sin, death, and the bondage of the devil (Heb. 2:14-18). By raising Christ from the dead God publicly declared that the sins of mankind had been fully atoned for and therefore forgiven, that sinful mankind now stands justified in the sight of God (Rom. 4:25; 5:15-19; I Cor. 15:14-20; II Cor. 5:19).

The death of Christ on the Cross was the payment, once and for all time, for the sins of man; it was the mighty proof of God's love for man, the device by which God could get His love to man (I John 4:9-16). But the resources of God's love are not therewith exhausted. God now sends His Spirit to make this His love in Christ Jesus effective in the individual who is still in the toils of death and sin. Actually, this process likewise has been planned from eternity.

Already in the Old Testament the Spirit of God is portrayed as a living and complete personality, judging and punishing mankind (Gen. 6:3), speaking through David (II Sam. 23:1-3), moved to sorrow through the falling of the children of Israel (Is. 63:10), guiding His people (Ps. 51:13-14; 143:10); He is prophesied as standing by the Savior in His future work (Is. 11:2) and by God's people in the Gospel age (Joel 3:1—Pieper, *Christliche Dogmatik*, I, 476; Pardieck, Western, 1909, p. 34).

In the New Testament revelation of God we now find the Spirit of God with Christ as He begins His ministry at His Baptism (Matt. 3:16). But more, He becomes the Agent for making the redemption of Christ Jesus and the love of the Father operative in the heart of the individual. He turns the dead heart of man to the knowledge and faith which is necessary to accept the Gospel;

He imparts the mind of Christ (I Cor. 2:10 ff.; I John 2:27; 4:13; Gal. 4:6; Rom. 8:16).

To accomplish this mighty work of bringing spiritual light out of spiritual darkness and producing its fruits in the soul of man, the Spirit employs the means of grace, Gospel and Baptism (Rom. 5: 5, 8; I Pet. 1:18-25; Rom. 1:16; Gal. 3:5; I Cor. 4:15; John 3:5; Acts 2:38; Tit. 3:5-7).

Thus, then, God comes to the end of the road in the process which He had planned before time for the restoration of man to His image. For the gift of faith through the Spirit of God means the gift of life. The believer not only acknowledges certain facts about God and Christ to be true; but he feeds on Christ, he draws upon the life of God as his own life (Gal. 2:20; 3:13-14). That new life through the Spirit sets up in the believer the very qualities of God for which God originally made man (Gal. 5:16 ff.; II Cor. 4:11; I John 3:14).

Not only does this complete life which the Spirit sets up in the individual prove itself in actions; but the heart and soul are set to rejoice in God, to trust in Him, to know Him truly as the one Life and Light for this world and for the life to come (Ps. 36:9; 84:11; Is. 60:20; Dan. 12:3; II Cor. 3:18; 5:5 ff.).

Conclusion

The practical inferences of our study of God are obvious. To know God means more than to recite the correct words about Him. It means to trust in Him with the true insight into His meaning for our life and soul in this world and in the life to come. It means to cling to Him as a Father; to trust in Him as the great God who yet is mindful of our needs; to be confident that even in our sin He will not leave us, and that nothing can come between us and the love of God, which is in Christ Jesus, our Lord (Rom. 8). It means to worship and adore Father, Son, and Holy Ghost, knowing that they are one, and that we are in the world to that end and have the right to do so as sinners reconciled to the Father by the blood of the Lamb. It means to realize that the life of God is true and real, far beyond every lowly counterpart of this present physical existence, and to cherish the supply of that life to us which is unfailing, the Gospel and Sacraments of the redemption of Christ, our Lord.

The Providence of God

As we gather to discuss and to plan ways and means of carrying forward the banners of our King in a land which like Canaan flows with milk and honey and meet near the territory where some of the mighty works of the Creator invite the soul to reverence and the body to relaxation, the subject assigned for consideration is a challenge to fathom some of the deep things of God. Before concluding these meditations we shall have occasion more than once to exclaim with the Apostle: "Oh, the depth of the riches, both of the wisdom and knowledge of God! How unsearchable are His judgments and His ways past finding out!" (Rom. 11:33.)

As we probe into the providence of God and in small measure attempt to trace out its many ramifications, we shall come upon questions and problems that make us confess: Finite mind cannot grasp the infinite God. Still our meditations are not rash presumption. Also regarding His divine providence God has made revelation of Himself. These things also have been written for our admonition and are profitable for instruction in righteousness. To this doctrine also applies the promise of the First Psalm: "Blessed is the man . . . whose delight is in the Law of the Lord and who meditates in His Law day and night." By meditating on the providence of God, we, too, shall be planted beside the rivers of water. Under the direction and guidance of the Holy Spirit such meditation will cause us to drive the roots of our faith deeper into the goodness of God so that we may bring forth fruit in due season.

Acknowledging our unworthiness, we then direct a prayer to the Spirit of Wisdom to guide us as we ponder upon and seek to fathom, as far as revelation permits — God forbid that we mingle our speculations with His thoughts — *The Providence of God.*

I. THE NATURE OF DIVINE PROVIDENCE

Divine providence is that activity of God whereby He uninterruptedly upholds, governs, and directs the world which He has created.

The world is not self-sufficient. It does not maintain itself. It is not an automaton which runs its course by its own inherent powers. When God created the world, He did not implant in the world the powers to continue an independent existence. God did not act like a builder, who leaves the house he has completed, nor like a watchmaker, who first constructs a watch, then winds it up, and lets it run down without more concern. God, who created the world, is the cause of its continued existence and growth. This fact we confess in our Catechism. "I believe that God has made me and all creatures . . . and still preserves them."

TESTIMONY OF REASON

The fact that the world depends on God can be deduced by reason. He who believes that there is a God must logically also believe that God exercises divine providence. God is the Supreme Being. If the world existed independently of God, then there would exist beside God something that is uncreated, something that is therefore just as eternal as God Himself. If such a thing exists besides God, then God is no longer the Supreme Being — no longer God. Hence whoever grants a God must grant a dependent world.

If God does not govern the world according to His will, this must be due to one of four reasons.

1. God is remote from the world — then He is not omnipresent;

2. God is near to the world but knows nothing of the world — then He is not omniscient;

3. God knows of the world but is unwilling to interfere in the course of the world — then He is morally indifferent, cares neither for right nor wrong;

4. God would like to interfere, but is unable to do so — then He is not omnipotent.

To apply the name God to a being who is not omnipresent, not omniscient, not concerned about right and wrong, not omnipotent, is to indulge in a self-contradiction. Such language is just as reasonable as to speak of a round triangle.

Furthermore, every man is born with the capacity for moral and ethical judgment and conduct. The Augsburg Confession also makes the point that natural man as opposed to the regenerate Christian has a capacity for civic righteousness. Every man is born with a conscience and with an instinctive knowledge of the Law. The Gentiles, which have not the Law, do by nature the things contained in the Law, thereby proving that the Law is written in their hearts (Rom. 2:14). Their thoughts accuse and excuse them for their conduct. This deeply ingrained characteristic of human nature makes sense only if there is a God, who takes account of our actions and metes out reward or punishment. That again implies that God rules and governs in the affairs of men; it makes sense only if God's providence is a reality.

Evidence from Nature

Evidence for the divine providence can be drawn from nature. If a person observes nature carefully, he soon learns that it maintains a marvelous balance. Plants and animals are so arranged that they serve for mutual support and supply each other's needs. Animals derive nourishment from plants and again serve to spread the seed of the plants. The species are carefully fixed — "each after its kind." Crossbreeding has developed many lateral varieties, but has never developed one species into another. Some of the latest researches reveal that such transmutation of species is physically impossible. Often the dumb creation achieves its goal far better than do the rational human beings. Astonishing co-operation exists in a beehive or in an anthill. How far behind them do men lag in achieving co-operation in national, not to mention international, affairs! How remarkable the instinct of bees and wasps, whose every action is directed toward the end of continuing the species! Now, when the dumb, unreasoning creatures act rationally, does not the fact testify mightily of a rationality behind the entire operation? Thus again common sense and careful reflection force one to the conclusion that there is a God and that God directs and controls the world He has created.

The Providence of God 81

The great miracle of life has escaped all attempts of biochemists at analysis. "The farther we advance, the greater is the mystery which faces us. If the cell reproduced itself always identically, each being would be a formless mass of flesh without differentiated organs. In order that each organ be formed in the embryo which develops in the mother's womb, the first cell or product of the fertilization must produce cells differing from one another, according to the part which they will be called upon to play in the upbuilding of the future body. If they are to make up the bones, they will be starlike in shape and secrete a fluid or cement which will solder them firmly. If they are to become blood corpuscles, they will be oval and not combine but float separately." (*The Cresset*, February, 1946, p. 21.) All of this argues mightily that there is an intelligent and rational Being, of infinite wisdom and power, which directs the actions of the cells in the body.

In short, whether we look within ourselves or without ourselves, we encounter clouds of witnesses which testify unanimously: The world does not uphold and rule itself by its own innate reason and strength; the world is maintained and ruled by One greater than the world — by God. To that extent the divine providence of God belongs to the things that may be known of God (Rom. 1:19).

Revelation Needed

However, if we were forced to depend on our reason for this truth, it would forever remain hidden from us except in barest outline. Our reason is too blind to read the record of divine providence in nature and history, even though it is written in large clear letters. To make matters worse, since the Fall reason is no longer the master of our thinking. By nature our reason lies enslaved under the total domination of the prince of darkness, "the spirit that now worketh in the children of disobedience" (Eph. 2:2). He persuades men that it is foolish to believe in divine providence. Even though glimpses of the truth force themselves into consciousness and even though men occasionally have lucid moments, yet the miserable wretches are again deceived — and that all the more inevitably because they desire to be deceived and, as St. Paul says, "hold down the truth in unrighteousness" (Rom. 1:19. R. V.). Beyond question, men would forever remain in darkness about divine providence if the Holy Spirit did not illumine their hearts and give us on the sacred pages of the Scriptures a revelation of divine providence, and then give us, in addition, believing hearts that tremble at God's Word. The divine providence remains, in the last analysis, an article of faith. To it also applies the Savior's word "Blessed are they that have not seen and yet have believed."

SCRIPTURE CLEAR

One thing is clear — the Scriptures ascribe the continued existence of the world, and all that is in the world, to God's influence and power. He upholds all things by His mighty word and keeps them from falling apart. (Heb. 1:3.) According to Psalm 104, God makes the earth fruitful and causes sun and moon to rise and set at their appointed times. "These wait all," the Psalm then continues, "upon Thee, that Thou mayest give them their meat in due season. That Thou givest them they gather; Thou openest Thine hand, they are filled with good. Thou hidest Thy face, they are troubled. Thou takest away their breath, they die, and return to their dust." (Vv. 27-29.) To the Athenian philosophers Paul declared: "He giveth to all life and breath and all things" (Acts 17:25). "In Him we live and move and have our being" (v. 28). God is the ultimate Cause of our origin and of our continued existence. Man lives not by bread alone, but by every word that proceeds out of the mouth of God (Matt. 4:4). "By Him," St. Paul writes to the Colossians, "were all things created . . . and by Him all things consist (*synesteken* = cohere, hold together), i. e., by the force He supplies, by the will He exerts, they hold together (Col. 1:16-17). That the world does not disintegrate is due to the will of God.

Scriptures indeed testify clearly that as the power of God called forth the world out of nothing, so the will of God and the power of God are the cause of its continued existence. "Were God to withdraw Himself from the world, the world would disappear without a trace. Were God to withdraw Himself from a portion of the world, that portion of the world would cease to exist." (F. Pieper, *Christliche Dogmatik*, I, p. 588.)

Nor is this activity of God in any way contradicted by the statement that "God rested on the seventh day from all His work" (Gen.

2:2). For, as Luther aptly remarks, this passage means simply that God created no new heaven and earth. "He rested from the work of creation and not from the work of preservation and governing" (St. Louis, I:91 ff. Quoted in Pieper, *Christliche Dogmatik*, p. 588).

II. THE SCOPE OF DIVINE PROVIDENCE

Divine providence extends over the entire creation. It provides for the continued existence of all individual creatures, directs their actions, and controls their destinies.

"Thou art the God of an infinite majesty." So we exclaim with the ancient *Te Deum Laudamus* as we peep into the wonders of divine providence. But our wonder and astonishment grow as we attempt to visualize in some detail the

VAST SCOPE OF DIVINE PROVIDENCE

The providence of God regulates and controls all creatures. None so great as to be independent of Him; none so small as to escape His attention. The Scriptures are very explicit on these matters. "In Him all things [not just some things] consist" (Col. 1). The eyes of all wait upon Him (Ps. 145). He is "the King of all the earth" (Ps. 47:7).

THE LIFELESS CREATION

The providence of God extends over the lifeless creation. Job declares of God: "Which removeth the mountains, and they know not [literal translation: suddenly, unexpectedly, before they are aware of it], which overturneth them in His anger; which shaketh the earth out of her place, and the pillars thereof tremble" (Job 9:5-6). He makes the "weight for the winds" [i. e., determines how gently or how furiously the wind shall blow], and He "weigheth [i. e., fixes the boundaries of] the waters" in the clouds above and on earth below (Job 28:25). He makes a decree for the rain and a way for the lightning of the thunder" (v. 26). He rules the raging of the seas (Ps. 89:10). Fire and hail, snow and vapor, stormy winds — all fulfill His word (Ps. 148:8). No man has yet explored, and no human mind has envisioned, the scope of His providence.

Unbelievers have made merry over the idea that God controls and governs the lifeless creation. In particular have they ridiculed prayers to change the course of nature — prayers for rain, for deliverance from flood, from fire and water. And yet who would control if God did not control? Eddie Rickenbacker tells how he and his companions, adrift on the Pacific, prayed for rain, saw a shower pass by a short distance away and, as they kept on praying, turn against the wind and overtake them, providing the water they needed to preserve their lives. Who would have prevented Spain from conquering England in 1588 if God had not destroyed the Spanish Armada with a frightful storm? Indeed, if God did not control the lifeless creation, then woe to the living creature! If the uranium atoms did not hold together, but split apart at will and released their incalculable energy, how completely and instantaneously would the life of men and animals be destroyed! The story of the atom bomb gives us a glimpse of the terrifying dangers that would threaten if God did not control and direct the atoms.

Plant Life

Of equal concern to God is the world of plants. "He maketh the grass to grow" (Pss. 147:9; 104:13-14). All plants must receive their nourishment — some from the soil, some from the air, some from decaying wood, some from insects. Some require special arrangements that their kind may be reproduced. Each of these plants, furthermore, has its own garb. Botanists count over 250,000 species; the individual varieties no one has attempted to count.

The Animal World

To this must now be added the entire animal world. "The eyes of all wait upon Thee; and Thou givest them their meat in due season" (Ps. 145:15). "He sendeth the springs into the valleys, which run among the hills. They give drink to every beast in the field; the wild asses quench their thirst. . . . He causeth the grass to grow for the cattle. . . . The young lions roar after their prey and seek their meat from God." In the great wide sea "are things creeping innumerable, both small and great beasts. . . . These wait all upon Thee, that Thou mayest give them their meat in due season. That Thou givest them they gather; Thou openest Thine hand, they are filled with good." (Ps. 104:10-25.) In counting up the reasons for sparing Nineveh, God included also the cattle (Jonah 4:4). Such is the concern of God for the animals that Satan and his cohorts could not enter even into the swine at Gadara without first securing the Lord's consent.

The World of Men

All this is recorded to inspire us with the confidence that God will never fail to provide for us. "Behold the fowls of the air, for they sow not, neither do they reap, nor gather into barns; yet your heavenly Father feedeth them. Are ye not much better than they? . . . Wherefore, if God so clothe the grass of the field, which today is and tomorrow is cast into the oven, shall He not much more clothe you, O ye of little faith?" (Matt. 6:26-28.) In truth, man is the prime object and chief concern of God's providence. God placed man into the focus of creation. There he stands to the present day, despite the Fall. The goodness of God does not demote the prodigal son from his primacy. Even though men have turned their backs on God in rebellion, "He maketh His sun to rise on the evil and on the good and sendeth rain on the just and on the unjust" (Matt. 5:45). Whatever their color, race, or social standing, "it is not the will of your Father which is in heaven that one of these little ones should perish" (Matt. 18:14).

The providence of God governs not only mankind in general, but directs and controls the fortune of each individual from the moment of his conception to his death. No man can be born without the will of God. David declares:

> For Thou hast formed my reins,
> Thou hast woven me in my mother's womb.
>
> My bones were not hidden from Thee
> when I was made in secret [i. e., the womb]
> (and) knit together in the depths of the earth [i. e., the womb].
>
> Thine eyes saw mine unformed substance [i. e., foetus];
> and in Thy book [i. e., omniscience] they [i. e., my days]
>   were all written,
> the days (which) were ordained
> while not one of them yet existed.
>
> (Psalm 139:13, 15-16. Translation of Emil Lund in
> *The Psalms*. Rock Island, Ill. 1908)

God's providence directs the course of each man's life. To each man God has appointed his particular task and work. For that work God equips him with all necessary gifts. Moses was ordained to lead Israel out of Egypt. Accordingly, God not only protected his life when the lives of all Jewish children were forfeit, but also caused him to be brought up at the Egyptian court, where he was able to learn the science of government. To Jeremiah the Lord declared: "Before I formed thee in the belly, I knew thee; and before thou camest forth out of the womb, I sanctified thee and ordained thee a Prophet unto the nations" (Jer. 1:5). In lives of men like Luther and Walther one can trace how God led them step by step to that work for which He had appointed them and for which He equipped them with exceptional gifts and in which they performed supreme services to the Church.

Includes Everything

The providence of God includes all that concerns men. It controls our thoughts and emotions. "The king's heart is in the hand of the Lord, as the rivers of water; He turneth it whithersoever He will" (Prov. 21:1). Thus God directed Cyrus to permit the Israelites to return to Jerusalem to rebuild the Temple (II Chron. 36:22-23; Ezra 7:27). God's providence regulates the slightest details of our lives. "The very hairs of your head are all numbered" (Luke 12:7). It governs the issues and problems of our lives. Man's time is in God's hands (Ps. 31:15). "The way of man is not in himself; it is not in man that walketh to direct his steps" (Jer. 10:23). Man's goings are of the Lord (Prov. 20:24). Psalm 139 assures us that God takes note even of such insignificant matters as our downsitting and our uprising.

God exercises His divine providence by providing the means that serve to preserve our body and life. As Luther teaches us to confess, God "provides us with all that we need to support this body and life": food, clothing, shoes, house, home, goods. He opens His hands and satisfies our desires. Sometimes He supplies the means of our sustenance in supernatural manner. During the forty years that Israel journeyed through the wilderness their clothing did not grow old nor their shoes worn. God fed them with manna and with quail, and fed them abundantly. To quench their thirst He made water gush out of the rock when Moses struck it with his staff. Ravens fed Elijah at the brook Cherith. Later on, Elijah, the widow of Zarephath, and her son lived for three years on a handful of meal and a little oil — normally not enough to provide one meal for two people. No means is so small that the power of God cannot make it do for any emergency. It makes no difference to God whether He feeds one person or a billion and a half. Usually, however, God supplies our needs by means of our own work and industry.

The providence of God, as Luther furthermore teaches us to confess, "guards and defends us against all danger and protects us from all evil." Many passages of Scriptures stress this truth. "He that dwelleth in the secret place of the Most High shall abide under the shadow of the Almighty. Surely, He shall deliver thee from the snare of the fowler and from the noisome pestilence." (Ps. 91:1, 3.) "I will lift up mine eyes unto the hills from whence cometh my help. My help cometh from the Lord, which made heaven and earth. He will not suffer thy foot to be moved [i. e. to slip, so that you fall and take hurt in dangerous duties]. He that keepeth thee will not slumber. Behold, He that keepeth Israel shall neither slumber nor sleep. . . . The Lord shall preserve thee from all evil; He shall preserve thy soul. The Lord shall preserve thy going out and thy coming in from this time forth and even forevermore." (Psalm 121.)

Divine Protection

This promise God carries out in two ways. Usually He wards off dangers, so that we are rarely even aware they threatened our safety. Just how hazardous life is, at home or abroad, we begin to realize when we stop to consider the accident statistics. Actually we do not draw a single breath in absolute safety. Still how seldom do we catch ourselves saying, That was a narrow escape! Even though accident statistics are constantly dinned into our ears, the hazards of life make next to no impression on us — so perfect is the protection of God's providence.

Sometimes God uses extraordinary measures, striking and noticeable; for want of proper consideration we call them lucky accidents. They are anything but accidents. They are God's providence in action. Thus an angel warned Joseph in a dream to take the Child Jesus to Egypt, where Herod could not take His life. Paul's nephew "happened" to overhear forty Jews swear to kill Paul, and he revealed the plot, so that the evil purpose was foiled. The Book of Esther relates how God employed apparently insignificant matters — Queen Vashti's self-respect, Esther's beauty, courage, and loyalty, Ahasuerus's insomnia — to thwart the evil schemes of Haman against the Jews. Dr. C. F. W. Walther had booked passage aboard the *Amalia* en route for the United States. Circumstances compelled him to transfer his passage to the *Johann Georg*, which sailed a few days earlier. That transfer saved his life, for the *Amalia* was never heard of again. Times without number has the promise: "He shall deliver thee in six troubles, yea, in seven there shall no evil touch thee," been fulfilled (Job 5:19).

Includes Heaven and Hell

The providence of God includes also the kingdom of woe and gnashing of teeth, inhabited by Satan and the evil spirits, who are not flesh and blood, but principalities and powers, rulers of the darkness of this world, spiritual wickedness in high places (Eph. 6:12). One clear look into the gloomy habitations of these evil spirits, revealing to us their superhuman strength, their raging fury against God, and their acid hate of mankind, making clear what all is required to control and keep them in subjections, would dispel all doubt of the omnipotent power and the gracious providence of God.

Providence and the Kingdom of Glory

Still another kingdom is under the providence of our God. It is the Kingdom of Glory. To give us a slight conception of what that kingdom is like — where there are things that eye has not seen, that ear has not heard, and that have not entered into the heart of man — Scripture strains language and imagination to the uttermost. The most precious metal is there used to pave the streets. What we call jewels are there used to erect walls. Pearls are as common as iron. This kingdom is inhabited by blessed spirits, who also direct their eyes to God and expect from Him the satisfaction of all their wants. That requires an abundance which we cannot visualize. Here we receive joy bit by bit; there joy comes in streams.

Here our delight never lasts a day without interruption. There is fullness of joy and pleasures forevermore. What miracles of God's providence! If for a single moment we could sojourn in this kingdom, our worries and fear would end at one stroke.

PROVIDENCE AND MINUTE CREATURES

A curious phenomenon occurs when we consider these matters. That God should be at pains to direct great and important matters we readily concede. But that God, with equal attention, directs small and insignificant matters appears unreasonable and ridiculous. There our faith stumbles. An important executive concerns himself with policies and fundamental plans; the details he entrusts to subordinates. Similarly, we think it plausible that God should be concerned to preserve the different species of animals, birds, and plants. But that God should determine the fortunes of individual storks, swallows, and sparrows, that He should bother to note the exact number of rabbits, gnats, and fleas living upon earth at a given moment and where each is — like the heathen philosopher Pliny and the old Church Father Hieronymus (Jerome), we are apt to consider that beneath the dignity of God and a blemish upon His majesty.

In war and great calamities men recognize the hand of God; but that a slight mishap should also be under the direction and control of God seems foolish. We readily praise the providence of God which preserved the garments of Israel fresh and strong during the forty years of journey in the wilderness, but incline to consider it a ridiculing of divine majesty to say that God is concerned also with the rents in a beggar's coat. That God should have special care of great men like Martin Luther or Doctor Walther appears sensible, but not that a man as insignificant as one of us should get similar care. How often has such a spirit caused us to forget to thank Him for small gifts and favors!

All such thoughts, however, contradict many clear and strong words of Holy Writ. Christ assures us: "The very hairs of your head are all numbered" (Luke 12:7). Sparrows were cheap enough in the days of Christ: five for two farthings. Still "not one is forgotten in the sight of God" (Luke 12:6). As the sun does not disdain to shine upon a worm, so the providence of God does not scorn to provide for it.

A little consideration will reveal that what seems ridiculous and unreasonable at first glance is perfectly logical and inevitable.

1. If God is honored by creating little things — gnats, sparrows, worms — He is honored also by preserving them. If He took the pains to create swallows and rabbits, why should He decline to concern Himself with preserving them?

2. Before God nothing is small, nothing is great. To distinguish between small and great, honorable and dishonorable, important and unimportant, when considering creation from the point of view of God, is to think of God in the way we think of men.

3. God is present everywhere, and that entirely. Since God cannot be divided, He is altogether present within and without each creature — the smallest leaf or insect and the greatest forest or animal. How, then, can the preservation of the least be of less concern to Him than that of the greatest?

4. It is a great error to think that the energy or the strength of God is in any way reduced by preserving hosts of creatures. St. Augustine says: "God knows how to be at rest in activity and to be active in resting." Finite mind and finite strength are exhausted by trifles. The infinite mind and power find activity no drain upon their strength or resources. To illustrate: The sun is no more weakened by shining upon a molehill than upon a mountain.

5. If God did not control small things, He could not uphold and direct the large matters, for large matters always consist of a great number of details. How would the garments of Israel have lasted if God had not cared for the individual threads? How would He maintain the race of sparrows if he did not consider the individual birds? How could He direct the course of wars if He had no control over the individual bullet? How govern a pestilence or an epidemic if the germs that cause the disease were beyond His control or outside His interest?

6. Nor can we say that small things are of no import. They can have the most important consequences. All the world is atremble today because man has unleashed the power of the atom — an object so small that only a trained scientist can form a concept of it. To date the only method suggested for controlling this atom is a world government stronger than any combination of governments,

Such considerations help us realize that God's care for minute creatures affords striking instances of His majesty and power. But even though it is illogical to deny God's providence in small matters, rational arguments will never persuade anyone to believe. As the Psalmist says: "Such knowledge is too wonderful for me; it is high, I cannot attain unto it" (Ps. 139:6). To the providence of God also are applicable the words of St. Paul: "Oh, the depth of the riches both of the wisdom and knowledge of God! How unsearchable are His judgments and His ways past finding out! For of Him and through Him and to Him are all things." (Rom. 11:33-35.) Only the man who knows the boundless grace and goodness of God, which provided salvation in the Beloved, and who has become a child of God, also in this matter will become as a little child and recognize the fact that Love, which finds no sacrifice too great, finds no trifle too small.

III. THE PRINCIPLE OF DIVINE PROVIDENCE

Divine providence normally expresses itself in definite laws.

Although a King of infinite majesty, God does not exercise His divine providence by caprice and catastrophe. God is not constantly changing His mind as to what He wants the world to achieve. Nor does He consider it essential to His majesty and glory constantly to be issuing new directions in order to see His subjects skip to His pleasure. Neither does He ordinarily resort to catastrophe to execute His will. Once indeed He interrupted the even tenor of His government and swept the earth clean of all inhabitants except those carried to safety in the Ark of Noah. Ever since, however, all has been law. After the Flood, God covenanted with Noah on behalf of the human race: "While the earth remaineth, seedtime and harvest, and cold and heat, and summer and winter, and day and night shall not cease" (Gen. 8:22). Even catastrophes like tidal waves, volcanic eruptions, and earthquakes, eclipses, and other unusual phenomena of nature obey and follow definite laws of cause and effect. Father Lynch, world-famous seismologist of Fordham University, New York, asked how he could find satisfaction in studying every great and small vibration that happens in the earth, answered: "The laws of nature are written deep in the folds and faults of the earth. By encouraging men to learn those laws one can lead them further to a knowledge of the Author of all laws." (*Life*, April 15, 1946, p. 66.) "By Him all things consist" (Col. 1:17).

The Scriptures report: "In the beginning God created the heaven and the earth." In and by that act of creation, God established the laws of nature, which have remained in force ever since. He commanded, "Let there be light!" — and into operation went the laws of optics. He separated light from darkness and made the first day — then were fixed the laws of time. God made the firmament and divided the waters above the firmament from those below it — that act established the law of gravity. He separated the water from the dry land, establishing the laws of chemistry, of physics, and of geology. The heavenly bodies appeared, and with them went into operation the laws of astronomy. Fish, fowl, and beasts were made and received their special law — to reproduce each after its kind. Modern scientific study has revealed the fact that no cell has ever deviated one iota from that law. "Research has developed the fact that the chemistry of the tissues of every species has definite differences. The hemoglobin of each species has its own crystalline form; each has its own fat molecule; proteins are specific for each; and the carbohydrate metabolism varies greatly. . . . In the Vitamin G investigations a separate G molecule has been identified for each species so far studied, and of the eight forms of Vitamin D so far known, each species has its most effective and least toxic one." (*The Cresset*, February, 1946, p. 23.) "Each after his kind," so far all scientific research points to the immutability of that law.

Finally, God fashioned the crown of His creation — man. By that act He established the laws of psychology, which by reason of sin are now chiefly identifiable through the study of abnormal psychology. At the side of man He placed an help meet for him, and thereby established the laws of ideal family relationship and of an ideal commonwealth.

These ordinances of creation are not the sort of statutes we think of when we speak of laws — regulations enforced upon unwilling subjects. They represent the inner urges and drives which God implanted in His creatures, so that all creation expresses in its activity its innermost urge and its most essential nature. The stars run their courses uninfluenced by the turmoil of the world of men; the sun shines and warms the earth, making it fruitful; trees put forth their leaves and blossom and bear fruit. All nature operates according to its innermost character — the heavens proclaiming the glory of God and the earth showing His handiwork.

That is, all except men. Only men, whom God left free to exercise the choice of obedience, elected to rebel. Their rebellion would speedily have returned them to dust had not God immediately established two additional laws: (1) The law of obedience and subjection — wife to husband, children to parents, subjects to their rulers; and (2) the most important of all laws — the law of grace, according to which God for Christ's sake does not impute trespasses, but forgives all sins and sets men free from the evil consequences of their sins.

ALL'S LOVE, AND ALL'S LAW

All this establishing of laws proclaims the benignity of divine providence. How wretched our life if the laws of nature were as changeable as the theories of scientists! Suppose the stars and the sun had for fifty-five hundred years run their course according to the system of Ptolemy and had then suddenly switched over to that of Copernicus? Would the world have survived? If the first cell, or the product of fertilization in the womb of the mother, were to reproduce itself identically, what a shapeless mass of flesh would result — a being without differentiated organs! (*The Cresset,* February, 1946, p. 21.) What a terrible mess this world would have been if the laws of reproduction had actually changed every time the Darwinian theory was modified! As Paul said to the men in Lystra, God "left not Himself without witness, in that He did good and gave rain from heaven and fruitful seasons, filling our hearts with food and gladness" (Acts 14:17).

Happily the laws of creation stand fast and immovable. "All's love, and all's law." Human theories and formulations come and go; the laws remain. In and by these laws of creation God expresses His divine providence.

IV. THE MODE OF DIVINE PROVIDENCE

Divine providence is ordinarily exercised through secondary causes, which, however, are operative only so long as God works through them.

This divine providence is exercised through certain means which theologians call secondary causes to distinguish them from God, who is the prime Cause. "Thou visitest the earth and waterest it;

Thou greatly enrichest it with the river of God, which is full of water. Thou preparest them corn when Thou hast so provided for it. Thou waterest the ridges thereof abundantly; Thou settlest the furrows thereof; Thou makest it soft with showers; Thou blessest the springing thereof. Thou crownest the year with Thy goodness, and Thy paths drop fatness." (Ps. 65:9-11.) According to these words, God is operative. In Isaiah we read: "For as the rain cometh down, and the snow, from heaven, and returneth not thither, but watereth the earth and maketh it bring forth and bud that it may give seed to the sower and bread to the eater, etc." (Is. 55:10). According to these words, the means are operative. Thus Scriptures clearly testify that both are operative — God and the means. The Lord builds the house, and the laborers build it (Ps. 127:1). Both views must be held.

The means or secondary causes, however, are not co-ordinate with God. They depend on the operation of God to such an extent that the moment God ceases to operate through them they lose all efficacy. For "except the Lord build the house, they labor in vain that build it" (Ps. 127:1). "We may indeed speak of a natural character, movement, power, and effect of the creatures. But what is natural to the creatures — that the worm crawls, man walks erect, the sun shines, a tree grows and bears fruit according to its kind, that medicine cures, bread nourishes, a watchman protects, etc. — is God's influence upon the creatures (Pieper, *Christliche Dogmatik*, I, p. 592). As Gerhard points out, it is natural for a man to move; yet we move and have our being in God (Acts 17:28). It is natural for the sun to rise; yet "He maketh His sun to rise" (Matt. 5:45). We must be careful not to separate the working of God from the working of the means, as if there were two separate workings and not one working. The result is not to be attributed one half or three fourths to God and one half or one fourth to the creature. One and the same action is ascribed entirely to God and entirely to the creature: "Thou preparest the corn" (Ps. 65:9), and the earth gives "seed to the sower and bread to the eater" (Is. 55:10). Nor are these actions to be thought of as separated in time. God does not first act upon the creature and put into it a certain power which the creature subsequently exerts by its own strength — like a storage battery, which is first charged and subsequently gives off the charge independently of the activity of the source of the stored electricity.

Co-operation a Mystery

The manner in which this activity takes place, how God and the secondary causes operate together and still remain distinct, is a deep mystery. "The same God which worketh all in all" (I Cor. 12:6) seems to indicate that somehow God with His power courses through the secondary causes whereby they become operative. Two examples may prove serviceable: 1. The induction coil in which the iron is magnetic only when an electric current passes through it; 2. Writing, which is not carried on one half by the human hand and one half by the pen, but entirely by the hand and entirely by the pen. Still no analogy will clarify this matter. It belongs to the deep things of God, which only the Spirit of God can search out.

Though incomprehensible, this truth has a practical value for life and faith. The conviction that the operation of God and the operation of the means must not be separated teaches us to pray with Job: "Thine hands have made me and fashioned me together round about," and to confess with our Small Catechism: "I believe that God has made me (not only Adam, but me) and all creatures, that He has given me my body and soul, eyes, ears, and all my members, my reason and all my senses, and still preserves them." "Though from our parents as from secondary causes we receive our souls and also our bodies with all their parts, yet we know at the same time that God is our Creator and our Father" (Pieper, *Christliche Dogmatik*, I, p. 594).

This concept will also shield us from the deistic error that, after making the world and charging it with powers that enable it to carry on, God subsequently withdrew Himself from the world and now allows it to run out its course without interference. It guards also against the pantheistic error that since God is operative in His creature, the creature is God, and God is responsible also for the evil that exists in the world. It disposes of the vexing question — sophistical rather than profound — Is God bound to the laws of nature? The answer is simple: The laws of nature are God's will as to the manner in which He chooses to operate in and through His creatures. Thus the question really amounts to asking: Is God bound by His own will? Answer: So long as He chooses and no longer. Can God change the laws of nature? That is the same thing as asking, Can God change the manner in which He operates in and through His creatures? Self-evidently if He so decides.

Far from invalidating prayer, the Scriptural teaching of the divine providence shows us the importance of prayer. We direct our petitions to the supreme Master of the universe, who is the Source of all the good and the blessings that come to us by the operation of the secondary cause — who makes food nourishing, medicine healing, and is, in fact, the Source and Fountain of every blessing.

V. DIVINE PROVIDENCE AND HUMAN FREEDOM

Divine providence deprives men neither of their liberty nor of their responsibility; it neither reduces men to automata nor makes God responsible for sin.

Among the secondary causes which God employs to govern the world are also men — good men and evil men. The proud king of Assyria is an ax in the hand of the Most High (Is. 10:12-15). King Herod becomes the agent by whom God fulfills His prophecy regarding Jesus "Out of Egypt have I called my Son" (Matt. 2:15). When Jezebel persecuted the prophets of the Lord, pious Obadiah became the agent by whom the Lord saved the lives of a hundred prophets (I Kings 18:4). Ebed-melech, the Ethiopian, was the instrument of God by whom the Prophet Jeremiah was rescued from the miry dungeon (Jer. 38:4-13).

Men become the causes through which God works. Balaam may accept the bribe of Balak to curse Israel, but as Balaam later explained to Balak: "Have I now any power at all to say anything? The word that God putteth in my mouth, that shall I speak." "If Balak would give me his house full of silver and gold, I cannot go beyond the commandment of the Lord to do either good or bad of mine own mind; but what the Lord saith, that will I speak." (Num. 22:38; 24:13.)

These facts give rise to the following question: Can one under such circumstances still speak of human freedom of action and of human responsibility? If God controls the thoughts and acts of men, can men still be held accountable for their actions? Does not God, at least in part, become responsible for their wickedness?

In approaching this question let us note at the outset that Scripture very definitely and unequivocally teaches that each man is fully accountable and fully responsible for his own acts. Acts 17:31

declares that God will judge the world in righteousness. Beyond question, righteous judgment presupposes responsibility for actions. To hold a man accountable when he is not responsible is unrighteous judgment. Hence the passage indicates that God considers men responsible beings. The same thought lies at the bottom of the prayer: "Enter not into judgment with Thy servant, for in Thy sight shall no man living be justified" (Psalm 143:2). Man's responsibility for his acts appears also from the activity of his conscience — "their thoughts the meanwhile accusing or else excusing one another" (Rom. 2:15). The actions of conscience show that sinners know the "judgment of God, that they which practice such things are worthy of death" (Rom. 1:32).

Complete Answer Not Given

The complete answer to the question how men remain responsible when divine providence directs and controls everything has not been revealed in the Bible. It is therefore impossible to resolve all the apparent contradictions. Here we touch upon mysteries the knowledge of which God has reserved for Himself. We shall not know until we see Him face to face. Now it is for us to believe, or, as Luther once put it, take off our hats and say: The Holy Spirit is wiser than I.

Some hints God has, however, given us. Scripture reveals that God does not, except on rare occasions, deal with men by sheer omnipotence. His usual method is to set before men a choice between good and evil and then to stimulate the choice of good. In the last analysis, God leaves men free to choose, so that men may experience joy in serving God by freely doing the will of God. Thus God dealt with Adam in Paradise.

Although Adam fell into sin, lost his ability to choose in spiritual matters, and passed this spiritual death on to his descendants, God still preserved in men the ability to choose in matters of civic righteousness. He preserved in them the ability to choose between stealing and not stealing, murdering and not murdering, getting drunk and staying sober (Alcoholics Anonymous rescues drunkards by mobilizing the mental and emotional resources of drunkards, without recourse to religion, although they agree that religion helps).

God preserved in men also the ability to recognize some truths about God — that He is righteous and demands righteousness from men; that He is almighty and demands obedience; that He is wise and demands homage; that He is God and expects our love. (Rom. 1:20; Acts 16:17.) The invisible things of God are clearly seen from the creation of the world. "The heavens declare the glory of God, and the firmament showeth His handiwork. . . . There is no speech nor language where their voice is not heard." (Psalm 19:1.) God gave to all men the ability to understand these things and constantly prompts men to grasp them.

Freedom Abused

But how do men exercise this choice? What have they done with their freedom? St. Paul tells us that "when they knew God, they glorified Him not as God" (Rom. 1:21). Instead, they hold down the truth; they suppress the truth by their unrighteousness, by their wickedness (Rom. 1:19). They "do not obey the truth, but obey unrighteousness," or as Goodspeed's translation expresses the thought, they "are disloyal to the truth and responsible only to what is wrong" (Rom. 2:8). "They refused to have God in their knowledge" (Rom. 1:28, R. V.). As Dr. Stoeckhardt remarks in his *Commentary on Romans* (p. 56), "they have become vain and futile in their thoughts by directing their thoughts toward vain, futile, and transitory things. By their thinking and reflecting they have immersed themselves and lost themselves in created things; and separated from God, the true Reality, all creation is vain." They did not consider God of sufficient importance to give Him that place in their life and thought which is due His majesty and worth. In fact, they tried to rule Him out of their thought and to rob Him of all influence. "Men closed their hearts and inmost selves against the light which streamed in upon them, refusing to let it exercise any influence upon their ethical thinking, feeling, and willing; thus their irrational hearts became darkened. Such blinding is an intensification of natural ignorance and blindness (Eph. 4:18). Rays of light fell into their hearts from the creation; they know some things about God and cannot escape this knowledge. But this light and knowledge does not in the least influence their ethical personality, the movement of their thoughts, the direction of their

The Providence of God

wills, for they constantly thwart such influence." (Stoeckhardt, *Romans*, p. 56.) Deliberately they follow their base passions and take especial delight in those who commit the old sin in a new way.

Balak is an example of how the heathen kept the truth in subjection to their wickedness. He knew of Israel's might; he knew it took more than human power to withstand Israel. Hence he hired Balaam to curse Israel. But when Balaam, instead of cursing, found himself compelled to bless and explained this fact to Balak, Balak left in anger, willfully resisting the truth to which his conscience testified.

The fact is that men steadily abuse the freedom God preserved to them after the Fall. Hence they are, as the Apostle says, "without excuse" (Rom. 1:20). They remain responsible for their actions.

Of course, this explanation does not answer fully the question how it is possible for man's activity to be entirely dependent on God for its energy and yet proceed against the will of God. We know only this: God is such a Master that He can work in His creatures without destroying the individualities which He has given them.

God and Sin

Closely related to the question just discussed is the following question: Does the fact that God overrules all human actions in any way make God in the last analysis the Cause of sin? If at creation God gave man the ability to rebel against the will of God, and if man then actually used this ability to rebel and as a result fell into sin, and if God still continues to uphold man in sin and even works in man while he sins, does not God thereby make Himself a participator in the sins of men? A thief cannot even desire another man's property, let alone scheme how to get it and actually take possession of it, if God did not keep the thief's eyes, mind, and hands operative and supply them with the power to act. Now, if God knows that His co-operation will be abused for sinful purposes, does He not become stained with sin and thus lose His attribute of holiness? That is the problem.

Again the complete answer is not available. Some things, however, have been revealed.

1. God does not want sin, but with all His holy nature is opposed to sin. To the wicked He says: "Thou thoughtest that I was alto-

gether such an one as thyself, but I will reprove thee" (Ps. 50:21). Against sin God gave His Decalog, which threatens punishment upon sin and promises reward to righteousness.

2. God often thwarts the evil intentions of others. Thus He kept Abimelech from debauching Abraham's wife Sarah (Gen. 20:1 ff.). He caused the evil plan of the Jews to assassinate Paul to become known and thus made its execution impossible (Acts 23:12 ff.). He turned Balaam's proposed curse into blessing (Num. 23:8-12).

3. God makes a sin which has actually been committed to serve a good end — as in the sale of Joseph (Gen. 50:20).

4. God sometimes permits sin as a punishment for sin. Paul declares that since men "changed the glory of the uncorruptible God into an image made like to corruptible man, and to birds, and fourfooted beasts, and creeping things" ... God also gave them up to uncleanness through the lusts of their own hearts" (Rom. 1:23-24). The unspeakable wickedness and depravity of the heathen world was God's judgment upon, and punishment for, their iniquity, in particular for their idolatry, which debased God.

5. Satan is operative in men. He works "in the children of disobedience" (Eph. 2:2). The corrupted nature of man has opened the way for satanic direction, which perverts the God-given energy and has closed the way for divine direction to what is good. Carnal mind is enmity against God. Man's will is completely under Satan's control. Thus there is in men a power of will and an emotional urge which constantly directs into evil channels the energy that God furnishes through the food we eat, the air we breathe, and the operation of the glands that pour hormones into the blood stream. When Balak asked Balaam to curse Israel, God gave Balaam the power to weigh and to decide. The slanting of the decision was Balaam's contribution. Pilate was entirely correct when he said to Jesus, "I have power to crucify Thee and to release Thee." God gave him the energy to weigh the evidence and to pronounce the judgment. But the bias and the direction which the sentence took arose not from God, but from Pilate's eagerness to content the Jews and his fear of being thought an enemy of Caesar.

6. The fact must, however, not be overlooked that God is operative in men and acts through and in men also when their deeds are

evil. II Samuel 24:1 we read: "And again the anger of the Lord was kindled against Israel, and He moved David against them to say, Go number Israel and Judah." Similarly David, speaking of Saul's enmity to himself, said: "If the Lord have stirred thee up against me" (I Sam. 26:19), thus indicating that God might have been the Author of Saul's hate. When Shimei cursed David and one of David's servants offered to kill Shimei, David answered: "So let him curse because the Lord hath said unto him, Curse David" (II Sam. 16:10).

Statements like these declare clearly that God has a hand also in the sinful acts of men. How shall we picture this to ourselves?

God's and Men's Acts

Certainly the influence which God exerts in a good and pious act differs from the nature of the influence which He exerts in an evil act. In good acts God makes both to will and to do, supplies both the energy and the direction and purpose of the act. There the entire credit is His alone. From Him proceed "all holy desires, all good counsels, and all just works." (Cf. Ps. 115:1.)

It is different with sin. Sin does not originate with God, but with Satan, who seduces men into "misbelief, despair, and other great shame and vice." Furthermore God is ready with His grace to effect repentance for sin in every man. If a man refuses to repent, however, and chooses to remain in his sins, then he loses also the ability to decide the particular forms which his sins will assume — that evil lust ends in rape or adultery or some other sex crime; that greed ends in robbery or embezzlement or in fraud; that hate results in slander or in murder; that disobedience to parents grows into crime and ends on the gallows. Once a man has yielded to Satan and has determined upon wickedness, then God takes his wickedness and directs it in such course that the wickedness is made to serve God's plan of world government, God's honor, and at times the welfare of the sinner himself, whose death God at no times desires, preferring that he repent and live. Once evil lust springs up in a man and, instead of combating this evil lust, he coddles it and takes delight in it, the form into which the evil lust develops, the actual sin which it brings forth, no longer depends on the man's discretion, but comes under divine providence. Thus Satan filled David's heart with pride and ambition, and David took delight in this pride so that he overruled all attempts to dissuade him from his undertaking (I Chron. 21:1). But that this pride was directed toward taking a census was divine direction. God made it subservient to the purpose of His divine providence, which found that Israel needed punishment at the time (II Sam. 24:1). The evil lust which led to David's adultery was the product of Satan and David. Instead of putting this evil lust out of his heart and abhorring it — as, for example, Joseph did — David fostered it. That was David's share. But that his eye fell just upon Bathsheba, perhaps the only woman in Israel whose husband would refuse to be compliant, so that David's sin became public — that was the providence of God, seeking to bring David to repentance, and to teach him, and through him all men, to pray: "Thou desirest truth in the inward parts." (II Samuel 11.)

What God supplies when men commit sin is only the capability of action — that they think, that they see, lift their hands, discharge a revolver. God does not work along in determining the direction the act takes — that they think blasphemy, look at indecent pictures, aim the revolver at an enemy. Theologians call the former the *materiale* of action; the latter, the *formale*. God supplies the *materiale*, which in itself is neither good nor evil; men supply the *formale*, which gives character to the activity.

Complete Explanation Not Possible

Of course, we understand that these distinctions and explanations do not satisfy our reason and answer all questions. But farther we cannot go. They set the limits within which we must confine our thinking. Any attempt to go farther will result in a denial of one of the following Scripture teachings: (1) God co-operates in all acts. We dare not deny that, for Acts 17:28 declares of all men, including thieves and murderers, etc., that in God "we live and move and have our being." (2) God does not tempt anyone to evil, but every man is tempted when he is drawn away of his own lust and enticed (James 1:13-14). (3) Not God, but man perverts the God-given power to act to evil ends. "Unto the wicked God saith . . . *thou* givest thy mouth to evil, and thy tongue frameth deceit. *Thou* sittest and speakest against thy brother; *thou* slan-

The Providence of God

derest thine own mother's son. These things hast *thou* done." (Ps. 50:16-21.)

Nor will the fact that we are unable to answer all the questions that arise in this connection disturb us unduly so long as we remain properly humble and remember that our finite minds are here attempting the impossible — to grasp the infinite God. It is like trying to live in a fourth-dimension world. Instead of caviling let us learn to keep silence and to adore the depth of the riches of the wisdom and knowledge of God, and accept with gratitude such explanation as God has granted. After all, it is love and grace that God has offered us some explanation. He could rightfully have retorted: "Yours not to reason why." "Where wast thou when I laid the foundations of the earth? Declare if thou hast understanding." (Job 38:4.)

> Hold, then, the good, define it well,
> For fear divine Philosophy
> Should push beyond her mark and be
> Procuress to the Lords of Hell.
>
> Alfred, Lord Tennyson, *In Memoriam*, LIII

Nor should the fact that God is operative in men when they sin disturb us in our adoration of God. It in no way smirches God's holiness. An analogy may help. When the sun's rays fall on a manure pile, they speed up the process of fermentation and decay and make the pile more offensive than it was. Yet this fact does not corrupt the warmth of the sun. It remains pure. If the warmth of the manure pile is passed through glass, which keeps out the offensive odor, the warmth will be just as pleasant and genial as that of the sun direct. So God's power does not become impure because through wicked men it produces evil.

Finally, this teaching is not without profit for instruction in righteousness. What an earnest exhortation to root out of our hearts all hypocrisy and all tenderness toward sin! All men are inclined to toy with sin, flattering themselves that they are able to take care of themselves, that they know how far to go and when to stop. But if we realize that once we indulge sin in our imagination — something that is just as surely sin as an actual sinful act — we may be swept into great sins and vices, affecting not only our own life but that of untold human beings in time and eternity, we shall learn to pray with greater ardor: "Create in me a clean heart, O God, and renew a right spirit within me," and having prayed thus, to flee temptation and with God's help work at filling our hearts with holy desires and pure thoughts.

No Fatalism

Another question that will not down: Is the course of events immutably fixed? Must things happen as they do, so that no variation is possible? Will things turn out as they are destined to turn out, irrespective of what we do? In short, does the doctrine of divine providence make fatalism the only logical philosophy of life?

The Scriptures, as Dr. Pieper ably sets forth in his *Christliche Dogmatik* (I, p. 598), teach us to hold both the immutable fixation of all things and man's responsibility. All depends on the point of view. When we consider how things happen from the point of view of divine majesty, we must say that they are all immutably fixed. Thus Scripture tells us: "For of a truth against Thy Holy Child Jesus, whom Thou hast anointed, both Herod and Pontius Pilate, with the Gentiles and the people of Israel, were gathered together, for to do whatsoever Thy hand and Thy counsel determined before to be done" (Acts 4:27-28). From the point of view of God it was all predetermined. Christ permitted Himself to be taken captive so that the Scripture might be fulfilled (Matt. 26:54). In Him we see how God lives up to His own prophecies and recognizes them as immutable. That is the divine point of view.

From the human point of view, however, we must, according to the Scriptures, recognize that things happen contingently, that events can be modified and depend on circumstances and upon decisions that we make, for which decisions we are responsible. Thus Christ dealt with both Judas and Pilate for the express purpose of swerving them from their evil intentions. And His words made such an impression on Pilate that "from thenceforth Pilate sought to release Him" (John 19:12). Accordingly Christ instructs His disciples, when persecution comes, not to attempt to view the outcome from the point of view of divine providence and to deliver themselves over to their persecutors as Christ did, but to flee into another city (Matt. 10:23). When the hostile Jews sought Paul's life in Damascus, he had himself let down the walls in a basket by night (Acts 9:25). In fact, whenever the enemies threatened Paul, it was his standard practice to exhaust all measures to keep himself out of their hands, including appeals to his Roman citizenship and an appeal to the judgment seat of Caesar.

Hence our principle must be to protect our lives with such means as God puts at our disposal. In sickness we employ a physician and take medicine. To secure food and clothing for ourselves and our families, we engage in daily occupation. To obtain salvation, we employ the means of grace. Doing that, we shall find out what God has decreed. Any attempt to search out divine providence apart from the means which God has ordained is folly and wicked presumption. Thereby we try to pry into the mysteries which God has wisely hid from our knowledge.

The End of Life

This is particularly important for the end of life. Scriptures teach, on the one hand, that the end of each man's life is immutably fixed. "His days are determined, the number of his months are with Thee, Thou hast appointed his bounds that he cannot pass" (Job 14:5). Not even a sparrow falls without the will of the Father in heaven; how much less shall men die without God's willing it? On the other hand, Scripture teaches with equal emphasis that human life may be lengthened. When Hezekiah prayed, the Lord extended his life by fifteen years (Is. 38:1-5). And Psalm 55:23 declares that "bloody and deceitful men shall not live out half their days." The former is stated from the point of view of God; the latter from that of man. (Pieper, *Christliche Dogmatik*, I, pp. 598—599.)

It is gracious condescension that God speaks to us concerning the hour of death from the human point of view and directs us to those means which He has ordained for the preservation of life. Few could live courageously if they knew the day of their death. Few would undertake new projects if they knew in advance that they could not complete them. Few men can say as did St. Paul, when heading for Jerusalem and knowing that bonds and affliction awaited him there: "None of these things move me . . . so that I might finish . . . the ministry . . . to testify the Gospel of the grace of God" (Acts 20:24). Men live by hope. It shows the goodness of God that He speaks to us in language which permits hope to spring up in our breast.

VI. THE GOALS OF DIVINE PROVIDENCE

The ultimate goals of divine providence are (1) the temporal and eternal welfare of man, particularly the salvation of the elect; (2) the spreading of the Gospel; (3) the promotion of the glory of God.

At creation God said: "Have dominion over the fish of the sea and over the fowl of the air and over every living thing. . . . I have given you every herb, bearing seed . . . and every tree in the which there is the fruit of a tree yielding seed." (Gen. 1:26-29.) After the Flood God declared: "While the earth remaineth, seedtime and harvest, and cold and heat, and summer and winter, and day and night shall not cease. . . . Every moving thing that liveth shall be meat for you; even as the green herb have I given you all things." (Gen. 8:22; 9:3.) St. Paul declares: He "gave us rain from heaven and fruitful seasons, filling our hearts with food and gladness" (Acts 14:17).

This earth, with all its beauty, wealth, and resources, was called into being and is steadily maintained by God for the benefit of men, to whom He gave dominion over all creatures.

The Scriptures tell us, furthermore, that all God's blessings, and all God's dealings with men, have one purpose — the conversion of men. God has appointed to all nations their times and the bounds of their habitation (Acts 17:26). He has determined where they shall dwell and how long they shall flourish and when their influence shall wane. And all this "that they should seek the Lord, if haply they might feel after Him and find Him" (Acts 17:27). Not soil, climate, and nationality determine the boundaries of nations, but God's plan for His kingdom and the conversion of men, which are the prime factors in the history of the world. The throne of God is exalted above the thrones of kings and potentates.

God chose Israel to be His own peculiar people in order to publish His name among the heathen. As Israel came into contact with different peoples on the journey to the Promised Land, they learned that in Israel was a God mightier than their idols, a God before whom their idols were helpless. That was definitely understood. The victories of Israel were ascribed to the power of Jehovah. Hence Balak was eager to have Israel cursed. When the statue of Dagon, the idol of the Philistines, fell from its base and was broken because the Ark of the Covenant had been installed in the heathen temple, the Philistines eagerly returned the Ark to Israel.

When the friends of Haman learned that his bitter enemy Mordecai was a Jew, they told Haman: "If Mordecai be of the seed of the Jews . . . thou shalt not prevail against him, but shalt surely fall before him" (Esther 6:13). And when the Jews received permission to defend themselves, "the fear of the Jews fell upon" the people (Esther 8:17). Every contact the heathen made with Israel brought home to them the realization: There is a God in Israel.

Israel was scattered among the nations before the birth of Christ, so that the good news of Christ could be more readily brought to all lands and that the first missionaries could find centers where to proclaim the Gospel and where congregations could be formed. Invariably Paul began his preaching in one of the synagogs of the Jews and made his first contacts and converts there. But when Israel rejected the Gospel, God so arranged matters that "through their fall salvation is come unto the Gentiles" (Rom. 11:11).

God and World History

If we consider the history of the world in the light of God's Word, we get glimpses of the workshop of the Almighty and are able faintly to trace the pattern of the providence of God. Alexander the Great conquered the world, a tool in the hand of God, to bring the world a common language — Greek — so that the Gospel could at once be read the world over. The history of England split off from the history of the European Continent in order that the concept of individual liberty under law, which was to be planted in the New World, might develop. God permitted England to gain control of North America in order to make North America a place where the Gospel could escape oppression by the Roman Catholic Church. God permitted the United States to break away from the British Empire in order to establish before all the world the fact that a nation dedicated to the principle of religious liberty — the only atmosphere in which Christianity can flourish without being oppressed by state regulations and persecutions — can become powerful and strong. Thus He provided a place where the Lutheran Church was able to develop according to its innermost genius without outside interference. Furthermore, until that genius was fully developed into a visible Church, the Missouri Synod remained primarily a German-speaking organization, whereby it was in large measure insulated from the sectarian influences round about. When this development had been completed, God used the First World War to force Missouri to turn English, so that the glorious Gospel could be brought to others. And God permitted Canada to remain in the British Empire in order to establish a closer contact between the British Empire and the United States, so that these two countries could stand shoulder to shoulder and become the agency that would prove responsible for the spread of religious liberty in other parts of the world, especially during the trying days of the present, when religious freedom is restricted in most quarters — something that always results in the persecution and oppression of the Gospel of salvation by grace alone through faith in Christ.

The history of the world is regulated in the interest of the Gospel. One people is brought into subjection to another in order to bring them under the gentle yoke of the Gospel — the colonies of England, the slaves in the United States. God makes a people famous — Israel under Solomon, when the Temple at Jerusalem was the most beautiful house of worship in all the world — in order to induce other people to inquire about its God, for example, the Queen of Sheba. The victory of the Second World War and the great discoveries of this war, especially the discovery of the atom bomb, were reserved to the Western World, which is also the center of Christianity, in order to draw attention to the salvation in Christ.

Of course, it is not possible to trace out exactly how and when God provides each people with opportunity to know the true God. It is not possible to construct a complete blueprint of God's operations. After all, as the Lord said to Job out of the whirlwind:

> Where wast thou when I laid the foundations of the earth? . . .
> Hast thou commanded the morning since thy days began
> And caused the dayspring to know its place? . . .
> Knowest Thou the ordinances of the heavens?
> Canst Thou establish the dominion thereof in the earth?
> (Chap. 38:4, 12, 13. R. V.)

But our ignorance of all the facts dare not become the occasion of denying what is clearly taught. Of one thing we can rest assured: When at last all things are revealed, we shall say from knowledge what we now say by faith: "The ways of the Lord are true and righteous altogether."

Preservation of Faith

A further purpose of divine providence is to preserve in faith those whom God has converted. Says St. Paul: "All things work together for good to them that love God, to them who are the called according to His purpose" (Rom. 8:28). Cp. I Cor. 10:13; Jer. 29:11.

Whatever happens to us Christians, these promises, and the many other promises that God will guard and protect us against all evil, assure us that God will so guide and direct all things that they must contribute to our salvation. His goodness and mercy, His abundant blessings, the happy coincidences of our life should serve as a constant reminder that God is good and that above all else He desires our happiness and welfare. They should teach us to recognize God as the Author of every true and perfect gift.

This is true also if the things that happen are painful and bring tears to our eyes and raise murmuring in our hearts. The purpose of all such divine dealings is to wean us away from this world, with its lusts of the flesh, lusts of the eye, and its pride of life, and to draw us closer to our God. Cp. Heb. 12:5-11.

The fact that Christians are called upon to bear crosses, heavy, severe crosses, does not mean that God has become their enemy, even though Satan likes to persuade them to that effect. It means that God has special use for them, sees in them special values, and that He goes to great lengths and takes unusual pains with them to present them to Himself without blemish or spot. Paul was sorely stricken at his conversion. After he saw the vision and heard the dread voice: "Saul, Saul, why persecutest thou Me? ... I am Jesus, whom thou persecutest," he was smitten with blindness and was unable to eat or to drink for three days before the Lord sent help. And the reason? The Lord answered: "He is a chosen vessel unto Me to bear My name before Gentiles and kings and the children of Israel, for I will show him how great things he must suffer for My name's sake." (Acts 9:1-16.) This experience qualified Paul to carry out the work to which he was appointed. Here he learned that "tribulation worketh patience; and patience, experience; and experience, hope; and hope maketh not ashamed," so that he was able to say, "We glory in tribulations." (Rom. 5:3-5.)

Nor was the cross entirely removed. Besides enduring hostilities, imprisonments, hardships, and beatings, Paul was afflicted by the special cross which he described as a "thorn in the flesh, the messenger of Satan to buffet me." Three times he asked to be delivered, but received only the answer "My grace is sufficient for thee." And Paul recognized that the affliction served the wholesome purpose of keeping him from being "exalted above measure." (II Cor. 12:7-9.)

The kind of love which God lavished on Paul, schooling him in trials and tribulations, He shows us also. Hence we, too, can know: "There shall not evil overtake thee." The great and mighty God, who governs, directs, and controls all things, will overrule all the evil counsels of the enemy and direct all the misfortunes and hardships that come upon us, all the storms of our lives so that they must serve to drive and hasten our ship into the haven of Paradise.

Both the Scriptures and experience teach us that a Christian is never so well armed against the danger of falling from grace as when he is afflicted and oppressed. Never is a Christian's confidence in God stronger than when he sees how vain and frail his own strength is. On November 30, 1939, the Russians bombed Luther Church in Finland. The entire building collapsed into ruins. But on the altar stood a glowing cross and above it a painting of Christ, His arms extended in blessing. "In this," said Bishop Lehtonen, "we saw a gripping testimony of the truth, mercy, and compassion, the forgiveness of sins. . . . Only in this assurance are we able to endure. With the conviction that nothing can separate us from the love of God, we have peace in our hearts in the midst of the storm. God suddenly becomes living and real when all the supports to which we have been accustomed crumble to pieces and God alone becomes our Refuge and Strength."

By trials and tribulations God may seek to cleanse the Christian of the secret faults of which David speaks. God may have special work for him, work that requires unusual fortitude, and on that account puts him through the gymnastics of tribulation. Perhaps others are to draw inspiration and comfort from his experiences, as the Christian world has for thousands of years drawn from the experiences of Job, David, and Paul. But whatever the purpose may be, whether the Christian understands or not, the promise remains: "Fear thou not, for I am with thee; be not dismayed, for I am thy God; I will strengthen thee; yea, I will help thee; yea, I will uphold thee with the right hand of My righteousness" (Is. 41:10).

The Glory of God

The ultimate goal and purpose of God's divine providence goes even beyond the final salvation of the elect. It is nothing less than the glory and honor of God. "Be still, and know that I am God; I will be exalted among the heathen, I will be exalted in the earth" (Ps. 46:10). For the sake of His honor God is in the midst of His Church and helps her right early. That is why "He uttered His voice," and "the earth melted." Hence He made desolations in the earth and made wars to cease. All His judgments, all His dealings are to make "men say among the nations: The Lord reigneth" (I Chron. 16:31). Verily, "of Him and through Him and to Him are all things; to whom be glory forever. Amen." (Rom. 11:36.)

Conclusion

Indeed, marvelous beyond words is divine providence! How can we give adequate expression to its wonders? If we remember how many and numerous are the objects over which it extends, we exclaim with the Psalmist: "How precious also are Thy thoughts unto me, O God! How great is the sum of them! If I should count them, they are more in number than the sand." (Ps. 139:17.) Remembering that God's providence upholds each being on earth, we confess: "Such knowledge is too wonderful for me; it is high, I cannot attain unto it" (Ps. 139:6). If we note how well God directs all things, we exclaim: "O Lord, how manifold are thy works! In wisdom hast Thou made them all." (Ps. 104:24.) If we attempt to probe the divine providence and learn its purposes, we confess: "Oh, the depth of the riches, both of the knowledge and wisdom of God! How unsearchable are His judgments and His ways past finding out!" "Great is our Lord and of great power; His understanding is infinite" (Ps. 147:5). But if we look into the holy of holies of God's divine providence in order to learn the motive of it all and see rising to meet us the lovely person of our Redeemer, we can only fall down and adore: "My Lord and my God!"

Great is our God and greatly to be praised, the God of an infinite majesty! To Him be glory and honor forevermore!

Office, or Work, of Christ

I
THE TWO STATES IN THE PERFORMANCE OF CHRIST'S OFFICE

THE Christology and Soteriology of the Lutheran Church begin and end with the Scriptures. Though our Lutheran theologians have spoken at great length, and at times with monumental learning, on every aspect of the subject, again and again they urge that we renew our understanding through a study of the "prophetic and apostolic Scriptures" themselves. (Epitome of the Formula of Concord, par. 1. *Triglot*, p. 777: also par. 3, p. 779.)

The triumphant cry of our dying Lord, "It is finished," brought to a close a great chapter in the history of the world as well as in the life of our Lord. This change which occurred in Christ's life and activity between Good Friday and Easter, clearly foretold already in the Word of Prophecy, e. g., Ps. 8:6-10; 110; Is. 53, has given rise to theological descriptions which are current in both Reformed and Lutheran theology — the States (Staende) of Exinanition, or Humiliation, and of Exaltation.

The Lutheran and Reformed definitions of these terms, however, have been constantly at variance. Reformed theology denies the communication of the divine majesty to Christ's human nature and teaches that the humiliation as well as the exaltation took place according to both natures in Christ, the human and the divine. The humiliation of the divine nature consisted in its becoming man and in hiding its divinity before man, while in the state of exaltation it fully revealed its majesty. The humiliation according to the human nature did not consist in refraining from the full use of the divine majesty (which was never communicated to the human nature), but in the endurance of unusual shame and suffering, while the exaltation consisted in the bestowal of great, but only created, finite gifts.

We shall see that this teaching is not in accord with the clear Word of Scripture.

The Lutheran doctrine, on the other hand, gives full prominence to all the facts of Christ's life and work as recorded in Scripture without any attempt to produce a logical harmony satisfying to human reason from the seeming dissonances inherent in the life of One who was at the same time God and man.

The Lutheran statement of the States gives full prominence to a fact which is immediately evident in the Scriptures: that the human nature of Christ was in constant possession of the divine glory from the first moment of the personal union (Atlantic District, 1946, p. 26). The synodical literature of the Missouri Synod is in complete agreement with the old Lutheran position that in the State of Humiliation Christ, although God in the fullest sense of the word, did not according to His human nature make full use of the divine attributes communicated to the human nature, in so far as such "hiding" was made necessary by His obligation to fulfill the Law (Gal. 4:4) and to suffer and die (Gal. 3:13). The State of Exaltation is simply the expression of the fact that, beginning with the descent into hell, Christ according to His human nature employed to their full extent the attributes communicated by the divine to the human nature.

Lutherans, therefore, hold that humiliation and exaltation occurred only in the human nature of Christ and that His divinity, untouched by humiliation and exaltation, participated integrally and unreservedly in the entire office and work of Christ. For the Godhead, said the Lutheran theologians, cannot be changed.

These two definitions, which we teach in our Catechism to our children and prospective communicants, are in full keeping with such extraordinary statements as that of Christ about Himself: "I lay down My life, that I might take it again. No man taketh it from Me, but I lay it down of Myself. I have power to lay it down, and I have power to take it again" (John 10:17 b-18 a; cp. John 3:13, 31-32; 1:18); and, on the other hand, that of the disciples about Him: "We beheld His glory, the glory as of the Only-Begotten of the Father" (John 1:14 b).

The Lutherans were careful to note that while in the State of Humiliation Christ did not make full use of the divine glory, He was at all times in full possession of it according to His human nature also, since they were met on every page of the Gospels by an authority, power, and radiance which was more than human.

Evidently, then, when Christ *chose* to conceal, He concealed; and when He *chose* to reveal, He revealed the divine glory. Luther could discover but one motive for this great transaction of the human and the divine, *the love of Christ*. First of all, love for His Father: "The prince of this world cometh and hath nothing in Me. But that the world may know that I love the Father," said He as He went forth to crucifixion, "and as the Father gave Me commandment, even so I do. Arise, let us go hence." And then, *love for men*: "Greater love hath no man than this, that a man lay down his life for his friends." (John 14:30 b-31; 15:13; cp. Luther, St. Louis, VIII, p. 551.)

Lutherans have also looked to Christ Himself for expression of the purpose of it all: "The Son of Man came not to be ministered unto but to minister and to give His life a ransom for many" (Matt. 20:28).

The doctrine of the two States, the State of Humiliation and the State of Exaltation, has been stated in greatest detail and clarity in that well-known passage Phil. 2:5-11: "Let this mind be in you, which was also in Christ Jesus, who, being in the form of God, thought it not robbery to be equal with God; but made Himself of no reputation and took upon Him the form of a servant and was made in the likeness of men; and being found in fashion as a man, He humbled Himself and became obedient unto death, even the death of the Cross. Wherefore God also hath highly exalted Him and hath given Him a name which is above every name, that at the name of Jesus every knee should bow, of things in heaven and things in earth and things under the earth, and that every tongue should confess that Jesus Christ is Lord, to the glory of God the Father."

The Apostle very clearly states that Christ Jesus, the incarnate Son of God, was in the form of God, just as John confesses: "The

Word (which was God, John 1:1) was made flesh and dwelt among us, and we beheld His glory, the glory as of the Only-Begotten of the Father" (John 1:14). But Christ Jesus "thought it not robbery to be equal with God." He did not regard His equality with God, His Godhead, as a prize obtained for the purpose of being constantly exhibited, continually to be manifested to the gazing eyes of people. No, He "made Himself of no reputation," or, as it may be translated literally, "He emptied Himself." What this emptying implies is explained by the participial phrases immediately following, "taking upon Himself the form of a servant" and "being made in the likeness of men." He who was God appeared in the form of a servant, was made in all things like unto His brethren, the seed of Abraham, and was in all points tempted as we are, yet without sin, as the Letter to the Hebrews puts it (Heb. 2:16-18; 4:15). "Being found in the fashion of man," although always in full possession of His deity, His divine nature, "He humbled Himself" even below the usual standard of human beings, by "becoming obedient unto death, even the death of the Cross," the death of a criminal. What Paul here states very clearly is that Christ Jesus, while never yielding one iota of His deity, while at all times being One with the Father (John 10:30), did not always during the days of His flesh manifest the fullness of the Godhead dwelling in Him bodily (Col. 2:9), did not continually and to the full extent make use of His divine majesty, but lived the life of all the sons of Adam. "No garb of pomp or power He wore." He permitted Himself to be regarded and treated as a slave having little if any right of his own. He was sentenced to death as a criminal, was subjected to cruel mockeries, died, and was buried. As true man, He felt keenly all the shame and agony heaped upon Him, yet not for a moment did He cease to be equal with God, the majestic Lord of Hosts.

That is the simple, clear sense of this passage; and that has been the doctrine of our Lutheran Church from the time of Luther. Says the Augsburg Confession: "Christ *truly* suffered, was crucified, dead, and buried, that He might reconcile the Father unto us and be a sacrifice, not only for original guilt, but also for all actual sins of men. He also descended into hell and *truly* rose again the third day; afterward He ascended into heaven that He might sit on the right hand of the Father and forever reign and have dominion over all creatures." (Augsburg Confession, Art. III. *Triglot*, p. 45.)

THE STATE OF HUMILIATION

Historically, the State of Humiliation embraces that period of our Lord's life from His conception to the moment He was "made alive in the spirit" (I Pet. 3:18). The Augsburg Confession, following that of the ecumenical creeds, speaks of His conception and birth, suffering, Cross, death, burial.

Conception and Birth.—The conception of Christ was supernatural; His birth was natural. If there ever were any misconceptions about His humbling Himself, His birth certainly would dispose of them for all time. The very fact that the Son of God became man by being born of a human mother, while He might have chosen a different manner of becoming flesh, is proof sufficient of His humiliation; and can there be stronger proof for His taking on the form of a servant than the fact that He was born in a borrowed home, a stable? Lutheran theology has never attempted to hide the humiliation of this lowly birth for the Christ. Recognizing the reality, it has discovered the real joy of that natal event.

The immediate purpose of it? Together with Gal. 4:5, Kromayer is quoted by Dr. Pieper with approval: "Christ has passed through all stages of our human life in order thoroughly to cleanse our unclean conception and birth" (Theol. pos.-pol. II, 91. Quoted by Pieper, *Christliche Dogmatik*, II, p. 365, note 836). Brockman understands its purpose in the same practical fashion: "We adhere to the confession 'truly begotten (born)', and find comfort in the fact that by His conception and birth He has purified and sanctified our sinful conception and birth." (Quoted in *Central Illinois Report*, 1913, p. 61.)

Suffering.—"The story of Christ's earthly sojourn from birth on is a constant Passion story" (Pieper, *op. cit.*, II, p. 370).

Summary of Heinrich Frincke, "Gelitten unter Pontio Pilato, etc.," Michigan, 1906, pp. 14—35: Living in extreme poverty, Matt. 8:20; forced to flee into Egypt, dubbed with a name of derision (Nazarene, John 1:46); blasphemed and persecuted by His opponents

(Matt. 9:3, 34; 11:19; John 8:48); tempted by the devil (Matt. 4: 1-11; Mark 1:13; Luke 4:1-13); plagued by the weakness of those about Him, surrounded on all sides by the blind, the dumb, the lame, the paralyzed, the leprous, the crippled, the dead, whose sufferings only caused Him to agonize the more with them, He knew perfectly the meaning of suffering.

All this was merely the prelude to that great suffering endured at the hands of churchmen and a politician whose name the Apostles Creed has perpetuated in infamy: Suffered under *Pontius Pilate* (*passio magna*).

The Lutheran doctrine of Christ's suffering does not shy away from the thought of degradation and of blood. Believing the Word of Scripture that mankind is redeemed by the blood of Christ (Acts 20:28; I Pet. 1:18-19), and that without shedding of blood there is no remission (Heb. 9:22), our Church has always made Luther's confession its own: "Christ has redeemed me . . . not with gold or silver, but with His holy, precious blood and with His innocent suffering and death."

Cross.—"He was obedient unto death, even the death of the Cross" (Phil. 2:8). When Christ chose to conceal the divine majesty, He concealed it. The Cross is the culmination of that concealment.

"The rulers also with them derided Him, saying: He saved others; let Him save Himself if He be Christ, the Chosen of God" (Luke 23:35). The soldiers came mocking: "If Thou be the king of the Jews, save Thyself" (Luke 23:37). The reviler joined the chorus: "If Thou be Christ, save Thyself and us" (Luke 23:39). Those that passed by wagged their heads: "Thou that destroyest the Temple and buildest it in three days, save Thyself. If Thou be the Son of God, come down from the Cross" (Matt. 27:40). The chief priests, scribes, and elders finally could not refrain from entering the game personally: "He saved others; Himself He cannot save. If He be the King of Israel, let Him now come down from the Cross, and we will believe Him. He trusted in God; let Him deliver Him now if He will have Him; for He said, I am the Son of God." (Matt. 27:42-43.)

Completely in the hands of His enemies, numbered with the transgressors (Luke 22:37), and then cut off from God! Such is the tale of the Cross.

"My God, My God, why hast Thou forsaken Me?" This cry, mysterious, incomprehensible to human reason, speaks of an unfathomable suffering. The Son of God is forsaken by His Father! To be forsaken of God is to be cast out of God's presence, into hell, as Christ tells us (Matt. 8:12): "The children of the Kingdom shall be cast out into outer darkness" and (Matt. 25:41): "Depart from Me, ye cursed, into everlasting fire." The Lutheran Church therefore teaches, in keeping with Scripture, that Christ upon the Cross actually endured the pangs of hell. (Cp. Pieper, *op. cit.*, p. 371.) They saw in this event upon the Cross the real climax of the passion of our Lord. Luther's deep spiritual insight into the meaning of the Cross is nowhere more evident than in his comment on this passage: "No one can by the use of words describe this as well as it is plainly, briefly, and simply stated by David. It does not treat of the physical suffering of Christ, which likewise is great and severe, but rather of His sublime (great) spiritual suffering, which He experienced in His soul, a suffering that far exceeds all bodily suffering.—No mortal man here below comprehends what that means, nor can any human being adequately describe it in words, for to be forsaken of God is much worse than death. They who have tried and experienced a little thereof may give it some thought. But self-sufficient, coarse, untried, and inexperienced people know and understand nothing of it. From the example of Job one can in a measure comprehend what it means to be forsaken of God. Christ was truly forsaken of God, not indeed by the separation of the Godhead from His human nature, but in this, that the Godhead retired and hid itself. Thus this just and innocent Person must tremble and quail in trepidation as a poor condemned sinner and in His tender, innocent heart experience God's anger at and judgment of sin; also external death and damnation in our stead, and, in general, suffer everything that a condemned sinner deserves and must suffer forever. He had to suppress and extinguish in His soul the terrible temptation of being forsaken of God, the fiery darts of the devil, hellish fire and anxiety, and everything that we deserved because of our sins. Thereby heaven, eternal life and bliss, was gained for us, as Isaiah declares, ch. 53: "He shall see of the travail of His soul and shall be satisfied." (St. Louis, V: 223–227.)

Office, or Work, of Christ

Death and Burial.—Pilate was astonished that the Troublemaker was so soon dead and verified the fact by calling in the centurion (Mark 15:44). Still in the form of a servant, Christ had turned to His Father: "Father, into Thy hands I commend My Spirit," and had died (Matt. 27:50; Mark 15:37; Luke 23:46; John 19:30).

The Lutheran Church has always affirmed unqualified adherence to the literal reports of Christ's death: that He really died and His spirit fled the body in the same way as any man's spirit takes its flight at the moment of death; that He died as God-Man in the complete sense of the *unio personalis;* that the sundered soul and body remained in the relationship of *unio personalis* though the former was with God and the latter in the grave.

Admittedly, this entire relationship constitutes an insoluble mystery.

Seldom has a hymnologist touched a greater mystery of theology than Johann Rist, who in 1641 published stanzas 2 to 7 of the hymn "O Darkest Woe." His words have been quoted with approbation, and with no attempt at explanation, in all the synodical literature, as the complete statement of a Biblical truth by a poet and preacher: "O Sorrow Dread, Our God Is Dead!"

With Christ's burial, the state of humiliation comes to a close. His burial is the last and lowest stage to which He could carry His human nature. Corruption of Christ's body could not take place, "because it was not possible that He should be holden of death," Acts 2:24, as Christ Himself in the word of prophecy had foretold. Thou wilt not suffer Thy Holy One to see corruption," Ps. 16:10. His dying bed was a cross, and His last resting place a borrowed tomb. His life ended, as it had begun, in borrowed quarters. "He took upon Him the form of a servant," and as a servant He was buried through the kindness of His wealthy friends Joseph and Nicodemus.

THE STATE OF EXALTATION

If the state of humiliation involved the partial concealment of the divine attributes communicated to the human nature, the state of exaltation is the full and uninterrupted revelation of the divine attributes communicated to the human nature. The *sedes* on Christ's State of Exaltation is clear and explicit: "Wherefore God also hath highly exalted Him and given Him a name which is above every name, that at the name of Jesus every knee should bow, of things in heaven and things in earth and things under the earth, and that every tongue should confess that Jesus Christ is Lord, to the glory of God the Father" (Phil. 2:9-11).

Since God cannot change (Ps. 102:27), exaltation, too, occurred only in Christ's human nature; just as humiliation had occurred before only in the human nature. "The *same Christ*," says the Augsburg Confession, "descended into hell and truly rose again the third day; afterward He ascended into heaven that He might sit on the right hand of the Father and forever reign and have dominion over all creatures. . . ."

"The same Christ shall openly come again to judge the quick and the dead, etc., according to the Apostles' Creed." (Augsburg Confession, Art. III. *Triglot*, p. 44. Compare also Formula of Concord, Thorough Declaration, Art. IX, *Triglot*, pp. 1023, 1025.)

The confessions record five stages in the State of Exaltation: descent into hell, resurrection, ascension, session, and return to Judgment. To be exact, these are rather five stages in the revelation of Christ's exaltation than in the exaltation itself.

Descent into Hell. — Every time we confess the Apostles' Creed we affirm our belief that "He descended into hell." This statement is included in all the Lutheran Confessions, with explicit testimony that we acknowledge not only its traditional position in the Christian creed, but also its truth.

The declaration first appears in the old Roman symbol known to us as the Apostles' Creed; it is not found, however, in many of the earliest manuscripts of that symbol. Dr. F. Bente's introduction to the *Triglotta* recognizes that the version of Bishop Marcellus of Ancyra is the oldest extant (c. 337 A. D.) and that it does *not* contain these words. The version to which we are accustomed, "evidently the result of a comparison and combination of the various preexisting forms of this symbol, may be traced to the end of the fifth century and is first found in a sermon by Caesarius of Arles in France, about 500 A. D." (*Triglot*, p. 12, par. 13.)

The crucial question in Lutheran theology, however, has never been: "When did the doctrine become a part of the creed of the

Church?" When all questions of historical precedent have been settled, the great Lutheran question still must be answered: "What do the *Scriptures* say about the descent into hell?"

The *sedes doctrinae* of the entire teaching is I Pet. 3:18-20: "For Christ also hath once suffered for sins, the Just for the unjust, that He might bring us to God, being put to death in the flesh, but quickened by the Spirit, by which also He went and preached unto the spirits in prison, which sometime were disobedient, when once the long-suffering of God waited in the days of Noah, while the ark was a preparing, wherein few, that is, eight souls, were saved by water."

The allegation has been made that this passage never was associated by the early Church with the descent into hell. This common argument was advanced particularly in Norwegian Lutheran circles. J. A. O. Stub demonstrated by copious citations that Clement of Alexandria, Origen, Eusebius, Pamphila, Hilarius, and the Peshito distinctly refer to this passage when discussing the descent. (Cp. *Theological Quarterly*, XII, 1908, p. 30.)

The additional assertion was made that this passage does not speak of a descent into *hell,* but rather into prison. Three terms are commonly used in the New Testament for hell: *Gehenna, Hades,* and *Phylake.* Some contend that Hades is a general term for the place of the dead; *Gehenna* and *Phylake* are then understood as synonyms for a certain section of Hades. The theory does not agree with Biblical usage. If it were to be followed consistently, Christ would be put in the position of saying: "The gates of Hades shall not prevail" against the Church (Matt. 16:18), and if the souls of the wicked are in an intermediate place, in the Phylake (I Pet. 3:19) with their fate to be decided on Judgment Day, then Satan and his hosts are in the same position, in Phylake (Rev. 20:7).

In the synodical literature these terms were all regarded as descriptions of hell in its various aspects: *Gehenna,* for its fiery quality (Matt. 5:22); *Hades,* for the place of punishment (even though in the story of Lazarus and the rich man it appears almost as a synonym for *Gehenna* (Luke 16:23-24); and *Phylake,* because, once a man is interned there, escape becomes impossible (Matt. 5:26).

The tendency of the attempts to distinguish between these terms was clear: to read into the statement "He preached" (I Pet. 3:19) the sense "He preached the Gospel." The use of the word is not decisive one way or the other, since it is used for the preaching of the Gospel (Matt. 4:23; 9:35; 24:14; etc.) and for the preaching of the Law (Matt. 3:1; Acts 15:21; Rom. 2:21). The further argument that v. 20 restricts the preaching to the people who died in unbelief before the flood was rejected by the Lutheran Church as incompatible with the context.

One uncertainty remains: What is the meaning of the two phrases: "put to death in the flesh" and "made alive in the spirit"? Several interpretations have been offered:

1. *Flesh* means "humanity"—*spirit* means "deity" when employed in connection with the person of Christ. Christ was put to death according to the flesh, His human nature; He was made alive according to the spirit, according to His divine nature.

The difficulty of this rendering is that it does not take into account the fact that the two phrases, "in the flesh" and "in the spirit," are not used in the same relation. This difficulty was acknowledged by those who offered it as their interpretation. Cp. E. A. Mayer, "Am dritten Tage, etc.," Michigan 1903, p. 17.

2. *Flesh* means "earthly mode of existence"—*Spirit* means spiritual mode of existence" (*irdisches Wesen—geistliches Wesen*)— Luther and Pieper (*Chrisliche Dogmatik*, II, p. 378) and others prefer this interpretation.

3. Bellarmin's interpretation, followed by most Romanists, that *flesh* means "body"—*spirit* means "soul," was completely rejected.

The statement of the Formula of Concord on the Descent (Art. IX) is based largely on Luther's famous sermon delivered at the castle of Torgau in 1533. Luther said: "Before Christ arose and ascended into heaven, and while yet lying in the grave, He also descended into hell in order to deliver also us from it, who were to be held in it as prisoners. However, I shall not discuss this article in a profound and subtle manner, as to how it was done or what it means to 'descend into hell,' but adhere to the simplest meaning conveyed by these words, as we must represent it to children and uneducated people.

"Therefore, whoever would not go wrong or stumble had best adhere to the words and understand them in a simple way as well as he can. Accordingly, it is customary to represent Christ in paintings on walls, as He descends, appears before hell, clad in a priestly robe and with a banner in His hand, with which He beats the devil and puts him to flight, takes hell by storm, and rescues those that are His. Thus it was also acted the night before Easter as a play for children. And I am well pleased with the fact that it is painted, played, sung, and said in this manner for the benefit of simple people. We, too, should let it go at that, and not trouble ourselves with profound and subtle thoughts as to how it may have happened, since it surely did not occur bodily, inasmuch as He remained in the grave three days.

"However, since we cannot but conceive thoughts and images of what is presented to us in words, and are unable to think of or understand anything without such images, it is appropriate and right that we view it literally, just as it is painted, that He descends with the banner, shattering and destroying the gates of hell; and we should put aside thoughts that are too deep and incomprehensible for us. But we ought . . . simply to fix and fasten our hearts and thoughts on the words of the Creed, which says: 'I believe in the Lord Jesus Christ, the Son of God, dead, buried, and descended into hell', that is, in the entire person, God and man with body and soul, undivided, 'born of the Virgin, suffered, died, and buried'; In like manner I must not divide it here either, but believe and say that the same Christ, God and man in one person, descended into hell, but did not remain in it; as Ps. 16:10 says of Him: 'Thou wilt not leave My soul in hell, neither suffer Thine Holy One to see corruption.' By the word 'soul,' He, in accordance with the language of the Scripture, does not mean, as we do, a being separated from the body, but the entire man, the Holy One of God, as He here calls Himself. But how it may have occurred that the man lies there in the grave, and yet descends into hell—that, indeed, we shall and must leave unexplained and uncomprehended; for it certainly did not take place in a bodily and tangible manner, although we can only paint and conceive of it in a coarse and bodily way and speak of it in pictures.

"Such, therefore, is the plainest manner to speak of this article, that we may adhere to the words and cling to this main point, that for us, through Christ, hell has been torn to pieces and the devil's kingdom and power utterly destroyed, for which purpose He died, was buried, and descended—so that it should no longer harm or overwhelm us, as He Himself says Matt. 16:18." (*Triglot*, Introduction, pp. 192–193.)

Resurrection.—The remarkable thing is not that our Lord conquered death, but that He carried our nature in victory over death. If it was the same Jesus who descended into hell, it was most certainly the same Jesus who rose from the grave. In fact, it was the same body that lay in the grave which came forth on Easter morning (Matt. 28:6; John 2:19). Still, the closed sepulcher and the locked doors tell the story of a body now sharing in the full divine perfections communicated to the human nature (Matt. 28:2; John 20:19, 26).

Lutheran scholarship has decided that Lessing, Schleiermacher, Strausz, Renan, Harnack, and all the host of those who deny the resurrection, have come a little too late to assume complete authority. It rather trusts the eyewitnesses of the events themselves, one of whom was careful to note when he reported the resurrection: "Many other signs truly did Jesus in the presence of His disciples, which are not written in this book. But these are written that ye might believe that Jesus is the Christ, the Son of God, and that, believing, ye might have life through His name." (John 20:30-31.)

Scripture connects the resurrection with the demonstration of three incontrovertible truths about Christ:

1. Christ is God's Son and His teaching is true (Rom. 1:3-4; I Cor. 15:14-15, 20).

2. God has accepted the sacrificial offering of His Son for the reconciliation of the world, and all enemies of our salvation have been overcome (Rom. 4:25; I Cor. 15:55).

3. All believers in Christ will rise to life at His coming (I Cor. 15:23; Phil. 3:20 b-21).

Ascension and Session.—It was an easy, composed homegoing as He lifted His hands in blessing upon the beloved eleven and those with them. With His words "Lo, I am with you alway" ringing in their ears, they returned rejoicing to the Holy City.

G. A. Bernthal's "Theses on the Ascension of Christ and His Session at the Right Hand of God" are a complete statement of the Lutheran and synodical position on the subject:

Thesis I

The ascension of Christ and His sitting at the right hand of God belong to the State of Exaltation, in which state Christ, the God-Man, according to His human nature, makes complete and uninterrupted use of His divine majesty, which He has always possessed according to His human nature.

Thesis II

By the ascension of Christ is meant the one definite event by which Christ withdrew His visible presence here on earth from His disciples and in His true human body rose visibly to the heaven of beatitude and glory.

Thesis III

According to Scripture, sitting at the right hand of God is the exercise of the infinite power and majesty of God by Christ according to His human nature, by virtue of which Christ now fills, rules, and governs all things unrestrictedly also according to His human nature.

Thesis IV

Sitting at the right hand of God, Christ discharges His threefold office until the end of days, in order to make us partakers of the salvation wrought by Him. (Michigan, 1900, p. 13.)

Luther was particularly solicitous about the relationship between this teaching and the correct understanding of the Lord's Supper. In a sermon of the year 1527 he writes: "In the first place, we consider the article that Christ is sitting at the right hand of God, concerning which the heterodox teachers (dreamers, fanatics) hold that it precludes the presence of Christ's body in the Holy Supper. If we were to ask them what they mean by the right hand of God, where Christ is sitting, I believe they would present a visionary picture to us, just as one pictures a supposed heaven to children, in which there is a golden throne, with Christ sitting beside the Father, wearing a robe and a golden crown, as artists depict the scene. For if they entertained no such childish, carnal thoughts regarding the right hand of God, they assuredly would not assail the presence of Christ's body in the Sacrament or make so much of the statement of Augustine (to whom they otherwise give credence as little as they give to anyone else) that Christ is necessarily confined in body to one place, while His truth is present everywhere." (Luther, St. Louis, XX. 802.)

The Scriptural teaching has been consistently upheld by the Lutheran Church that Christ now fills and rules all things and is with us here on earth according to His human nature, the convincing authority for which is found in such passages as Matt. 28:20 and Eph. 4:10.

Return to Judgment.—This subject will be treated under another topic in the series arranged by our Centennial Committee.

The Judgment will bring to an end the work of Christ in time and space as known to us (I Cor. 15:24-28).

Luther's thorough theological understanding is apparent in his comments on this passage: "However, Christ will nevertheless continue in His dominion and majesty, for He is the same God and Lord, eternal and almighty with the Father. But because He now governs by means of His Word, the Sacraments, etc., so that the world does not see His dominion, it is called the kingdom of Christ, and everything must be subject to Him except Him who subjects all things to Him until the Last Day, when He will put an end to all things and when He, with His entire Kingdom, will commit Himself to the Father and say to Him: "Until now have I ruled with you in faith. I now turn it over to you in order that all may see that I am in Thee and Thou in Me, together with the Holy Ghost, in the same divine majesty, and in order that they may freely have and enjoy everything in Thee which until now they have believed and for which they have waited. Then (He says) God will be All in all, i. e., each will have in God everything that he now has in all things, so that at His revelation we shall all have a sufficiency in soul and body and no longer need so many things as we now of necessity must have in this world." (St. Louis, VIII, 1187.)

II

CHRIST'S OFFICE, OR WORK, IN THE TWO STATES

"Everything which Christ, the God-Man, *did* for the salvation of men in the state of humiliation and *still does* in the state of exaltation belongs to His office or work" (Pieper, *Christliche Dogmatik*, II, 388).

"I have finished the work which Thou gavest Me to do" (John 17:4). He said to the Father in His final public prayer before the crucifixion: "My meat is to do the will of Him that sent Me and to complete His work" (John 4:34).

His work, according to the Scriptures, was not to complete the creation, but to restore what had been destroyed, to save that which was lost, to save sinners (Luke 19:10; I Tim. 1:15).

Augustine's sentence is the complete statement of the necessity and the purpose of Christ's work: If man had not perished, the Son of Man had not come (quoted by Pieper, *op. cit.*, II, 391).

The very name Jesus, which God gave His Son, is a divine pronouncement of His mission. Joseph it was who received the final prenatal announcement: "She [Mary] shall bring forth a Son, and thou shalt call His name Jesus; for He shall save His people from their sins" (Matt. 1:21).

Chemnitz especially emphasized the importance of the name, for, he said, on God's own authority we address Christ as "Jesus," as the Salvation from our sins (Chemnitz, Harm. ev., c. 9, quoted in part by Pieper, *op cit.*, II, p. 388, note 926).

Chemnitz felt the same way about the name "Christ," the Greek equivalent for the Hebrew "Messiah." Both names mean "The Anointed." The great Jewish tradition from the Old Testament was well acquainted with the anointing of priests (Ex. 29:7, Aaron), of kings (1 Sam. 16:13, David), and sometimes even of prophets (1 Kings 19:16, Jehu, Elisha). So Christ was anointed by God Himself with the Spirit, in Chemnitz's words: "at the same time as King, Priest, and Prophet" (Harm. ev., c. 23, p. 304).

This threefold division of the work of Christ has good Scriptural and historical foundation.

The Old Testament was explicit in identifying the One who was to come as a Prophet (Deut. 18:15-19), Priest (Ps. 110:4), and

King (Ps. 110:1, 5-6; Ps. 2:6; Ps. 72:8-9, 11). The mission of Christ is described by the New Testament in similar terms:

1. Prophet: "to *preach* the Gospel to the poor" (Luke 4:18).

2. Priest: "Christ is come a High Priest of good things." Heb. 9:11; Cp. Matt. 20:28; I Pet. 2:24.

3. King: "He shall reign over the house of Jacob forever, and of His kingdom there shall be no end" (Luke 1:33).

Some Lutheran theologians have divided the office, or work, of Christ into two divisions, combining the prophetic and priestly offices (compare Quenstedt, Syst., II, 304; Pieper, *op. cit.*, II, p. 393, note 392). Eusebius (died 340) noted that the Scriptures describe Christ as "alone the High Priest of all the world, alone the King of all creation, and alone the chief Prophet of His Father among all other prophets" (*Ecclesiastical History*, I, 2).

All three offices are directly related to the purpose of Christ's coming. All three appear in direct relationship to the facts of Christ's humiliation and exaltation. Logically the order would be Priest, Prophet, King; such order, however, would be merely a matter of emphasis. In reality, and point of time, the three are coextensive. For that reason the traditional order of Prophet, Priest, King has been generally preserved.

A. The Prophetic Office

Prophecy, an Old Testament Institution. — God Himself defined the duty of a prophet in two very interesting passages recorded in Exodus. Both are a part of God's conversation with Moses and Aaron after the former's fancied or real inability at public speaking prompted his refusal to carry out the mission assigned to him. "And the Lord said unto Moses: See, I have made thee a *god* to Pharaoh; and Aaron thy brother shall be thy prophet" (Ex. 7:1). "Thou shalt speak unto him and put words in his mouth . . . and he shall be to thee instead of a mouth, and thou shalt be to him instead of God" (Ex. 4:15-16). The function of a prophet, therefore, might be described simply: God spoke to the prophet, and the prophet reported to the people.

An important question in the minds of a prophet's contemporaries, as well as in ours today, was that of his authority. Occasionally a man's designation as a prophet was announced through a formal act of anointing. Compare I Kings 19:15-16 (Elisha). Usually the office was conferred through an immediate divine call which the prophets themselves describe in such terms as: "I am full of power by the Spirit of the Lord, and of judgment and of might, to declare unto Jacob his transgression and to Israel his sin" (Micah 3:8); or: "The Spirit of the Lord fell upon me and said unto me, Speak: 'Thus saith the Lord.'" (Ezek. 11:5.) The prophets were often endowed by God with wonder-working powers to establish the authority of their message (Ex. 4:31; I Kings 17:24). Occasionally the marvelous fulfillment of the prophecies was enough to establish the authority of their message (Jer. 28:9, 16, 17).

The message, however, was the important thing, and that was to be the Word of God. Every Israelite was aware that this was the true test of a prophet's authority, for the law was pointed and clear: "If there arise among you a prophet, or a dreamer of dreams, and giveth thee a sign or a wonder, and the sign or the wonder come to pass, whereof he spake unto thee, saying: Let us go after other gods, which thou hast not known, and let us serve them; thou shalt not hearken unto the words of that prophet, or that dreamer of dreams; for the Lord your God proveth you, to know whether ye love the Lord, your God, with all your soul" (Deut. 13:1-3).

Even if the prophetic office of Christ had not been explicitly foretold and carried out, the resemblance is close enough to make it inevitable that one of the New Testament writers should have noted: "God, who at sundry times and in divers manners spake in time past unto the fathers by the prophets, hath in these last days spoken unto us by His Son" (Heb. 1:1-2).

CHRIST THE PROPHET

The people of God were looking for a prophet. Those who saw Jesus feed the five thousand exclaimed: "This is of a truth that Prophet that should come into the world" (John 6:14). Hearing Him quote the Old Testament with an authority to them hitherto unknown, some said: "Of a truth this is *the* Prophet. Others said: This is the Christ". (John 7:40-41.) Even the woman of Samaria was aware that Christ was a Prophet: "Sir, I perceive that Thou art a Prophet" (John 4:19). She also had knowledge that a great prophet was coming, whom she associated with the Messiah: "I know that Messias cometh, which is called Christ. When He is come, He will *tell* us all things." (John 4:25.)

Early in His public ministry people recognized that Jesus was a "teacher come from God" (John 3:2). As late as the last week the multitude which accompanied Him with palm branches acclaimed Him: "This is Jesus, the Prophet of Nazareth of Galilee," and the leaders did not arrest Him, for "they feared the multitude, because they took Him for a Prophet" (Matt. 21:46). The two mournful disciples on the Emmaus road were possessed of a glorious memory, only heightening the tragedy of their disillusionment, that He had been "a Prophet mighty in deed and word before God and all the people" (Luke 24:19).

Though the people, and even His disciples, undeniably had a very imperfect conception of His prophetic mission, Christ Himself was never in doubt about it. How little they understood, and how well He was aware of, that mission is evident from the incident in the synogog at Nazareth, where, having quoted the prophecy of Isaiah: "The Spirit of the Lord is upon Me to preach the Gospel to the poor," He boldly stated: "This day is this Scripture fulfilled in your ears" (Is. 61:1-2; Luke 4:16-29).

That the holy writers were constantly aware of Christ's prophetic office is evident from the terms they apply to Him: Teacher (John 3:2), Witness (Rev. 1:5), Word (John 1:1), Truth (John 14:6), Light of the World (John 1: 8-9) Servant of God (Is. 42:1; 49:6), Angel of the Lord (Gen. 22:1), Angel of the Covenant (Mal. 3:1), Apostle (Heb. 3:11), Good Shepherd (John 10:12), Bishop (I Pet. 2:25).

It was no accident, nor was it an interpretation of the Church, which made Christ a Prophet. "To this end was I born," said He Himself, "and for this cause came I into the world, that I should bear witness unto the truth" (John 18:37 b).

Christ was *anointed* to be a Prophet. "God anointed Jesus of Nazareth with the Holy Ghost and with power" (Acts 10:38), said Peter to Cornelius. Indeed, this fact was one of the marks which prophecy had given, whereby He might be recognized (Ps.2: 2; 45:7; Is. 61:1). It was the mark Christ Himself most readily acknowledged (Luke 4:18). This was His divine call. Lutheran theologians have recognized the Baptism of Jesus as the public confirmation of the original call and anointing. Thus He was publicly called. (Cp. Northern Illinois, 1916, p. 25.)

The Father Himself "sealed" the call of Christ (John 6:27) as the voice came from the brightness on the Mount of Transfiguration: "This is My beloved Son, in whom I am well pleased. Hear ye Him." (Matt. 17:5.)

Christ the Unique Prophet

Moses was the Mediator of the First Covenant and is so revered by the Jews today. Indeed, of all the Old Testament prophets, only Moses spoke to God "face to face," and "there arose not a prophet since in Israel like unto Moses, whom the Lord knew face to face" (Deut. 34:10). The great Prophet to come was to be like unto him!

So Jesus Christ "was faithful to Him that appointed Him, as also Moses was faithful in all His house. For this Man was counted worthy of more glory than Moses, inasmuch as he who hath builded the house hath more honor than the house. For every house is builded by some man; but He that built all things is God. And Moses verily was faithful in all His house, as a servant, for a testimony of those things which were to be spoken after; but Christ as a Son over His own house, whose house are we if we hold fast the confidence and the rejoicing of the hope firm unto the end." (Heb. 3:2-6.)

1. Moses proclaimed what he received in direct conversation with God, and so did Christ (John 7:16; 8:28). Yet when Christ spoke, His own Word was God's Word in a higher sense. He Himself was God's Word (John 1:1), the incarnate, visible Word. When He spoke, "Thus saith the Lord" became "Verily, verily, I say unto you."

2. Moses prophesied of Jesus Christ, and in a higher manner Christ testified of Himself. Christ's testimony of Himself, in fact, would be sheer arrogance if it were not the higher testimony of the Son of God.

3. Moses was a man "mighty in words and in deeds (Acts 7:22), and so was Christ. Indeed, the Old Testament had seen no demonstration of divine power such as Christ showed to His generation.

"And thou, Capernaum—if the mighty works which have been done in thee had been done in Sodom, it would have remained until this day" (Matt. 11:23).

4. Moses was the mediator of the Old Covenant; Christ is the Mediator of the New.

Thus the hope that the unique Prophet of the Gospel would come was made graphic and was kept alive by His prophetic attachment to the unique prophet of the Law.

CHRIST'S PROPHETIC WORK

1. In the Old Testament

In the Old Testament we meet frequently with the Angel of the Lord, the Messenger sent by the Lord to reveal His will, a Messenger in whom was the name of the Lord (Ex. 23:20-21); who is called Lord, (Gen. 16:13; 22:14); and speaks of Himself as God (Gen. 31:11-13); as the Lord (Gen. 22:15, 16; Ex. 3:1, 13-15). This Angel of the Lord brought messages of the Lord to Hagar, (Gen. 16:7-10; 21:17-19); to Abraham (Gen. 22:11-19); to Jacob (Gen. 28:11-22; cp. 31:11-13); to Moses (Ex. 3:1-22), and others. In these instances Christ performed His prophetic work personally. The New Testament, however, informs us that it was Christ who also spoke through other persons, the holy Prophets, the Spirit of Christ, which was in them, testifying "beforehand the sufferings of Christ and the glory that should follow" (I Pet. 1:11).

2. In the State of Humiliation

When the Prophet appeared in the flesh, His message did not change. Invariably He referred His interrogators to the Old Testament Scriptures: "What is written in the Law?" (Luke 10:26.) "Ye do err, not knowing the Scriptures nor the power of God. . . . As touching the resurrection of the dead, have ye not read that which was spoken unto you by God?" (Matt. 22:29, 31). "Search the Scriptures . . . They are they which testify of Me" (John 5:39).

People cried out in wonder at His knowledge of the Scriptures although, as they put it, He had "never learned" (John 7:15); their hearts burned within them as, "beginning at Moses and all the Prophets, He expounded unto them in all the Scriptures the things concerning Himself" (Luke 24:27).

When the Lutheran Church asserts that Christ was a preacher of the Gospel, it does not mean to say that He did not preach the Law. To do so would be to ignore the record of the Scriptures. The Sermon on the Mount is an interpretation of God's Law by the Prophet sent by God (Matt. 5—7); and in Matt. 23 Christ invokes the curse of God's holy Law upon the unbelieving Jews and their leaders.

Yet the chief and proper function of the prophetic office of Christ is the preaching of the Gospel. "The Law was given by Moses, but grace and truth came by Jesus Christ," said John (ch. 1:17). Whenever Christ preached Himself, He preached not Law, but Gospel—a term which Lutherans understand as "the good news of the grace of God in Christ Jesus." Whenever Christ preached the Law, He preached it solely for the sake of the Gospel.

All His miracles, signs, and wonders had but one object: to make it easier for people to believe His message. He was not in the least bit interested in impressing people (Matt. 4:1-11; 13:58). He cautioned against too great publicity of the deeds themselves, for fear that they might throw His mission out of its true perspective (cp. Matt. 12:15-19; Mark 7:36). The reaction Jesus was looking for was that of his fellow townsmen in Capernaum who, astonished at the casting out of an unclean spirit, "questioned among themselves, saying: What thing is this? What new doctrine is this? For with authority commandeth He even the unclean spirits, and they do obey Him" (Mark 1:27). "Lord, I believe. Help Thou mine unbelief!" (Mark 9:24.)

And while many rejected His message, yet there were always some who accepted His Word and believed that He was the Christ, the Son of God, the Savior of the world (John 4:1-54; 6:64-69; 9:1-38).

So He moved humbly onward, preaching Himself as the Fulfillment of the long-promised Hope of Israel, yet with an authority that left His contemporaries spellbound (Matt. 7:28-29). As Ezekiel's before Him, His mission was "to speak (God's) words unto them [the people], whether they will hear or whether they will forbear; for they are most rebellious" (Ezek. 2:7).

There was nothing more that He could do when people refused to believe. He carried this suffering to the grave, for He had taken upon Him the form of a servant.

3. In the State of Exaltation

It was the same message of the Gospel, however, which the Apostles received as a sacred trust to carry to the ends of the world: "Go ye into all the world, and preach the Gospel to every creature" (Mark 16:15).

"As My Father hath sent Me, even so send I you" (John 20:21), was His mandate to the disciples on that first Sunday behind locked doors. Luke tells us that, on the same evening, Christ said unto those that were assembled: "These are the words which I spake unto you while I was yet with you, that all things must be fulfilled which were written in the Law of Moses, and in the Prophets, and in the Psalms, concerning Me. Then opened He their understanding, that they might understand the Scriptures, and said unto them: Thus it is written, and thus it behoved Christ to suffer and to rise from the dead the third day; and that repentance and remission of sins should be preached in His name among all nations, beginning at Jerusalem. And ye are witnesses of these things" (Luke 24:44-48).

Christ, therefore, has now entrusted His prophetic office to the Church—the community of those anointed through Him to be priests and prophets. "Ye are a chosen generation, a royal priesthood, an holy nation, a peculiar people, that ye should *show forth* the praises of Him who has called you out of darkness into His marvelous light" (I Pet. 2:9).

Witnessing to Christ is the prophetic duty of the Church. It is the spiritual sacrifice of the holy priesthood. The great promise "I am with you alway" was given to those who would undertake this duty and carry out the missionary command. The Lutheran minister is, therefore, nothing more than a witness for Christ; the Lutheran layman is nothing less than a witness for Christ.

All of us together are bound by but one cord in our witnessing — the Word of Christ. He said: "Teach them to observe all things whatsoever I have commanded you" (Matt. 28:20). The Lutheran Church has always found in John 17:20 the statement of Christ that the Word of His Apostles is His own Word: "I pray for them which shall believe on Me through their [the Apostles'] Word."

The Lutheran Church, therefore, through its loyal adherence to the Scriptures as the inspired Word of God, rightly claims that it preaches the Word of Christ and exercises His prophetic office. Luther complained of a careless, negligent attitude toward the preached Word even in his own time: "Human nature is so completely perverted and corrupted that we do not believe that we are hearing God's Word when He happens to speak to us through some human being, for we judge the Word according to the eminence and reputation of the speaker. We hear the speaker speaking as a mere human being, and consequently we consider the Word that he speaks as that of a human being. And so we despise it and grow tired of it, while we should thank God for putting His divine Word into the mouth of a man, His servant, who is like us in all things and who can speak to us, comforting and cheering us with the Word. And so it is not the word of the clergyman, or of St. Peter or some other servant of the Word, but that of divine Majesty itself." (Pieper, *Christliche Dogmatik*, II, p. 402, note 970.)

If the Lutheran Church is to be true to its prophetic mission, it will have to preach His Word. "Let us not wrap our talent in a napkin, let us not bury it in the earth, but let us prove ourselves to be the bearer of good tidings upon the high mountain, to lift up our voice with strength and say to the cities of Judah, 'Behold your God'" (Northern Illinois, 1916).

B. The Priestly Office

The priestly office of Christ is the heart of the Christian faith. It has happened on occasion that theology has left Christ the head and the tongue but has taken away the heart. Christ the Priest looses the tongue for Christ the Prophet and provides the subjects for Christ the King of His Church.

This topic takes us back to the climax of Old Testament worship and the silence of the multitude in the moment of reconciliation with God through the hands of a mediator.

The function of the Hebrew high priest is succinctly stated (Heb. 5:1): "Every high priest taken from among men is ordained for men in things pertaining to God, that he may offer both gifts and sacrifices for sins." It is evident from this passage that there was a sharp contrast in the Hebrew conceptions of the prophetic and priestly functions. While the prophet was the representative of God, the priest was the representative of the people. The prophet stood with God toward man; the priest stood with man toward God. In the same sense Christ, as a Priest, was man's representative, not God's. God gave the Priest, it is true. Since men were not looking for a representative, God sent one; for where *satisfactio* is required, there a priest is required, too.

So it happened that "God was in Christ, reconciling the world unto Himself" (II Cor. 5:19) and, "having made peace through the blood of His Cross, by Him reconciled all things unto Himself" (Col. 1:20). Reconciliation of two disunited parties, God and man, was the priestly function; and it was the function of the high priest.

Need for Reconciliation.—Reconciliation presupposes a time when things were different. Lutherans have always accepted the Scriptural accounts that there was such a time when man loved God spontaneously and not as a duty to be wrung from him contrary to his inclinations and his very nature. But man became a sinner. What this brief word implies is brought out by Scripture in stark reality. Scripture never becomes sentimental about sin so as to tone down its nature or its consequences. It portrays sin for what it is in its actuality (I John 1:8) and universality: a deed of transgression (Rom. 5:12; II Cor. 5:10), an unconscious depravity (Ps. 51:7), a sleeping lust (Rom. 7:7), a thought of the mind (Matt. 15:19; Mark 7:21), and idle word (Matt. 12:36), a deed undone (James 4:17).

The Scriptures are just as clear about sin's consequences: the prevention of God's blessing (Jer. 5:22-25), a cleavage between God and man (Is. 59:2), temporal punishments, one worse than the other (Deut. 28:16-40), enmity of men toward God (Rom. 8:7), and wrath of God toward men (Rom. 1:18), and finally death (James 1:15).

At the base of sin lies an enmity of man toward God which the Scriptures throughout regard as an incontrovertible fact. The carnal mind is enmity against God. "You that were sometime alienated and enemies in your mind by wicked works, yet now has He reconciled in the body of His flesh through death" (Col. 1:21-22 a). The enmity of men toward God may come, as Bente suggests (Canada, 1898, p. 34), from the knowledge that God in His justice and holiness will not stand idly by while a rebellion is going on. It may arise, too, from a sense of indebtedness to God in the matters of (1) punishment for transgressions and (2) the duty to fulfill the Law, which soon becomes apparent as an impossible task (Northern Illinois, 1918, p. 29).

Man's enmity against God has made God the enemy of man. "The wrath of God is revealed from heaven against all ungodliness and unrighteousness of men," says Paul (Rom. 1:18). The suffering which the holy and just God imposes upon men in His anger is the suffering of a curse, of wrath, of punishment, of retribution, of damnation. These sufferings are not intended to improve the sinner, nor to bring him to repentance, but rather to destroy him in hell. (Canada, 1898, p. 46.)

The sinner stands condemned before God, the witnesses for the prosecution having been the Law of God and his own conscience. "The sinner becomes an enemy of his own God-given moral nature." "Man cannot thrust God from the throne of his heart without being condemned by his own conscience." (Canada, 1898, p. 50.)

Enmity between God and man is, therefore, a reciprocal relationship. According to Scripture, this enmity is the real illness; sinful acts and suffering are just the symptoms. No medication for the symptoms will cure the illness. Salvation depends on a real cure, and that means reconciliation of God with men and of men with God. To deny, with V. Hoffmann, the hate of God toward sinners, or, with Ritschl, the wrath of God altogether, was always rejected by Lutherans as a solution to the problem.

Thank God that Christ faced the whole ugly reality of the problem and became our High Priest. We changed the friendship of God into enmity, and He changed it back to friendship. We changed the wine into vinegar, and He made it wine again. This is the "reconciliation" of the Scriptures which Christ has performed as our High Priest.

1. Christ's Priesthood Foretold in the Old Testament

Like the prophetic office, the sacerdotal work of Christ was foretold in Old Testament prophecy and foreshadowed in types prefiguring Christ as the perfect High Priest. "Thou art a Priest forever," says the Lord to Him whom He had told: "Sit Thou at My right hand" (Ps. 110:1, 4). The entire priestly cult of the Old Testament pointed forward to Him who was to be the Fulfillment of all these figures and shadows. Concerning the priests, God had told Moses: "They shall be holy unto their God and not profane the name of their God; for the offerings of the Lord made by fire, and the bread of their God, they do offer; therefore they shall be holy" (Lev. 21:6). This inner holiness was to be symbolized by the many washings and purifications incumbent upon them before they were to perform their work (Ex. 29:4; 30:18-21; Lev. 16:4, 24; etc.); by their holy garments (Ex. 28:2 ff; Lev. 16:4); by refraining from wine and strong drink (Lev. 10:9); by avoiding all defilement (Lev. 21:1-15). No descendant of Aaron having any physical blemish was permitted to function in the priestly office (Lev. 21: 16-23). In spite of all these prescriptions, the high priests of the Old Testament were and remained sinful beings (Heb. 7:28), who had to offer sacrifices for their own sins (Heb. 5:3; 7:27); feeble, imperfect types of Him who is holy, harmless, undefiled, separate from sinners (Heb. 7:26), because He is the everlasting Son of God.

As the person of the Old Testament priests, so their sacrifice, no matter how carefully selected (cp. Lev. 1:3, 10; 3:1, 6; etc.), was only an imperfect shadow of that High Priest who offered up Himself as the Lamb without blemish and without spot, foreordained before the foundation of the world (I Pet. 1:19-20).

Here we have the perfect High Priest, offering the perfect sacrifice. Being true man, He could take man's place; being sinless, He could take upon Himself another's sin; being the eternal, omnipotent God, He could become the Substitute for all mankind. By His sacrifice, once offered, He has obtained an eternal redemption (Heb. 9:12) and has perfected forever them that are sanctified (Heb. 10:14).

2. Passive and Active Obedience

In Christ's performance of His sacerdotal office we usually distinguish between His passive and His active obedience. By His passive obedience we mean His substitutionary work of freeing men from the penalties provided by the Law of God for all sinners. He did this by taking our sins upon Himself and suffering in our stead our punishment. Isaiah 53 describes this passive obedience, as does practically the entire Letter to the Hebrews. The Epistles of the Apostles are replete with references to this passive obedience (cp. Rom. 5:25; Gal. 3:13; Eph. 5:2; Col. 1:14; John 1:7; I Pet. 2: 21-24; etc.).

The active obedience of our High Priest consists in His substitutionary work of freeing us from the demands of the Law and obtaining for us a perfect righteousness by perfectly fulfilling, as our Substitute, the entire Law in all its demands, so that His Righteousness may be made our own by faith. "Think not," says Christ, "that I am come to destroy the Law or the Prophets. I am not come to destroy, but to fulfill." (Matt. 5:17.) Paul says: "Christ is the end of the Law for righteousness to everyone that believeth" (Rom. 10:4), and, again, "God sent forth His Son, made of a woman, made under the Law, to redeem them that were under the Law" (Gal. 4:4-5).

Thus by fulfilling the Law as our Substitute and suffering in our stead all the penalties we had deserved, Christ, our High Priest, rendered full satisfaction to the mandatory as well as the punitive justice and holiness of God and thereby reconciled the world unto God as our Proxy, our Substitute, by vicarious atonement (II Cor. 5:18-21).

Philippi has left us a remarkable personal testimony of what the vicarious atonement meant to him in his own life. In refutation of von Hofmann, who denied the Biblical Lutheran doctrine of reconciliation and justification, i. e., of the vicarious atonement of Christ, Philippi said: "If the assumption that Hofmann's teaching concerning reconciliation and justification were proved to be in agreement with Scripture, I would immediately cease being, not only a Lutheran theologian, but even a member of the Lutheran Church, for it is precisely because of the Lutheran doctrine of reconciliation and justification in its confessional form and wording that I am a Lutheran theologian, a Lutheran Christian, indeed, a Christian at all. For whoever takes away from me the propitiatory blood of the Son of God, which was offered as a ransom to appease God's wrath, i. e., the vicarious atonement of our Lord and Savior Jesus Christ, made to satisfy the penal justice of God, and thereby deprives me of justification or forgiveness of sins solely by faith in the merits of this my Warranter and Mediator, in other words, the imputed righteousness of Christ, he deprives me of Christianity altogether. I should then just as lief have remained an adherent of the religion of my fathers, the seed of Abraham according to the flesh." (Philippi was a baptized Jew.) (Eastern District, 1903, p. 59.)

3. In the State of Exaltation

"They truly were many priests, because they were not suffered to continue by reason of death, but this man, because he continueth ever, hath an unchangeable priesthood" (Heb. 7:23-24).

Christ rose from the dead with the sanction of God upon His high-priestly sacrifice. "It is Christ that died, yea rather, that is risen again" (Rom. 8:34). The same Christ who was put to death for our sins was "raised for our justification" (Rom. 4:25).

He ascended to heaven with the blood of the covenant, as the God-Man, who had offered the high-priestly sacrifice. By virtue of that blood He speaks today in intercession for His own. "He is also able to save them to the uttermost that come unto God by Him, seeing He ever liveth to make intercession for them" (Heb. 7:25). "He is even at the right hand of God, who also maketh intercession for us" (Rom. 8:34 b).

It is not merely the blood of Christ, or only His merit, which intercedes for us at the throne of God, but Christ Himself on the basis of His blood and merit. He intercedes, even as He atoned for us, as our High Priest.

His intercession is authoritative, wise, and understanding, righteous, compassionate, unique (He is the only Intercessor), and perpetual. "If any man sin, we have an Advocate with the Father, Jesus Christ, the Righteous; and He is the Propitiation for our sins, and not for ours only, but also for the sins of the whole world" (I John 2:1-2).

C. The Kingly Office

1. Old Testament Prophecies

In the hope of Israel there lay the promise of a king. "The Lord said unto my Lord: Sit Thou at My right hand, until I make Thine enemies Thy footstool. The Lord shall send the rod of Thy Strength out of Zion; rule Thou in the midst of Thine enemies" (Ps. 110:1-2).

To David had been given the promise: "The Lord telleth thee that He will make thee an house. And when thy days be fulfilled, and thou shalt sleep with thy fathers, I will set up thy Seed after thee, which shall proceed out of thy bowels, and I will establish His kingdom. He shall build an house for My name, and I will

Office, or Work, of Christ

establish the throne of His kingdom forever" (2 Sam. 7:11-13; cp. also Ps. 8:8-9; Is. 9:7; Dan. 7:13-14).

A large section of the population emphasized the kingly function of the Promised One almost to the exclusion of his prophetic and priestly functions. They were looking not for spiritual blessings, but for material prosperity and peace. Conflict with an occupying foreign power only heightened the hope and hence the expectation that when He came, He would be a political deliverer. Needless to say, those who expected an apocalyptic king were disappointed in Christ. After the feeding of the five thousand they were willing to crown Him, but soon disowned Him in resentful disappointment (John 6:1-66). Some, no doubt, followed Him until the road led to Calvary. Their hopes crushed there, they returned in disillusionment.

Christ passed to glory not simply *after*, but because of, and through, His sufferings. The ground of His kingly dominion is to be found in His obedience unto death, even the death of the Cross.

2. In the State of Humiliation

Christ certainly had not given any of His followers false hopes about the Kingdom. Yet even they consistently misinterpreted the purpose of the great demonstrations of divine authority which caused them to cry out in astonishment: "What manner of man is this that even the winds and the sea obey Him?" (Matt. 8:27).

Even in the State of Humiliation, Christ was King. Lutherans have always found in Christ's miracles the complete proof of His divine kingship. Christ was ruling the world as He Himself testified: "My Father worketh hitherto, and I work." (John 5:17). The Babe in the Manger, and the Man who walked the roads of Judea, ruled the world. "All things have been delivered to Me by My Father" (Matt. 11:27), He said in the days of His Galilean ministry.

The men who walked with Him freely admitted later on that they had not seen in this unprepossessing figure the king of Israel and of the world. As the crowds shouted: "Hosanna, blessed is the King of Israel that cometh in the name of the Lord," the disciples who knew Him best stood by in amazement. John's account describes the situation perfectly: "These things understood not

His disciples at the first; but when Jesus was glorified, then remembered they that these things were written of Him and that they had done these things unto Him" (John 12:16).

The kingly office of Christ, however, was fully revealed only after His resurrection and ascension.

3. In the State of Exaltation

The powers of government which Jesus exercised in a hidden way during the State of Humiliation, He used fully, used continually during the period between the Resurrection and Ascension. "All power is given unto Me in heaven and on earth" (March 28:18) was the way He expressed it.

The particular revelation of the divine powers became manifest, of course, as the Scriptures testify, with His ascension and His sitting down at the right hand of God. "Now, O Father, glorify Thou Me," prayed Christ in the last days of the Humiliation, "with Thine own Self with the glory which I had with Thee before the world was" (John 17:5). He sat down at the right hand of God, as He had risen from the dead, with His human nature fully participating in all the functions of the Godhead as King of the *world* and of His *Church*.

The Scriptural teaching that Christ rules the world and His Church has given rise to the old distinctions of the Kingdom of Power, the Kingdom of Grace, and the Kingdom of Glory. These distinctions have been retained in our Catechism. The Kingdom of Power is the term applied to Christ's rule of the entire world; the Kingdom of Grace, or Church Militant, to His rule of the Church; and the Kingdom of glory, or the Church Triumphant, to His rule in the world to come.

These distinctions do not imply that Christ's kingdom is divided. From the viewpoint of the King, they simply recognize a Scriptural fact that Christ rules the world in the interest of His Church. The working of Christ's power in His believers is a direct result of His having been set down at God's right hand in the heavenly places, according to Paul, "far above all principality, and power, and might, and dominion, and every name that is named, not only in this world, but also in that which is to come; and hath put *all* things under His feet, and gave Him to be the Head over all things to the Church, which is His body, the fullness of Him that filleth all in all." (Eph. 1:21-23.)

God gave His Son dominion over all the world that His Church might be gathered from the four corners of the earth. Christ Himself has given us the assurance of that fact: "All power is given unto Me in heaven and in earth. Go ye *therefore*, and teach [make disciples of] all nations" (Matt. 28: 18-19).

From the viewpoint of the subjects, the distinction between the Kingdom of Power and the Kingdom of Grace is simply that the adherents of the latter are "in the world but not of the world." (John 17:11, 15.) Christ rules the world by exerting His power in the social structure; He rules and builds His Church through the means of grace, the Word and the Sacraments. In the Kingdom of Grace He rules not with the Law, but with the Gospel. Here all His subjects call Him Lord and King, and He calls them His friends.

The practical implications for the life of the Christian in the Scriptural distinctions of the two kingdoms are tremendous. On the one hand, the Christian discovers that he belongs to a commonwealth of the world in which He is urged to offer "supplications, prayers, intercessions, and thanksgivings . . . for all men, for kings, and for all that are in authority; that we may lead a quiet and peaceable life in all godliness and honesty" (I Tim. 2:1-2). On the other hand, He is constantly aware of His citizenship in a commonwealth which is not of this world, of which our Lord stated clearly that its aims and methods were totally different from those of the world: "If My kingdom were of this world, then would My servants fight that I should not be delivered to the Jews. But now is My kingdom not from hence" (John 18:36).

The solution of this practical difficulty lies in a hearty participation by the Christian in the affairs of state, for He knows the purpose for which the state is organized. At the same time he dare not expect the state to demand anything of its citizens which requires the operation of the Holy Spirit, for that belongs to the Kingdom of Grace. This is the truly Scriptural position, occupied alone today by the Lutheran Church.

The reason why the world does not know us, said John to the faithful of his time, is that it did not know Christ. But Christ has a great promise for just those whom the world does not know: translation into the Kingdom of Glory. "Beloved, now are we the sons of God, and it doth not yet appear what we shall be. But we know that when He shall appear, we shall be like Him, for we shall see Him as He is" (I John 3:1-2).

This other world, too, is called Christ's kingdom in the Scriptures: "We must through much tribulation enter into the Kingdom of God" (Acts 14:22). The Kingdom of Grace and the Kingdom of Glory, however, are a unit, even though being with Christ will take the believer from a world of faith into a world of blessed vision, from the cross to the crown.

Conclusion

Thus Christ the Prophet, Priest, and King remains the Hope of the New Covenant, as He was the Hope of the Old. "These three names represent to us the full extent of the work of redemption, without its being possible for one of them to be either wanting, or transplaced, or replaced by another," said the Reformed theologian Van Oosterzee. "He who will acknowledge only one or two of these offices, to the exclusion of the third, fails to do justice to the fullness of the Gospel and becomes one-sided, if he does not altogether lose the track. Lay stress on the prophetic office, at the expense of the other two, and you become a rationalist; on the high-priestly alone, and you become a mystic; on the kingly, overlooking the other two, and you split on the rock of the Chiliastic reveries." (Van Oosterzee, *Christian Dogmatics*, II, p. 585.)

With that we Lutherans agree. In our homes, churches, and schools we offer our adoration to "Jesus Christ, who is the faithful *Witness* [Prophet] and the First-begotten of the dead and the Prince of the *kings* of the earth [King]. Unto Him that loved us and washed us from our sins in His own blood [Priest] and hath made us kings and priests unto God and His Father, to Him be glory and dominion forever and ever (Rev. 1:5).

Sin

CHRIST's vicarious atonement is the chief and fundamental doctrine of Holy Writ. Speaking of Jesus of Nazareth, crucified, dead, buried, raised from the grave by the power of God, Peter says: "Neither is there salvation in any other; for there is none other name under heaven given among men whereby we must be saved" (Acts 4:12). However, no one can properly understand or fully appreciate this Gospel who has not first learned to know his sin. "Without a real knowledge of what an awful thing sin is, man cannot understand and accept the Gospel," says Walther (*Law and Gospel*, p. 325).

In realization of this truth, our fathers gave an important place in their theology, in their writings, and in their conventions not only to the doctrine of grace, but also to the doctrine of sin. As we shall summarize their teaching, we shall follow their example and treat this doctrine under three heads: *I. The Doctrine of Sin in General. II. The Doctrine of Original Sin. III. The Doctrine Concerning Actual Sin.*

I. THE DOCTRINE OF SIN IN GENERAL

A. What Is Sin?

To the average person that is sin which to him seems horrible and wicked, the Lindbergh kidnaping, the Bataan death march, or the wartime atrocities; but before God every form of lawlessness is sin, for according to Scripture, "Sin is '*anomia*,' lit., "lawlessness" (I John 3:4). Anything, therefore, which fails to measure up to the standard of God's Law or is opposed thereto, whether it seems horrible to man or no, is sin and wickedness.

While the word "lawlessness" is etymologically a negative term, denoting merely lack of harmony with God's will, Scripture uses it to indicate a positive opposition to the Divine Law, since it describes sinful man as one who "does lawlessness" (I John 3:4), and sinners as them "that work lawlessness" (*anomia*, Matt. 7:23); hence the definition of our Catechism: "Sin is the transgression of the Law" (p. 86) is Scriptural and correct.

But are also the evil thoughts, desires, and deeds which are done in ignorance and without deliberation to be designated as sin? the anger of an infant? the unbelief of the heathen who does not know the Gospel? the sudden flare-up of an uncontrollable passion? We reply: All lawlessness, whether a condition or an act, whether done knowingly or unknowingly, with deliberation or no, is a transgression of God's Law, for the Scriptures call the inner emotions of the flesh sinful, so that we are "by nature the children of wrath" (Eph. 2:3), and the promptings of the flesh which arise in the Christian against his will are called sin, for the Apostle says: "The evil which I would not, that I do," and adds: "Now it is no more I that do it, but sin that dwelleth in me" (Rom. 7:19-20). Moreover, in describing his attacks upon the Gospel, which were made in ignorance and before his conversion, the Apostle not only acknowledges them to be sins, but on account of them calls himself the "chief" of sinners (I Tim. 1:13-16).

Romanists, Pelagians, Calvinists, and other Reformed writers err, therefore, when they declare only such acts to be sinful which are done knowingly and with deliberation. (F. Pieper, *Christliche Dogmatik*, I, p. 633, Note 1564.)

B. The Cause of Sin

There is in every one of us the natural tendency to place the blame for our sins on others, yes, even on God Himself. Adam did this when in presumptuous insolence he dared to say to his Creator: "The woman whom Thou gavest to be with me, she gave me of the tree, and I did eat" (Gen. 3:12), and thus laid the blame for his fall, first, on his wife, but secondly and chiefly on God, who in His goodness had given her to him, not as a stumbling stone for sin, but as "an help meet for him" (Gen. 2:18).

The ranking leaders of Reformed Protestantism also blame God for the existence of sin by declaring Him to be its original and moving cause. Calvin did this when he said: "The first man fell because God looked upon it as a good thing. . . . Accordingly man fell into sin, because God in His providence *decreed it so.*" (*Institution of the Christian Religion,* Book III, c. 23, 8.) And Zwingli, when speaking of the wickedness of Esau, said: "God in His providence created (Esau) for the purpose he should live, indeed, that he should live wickedly." (*Elench. vs. Catabapt.,* f. 36 A.) Thus these men actually held God to be the cause of sin.

The Scriptures expressly declare that God is not the cause of sin, for God "saw everything that He had made, and behold, it was very good" (Gen. 1:31), and "all that is in the world, the lust of the flesh and the lust of the eyes and the pride of life, is not of the Father, but is of the world" (I John 2:16), and again: "A God of truth and without iniquity, just and right is He" (Deut. 32:4). The Formula of Concord therefore declares: "He (God) is not a creator, author, or cause of sin." (Thorough Declaration, I, 7, *Triglot,* p. 861.)

Furthermore, the Scriptures tell us explicitly that sin came into this world, first, through *the devil,* and secondly, through *man himself.* Satan is called the "murderer from the beginning" (John 8:44), "which deceiveth the whole world" (Rev. 12:9), on whose account the Christians are also constantly in danger of being "corrupted from the simplicity that is in Christ" (II Cor. 11:3). And man is held responsible for his sin, both by his conscience (Gen. 3:8) and by his God, because, like Adam, he willingly permits himself to be enticed thereto (Gen. 3:12, 17; Eph. 2:2-3; II Thess. 2: 9-10). Jesus charges His adversaries: "The lusts of your father ye *will do*" (John 8:44). Wherefore God also, in disavowing the responsibility for sin, says: "They have corrupted *themselves*" (Deut. 32:5; cp. v. 4).

Reason, however, is not satisfied with this teaching of Scripture and asks: But why did God make it possible for man to fall? Why did He not in His Omnipotence prevent the approach of Satan and, consequently, the fall of our first parents? We confess that we are not able to answer these questions. Nor can any man. Paganism, in the forms of Zoroastrianism and Manicheism, tried it by teaching the doctrine of dualism, namely, that evil has always existed alongside of God and is an eternal principle. But this doctrine contradicts Scripture and leaves the question unsolved: "How did evil originate?" and "Why does God permit it to continue?" Mary Baker

Eddy, founder of Christian Science, sought to solve the problem by the simple expedient of saying that sin does not exist, that it is merely an idea, an error of the mind. "If God is real," she says, "the *evil*, the opposite of God, *is unreal*," and: "There can be but one Mind, because there is but one God, and if we claimed no other and accepted no other, sin would be unknown" (*Key to the Scriptures*, pp. 469–470, 1902 Ed.). According to Mrs. Eddy the idea of sin is here only because we *claim* it is here. But this does not answer our questions, for then we ask: "How did this idea of sin originate? Why did God permit such an idea to enter our minds? And why does He not now expunge it from the voice of conscience?"

There simply is no satisfactory answer to the question: How could sin get into the world? for "we know in part, and we prophesy in part, but when that which is perfect is come, then that which is in part shall be done away" (I Cor. 13:9-10). The fact is, however, that sin did get into the world, that it is here. And the fact is that in Christ, God has blotted out our transgressions and forgiven them and has assured us that, if we believe this, we shall be saved (John 3:16). Shall we, then, reject this message of salvation just because we cannot now find all the answers to certain problems connected with the origin of sin?

C. The Seat of Sin

The seat of sin is primarily the soul with its intellect and will, the body sharing therein since it is the organ of the soul, for Jesus says: "Out of the heart" (that is, out of the soul, which is the seat of thought and will) "proceed evil thoughts, murders, adulteries," etc. (Matt. 15:19). By taking its seat in the soul of man, sin has corrupted all men in their highest powers so that "there is none that doeth good, no not one" (Ps. 14:3). Only of One can it be said: "He was holy, harmless, undefiled, separate from sinners" (Heb. 7:26), for He was conceived by the Holy Ghost (Matt. 1:20). And thank God, He became incarnate for us "that we might be made the righteousness of God in Him" (II Cor. 5:21).

D. The Consequences of Sin

It is when we see the exceedingly dreadful and everlasting consequences of sin that we begin to realize how horrible sin really is, for, as the Apostle declares, by sin came death (Rom. 5:12), which has "passed upon all men," — spiritual, temporal, and eternal death. Now death is not an annihilation, but a separation. Thus spiritual death is the spiritual separation of man from God, from the original image of righteousness, from all that is good, and from the hope of eternal life (Eph. 2:1). And with this spiritual death there comes into our lives a catastrophe the enormity of which is never fully realized because it is so common before us, namely, the continuous and general dissolution of our mortal bodies, the constant corruption and decay of strength and health, ending finally in the separation of the soul from the body in physical death; and — unless we accept Christ — this physical death will finally end in the eternal separation of the creature from its Creator in the torments of the damned, for, according to Scripture, those who "obey not the Gospel of our Lord Jesus Christ . . . shall be punished with everlasting destruction from the presence of the Lord and from the glory of His power" (II Thess. 1:9).

But why is sin visited with punishments so utterly dreadful? The answer is: Because sin is always a transgression of the Law of God, a capital crime, a flying into the face of the divine Lord, a lese Majesty crime. As one of our synodical writers puts it (Central District, 1877, p. 35): "It is one thing to strike down a poor beggar who has no friends to plead his cause and who is able to do little about it in the courts of men; but it is quite another thing to strike the king, who has the power over life and death and therefore can execute a speedy sentence. Every sin is always an affront to the Most High God, the King of Kings, and is for that reason incalculably wicked. Surely man's biting into the fruit of the first Garden was not in itself horrible, for he was not only permitted but commanded to eat of the fruit therein. The true heinousness of Adam's sin consisted in this that he ate despite a clear and definite command of God concerning this particular tree and its fruit and thus defied the divine Lord, for 'sin must be gauged,' as Dr. Luther says, 'not according to itself . . . but according to Him who has been violated and put to shame thereby'" (Luther, Ps. 112:5; quoted, Central District, 1877, p. 35, in footnote).

The heinous nature of our sins is evident also from their effect upon our fellow men. Let a soldier, while on watch at night and on a field of battle, carelessly light just one match for the purpose, let us say, of reading his instructions, and he is at once subject to the extreme penalty of death. Why? Not because this act is dangerous in itself, but because it exposes his position to the enemy, because it may, under the circumstances, endanger the lives of countless others, and because it may pave the way for the loss of an important battle and ultimately cost the war. Thus one such careless and forbidden act could actually bring desolation and ruin over an entire nation. Even so the one sin of Adam affected the world. It brought with it thorns and thistles, sickness and sorrow, poverty and crime, war and bloodshed, yes, all the horrible iniquities of this whole world throughout all her generations. It was, therefore, an indescribable evil, deserving an inexpressible punishment. Consequently every sin, whether it seem ever so slight, is always infinitely dangerous and indescribably evil, and "a true Christian manifests himself as a person who *fears to commit a single sin*" (Walther, *Law and Gospel*, translated, p. 327).

However, the complete devastation caused by sin is seen even more clearly as we examine the Scriptural doctrine of original sin.

II. THE DOCTRINE OF ORIGINAL SIN

A. THE IMPORTANCE OF THIS DOCTRINE

The doctrine of original sin is vital. It touches the very heart of Christianity. It gives answer to such important questions as the following: Can man save himself? Is he able to help along in his conversion? Does he possess the power of free will in spiritual matters? Is total corruption the very essence of man's nature? As Dr. Pieper points out, an error in reply to these questions invariably affects the doctrines of salvation, of conversion, of sanctification, of creation, and of the incarnation of the Son of God, and may utterly corrupt them (*Christliche Dogmatik*, I, p. 657, note 1605). How important, then, for us to know the doctrine of original sin!

B. THIS DOCTRINE IS FULLY UNDERSTOOD ONLY BY DIVINE REVELATION

While human reason is able to perceive somewhat that there is in the nature of every man an innate propensity towards evil, as Horace, Cicero, and other pagan writers testify (quoted by Dr. Pieper, *Christliche Dogmatik*, I, p. 649), nevertheless, because of the corruption of man through sin, this knowledge is so utterly inadequate that a full and complete understanding of all that is involved in this sin can be attained only by divine revelation, for according to Scripture, "the heart is deceitful above all things and desperately wicked; who can know it?" (Jer. 17:9). The Smalcald Articles, therefore, declare: "This hereditary sin is so deep and horrible a corruption of nature that no reason can understand it, but it must be learned and believed from the revelation of Scripture" (Part III, Art. I, 3, *Triglot*, p. 477).

C. THE SCRIPTURAL DOCTRINE CONCERNING ORIGINAL SIN

1. Terms and Definition

To describe this sin, the Bible uses such terms as: "indwelling sin" (Rom. 7:17), a "law in the members" (Rom. 7:23), and "lust," literally, "a desire for that which is forbidden," or "concupiscence." All that is embraced in these terms the Church has embodied in a word of her own coinage, namely, "original sin," an expressive designation pointing to the fact that this sin has its origin in Adam, is connected with the origin of each of his descendants, and is the origin of all actual transgressions. (Hollaz; see *Christian Dogmatics*, Mueller, p. 216.)

What, then, is original sin? Our Catechism replies: "Original sin (inherited sin) is the *total corruption* of our *whole human nature*," so that "man is by nature without true fear, love, and trust in God. He is without righteousness, is inclined only to evil, and is spiritually blind, dead, and an enemy of God" (p. 87, Questions 94, 95). It is not an act, but a condition into which all men since the Fall are born. It embraces a) hereditary guilt, and b) hereditary corruption. Let us study these two phases of this sin separately:

2. The Hereditary Guilt of All Mankind

In the first place, then, original sin embraces hereditary guilt, that is, every man, woman, and child is by nature charged with the guilt of Adam's transgression. Now, all the logic of man's carnal mind has been enlisted to make a concerted attack upon this phase of our doctrine, for all that is in us by nature rebels against the idea that we should be held responsible for what Adam did in that first sin. Pelagians, Arminians, Socinians, and even neo-Lutherans have lifted up their heels to kick against it, their opposition ranging, as Dr. Pieper shows, from a mere denial to veritable blasphemy. (*Christliche Dogmatik*, I, p. 646, note 1581.) However, the "stubborn facts" are that Scripture teaches it, for in Rom. 5:18 the Holy Spirit declares: "By the offense of one, judgment came upon all men to condemnation," lit., "by the offense of one (namely, Adam) there came to all men a damnatory sentence." And in Rom. 5:19 we read: "By one man's disobedience many were made sinners," lit., "by the disobedience of one the many were placed into the category of sinners." Furthermore, the Lord has given us also visible evidence of this universal condemnatory sentence by permitting all men, as a consequence thereof, to be born in a state of total corruption, for we are "by *nature* children of wrath" (Eph. 2:3). Moreover, in the passages cited above (Rom. 5:18-19) God has inextricably bound up the universal sentence of condemnation with the universal declaration of justification, for we read (Rom. 5:18, lit.): "As by the offense of one there came upon all men a condemnatory sentence, even so by the righteousness of One there came upon all men a sentence of acquittal unto life." Hence, to deny the universal sentence of guilt is to deny also the universal sentence of pardon and acquittal and constitutes an attack upon the central doctrine of Scripture, the doctrine of objective justification.

Because original sin is, therefore, real guilt, it brings with it also real punishment, for the Scriptures declare that we are the "children of *wrath*," not first by deeds of actual transgression, but already "*by nature*" (Eph. 2:3).

The question has been asked: But is it right and just of God to charge us with Adam's sin and to punish us for it? Various efforts have been made to answer this question to the satisfaction of human reason. But it is neither right nor necessary for us to vindicate God. Who are we to challenge His righteousness who says: "As the heavens are higher than the earth, so are My ways higher than your ways, and My thoughts than your thoughts" (Is. 55:9). Moreover, God has already imputed to the whole world the obedience of Christ and thus by grace has removed the imputation of Adam's guilt. When Israel, therefore, challenged God for visiting the sins of the fathers upon their children, God reminded His people that whenever the son shall turn from all his sins, he "shall not bear the iniquity of the father" (Ezek. 18:20). God has also promised that "all things," including the evils of this world which have come down to us on account of Adam's sin, shall "work together for good to them that love God" (Rom. 8:28). To question the justice of God for imputing to the world the sin of our father Adam, is therefore both unnecessary and wicked.

3. The Hereditary and Total Corruption of All Mankind

According to Scripture, every human being, because of the guilt of Adam's transgression, is by nature corrupt and utterly sinful. David wrote: "Behold, I was *shapen* in iniquity, and in *sin* did my mother *conceive* me" (Ps. 51:5). And Jesus calls natural man "*flesh*," that is, a being *outside* the Kingdom of God and in need of regeneration (John 3:3, 5), for "ye *must* be born again," He said, "and except a man be born again he cannot enter into the Kingdom of God." And this description He applies to us all since He declares: "That which is born of the flesh is flesh" (John 3:6).

A. THE NEGATIVE AND POSITIVE SIDE OF ORIGINAL CORRUPTION

This total corruption of man by nature is first of all a negative concept, that is, it describes man as being without those attributes which he possessed before the Fall. Our Confessions state that man "is destitute of the righteousness wherein he was originally created, and in spiritual things dead to good" (*Popular Symbolics*, p. 39). And in Ephesians the Holy Spirit declares the unregenerate to be "dead in trespasses and sins" (Eph. 2:1), lit., "*dead* on account of trespasses and sins." Hence man is by nature so totally corrupt that he is without that original concreated righteousness, holiness, and happy knowledge of God which he originally possessed in the "image of God."

But this total corruption of man is also described in Scripture as a *positive wickedness*, a "constant, vicious disposition to evil" (*Popular Symbolics*, p. 85), which the Apostle calls "lust," lit., "concupiscence," a "craving for that which is forbidden" (Thayer; Rom. 7:7 ff.; James 1:14). This wickedness adheres even to us as Christians, for St. Paul says: "I see another law in my members *warring*" (present participle, "*continuously fighting*") "against the law of my mind" (Rom. 7:23), for "the flesh *lusteth* against the Spirit" (Gal. 5:17).

However, in describing the total corruption in man as something positive in him, we do not wish to be misunderstood as teaching what Flacius did, namely, that it is the substance of man as such, or his very nature. If we distinguish properly between a substance as that which exists by itself, and an accident as a quality which clings to an object but is removable therefrom, then the inherited wickedness of man is certainly not a substance, but an accident, for as the rottenness of an apple is not the apple itself, even so the corruption of nature is not nature herself. In order to guard against the errors of those (Romanists, Reformed, and particularly Strigel) who called original sin only a slight *stain* or *sickness*, Flacius (Historical Introduction, *Triglot*, p. 144, No. 167) held that original sin is *not an accident*, but the very *substance* of man. While this error of Flacius has now been somewhat exaggerated by many who are unaware of his real position (for he made distinctions which can be understood as in harmony with our doctrine, Pieper, *Christliche Dogmatik*, I, p. 658, note 1607), yet the statement that original sin is not an accident, but the very nature of man, should not have been defended by him, nor can it be defended without violating the Scriptural doctrines of creation, redemption, sanctification, and resurrection (*Christliche Dogmatik*, I, p. 658, note 1605), for human nature, though corrupted by sin, is nevertheless still a creation of God, and, therefore *in itself (per se)* good.

B. THE TOTAL CORRUPTION AND THE MIND AND WILL OF MAN

But what is the effect of such total corruption on the mind, and will of man? This question is, as we shall see, vital to the doctrine of conversion. With respect to the intellect, Scriptures describe man as "having the understanding darkened," as being "alienated from the life of God because of the blindness of their heart" (Eph. 4:18), as being in a state of "darkness" (Eph. 5:8) and as "dead" (Eph. 2:1). Furthermore the Holy Spirit expressly says: "The natural man receiveth not the things of the Spirit of God, for they are foolishness unto him; neither can he know them, because they are *spiritually discerned*" (I Cor. 2:14). As one writer puts it: "The unspiritual are out of court as religious critics; they are as deaf men judging music" (*Expositor's Greek Testament* on I Cor. 2:14, Note, p. 784). In fact, man by nature is so dead in his blindness that he regards the Gospel as foolishness (I Cor. 2:14), while he looks upon the Law, which condemns him (Gal. 3:10-12), as the true way to salvation (Gal. 3:1, 3, 10-12). Yes, man's natural intellect is more than blind, it is, as the Holy Ghost declares, "enmity," lit., hatred, "against God" (Rom. 8:7), so that it is always inclined to pass "rash, false, and corrupted judgments" on matters spiritual. The Formula of Concord describes this fully when it says: "Man's reason or natural intellect indeed still has a dim spark of the knowledge that there is a God, as also of the doctrine of the Law (Rom. 1:19 ff.), yet it is *so ignorant, blind, and perverted* that, when even the most ingenious and learned men on earth read or hear the Gospel of the Son of God and the promise of eternal salvation, *they cannot from their own powers perceive, apprehend, understand, or believe and regard it as true,* but the more diligence and earnestness they employ, wishing to comprehend these spiritual things with their reason, the less they understand and believe, and before they become enlightened and are taught by the Holy Ghost, they regard all this only as foolishness or fictions. (I Cor. 2:14; Eph. 4:17; Matt. 13:11 ff.; Luke 8:18; Rom. 3:11-12.) Accordingly, the Scriptures flatly call natural man in spiritual and divine things *darkness.* (Eph. 5:8; Acts 26:18; John 1:5.) Likewise the Scriptures teach that *man in sins is not only weak and sick, but defunct and entirely dead.*" (Eph. 2:1, 5; Col. 2:13. Thorough Declaration, II, 9, 10. *Triglot,* p. 883 f.)

As the mind, so the will of man is likewise totally depraved. It is not only spiritually dead and hence unable to will anything that is pleasing to God, but it is also carnally alive in active opposition to the Law of God, so that it can only oppose it. As Dr. Pieper states: "It cannot but sin" (*Christliche Dogmatik,* I, p. 652), for, according to Scripture, the "carnal mind is enmity against God; it is not subject to the Law of God, neither indeed *can* be" (Rom. 8:7). Even when natural man chooses that which is outwardly good in the eyes of the world, civic righteousness, feeding the hungry, caring for the destitute, etc., he is never able to will and do them out of a right and God-pleasing motive, namely, out of fear and love of God, as ordained in the First Commandment. That is impossible for him, for how can poor sinful man, "having no hope, and (being) without God in the world" (Eph. 2:12), love that God whom he by nature does not know or fear? (Rom. 3:17-18.)

Moreover, on account of his trespasses and sins man is also constantly smitten by conscience and driven to flee from before the presence of the Lord. In his own inimitable way Dr. Luther illustrates this total perversity of mind and will in our first parents immediately after the Fall. He shows the sheer stupidity of their minds, as they sought to do the impossible in trying to flee from the omnipresence of God; in seeking to hide from Him among the trees of the Garden; and in trying to deceive His omniscience as to the cause of their fear and flight. He shows the utter perverseness of their wills in daring to lie to the very face of God and in ultimately laying the blame for their fall at His feet. "Is not that," says Luther, "charging the Creator and disavowing one's own guilt?" (St. L. I:199—223.) And yet, behold the mercy of God! Even in the face of their willful and utter depravity He brought to them in the promise of the Woman's Seed the first word of absolution, the first message of grace and pardon.

C. THIS HEREDITARY CORRUPTION AFFECTS ALL MANKIND

However, this depravity of mind and will has by way of natural generation and birth (Eph. 3:6) come down to us all, so that God says of man: "Every imagination of the thoughts of his heart is only evil continually" (Gen. 6:5), and: "They are all under sin; as it is written: There is none righteous, no not one; there is none that understandeth, there is none that seeketh after God. They are all gone out of the way, they are together become unprofitable; there is none that doeth good, no, not one" (Rom. 3:9-12). So complete is the corruption of man that the Scriptures describe even the various members and functions of the body and soul as placed into the service of sin. For men as they are by nature are depicted as "having *eyes* full of adultery and that cannot cease from sin" (II Pet. 2:14; cp. also Rom. 3:13-18). We behold, therefore, the whole world of mankind by nature totally depraved in body and soul in the highest and noblest powers of intellect and will.

D. THE CONSEQUENCES OF THE HEREDITARY CORRUPTION

1. *The Loss of Free Will in Spiritual Matters.* — In a sense the will of natural man is free, free to reject God's grace, free to move in the realm in which it lives. But since it is dead to the spiritual

world, it has no life therein. When we therefore speak of a man as having lost his free will, we do not mean that he has no will at all, or that he cannot choose between good and evil on the level of civic righteousness. We mean that he has no power to choose on the higher level of God's realm and God's world, because to that world he is totally dead. While he, therefore, can choose to go to church, he cannot by his own powers choose to accept the Gospel which he hears there, nor can he set his will in motion in the direction of conversion, for in that sphere he has no life. He can choose to steal or not to steal, but to refrain from stealing on the higher spiritual level of love to God is not within his power, for to such love he is dead. The Apology of the Augsburg Confession admits this "freedom of the will" on the lower level of civic righteousness when it says: "The human will has liberty in the choice of works and *things which reason can comprehend of itself.* It can to a *certain extent* render civil righteousness." However, when speaking of the higher level of spiritual righteousness, the Formula of Concord denies any freedom of action to the will when it declares: "In spiritual and divine things the intellect, heart, and will of the unregenerate man are utterly unable by their own natural powers to understand, believe, accept, think, will, begin, do, work, or concur in working anything; but they are entirely dead to that which is good, and (they are) corrupt so that in man's nature since the Fall, before regeneration, there is not the least spark of spiritual power remaining or present by which . . . he can prepare himself for God's grace or accept the offered grace . . . or by his own powers be able of himself . . . to aid, do, work, or concur in working anything towards his conversion, either wholly or half, or in any, even the least or most inconsiderable part . . . he is the servant (and slave) of sin, John 8:44, and a captive of the devil, by whom he is moved, Eph. 2:2; II Tim. 2:26. Hence natural free will according to its perverted disposition and nature is strong and active only to what is displeasing and contrary to God" (Thorough Declaration, II, 7. *Triglot,* p. 883. Cp. also *The Abiding Truth,* Vol. I, "Conversion," p. 168, and Vol. II, "Synergism," p. 299 ff.

2. *Eternal death.* — Other consequences of inherited corruption are the sins that flow therefrom, and the final eternal condemnation,

called "the second death" (Rev. 20:14), which is the ultimate end of all sin. Since we have already discussed eternal death in a previous chapter (I, D), we shall proceed at once to a study of the Scriptural doctrine concerning actual sins.

III. THE SCRIPTURAL DOCTRINE CONCERNING ACTUAL SINS

A. NAMES AND DEFINITIONS

While original sin is a sinful *condition,* actual sins are the *deeds* which in the form of commission and omission result therefrom. Holy Scripture characterizes these sins by such terms as the following: "works of the flesh" (Gal. 5:19), "unfruitful works of darkness" (Eph. 5:11), "deeds of the old man" (Col. 3:9), "dead works" (Heb. 6:1; 9:14), "unlawful deeds" (II Pet. 2:8).

B. THE CAUSES OF ACTUAL SINS

1. *Internal (Inherent Ignorance and Corruption)*

Now, what are the causes of actual sins? The real, internal cause, as already indicated above, is the flesh, for the Holy Spirit calls actual sins "works of the *flesh,*" and "deeds of the *old man.*" But the Scripture mentions also other secondary causes within us, such as *spiritual ignorance* (for concerning those who reject Him, Jesus says: "They know not what they do," Luke 23:34); *sinful emotions and passions,* such as fear, wrath, love, etc., which cause man to put his personal safety and personal desires before the will of God; and *sinful habits,* which so accustom one to sinning that he cannot do good, as the Lord also warns when He says: "Can the Ethiopian change his skin, or the leopard his spots? Then may ye also do good, that are *accustomed to do evil*" (Jer. 13:23).

2. *External Causes of Actual Sins*

As external causes of actual transgressions, Scripture points to the devil and to our fellow men. The devil is described not only as the "spirit that worketh in the children of disobedience" (Eph. 2:2), but also as the "adversary" of the children of God (1 Pet. 5:8-9). His method of attack is illustrated in the Fall and in the temptation of Christ, and we are exhorted to resist him by remaining "steadfast in the faith" (I Pet. 5:9). Our fellow men also become the cause of sin in us when they entice us thereto by word and deed.

3. Actual Sins and the Providence of God

In this connection the question arises: but what of the providence of God and its relationship to actual sin? Does He, in ruling this world and guiding the details of men's lives, permit their sins and thus become a partaker thereof? We have already pointed out (see I, B) that God is not the cause or the author of sin. The Bible teaches, however, that the Lord *does* permit sin to occur, for He Himself says: "*I* gave them up unto their own hearts' lust" (Ps. 81:12), and the Holy Ghost tells us that *God* "suffered all nations to walk in their own ways" (Acts 14:16; cf. also Rom. 1:24, 26, 28). But while the Lord allows sins to take place, He does not accept the blame for them, for in these very passages He calls the sins of men "their *own* hearts' lust" and a walking "in their *own* ways." The dogmaticians, therefore, point out that God concurs in sinful acts *only in so far as they are* ACTS *(quoad materiale), but not in so far as they are* SINFUL *(quoad formale)*. Because the Scriptures say of God that "in Him we live and move and have our being" (Acts 17:25-28), it follows that God certainly participates in all we do; but since the Scriptures also tell us that God is holy (Lev. 19:2; Is. 6:3) and that He hates "all workers of iniquity" (Ps. 5:6-7), it also follows that He does not participate in that which makes our deeds sinful.

We know that this distinction of our dogmaticians between the *act as such (quoad materiale)* and *its sinfulness as such (quoad formale)* does not altogether satisfy human reason, but it does serve the very definite purpose of restricting our thoughts on this matter to what the Scriptures say. All further speculations on this point lead only to a denial of Scripture; for, if we say that God has nothing at all to do with the deeds of sin, we deny the Scriptural teaching of the providence of God and His concurrence in the acts of men; and if we hold that God concurs, not only in the *acts* of sin, but also in their *sinfulness*, we contradict those Scriptures which place the full guilt for sin, not on God, but solely on man. (Cp.

Hos. 13:9: "Thou hast destroyed *thyself.*") Moreover, the voice of conscience does not excuse man from his sin, but accuses him instead. (Cp. Bente, The Providence of God, *The Abiding Word,* II, p. 96 ff.)

C. THE CLASSIFICATION OF ACTUAL SINS

1. The Reason for Such Classification

The cataloging of the different kinds of sin under specific heads serves a very useful and necessary purpose. Thereby we are made to realize more keenly the multitude of our transgressions, how incalculably great and manifold they are; and as a consequence of such knowledge, the Gospel, which assures us that God has forgiven our sins for Jesus' sake, will become to us the more a priceless treasure of infinite and inestimable worth. We shall classify the various kinds of sins under thirteen different heads.

2. The Various Kinds of Actual Sins

A. THE SINS OF OFFENSE

The Bible distinguishes between the sin of *giving* offense and the sin of *taking* offense. To *give* offense does not mean to hurt another's feelings, but according to Rom. 16:17 it is *skandalon poiein,* lit.: "to make a snare or a trap" for another. Hence to say, to teach, or to do anything whereby I place a snare before another so that he may be entrapped in unbelief, error, or a wicked life, is to give offense. Our Savior has uttered most solemn warning against this sin. (Matt. 18:6 ff.; Mark 9:42; Luke 17:1-2.) Verily, with what care we ought, therefore, to speak and to teach doctrine, lest by the snares of error we set traps for souls and bring this woe upon ourselves! With what earnest scrutiny we ought to be on our guard against sin in our lives, lest by our wickedness we give offense, place a snare before others, and so come under the condemnation of this dreadful curse!

However, offense is given not only by false doctrine and sin, but also when through the loveless use of our liberties in adiaphora (eating of meats, drinking of wine, etc. Rom. 14) a weak brother is encouraged by our example to do something which his *erring* conscience regards as wrong; for according to Rom. 14:20 "it is evil for that man who eateth with offense" (lit.: "while recoiling at it"), and again: "He that doubteth is damned if he eat, because he eateth not of faith," that is, he is damned because, lit., "he eateth not with the conviction that he has a right to eat" (Rom. 14:23). Because it is wicked ever to cause our fellow men to stumble into sin, we Christians ought to be extremely careful in the full and unrestricted use of our Christian liberties, except where the truth of the Gospel is at stake. (F. Pieper, *Christliche Dogmatik*, I, p. 673; Mueller, *Christian Dogmatics*, p. 226, 3. Cp. Gal. 5:1, 13.)

Taking offense is the sin of finding fault with the doctrines or ethics of Scriptures or the crosses of Christianity and using these or other matters as an excuse to reject the Gospel and live in sin. The self-righteous do that when in their overweening pride they stumble at the doctrine of salvation by grace through faith (Rom. 9:31-33). The worldly wise do that when they are offended at the "foolishness of the Cross" and the "theological problems" involved in Scripture (I Cor. 1:22-23; I Cor. 13:9). And the Christians can also become guilty of this sin when they fault Christianity for its crosses and tribulations and consequently renounce it (Matt. 24:10; 13:21). Therefore Jesus says: "Blessed is he whosoever is not offended in Me" (Matt. 11:6; cp. also vv. 25-26).

B. VOLUNTARY AND INVOLUNTARY SINS

The will of man plays a part in every sin, whether he is aware of it or not. (Pieper, *Christliche Dogmatik*, I, p. 676.) Hence all sins can properly be called willful, or voluntary, sins. However, sins committed through blind ignorance and as a result of violent passions, natural affections, a strong party spirit, etc., because the exercise of the will is thereby pushed into the background, are properly called involuntary, or precipitate, sins. When, because of the indwelling lust, such sins are found also in believers, we call them sins of infirmity or sins of weakness. This term should, however, be restricted only to believers, since unbelievers sin, not because they are weak, but because they are spiritually dead. Little children and infants are, of course, less blameworthy than adults. While, because of the corruption of the flesh, the acts of their emotions and wills are truly actual sins, they are not to be classed as deliberate sins, that is, sins done with the knowledge of evil, for the Lord speaks of little children and infants as such "which have no knowledge between good and evil" (Deut. 1:39).

C. SINS AGAINST CONSCIENCE

Closely related to voluntary sins are those which are done against conscience. These our theologians have divided into four classes (Pieper, *Christliche Dogmatik*, II, p. 677): 1) the sins against a *correctly informed conscience* (right conscience); 2) the sins against a *misinformed conscience*, more frequently called an *erring conscience*. A misinformed conscience is one which causes unnecessary and mistaken scruples because of false indoctrination. The pagan who believes that he must pray to an idol is, by his misinformed conscience, actually placed into a dilemma. He is in a position where he sins no matter how he turns. If, to satisfy the voice of his misguided conscience, he prays to the idol, he transgresses God's First Commandment and brings damnation upon himself; if, on the other hand, he disobeys the voice of his conscience and neglects his idol worship, he violates the Word of God, which forbids any act against the voice of conscience, and thus he again brings damnation on himself, for, says the Scripture: "He that doubteth is damned if he eat . . . for whatsoever is not of faith," lit., of the conviction that it is proper, "is sin." (Rom. 14:23.) There is no possible escape for such a one except his conscience be instructed through the Word. False doctrine for that reason is a horrible and damnable thing, because it corrupts conscience and brings man into damnation no matter in what direction he walks. 3) There is also the sin against a *probable conscience*, that is, against the conscience which has been neglected, which could and would have warned us against sin if we had taken the trouble to give it the necessary information and instruction according to God's Word, or if we had granted ourselves more time for reflection. 4) We speak also of the sin against a *doubting conscience*, for "he that doubteth is damned if he eat, because he eateth not of faith; for whatsoever is not of faith," that is, of the conviction that I may do it, "is sin" (Rom. 14:23).

It is when we study the sins against conscience that we realize with a start how very important is right indoctrination from the cradle to the grave. May we, therefore, never deprecate the emphasis which our fathers placed on pure doctrine. Let us rather emulate them therein, for a right conscience can be wrought only by right doctrine.

D. SINS OF COMMISSION AND OMISSION

In sins of commission that is done which God has forbidden, while in sins of omission that is omitted which God demands. It is the sins of omission to which we shall give special attention, since they are the more frequently glossed over. The Holy Spirit tells us that, "to him that knoweth to do good and doeth it not, to him it is sin" (James 4:17), and Jesus calls that servant who buried his one talent a "wicked and slothful servant," condemning him with the fearful sentence: "Cast ye the unprofitable servant into outer darkness: there shall be weeping and gnashing of teeth" (Matt. 25:30). Moreover, sins of omission are weighed in the balance of our talents, for our Savior says: "Unto whomsoever much is given, of him shall be much required" (Luke 12:48).

E. SINS AGAINST GOD, NEIGHBOR, AND SELF

All sins are violations of God's Law, hence they are all done against God. However, the transgressions of the first part of the Decalog are sins against the Lord in a special sense, since they violate His person and being, His name and doctrine, His Word and His servants. They constitute a crime of lese majesty and will meet with the direst consequences. Sins against our neighbor include all those against the Second Table, especially also the sin of failing to rebuke our brother's error, his false doctrine and wrongdoing, for the Lord says: "Thou shalt in any wise rebuke thy neighbor and not suffer sin upon him," lit., "that thou bear not sin on his account" (Lev. 19:17). Sins against self are such as fornication and impurity, which, God tells us, "defile the temple of God" (I Cor. 3:17; 6:18).

F. GRIEVOUS AND LESS GRIEVOUS SINS

Every transgression of the Law is always a grievous sin, because it offends God and brings everlasting condemnation (Ezek. 18:20; Rom. 8:13; John 8:21). But some sins are more so than others, for example, the sins of adults are more grievous than those of little children who have not yet arrived at the age of discretion and knowledge (Deut. 1:39); and the trespasses of Israel, of the scribes and Pharisees in the days of Jesus, were far more heinous than even those of Sodom and Gomorrah, because of the greater measure of grace which had been bestowed on them in the fulfillment of Old

Testament type and prophecy and in the coming of the Christ. Wherefore Jesus also said: "It shall be more tolerable for Sodom in the Day of Judgment than for thee" (Matt. 11:24; Luke 10:14; Matt. 23). And now, with the New Testament in our hands, its many prophecies fulfilled before our eyes, the sins of our day by far exceed those of previous generations. This is especially true of us who have been so signally blessed by God. We have been cradled and nurtured in the purity of Christian doctrine and practice, as, perhaps, no other church body in the world. Verily, if we, who are not worthy of the least of all these mercies, now despise, neglect, or forsake them; if we do now turn from the ways in which our fathers trod, then our sin will be grievous indeed, for the Scriptures warn that the servant "who knew not" his master's will and "did commit things worthy of stripes shall be beaten with few stripes," but "that servant which knew his lord's will and prepared not himself, neither did according to his will, shall be beaten with many stripes" (Luke 12:48, 47).

G. MORTAL AND VENIAL SINS

Potentially, all sins are always mortal, for "the soul that sinneth it shall die" (Ezek. 18:20; John 8:21). But the moment we turn to Christ, accepting Him as our Savior, our sins can no longer destroy us, for "Christ has redeemed us from the curse of the Law" (Gal. 3:13). The evil deeds of the believing child of God, therefore, are no longer called mortal but venial sins, not because they are in themselves of a less sinful nature, but because they are always fully pardoned and for that reason have no power to accuse or destroy. Mortal sins, in the narrower sense, are sins that destroy faith.

The doctrine of the Roman Catholic Church, whereby venial sins are described as only a "slight offense against the Law of God," which merely "lessen but do not deprive us of God's friendship" (*Baltimore Catechism*, No. 2, p. 20, Questions 57 and 58), is vicious, because it deceives man about the enormity of his smallest sin and deadens his conscience. It is unscriptural, because the Bible states: "Cursed is everyone that continueth not in all things which are written in the Book of the Law to do them" (Gal. 3:10) and: "Whosoever shall keep the whole Law, and yet offend in one point, he is guilty of all" (James 2:10).

Sin

H. DOMINANT AND NON-DOMINANT SINS

According to Eph. 2:2, unbelievers are always under the rule of Satan and sin, but of believers the Apostle says: "Sin shall not have dominion over you; for ye are not under the Law, but under grace" (Rom. 6:14). Dr. Walther's comment on this passage deserves attention. He says: "What the Apostle actually says, is that sin shall not be able to dominate Christians. It is absolutely impossible that a person who is in a state of grace should be ruled by sin. A pilgrim traveling on a lonely road, when attacked by a highwayman, escapes from him at the first opportunity. He does not want to be overcome and slain. Christians are like pilgrims through this world on their way to heaven. The devil, like a highway robber, assaults them, and they go down before him because of their weakness, not because they meant to go down. To a true Christian his fall is forgiven him, since he turns to God in daily repentance with tears or at least heartfelt sighings for pardon. If a person allows sin to rule over him, this is a sure sign that he is not a Christian, but a hypocrite, no matter how pious he pretends to be." (*Law and Gospel*, p. 320.) Dr. Walther warns, therefore, that "the Word of God is not rightly divided when the universal corruption of mankind is described in such a manner as to create the impression that even true believers are still under the spell of ruling sins and are sinning purposely" (*Law and Gospel*, Thesis XVIII, p. 318). In agreement with Scripture, we, therefore, call the sins of unbelievers dominant or ruling sins, whereas the sins of Christians are called non-dominant or non-ruling sins.

I. SECRET AND OPEN SINS

Secret sins are a) such as are not known to the offender, for which we ask forgiveness of God when we pray: "Cleanse Thou me from secret faults" (Ps. 19:12); b) those transgressions which are known to the transgressor and God alone, namely, evil thoughts, lies, private vices, etc.; and c) such offenses as are known to the guilty party and to one or a few others, but are not publicly known.

The secret sins of our fellow men which are known to us should never be exposed, except when the duty of love compels it. "Charity shall cover the multitude of sins" (I Pet. 4:8). Dr. Luther says: "Whatever is secret should be allowed to remain secret. . . . For honor and good name are easily taken away, but not easily restored" (Large Catechism, *Triglot,* pp. 657, 272). Secret sins of this sort must be reproved (Lev. 19:17), but always in the spirit of humility and love and for the purpose of winning the offender (Gal. 6:1; Matt. 18:15-17).

Concerning open, or public, sins, such as false doctrine, living in adultery, etc., Dr. Luther, in his explanation of the Eighth Commandment, says as follows: "When the matter is public in the light of day, there can be no slandering or false judging or testifying; as when we now reprove the Pope and his doctrine, which is publicly set forth in books and proclaimed in all the world. For where the sin is public, the reproof must also be public, that everyone may learn to guard against it." (*Triglot,* pp. 659, 276.)

Scripture mentions the case of Peter, who in Antioch refused to eat with the Gentiles for fear of the Jews, whom Paul rebuked "before them all" (Gal. 2:11-14). Public reproof should also be administered against such leaders of the Church, particularly pastors, as continuously sin, for the Apostle says: "Them (the elders or pastors) that sin (lit., present participle: "are continuously sinning") rebuke before all, that others also may fear" (I Tim. 5:20). Continuous sinning includes, of course, the promulgating of false doctrine in writing, since such error, as long as it is not withdrawn, constitutes a menace to unstable souls.

J. PARTAKING OF OTHER MEN'S SINS

The Lord says: "Neither be partaker of other men's sins" (I Tim. 5:22). We violate this command of God when we practice Christian fellowship with prophets who do not cling faithfully to the doctrine of Jesus as the Christ (II John 9), "for," says the Apostle, "he that is continuously bidding him (that is, the false prophet) welcome, is partaking of his deeds, his evil deeds" (verse 11). The present participle in the original (which denotes durative action) indicates the fact that the Lord is here speaking not of a mere casual and civil greeting, but of a state of fellowship whereby one is constantly and repeatedly bidding such a false prophet brotherly welcome. The text actually forbids receiving a false prophet with a greeting of fraternal approval at any time, for, "if there come any unto you and bring not this doctrine" (namely, that Jesus is the Christ), "receive him not into your house, neither bid him Godspeed" (verse 10). When despite this command of God we continue to greet such a false prophet with brotherly approval, we make ourselves partakers of his evil deeds.

We also participate in the wickedness of others when we are "unequally yoked together with unbelievers" (II Cor. 6:14-18). The Lord does not forbid our being one with unbelievers under the *equal* yoke of social fellowship and state citizenship, but He does prohibit the *unequal* yoke of religious fellowship, as in anti-Christian lodges and such fraternal organizations as unite in idolatrous worship and in the promulgation of error.

In Lev. 19:17, the Lord says that if we fail to rebuke our neighbor for his sin, we also shall bear responsibility for it. Dr. Mueller summarizes all that is included in this sin when he says: "We participate in the sins of others if we command, counsel, consent to, or connive at, their evil deeds, or do not oppose them, nor give information concerning them, so that we become morally responsible for such sins." (Mueller, *Christian Dogmatics*, p. 235.)

To know that we so easily are made partakers of other men's sins, would be a burden too great to bear, were it not that by faith we are made partakers of another's righteousness, even the righteousness of Christ. Wherefore we sing: "Jesus, Thy blood and righteousness My beauty are, my glorious dress."

K. SINS THAT CRY TO GOD FOR VENGEANCE

These are the crimes against the helpless, the widows, and the orphans, the poor and the oppressed, also murder, the persecution of Christians, the refusal to give to a laborer his just pay, and such sort. (Cp. Gen. 4:10; Ex. 22:21-24; James 5:4; Rev. 6:9-10.) In short, all sins against the defenseless cry to God for vengeance and will be punished by Him.

L. THE SIN OF HARDENING ONESELF

Hardening oneself is the deadly sin of persistently and stubbornly resisting the call of the Holy Spirit and the testimony of the Word of God. It is demonstrated in the life of Pharaoh, who again and again steeled himself against the will of the Lord, growing step by step in obdurate defiance. (Laetsch, *Theological Monthly*, III, p. 7 ff.) Natural man can of his own accord only harden himself in sin and enmity against God. St. Paul describes this sin in his Letter to the Romans, chap. 1:20-23. The Christian is not immune to the danger of self-hardening. He still has his old Adam to contend with, his natural inclination to love sin and to serve it, to follow the perverse will of his wicked heart in spite of all warning by the voice of conscience, of his fellow Christians, of God Himself in nature, in history, in His holy Word. Our Lord warns against this sin by picturing its dire consequences (Matt. 13:14-15). And Paul describes the terrible judgment of obduracy which God visits upon all that harden themselves in unbelief and service of sin in his Letter to the Romans, chap. 1:24-32, where Paul describes the whole gamut of sins which as a recompense for his persistent rebellion (Rom. 11:9) the sinner is allowed to run unto his eternal ruin.

By this fearful judgment of obduracy may we be moved to see how dangerous it is to reject even an iota of God's Word, for it is the testimony of His Spirit. May we tremble at the slightest jot of sin, lest it be the first step towards a hardened heart and its fearful consequences! But by contrast, let us realize how precious and blessed is our lot as Christians, for by faith in Christ as my Savior, I am free from the curse of sin, a child of God, an heir of eternal life.

M. THE SIN AGAINST THE HOLY GHOST

Whereas the sin of hardening one's self can still be forgiven as long as the Lord has not yet pronounced His judgment of obduracy upon it, the sin against the Holy Ghost can never be forgiven, for it is the one "unpardonable sin." How very important, then, for us to know precisely what this sin is. There are six texts in the Scriptures which speak of it. The chief texts are Matt. 12:31-32; Mark 3:28-29; Luke 12:10; I John 5:16; additional passages are Heb. 6:4-6; 10:26-27. From these words of the Lord we gather the following information with respect to this transgression:

1. It constitutes an act, not against the person of the Holy Ghost, but against His office. Dr. Walther says: "Now it is certain that the Holy Spirit is not a more glorious and exalted person than the Father and the Son, but He is co-equal with them. Accordingly, the meaning . . . cannot be that the unforgivable sin is blasphemy against the person of the Holy Spirit; . . . it is directed against the office, or the operation, of the Holy Spirit; whosoever spurns the office of the Holy Spirit, his sins cannot be forgiven." (*Law and Gospel*, p. 393.)

2. It is not a mere blasphemous thought, but an utterance against the Holy Ghost, for Jesus calls it the sin of one who *"speaketh against the Holy Ghost"* (Matt. 12:32; *Law and Gospel,* p. 394; *Christliche Dogmatik,* I, p. 685), and it is an utterance whereby the operation of the Holy Ghost is called the work of an unclean spirit, for Jesus accused certain of the Pharisees of this sin, "because they said, 'He hath an unclean spirit.'" (Mark 3:30; *Christliche Dogmatik,* I, p. 685; *Law and Gospel,* p. 394.)

3. It is a sin which is done willfully (Heb. 10:26) and against better knowledge (Heb. 6:4-6).

4. It is a wickedness which is persisted in, for those who do this sin are described as "continuously sinning" (Greek, Heb. 10:26: *'hamartanonton,* present participle, denoting durative action) and as "constantly crucifying . . . the Son of God afresh," and as "constantly exposing Him to public shame."

5. It is called the sin unto death, in behalf of which St. John says no intercession is to be made (I John 5:16; cp. Heb. 6:6).

Wherein, then, does the sin against the Holy Ghost consist? In order to preclude any possible misunderstanding, let us eliminate all those sins which are *not* to be designated as such: a. The blasphemy against the Holy Ghost is *not* the sin of final impenitence and unbelief, for the Scriptures do not charge all who die in unbelief with having committed this transgression. (*Christliche Dogmatik,* I, p. 684.) b. Nor is it every act of willfully resisting the Holy Spirit, for all men resist the Holy Ghost willfully until they are converted. (*Christliche Dogmatik,* I, p. 684 b.) c. Nor does this sin consist in a blasphemy uttered against the truth of the Gospel while a man is still in a state of unbelief and ignorance. St. Paul, prior to his conversion, *did* utter such blasphemies (I Tim. 1:13), and yet "obtained mercy," for, as he says: "I did it ignorantly in unbelief." (*Christliche Dogmatik,* I, p. 684.) d. Finally, the sin against the Holy Ghost is *not* every public renunciation of Christ by an oath and every sin against conscience, as in the case of Peter; for Peter was converted again. (Matt. 26:72; *Christliche Dogmatik,* I, p. 685.)

What, then, is the sin against the Holy Ghost? When has it been committed? Dr. Pieper quotes Hollaz: "The sin against the Holy Ghost consists in maliciously renouncing, viciously opposing, horribly blaspheming the divine truth one has clearly recognized and approved in his conscience, together with an obstinate and unceasingly persistent rejection of all the means of salvation." (Examen, p. II, cap. IV, par. 38. Quoted by Pieper, *Christliche Dogmatik*, I, p. 685.) And Baier says: "The most grievous of all actual sins, which is called the sin against the Holy Ghost, consists in a malicious renunciation and blasphemous and obstinate assaults upon the heavenly truth which had once upon a time been known by the person committing this sin." (Quoted by Walther, *Law and Gospel*, p. 399.)

This is the unforgivable sin (Matt. 12:31-32). It is unpardonable, not because of its magnitude, as though the blood of Christ were not sufficient to cover all sin, but because it rejects the very offer of the blood by the Spirit. (Walther, *Law and Gospel*, Thesis XXIV, p. 393.) If, therefore, any man falls into this sin, it is not due to any deficiency in God or in the merits of Christ or in the operation of the Holy Ghost, but solely and alone to man's own great wickedness (*Christliche Dogmatik*, I, p. 689), wherefore God also says to him: "Thou hast destroyed *thyself*" (Hos. 13:9). On the other hand, if by God's grace we have escaped this sin and are still children of God by faith in Christ Jesus, then the credit for this fact belongs not to us, but altogether to God, for He says: "In Me is thine help" (Hos. 13:9). And if, by God's mercy, there is in us only the smallest desire for faith, the mere wish to believe in Christ and to escape this horrible sin, then we have the divine and certain assurance from God Himself that we have not become guilty of this great iniquity and that we are still His children, for, as the Scriptures state, "it is God which worketh in us both to will and to do of His good pleasure" (Phil. 2:13).

Temptation

INTRODUCTION

THE average human being has a rather narrow concept of "temptation." He uses the word to describe an overwhelming lure to do wrong. He is apt to presume temptation to be the area of behavior in which he is least mindful of God.

God through His Word, however, has a great deal to tell us about temptation. He says it specifically to people who are His children, and people who wish to be mindful of His will. Temptation has vital significance for every step of their earthly journey.

The age in which we live is the climax of a long period of materialism and secularization. Men have shaped habits and fashions of thinking in which they leave God out. The modern Christian, too, is apt to try to live many moments of his life without reference to the love of God for him and his responsibility to God. Rapidly we are drifting into an age of thorough immorality and irresponsibility toward God. In such evil times the Christian's heart also tends to become more and more sluggish toward the approach of temptation, and more and more unaware of the great aims of his Father. May our consideration of this subject refresh in our minds the understanding of this common experience, this everyday fact in our lives. May that understanding be one not merely of the teaching of the Word of God about it, but one of its meaning and application to our own daily lives.

I

Temptation is the testing of the believer's life in God through Christ. It is a permanent fixture of every Christian's life this side of eternity.

Temptation means more than falling into trouble, or lure to sin. Temptation means testing. The Word of God uses various words to describe the idea; but all of them imply a putting to the test of the Christian's life in God.

God gave the first man a body constructed with special care. Into this body God breathed His own Spirit, and man became a living soul. God made man in His own image. This divine image meant man's likeness to God in his knowledge of God (Col. 3:10), in righteousness and true holiness (Eph. 4:24), which manifested itself in love toward God and His fellow man.

Adam and Eve had the power for this righteousness, holiness, and love only as they drew upon God for it. God made this clear to the first human pair by a simple test. He designated one tree of the Garden to be a test of their devotion to God's will, of their desire to put God above everything else and make God the sole source of their life. If they went contrary to God's will and if they turned to another source of life and happiness, they would automatically cut themselves off from the life of God, and die (Gen. 2:17). This death was in the first place not to be a mere stopping of the bodily and mental processes; but it was to be a stopping of the life of God in man.

Man chose a life other than that of God, tempted thereto by Satan. In making his choice, he was moved by impulses completely other than those of the Spirit of God (Gen. 3:6). At once man's entire nature changed. He was moved by fear of God and by lust toward his fellow man. The physical body became hampered by the curse upon sin, doomed to physical death and decay (Gen.3: 16-24). Moreover, this death and curse was not only for the first human pair. In them, all humanity diverged from God, mankind died (Rom. 5:12, 15, 17). The life passed on from generation to generation was not life at all, but it was death; from the beginning on mankind is born into sin (Rom. 5:19; Ps. 51:5; Eph. 2:1-3).

Before God ever made the world and before man fell away from Him, God planned a way that men might nevertheless be "holy and without blame before Him in love" (Eph. 1:5). He foresaw that man would lust and sever the supply of God's life in himself; but He conceived a plan for restoring this life (II Pet. 1:3-5), and when the first human pair fell into sin and away from God, God was there with the announcement of the plan for rescue from Satan's power, a way of life (Gen. 3:15-16). This promise was made in many ways and with ever greater detail during the long waiting time of the Old Testament (I Pet. 1:10).

The way of life which God planned was Jesus Christ (Gal. 4: 4-5). Sin not simply makes God angry, but it is revolting to His very being; it is an affront and an offense. Still the love of God devised a way of life that was in full accord with His holiness. This way He found in His own Son. He made Him the means by which He would be reconciled to mankind (II Cor. 5:19-21). Jesus Christ, true man as well as the only-begotten Son of God, lived the life that was completely in accordance with the will of God. He was one with the Father, not only in His divine being, but in His accord with the holiness of God (John 7:18). He withstood every test of this relation and this holiness (Heb. 4:15). And then, in the agony on the Cross, God forsook His Son and directed the full wrath and revulsion over man's sin upon His sinless Son (Ps. 22; Mark 15:34). Thus Christ took upon Himself the penalty of man's sin (Is. 53:5; Heb. 2:14-15). Through Adam's sin death and guilt and continued sin came upon all the world. But by Jesus Christ "the grace of God and the gift of grace hath abounded unto many. . . ." (Rom. 5:15 ff.)

So it is that God's purpose and grace has restored life to man (II Tim. 1:9-10). It is there for them; now, through the Spirit of God at work in the Gospel and the Sacraments, the mind of man has to be changed from death to faith and life (Luke 24:46-47). That Gospel witness makes men born of the Spirit to a new life, the life that is in the plan of God (I Pet. 1:23 ff.). That life means the hold on God through faith and the exercise of the restored powers in love (Gal. 2:20; 5:6).

Hence the emphasis in the life of the Christian restored to God by faith in Jesus is upon the maintaining and preserving of this new relation. This problem is complicated by the fact that the newborn man is not perfect. St. Paul describes the clash between the new life of the Spirit of God and the remnants of the dead mind and sinful self which are still left at our new birth (Rom. 7:21 ff.). The Christian is not automatically beyond the reach of sin (I John 1:8; I Cor. 10:12; 16:13; I Pet. 5:8-9). Everything depends upon the maintaining of his spiritual life, the supply of his life from God (John 15:6).

The testing of faith and life is, therefore, all-important for the Christian. Where this testing reveals inadequacy, it should drive him to the sources of supply of God's grace and Spirit.

A. *The Christian should continually apply tests to his faith: confession of faith, the standard of the Law, the production of works of love.*—We cannot adequately discuss temptation in the life of the Christian without reminding ourselves that the Word of God points out more tests of faith than those which we call "temptation." Temptation comes from outside of our renewed and godly nature. But God urges us as renewed men continually to employ tests of faith which are at our own disposal.

The most immediate token of faith is confession. That means that the Christian man says in words the fact of his hold on God and the life surging through him. Hence the Savior and the Apostles link this witness directly with saving faith (Matt. 10:32; Luke 12:8; Rom. 10:9; I John 4:15). It expresses itself in worship, and the opportunity for worship with the brethren of the faith (Col. 3:16). It expresses itself in prayer, the desire to communicate with God and to lay all the joys and all the problems of life before Him (Ps. 119:82). As the Christian marks his own readiness to confess and to witness, or as the danger signals arise before his scrutiny, he should sense renewed impulse to "seek first the Kingdom of God and His righteousness" (Matt. 6:33) and to devote himself to the One Thing Needful (Luke 10:42), the restoration of the Spirit of God through the Gospel of Christ and the Sacrament of His blood.

That same renewed devotion to the sources of the spiritual life should be the result of the Christian's applying to himself of the standard of the Law of God. Before the Christian it stands as a constant reminder of the presence of the flesh in him, an unmasking of the lusts that still beset his spiritual life. The alert and true Christian, therefore, will seek not only to hear the will of Christ, but also to do it (Matt. 7:24-27); he will courageously face the problem of the flesh in himself, and he will discern and acknowledge his sins and shortcomings, with sorrow of heart and with earnest turning to God for restoration and improvement of the spiritual life (I John 1:9; II Cor. 7:9 ff.).

A further means of testing and improving spiritual life is the record of the life of God in the characters of Holy Writ (I Cor. 10:11). Examples for testing purposes are for warning and for imitation (I Cor. 10:11; Phil. 3:17). At the apex of the godly company of the saints is Christ Himself, whose mind is to be in us and who left us an example (Phil. 2:5 ff.; I Pet. 2:21; Heb. 12:1-2).

God calls upon us ever to test the spiritual life within us by the production of our works of love. For the sake of love and for the sake of the spiritual life at work toward others our heavenly Father gave Christ as our Redeemer and gave us new birth through the Spirit (Eph. 2:10; John 15:8). The pondering of that fact should stimulate the disciples to abide in Him through the Word (vv. 3-5). In the Judgment our record of works will be our Lord's test of those who are the blessed of His Father (Matt. 25:31-46; cf. John 3:18 ff.; 4:12 ff.).

So important is the steady supply of spiritual nurture for the Christian, and so important is the Christian's spiritual life for this world, that our heavenly Father demands an unflagging program of self-testing of this life (Eph. 5:15-16). The clearheaded application of the standard of God's will and the use of the divine power for spiritual life the Word of God calls soberness (I Thess. 5:8; Tit. 2:11 ff.; I Pet. 1:13). The Christian's testing of his own faith demands watchfulness in view of the end of the world and the coming of Christ to Judgment (I Pet. 4:7; Heb. 10:25; Matt. 24: 45 ff.; 25:14-30).

B. *The term "temptation" concerns tests which the Christian does not apply to himself, but which come from outside his regenerate self.*—Despite the abundant exhortations of the Word of God to every Christian to test his faith and see to it lest he fall, to utilize every means for the quickening of spiritual life and to do so to the very end, also the instructed Christian tends continually to lag in this regard. For the Christian is beset by enemies of his life and faith, by the flesh within him, by sin, by apathy, by the pride of achievement and satisfaction with Christian accomplishment. The Pharisees were men learned in religion and outwardly abundant in good, yet their pride had severed their supply of life from God and literally killed their souls (Luke 18:11 ff.; John 9:41). The same spiritual torpor beset the outwardly Christian Laodiceans

(Rev. 3:14 ff.). Also our Church is beset by the problems of its time. It has not always been a city set on a hill and a light unto the world; but too often has it been immersed in the accumulation of property and prestige, in the managing of a human system. We, too, as we approached the Centennial of our Synod, are mindful of the handicaps for the testing of spiritual life which our very age and bulk and wealth bring with them.

Our heavenly Father is not limited, however, by our own shortcomings. When we become sluggish and we actually lose our clearheaded capacity for judging our spiritual life, God has other devices. They are not merely words. They strike where we feel them and give heed. They are calculated to make clear the bankruptcy of life without God. They are designed to set in bold relief the weakness and waywardness, the unhappiness and the helplessness of the Christian who begins to think he can get along without God. We usually call these the chastisements of God.

In this paper we discuss not simply God's chastisement, but temptation. We shall see that the tests of faith are not only designed as tools of God; but the devil, world, and flesh have their hand in many of them, proposing not simply to test faith, but to destroy it. It is the marvelous lesson before us, however, that God is not hampered even by the enemies of our souls. God employs the entire plot and pattern of our life in the world to the end that we be held close to Him.

II

The believer's faith and life is effectively tested by sin and the consequences of sin.

Since man's fall into sin, man lives in a world which is filled with sinning people. The Scriptures simply term them "the world." The world has a branch agency in every Christian; the Scriptures call it "the flesh." The world and the flesh are the forces which beat in upon the regenerate nature of the Christian. They are the instrumentality of the opponent of God, Satan himself. They are his kingdom.

The world and the flesh commit sins. But behind the isolated sins are great standard attitudes, ways of thinking, drives, and interests. They are directed against God, and against the nature of God; they are wholly selfish, completely unholy (Matt. 15:19;

Rom. 1:25). The world carries the flesh of the individual along in its fateful toils. The unregenerate flesh of man—and it dwells also in the Christian—is driven by lust. Lust is the drive of the flesh to make all things, even those innocent in themselves, serve the purposes of the flesh alone. It is so close to man, so much a part of him, that he hardly senses how it works (Rom. 7:7). The world without God finds lust self-evident and natural; it adorns it and praises it, it gives it priority in the domains of sex, of art, of business, of politics (I John 2:15 ff.).

Man's sinful lust has brought with it a vast train of evil. Scripture gives a sordid picture of human nature riddled by the drives for self-preservation and self-interest, shaken by inferiority and fear, compensating by lying or pugnacity or self-assertion. The first human pair revealed the twin signals of the loss of the life of God: lust and fear, in the first moments of their fall (Gen. 3:1 ff.).

St. James very vividly describes the insidious work of the lust inherent in man and its truly appalling consequences in the words familiar to every churchgoer: "Every man is tempted when he is drawn away of his own lust and enticed. Then when lust hath conceived, it bringeth forth sin; and sin, when it is finished, bringeth forth death" (James 1:14-15). The truth of this word is taught by the Scriptural record of the fall of our first parents. Eve listened to Satan, she doubted God's word, God's love. "When the woman saw that the tree was good for food and that it was pleasant to the eyes and a tree to be desired to make one wise, she took of the fruit thereof and did eat and gave also unto her husband with her; and he did eat" (Gen. 3:6). That is the truth God impressed upon Cain, who was angry because his offering did not please the Lord. "Why art thou wroth?" the Lord asked Cain, "and why is thy countenance fallen? If thou doest well, shalt thou not be accepted? And if thou doest not well, sin lieth at the door. And unto thee shall be his desire, and thou shalt rule over him" (Gen. 4:6-7). In disregard of this warning Cain followed the impulse of his wicked lust and killed his brother. This is the tragic lesson taught in the lives of Samson and Saul and Judas and Demas. To overcome temptation, accordingly, demands advance scrutiny of even inoffensive items in the Christian's range of experience (Matt. 26:41). But to overcome temptation demands also knifing into and interrupting the chain of sinful reactions which any one temptation sets up (Rev. 3:1 ff.).

For the purpose, therefore, of our discerning danger in advance and of breaking the force of sin when tempted, the Holy Scriptures in precept and example set before us a vast panorama of temptation. We are to employ this counsel in the safeguarding and purifying of our own spiritual life and in our program of personal admonition and mutual assistance in the fellowship of brother Christians.

A. *Consequences of sin which serve as temptations may be discomfort or hardship to body or mind and the threat of death.—* The unregenerate flesh too easily lulls to security, too easily blunts the Christian's self-testing. Temptation, on the other hand, works so that the Christian can notice it, and notice it not only with his regenerate spirit, but with his flesh. Temptation is a test of faith, but it tests it by revealing the strength of the counterpoise of the flesh.

Satan's first temptation of our Lord attached itself to the problem of His physical hunger and sought to give rise to the idea that its stilling was His greatest need and goal (Matt. 4:1 ff.). The problem of food and drink and clothing is particularly tormenting where the world is given to appreciation of earthly possessions and where the Christian becomes conscious of his own handicaps and poverty by comparison. It sets up its weakening of the faith and its chain-reaction of sin through worry, the attempt to solve a problem without help from the outside. It is a variety of fear and becomes a potent source of spiritual malnutrition and undernourishment (Matt. 6:19 ff.; Ps. 127:2; Luke 12:16 ff.; Prov. 30:9). The fact that worry is foolish does not make it unusual. Our time with its machine production and its specialization of tasks, with its stresses between classes and its derangements of the means of living throughout the world, has stepped up the temptation to worry. It is a potent invitation to forget God and to heed the devil's "Yea, hath God said?" of the first temptation in the Garden.

The instability of human achievement, the constant backward slipping of human thinking, the disappointments in the quest for personal gain and growth, likewise drive in upon the Christian with a fearful pessimism, turn him to the thought that caprice and blind fate rule all and thwart his drawing upon God's own resources for his spiritual life (Eccl. 9:11 ff.). The irksomeness to the Christian of the prosperity and success of those who deserve the opposite is a fertile source of fleshly thinking. The grinding wear of resistance against evil men, particularly those who disgust and destroy through falsehood and slander, produces irritation and resentment (cf. Job 21: 7-15; Pss. 37; 52; 56; 57; 58; 64; 73). One of the great promises of deliverance in temptation is against that caused by the uncharitable man (Is. 29:20).

Another potent temptation is doubt. Like worry, doubt is a direct matching of the flesh against the believer's faith and trust in God. It is the flesh in action; it is the signal of unbelief existing side by side with faith. Doubt is always a symptom of materialism, of human reason or judgment. This trend the Savior castigated frequently in His disciples (Matt. 17:17; Luke 24:25; John 20:29). Right in a faithful and eager Christian this temptation may take hold most tenaciously. The Christian who holds to the Word of God as his one source of strength and wisdom becomes perturbed by its difficulties or seeming discrepancies; he forgets that his own prejudices or those of others may have been the cause of his difficulty rather than the Word itself; and thus needed areas of instruction and supply of faith are rendered inoperative (II Pet. 3:15 ff.).

The most uncomfortable consequence of sin in the life of the Christian is the bad conscience. Normally the Christian will silence it by the assurance of Christ's forgiveness and grace. But under the drag of the flesh the bad conscience may become a temptation to turn to human anodynes and anaesthetics, to invent human devices for self-righteousness and the quenching of the conscience (I Tim. 4:1 ff.).

In the chain-reaction set up by temptation occurs the fear of death and judgment. It may be a panic of physical disaster, as was Peter's in the court of the high priest's house, leading him to forswear his Lord; or it may be a panic of everlasting damnation, in turn cutting off from the means of grace and the supply of forgiveness (Heb. 10:26-27; Job 2:9). It may try to effect a doubt about all the work and care of God, endeavoring to break off the relation of the Christian's life with God and fostering the existence of his flesh (Ps. 10:1 ff., 14). The attitudes of the world round about the Christian set up reactions of pain and torment which cannot be overlooked and which probe relentlessly the answering of the question: "Do I have a faith sufficient to hold to my Savior for every need?"

B. *Material advantages or comforts may as consequence of sin dwelling in us become temptations to the Christian.*—In themselves, the good things of life are not sin. The life of the body—eating and drinking, marriage and labor, satisfaction and success—is all a gift of God (James 1:17; Heb. 13:4; Eccl. 9:10; Ps. 139:14). Nevertheless, the fall of man into sin and the presence of unregenerate flesh existing in the Christian side by side with his new life has made possible that these very gifts of God can become temptations, encouragements for sin, tests of faith. Since they are in the domain of the innocent and the godly, the Christian may frequently be unaware of the testing quality in them. Here it is especially necessary to recognize the characteristic of progressive action, the chain-reaction quality of temptation, and to be sensitive to the trends and drives of the unregenerate flesh.

The very first temptation of Satan operated with the pleasurableness of something to eat and proceeded from that simple beginning to a questioning of the very intentions of God and a desire to be independent of His will (Gen. 3:1 ff.). The possession of earthly goods may swiftly proceed into an earthly-mindedness and a forgetting of God which is sheer disaster. Our Lord Himself put before the faith of the rich young ruler the prospect of life without his possessions; and when he failed the test, the Savior said (Mark 10:23 ff.): "How hardly shall they that have riches enter into the kingdom of God!" The Savior describes the deadly process of this temptation more specifically in the Parable of the Sower (Mark 4:19). Moses had warned against this reaction long before (Deut. 8:11 ff.). St. Paul speaks just as bluntly (I Tim. 6: 8 ff.). In Judas Iscariot the full train of reaction is most luridly apparent (Matt. 26:14-15); the stories of Lot (Gen. 13:10 ff.) or Achan (Joshua 7), or the parables of the Rich Fool (Luke 12:16 ff.) or the Rich Man and Lazarus (Luke 16:19 ff.) are in the Scriptures to illumine the same disastrous sequence.

Other earthly advantages, catering to the lusts of self-satisfaction and power, are temptations in similar manner. The second and third temptations of Jesus in the wilderness operated with this presumption that possession of worldly power or prestige can deflect from obedience to the will of God (Luke 4:5 ff.).

Fleshly lust has its hold on man because of its seeming enjoyableness. It seems easier and more pleasant to yield to it than to direct the physical appetite underlying it into the aims which God intended. It is noteworthy that every decadent civilization, including our own, exaggerates and stimulates the hunger of the flesh, chiefly of sex and the palate, to an enormous degree. St. Paul gives a harrowing survey of this fact in the world of his time (Rom. 1 and 2). The problem of temptation lies not merely in the fact that the unregenerate individuals yield to fleshly appetite, but that they with their fashions and emphases of living surround the Christians (Phil. 3:18 ff.). St. Peter describes this seducing power of the unregenerate world attacking the Christian's flesh (II Pet. 2:14 ff.). Hence the Word of God frequently discusses this type of temptation in conjunction with the power of evil companionship. The Old Testament is full of the portrayal of evil resulting from the mingling in marriage of Israel and the heathen. Solomon's admonition is not extreme puritanism, but an analysis of the temptations of evil companionship (Prov. 1:10 ff.; cf. also 4:14 ff.; 22:24; 24:1-2).

Just as fear operates with the prospect of impending disaster and pain, so lust operates with the prospect of future ease. This is a particularly insidious guise in which the true resources of faith are confronted by temptation. Hardly had the Savior completed His warning against the lust of riches, when Peter says, "Lo, we have left all and have followed Thee" (Mark 10:28) — what gain shall we get out of it? As the Church becomes an established institution, an agency for the paying of obligations to God, also Christians tend to settle into the comfortable grooves of ritual and membership and to shrink from thinking through the ends of their worship and the meaning of the Word with which they busy themselves. The familiar instance of the succumbing to this temptation is Martha (Luke 10:41); actually it was not only care for unfulfilled tasks, but complacency with an accepted mode of thought, that menaced her supply of the means of grace. This complacency is richly illustrated in the Seven Letters of Revelation: Ephesus is busy with a strict campaign against falsehood, but has left its first love (Rev. 2:1 ff.); Pergamos has preserved a pure confession, but has been sluggish in disciplining unbelief in its own midst (2:12 ff.); Thyatira is active in charity, but similarly sluggish in discerning the seduction of false teaching (2:18 ff.); Sardis is reputed to be vigorous, but underneath is dying (3:1 ff.); Laodicea regards itself as rich and powerful, but is actually in bitter want (3:14 ff.); only Smyrna and Philadelphia have a cleaner bill of health, the one because it is tested by trouble, the other because it is truly alive in the use of the Word (2:8 ff.; 3:7 ff.). St. Paul warns against those who "have a form of godliness, but deny the power thereof" (II Tim. 3:5). Easily the forms of religion become an insurance, in the practicing Christian's mind, of ease and prestige in this present life and of prerogative and material glory in the life to come. The aspiration of the sons of Zebedee and their mother for prestige in the kingdom of Christ is symptomatic of this temptation, which strikes at the very heart of the true life of God in the Christian (Matt. 20:20 ff.). The Savior thrust out sharply at this attitude in His teachings (Luke 17:7 ff.). The Christian lives in the world. But the Christian has a piece of the world in him, in his flesh, and he is ever ready to react to its thoughts and fashions. The Church itself stands in continual danger, through this process, of being perverted from the purpose of quickening and guiding the spiritual life of its members, to an agency for lulling them to complacency and assuring them that all is well (Jer. 6:13 ff.).

III

Temptation, therefore, can be the attempt of devil, world, and flesh to ruin the believer's spiritual life and to weaken or destroy his faith; or it can be God's attempt to drive him to faith and restore life.

The Christian man is two men. His flesh is allured by temptation and finds it congenial, interesting, enjoyable. His true self, his new self, is not lured by it, but neither is it oblivious of it. The true Christian seeks to recognize the danger, and the value, of temptation. The Christian prays at the direction of his Lord: "Lead us not into temptation, but deliver us from evil." He faces the unseen menace of Satan and senses the hostility of the unbelieving world for his own faith and life. But he also notes with James: "My brethren, count it all joy when ye fall into divers temptations, knowing this, that the trying of your faith worketh patience" (James 1:2-3). This raises a number of questions in the Christian's mind. Does God ever take the initiative in temptation, or does He always deliver and rescue out of situations in which the Christian is already entangled? When devil, world, and flesh attack the Christian with their temptations, are they stronger than God, or are they used by God?

Our Church has approached these questions by distinguishing between the temptations for evil and the temptations for good (F. Pieper, *Christliche Dogmatik*, I, p. 674; New Synodical Catechism, p. 164; Old, p. 120, question 256). The word "temptation" thereby undergoes a subtle change in meaning; but this twofold connotation of the word is in keeping with the usage of the Word of God.

A. *Temptation for evil.*—In temptation for evil, the devil, the world, and the flesh are the prime movers, frequently in a triple onslaught. Before we observe their activity, let us realize what they are really trying to do. We usually simply say "tempt," or "deceive," or "seduce into misbelief, despair, and other great shame and vice" (Explanation of the Sixth Petition, Small Catechism). Temptation to evil means that the Christian's faith is being put in jeopardy. It throws itself against faith in various ways. It may seek to weaken the object of faith in the Christian's mind, to make him uncertain of what he is holding to in faith; or temptation to evil may weaken the supply of faith; or it may assault the purpose of faith in the Christian's mind. Temptation is not merely the process of inciting an army to direct rebellion or insurrection, but temptation flings itself at an army's supply lines. It seeks to confuse the maps which show where the supplies come from; it seeks to interrupt the flow of supplies, the transport and communication; or it seeks to confuse and reduce the sense of importance for an ample supply of munitions and rations.

"Then comes the devil, inciting and provoking in all directions, but especially agitating matters that concern the conscience and spiritual affairs, namely, to induce us to despise and disregard both the Word and works of God, to tear us away from faith, hope, and love, and bring us into misbelief, false security, and obduracy, or on the other hand to despair, denial of God, blasphemy, and innumerable other shocking things" (Large Catechism, *Triglot*, 727, 104). This enterprise of Satan is apparent in his method of temptation. Satan endeavored to confuse our Lord's attitude toward His own heavenly Father, to shift His attention away from the will of God that He should be our Redeemer, and to concentrate it upon the opportunities for his own earthly control of humanity (Matt. 4:1 ff.). Satan's temptation in the Garden operated by beclouding the knowledge of the Father's will—"yea, hath God said, ye shall not eat of every tree of the Garden?"—and by reducing the desire to cling to God as the one source of life (Gen. 3:4 ff.). "Satan stood up against Israel and provoked David to number Israel" (I Chron. 21:1); thus he weakened David's desire to trust in God for help, and made him concentrate on his and his people's power (I Chron. 21:1). The spiritual collapse of the Pharisees and capitulation to Satan came via the delusion that being Abraham's descendants meant spiritual life, with the result that they were unable to understand the Scriptures or to hear Christ's Word (John 8:37). Satan's power over Judas operated with the chain-reaction of lust engendered in avarice, leading him progressively away from any thought for the meaning of Christ's work and word. Satan's conquest of Ananias and Sapphira progressed by means of their desire for property as well as prestige in the eyes of their fellow Christians, to the point that they repudiated the Holy Spirit in their own hearts (Acts 5:1 ff.). When Peter sought to deflect the Lord Christ from His program of redeeming the world through His suffering and death and persisted in this uncertainty concerning the work of Jesus, the Lord said: "Get thee behind me, Satan," and "Simon, behold, Satan hath desired to have you, that he may sift you as wheat; but I have prayed for thee, that thy faith fail not" (Matt. 16:23; Luke 22:31 ff.). The ultimate objective of Satan in tempting the Christian is to render the Gospel ineffective (II Cor. 4:3 ff.).

The unbelieving world operates with a similar strategy of temptation. The world is the sum total of human minds unstirred by the Spirit of God. Hence its companionship, its speech and amusements and business and culture and philosophy tend to move the Christian into pursuits and channels which weaken the hold on God; they tend to make God unimportant (I Cor. 1:33; 2:11 ff.).

The objectives of natural human life are not for God, but always for man (James 4:4). Making money, competing for existence, enjoying the sensual stimuli of food and drink and sex and success and approval are activities common to the unregenerate life of the Christian also, and hence potent devices for destroying the will to live for God (Luke 21:34; I Cor. 7:33). Our own civilization is particularly subject to the temptations of this sort. It stresses material wealth as a standard of happiness and worth, and physical enjoyment as an objective for wealth. It is thus a vast conspiracy for belittling the power of God and the life for God, a shouting down of the Savior's reminder: "What is a man profited if he shall gain the whole world and lose his own soul?" (Matt. 16:26). Furthermore, many Christians fall out of the ranks and, like Demas, forsake the company of the faithful, "having loved this present world" (II Tim. 4:10). Many Christians retain connection with the Church, but actually are driven by the motives of fleshly lust as are the men of the world. This causes confusion and becomes a temptation to evil for those who are unwary. The Epistle of James is the great document in Scripture on the world in the Church. It attacks the spectacle of men in the visible Church with respect of persons (2:1 ff.), evil speech (3:2 ff.), envy and strife (14 ff.), accumulation of property by fleshly means (4:13 ff). All of that, James would say, is a confusion of the very foundation of the Christian faith and religion, a temptation to evil which is an erring from the truth (1:20 ff., 27).

Ultimately all temptation to evil roots in the flesh of the Christian himself. "Every man is tempted when he is drawn away of his own lust and enticed" (James 1:14). Devil and world seek to move the Christian away from God; but they bore from within. Here, too, the strategy of temptation attacks the supply lines of the Spirit. Since the natural reactions of the body are so close to the individual and his thinking, it is doubly important that he recognize their impact for evil due to the remnant of the flesh within him (I Cor. 9:27; Matt. 5:29; I Pet. 2:11). The story of Old Testament Israel is given us to warn us against the succumbing to earthly lust and the blotting out of the power of the means of grace (Hos. 4:6; I Cor. 10:1-12). The Corinthians allowed a similar lust for physical indulgence and advantage to limit the meaning of the Sacrament of Holy Communion (I Cor. 11:20-30). To those who followed Him for reasons of mere fleshly gain, Christ sketched the alternative of life or death, which is difficult for the flesh to face (John 6:26; cf. Rom. 7:19).

Temptation for evil, therefore, is a steady accompaniment of the life of every Christian. "Great and grievous, indeed, are these dangers and temptations which every Christian must bear, even though each one were alone by himself, so that every hour that we are in this vile life where we are attacked on all sides, chased and hunted down, we are moved to cry out and to pray that God would not suffer us to become weary and faint and to relapse into sin, shame, and unbelief" (Large Catechism, *Triglot*, 727, 105). Every Christian, beginner or veteran, is engaged in a struggle against an unrelenting and insidious foe.

B. Temptation for good.—Devil, world, and flesh tempt the Christian in order to destroy his hold on the grace of God and his life in the Spirit. The Word of God tells us, however, that God is also interested in the temptations that beset the Christian. He is not merely interested in extricating the Christian from them, but He is interested in sending them. But God has no pleasure in the death of the wicked. When God sends or allows temptation, therefore, it is for good and not for evil. It is not intended to disrupt communication with God and faith in God, but to lead to the opposite result (Ps. 145:17; James 1:13).

To the worldling it is a paradox that a benevolent God would cause trouble and pain. But it would be a greater mystery if trouble and pain could exist side by side with a God who did not want them. When we grant the existence of God at all, then we grant Him the power to inflict pain, and we grant that behind the thrust of pain and sorrow, God is at work (Is. 45:5 ff.; Ps. 46:8 ff.). True, God is not capricious or bullying in the exercise of this power; it is always for the good of man, for the rebuke and the unmasking of waywardness, for the gathering and the strengthening of His people (Deut. 32:29, 39).

So it is that we can speak of God's tempting, that is to say, testing the Christian to reveal his relation to God in its true light, to make the Christian's need for God clear to him, and to refresh in the Christian's program of life the use of the means of grace and the

Temptation 187

drawing on the life of God. The Bible does not always call this process tempting or testing; but it gives abundant illustrations of God at work toward His people toward those ends.

As temptation for evil strikes at the disrupting of the supply lines of the Spirit, so temptation for good seeks to make the need for uninterrupted supply apparent. The simplest and most frequent temptation for good on the part of the heavenly Father is pain for body or for mind. The very curse on the earth and banning of Adam and Eve from the Garden was to keep them awake to their need of God's grace in the Woman's Seed (Gen. 3:22, 23; cf. Luther, I, p. 274). The classic illustration of temptation for good is the trial of Abraham's faith by commanding him to offer up Isaac (Gen. 22:1-18).

In the carrying out of this design the heavenly Father utilizes tools that seem evil indeed; and yet His good purpose holds to its end. He tells us that even the emergence of false prophets among His people shall serve the purpose of testing their love to Him and His truth (Deut. 13:3). God sends Satan out to ravage Job and test his faith and love for God (Job 1 and 2). When the Lord tells Peter that cross-bearing has its compensations, He lists among them "persecutions" (Mark 10:30). It was Peter himself whose First Epistle became the great textbook on the meaning to the Christian of trouble and persecution (2:19 ff.; 3:14 ff.; 4:12 ff.). St. Paul likewise had much to say about temptation for good. God utilized "the messenger of Satan" to the end that Paul could learn to say: "I take pleasure in infirmities, in reproaches, in necessities, in persecutions, in distresses for Christ's sake; for when I am weak, then am I strong" (II Cor. 12:7-10). Describing the justified Christian, St. Paul says: "We glory in tribulations also, knowing that tribulation worketh patience, and patience, experience, and experience, hope" (Rom. 5:3-4; cf. 8: 28 ff.).

God's temptations are to teach the Christian to put his whole confidence in God and His Word. This is the meaning of Christ's words to Philip at the feeding of the five thousand (John 6:5-6). This is the meaning of that most agonizing of all spiritual tests, that God seems to delay His answer and to be far from His child (Pss. 27; 42; 11). He searches not simply for a faith that is there; but He looks for faith that holds on, that grows and flourishes, that uses God and His Word and knows God as all in all. Here are revealed the purposes of Christ in the incident of the Syrophoenician woman (Matt. 15:22-28), or the raising of Lazarus (John 11:1-26; cf. James 1:2, 3, 12).

When the Christian ponders the influence of evil in the world and the threats of temptation to evil, he is sobered and chastened in mind. But the Christian does well to remember that God is just as restlessly at work as Satan. Grace abounds much more than sin. God dwells about us and in us, stirring and moving with His Spirit; and He seeks to get at our sluggish souls by the devices that reach just them (Heb. 12:5-11). Every Christian in his inner thinking about the ways of God, every pastor to his people, every Christian to his brother or sister, must ever be alert to the answer for these questions: What is this trouble all about? What is God trying to say to me? Who is getting at me in this incident of my life? Whose man shall I be, God's or Satan's? Where are my resources for the struggle? The whole purpose of our life and being lies in these questions.

IV

God's purpose in temptation is to make the believer aware of his need for God and thereby indirectly to strengthen his hold on grace.

A familiar figure of speech for temptation for good is that of the refining of precious metal by fire; it is employed for the chastening and testing of God by Job (23:10), the Psalmist (66:10), Isaiah (1:25; 48:10), Jeremiah (9:7), Zechariah (13:9), Malachi (3:3), and St. Peter (I Pet. 1:7; 4:12). The figure is apt, for it emphasizes changing an impure being into a purer one by means of a painful process. Another such figure is that of a parent punishing a child; it is used by Moses (Deut. 8:5), Job (33:19), the Psalmist (94:12), Solomon (Prov. 3:11-12; quoted Heb. 12:5 ff.). Again the figure is most apt, for it stresses a change through pain to a better state and implies the fatherly and correcting relationship. The Savior employs the picture of a husbandman pruning his vines so that they bear more efficiently; and again the analogy emphasizes the great concern of God for results and the pain involved in the process (John 15:1 ff). The writer to the Hebrews uses the analogy of a runner stripping off every garment or baggage hindering his most effective pace (Heb. 12:1 ff.).

We may call temptation for good or "testing of faith" an enforced audit or inventory of our spiritual resources. We may be remiss in applying the standard tests of faith and life to ourselves. But here comes a test that cannot be shrugged off. God means it for good; and He is not going to relent until its purpose has been achieved. He will succeed either in drawing our attention back to the resources for life and stimulate us to employ them; or He will make us aware of our shortcomings and deficiencies in these resources and prompt us to replenish them.

The most central fact in the supply of God's spiritual life to the individual is his trust in Jesus Christ as his Savior. When the Christian turns his mind away from that fact, his entire spiritual life is threatened. "Without Me ye can do nothing," says Christ (John 15:5). The tests of faith operate by bringing to light the fallacy and emptiness of any competing trusts or conviction and by turning the Christian's mind to the centrality of Christ's redemption. Thus the Syrophoenician woman was forced to think through the very foundations of Christ's atonement for the sins of the whole world (Matt. 15:24, 26). When she had founded herself solidly on the fact, then the Savior could say: "O woman, great is thy faith." The Savior seeks to lead Martha forward, through the object lesson of her brother's death and resurrection, from a formal and general recognition that He had the power to do miracles or that Lazarus would rise at the Last Day, to the point that she thinks through His meaning for life of the Spirit and resurrection of the body in terms of His redemption, of His being the Savior from sin (John 11:25 ff.).

The tests of faith search out not merely what we call saving faith, the understanding and trust that through the work of Christ we are saved, but faith in its wider sense likewise, namely the trust in God for every need. That trust is actually a fruit of the faith in Christ; and so the trials and tests of faith again drive to a clearer recognition of Christ as Savior. Job is the prime illustration in Scripture of this type of testing. His friends, "miserable comforters" he called them (16:1), tried to interpret his whole trouble as a manifest proof of some special wickedness in his life. But Job senses in that interpretation a device to shake his trust (16: 17 ff.). He is fully aware of the magnitude of his suffering; but it makes him all the surer of God, who is his trust through the

Redeemer (Job 19), and it leads him to test the results of this relation to God in every domain of life (Job 31). St. Paul chafed under the thorn in the flesh; God Himself interpreted its purpose to him, namely, to turn away from satisfaction simply in his revelations of God, and to apply himself to God in trust that God's grace was his greatest need (II Cor. 12:1-10). The whole Old Testament visitation upon the Children of Israel had this purpose for its process (Deut. 8:2-3). That is the function of material tests of faith, then, to make man aware of the vanity of his earthly gains, to the end that he concentrate on the real source of spiritual life.

The Savior promised a special type of suffering and testing which would specifically reveal the Christian's faith in God through Christ. This is persecution (Luke 21:12-13; John 16:2 ff). The function of persecution was not to provide merit in the persecution itself or in the enduring of suffering, but to achieve the effect of the Christian's own greater hold on God.

The Christian's faith clings to God with endurance and hope. His faith is not a one-time subscription to truth, but a continued use of God's grace and a reliance upon God's nearness and His promises. To reinforce the foundation of such faith and hope, the heavenly Father frequently inserts delay into the carrying out of His promises and forces the individual to review the bases for such faith and hope (Pss. 13 and 69). St. Paul describes this process of testing in a chain reaction for good (Rom. 5:3 ff.). St. Peter discusses the seeming delay of the coming of Judgment Day, and attacks the materialistic judgments of unbelievers (II Pet. 3:1 ff.).

This review of the temptation or testing for good reveals that our heavenly Father does not send it indiscriminately, merely for the sake of discomfort, but always in a careful plan directed to the increase of spiritual life. God suits and apportions tests to their purpose (I Cor. 10:13). This wise and loving control of the Father is especially important, since so many devices for the testing of faith are at the same time devices by which devil, world, and flesh seek the destruction of spiritual life (II Pet. 2:9; Job 5:8 ff.). Peter, the headlong and proud disciple, needed much disciplining and testing; but before it began, the Savior said: "I have prayed for thee, that thy faith fail not; and when thou art converted, strengthen thy brethren" (Luke 22:32; cp. John 16:33; 17:15; cf. Matt. 24:22).

Temptation

Thus Scripture teaches that God's purposes in temptation are always for good. It behooves us to recognize those purposes in every attack of difficulty and trial; to look upon them not merely as pricks and pains, but as prods and directives (Deut. 32:26 ff.). Every item of testing and temptation is a fruit of the limitless planning and wisdom of God; every item is an indication of grave needs of the Spirit; every one is an invitation to get busy with salvage and remedy.

V

Actually it is not the temptation which strengthens faith, but God's grace, conveyed through the Gospel and the Sacraments. Their use gives the power to withstand and to profit from temptation.

Christians are in danger of imagining that in a test of faith or a temptation for good that good has been done through the very endurance of pain. The Christian may thus imagine that he contributes something, even if only through suffering, to the health of his soul. Hence at this point it behooves us to emphasize the Apostle's words: "It is God which worketh in you both to will and to do of His good pleasure" (Phil. 2:13; cf. also James 4:4 ff.). Through Jesus Christ the Christian is to reach a salutary end and a useful purpose of every one of God's tests (Heb. 2:18). What are the means which He employs for strengthening faith?

In our initial study we reminded ourselves of the fact that God is our Father for the sake of Jesus Christ, His Son, who suffered and died in order to take man's sin upon Himself, redeem us, and thus convert God's wrath to grace and reconcile us with Him. Faith is the hold of the individual upon this grace of God. It is the coupling by which the Christian is attached to the flow of God's life in himself again for the sake of Jesus Christ (John 15). Everything in this spiritual life depends upon the sureness and the permanence of that coupling. The Holy Spirit works this faith. The faith is not only the mark of the new life which the Spirit implants; it is the beginning and the one support of the new life (I John 5:4).

The Holy Spirit works faith through the means of grace, the Gospel of Jesus Christ and the Sacraments. The Gospel is the message of the plan of God for the salvation of the world, worked out through the coming into the world of Jesus Christ and His death and resurrection. Through that message and invitation, as it reaches the mind of man, the Holy Spirit works the faith to trust in Jesus Christ for the forgiveness of sins (Luke 24:45 ff.). So also Baptism is a means of making us shareholders in the benefits of Christ's death and resurrection (Rom. 6:3 ff.; Gal. 3:27; I Pet. 3:21). And the Sacrament of the Breaking of Bread conveys to us the forgiveness of sins through the death of Christ, imparting the very body and blood of Christ to the end that the spiritual shortcomings of the Christian be remedied (I Cor. 11:23 ff., 29-30).

Through the means of grace the Holy Ghost initiates and maintains the new birth. Thus the Gospel is a seed of this new birth (I Pet. 1:22 ff.). The Sacraments are the means of partaking of the life in Christ (Rom. 6:1 ff.; Gal. 3:27; I Cor. 11). Through the means of grace, accordingly, the new life with all of its phases and all of its purposes is maintained. The means of grace become the support for the snuffing out of the flesh and the overcoming of its power in the Christian (Rom. 6:6, 11, 17-18).

The means of grace become the support for the performance of good works. Love and all the activities of the new life—loyalty, meekness, faithfulness, purity—are the gifts of the Spirit as He operates through the Gospel and the Sacraments (Gal. 5:16 ff.; John 15:3 ff.).

The Christian, as he trusts in God for forgiveness and life, envisions that life as permanent, outlasting this present world and moving on in a glorious and perfect eternity with a complete exercise of every faculty in the service of love (I Cor. 13:8; 15:54). That Christian hope is the fruit of the Spirit's work through the Sacrament (I Cor. 15:58; Col. 1:3 ff.).

Our purpose in these discussions is not, however, simply to chronicle the unique importance of the means of grace. Rather do we wish to note the significance of temptation, of tests of faith, in stimulating the Christian to the richer use of the means of grace. For all temptation for evil seeks to relax the Christian's hold on God through faith; that is another way of saying, to relax the Christian's use of the means of grace. All temptation for good seeks to stimulate the Christian's hold on God through faith, to make him conscious of his tremendous need for God's grace and that alone, and thus to have Him replenish that grace through the use of the means of grace.

When we observe our Savior at work in warding off the temptation of the devil, we find that each assault of the devil drove Christ to exalt the supremacy of God's Word (Matt. 4:4 ff.). As St. Paul wrestles with God for an answer to the meaning of his thorn in the flesh, he receives this answer: "My grace is sufficient for thee, for My strength is made perfect in weakness" (II Cor. 12:9). Chastisement forces the Christian to concentrate upon the one source of his help and comfort, God and His Word. The Father describes the purpose of all of the suffering which He inflicts upon the world, and its removal, in the light of that truth—"Be still, and know that I am God" (Ps. 46:10). That grace, and the means by which it is purveyed to the individual, becomes all-important (John 6:63). The great Psalm of the Word, 119, makes much of the function of sorrow and suffering in making clear the essential need and the power of the Word of God's grace (cf. 5, 19, 21, 22, 23, 25, 28, 31, 37, 39, 41 ff., 50, 61, 67, 69, 75 ff., 81 ff., 92, 95, 107, 110, 115, 119, 121, 134, 143, 150, 153, 161, 176). It is a major purpose of this Psalm to show the one pervading purpose of all the testing of faith: to drive to the grace of God extended through His Word. It is very easy for the Christian to become formal and mechanical in his use of the Word of God, and thus actually to insert resisters between himself and the source of grace in God. Trouble and temptation has the purpose of making the unique need of God's grace and the transcendant importance of the means of grace clear in the Christian's every moment. Our heavenly Father is ceaselessly busy with the tests and trials that are to hold us to the one source of His life in Christ, namely, the Gospel and the Sacrament of His blood.

The function of temptation is not merely to slip a memorandum before us concerning the means of grace. It works not in a formal and mental manner. But it literally drives to grace. It makes clear that we are suffering from a deficit of spiritual power, owing to lack of supply of the bread of life, or malnutrition induced by our own preoccupation. In the Sermon on the Mount the Savior describes the sphere of worry for daily existence in our lives as a device to spur us to priority for the things of the Spirit

(Matt. 6:32-33). The Parable of the Sower is a warning of the Savior to people listening to His words, to point out the handicaps for the effective use of the Word—the devil, temptation which causes men to fall away, cares and riches and pleasures of this life (Luke 8:12 ff.). Thus the Christian has the opportunity in his very attention to the Word and thirst for the Gospel to gauge and verify the status of His own spiritual life. Similarly the lack of love, the preoccupation with worldly and selfish interests, are a testimony to the individual that the means of grace are not coming into their own and that he is in need of new and genuine supply (I Tim. 6: 17 ff.). As the heavenly Father stabs and thrusts with the reminders of the vanity and uselessness of temporal things and the Christian's heart becomes aware of how strongly he has been holding to them, the richer influx of the grace of God through the supply of Gospel and Sacrament becomes most literally the One Thing Needful (James 5:1 ff.; Rev. 3:18-19).

Thus every temptation for good should climax in the actual use of the means of grace. We repeat the core verses from the 119th Psalm: "Before I was afflicted, I went astray; but now have I kept Thy Word" (67); "Mine eyes fail for Thy Word, saying: When wilt Thou comfort me?" (82.) St. Paul holds a harrowing prospect before Timothy of the temptations and persecutions of the faith that will beset the Church and perplex him; he urges him to continue in the use and the power of inspired Scriptures, able to make wise unto salvation which is in Christ Jesus, able to perfect the man of God to all good works (II Tim. 3:15-17). James sets forth the blessed issue of temptation in the victorious Christian: he lays apart all filthiness and superfluity of naughtiness and receives with meekness the engrafted Word, which is able to save his soul (James 1:21; cf. also I Pet. 2:2; I Cor. 11).

The enlarged use of the means of grace and the renewed supply of the grace of God for every need and demand of life make the Christian recognize that the test of faith was a salutary thing. He is not always sure of this when he is caught in the toils of the testing device; but when it is over, he recognizes it for what it was, a means toward good (II Cor. 4:8 ff; Phil. 3:8).

The temptation succeeds in its total purpose, accordingly, when it has been the occasion for the enlarging of the spiritual vitality of the Christian and that vitality applies itself to the needs and

Temptation 195

opportunities of the Christian life. Temptation leads to the use of the Word, and the hearing of the Word must be coupled with the doing of the Word—so James schedules the process (James 1:12-27; Ps. 17:3, 5). The result of temptation is the improving of the total Christian life, because of this supply of the grace of God, and thus the improving of faith itself to ever new fruits of faith (Luke 6: 47-48; Rom. 5:1-5). The process constantly involves the reducing and weakening of the flesh and the enhancing and strengthening of the Spirit (Col. 3:5 ff; I Pet. 4:1-2; Eph. 6:10 ff.). All of the function of temptation and trouble in life heads toward this end, the use of the means of grace. All of the fruits of temptation and trial, in the plan of God, stem from this source, the use of the grace of God through Christ Jesus and the means of giving us the results of His redemption.

The Christian is associated with his brother in the business of making this use of the means of grace and this help against temptation a mutual task. One Christian is to help the other. The Savior was at work toward His disciples in that task (Luke 22:32). James speaks of it 5:19-20. The chain reaction of temptation for good does not end inside of the Christian, but goes on, through the mutual intercourse and admonition of the Christian, to influence the souls around him (I Tim. 1:16; Job 32:1 ff). Hence every Christian, stirred by the new gift of love in his heart, will be anxious to guide the faltering footsteps of his brother, or to be helped by him. That is one of the chief purposes of the organization of the Christian congregation, that it be a fellowship of people concerned about each other's welfare and serving the spiritual vitality of one another in the midst of all the tests and reminders of trouble (James 5:16; I Pet. 5:5 ff.).

VI

The Christian should pray in time of temptation. Such prayer will be a mark of his sense of need for the grace of God and of his readiness to apply the means of grace to himself in time of need.

God wants the Christian to pray in time of temptation. When the disciples asked our Savior to instruct them in prayer, He gave them a list of the great aims and goals of prayer which should always be before them; we call it the Lord's Prayer. It climaxes in the words: "Lead us not into temptation, but deliver us from evil" (Matt. 6:13; Luke 11:4). As the Christian prays that prayer, he reminds himself of the constant activity of temptation and testing of his faith going on around him and in him; and he spreads the matter out before God in prayer. Our Lord Himself is the great example of this process in action in Gethsemane (Matt. 26:38 ff.); and in connection with that incident He reinforced the place of prayer in the life of His disciples (v. 41). The ancient record of Jacob at Peniel remains forever an inspiration to the child of God in the day of trial to bring the problem and the need to God in prayer (Gen. 32).

God wants the Christian to pray in temptation. But God also wants the Christian to understand what He means by prayer and why He promises to hear prayer. Prayer is not simply the cry of man for help from a god. It is not merely a ritual by which God is wheedled into an attitude of complaisance or indulgence toward man. But prayer is an act of the Christian's faith. That faith is not simply a kind of general assurance about God. "All things whatsoever ye shall ask in prayer, believing, ye shall receive," said the Savior to His disciples (Matt. 21:22). And "believing" means being sure of being God's children because of the redemption of Jesus Himself and therefore confident that God will grant them whatever they desire in accord with the will of God (John 14:11-12; John 15:6-7). In the light of that fact concerning prayer must we also consider prayer in temptation. It is not simply a formula that is to rid us magically of the evil of temptation. When the Christian says: "Lead us not into temptation," he is not suggesting that God lies in wait to plunge him into misery. But he has already acknowledged that God is his Father, that all of his trials and problems are in God's hand, and that he counts on God for Jesus' sake to appoint and to apportion them for his good. He prays for deliverance from the evil of temptation in that faith (Luther, Large Catechism, *Triglot,* p. 731).

The Christian, to the extent that he is a Christian, is a child of God, driven by the will and impelled by the interests of God (John 15:7; Ps. 37:4 ff.). The plea to escape temptation is hence always the plea at the same time to be filled with the power of God to do His will (Rom. 8:23 ff.). As the praying Christian confronts fleshly motives and lusts battling for the mastery of his soul, he calls on God for the help to overcome the power of the flesh with the power of the Spirit (Matt. 6; 5:44). St. James bids the Christian who is ridden by lust to pray (James 4:2 ff.).

The prayer of the Christian in temptation, moreover, does not merely ask God not to permit him to succumb to devil, world, and flesh. It asks God to strengthen his faith through the means of grace so that he will be able to overcome his enemies. The whole 119th Psalm is a prayer in which the Psalmist beseeches the heavenly Father to make the Word of God a power to him in the overcoming of his difficulties and the turning to good of his chastisements. The Savior taught prayer as the response of the Christian to need and made clear that its real goal, if it was true prayer, was the growth in the Spirit of God (Luke 11:13) given to us in the Gospel.

It is easy for the Christian to imagine that as he progresses in Christian life and experience, the thrust and menace of temptation will become less and less. Conversely, the Christian may sometimes imagine that just because he is attacked by devil, world, and flesh, he may be deteriorating in his spiritual life, and he may become discouraged. Luther corrects both errors concisely: "Every hour that we are in this vile life where we are attacked on all sides, chased and hunted down, we are moved to cry out and to pray that God would not suffer us to become weary and faint and to relapse into sin, shame, and unbelief. For otherwise it is impossible to overcome even the least temptation. This, then, is leading us not into temptation, to wit, when He gives us power and strength to resist, the temptation, however, not being taken away or removed. For while we live in the flesh and have the devil about us, no one can escape temptation and allurements; and it cannot be otherwise than that we must endure trials, yea, be engulfed in them; but we pray for this, that we may not fall and be drowned in them. To feel temptation is therefore a far different thing from consenting or yielding to it. We must all feel it, although not all in the same manner, but some in a greater degree and more severely than others; as, the young suffer especially from the flesh, afterwards they that attain to middle life and old age, from the world; but others who are occupied with spiritual matters, that is, strong Christians, from the devil. But such feeling, as long as it is against our will and we would rather be rid of it, can harm no one. For if we did not feel it, it could not be called a temptation. But to consent thereto is when we give it the reins and do not resist or pray against it" (Large Catechism, *Triglot*, pp. 728—729). Hence the Christian is not surprised when the tests of faith continue; in fact, he prays for them and for the power to bear them (Ps. 139:23-24). St. Paul sets up constant prayer as a central signal in the busy and fruitful Christian life (I Thess. 5: 14 ff.; I Tim. 2:8).

Conversely, the collapse in the life of prayer is the signal that temptation has become, not temptation for good, but temptation for evil. David describes the spiritual deterioration of the man who seeks to live without God and persuade himself that He does not exist (Ps. 53:3-4). Through Isaiah God pleads with sluggish Israel to pray (Is. 43:22, 27). Daniel in his confession of sins to God summarizes the sin of Israel: "Yet made we not our prayer before the Lord our God" (Dan. 9:12-13).

The Christian is left in the world, despite his conversion and his conversation in heaven, to be a witness of his life in Christ to others, and to be a helper of that life in his brother. Temptation is the act by which devil, world, and flesh would destroy that life by severing it from its source of supply in the redemption of Christ Jesus. Temptation is permitted by God to sound the danger signal and to drive the Christian to the rebuilding of his spiritual life through Gospel and Sacrament. It is God's summons to the Christian to become busier day by day in that task for himself and for his fellow Christian. Philippians is the illustration of Christians, though separated by distance, working together in prayer for the turning of trouble to benefit, for the overcoming of trials of faith through victories of faith (Phil. 1:3 ff., 9, 19, 29, 30; 4:6). The Book of Acts displays Christians at work in prayer in the midst of affliction, not only individually, but in company with fellow believers by way of mutual strengthening, always coupled with the supply of the Word of God (Acts 2:42; 4:23-29; 6:4; 16:25). Both St. Paul and St. Peter counseled husbands and wives so to guide their lives together that their prayers would not be hindered (I Cor. 7:5; I Pet. 3:7); and Peter climaxes his great Epistle on the suffering of the Christian with the encouragement: "The eyes of the Lord are over the righteous, and His ears are open unto their prayers" (3:12). The writer to the Hebrews admonishes the congregation of Christians to pray for and with each other (10: 19 ff., 35 f.).

Conclusion

A thousand events great and small in our lives, from vagrant impulses of physical appetites to harrowing crises of pain and perplexity, from the enjoyment of the good things of life to climactic miseries and the threat of death itself, from activities out in the world to those among our fellow believers, thus suddenly assume new meaning to the Christian. Death to the soul lurks in many of them. Our world stands at the end of a long line of years in which it has trained men to be less conscious of the life of God, more ready to dally with the lusts of the flesh and the eyes and the pride of life, less mindful of the judgment to come; and so it has been fashionable to toy with temptation or even to overlook its presence and disregard its danger.

Likewise the long sequence of undisturbed years in the Church, the rich supply of the pure Gospel, the ample provision of churchly prayer and praise, and the similarity of the fellowship of the Church to that of many secular groups tends to make also us Christians unaware of the purposes of God in many of the problems and trials of life. We find it easy to see God at work in the church building and confirmation instruction and religious service; we are apt to overlook Him probing for our souls and searching our hearts in the details of everyday life.

One life line binds us to God — the Gospel of Jesus Christ, which is to this day the power of God unto salvation to every one that believeth. (Rom. 1:16.) May we cultivate our use of Word and Sacrament, not as dreary and haphazard tokens of church membership, but as carriers for the current of the Spirit of God. May we apply ourselves to them in the precious habit of prayer and the joyous fellowship of worship. May we bind ourselves in our earthly pilgrimage to Christ Jesus, the Author and Finisher of our faith and the Captain of our salvation. For He has prayed for us, too, that our faith fail not; He has said: "In the world ye shall have tribulation; but be of good cheer; I have overcome the world" (John 16:33).

The Grace of God

THESIS I

The foundation on which our Christian faith rests is the grace of God in Christ Jesus.

ALL our hope for eternity rests on the grace of God which bringeth salvation. This is the one essential truth which every man must learn if he is to be saved from the just results of his sin. That is the truth which we must preach and teach without end if we at all are to serve the purpose for which our Lord has left us in this world, the great work of building His kingdom on earth and winning souls for His Kingdom of Glory. That is nothing new to us; in fact, we remember in these days that for a hundred years now our Synod has preached this truth in this our land. Wherever you go, all our churches re-echo with this blessed truth, and every sermon on every Sunday and every festival day presents it in one way or another.

Our Church is right in placing such emphasis on this truth. The grace of God is the underlying cause of our salvation. God was gracious toward sinners before He sent His Son, aye, before He planned the redemption of man; for His grace prompted Him to send His Son into the world. In order that He might be gracious toward us without violating His justice, God sent His Son into the world that He might render satisfaction to His justice. Without the grace of God there never would have been a redemption by Jesus Christ. Without the grace of God we could never speak of a forgiveness of sin. Without the grace of God there could be no Gospel. Baier in his Dogmatics says: "Whatever there may be by which our salvation is secured to us sinners, that depends on, and flows from, grace" (Dau, *Doctrinal Theology*, II, p. 4). His grace is "that which prompts God to enter upon and carry out the plan of salvation viewed as a whole and in every particular instance. There is nothing prior to His own grace that prompts God to save" (Dau).

It must, of course, be noted that, speaking thus of God, we are following human conceptions. Thus, when we say, God is prompted, we do not mean that God is "put under a constraint from some outside source. God never answers to force or to the law of necessity." "God's grace is not anything distinct and separate from God Himself. God's grace is simply the gracious God. And God's grace prompting God practically means: The gracious God determining Himself to a certain action" (Dau).

Hence, the Formula of Concord says: "Faith lays hold of God's grace in Christ, by which the person is justified" (Formula of Concord, II, 3, 41. *Triglot*, p. 929); and we rightly say in our thesis: The foundation on which our Christian faith rests is the grace of God in Christ Jesus.

> What saints have penned by inspiration,
> What in His Word our God commands,
> What our whole faith must rest upon,
> Is grace alone, grace in His Son.

Thesis II

The grace of God on which our faith rests is God's favor or favorable disposition to sinners.

What does that mean: God is gracious to us? That grace of God on which our faith rests, the saving grace of God, the grace of God which prompted Him to send His Son into the world to redeem and to save us, what is it? To ascertain that we must examine the Scripture passages in which the word "grace" is used.

Here we note at the outset that Scripture not only uses various words to express this conception of grace (*chesed, charis, eleos, agape, chrestotes*), but also uses these words to denote different meanings. In Psalm 136 each verse ends with the refrain "For His mercy (*chesed*) endureth forever"; mercy is God's compassion upon those who are in misery, affliction, and suffering, Job 10:12: "Thou hast granted me life and favor (*chesed*)," that is, kindness, which prompts Him to shower blessings upon us. Acts 15:40 the brethren commend Paul and Silas to the grace (*charis*) of God;

evidently that means the protection of God. James 4:6: "God resisteth the proud, but giveth grace (*charis*) unto the humble"; but James does not mean to say that God's saving grace is extended to only those who, as it were, acquire worthiness by being humble, but that He grants help to the humble particularly in leading an upright life, which the proud do not receive because they reject it and as a result in their pride fall into the snare of sin. There is, it is true, a certain connection between this goodness and mercy of God and His saving grace. Matt. 24:14 Jesus says: "This Gospel of the Kingdom shall be preached in all the world for a witness unto all nations; and then shall the end come." That is the final purpose of all that God does in the world, that through the preaching of the Gospel all men might be saved; for that purpose He extends His goodness to men through all these centuries, gives them all that they need for the support of life, in His mercy protects them from evil, so that they may hear and accept the Gospel; and that is the purpose of His saving grace.

Then the Scriptures use the word "grace" metonymically. I Pet. 4:10 the Apostle says: "As every man hath received the gift, even so minister the same one to another, as good stewards of the manifold grace (*charis*) of God"; then, in verse 11, he mentions various examples of this grace of God, the gifts of grace to Christians, that enables them to speak, to minister to the glory of God. Grace, then, in this case means the gift of grace, the fruit of the new spiritual life planted in men by the saving grace of God. Rom. 15:15-16 St. Paul calls it "the grace (*charis*) that is given to me of God, that I should be the minister of Jesus Christ to the Gentiles, ministering the Gospel of God." But again, the office of the ministry and the ability to perform the duties of this office are a gift of God's grace, not the grace itself. Just so various specific gifts of grace are simply called "grace," for example, the gift of prophesying, of speaking with tongues, etc. In general, "grace" in this sense means the ability imparted by God's grace to Christians to do good works, to serve their fellow men, to bear their cross patiently, etc.

Right here, in the definition of saving grace, we part company with the Church of Rome. Rome always calls this grace in the metonymic sense "saving grace." God's grace that saves men according to their teaching is a quality which in part is inherent in man, partly is imparted to man, by which they love God. That inherent grace is a fiction of which Scripture knows nothing; Pelagius started the teaching that there is in natural man an ability to do good, to decide for good; what he meant was a free will in spiritual things; it was an accommodation to Christian phraseology that he called it "grace." On the other hand, that God does impart to man the quality by which he can and does love God is Scriptural; but that is an effect of saving grace, not saving grace itself. And that is the fundamental error of the Roman Church and of many of the sects that they make the *effects* of divine grace in man the basis of man's justification and salvation. Papists urge that man must become contrite, fast, confess, do works of penance, in order to have the grace of God in him. Sects maintain that man must base his faith in the grace of God on sensations of grace in the heart. Both undermine the very foundation on which rest our justification and salvation. That is the reason why we must be careful when speaking of saving grace to make it plain: We are not speaking of the gifts of grace. Luther points out the difference between the two in his Introduction to Romans (XIV:113 f.).

In this treatise we speak only of the "grace of God that bringeth salvation," the saving grace of God. What is it? It is not something in man. "By grace are ye saved through faith; and that not of yourselves; it is the gift of God" (Eph. 2:8). Grace is never any merit in man winning the favor of God, but, as Luther said, it is a thought which God entertains in His own mind and by which He prompts Himself to approach the sinner. All that we as Christians possess we owe to the grace of God. Eph. 1:7-8: "In whom we have redemption through His blood, the forgiveness of sins, according to the riches of His grace; wherein He hath abounded toward us in all wisdom and prudence." That we are redeemed by the blood of Christ, we owe to the grace of God; God's favorable disposition toward us moved Him to send His Son into the world to redeem us. Rom. 3:24: "Being justified freely by His grace through the redemption that is in Christ Jesus." This favor of God toward us is the motive that induced Him to justify us. The grace of God extends back into eternity. II Tim. 1:9-10: "Who hath saved us and called us with an holy calling, not according to our works, but according to His own purpose and grace, which was given us in Christ Jesus before the world began, but is now made manifest by the appearing of our Savior Jesus Christ." Redemption and salvation in Christ has been revealed to us now, in time; it has been given to us by the Word of the Gospel; but all of this issues from His eternal grace. There was grace in God before Christ came into the world, before the world began; God was gracious to us in eternity; and that was the motive for that resolution to save man by the blood of Christ.

It is the saving grace of God which forms the subject of our discussion. It is, therefore, evident that it is directed toward those who need saving. The grace of God deals with sinners. Had there been no sin, there would have been no need of saving grace, for then there would be no sinners who are in need of being saved by God's grace. The underlying meaning of the term therefore is: The love of God to sinners; it is the goodness of God extended to utterly unworthy objects, who have not only not merited it, but have merited the very contrary. In so far as the good God disregards these unfavorable qualities in the objects of His love, His goodness is called grace (*chesed, charis*). Grace always has as its proper object the befriending of sinners. Ex. 34:7 Moses says that God keeps "mercy (*chesed*) for thousands," and explains: "forgiving iniquity and transgression and sin." Psalm 103 David admonishes his soul to bless the Lord because He is "merciful and gracious, slow to anger, and plenteous in mercy"; and that mercy consists in this, that "He hath not dealt with us after our sins, nor rewarded us according to our iniquities"; "as far as the east is from the west, so far hath He removed our transgressions from us." I Tim. 1:14-16 St. Paul testifies that it is the grace of God that Jesus Christ came into the world to save sinners, of whom he was chief. (Luther, XXII: 434: XII: 1493.)

We are, therefore, not properly stating the case when we say God is gracious to all men, even to sinners. God extends His grace to all men because they are sinners. That is their only hope. And that is God's true purpose and intention, to be gracious and merciful to sinners. Only sinners have claim to the grace of God.

Only sinners, and all sinners. "The grace of God that bringeth salvation hath appeared to all men" Tit. 2:11. This truth we shall consider in a special chapter (ch. VI).

Since grace is extended to sinners because they are sinners there is another characteristic of grace which is essential. St. Paul says: "If by grace, then it is no more of works; otherwise grace is no more grace. But if it be of works, then is it no more grace; otherwise work is no more work" (Rom. 11:6). Grace and merit absolutely exclude each other. Again and again that contrast is emphasized. "By grace are ye saved through faith; and that not of yourselves; it is the gift of God; not of works, lest any man should boast" (Eph. 2:8-9). "Not by works of righteousness which we have done, but according to His mercy He saved us" (Tit. 3:5). "Who hath saved us and called us with an holy calling, not according to our works, but according to His own purpose and grace, which was given us in Christ Jesus before the world began" (II Tim. 1:9). So the justifying, saving grace of God is free grace. It excludes all merit of man and all obligation on the part of God. Whatever God does by grace, He does not owe, He gives freely (Rom. 4:4).

God's grace is not indifference to sin. There are those who confuse the two concepts. They admit they are sinners; they have not done what they should have done; but, they conclude, God is gracious and merciful; He will bear with their weakness, will regard their good intentions, their remorse, their occasional resolution to do better; He will forget His justice and give way to His grace. They think that God, like Eli, in love to His children will deliberately overlook many things which in strict justice He ought to punish. Similar thoughts will come to Christians; it appears to them that their very weakness, their spiritual misery and helplessness, should incite and stimulate the love of God, as though they had a certain claim on the love and pity of God because they are helpless, because they are sinners. That is a perverted conception of God's grace. Scripture tells us two things: We are not worthy of any pity, of any love; we deserve nothing but punishment; we would have not the least reason to complain if God were to condemn us outright to eternal perdition; we could not charge Him with injustice, no, not even think of Him as hard and unfeeling. On the other hand we are told that God did have mercy upon us who are not worthy of any mercy, that God has saved us from our miserable and lost condition, not because He owed us anything, but freely by grace. God is perfectly just, and He is altogether gracious. He never forgets His justice, and He never overlooks a single sin; He always thinks of us in mercy, and He forgives every sin. How that is possible, we shall hear later. Here our object is to establish that God's saving grace is His gracious disposition toward sinners.

Thesis III

The saving grace of God is active grace: His grace prompts God to save men, who cannot be saved in any other way, in the way of grace.

The saving grace of God is active grace. God is gracious toward sinners; that does not merely mean that God is pleased when sinners are saved despite their sins; that He hopes men will in some way manage to escape damnation and secure entrance into heaven. God's grace is not such an idle compassion; it prompts Him to action. God's grace is "a thought which God entertains in His own mind and by which He prompts Himself to approach the sinner. . . . Out of this unlooked-for disposition of God toward the sinner springs the first thought and the possibility of a salvation for man. God, not man, starts this business. God proposes to restore man and does not wait for man to rehabilitate himself with God" (*Theological Quarterly*, XXI, pp. 70—71). God's grace is active and moves Him to do all that is necessary that men might be saved.

His grace, and nothing else. We have heard before that no work of man, no attitude of man, nothing in man or proceeding from man, may in any way be considered as prompting or in any way influencing God to justify and save the sinner; the very concept of grace excludes that. But modern theologians, ever anxious to substitute something more modern and "scientific" for the old Biblical motive for man's salvation, the free grace of God, advance such a notion under the term "necessity of God's grace." Now we speak of a necessity of God's grace, too; Dr. Pieper (*Christliche Dogmatik*, II, p. 5): "When we speak of a necessity of grace, we of course do not mean a necessity on the part of God, but a necessity for man, if man is to come into possession of salvation." In other words, if there were no grace of God, man would never be saved. But Modernists, when they speak of the necessity of grace, mean just that: a necessity in God. As in everything else, they say, there is an evolution in God. This evolution brought about the sending of the Son of God; Christ would have become man even if man had not fallen into sin. Others argue, God would have denied His own being, His very essence, had He suffered His creatures to perish in sin and misery; such hardness and cruelty is unworthy of God; so their very misery and helplessness required that He save them; not only His love, but His justice, demanded a redemption; hence the necessity of grace on God's part.

Rom. 3:24-26 is quoted for this view: "Being justified freely by His grace through the redemption that is in Christ Jesus, whom God hath set forth to be a Propitiation through faith in His blood, to declare His righteousness for the remission of sins that are past, through the forbearance of God; to declare, I say, at this time His righteousness; that He might be just and the Justifier of him which believeth in Jesus." God declared, manifested His grace and His righteousness in redeeming men through Christ. That is Bible truth. But to set grace and justice of God side by side as a *motive* in God for our redemption and salvation, to say that in procuring our salvation God was prompted in part by His grace, in part by His feeling of justice, that is not Biblical. Our redemption was not a compromise between the love and the justice of God; in a compromise both opponents give a little and take a little, and both fall a little short of what they are convinced is right. There is on God's side no necessity of grace toward fallen man. God did not owe men the redemption; their condemnation was right and just. Nor did God owe this deliverance to Himself; had He never thought of a redemption, had He condemned sinners without further hesitation, He would not have denied Himself or His truth and justice, no, not His love and goodness; nor would that have been unworthy of His divine being. It was a totally free move of His divine love which prompted Him to redeem sinners; and this impulse of His love we call grace. To be sure, God did not forget, did not set aside His justice even in this action of His grace. It is a manifestation of divine justice that Christ bled and died. Penalty must follow sin; that's justice, even though it strikes the Son of God. But that Christ took the place of man, that the Lord laid on Him the iniquity of us all, that was grace. Justice did not require that; justice requires penalty for sin, nothing more. God could have satisfied justice in another way, by making the sinner bear his own penalty; He could have damned the whole world of sinners, and not a one of them would have suffered more than he deserved; justice would have been done and God's whole action justified. But that God did not do what He had a perfect right to do, that He took our sins from us and laid them on Jesus Christ, that is free grace.

So there is no necessity of grace in God; God did not have to save us in Christ or else cease to be God. But for man God's grace is an absolute necessity. If the sinner was to be saved, God had to be gracious toward him and save him. There is no other way of salvation but the way of grace. Two errors are rejected by that statement: 1) that man can enter heaven as he is, irrespective of what he is or does, or despite everything he is and does; 2) that man by his own endeavors can undo the harm that was done and save himself.

St. Paul wrote a word to the Galatians which is, as it were, a *summa summarum* of all that Scripture says on the subject; he says (Gal. 3:22): "The Scripture hath concluded all under sin." As fishermen out at sea pull in their net and enclose all the fish they have caught, large and small, good and bad, in one net, so the Scriptures take all men, large and small, old and young, respectable people and bloodiest criminals, all of them together, and stamp them all with one term: sinners.

And the Scriptures are, of course, right. It is the result of Adam's fall. By one man sin entered into the world. Previously there was no sin in the world; now there is no man living who is not tainted with sin. The first sinners were at the same time the parents of the human race and bequeathed their sinful nature to all their children. Adam had lost his holiness, his concreated righteousness; and Adam could not give to his children what he himself did not possess. Adam "begat a son in his own likeness, after his image" (Gen. 5:3). Now it is the rule without exception:

> All mankind fell in Adam's fall,
> One common sin infects us all;
> From sire to son the bane descends,
> And over all the curse impends.

"That which is born of the flesh is flesh" (John 3:6).

Now, a corrupt tree cannot bring forth good fruit (Matt. 7:18). Every man is sinful, and the result is, every man sins. "There is none that doeth good, no, not one" (Ps. 14:3). "There is not a just man upon earth that doeth good and sinneth not" (Eccl. 7:20). "If we say that we have no sin, we deceive ourselves, and the truth is not in us" (I John 1:8). St. Paul, writing to the Romans, ch. 1:18—2:29, paints a gruesome picture of mankind; but it is true to nature. Man who issued from the hand of the Creator in the image of God has become a grotesque caricature.

Sin has brought a dreadful change in man and a fateful change in his relation to God. God hates and abhors sin. "Thou art not a God that hath pleasure in wickedness, neither shall evil dwell with Thee" (Ps. 5:4). And He abhors the person that sins. "Thou hatest all workers of iniquity" (Ps. 5:5). "The wicked and him that loveth violence His soul hateth" (Ps. 11:5). "They that are in the flesh cannot please God" (Rom. 8:8). It is evident that a sinner cannot enter heaven, that he is lost, helplessly lost, under the wrath of God. God's curse pronounced in the Old Testament Deut. 27:26 is repeated in the New Testament: "Cursed is every one that continueth not in all things which are written in the Book of the Law to do them" (Gal. 3:10). "Whosoever shall keep the whole Law, and yet offend in one point, he is guilty of all' (James 2:10). You can't pick and choose which you will keep, which not. "Thou shalt," God says; that means the whole man, including the heart, particularly the heart, as Jesus tells us in the Sermon on the Mount. And this not only for a time, but for your whole life; not only on Sundays, but in business, in your most private life; not only in old age when death threatens, but from the first breath to the last. More than that; the Law judges not only your actions, but your very being; every evil tendency is condemned. "Ye shall be holy, for I the Lord your God am holy" (Lev. 19:2; I Pet. 1:15-16). That demand includes Christians. They begin indeed to keep God's Law; but to keep the whole Law, that is beyond their power. Everyone of their good works is tainted with sin. And there remains the corrupt heart. Surely, "that no man is justified by the Law in the sight of God, it is evident" (Gal. 3:11).

But who can then be saved? With men this is impossible; but with God all things are possible. "What the Law could not do in that it was weak through the flesh, God, sending His own Son in the likeness of sinful flesh and for sin, condemned sin in the flesh, that the righteousness of the Law might be fulfilled in us" (Rom. 8:3-4). God did not create men for hell, but for heaven; in His grace

He resolved to save them in spite of their sin; and in His unfathomable wisdom He found a way to save them. It is the way of forgiveness of sin. Sin is a fact; it cannot be made undone. And sin requires punishment; the justice of God demands that. So God in eternity resolved to lay all our sin on His Son Jesus Christ, to let Him pay the wages of sin, and then forgive men their sin for Christ's sake and take them into heaven, solely by grace, without any merit of their own. And in the fullness of the time this plan was carried out. Now it is the will of God: Since the way of the Law is impossible, man is to be saved by the way of grace, only by grace, and in no other way.

Thesis IV

The way of grace to life consists in this, that God declares men righteous and saves them without the Law, hence without good works on their part.

Sin is a fact. God can and will not change that record. But God resolved to save men despite their sin by forgiving their sins, by not imputing their sins to them, not charging them with this debt, by justifying them, or declaring them righteous. Scripture, viewing this act of God from different viewpoints, uses all these and other expressions; but they all mean: God declares the sinner righteous.

That does not mean: God makes sinners righteous. Here we part company with the Church of Rome and with many of the sects. "It is characteristic of good Papists and poor Protestants to set up the principle that God can declare only such people righteous as are actually inherently righteous, either entirely or at least in a measure or, at any rate, have made a start. Any other mode of justification would not be proper for God" (Pieper). There is, it is true, a difference. Romanists hold that God infuses righteousness into the heart of the sinner so that he can live right and so become righteous before God. The Canons and Decrees of the Council of Trent declare: "The alone formal cause (of justification) is the justice of God, not that whereby He Himself is just, but that whereby He maketh us just, that, to wit, with which we, being endowed by Him, are renewed in the spirit of our mind, and we are not only repentant, but are truly called, and are, just, receiving justice within us, each one according to his own measure which the Holy Ghost distributes to every one as He wills, and according to each one's proper disposition and co-operation. For although no one can be just but he to whom the merits of the Passion of our Lord Jesus Christ are communicated, yet is this done in the said justification of the impious, when by the merit of that same holy Passion the charity of God is poured forth by the Holy Spirit in the hearts of those that are justified, and is inherent therein; whence man, through Jesus Christ, in whom he is ingrafted, receives, in the said justification, together with the remission of sins, all these (gifts) infused at once, faith, hope, and charity." (Session VI, Ch. VII. Waterworth, p. 35.) Many of the sects, that is evident to everyone, revert to the natural religion of man and hold that man must work out his own righteousness. Both, then, teach that man is justified by God because of his works, because he has, more or less, become righteous; the Romanist says: through powers bestowed by God; the sectarian: by his own powers.

It marks the turning point in Luther's life that he learned the true meaning of justification, chiefly in connection with Rom. 1:17. He had been taught, as everyone was taught by the Church of that day, that he must be good and do good before he could attain the favor and the pardon of God. When by God's own enlightenment he learned that the righteousness that avails before God is not man's own, but the righteousness of Jesus Christ imputed to the sinner by faith, that in the justification of the sinner his own works, good or bad, are entirely excluded, he said: "I felt as though I had been born anew and believed that through wide-open doors I had entered Paradise!" And surely it is easy to understand that; what a vast difference it makes whether you read the promises of the Gospel with Sinai in the background or Calvary; whether your heart tells you: You must earn the forgiveness of your sin by your own good works — leaving you forever uncertain whether you have done enough to satisfy God — or whether your heart rejoices: It is finished, all done since Jesus died on the Cross! It was natural, therefore, it was inevitable that the doctrine of justification by faith without the deeds of the Law became, and still is, the center and heart of Lutheran teaching as well as that of the truly Protestant portion of Protestantism. This is the basic point of difference between Lutheranism and true Protestantism on the one side, and the pre-Reformation Church and the present Roman Catholic Church on the other side: "Justification is not a *physical* or medicinal act, *changing man internally* from an unrighteous to a righteous man, but a *juridical* act in this sense, that a person who is *in himself unrighteous* is *declared* righteous" (Pieper, W. Albrecht's translation, II, p. 307 f.). The question here is not at all whether God could *make* the sinner righteous; whether the God who in the beginning created man pure and holy, could or could not now recreate man in His own image. When God wanted a holy, harmless, undefiled man, a man who knew no sin, whom He could make to be sin for us, He created Him; He created the sinless humanity of Jesus. But here the question is not what God can do, but what God did do when in His mercy He wanted to undo the effect of man's fall into sin, to justify and save him. And no one can answer this question but God Himself, and He has answered it thus, that He by grace, that is, without any works on their part, declares men righteous.

The detailed consideration of this doctrine belongs to the article of Justification. Since here, however, we speak of the way of grace in which God saves man, it is necessary to show briefly what Scripture says on this point. The word which Scripture uses to designate God's act of justifying the sinner always, even in profane literature, means "to declare righteous," and not "to make righteous." Thirty-eight times the word occurs in the New Testament; without exception it means "to declare righteous." But Scripture also describes this act of God so clearly that it cannot be misunderstood. II Cor. 5:21 St. Paul says: God "hath made Him to be sin for us, who knew no sin; that we might be made the righteousness of God in Him." We are made righteous in the same way, by the same act, by which Christ was made sin. Christ in Himself was holy, He "did no sin, neither was guile found in His mouth" (I Pet. 2:22). Nor was He made to be sin in this way that He was essentially changed, recreated a sinner. "The Lord hath laid on Him the iniquity of us all" (Is. 53:6) — so was He made sin. God charged our sin to Him, so really and actually charged them to Him that "He was wounded for our transgressions, He was bruised for our iniquities" (Is. 53:5).

Says the Formula of Concord, III, 17: "The word *justify* here means to declare righteous and free from sins and to absolve one from eternal punishment, for the sake of Christ's righteousness, which is imputed by God to faith, Phil. 3:9" (*Triglot*, p. 921). We are accustomed to call this a forensic act of God, that is, a judicial act; and Scripture clarifies the meaning by using as synonymous of justification the phrases *forgiveness or remission of sin, covering sin, not imputing sin.*

The fact that the Scriptures present this act of God as a forensic, a judicial, act of God must impress us with the seriousness, the solemnity, of the situation. Our sin is not an indifferent matter which God might overlook in passing and forget in His love and mercy. Nor can His righteousness be satisfied with anything less than that sin receive its full due. Hence the Lord pictures the justification of a sinner, as it were, as a solemn procedure in His divine court; the great Judge on His throne; the accusers, Law, conscience, Satan, presenting their case; the criminal conscious of his guilt; the prison gates, the jaws of hell, open for him. And then enters One who has the marks of nails in hands and feet; He intercedes for the sinner; and for His sake the Judge declares the sinner righteous.

In a thousand passages Scripture speaks of this way of salvation by the grace of God. First directly (Rom. 3:24; Eph. 2:5; Tit. 3:7). Then in the innumerable passages stating that we are saved by faith, for the Apostle says (Rom. 4:16) that righteousness "is of faith, that it might be of grace." Grace and faith go together; they complement each other; the one gives, the other takes, the righteousness that avails before God. Then we are told that eternal life is a gift of God (Rom. 6:23). The same truth is stated in all those passages in which works of every kind are excluded from the way of salvation; "without the deeds of the Law" (Rom. 3:28), "no more of works" (Rom. 11:6), "without the Law" (Rom. 3:21), "not of works" (Eph. 2:9). God justifies us "freely by His grace" (Rom. 3:24). You pay no toll, no fee on the way of grace, neither at the gate nor anywhere along the road. Works and grace exclude each other absolutely. If I believe that God gives me heaven and eternal life by grace, I cannot at the same time believe that I must earn heaven; and if I set out to climb to heaven by the ladder of the Law, it is no longer grace but merit; and if it is only one single rung of the ladder, it is no longer grace, but in part merit.

And then that great word which alone would suffice, not only to prove, but completely to clarify, this doctrine (Eph. 2:8-9): "By grace are ye saved through faith; and that not of yourselves; it is the gift of God; not of works, lest any man should boast." Read that whole chapter; it sounds as though the Apostle is urged on by the thought: I have not yet said enough, I must add more to make misunderstanding impossible, to keep my readers from self-righteousness, to impress upon them the glorious fact that salvation is a free gift of God's grace. The same truth is taught with equal force and clarity in the Letter to the Galatians.

A common modern contention is that this was a Pauline foible, something that Paul injected into the teaching of Christ and the other Apostles. This is, of course, pure invention; and you needn't look far to prove that. At the council of the Apostles, Acts 15, "there rose up certain of the sect of the Pharisees which believed, saying, that it was needful to circumcise them" (the Gentile Christians) "and to command them to keep the Law of Moses." Then "Peter rose up and said unto them: Men and brethren, ye know how that a good while ago God made choice among us that the Gentiles by my mouth should hear the Word of the Gospel and believe. And God, which knoweth the hearts, bare them witness, giving them the Holy Ghost, even as He did unto us; and put no difference between us and them, purifying their hearts by faith. Now, therefore, why tempt ye God, to put a yoke upon the neck of the disciples, which neither our fathers nor we were able to bear? But we believe that through the grace of the Lord Jesus Christ we shall be saved, even as they. Then all the multitude kept silence"; they listened to Barnabas and Paul; then James spoke at length, advising them "that we trouble not them, which from among the Gentiles are turned to God." Not only Paul, but all the Apostles and the early Christians are of one mind in the truth which St. Paul stated so emphatically to the Galatians. "Whoever before God appeals to the Law and the works of the Law, rejects and annuls the grace of God . . . God's grace is exclusive, it will not tolerate the least alien addition. Whoever mixes with it the smallest dose of his own righteousness, of the works of the Law, rejects grace entirely and annuls it totally" (*Lehre und Wehre*, 31, 98). Cp. Luther's fine exposition of Gal. 4: 21-31, IX; 565—601.

To this day many within the visible Church, like the Galatians, mix Law and Gospel and hope to be saved by both. Actually they propose to earn heaven, but they hope the Savior will serve as a stopgap, supply what in the end they will lack. It appears in their very language; they call Gospel what actually is Law; the Golden Rule to them is sum and substance of Christ's teaching; the Sermon on the Mount, they proclaim, is the essence of the Gospel. The basic error of many among the sects is this, that the sinner's justification and salvation is made dependent on his life before or after conversion. Romanists in this case are at least honest; they never deny that they consider man's co-operation necessary to salvation. Among sectarians you frequently hear orthodox phrases: By grace alone, through faith, for Christ's sake; but behind it hides the error of the Judaistic teachers in Galatia. Against all of them we must firmly uphold the truth as did Paul.

It need only be mentioned briefly that even the truly good works of Christians must be excluded from the way of grace to salvation, from the justification of a sinner before God. Our confessions state "that neither renewal, sanctification, virtues nor good works are *tamquam forma aut pars aut causa justificationis,* that is, our righteousness before God, nor are they to be constituted and set up as a part or cause of our righteousness or otherwise under any pretext, title, or name whatever to be mingled in the article of justification as necessary and belonging thereto" (Formula of Concord, III, 39. *Triglot,* p. 929). You could not well speak more plainly. And that is Bible truth. "By grace are ye saved through faith; and that not of yourselves; it is the gift of God; not of works, lest any man should boast." St. Paul wrote that to Christians whom he praises for their faith and their love to all the saints (Eph. 1:15). It excludes all human actions and attitudes from justification. Romanists, who want to include the good works of Christians in the causes of justification, say that St. Paul, when he excludes the deeds of the Law from justification, means only the keeping of the Jewish ceremonial Law. Would not that be a peculiar limitation of the Law? St. Paul should speak of God's Law, but wants to exclude God's chief Law, the Moral Law, the Ten Commandments, and that without a word to indicate this limitation? Deeds of the Law are all the deeds which God has ordered in His Law, chiefly in the Ten Commandments. And that includes the good works of Christians, for "a good work is everything that a child of God does, speaks, or thinks in faith according to the Ten Commandments" (Catechism). All that men can do or speak or think or imagine or will, no matter what it may be, no matter what you may call it, it is all excluded from the way of grace.

Nor is it the purpose of the Law to assist in leading man along this way of grace. That was the old Judaistic error which the Roman Catholics have again revived: "It was a false, misleading dream That God His Law had given That sinners could themselves redeem And by their works gain heaven." That false, misleading dream was prevalent in Christ's day; one after another they came to Him and asked Him: "What must I *do* to be saved?" God tells us, "By the Law is the knowledge of sin," (Rom. 3:20). As far as the way of salvation is concerned, the Law can act only negatively: it shows us how we cannot be saved. The only way of salvation is the way of grace; the Law is excluded. "Useless were for thee My Passion If thy works thy weal could fashion."

What has been said of the way of salvation in general applies to every part of it. Every step on this way is marked by the grace of God. "God has called us with an holy calling, not according to our works, but according to His own purpose and grace, which was given us in Christ Jesus before the world began" (II Tim. 1:9). There is nothing in man that might move God to call them to the supper of His salvation; on the highways and in the hedges they lurk, ragged and totally depraved; yet He invites them: "Come, for all things are now ready." There is no co-operation on their part; they want none of His hospitality; they are carnally-minded, and that is enmity against God. God knows that most of them will never answer His call, will always despise the riches of His goodness in forbearance and longsuffering; yet He sends out His servants with the instruction: "Thou shalt speak My words unto them, whether they will hear or whether they will forbear; for they are most rebellious" (Ezek. 2:7). There is nothing in man that might move God to call him, no natural beauty or amiability in man, no desire for the help of God. Nothing but His grace moves God to call the sinner to repentance.

Again, it is the grace of God that makes out of stubborn and unwilling men willing ones (Formula of Concord, Epitome, *Triglot*,

p. 791), enlightens them with the gifts of the Holy Ghost, leads them to know Jesus Christ as their Savior, to believe in Him, trust in Him, and find peace and joy in Him. When the gracious call of God comes to man, he is blind and deaf; he "receiveth not the things of the Spirit of God; for they are foolishness unto him; neither can he know them, because they are spiritually discerned" (I Cor. 2:14). He cannot even think anything that is good (II Cor. 3:5). He is an enemy of God (Col. 1:21). Scriptures multiply descriptive terms and figures and illustrations to make this point clear. "Ye were sometimes darkness," St. Paul says Eph. 5:8; not twilight, not dusk, or dawn, but darkness; there is no light in natural man, neither the last gleam of the old light nor the first ray of a new light. He is blind (Eph. 4:18); not nearsighted, but blind. He is dead (Eph. 2:5); not merely weakened, there is not the faintest breath of spiritual life in him.

But the call of God is mighty, almighty; He calls, and what was not, is. He said: "Let there be light!" And the light which was not, shone out of darkness; so He has called us out of darkness into His marvelous light. He said: "Ephphatha!" and the blind man, whose eyes had never seen, saw; so He enables us to see and know that Christ, who was a stone of stumbling and a rock of offense to us, is our Savior. He calls Lazarus, in whom death had done its work to such an extent that his own sister did not want him uncovered; and Lazarus came forth living. "But God, who is rich in mercy, for His great love wherewith He loved us, even when we were dead in sins, hath quickened us together with Christ (by grace are ye saved) and hath raised us up together and made us sit together in heavenly places in Christ Jesus" (Eph. 2:5-6). Therefore faith is directly called a gift of God, a gift of God's grace (Phil. 1:29): "For unto you it is given (*echaristhe*, a gift of grace) in the behalf of Christ, not only to believe on Him, but also to suffer for His sake."

It follows necessarily that the evidence of the new life in man, sanctification, is a result of God's grace. St. Paul says that the new man is *created* after God in righteousness and true holiness (Eph. 4:24); again, that he is renewed in knowledge after the image of Him that created him (Col. 3:10). A Christian is God's workmanship, created in Christ Jesus unto good works, which God hath before ordained that he should walk in them (Eph. 2:10).

There was no nucleus out of which God formed the chaos in the beginning; He created the universe out of nothing. It is not true that there is a good kernel in man which then unfolds; the new man is a creation of God. And so little as the chaos co-operated in its creation, so little does man assist God in this creation. To be sure, this new man now uses the powers given him by God. Christians in the strength given to them work out their own salvation with fear and trembling; but it is God who worketh in them both to will and to do of His good pleasure (Phil. 2:12-13). This co-operation in regenerate man is also clearly attested in Scripture; but we must guard against applying to unregenerate man the words directed to Christians; that would be like prescribing medicine and diet to a corpse.

And God keeps us in the faith. Man can destroy life, spiritual as well as physical; God alone can preserve it. Here, too, a Christian can and does use the powers God has given, particularly since God has given us means by which He preserves faith, the Gospel and the Sacraments; there it is in our power to use or to neglect. In the end, however, it is God who has begun the good work in us and who must perform it until the day of Jesus Christ. (Cp. Formula of Concord, II, par. 65, 66. *Triglot*, p. 907.) Finally, this which God's grace here in time begins, continues, and completes in us, has a background in eternity; for our calling, conversion, sanctification, preservation, and final salvation is but the performance of an eternal resolution of God. St. Paul speaks of this Eph. 1:3-6; Rom. 8:28-30; II Thess. 2:13; II Tim. 1:9; and St. Peter in his First Epistle, ch. 1:2. God has, in eternity, before the foundation of the world, chosen us, who are kept by the power of God through faith unto salvation, to be His children by Jesus Christ and to be glorified in heaven. And this determination of God cannot fail. Again, this eternal election of God characterizes the way of salvation as the way of grace. Those who walk this way, who are brought to faith in the Savior by the Gospel and are finally saved by this faith, are the same people whom God in eternity elected that they should be saved in this way. This election by grace is the cause of all that God in time does for us to bring us into heaven. Because He has chosen us, therefore He calls us by the Gospel, kindles faith in the Savior in our hearts, and keeps us in that faith until we have taken the last step and are safe in heaven. God has not chosen us because we believe, but we believe because God has chosen us. Formula of Concord, Thorough Declaration, XI, 8. *Triglot*, p. 1065: All the good in us is a result of God's election; how could anything in us be a cause of election? Paul stresses the part that God's grace takes in this election when, Rom. 9, he adduces the example of Jacob and Esau; and he concludes: "So, then, it is not of him that willeth nor of him that runneth, but of God that showeth mercy" (Rom. 9:16).

Thesis V

The saving grace of God is grace for Christ's sake

The saving grace of God is free grace. His grace has moved Him to do all that is needful to save sinners. It opens before our mind's eye an abyss of love that is incomprehensible. That the father in the parable longs for the return of his prodigal son is natural; that Hagar's heart yearns over her dying son we can understand; that the blessed holy God should yearn for sinful, totally depraved men, who have turned against Him in hatred and enmity, that is superhuman, that is beyond our conception.

> It is that mercy never ending,
>   Which human wisdom far transcends,
> Of Him who, loving arms extending,
>   To wretched sinners condescends;
> Whose heart with pity still doth break
> Whether we seek Him or forsake.

But God's grace is not indifference toward sin. His justice demands atonement. It is useless speculation to wonder whether God in His absolute authority could not merely pass by the sin of mankind as though it had never been done. Quenstedt rightly says: "It is needless to dispute about the power of God when His will is plainly evident in revelation." Why argue about possibilities when the fact is definitely stated in God's Word: God is just and will let no sin go by unpunished.

Atonement is necessary. Who should atone for sin? Why, man; the guilt is his. But man could not. The guilt is too great (Ps. 49: 7-8). The punishment must be equivalent to the guilt; and God is not vague as to what that was: the punishment for sin, for each sin, is eternal death. The man on whom his sin is visited is forever beyond the reach of divine grace. And atonement was beyond the ability of any man living because of his own natural condition. "Ye were dead in trespasses and sins." Can a dead man earn money to pay his debts? They are the children of wrath (Eph. 2:3); could a child of wrath do something that is pleasing to God? Remorse, many think, will cancel sin; but the remorse of a thief will not pay back a penny of his debt. Remorse may dispose a judge to be lenient, but atonement it is not. And what is the remorse of unregenerate man but anger because of the predicament in which he finds himself? Or shall good resolutions satisfy God? Try it on your grocer whether the resolution to pay cash in future will cancel past debts! Love to God, prayer, is to atone for sin. But you cannot love God, you cannot acceptably pray to God until your sins are put out of the way; and God cannot forgive sin without atonement; atonement must precede love and prayer and all good works. Besides, all that you could do in the way of loving God and your neighbor, all good works, and this includes all that Christians can do, you owe God beforehand. And if a man could live a perfectly holy life, he would still be an unprofitable servant who has only done his duty, but has not atoned for a single sin. And even an angel could do no more.

Was it at all possible to solve this apparent contradiction in God: Justice and grace? God is just and must punish sin; God is love and wants to forgive sin. Six thousand years of groping paganism bears testimony that man can find no solution of that problem. Heathen religions never got farther than devil worship and suicide. The reason for this failure was not lack of intellectual development. Some of their philosophers have produced works which are still models of keenest thinking and are used in modern universities. Nor was it lack of serious intention; when a tortured pagan throws himself under the crushing wheels of the Juggernaut so that nothing of him is left when the procession has passed but a spot on the pavement; when the Hindu mother throws her babies to the sacred crocodiles to pacify her gods; could they possibly take their religion more seriously? No, the reason for pagan failures to solve the problem of religion lies deeper. Solving this problem was beyond human ingenuity; working out a solution was beyond human ability.

What man could not do, God did. Paul writes to Timothy (II Tim. 1:9-10): "God hath saved us and called us with an holy calling, not according to our works, but according to His own purpose and grace, which was given us in Christ Jesus before the world began, but is now made manifest by the appearing of our Savior Jesus Christ, who hath abolished death and hath brought life and immortality to light through the Gospel." God in His grace wanted man saved; but His grace was not an idle emotion; it is active grace. He made our salvation possible by Himself furnishing the atonement which His justice demanded, so that His grace could forgive sin. "God so loved the world that He gave His only-begotten Son." (Luther XI; 1085 ff.) So God in His wisdom found a way to solve the great problem: He sent His Son to do for us what we could not do: "The Lord hath laid on Him the iniquity of us all." He bore the punishment for our sin. His atonement was perfect, completely valid; He paid for all sins of all men, and He satisfied divine justice. It is not our object here to consider how Christ did this; our object is to establish that atonement was necessary; Christ made this atonement; there is now nothing in the way of God's grace; God can forgive sin without violating His justice; but we must now never think of God's grace without the atonement of Christ.

The work of Christ was in deed and in truth a full atonement for our sin, complete satisfaction of divine justice. We use the term vicarious atonement, substitutional satisfaction. You will not find these terms in the Bible; but that is immaterial; these are terms expressing perfectly what God's Word tells us of Christ's work.

Christ became our Substitute. God considered Him as standing in our stead, as taking our place. He, the Son of God, was not under the Law; but God put Him under the Law (Gal. 4:5) to fulfill it for us and to bear all punishment which we deserved for transgressing the Law. And Christ did that. He fulfilled all righteousness for us (Matt. 3:15). He bore for us the curse of the Law (Gal. 3:13). "The Lord hath laid on Him the iniquity of us all" (Is. 53:6). So great was the bulk of this sin that He, as it were, was made sin for us (II Cor. 5:21). He bore the sin of the world (John 1:29); for thirty-three long years he bore them. He suffered for us (I Pet. 3:18; Is. 53:4-5). He, "His own self bare our sins in His own body on the tree" (I Pet. 2:24). For us He was put to death (I Pet. 3:18). Eternal death, damnation, He suffered for us (Matt. 27:46). And so He restored what not He, but we, had taken away. He paid our debt to God (Ps. 69:4). "He gave Himself a ransom for all" (I Tim. 2:6). So we were bought with a price (I Cor. 6:20; 7:23), with His own blood (Acts 20:28; I Pet. 1:18-19), the blood of the Son of God, a price worth more than all the debt that humankind had incurred with God. So full and complete was this satisfaction rendered by Christ that he who can claim Christ's merits as his own may not only depend on God's grace and truth, but can appeal to the justice of God to absolve him; so says John: "If we confess our sins, He is faithful and just to forgive us our sins and to cleanse us from all unrighteousness" (I John 1:9). A creditor has no claim on a debtor if another has paid for him; any further demand would be dishonest; God can demand nothing more of us, says St. John, since Christ has paid for us; to demand more would be unjust. — It's another matter entirely if the debtor rejects this payment and obstinately insists on paying for himself; he is responsible for his own obligation. — Finally, this atonement of Christ was made for all men to the end of time (Heb. 9:12; 10:14; I John 2:2).

People take offense at this "blood-and-wounds theology." They ask: Could not God have found another way, a more "aesthetic" way of satisfying His justice and opening the way for His grace? Luther answers (XX: 882 f.): "Who are you supercilious, ungrateful devil, that you dare to ask why He has not done this in another and not in this way? Will you set and choose manner and measure for Him? You should leap for joy that He does it in whatsoever a manner He pleases as long as you receive the benefit." Those are hard words; but they are needed when dealing with people who attack the very heart of the Gospel.

It's the old story: Christ the Crucified the sign that is spoken against; unto the Jews a stumbling block, unto the Greeks foolishness. And the Church of our day has lost the courage to battle with the devil and the world. They seek favor with the world, would like to bring the world, especially the rich and powerful world, the "leaders of thought," unto the fold of the Church, to boast of large numbers. They are tired of being the little flock, of being despised and ridiculed as fools and fanatics or people who

The Grace of God

are still living in the Middle Ages. Hence, away with everything that is obnoxious to human reason, that humbles the natural pride of man! And that means chiefly the vicarious, substitutional work of Christ; that will allow no pride; it humbles man into the dust. And there is no way of making the vicarious satisfaction plausible to human reason. If a human judge condemns and sentences an innocent man in place of a criminal, we call it unjust; that judge would soon lose his job. A material debt may be paid by a substitute; but moral guilt cannot be transferred. But that is exactly what God did: The moral guilt of our sin He transferred to Christ, charged Him guilty and us innocent, when as a matter of fact He was innocent and we were guilty; and reason, your reason, too, calls that unjust; and by no manner or amount of arguing can you change that! It is, of course, the devil operating with our false conception of justice; we say: This or that is just, and so God must act. We should say: This is what God does; consequently it is just. But it takes a mind enlightened by the Holy Ghost to take that attitude.

Then, and then only, do we stand sure and safe when we can say: Thus saith the Lord. Men who do not believe the divine relation will never find the substitutional merits of Christ acceptable. He whose faith rests on the divine Word knows that he must not, cannot think of divine grace without the redemption wrought by Christ. (Luther XII: 261 ff.) That is the Scriptural and, therefore, the Christian conception of the saving grace of God: it is grace for Christ's sake. It still remains unmerited grace, as far as we are concerned. Human merit and God's grace exclude each other (Rom. 11:6). But divine grace and the merits of Christ do not exclude each other; they are indissolubly connected. When St. Paul says that we are justified freely by God's grace, he at once adds: "Through the redemption that is in Christ Jesus" (Rom. 3:24). God's favor toward sinners does not exclude, but includes the satisfaction of the demanding and condemning justice of God rendered by Christ's vicarious work, suffering, and death (Rom. 3:25). Mixing human efforts with God's grace nullifies it; thinking of God's grace without the work of Christ is mere imagination. Hence in Scripture the Gospel of God's grace and the Gospel of Christ the Crucified are interchangeable, equivalent expressions (Acts 20:24 and I Cor. 2:2). To speculate about an absolute will of God, separate from the work of Christ, is foolish because Scripture knows nothing of that; Scripture links God's will toward us with the redemption of Christ. To ask impertinent questions, why God did so and not otherwise, why Christ could not redeem us some other way, is foolish and useless. "When a man begins to criticize God, he can be sure that he is a great fool" (Pieper). On our knees we should thank God that He has found any way to save us. He who despises the grace of God in Christ Jesus has no comfort in life or in death. Our only comfort is to say with the children:

> Jesus, Thy blood and righteousness
> My beauty are, my glorious dress;
> Midst flaming worlds, in these arrayed,
> With joy shall I lift up my head.

THESIS VI

The saving grace of God is universal.

God is gracious. Christ has earned the favor of God for men; God can now, in Christ Jesus, forgive sin without violating His Justice. But is God gracious to me? Will He forgive my sin? That is the great question which every man must have answered satisfactorily. Can we be sure of that? Can we assure every other man of that fact?

Scripture answers: The saving grace of God in Christ Jesus is universal. God is gracious to all men, to every individual man, even to those who finally are lost.

The saving grace of God embraces all men. The Scriptures state this directly. "The grace of God that bringeth salvation hath appeared to all men" (Tit. 2:11); "God hath concluded them all in unbelief, that He might have mercy upon all" (Rom. 11:32). Jesus Himself says that the object of God's love is the world (John 3:16); and no man, not even Calvin, has the right to limit that word "world" to the world of the elect, and to eliminate from that word any single soul that ever lived or will live in the world. (Luther XI: 1107.)

The Scriptures further testify: All that God in His grace has done for mankind He has done for all men. Christ has redeemed all men. "In thee shall all families of the earth be blessed" (Gen.

12:3). "The Lord hath laid on Him the iniquity of us all" (Is. 53:6). "Behold the Lamb of God, which taketh away the sin of the world" (John 1:29). "He is the Propitiation for our sins; and not for ours only, but also for the sins of the whole world" (I John 2:2). "As by the offense of one judgment came upon all men to condemnation, even so by the righteousness of One the free gift came upon all men unto justification of life" (Rom. 5:18). "God is not willing that any should perish, but that all should come to repentance" (II Pet. 3:9); that all men be saved and come unto the knowledge of the truth (I Tim. 2:4). He commandeth all men everywhere to repent (Acts 17:30). He invites all: "Come unto Me, all ye that labor and are heavy laden" (Matt. 11:28). His general commission to the Church is: "Preach the Gospel to every creature." Luther says: "That means: Open your mouth wide, preach not in the corners, but freely, openly, so that all creatures, sun, moon, etc., may hear it" (XIII: 2020). All are to be invited; therefore He calls, not once, but often. It is sad that that is necessary. Not many come at the first invitation. But He calls again and again. "How often would I have gathered thy children together, even as a hen gathereth her chickens under her wings, and ye would not" (Matt. 23:37; cp. Rom. 10:21). Surely, it is God's will that all should come to His great supper. And for everyone who comes the angels in heaven celebrate in the presence of God (Luke 15:10). Cp. Formula of Concord, Thorough Declaration XI, 28. *Triglot*, 1071.

Romanists and many others teach that God will be gracious to you, but you must by penances and good works show that you are worthy of divine grace. God will be gracious to you if you repent and lead a respectable life. That means—doesn't it?—Heaven's gates are open; God invites you to come; but when you get there, you are told: Entrance costs you so and so much; you must pay remorse, repentance, good works, before you can enter. Such teaching certainly denies the universality of divine grace; it is actually extended only to those who fulfill the conditions. And so the Papacy deliberately, and many of the sects, perhaps not with premeditation, yet actually, keep untold numbers of poor souls in doubt and terror of conscience. The careless, the indifferent are not greatly disturbed, it is true; but the best among them, those who are seriously concerned about their salvation, suffer under the thought: Before you can rely on God's promises and find comfort in the assurance of His grace, you must do your part and prove that you are worthy of receiving His grace; God will remit the 10,000 talents you owe Him, but before He will do so, you must pay Him 10 or 20% interest on the debt. That is a frightful error; it almost drove Luther to despair. It was Staupitz at that time who told Luther that he had resolved to forget all about such limitations of divine grace and to trust His soul to the care of the Savior. And so no doubt many souls who are nominally members of the Roman Church, and others who teach that error, by a fortunate inconsistency actually do rely on the grace of God in Christ, forgetting all about such conditions, and so save their souls. But for the soul that follows such teaching only two ways are open: Either despair, because he cannot do what is required of him, or self-righteous reliance on his own works, which again will cost him his salvation.

It is, of course, a contradiction in itself to say: You must make yourself worthy of God's grace; you must earn it. God's grace is free grace or no grace at all. And God's grace embraces all men. God comes to us like that father to the prodigal son; he did not say: You must patch your poor rags before we go to the house so that I need not be ashamed of you before your big brother; you must wash yourself and your rags that you do not smell quite so much like a pigsty! He loves him as he is. The good Shepherd does not expect the lost sheep to meet Him halfway; He loves it while it is running away; in fact, the faster the sheep runs, the faster He follows to catch it. "Ho, everyone that thirsteth, come ye to the waters, and he that hath no money; come ye, buy, and eat; yea, come, buy wine and milk without money and without price" (Is. 55:1). God offers His grace to all men, and does not then nullify His offer by adding any condition. We need only come and take what He offers, believe what He says: "Come, for all things are now ready."

But, says someone, do not you yourself set a condition when you say: God is gracious to you if you believe His promises? God is gracious to believers, but not to unbelievers? — But we do not say that. Nowhere is it written that God is gracious to believers, but not to unbelievers. God is gracious toward all men, whether they believe it or not. He offers His grace to all and sets no condition. He does not even say: My grace is yours if you accept it. No, He says: My grace is yours whether you take it or not. To be sure, to receive what the grace of God has in store for you, you must accept it; and faith is the hand that accepts, that takes what God offers. But faith does not make it possible that God can be gracious to us. The grace of God embraces all men, whether there is faith or not. Faith does not earn the grace of God. Faith does not effect or procure the grace of God. But faith is the hand that receives what the grace of God offers. The good Shepherd loves His sheep; if the sheep deliberately squirms out of the arms of the Shepherd, jumps off the precipice and breaks its neck, the Shepherd's love is vain; but He loves the sheep nevertheless.

Rom. 10:21 St. Paul cites the words of Isaiah: "But to Israel He saith: All day long I have stretched forth My hands unto a disobedient and gainsaying people." God is speaking of people who seek Him not, who ask not after Him, people who are, as Stephen said, stiff-necked and uncircumcized in heart and ears; yet God stretches forth His hand to them all day long; He wants to save them. And on the Mount of Olives stands the Savior Himself shedding tears, and He says: "O Jerusalem, thou that killest the prophets and stonest them which are sent unto thee, how often would I have gathered thy children together even as a hen gathereth her chickens under her wings, and ye would not!" (Matt. 23:37.) Dare anyone say that His tears were hypocritical? The saving grace of God is extended even to those miserable wretches who seduce others into misbelief and unbelief. St. Peter writes (II Pet. 2:1-2): "But there were false prophets also among the people, even as there shall be false teachers among you, who privily shall bring in damnable heresies, even denying the Lord that bought them and bring upon themselves swift destruction. And many shall follow their pernicious ways!" These, then, are teachers who not only deny Christ and to the end obstinately reject the grace of God and are finally damned, but they lead many others into eternal perdition; yet the Apostle says: The Lord whom they deny has bought them, redeemed them. (Luther VII: 1717 ff.)

In view of this overwhelming testimony of Scripture for the universal grace of God in Christ one would hardly deem it possible that it should ever be questioned in the Christian Church. Yet this has been done. This denial of God's universal grace appeared early in the history of the Church, and it is more widely spread than ever. It is the official teaching of all Calvinistic Reformed church bodies. Calvin taught that God did not create all men for the same fate, but predestined some unto life, others to eternal damnation. The Westminster Confession of Faith contains this statement: "Neither are any other redeemed by Christ, effectually called . . . but the elect only. . . . The rest of mankind God was pleased according to the unsearchable counsel of His own will, whereby He extendeth or withholdeth mercy as He pleaseth for the glory of His sovereign power over His creatures, *to pass by,* and to ordain them to dishonor and wrath for their sin, to the praise of His glorious justice." The reason for this denial lies not in lack of Bible testimony for universal grace nor in lack of clarity in the adduced passages, but in man's depraved reason. Reason argues thus: Not all men are actually saved; if therefore God wants to save all, there must be something in man or in what man does that is added to God's grace and so decides why some are saved, others not. — We call that synergism; it denies the "by grace alone" and gives some merit for man's salvation to man himself. — Or, reason says, if man is saved by grace alone, then God cannot extend the same grace to all, otherwise all would be saved. — That we call Calvinism; it denies the universal grace of God. — We must not allow the apparently straight logic of either side to sway us, but hold firmly to plain Bible truth, that man is saved by grace alone and that God's grace is universal. This presents a problem, it is true; and this problem will be considered in the next thesis.

Thesis VII

The saving grace of God is serious and efficacious.

It is an "un-Lutheran and false principle" that it is the office of a theologian, when doctrines of the Scriptures seem to contradict one another, to harmonize them with each other by drawing inferences and that such inferences are just as well and as much divine truth as the written Word. It is also a most dangerous and destructive principle, whereby the theologian is made master over the Scriptures. It is dangerous to follow this principle when Scripture and experience do not seem to harmonize. At times this is the case; then, instead of following above principle, we should say: We must judge experience by Scripture; and if we strike problems which we cannot solve, we must leave them unsolved and regard them as mysteries which are beyond our reason and understanding in our present imperfect condition, which we shall comprehend in the future perfection in heaven.

This does not satisfy our reason, nor those who prefer to follow reason rather than the Scriptures. A problem of that kind we have here in the doctrine of the saving grace of God. Experience teaches us — and this is corroborated by Scripture — that not all men are saved; Scripture teaches that salvation is by grace alone. Reason says: The only solution is: God does not seriously want all men to be saved, not even all those who hear the Gospel. While the Gospel is to be preached to all, God's intention is not that all shall accept it unto salvation. He calls all, but for some the call is only external; serious and efficacious, this call is only for the elect. More than that: To some God even gives faith for a time, then deserts them, and their penalty will only be the greater.

Calvin himself calls this a horrible doctrine. Thank God, it is not Scriptural; it is not only not revealed in Scripture, it is flatly contradictory to Scripture; it has its foundation only in the depraved reason of false teachers. The Scriptures teach that this universal grace of God in Christ is earnest, active, efficacious.

In the first place, Christ has commanded that the Gospel, the good news that God is gracious to all, that God was in Christ, reconciling the world unto Himself (II Cor. 5:19), should be preached to all creatures. This great work of reconciling the sinful world with God was not done in secret nor kept a secret; all the world is to be informed of the finished redemption of Christ. That should suffice. When a man tells me something, I cannot be absolutely sure; men are sometimes in error; they may think they know what they are talking about, but they deceive themselves or are deceived by others; and there are hypocrites, who deliberately tell the untruth with the purpose to deceive. And when Satan tells us something, we know *a priori* that it is a lie. But God! "God is not a man, that He should lie; neither the son of man that He should repent; hath He said, and shall He not do it? Or hath He spoken, and shall He not make it good?" (Num. 23:19.)

God is the essential truth; and on His oath He assures us that He wants to save all men (Ezek. 33:11). He has instituted Holy Baptism, "the assurance of a good conscience toward God" (I Pet. 3:21), a pledge for the truth of His promises. It is incredible that Christians should doubt the truth of this testimony. Nor can there be any reason to doubt that this grace of God extended to all is efficacious. Whenever and wherever the Gospel is preached, God wants to work faith in the hearer; (Matt. 23:37: "I would have gathered thy children together, even as a hen gathereth her chickens under her wings." (Luther VII: 1260 f.) This faith He wants to preserve in all who have come to the knowledge of their Savior until they reach the goal in heaven (Phil. 1:6).

It is a pity that we must discuss this question whether God means what He says in His Word. Wouldn't you be highly insulted if a man called you two-faced? And men can imagine that of God! He prepares His great supper, He opens His doors, He calls, He sends His servants, millions of them, to call: "Come, for all things are now ready!" When at first the invitation is ignored, He sends them out again and again. He is angry when men reject His invitation (Luke 14:21); He cries out: "Turn ye, turn ye from your evil ways; for why *will* ye die, O house of Israel?" (Ezek. 33:11.) Jesus sheds tears when men refuse to come to Him. Is all of that mere sham, nothing but pretense? Shall we charge Him with hypocrisy? That would be blasphemous!

No, the call of God's grace is no jugglery, but "Christ calls to Himself all sinners and promises them rest, and He seriously wills that all men should come to Him and suffer themselves to be helped, to whom He offers Himself in His Word and wishes them to hear it and not to stop their ears or neglect and despise the Word. Moreover, He promises the power and working of the Holy Ghost and divine assistance for perseverance and eternal salvation" (Formula of Concord, Epitome, XI, 8. *Triglot*, 833).

Another emphatic proof for the truth that the saving grace of God is serious and efficacious appears in those passages which tell us why not all who are called by the Gospel are actually saved. The reason for this is not a lack of serious intention on the part of God; God does not pass them by with His grace. The reason lies altogether in man. "Ye would not," Jesus says to Jerusalem

The Grace of God

in the repeatedly adduced passage, Matt. 23:37. And Stephen tells the Jewish council (Acts 7:51): "Ye do always resist the Holy Ghost." A very significant word we find Acts 13:46-48. St. Paul tells the unbelieving Jews at Antioch in Pisidia: "It was necessary that the Word of God should first have been spoken to you; but seeing ye put it from you and judge yourselves unworthy of everlasting life, lo, we turn to the Gentiles." Rightly Dr. Pieper points out that if words really mean what they say, then the reason why some are lost lies not in God, but in man; "Ye do always resist"; "ye put it from you."

Is it possible that man can successfully resist Almighty God? Yes, that is possible. It is indeed the omnipotence of God that is active in the means of grace, the Gospel and the Sacraments, the same power which created the world, the same power which on the Last Day will raise the dead. It is not true that the power of God in the Gospel is less than His creative power. Eph. 1:19-20 speaks of those "who believe according to the working of His divine power which He wrought in Christ, when He raised Him from the dead." Again, II Cor. 4:6: "God, who commanded the light to shine out of darkness, hath shined in our hearts, to give the light of the knowledge of the glory of God in the face of Jesus Christ." Yet there is a difference. Luther says: God working through means, can be resisted; God operating without means in uncovered majesty, cannot be resisted. Again, the question is not whether God could work irresistibly in conversion as well as in creation; we merely state what God Himself has revealed in Scripture, and that is that man has the sorry ability to resist successfully the almighty power of God working in the Gospel. And if someone asks: Why does God do that? The simple answer is: It has pleased Him to do so and not otherwise. Where He has not told us the reason for His actions, we keep our mouth shut. That we are here dealing with a mystery no one need tell us; we know that. But whoever thinks that we must now solve these mysteries of God and find a way to harmonize these seeming contradictions, mistakes entirely our business here on earth; our business is to learn and to believe what the Scriptures say.

It has been pointed out that there is an analogy in nature, that God working through means can be resisted. The almighty God alone can produce life in plants, animals, and in man; but anyone can destroy this life. Isn't it ridiculous to draw the conclusion: Since man can destroy a living being, he must also be able to produce one?

The Scriptures do speak of obduracy. God does at times inflict this terrible judgment on individuals that they can no more repent and believe. That is Scripture truth. John 12:39 says of certain Jews: "Therefore they could not believe." But to adduce such examples as proof that God does not seriously want to save all men is again a fallacy. The conclusion would be true if God had resolved: This and that person I will harden so that he cannot believe what he hears. But that is not true. Obduracy is a punishment which the wrath of God inflicts on people who have persistently hardened their hearts against the grace of God offered to them in the Gospel, who persistently resist the Holy Ghost working on their hearts to convert them; and obduracy consists in this, that God finally withdraws His grace from them, that the Holy Spirit finally stops working on their hearts. To all men comes the time when the day of grace ends; it is the day of their death. On the obdurate God inflicts the punishment that their day of grace ends before their death. But this fate befalls no man who has not persistently and for a long time hardened his heart against all the efforts of divine grace to save him. Compare the examples of Pharaoh (Ex. 7:3), Israel (Is. 6:9-10), the Jews (Luke 8:10).

To conclude: The reason for all the objections raised against the universal and the serious and efficacious grace of God is the desire to explain in a way acceptable to our reason the mystery: Why, then, are not all men saved? "'The same sermon,' says Calvin, 'is addressed to a hundred persons; twenty receive it with the obedience of faith; the others despise, or ridicule, or reject, or condemn it.' Here is the whole of it in a nutshell. Calvin explains the result of that sermon in this wise: The eighty are called only externally by the Word and therefore they cannot believe; the twenty are called with the effectual calling of the Spirit and therefore must believe. This would make the result very plain. Synergists explain it in this wise: The eighty are so desperately wicked as to regard the Gospel foolishness; the twenty are not quite so desperately wicked; they refrain from counting the Gospel foolishness and so enable God to have His work in them. This would also make the result very plain. Does the reader perhaps ask: How do you Lutherans explain this? Answer: We do not explain it at all; we let it alone. We only insist on these four things, but on these *we do insist*: 1. The same call comes to them all. 2. The same depravity is in them all. 3. The eighty despise the Gospel by their own wickedness. 4. The twenty are no better, of themselves they would do exactly the same as the eighty but for the work of divine grace in them. Here we stop, and let Arminians and Calvinists travel on flourishing the lantern of reason." (Kuegele, in *Theological Quarterly*, IX, 101 f.)

This, of course, does not satisfy our reason. But that must not disturb us. We teach the universal, serious, efficacious, grace of God because Scripture says so. That's all.

Thesis VIII

The saving grace of God is revealed to us in the Gospel, offered, given, and sealed to us in the means of grace, and made our very own through faith.

Saving grace is something in God; it is God's favorable disposition toward the sinner. It is not something in man, a saving quality, a noble core or nucleus, on which God then builds up man's salvation. It is, as Luther says, a thought which God entertains in His own mind and by which He prompts Himself to approach and to save the sinner.

Now "the things of God knoweth no man," says St. Paul (I Cor. 2:11). How should man know of this disposition of God toward the sinner?

There was only one way in which the sinner could come to the knowledge of this wonderful way of salvation: God had to tell him. And that God did. In the Gospel He "made known unto us the mystery of His will" (Eph. 1:9).

In the Gospel God approached man and revealed to him that He, God, is gracious to all men; that in His grace He has prepared this way of salvation; that in Christ He has reconciled "the world unto Himself, not imputing their trespasses unto them" (II Cor. 5:19). And this Gospel is the Word of the living God, a word whereby the God of Life offers to man, dead in trespasses and sin, life, spiritual life, eternal life, in Christ Jesus. And this Gospel is the power of God unto salvation (Rom. 1:16; I Thess. 2:13; James 1:18). Baptism is the washing of regeneration and renewing of the Holy Ghost (Tit. 3:5). And in the Lord's Supper He assures those who have been brought to faith by water and the Word of His continued grace and offers, conveys, and seals to all who partake of this Sacrament the forgiveness of their sin, life, and salvation. And everyone who believes these words has what they say and convey, the forgiveness of sins by the grace of God in Christ Jesus. In order to be sure of God's grace, the Christian will diligently use the means of grace.

(Compare the essays on Means of Grace, Gospel, Sacraments, Baptism, Lord's Supper, pp. 321—446.)

Conclusion

The doctrine of God's grace is the basic truth of Christian faith. All other doctrines are either presuppositions or censequences of this. It is the central doctrine of the divine revelation; and so it is and must remain the central doctrine of the religion which is founded on God's revelation. It is significant that whenever Christians began to drift away from divine revelation, their chief error always concerned the doctrine of grace. So the Jews in the day of Christ; so the Judaistic teachers in Apostolic times; so the Roman Papacy; and so it is today. The Church, therefore, which would cling steadfastly to the revelation of God, must guard this doctrine with particular care. Salvation by grace without works, that was the center of the Reformation. It is today the central doctrine around which are grouped all the articles of our confession, which therefore we must guard with utmost care, lest we, too, fall into the soul-destroying errors of so many of those who surround us. It is the object of this essay to show that, with the help of God, our Synod has guarded and upheld the doctrine of God's grace during these hundred years. For that we thank Him with all our heart. God has been good to us; despite all the changes in the world, we can testify that the old Word is still true: "The Word of the Lord abideth forever." And we add the prayer: Lord, preserve unto us Thy Word!

The Doctrine of Justification

WHEN in 1859 the Western District of our Synod assembled at Addison, Ill., at that time not yet the location of the famous normal school from which River Forest and Seward were to stem, the president of the body, Pastor Schaller, devoted his presidential address chiefly to the introduction of the subject which was to be the main theme of the doctrinal discussions. He said that it was the most comforting, the most indispensable, and the most difficult one that could be chosen. It was the subject which is to engage our attention these days—the doctrine of justification by grace through faith. In explaining why it is the most difficult subject, the venerable president pointed out that if this teaching is to be properly understood and taught, it must permeate the whole system of doctrines everywhere, and regardless of what teaching you present, say, for instance, in the doctrines concerning the Sacraments, the Church, and the Last Things, it must be the echo and the refrain. This meeting at Addison, incidentally, was the first one of our many conventions, now covering almost a century, at which the subject of justification was considered on the basis of a formal doctrinal essay. Needless to say, it had been taught and presented innumerable times before in sermons, articles, and in minor references at conventions. Moreover, since that time our conventions have frequently in formal discussions concerned themselves with this teaching, and the essays that were delivered on those occasions, several, for instance, either by Dr. Walther himself, or based on propositions drawn up by him, belong to the choice literature of our Church.

Are our hearts properly attuned for a renewed consideration of this doctrine? Somebody will probably say, We live in a modern age, our fields we plow with tractors, our mail we send by airplanes, our news we get through the radio, our enemies we blast into nothingness by the atomic bomb, our criminals we execute in the electric chair or the lethal chamber, our bodies we keep fit by vitamin pills—and you expect us to be interested in such a hoary subject as the doctrine of justification? Why not submit something new in the field of religion and morals—an examination of the teachings of Communism, the views of the Gloomy Dean and of the Red Dean of England, the need of new divorce laws, the United Nations Organization, price control, and the like?

The position of this objector is just as foolish as would be that of a person who said, "I refuse to hear anything said in my presence about liberty; that subject is worn and shabby." Shall we not say to such a man that if he does not want to hear about freedom any more, he had better leave this country and seek citizenship elsewhere, that we here are all interested in freedom and love it and wish to hear about it again and again.

For us Lutherans a renewed consideration of the teaching of justification should be as natural as in a physical way it is for us to breathe. This teaching is universally considered the characteristic doctrinal feature of our Church. Webster's Dictionary, when defining the term "Lutheran," after giving the titles of the Confessional Writings, says, "The cardinal doctrine is that of justification by faith alone." In China the Lutheran Church is largely known as the "justification by faith" Church. How grand if in our country everybody realized that the Lutheran Church is the denomination that teaches justification by faith! Believing that President Schaller in 1859 was right in his high evaluation of this doctrine, let us, grateful for our membership in the Lutheran Church, give some thought to this blessed teaching and view its cardinal features.

I

The Lutheran Confessions and the renowned Lutheran teachers of the past call the doctrine of justification the most important teaching of divine revelation.

In speaking of this doctrine, the Church and her eloquent theologians, like enthusiastic organists, pull all the stops and play fortissimo. It will do our matter-of-fact and sophisticated generation much good to listen to some of these outbursts of warm, admiring faith. The Apology of the Augsburg Confession, in the Fourth Article, calls this doctrine "the chief topic of Christian doctrine—an article which is of special service for the clear, correct understanding of the entire Holy Scriptures and alone shows the way to the unspeakable treasure and right knowledge of Christ and alone opens the door to the entire Bible" (Par. 2, *Triglot*, p. 121). "Of this article," says Luther in the Smalcald Articles, "nothing can be yielded or surrendered, even though heaven and earth and whatsoever will not abide should sink into ruin" (II, 1. *Triglot*, p. 461). Writing in a letter to Brenz, Luther says that this teaching is the chief thing, the cornerstone, and that it alone brings forth, strengthens, builds, and protects the Church, and that without it the Church cannot exist one hour (St. Louis, XIV: 168). In his comments on Gen. 21:17 Luther writes thus about this doctrine, "This is the highest article of our faith. If one removes it, as the Jews do, or adulterates it, like the Papists, the Church cannot stand, nor can God receive the honor due Him" (St. Louis, I: 1441). And in another passage he says, "Mohammed devastated the Church, and the Pope obscured the doctrine pertaining to faith, but where this article remained, there God preserved His Church." (Comments on Is. 53:11; St. Louis, VI: 721.) And again he says, "Hence this article of justification, which we alone today teach, must be learned and maintained with diligence, for if we have lost it, we shall not be able to withstand any heresy, any false teaching, be it ever so ridiculous. This happened under the rule of the papacy. There we believed things of which we now are ashamed and for which we feel sorry. Contrariwise, if we remain faithful to this article, we are secure against heresy and retain forgiveness of our sins, receiving pardon for our weakness in conduct and in faith" (St. Louis, XVI: 1664). Hearing these words of Father Luther, we can understand why our theologians have always said that this article is the article of the standing and falling Church, that is, that with this teaching the Church stands and if this article should fall, the Church would fall, too.

Martin Chemnitz, the second great Martin of the Lutheran Church, calls this article the citadel and main defense armament of the whole Christian doctrine and religion. If it is obscured or falsified, you cannot keep the other articles pure; if it is kept intact, then all idolatries and superstitions and whatever other adulterations in other articles may have occurred, will disappear. (Cf. *Loc. theol.* II, 200.)

And, finally, Balthasar Meisner (died 1626) calls it the center of true theology, to which everything tends, the sacred ocean where all the streams meet, the rock of faith which keeps everything safe and unharmed. (Cf. *Anthropolog.* D. 3, disp. 24, p. 139.)

It is a grand chorus singing not in strident, jarring confusion of voices, but in remarkable harmonies and with as perfect pitch as is humanly possible, extolling the unparalleled significance of this teaching for our whole Christian faith.—The following discussion will have to show whether we can follow the fathers in their jubilation and join them in that ecstasy of joy and gratitude with which they considered this doctrine.

II

The apprehension of this doctrine by Luther made him the Reformer of the Church, equipped by God for his great work.

As yet we do not discuss the doctrine itself, but certain preliminaries which, however, are indispensable and quite helpful. It is customary to say that what brought on the Reformation was the publication of Luther's 95 Theses, in which he protested against the indulgence traffic. That is only partly correct. The nailing of the 95 Theses to the door of the Castle Church at Wittenberg provided a spark which brought on a violent and most wholesome explosion. But it is important to see that if the Reformation was to occur, Luther had to find the heart of Christianity and the true meaning of the Gospel. The day or days when he grasped the full significance of Paul's message on justification by faith may fittingly be designated as the point of time when the Reformation was born. He himself in moving words tells us about this grand experience in his life. (Cf. his Preface to the Latin edition of his works, St. Louis, XIV: 446 f. This Preface was written in 1545.) The date of it is in dispute. Some put it as early as 1512 or 1513, others as late as 1518 or 1519. We shall not here occupy ourselves with the problem of chronology involved, but concentrate without delay on this happening, which furnished Luther a key to the Scriptures. Scholars refer to it as the *Turmerlebnis*, the tower ex-

The Doctrine of Justification

perience of Luther, because it was in the tower of the Cloister in Wittenberg, *schwarzes Kloster,* where he was sitting and meditating when the decisive illumination came upon him.

He was pondering the significance of Rom. 1:16, 17: "I am not ashamed of the Gospel of Christ, for it is the power of God unto salvation to every one that believeth, to the Jew first and also to the Greek; for therein the righteousness of God is revealed from faith to faith, as it is written, The just shall live by faith." Many a time he had looked at these words before and tried to understand them. What baffled him was the expression "righteousness of God." What did that term mean? He had been taught that it signified the righteousness or justice of God, that is, a quality in God through which He is personally righteous and just and punishes the sinners and the unrighteous. That this righteousness was said to be revealed in the Gospel, in the message of good news, seemed to be self-contradictory. It lacked plausibility. The sinner is frightened at the thought that God is righteous and just. And then to say that this is a part of the good news sounds like making sport of man in his predicament.

One day Luther again was pondering this problem, looking at it from all sides, and suddenly something happened. A thought flashed upon him which he had never entertained before. The righteousness which God speaks of, he said to himself, is not a quality in God, as he had been taught, nor is it something that God demands of us. It is something that God bestows on us sinners. It was an overwhelming idea. Scales fell, as it were, from his eyes. The whole passage now appeared luminous. Indeed, that was good news: God has prepared righteousness and in the Gospel hands it to us. Could it be possible that that was the meaning of Paul? Quickly in his mind he surveyed all the passages in which the Bible speaks of the righteousness of God and similar matters, and he said that indeed this very thing had to be the meaning of the term. There could be no doubt about it. Luther felt as if he had been born again. It was as if the gates of Paradise opened up to him. Never again did he lose sight of the great truth thus discovered, that the righteousness of God is a righteousness which God prepares through the sacrifice of Christ.

When he understood this passage, he had the key to the whole Scripture. Now Law and Gospel, the Old Testament and the New Testament, justification and sanctification, became understandable to him. It was then and there that he received the chief equipment which the Reformer of the Church needed—a true grasp of the fundamental teaching of the Gospel. Now he could set forth correctly the teaching of justification by faith.

III

The teaching of justification presupposes the doctrine that man both through his natural condition and his thoughts, words, and deeds is a transgressor of God's Law, subject to the divine wrath, and condemned to eternal death.

A great painting must have the proper background. An object that is bright will captivate you all the more if it is placed against a dark wall. Similarly, if we wish to understand the doctrine of justification and be moved by its grandeur to sing hallelujahs, we must see what made this justification important and necessary for the human race. Yes, there first have to be strains in a minor key before we thrill to the full beauty of the melody in a major key which is played for us on the harps of the inspired men of God as they convey to us the message of peace, joy, and hope. The fathers said correctly: First the Law must be preached; the doctrine of justification in its purity presupposes the teaching of the Law. Was justification required for man's bliss? It certainly was: both the human heart and Scripture testify to that truth. Man's natural condition ever since the Fall is sinful. Listen to Isaiah: "We are all as an unclean thing, and all our righteousnesses are as filthy rags," Is. 64:6. Our own heart confirms this and charges us with not being pure, loving, pious, devoted to the service of God and to our neighbor. When we look at what we do, our thoughts, words, and deeds, we see transgressions of God's commandments. "There is not a just man upon earth that doeth good and sinneth not," says the Old Testament Scripture (Eccl. 7:20), and the New Testament reiterates the thought. Our hearts in sadness and trembling have to say, Yes, so it is. It is a most appalling truth which we here face, brought before us in the teaching of original sin and of actual sin. Man by nature is corrupt and does that which is evil. The result is that he is subject to divine wrath. God is just; whatsoever

The Doctrine of Justification 241

is wrong offends Him. Sin is the very antithesis of God, because He is holy, righteous, without any imperfection. So it is inevitable that wrongdoing arouses His wrath. As the holy and just God He must punish what is evil. Even here on earth we find a household disgusting in which the father permits the children to do anything filthy, improper, unbecoming that strikes their fancy. And will the holy, perfect God look on with complacency as His creatures violate the laws concerning right and wrong which He has issued? When Paul prepares to set forth the doctrine of justification, he first in red colors paints man's sad state, Romans 1—3.

If all this is true, and it certainly is, because it rests on the divine statements of the Scriptures, there is no hope for man as far as his own resources are concerned. He is condemned at the tribunal of God. Can he not rescue himself? We reply, How could he who is ill himself perform the operation that is required? Man is corrupt. How can he pacify the holy God? As little as the servant in the parable who owed his king ten thousand talents could pay the debt, can we pay God for the evils that we have done. — What the Law demands is perfection, and we have nothing to offer but sins. The penalty for wrongdoing is eternal damnation. The penalty or its equivalent has to be borne. If we have to bear it, then we have to be condemned forever. — Is that perhaps merely our own construction, a logical conclusion which we draw, but which does not rest on reality? Not at all. We merely have to think of what Paul says Rom. 2:8 f., "Unto them that are contentious and do not obey the truth, but obey unrighteousness, indignation and wrath. Tribulation and anguish upon every soul of man that doeth evil, of the Jew first and also of the Gentile." And we think of the words of Jesus stating what the Judge will say to those on His left in the final Judgment, "Depart from Me, ye cursed, into everlasting fire prepared for the devil and his angels," Matt. 25:41. — Help is needed. Is there help? the human soul asks in terror.

IV

This doctrine includes as one of its chief elements the truth that God is moved to justify us by His grace.

In speaking of this matter one ardently wishes that tongues of angels and archangels would be at our disposal so that this point might receive the treatment it deserves. The grace of God! The subject makes us look upon an ocean of divine love, infinite, limitless, altogether beyond our powers of apprehension and our ability adequately to portray and praise. Whoever wishes to know the foundation of our justification, the foundation from which it flowed and flows, must look at God's grace. When Paul in the Epistle to the Romans sets forth this doctrine, he says that justification is by God's grace, Rom. 3:23 f., "For all have sinned and come short of the glory of God, being justified freely by His grace." Let us mark that well. Something must have motivated or induced God to bring about our justification. He does not always tell us why He did or does a certain thing. In this case, however, He gives us the information we seek. His grace induces Him to justify us.

What is grace? We use the word every day. It must be our endeavor to see precisely what it means. From the passages in which it occurs we see that it is a certain aspect of God's love. The Apostle could have said that God's love induces Him to justify the sinner. That would have been entirely correct. But using the word "grace," he goes a step farther. Grace is a particular kind of love. It is love directed toward those that are undeserving or unworthy. It excludes the idea that the love in question has been merited or earned. When Paul says that God's grace induces Him to bring about the justification of sinners, he says not merely that God's love operates here, but that this love is not based on some good quality, merit, or worthiness on our part. That we are not wrong in this teaching is confirmed by that little word "freely." We are justified freely, says Paul in the passage cited. Freely means: free of charge, gratis, no price was paid by us.

What Paul says, then, is this: God sees the sinner lying in misery brought on by his own wickedness, a rebel against God, a condemned creature, and still God bends down to him in love where only punishment had been deserved, and decides on the work of justification. "Where sin abounded, grace did much more abound," Paul exclaims triumphantly, Rom. 5:20. In eternity, when we shall have gathered around the throne of God and the Lamb with all the saints and angels, this boundless grace of God will be a theme of our ecstatic songs of thanksgiving.

The Doctrine of Justification

V

This doctrine next takes us to Calvary and teaches us the atonement of Christ which earned righteousness for all human beings (objective justification).

In speaking of God's grace, the foundation of our justification, we dwell on something that reaches far back beyond the creation of the world into eternity itself. Just as God exists always, so God's grace is from everlasting to everlasting. When the question arises, How did God's grace carry out its benevolent design to provide for us the help we needed? we are taken into history, into the very stream of happenings and events, and we are shown the central fact of everything that has or will come to pass. The task that had to be performed transcended all human wisdom. There were two attributes in God that had to be safeguarded, and in this case there seemed to be a conflict between them. These attributes were the justice and the love or grace of God.

For us finite beings it would be impossible to invent a way which would satisfy both the justice and the love of God. With respect to these two qualities, our poor understanding or intelligence says, there is an unavoidable collision. But, eternal praise be to God, He has a way which safeguards both qualities. He does it through the work of Christ.

We come here to what has been called the divine drama of redemption. God sends His Son, sinless, pure, spotless in every respect. He lets this Son become a human being and makes Him our Substitute. This Substitute fulfills all requirements of the Law in our place (active obedience). Besides, He suffers the pangs and woes which we had deserved (passive obedience). Divine justice is satisfied; and behold, divine love triumphs, too. The sins are paid for; God speaks the great word: The human race now is justified, it possesses righteousness, the sins of all men are forgiven. "God was in Christ," says Paul, "reconciling the world unto Himself, not imputing their trespasses unto them." Mark well these words of unspeakably great significance. God was in Christ. God was most intimately united with Christ and did His work through Him. What He performed can be designated by that one word "reconciliation." He reconciled the world to Himself. The world was His enemy, and His wrath was enkindled against it. Punishment had to be meted out. It was done when Christ suffered and died. This substitutionary, vicarious suffering of Jesus reconciled the world to God, made it acceptable to Him, induced Him to forgive its sins.

When Christ spoke the word on the cross which must have echoed through the whole universe, "It is finished," then all sins had been actually expiated. In heaven God said to the angels, as it were, Bring the books and cancel the debts of all human beings. I can again look upon the world with favor. And on the third day after the event of Golgotha, God made it known throughout the world that the demands of divine justice had been met and all sins had been forgiven—He raised Jesus from the dead. See Him rise from the grave, the One on whom all the sins of the world had been laid. In triumph He leaves the tomb. Where are our sins? They have all been canceled; they have been cast into the sea where it is deepest. Sin has been forgiven—the human race is acquitted— so rings the shout through the universe. Who can speak of these things without being deeply moved?

When Paul views the cross of Christ, he speaks of the wisdom of God, I Corinthians 2. At the cross we see how in God's plan of salvation both His justice and His love were maintained and made to triumph. Paul is in such ecstasy when he views this divine wisdom that he exclaims that here we consider what "eye hath not seen, nor ear heard, neither have entered into the heart of man, the things which God hath prepared for them that love Him."

The question is often asked, Are we really following the Scriptures when we call this act of God, in which He through Christ provided forgiveness of sins for the world, justification? There can be no doubt about it. "Christ was delivered for our offenses and raised again for our *justification*," says St. Paul, Rom. 4:25. Most convincing are the words of Paul when he in Rom. 5:12 ff. draws the stupendous parallel between Adam and Christ. What Adam did when he transgressed the command of God in the Garden of Eden affected the whole human race. So likewise what Christ did when He died for us on the cross affected the whole human race. Listen to these words, Rom. 5:18, 19: "Therefore as by the offense of one judgment came upon all men to condemnation; even so by the righteousness of One the free gift came upon all men unto justification of life. For as by one man's disobedience many were made sinners, so by the obedience of One shall many be made righteous." There the term *justification* is used to describe the act of God in which He grants forgiveness of sins to the world.

This is a convenient place to examine a little more closely the terms *justify* and *justification*. What does *justify* mean? The verbs ending in *fy* often signify "to place into a condition or state." *Clarify* means to make clear; *beautify* means to render beautiful; *glorify* means to render glorious. So *justify* means to make just or righteous. But this expression, to make just, can be taken in various meanings. It may signify: to make somebody a righteous, just being through education, training, admonition, and the like. But it may mean, too, to declare somebody just and righteous. It may refer to the act of a judge when he renders his verdict and states to the accused standing before him, "I acquit you," "I declare you innocent." The judge in such a case has made the defendant righteous or just in a legal sense; from the point of view of the law the accused is just. That Paul uses the term in the legal or forensic sense is very evident. God justifies the whole world. He makes the whole world righteous; that can only mean: He declares the whole world righteous. The world, generally speaking, is wicked, ungodly, opposing the Creator. But God declares the world innocent, acquitted. What a glorious act! (Cf. Section X for a further elaboration of this matter.) Is it not a fiction? Not at all, because we have the Word of God as a guarantee that actually the sins of the whole world were canceled when the sacrifice of Christ was offered. Forgiveness has been obtained for every human being. Who can worthily extol the greatness of God's love and the blessed results of the work of Christ on Calvary?

What we have just now considered is called objective justification. The term is intended to signify that, apart from the attitude of individual human beings, in a very objective way God has declared that the world is justified, that sins are forgiven, that all mankind has been redeemed. Another term used for this great act of God is *universal justification,* a justification that extends to everybody.

VI

This doctrine shows that God hands us the righteousness of Christ in the Gospel and the Sacraments.

The righteousness which men need was in existence the minute that Christ said "It is finished"; but it was, as it were, a hidden treasure, stowed away in the invisible realms, behind the curtain which hides God, the angels, and heaven from our view. As an illustration one might point to the conditions under which the battle of New Orleans between Andrew Jackson and the British was fought in 1815. It was a bloody struggle for the British, costing them one fifth of their whole force. But two weeks before it occurred, the peace treaty had been signed in Europe. The tragedy was that means of communication were lacking and our nation did not know about it. Hence, though peace had been declared, the poor soldiers at New Orleans fought each other bitterly as if the war were still on. (Treaty signed in Ghent, December 24, 1814; battle of New Orleans, January 8, 1815). Let this illustration remind us that if we were to enjoy true happiness for time and eternity it was required not only that righteousness be achieved for us, but, in addition, that we be made aware of it and become its possessors.

With joyful hearts we proclaim that God in His love has made provision to bring to mankind the treasure which His grace through the sacrifice of Christ prepared. It is one of the distinctive glories of our dear Lutheran Church that it has a clear Scriptural presentation of the ways that God employs for making us partakers of the righteousness of Christ. It teaches according to God's holy Word that the Lord employs the Gospel and the Sacraments, the so-called means of grace, to make us possessors of the heavenly gift which we require.

We have to analyze this a little. What the Word and the Sacraments do for us, in the first place, is that they bring to us information about the righteousness which Christ forged out for us through His holy life and His bitter suffering and death. The Gospel is the good news, the account of what divine love has accomplished in our behalf. Paul often calls it "the Gospel," that is, the good news of Jesus Christ. Similarly, Holy Baptism makes an important proclamation every time it is performed. It declares to all who witness it that justification has been brought about for sinners. That the Lord's Supper has the same significance is very obvious. Whenever we observe it, we are taken to the night when our Lord Jesus Christ was betrayed, and we are told how He labored in our behalf to achieve for us forgiveness of our sins.

But the Gospel and the Sacraments do much more. They not only inform; they convey, they bring, they present, they confirm, they seal. The means of grace may be compared to vessels, and vessels that are not empty, but filled with the heavenly treasure which we have to have, God's forgiveness, our justification. In these means the Holy Spirit is active, and through them He invites, urges, persuades, draws. One can best see what truths are here involved if we turn to the Scripture passages on which the teaching rests. Of the Gospel, St. Paul says Rom. 1:16, "I am not ashamed of the Gospel of Christ, for it is the power of God unto salvation to everyone that believeth; to the Jew first, and also to the Greek." You observe that Paul does not regard the Gospel as a bit of news satisfying people's curiosity, but as something strong, a dynamo having power from above. John 15:3 may well be quoted here: "Now ye are clean through the Word which I have spoken unto you." The disciples of Jesus addressed here are told by Him that through the Word they are clean, they have forgiveness of their sins. The Word has brought them God's pardon. That through Baptism we receive what Christ has earned for us St. Paul expresses beautifully Gal. 3:27: "As many of you as have been baptized into Christ have put on Christ." To put on Christ as we put on a garment signifies that we are clothed in His blood and righteousness, that is, that we receive forgiveness of our sins. That in the Lord's Supper the gift of justification is bestowed can be demonstrated in various ways. Let us here think of it that Jesus, in instituting the Sacrament, says of the cup, "Drink ye all of it; this cup is the new testament in My blood." The new testament means the new covenant; hence Jesus says that here He establishes a new covenant. The old covenant had been one of law. Here there is a new covenant, which is one of grace, bringing forgiveness of sins. We must remember that Jesus adds, speaking of His blood, "which is shed for you for the forgiveness of sins."

VII

This doctrine declares that we appropriate this righteousness through faith.

To discuss this matter intelligently, we first have to come to grips with an apparent difficulty. In raising Christ from the dead God justified the whole world, we heard before. That means that every sinner is justified, that all of us have forgiveness. What more is needed? Nothing, we say, from one point of view. But remember, God does not force His gifts on anybody. He does not compel a person to enjoy justification against his own will. He comes before us and says, I have justified you; here is your pardon, take it. If man then refuses to take it, he will be without it unless he changes his attitude.

The question then is of great importance, How is the justification of God received by us when He offers it in the means of grace? The Scriptures answer in a mighty chorus, Through faith. "Therefore we conclude that a man is justified by faith without the deeds of the Law," St. Paul says Rom. 3:28. He had shown that all men are under the sentence of condemnation on account of their transgression of the divine Law. Then, beginning Rom. 3:21, he sets forth that there is righteousness, forgiveness, to be had by man, a forgiveness provided by God's grace through the propitiatory work of Christ. And he ends the paragraph thus, if I may paraphrase: This is the conclusion which we reach, looking upon all the glorious facts that have been adduced, that a man is justified by faith without the deeds of the Law.

Our fathers called the means of grace the giving hand of God, and faith they called the receiving hand of man. Those are good, helpful expressions, describing quite well the processes which the Scriptures point to in this field.

We naturally inquire, What is faith? That is an important question indeed. If we are to find comfort in the teaching of justification by faith, we have to have the right conception of what is meant by faith. It is conceivable that faith involves the performance of such a tremendous task on our part that no human being can ever attain to it. But, God be praised, faith is such a simple matter that even a little child can have it. On the other hand, so we had better add at once, it is so difficult a matter that many of the wisest and most learned men fail to become possessors of it. Faith in Jesus is simply the trust that He, as the Gospel proclaims, is our Savior and that He has obtained for us forgiveness of our sins. That is what it meant for Paul. He had cruelly persecuted the Christian Church. But he was sure that God had forgiven him for Christ's sake. "Jesus loved me and gave Himself for me," Paul says in words of exquisite tenderness.

Faith, according to the root meaning of the word in English and in Greek, does not signify a guess, or a conjecture, or an opinion. It means confidence, assurance, reliance. It is well described as a taking of what God offers. Paul pictures it to us in Romans 4 through the case of Abraham. The patriarch had received the promise of a son to be born to him by Sarah, though he and she were superannuated by a wide margin. But while all likelihood and experiences were against him, he trusted in the truthfulness of God. That was faith. When it turns to Christ and relies on His work for the forgiveness of sins, life, and salvation, we speak of it as the justifying and saving faith.

The nature of this saving faith is easily determined if we hold to the Scriptural doctrine of the grace of God and the work of Christ. When you have learned that Christ has done for us what the Law requires, and that God has forgiven all our trespasses, the role of faith is clear. It merely has to take the pardon of Christ. It does not create, it appropriates. Several other important facts concerning faith will come before us as we proceed.

VIII

This doctrine declares that in the minute that we take this righteousness God pronounces us justified, free from sin, acquitted (subjective justification).

Here we ask, What according to the Scriptures happens when the sinner comes to believe the Gospel message of Jesus as his divine Savior and of God's forgiveness? The answer of the Bible is definite. When the sinner says, Jesus is my Savior, and puts his trust in Him, then God declares that his sins are forgiven and that he is righteous. One or the other of you will probably interpose the remark that the sinners already were forgiven. That is perfectly true. But the Bible tells us in addition that when faith springs up in the heart, then one is justified. "Abraham believed God, and it was counted to him for righteousness." It is undeniable that righteousness was in existence for him long before he believed. But, nevertheless, when he came to have faith, God declared, Abraham is righteous, his sins are forgiven. Similarly, Paul says, Gal. 2:16, "We have believed in Jesus Christ that we might be justified by the faith of Christ." You observe that here Paul says justification takes place when we come to be believers. It is at that time that God declares concerning us individually that we are righteous and acquitted.

In Luke 15 Jesus affords us a glimpse of what takes place in heaven when a sinner repents and as a result is justified. There He relates the three precious parables of things or persons lost and found, the lost sheep, the lost coin, and the lost son. When the sinner accepts the pardon of God, thereby returning to the heart of his heavenly Father, there is rejoicing in the heavenly mansions. The angels and God Himself manifest happiness when divine justice declares, "This sinner is justified."

We call this the subjective or individual justification. In the vast majority of instances where this divine act is referred to, subjective justification is signified. But the basis of it, we must not forget, is universal redemption, the forgiveness of sin earned for the whole world, the objective justification of all sinners.

The discussion of this subjective justification is, as it were, one of the brightest stars in our confessional writings and in the writings of Luther and other great theologians of our Church. There is a passage in the Apology which I should like to read (Art. IV, par. 84 f., *Triglot*, p. 145): "Remission of sins is something promised for Christ's sake. Therefore it cannot be received except by faith alone. For a promise cannot be received except by faith alone. Rom. 4:16: 'Therefore it is of faith, that it might be by grace, to the end that the promise might be sure'; as though he were to say, If the matter were to depend upon our merits, the promise would be uncertain and useless, because we never could determine when we would have sufficient merit. And this, experienced consciences can easily understand. Accordingly, Paul says Gal. 3:22: 'But the Scripture hath concluded all under sin, that the promise by faith of Jesus Christ might be given to them that believe.'

The Doctrine of Justification

He takes merit away from us, because he says that all are guilty and concluded under sin; then he adds that the promise, namely, of the remission of sins and of justification, is given, and adds how the promise can be received, namely, by faith. This reasoning, derived from the nature of a promise, is the chief reasoning in Paul and is often repeated. Nor can anything be devised or imagined whereby this argument of Paul can be overthrown. Wherefore let not good minds suffer themselves to be forced from the conviction that we receive remission of sins for Christ's sake, only through faith. In this they have sure and firm consolation against the terrors of sin and against eternal death and against all the gates of hell."

IX

This doctrine emphatically excludes all merit on our part in this matter.

If the Scriptures merely stated that our justification is brought about by God's grace through the sacrifice of Christ and that we become possessors of it through faith, they would thereby indicate indirectly, but nevertheless quite emphatically, that all merit on our part is excluded in this transaction; in other words, the absolute gift-nature of justification would be definitely implied. But the Scriptures have not left it to us to make and to rely upon inferences in this field. With unsurpassed clarity the truth is expressed that there is no room for human merit in our justification. Not only does Jesus tell us the parable of the publican in the Temple, who pleaded nothing but his sins when he appeared before God, but who went down to his house "justified"; not only does He place before us the parable of the unmerciful servant who owed his master ten thousand talents and who, when he was utterly destitute, appealed for mercy and received complete forgiveness, full justification; but the Apostle Paul expressly examines the question whether in justification there is any performance of man to which the latter might point as ground for boasting. In Rom. 3:27, after he has carefully, precisely stated how our justification is accomplished, he asks the question, "Where is boasting then?" And he answers, "It is excluded"; there is no room for any, and he continues, "By what law? Of works? Nay, but by the law of faith." Law here signifies principle or method. What principle or method was employed? The method of the law which prescribes good works? If that had been the case, then there might be an opportunity for boasting, but that was not the method. The way in which justification came about was by faith; and that excludes all merit and ground for boasting.

At this point there may be introduced the classic definition of the doctrine of justification which our Church has adhered to these many years and which is found in Article IV of the Augsburg Confession. The Article has the heading: "Of Justification." It reads: "Also they [that is, our churches] teach that men cannot be justified before God by their own strength, merits, or works, but are freely justified for Christ's sake through faith, when they believe that they are received into favor and that their sins are forgiven for Christ's sake, who by His death has made satisfaction for our sins. This faith God imputes for righteousness in His sight, Romans 3 and 4." (*Triglot*, p. 45.) — Here you find brought together in one statement all the various truths which we have dwelt on — a golden gem in our fundamental confession.

Before leaving this chapter there is one point which must be scrutinized and to which reference has not yet been made. When we say that no human merit at all enters into the transaction which we call justification, we imply that faith must not be considered as a meritorious act on account of which God might justify us. The famous dogmatician Johann Gerhard correctly says that we are justified through faith, but not on account of faith (*Loc. de Justif.*, par. 179). Faith is simply the taking of what God offers. No merit attaches to it. Would you say that a beggar must be praised for having performed a meritorious work when he accepts the ten-dollar bill which a charitable person hands him? The receiving is necessary, but no merit attaches to it. Faith is the instrument, not the cause of our justification.

There is an additional truth which must be mentioned and which totally annihilates all human pretensions to credit in the act of justification. The faith through which we are justified is not of our own creation, but it is a gift of God. We do not make ourselves believers; the Holy Spirit does it through the Word and the Sacraments. Hence, since faith is merely the instrument, we cannot even give ourselves credit for having and employing this instrument. It is bestowed on us from above. It is clear, then, that from beginning to end in our justification all glory belongs to God. How utterly, when we view this divine teaching, must all self-praise then be rejected as unfounded and unworthy of us who have been pardoned in the court of our heavenly Creator.

X

This doctrine shows that justification takes place outside of us, at the tribunal of God.

What we dwell on here has been variously touched on in the preceding discussions; but it seems advisable to give it special mention. Justification is a divine act—on that we are all agreed. Where does the act take place? Many a person, not giving the subject much thought, and considering that we are justified through faith, will be inclined to say, Its scene is the human heart; it takes place *in* us. But that is evidently not what the Scriptures teach. According to the instruction of Jesus and the Apostles, justification is a judgment which is rendered by the divine majesty. Viewing it correctly, we have to think of the courtroom in the invisible world. Using figurative language, we say, The Judge sits on the throne; the case of a sinner is called; it is stated that he has in true faith accepted Christ as his Savior; the Judge declares, "He is justified." To bring out this feature we say, as has been mentioned before, that justification is a forensic, judicial act of God, something that happens outside of us. When we speak of regeneration or conversion we indeed speak of something that takes place *in* us, in our hearts. But from this act of God in us we must carefully differentiate the act which is performed with reference to us in the heavenly courtroom. That the Bible actually teaches this conception we see, for instance, from Rom. 8:33 f.: "Who shall lay anything to the charge of God's elect? It is God that justifieth. Who is he that condemneth? It is Christ that died, yea rather, that is risen again, who is even at the right hand of God, who also maketh intercession for us." Evidently a court scene is before the eye of Paul. Can anyone successfully bring accusations against God's elect? Not at all. God justifies them. Whatever charges are presented the Judge will refuse to entertain. "These people are acquitted," He declares. And the basis is the work of Christ, who died and who arose from the dead, and who, besides, pleads for us at the throne of the divine majesty.

The Council of Trent in its Sixth Session (Chap. VII) declared, "Justification is not merely the remission of sins, but includes the sanctification and renovation of the inner man through the willing reception of grace and its gifts." One sees the totally different conception manifesting itself in these words of the Roman pronouncement. The Roman teaching confuses justification and sanctification, mixing the latter into the former, not differentiating between an act and the results or fruit of the act.

This Roman error is not merely an unfortunate departure from correct terminology; it is of the gravest consequence. If our eternal salvation depends on our justification, and if justification is an act in us, including the production of good qualities in our hearts and lives, how can we ever be certain that we have been justified and that salvation is ours? We shall constantly have to say to ourselves that our justification is not complete because sin is still dwelling in us. And there has to result a state of doubt, of inquietude and dread. The Roman Catholic position on this point is simply in keeping with the general tendency of their theology, which avoids leading the Christian to joyous certainty concerning his state of grace and keeps him in suspense with respect to his future. God be praised for the light of the Reformation, which makes us declare jubilantly with Paul, "If God be for us, who can be against us? He that spared not His own Son, but delivered Him up for us all, how shall He not with Him also freely give us all things? Who shall lay anything to the charge of God's elect? It is God that justifieth."

XI

The Scriptures tell us that when the sinner has been justified he has peace with God, enjoys Christian liberty, performs good works, and is filled with the hope of eternal life.

When God has justified us, saying that our sins are forgiven for Christ's sake, we have peace with God. "Therefore, being justified by faith, we have peace with God through our Lord Jesus Christ," Rom. 5:1. We no longer look upon God as an angry Judge, but we consider Him our dear heavenly Father, who has received us into His household and will take care of us in time and in eternity.

Furthermore, we enjoy Christian liberty. As long as a person is in the unjustified state, he is a slave of sin. Besides, he is in bondage to the Law, which condemns him to be cast into eternal death. But now hear what Jesus says John 8:36, "If the Son, therefore, shall make you free, ye shall be free indeed." Through faith in Christ we obtain forgiveness of our sin and freedom from its dominion and tyranny. The Christian, as far as he is a new man, serves his God and Savior in grateful liberty. Gone, too, are the bonds of the Law which held him in distressing servitude. Paul gives expression to both freedoms, freedom from the dominion of sin and freedom from the yoke of the Law, Rom. 6:14: "For sin shall not have dominion over you; for ye are not under the Law, but under grace."

Moreover, having been justified, the sinner performs good works. He leads a life of sanctification. Sin is still in him, the old Adam has not disappeared, but the Christian can say with Paul (Rom. 7:25 and 8:1 f.), "So then, with the mind I myself serve the Law of God; but with the flesh the law of sin. There is therefore now no condemnation to them which are in Christ Jesus, which walk not after the flesh, but after the spirit. For the law of the spirit of life in Christ Jesus hath made me free from the law of sin and death."

And, finally, whoever has been justified is filled with the fervent hope of everlasting life. His sins being forgiven, he belongs to God's family; he has received the Spirit of adoption which cries, "Abba, Father." "If we are children, then heirs, heirs of God, and joint heirs with Christ, if so be that we suffer with Him that we may be also glorified together" Rom. 8:17. In fact, all the bliss of heaven belongs to us now, salvation is ours, life everlasting is our possession; merely the full fruition of it is still lying in the future. What a chain of privileges and blessings having its foundation in the sentence of justification uttered in the courtroom of God!

XII

Additional truths about justification are that it is not a long-drawn-out process, but occurs in a moment of time; that it is never partial, but always perfect and complete; that it is alike in all that are justified; that it puts us into a state of righteousness which continues as long as we are believers; that it can be lost; and that it can be obtained anew when it has been lost.

Some of these truths or features are implied in what has been submitted before. That justification is not a long-drawn-out process like sanctification is clear from its nature. It consists in the verdict of God: This person is acquitted; and that verdict is issued in a moment. Compare the holding out of the golden scepter by King Ahasuerus to Esther, showing that she had found favor in his sight. It was an act requiring but a moment.

It follows, furthermore, that justification is never partial, but always complete and perfect. The sins are either forgiven, or they are not forgiven. Here there is no halfway state. When God says "Acquitted," then all the transgressions are wiped off the slate.

It is implied, furthermore, that there is no difference in the act of justification with respect to the various persons concerned. One cannot say that the justification of Peter was more effective or real than that of James. Whoever is acquitted is acquitted. The glorious sentence is alike in the case of every sinner who is justified. The amount of sinning that has preceded does not affect the nature of the sentence.

Moreover, we say that whoever is justified is thereby put into a state of righteousness which continues as long as he is a believer. Wherever there is true faith, the sinner is clad in Jesus' blood and righteousness. He possesses the favor of God; he belongs to the family of the heavenly Father.

In saying this we must not forget the sad fact that justification can be lost. When the sinner gives way to unbelief, when he ceases to be connected with his Savior and to put his trust in Him, then the sentence of acquittal falls too, and he reverts to the ranks of those who are subject to the wrath of God. We may here think of the words of St. Paul, Rom. 11:20: "Well; because of unbelief they were broken off; and thou standest by faith. Be not highminded, but fear." Paul is speaking of the Jews who had rejected Christ. They were branches of the olive tree once upon a time, but they were broken off because of their unbelief. What a warning to all of us not to indulge in carnal security!

But, God be praised! when the sinner has through unbelief lost the state of justification, he can through the grace of God obtain it anew if he repents and again seizes the helping hand of Christ. Speaking of the apostate Jews whose case was mentioned a moment ago, Paul says in the same connection, Rom. 11:23: "And they also, if they abide not still in unbelief, shall be grafted in; for God is able to graft them in again." Think of John 6:37: "All that the Father giveth Me shall come to Me; and he that cometh to Me, I will in no wise cast out." There is our anchor of hope, the love of Christ, which is ready to receive us every time we turn to Him. When the sinner repents, the sentence of acquittal is again pronounced. How ready God is to forgive, the parable of the prodigal son shows most eloquently.

Thus we have once more surveyed the sacred doctrine of justification. What a message it represents! It proclaims great events which angels were eager to look into. It is confessed by us every time we recite the Apostles' Creed, where we say that we believe in the forgiveness of sins. It is woven into the fabric of our most beloved hymns; our music masters have written for it their choicest melodies; it is the heart of the sermons preached in our churches on the great festivals of Christmas, Easter, and Pentecost; to it reference is made in every Gospel discourse; its sweet comfort comes to us every time we hear the words of absolution and partake of the Lord's Supper; it is taught by our teachers in day schools and Sunday schools, by our pastors in their catechetical instruction, by our mothers to the little ones on their knees as soon as they can teach them anything. It contains the truths that form the well of living water springing up into everlasting life. With it we vanquish doubts, put to flight the devil, overcome the world, and strengthen ourselves in the journey on the narrow way. With this truth in our hearts and the assurance it gives, we intend to face the last bitter foe, death, and depart this life in peace. May our dear Lutheran Church, in the future as in the past, be known as the denomination that teaches justification by grace through faith as its chief tenet, and thus continue to hold high the flag of the blessed Reformation. God grant it for Jesus' sake. Amen.

Repentance

MEN AND BRETHREN: "Repent ye!" What should you do? Repent. Who should repent? You. Could you imagine John the Baptist sitting down with the priests, the scribes, the laymen of Jerusalem, to give them an essay on repentance without making it at the same time a most earnest exhortation?

Dr. Walther in the year 1854, seven years after the founding of our Missouri Synod, preached a sermon to his congregation on the General Day of Repentance, in which he said: "We must fear that many of our members have never truly repented of their old sins. Miserable men that you are, take my words to heart, truly repent of your sins and wash your polluted hearts in the atoning blood of your Savior." — But Dr. Walther addressed this sermon on repentance to all his members, including himself. He said: "Let *us* confess our sin, show God our open sores with woebegone hearts and fervently beseech Him for healing." — In German: "Laszt uns mit wehmuetigem Herzen Gott unsere Wunden zeigen, und ihn um Heiligung inbruenstig anflehen." (Walther, *Epistelpostille*, pp. 484—485.)

LUTHER'S CALL TO REPENTANCE

Long before Dr. Walther, Dr. Luther had sounded the first Lutheran call to repentance, thus beginning the Reformation, especially in the first four of his Ninety-five Theses. He said in the first: "When our Lord and Master Jesus Christ said, Repent ye! He makes clear that the whole life of His believers is to be a constant or unending repentance." Now, Luther was even then thinking not only of that complete inner change which alone is true repentance, but also of those outward manifestations which alone prove it real, for he said in the third thesis: "He does not want us to think alone of inner repentance; yea, inner repentance is nothing and not repentance unless it outwardly effects all manner of crucifixions of the flesh." In these theses, as in a tightly folded flower bud, we have everything on repentance which by and by came to perfect blossoming in our Lutheran Church.

AN EPITOME OF THE TRUTH

Who could count what has been written since by Lutherans defending, amplifying, elucidating, evaluating, and driving home what Luther said at the beginning! The Missouri Synod has added much. This essay will abound in quotations, especially also from the words of men of our own Synod written during the past one hundred years. We have enjoyed the possession of the truth, have it still. Others are not so fortunate. The need of repentance is, to be sure, generally conceded. It is the true nature of it which is not understood. Someone recently wrote: "Even Soviet Russia can recognize sin in others." And who has not been able to recognize it in Germany and Japan! If men were only as willing to confess their own sin! Someone has written recently: "The old word 'repentance' rings strange in our ears. It is more natural to pray the prayer of the Pharisee than that of the publican. It is not the nature of salvation, but our own need of it which is questioned. We have developed a technique by which we are able to detach the sinfulness of sin from ourselves and fasten it upon those we dislike." The writer quoted denounces this attitude.

Rather humble is also the language of Harry Emerson Fosdick: "To our fathers, sin was a horrid reality, a deep-seated depravity in human nature, in which from birth we all shared and from which only the grace of God in Christ Jesus could save us. The old pictures of hell made lurid the endless horror of sin's consequence. Liberal Christianity, however, has on the whole been complacent about human nature. Modernism grew up in an era when progress was in the air. So our liberal Christianity has everywhere been characterized by an ideal view of human nature. To be sure, there were failures to be outgrown, inadequacies to be overpassed, ignorance to be illumined, selfishness to be corrected, but no such tragic depravity at the heart of human nature as made Pascal call man 'the glory and the scandal of the universe . . . a monster even beyond apprehension.' Now, however, we face a difficult era, with such cruel and depraved things afoot in the world as some of us have never seen before. We are up against a powerful antagonism, something demonic, tragic, terrific, in human nature. Our fathers called that sin. If you have a better name for it, use it, but recognize the fact." (*Living Under Tension,* p. 112.) Fosdick preaches "repentance." But does this mean a return to that old theology which in the words quoted he has so well defined and in which we believe? By no means, for in the same book (p. 120) he says: "I do not believe in the old theology. The old pictures of hell are to me an incredible anathema." Nevertheless he accuses both himself and his congregation of sin and says: "Saviorhood is the essence of Christ, and to face our deep needs in earnest, to repent sincerely and to seek forgiveness and power, to take seriously Him who for our sakes suffered, the just for the unjust, that He might bring us to God, that would be entering into the meaning of the Gospel." Strange language, this, from Fosdick, who in the same book repeats that he does not believe in the virgin birth of our Lord.

Just as disappointing is Mr. Henry Link's *Return to Religion,* to whom the return to God, or repentance, means only this: "My religion includes the belief in God as a Supreme Being, the belief in a divine, moral order expressed in the Ten Commandments and in the life of Christ, and the acceptance of the Church as the chief though imperfect vehicle of religious truth." Mr. Link is a psychologist, who found that people consulting him needed religion more than anything else.

DICTIONARY DEFINITIONS OF REPENTANCE

Also dictionary and encyclopedia definitions of repentance show that the world has much to learn. *Webster* defines repentance as "sorrow for what one has done or omitted to do, especially contrition over sin." The *Century Dictionary and Encyclopedia* says: "Repentance is a change of mental and spiritual habit respecting sin, involving a hatred of and sorrow because of it and a hearty and genuine abandonment of it in the conduct of life." As an illustration it quotes Tennyson:

> For what is true repentance but in thought,
> Not even in inmost thought, to think again
> The sins that made the past so pleasant to us.

That interesting little magazine *Reader's Digest* made a cute summary of what repentance is supposed to be when it quoted the words "Repentance is when you are sorry enough not to do it again." The *Jewish Encyclopaedia* says of repentance: "It is a change of heart which issues in better action. The rabbis insist that repentance and good deeds are at least as efficacious as the old sacramental methods of obtaining God's favor." In explanation it makes clear that it has in mind such things as were done on the Day of Atonement. In saying that repentance and good works are just as efficacious, it casts off the last vestiges of salvation by grace through the Redeemer. The *Catholic Encyclopaedia* says: "Repentance or contrition in both Protestant and Catholic theology, as defined by the Council of Trent, is a grief of mind and detestation of sin committed with the purpose of sinning no more." It also says: "Until the time of the Reformation no one ever thought of denying the necessity of contrition for the forgiveness of sin." But the Lutheran Church too has never denied the need of contrition, or sorrow over sin.

LET'S GET A TRUE PICTURE

So far we have been content just to toss out upon the table various definitions of repentance like so many pieces of a picture puzzle. The trouble is not that they are completely wrong, but that they say too much or too little and do it in a confused manner. We are reminded of words in our Apology: "We must say that before the writings of Luther appeared, the doctrine of repentance was very much confused." (Apology, Art. 12, *Trigl.*, p. 253.) As nowadays presented by most writers, it still is. Let's try to fit everything that is true into its proper place, that we may get a beautiful and comforting picture. As often portrayed, the picture of repentance drives troubled souls to despair.

REPENTANCE — NECESSARY TO SALVATION

Unsatisfactory definitions of repentance are exceedingly dangerous, because the Word of God declares that no one can have eternal life except he repent. In Luke 13:3 and also 5 our Lord said: "Except ye repent, ye shall perish." In Luke 15:7 we are told: "I say unto you that likewise joy shall be in heaven over one sinner that repenteth, more than over ninety and nine just persons which need no repentance." In Acts 17:30 we read: "And the times of this ignorance God winked at, but now commandeth all men everywhere to repent." St. Peter said (II Pet. 3:9): "The Lord is not willing that any should perish, but that all should come to repentance." — Repent or perish! — In all these passages the urgent need of repentance is stressed. What, then, is repentance?

WORDS TRANSLATED WITH REPENTANCE

True, not even we Lutherans make it a habit always so to use the word repentance. We don't do it in our Catechism, in our answer to the question "What is the work of the Holy Spirit called?" Answer: "This work of the Holy Spirit is called conversion, or regeneration." Could it be that even we are not fully satisfied that repentance is a good translation from the Hebrew and Greek? The word in the original tongues which seems to come closest to the English word repentance is the Hebrew *nacham*, meaning literally "to sigh," "to breathe heavily." It is translated by Gesenius with "to be sorry; to feel contrition." Another Hebrew word translated with "repentance" is *schub*. This literally means "to turn back," but is in at least four places translated in our English Bible with "convert." Is. 1:27: "Zion shall be redeemed with judgment and her *converts* with righteousness." Psalm 19:7: "The Law of the Lord is perfect, *converting* the soul." The same word is in the prayer of Solomon (1 Kings 8:47) translated with "repent." So also in Ezek. 14 and 18. So you see that "repentance" and "conversion" were to the translators of the Bible into English identical in meaning. In the Greek we have two words translated with repent: *metanoeo* and *metamellomai*. And what's the difference between them? I know of none. Green's *Handbook of the Greek Testament* defines *metamellomai* as "changing the mind" and *metanoeo* as "changing the view." This is the same thing! These are the Greek words for the English word *repent* and the German *Busse tun*.

Repentance 263

SORROW A PART OF REPENTANCE

It is good to have one word for that great change in man saving him which emphasizes the need of sorrow. There is no repentance without sorrow, no regeneration without sorrow, no conversion without sorrow. True, repentance is of two parts: sorrow over sin and faith in Jesus Christ. Our Augsburg Confession, which even Lutherans do not appreciate highly enough nor know well enough, says in Article 12: "Repentance consists properly of these two parts: One is contrition, that is, terrors smiting the conscience through the knowledge of sin; the other is faith, which is born of the Gospel, or of absolution, and believes that for Christ's sake sins are forgiven, comforts the conscience, and delivers it from terrors" (*Triglotta*, p. 49). By no means do we Lutherans question the need of contrition. To say so is slander. The difference between us and our opponents is in the definition of contrition.

Contrition to us is "terrors smiting the conscience through the knowledge of sin." That's all; that's enough. The contrite sinner knows that he has merited God's wrath, temporal and eternal punishment. There can be no love of God in him, no contrition which flows from this most noble well, before he has received through the Gospel the assurance of forgiveness. Love to God is a fruit of repentance, the most perfect fruit, but is not, strictly speaking, itself repentance. "Neither is love present before reconciliation has been made by faith" (Apology, Art. 12, *Triglot*, p. 261).

GRIEVOUS ERRORS CONCERNING REPENTANCE

The errors of Catholic theologians and others in defining that sorrow over sin before the sinner may rejoice in his Savior are many and grievous indeed and, instead of creating the better kind of sorrow, prevent it. The Catholic Church distinguishes elaborately between contrition and attrition. Concerning contrition the *Catholic Encyclopaedia* says: "It is a sorrow of soul and a hatred of sin committed, with the firm purpose of not sinning in the future." Their theologian Thomas Aquinas is quoted by them as follows: "It is requisite for the remission of sin that a man cast away entirely the liking for sin." In that kind of definition alarmed sinners can find no consolation. "Perfect contrition," we are further told, "springs from the love of God. Imperfect contrition (attrition) from some other motive, such as fear of hell." We want to be unjust to no one. Therefore we continue to quote: "Contrition ought to be prompted by God's grace and aroused by motives which spring from faith. All doctors insist on the absolute necessity of grace for contrition. If anyone says that without the inspiration of the Holy Spirit and without His aid a man can repent in the way that is necessary to salvation, let him be anathema." So, then, they plainly teach that there is no contrition created in man by his own efforts, without the Spirit's aid and God's grace. But it is well now to pursue our inquiry by asking how, according to them, the grace of God and the Holy Spirit effect contrition. The answer is in chapter 5, session 6, of the Council of Trent (Canons and Decrees of the Council of Trent, Symbolic Publication Society, Chicago, p. 32 f.): "The Synod declares that in adults the beginning of the said justification is to be derived from the prevenient grace of God through Jesus Christ, that is to say, from His vocation, whereby, without any merits existing on their parts, they are called; *that so they, who by their sins were alienated from God, may be disposed through His quickening and assisting grace, to convert themselves to their own justification.*" In simple words: God does not do it all. The sinner must convert himself, repent.

But what is the difference between this doctrine and that of Lutherans falsely so called in this respect, who ascribe the repentance, conversion, of men to their better behavior when the prevenient grace of God has come to them? Has this doctrine been given up? Dr. Reu, in *Lutheran Dogmatics*, 1941—42 edition, Vol. II, p. 138, indeed rejects the doctrine of prevenient grace, saying: "The fact that we have come to faith is due to nothing whatever in ourselves, nor to anything whatsoever that we have done or left undone, *with natural powers or with so-called powers of grace bestowed upon us here in this life*, but solely to the eternal election and purpose of God." However, also every other effort to explain why some are lost by ascribing to them a different kind of resistance, something in addition to the natural, smacks of the same thing. Therefore we object to such language as the following used by Dr. Reu: "God does not force salvation upon anyone and their resistance is a possible, though not a necessary, nor unavoidable aggravation of natural resistance. *The eternal saving will of God is universal, but in its enactment it becomes particular by the willful and persistent resistance of men.*" We say: "Every man's resistance was both persistent and willful until God converted him." Our Catechism answers the question "Why are not all men saved?" thus: "Because many in unbelief *stubbornly resist* the Word and Spirit of God and are thus lost by their own fault." True. But while it is true that those who are lost stubbornly resisted, so did those who were saved. There simply is no answer to the question why some are lost other than this, that it is by their own fault, even as the salvation of others is entirely God's work. Efforts of human reason to harmonize the doctrine of God's grace with the doctrine of predestination inevitably lead into error.

THE PART THAT SORROW PLAYS

We have admitted that sorrow is a part of repentance. Very true. But this does not mean that it atones for any sin or merits in any degree God's favor. Dr. Theodore Engelder read an essay on "Repentance" at the 1925 convention of the Central Illinois District, based on Article 12 of our Augsburg Confession. On pp. 16, 17 of *Central Illinois Proceedings,* 1925, he said: "Contrition is a part of repentance. This, however, does not mean that he who has come to the knowledge of his sin is then half converted. So long as he does not believe in Jesus Christ he is neither half nor in one thousandth part converted. Contrition on the part of Judas did not bring him closer to God. In the terrors of conscience he and Peter and David hated God. In what sense, then, is contrition a necessary part of repentance? Why are both contrition and faith inseparably connected in God's call to repentance, as, for instance, in Joel 2:12-13: 'Turn ye even to Me with all your heart and with fasting and with weeping and with mourning, and rend your hearts and not your garments, and turn unto the Lord, your God, for He is gracious and merciful, slow to anger and of great kindness and repenteth Him of the evil'? Why does Christ require first the preaching of contrition and then of the forgiveness of sins? Answer: Because the knowledge of sin is prerequisite to faith. And why can he only come to true faith who has true contrition? Not because contrition makes the heart morally better and in this sense more receptive, but only in this respect, that it makes the heart aware of its need, because they that think themselves whole want no physician. The Pharisee in the Temple despised the Gospel because he did not feel guilty and deserving of damnation. Only when a man has despaired of being able to save himself does he reach out for the saving hand of his Redeemer. This also makes clear that nothing depends on the degree of contrition, the depth of sorrow. Man has true contrition when he realizes that he is lost. To what has been said about the contrition of Judas this should be added: The reason why in his case conversion did not result is not to be sought in the assumption that his contrition was not of the right kind and did not come from the same source as that of Peter. There was no essential difference between their contrition. As our Apology declares, the difference in their repentance was that Peter came to faith. His contrition led to salvation because he accepted the Gospel. In both men God had created contrition because he wanted to bring both to true faith."

CONTRITION IS A SERVANT

In the October, 1904, issue of the *Theological Quarterly* Rev. J. A. Rimbach treated the subject "What Relation Does Contrition Bear to Repentance?" He answers: "It were a mistake to infer that contrition and faith are co-ordinate parts of repentance. It is evident from the Scriptures that contrition and faith are not coordinate parts of repentance, but contrition is, and of necessity must be, subordinated to faith. Faith is the *domina* [mistress], contrition the *ancilla* [maid]." Pastor Rimbach also wrote: "If a man could have faith without contrition, he could be saved without contrition. Contrition is not necessary in itself, but as a prerequisite of faith. Contrition plows up the hard soil of the human heart, so that the seed of the Gospel can be sown into it and bear the fruit of faith. If a farmer could sow his wheat and raise his crops without plowing his fields, he would surely do so. But under conditions that generally prevail this cannot be done."

WE MUST PREACH LAW

It is apparent from the foregoing that the preacher of repentance must preach God's Law in all its unmitigated fury and severity, as it was made manifest by such truly great preachers of repentance as Moses, Elijah, John the Baptist, and especially our Lord and Master Jesus Christ. True as it is that no one so preaches grace and truth as our Lord, He also said more about hell than any other preacher of the Bible. And the "repentance unto Christ" preached by such men as Fosdick is spurious when they refuse to preach hell as He did. Our Lord did not threaten only the gross sinners among men with hell's eternal flames, but also those who had been esteemed the best of men until He exposed them, the self-righteous Pharisees, who gave tithes of all that they possessed, fasted twice a week, avoided coarse deeds of crookedness and immorality; who were the patriots loathing those Quislings of their own time and nation the publicans, collaborators with cruel Rome; who, touching the righteousness which is in the Law, were supposedly blameless. These vain and loveless men, who despised others and even thereby exposed their sin, heard from the lips of the Holy One of God how they stood with Him, God's Judge eternal. His disciples were told that their righteousness must exceed that of the Pharisees if they were to enter into heaven. That condemns the Pharisees, and every self-righteous man of every other nation likewise. Who on earth can lay claim to a righteousness that satisfies Christ, in whose sight every sly look at a woman to lust after her is adultery, who condemns anger as murder, whose Law has emphatically said, Thou shalt not covet. Epaminondas of Thebes was called "the Righteous" because of his exceptional piety. But he said that the mere desire to sin is not sin, even as most men of today would pat themselves on the back if they wanted to sin, but resisted the impulse, intsead of lamenting with Paul: "The good that I would I do not" (not perfectly), "but the evil which I would not, that I do" (not avoiding it perfectly). – On an occasion when I served on a jury, we were told by the judge that we must apply the law as it is, not as we thought it ought to be. Even so must we preach God's Law, not the law of man, which may be something like this: "Do the best you can, and God will be satisfied." There is no such law in the Bible, which instead thunders at us with its verdict "Cursed is everyone that continueth not in all things which are written in the Book of the Law to do them" (Gal. 3:10). But even the kind of preaching just described does not do justice to its theme. The preacher of repentance must go into particulars with his people, exposing especially those sins of which they appear to be guilty still, which they wish to exclude from their confession and want to live in. It is poor advice, "Don't preach against the sins of the times (*Zeitsuenden*) lest you create an evil conscience for your people." Surely that is not the way to help your people repent, if you become a dumb dog that will not bark even if he could. It has been well said: "Wait not until you are backed by numbers. The fewer the voices on the side of the truth, the louder and the more emphatic should be your own." Whatever was at any time a sin against God's Moral Law is still a sin, whether it be birth control, the immorality associated with dance and theater and other amusements, unionism, or something else that is popular and virtue in the eyes of the world, which knows not God and His Law. "The prophet that hath a dream, let him tell a dream; and he that hath My Word let him speak My Word faithfully, saith the Lord. Is not My Word like as a fire? saith the Lord, and like a hammer that breaketh the rock in pieces?" (Jer. 23:28, 29.) Preacher, God has given you a hammer wherewith to make little ones out of the big ones of this world. He gave you a flaming torch. Are you setting the world on fire? Or have you lost your punch? Are you getting old or weak or both? Have you none of the stuff of which heroes, such men as John the Baptist and Luther, were made? Are you like unto old Eli, who could only weakly remonstrate against coarse sin, saying: "Nay, my sons, for it is no good report that I hear" (I Sam. 2:24). As if any report could have been worse than that brought to him about his sons, God's priests! If you are like him, the scathing sarcasm of Thomas Carlyle should be applied to you: "Annihilation, *Selbsttoetung*, as Novalis calls it; casting thyself at the footstool of God's throne; as Thou wilt, not as I will. Brother, hadst thou never in any form such moments in thy history? Thou knowest them not even by credible rumor? Well, thy earthly path was peaceabler, I suppose. But the Highest was never in thee; the Highest will never come out of thee. Thou shalt at best abide by the stuff, as cherished house dog guard the stuff, perhaps with enormous gold collars and provender. But the battle and the hero death and victory's chariot calling men to the immortals shall never be thine. I pity thee; brag not, or I shall have to despise thee."

PREACH ONLY AGAINST *SIN*

And yet the preacher of repentance, however willing to become a martyr for God, must also beware lest he preach what God does not want preached. Don't go too far out on a limb and then saw it off by your own folly and to your sorrow. You have no business denouncing as sin something you cannot prove to be contrary to God's will. To say that something is sinful because it may lead to sin is a specious argument. The prohibitionist uses it and becomes a fool. His way of arguing would convict our Lord of sin, who did no sin, for did He not change some 165 gallons of water into wine at Cana?

Let us, therefore, make no law for our people where God has made none. This will well suffice to bring men to the knowledge of their sin, to contrition. Where there is no sharp, clear, bitter condemnation of sin, the Gospel will soon lose its sweetness, as members will begin to regard it as the children of Israel their manna, which tasted like wafers made with honey even though they said: "Our soul loatheth this light bread." — The Catholic Church had done at least one thing for Luther, which many a Protestant church does not do for its hearers: it made him terribly aware of his sin. — The self-righteousness of men, their lack of contrition, is ever the chief obstacle in the way of Christ and of the Gospel. When my brother Otto was a missionary in India, he sent me a book, "Things as They Are, Mission Work in Southern India." One thing that I remember from it was the complaint of the writer that the heathen did not feel their sin and therefore paid no attention to the Savior. One day, however, an old woman kept her eyes riveted on the missionary's face. "At last," thought she, "a soul hungering for righteousness!" But when she had finished, the old woman said, "What? Don't you have any soap on your hair? Are you too poor to put any soap on your hair?" To overcome the false security of a world perishing in its sin and going to hell, tell the world where it is going.

THE GOSPEL FOR THE TERRIFIED

Contrition, then, is a part of repentance. But the main part is faith. How horrified were not our fathers when their opponents would not concede that faith is the main part of that repentance which saves! In the Apology, Art. 12, they say: "In the Twelfth Article they approve the first part, in which we set forth that those who have fallen after baptism may obtain remission of sins at whatever time and as often as they are converted. They condemn the second part, in which we say that the parts of repentance are *contrition and faith* [a penitent, contrite heart, and faith, namely, that I receive the forgiveness of sins through Christ]. They deny that faith is the second part of repentance. What are we to do here, O Charles, thou most invincible Emperor? The very voice of the Gospel is this, that by faith we obtain the remission of sins. [This word is not our word, but the voice and word of Jesus Christ, our Savior.]. . . We therefore in no way assent to the Confutation. . . . What else is the denial that by faith we obtain remission of sins than to treat the blood and death of Jesus Christ with scorn? We therefore beseech thee, O Charles, most invincible Emperor, patiently and diligently to hear us." (*Triglot,* p. 253.) Yes, indeed, as we too are willing to confess before all men, emperors, kings, and presidents, before Charles, Tom, Dick, and Harry, faith is a part, aye, the main and only saving part of repentance. John was the great preacher of repentance. But his name after all means "God is gracious." John was a good preacher of repentance chiefly because he preached the grace of God in Christ Jesus, the Lamb that takes away the sins of the world. He preached the remission of sins to all contrite, trembling sinners. He washed them from their sins in the waters of Holy Baptism, and his Baptism as well as that of Jesus was, as he saw it with the eyes of faith, "the blessed fountain red with the dear blood of Jesus, which from all sins inherited of fallen Adam frees us, and from our own transgressions." So preach repentance that faith is created in the hearts of your hearers. Make clear to them that God will forgive them as they are. Pastor C. Runkel of our California District, who read a paper on repentance for his District in 1901, said: "Whosoever thinks of repentance in such manner that he believes he must do something to reconcile God, acts like a man who wants to go north, but takes a train for the south. All the time he is only getting farther away from his goal. Instead of arriving in the Paradise of Divine Consolation, Peace and Joy, he lands in the Desert of Sorrow and Misery. Nothing will lead to God but this, and this alone, that you flee in faith to the word of the Gospel."

HOW TO PREACH THE GOSPEL

"How to Preach that Faith May Be Created in the Hearts of the Hearers" is the title of a series of lectures delivered before Concordia Seminary students by Dr. F. Pieper in 1909. Nothing has ever helped me more. So far as I know, the lectures were only mimeographed. Dr. Pieper, as you know, masterfully taught objective justification, the universal grace of God, who was in Christ and reconciled the world unto Himself. Dr. Pieper takes such precious assurances of the Gospel as 2 Cor. 5:19: "God was in Christ, reconciling the world unto Himself" and teaches the sinner to base on it the perfectly simple, logical, true argument of saving faith: 1. God is through Christ reconciled unto the world. 2. I belong to the world. 3. Therefore God is reconciled unto me. Dr. Pieper, in Lecture 5, p. 66, said: "If I were to make you this proposition, that you must react in a better way than others to the grace of God, or that your guilt must be smaller, I would make your salvation uncertain for you. And why? Because you would always wonder whether you have furnished what is required of you in the right quantity and quality, whether you have behaved better, been less guilty. I remind you of Luther's declaration, If the forgiveness of sins depended on a single Lord's Prayer rightly spoken, then it would be uncertain. Because of the weakness of his flesh, no Christian has ever spoken a perfect Lord's Prayer. To create faith, you must preach universal grace and say that God, purely because of His grace forgives sin and bestows on us life eternal. If you now declare with God's Word that His love is altogether free and makes no demands concerning worthiness and grace, that God's grace accepts the sinner exactly as he is, from the gallows, the highway, the hedges, then the sinner, condemned by the Law, is moved to say: 'In that case God is gracious to me also.' And this is faith, a spiritual reaching out for Christ, and you have preached it into men's hearts by your proclamation of a grace that is universal." — Let us tell sinners to go to the Lord Jesus just as they are, and waiting not to rid their soul of one dark blot, as Cesar Malan told Charlotte Elliott to do when she was worried about her salvation. She responded with her beautiful hymn

> Just as I am, without one plea
> But that Thy blood was shed for me
> And that Thou bidst me come to Thee,
> O Lamb of God, I come.

REPENTANCE IN THE NARROW SENSE

One reason why even some Christians may hesitate to call faith a part of repentance, in spite of all that has been said, is to be found in the fact that repentance is indeed also used in a narrow sense in the Bible. In such instances a distinction is made between repentance and faith, repentance and remission of sins. In Mark 1: 15 we read: "Repent ye and believe the Gospel." Dr. Pieper in his *Christliche Dogmatik*, Vol. II, p. 604, frankly concedes this and says: "The word repentance has, as the Formula of Concord reminds us, both a narrower and a wider meaning in the Bible. It sometimes speaks merely of the contrition created by the Law, the terrors of conscience." In the Formula of Concord we read: "The term repentance is not employed in the Holy Scriptures always in one and the same sense. For in some passages it is employed and taken for the entire conversion of man. . . . But in Mark 1:15, as also elsewhere, where repentance and faith in Christ (Acts 20:21) or repentance and remission of sins (Luke 24:46-47) are mentioned as distinct, to repent means nothing else than truly to acknowledge sins, to be heartily sorry for them, and to desist from them. This knowledge comes from the Law, *but is not sufficient for saving conversion to God if faith in Christ be not added, whose merits the comforting preaching of the Gospel offers to all penitent sinners* who are terrified by the preaching of the Law." (Thorough Declaration, Art. 5, p. 953 f.) Yes, as our Confessions here declare, repentance in the sense of mere sorrow does not suffice to save, even though the sinner gives up sin, the coarse outbursts thereof, as found in drunkenness, adultery, and the like. As Pastor Runkel said in 1901 in California, "A man may outwardly improve his morals and yet remain as far from God as ever. The state gains something by such a change, not the Lord. Outwardly decent

Pharisees end in hell just as well as openly vicious and sinful men." We may well add that also in true contrition even coarse sin is not always given up before faith and love to God has supplied the proper motivation and power.

THE FRUIT OF REPENTANCE

When in faith and love man gives up sin — that is the fruit of repentance. When John, the preacher of repentance, admonished those who came to him to "bring also the fruits meet for repentance" (Matt. 3:8), he sharply distinguished between repentance itself and its fruits. Everything really good that we think or say or do is the result of that complete renewal, that *metanoia*, which we know as repentance. If any man be in Christ Jesus, he, and he alone, is a new creature. Christ has come into his heart with "the expulsive power of a new affection." Yes, of affection, love. We love the Savior and the God and Father who has saved us, who opened His arms to the poor prodigal coming home, hugged him to His breast, adorned him with His jewels, wined and dined him with the priceless and invaluable food and drink of the Gospel. What a change the Savior's love quickly effected in Zacchaeus! By these fruits we indeed know Christ's disciples. Where they are missing, we detect no faith, no love, and the case of the professing Christian may become so bad, his farness from Christ so apparent, that we reluctantly resort to excommunication as to the last sermon on repentance we can still preach to such as him in hope. — So closely are repentance and its fruits associated that, as Dr. Engelder put it, our Apology does not care to argue much with him who wants to call it the third part of repentance. He is thus referring to what we find in the Apology, Article 12, 28 (*Triglot*, p. 259): "If anyone desires to add a third part, namely, fruits worthy of repentance, i. e., a change of the entire life and character for the better [good works, which shall and must follow upon conversion], we will not make any opposition" (German: "*gross fechten*"; Latin: "*non refragabimur*"). Dr. Engelder adds: "We would not stand for it that a Papist adds this third meaning, for he would mean the wrong thing thereby. But if one does it who knows the true essence of repentance to be contrition and faith alone, then we know what he has in mind: he wants to emphasize as strongly as possible the inseparable connection between good works and conversion. Why does the Holy Scripture do this at times, as in Ezek. 18:21: 'If the wicked turn from all his sins that he hath committed and keep all My statutes and do that which is lawful and right, he shall surely live, he shall not die,' thus describing repentance by its fruits as a turning from sin? It does this for two reasons: 1. On account of those who live in carnal security. We prove to them thus that they have not yet really repented. 2. It does so also for the sake of those truly penitent, whose careless, lazy flesh has to be spurred on to righteousness. We, as it were, say to him: 'Consider what has been done for you. Forget not your Savior's love. Let the new man prevail.'" (*Central Illinois Proceedings*, 1925, p. 25.) — It cannot be otherwise — in the truly penitent sinner there is also the fruit worthy of repentance.

DAILY CONTRITION AND REPENTANCE

Luther says that the old man must by daily contrition and repentance be drowned and die with all sins and evil lusts. Pastor Runkel observes: "The daily contrition and repentance of which Luther speaks is a constant repetition of that which constitutes conversion. The same acts are there: sorrow over sin, so that we despair of being able to save ourselves and plead guilty of deserving God's wrath and eternal damnation. But the other is there also, that we daily reach out for the forgiveness in Christ, saying, 'The blood of Jesus Christ, God's Son, cleanses us from all sin.' This requires of us the diligent use of the means of grace, by which repentance is effected, Law and Gospel." It also requires that we make every effort to conform to God's will. As Pastor Runkel puts it: "The Old Adam argues that it is not necessary to be so painstaking. After you have been good for a while, he tells you that you may relax in your efforts. Beware! Awful are the words of Christ, showing the need of daily repentance, found in Mark 9:43: 'If thy hand offend thee, cut it off; it is better for thee to enter into life maimed than, having two hands, to go into hell, into the fire that never shall be quenched.'" — Men and brethren, repent ye. Remember from what you have fallen if you have fallen. And whatever the heights of holiness you may have reached, go excelsior, higher still, by God's grace!

Sanctification

THERE can be no question of the importance of the doctrine of sanctification to every one of us. In the first place, the Bible speaks frequently (the verb and the noun occur about 135 times in the Scriptures) and with decisive emphasis (John 17:17; II Tim. 3:16-17; Is. 45:24 a) concerning sanctification. This subject does not belong to the strong meat of God's Word, which we should offer to the advanced only; it belongs to the milk of the Word, which every Christian must imbibe. The teaching of Holy Writ concerning sanctification must become known to every Christian, even to Christian children.

But on this subject of sanctification there has been much confusion and misunderstanding also among members of the Christian Church. Lutherans are often charged with neglecting the subject of sanctification, while giving entirely too much attention to justification. We are accused of speaking too much about creeds and too little about deeds. Yet, in the Epitome of the Formula of Concord, our confessors say "that men may be damned by an Epicurean delusion concerning faith, as well as by a papistic and Pharisaic confidence in their own works and merits" (Formula of Concord, Epitome IV, Negativa 2, *Triglot*, p. 801). Paulist Father Bertrand L. Conway writes in the *Question Box*, p. 107: "The Lutheran Doctrine of Justification by Faith alone is essentially immoral and has led . . . logically to the reaction of the common Protestant creed of today, indifferentism."

Again, there are those even in our churches who are in danger of imagining that faith is simply a matter of knowledge of Bible history. For more than one reason, therefore, it is not only highly profitable, but also very necessary that we discuss this subject, meditate upon it, and gain a clear conception of what the Scripture teaches concerning sanctification. God grant us His blessing and the assistance of His Holy Spirit that our study of it on the basis of Holy Writ may help us all to grow in true sanctification.

I. THE MEANING OF THE WORD "SANCTIFICATION"

First of all, let us see what the Bible and the Confessions of our Church mean by this word *sanctification*. Like so many other words in Scripture, it is used in more than one meaning. Our Church has pointed out that it is used especially in two meanings, in a wider and in a more limited meaning. In its wider sense the term *sanctification* includes all those effects of God's Word produced in the heart and life of man beginning with his rebirth from spiritual death to spiritual life and culminating in spiritual perfection in life eternal. When used in this wide sense, sanctification includes the call, conversion, regeneration, illumination, justification, and renewing of the image of God in man. It is used in this sense, for instance, in Eph. 5:26 ("that He might sanctify and cleanse it with the washing of water by the Word," etc.), where we are told that Jesus did not simply come to begin a good work in us, but to complete it till in heaven His Church is at last the company of perfectly righteous, innocent, and blessed people. It is used in this sense also in Acts 26:18, where we are told that Jesus commanded Paul to go forth to be a preacher of the Gospel in order that men might receive "inheritance among them which are sanctified." In Heb. 10:14 ("For by one offering He hath perfected forever them that are sanctified") "the sanctified" are those who are being renewed entirely. Similarly Paul writes: "But we are bound to give thanks always to God for you, brethren, beloved of the Lord, because God hath from the beginning chosen you to salvation through sanctification of the Spirit and belief of the Truth" (II Thess. 2:13). In this passage sanctification is used in the wider sense. It is also used in the wider sense in I Pet. 1:2, where we read: "Elect according to the foreknowledge of God the Father, through sanctification of the Spirit, unto obedience and sprinkling of the blood of Jesus Christ."

Our Confessions use the word *sanctification* in this sense: In Luther's Large Catechism we read the following: "If someone asks: 'What do you mean by the words, *I believe in the Holy Ghost?*' you answer: 'I believe that the Holy Ghost makes me holy, as His name implies.'" (Par. 40. *Triglot*, p. 689.) "Makes me holy" has the same meaning as "He sanctifies me."

Sanctification

The teachers of our Church have also called attention to this wider sense of sanctification. Quenstedt writes concerning Eph. 5:26: "Sanctification is at times taken in the wider sense and includes justification" (*Theologia Didactico-Polemica*, III, p. 632).

However, the word *sanctification* is more frequently used in the Scriptures, in the Confessions, and in the writings of our teachers in the narrower sense, which expresses the work of God in the heart of one who is already a Christian, whom God is now leading on step by step in the renewing of the image of God, step by step in righteousness of life in thought, word, and deed, in holiness of conduct, in emotions, in wishes, in prayers, in devotions, and in charity toward everyone. When used in this narrower sense sanctification refers to the spiritual growth which follows upon justification. A person receives forgiveness, that is, he is justified immediately and perfectly just as soon as he repents of sin and by faith lays hold on the forgiveness of sins procured by the vicarious atonement wrought by Jesus Christ, the Savior. Justification is instantaneous and perfect. It is not a gradual process. It is like a sentence of the judge in court when he declares the accused "Not guilty." The judge's verdict "Not guilty" ends the matter perfectly. When the repentant sinner hears God say: "Son, be of good cheer, thy sins be forgiven thee" and believes that word, he is personally justified, that is, the forgiveness of sins, procured by Christ for all men and offered in the Gospel to all freely, is pronounced upon him individually. He is declared a saint. His record before God is perfectly clear and clean. But in his actual life there is still the old Adam, or his sinful nature. Even though a person be ever so good a Christian, he must confess with St. Paul: "I know that in me (that is, in my flesh) dwelleth no good thing" (Rom. 7:18). Therefore the Christian must fight a daily battle against sin. And here God, through the Word and the Sacraments, continues to pound away at, buffet, immerse, and drown the old Adam and the sinful nature. And the Christian by the grace of God co-operates in this work, and daily through the Holy Spirit's work faith is increased, love toward the brethren is strengthened, confidence in God and in His promises is confirmed and established, the image of God is renewed, the Christian becomes more and more righteous, more and more holy, more and more blessed, more and more firm in faith and godliness. That is *sanctification in the narrow sense.* It is used in this narrow sense in the Bible when it is pointed out as a consequence of justification and is thus carefully distinguished from justification. For instance, in Rom. 6:22, where St. Paul says that since the Christians have become servants of God, they are now made free from sin and are beginning to live in holiness and to receive the fruits of this holiness. When sanctification in the narrower sense is meant, it is pictured as *growth.* Peter writes (II Pet. 3:18): "But grow in grace and in the knowledge of our Lord and Savior Jesus Christ." There are so many passages of Scripture in which sanctification or one of its synonyms is used in this narrow sense that it would lead us too far afield to quote them all, even in part, or speak of them at length. St. Paul pictures this process of sanctification to us as a process of being made free from the service of sin and becoming more and more servants of righteousness (Rom. 6:15-23). One gets the definite idea of a growth by reading carefully this portion of Holy Writ. In the Small Catechism of Martin Luther, sanctification in the narrower sense is spoken of under the Fourth Part of Baptism, where the question is asked: "What does such baptizing with water signify?" With Scripture Luther answers: "It signifies that the old Adam in us should, by daily contrition and repentance, be drowned and die with all sins and evil lusts and, again, a new man daily come forth and arise, who shall live before God in righteousness and purity forever." At other times also the Confessions of our Church call attention to this meaning of sanctification in the narrower sense, although they frequently use the term *renewal,* which means the gradual restoration of the image of God in man.

Having called attention to the two meanings in which the Bible, our Confessions, and our teachers use the word *sanctification,* we now limit our discussion to the consideration of sanctification in the narrower sense, and we define it by stating that sanctification in the narrower sense refers to the operation of the Holy Spirit in the heart of the Christian (the regenerate) whereby the Christian, the believer, daily puts off more and more the old Adam and daily puts on the new man. In other words, sanctification in this sense refers to that work of the Holy Spirit in the hearts and lives of God's children through which they receive power to conquer the temptations of the devil, the world, and the flesh. Sanctification in this sense refers to that work of the Holy Spirit whereby the believers conquer more and more the works of the flesh, the sins which so easily beset us, which even the best of Christians still feel in themselves: envy, jealousy, discontent, murmurings, ingratitude, lack of love for God and His Word and our neighbor, and all other sins, in view of which even St. Paul confessed: "I know that in me (that is in my flesh) dwelleth no good thing" (Rom. 7:18). Sanctification in this narrow sense includes also the Holy Spirit's work whereby He produces in the Christian the fruits of the Spirit: love, joy, peace, long-suffering, gentleness, goodness, faith, meekness, temperance, so that the Christian grows in grace and in the knowledge of Jesus Christ, our Savior.

Now, concerning the work of the Holy Spirit called sanctification, let us note these four points: (1) This sanctification is the work of the Holy Spirit alone; it is the work of His grace and mercy; (2) This work is carried on only in the Christian, the believer, not in the unbeliever; (3) The Holy Spirit uses the means of grace to produce the effects of sanctification, and God also employs certain conditions which favor the application of the means of grace; (4) Sanctification is finally complete and perfect in heaven.

II. SANCTIFICATION IS THE WORK OF THE HOLY SPIRIT

To prove this point, that the Holy Spirit alone works, operates, and effects this sanctification, we may quote Phil. 2:13: "It is God which worketh in you both to will and to do of His good pleasure." Some imagine that we ourselves can decide to be obedient, God-fearing, holy, righteous. No; the Bible teaches: "It is God that worketh in you both to will and to do." God must make the unwilling willing. He must give strength and power to conquer sin. When a Christian fights against temptation, when with his heart he confesses his sin with sorrow, when he rejoices in Jesus Christ and in gratitude to His Savior wishes to glorify the Savior's name, when the Christian is moved to help his neighbor, to be forgiving, these are not the fruits of the flesh, nor are they the consequence of his own personal activity, it is God that works these things in him. Therefore Scripture also teaches (Gal. 5:22 f.): "The fruit of the Spirit is love, joy, peace, longsuffering, gentleness, goodness, faith, meekness, temperance." All these beautiful virtues are created in us, strengthened in us, developed in us, through the operation of the Holy Spirit. We must therefore remember that sanctification, just like redemption and creation, is a work of God. The Holy Spirit, promised to the believers as a precious gift by the Savior, teaches them and brings to their remembrance the words of Christ (John 14:26); guides them into all truth (16:13); glorifies Christ (v. 14); fills them with His gifts (I Cor. 12:7-11). As the Spirit of prayer (Zech. 12:10) He teaches the believers to pray, to cry, "Abba, Father" (Rom. 8: 15, 26). As the Spirit of adoption He strengthens their conviction that they are the children of God (Rom. 8:16). As the Spirit, not of fear, but of power and of love and of a sound mind (II Tim. 1:7) He strengthens them in their daily battle against their flesh (Gal. 5:16-18, 22) and works in them righteousness and peace and joy (Rom. 14:17). As the Spirit of the God of hope (Rom. 15:13) He enables them to abound in hope through the power of the Holy Spirit (Rom. 15:13). It is indeed God the Holy Spirit that sanctifies those whom He has brought to faith.

In our day also there are many who tell us Christian church members: "We are just as good as those people who go to church; we may not attend your church, we may not read the Bible, but we can point to our virtues and in some respects do better even than many of your church members." But we must keep in mind that the Lord Jesus expressly tells us: "I am the Vine, ye are the branches. He that abideth in Me, and I in him, the same bringeth forth much fruit; for without Me ye can do nothing. If a man abide not in Me, he is cast forth as a branch, and is withered; and men gather them and cast them into the fire, and they are burned" (John 15:5-6). In these words Jesus expressly tells us that no matter what we do, no matter what we undertake or accomplish, if we are not a branch in the vine Jesus, then we are withered and dead in the sight of God, and all our works are nothing but the glittering, shining vices of the heathen.

III. SANCTIFICATION IS CARRIED ON ONLY IN THE BELIEVER AND NOT IN THE UNBELIEVER

The work of sanctification is carried on in the Christian, only in the true believer, and never in the unbeliever. This is taught by our Lord Jesus, who says: "That which is born of the flesh is flesh, and that which is born of the Spirit is spirit" (John 3:6). The unregenerate are dead in trespasses and sins, so states the Bible. It is only after a man is born again that new spiritual life begins to exert itself. St. Paul also calls attention to this when he teaches: "For we are His workmanship, created in Christ Jesus unto good works, which God hath before ordained that we should walk in them" (Eph. 2:10). Man is born with natural powers, but they are corrupted by sin. He has inherited sin and corruption from his parents. He is, by his birth from these sinful parents, a sinner, a servant of sin. It is only after God has created in him new spiritual life that he begins to do spiritual, God-pleasing works. This is also taught by the Lord in His Sermon on the Mount (Matt. 7:16-18): "Ye shall know them by their fruits. Do men gather grapes of thorns or figs of thistles? Even so every good tree bringeth forth good fruit, but a corrupt tree bringeth forth evil fruit. A good tree cannot bring forth evil fruit, neither can a corrupt tree bring forth good fruit."

Luther also, in his forcible manner, taught that the so-called good works of an unbeliever are nothing more than vermin crawling in the filth. On the other hand, he taught that if you fear God and are regenerate, a child of God, all that you do, in accordance with the Ten Commandments, in your ordinary walk of life, even though it be nothing more than loading manure and driving donkeys, is pleasing to God. In order not to be misunderstood, Luther added: "We do not condemn good works, but we wish to have it understood that a person must be born again. First of all, new spiritual life must be created in him, and then good works will certainly follow. . . . Our opponents accuse us of ridiculing good works and forbidding them, but it is not true; for we preach very earnestly and clearly what good works are and that they must be done, and will be done, by those who have the life which God has created in them, the new spiritual life." (St. Louis, I:1,577.)

Those who are somewhat acquainted with Luther's works know how often and at what length he writes on this very subject.

This point that the *justified* child of God alone can do God-pleasing works is an important one also because even the believers' good works are not in themselves perfect. They are soiled with sin; but because of the Christians' faith in the forgiveness of God, these sins of weakness which cling even to their best good works are forgiven, and their imperfect works are accepted by God and are pleasing to God. Therefore God on Judgment Day will render this judgment concerning the *imperfect* works of the believer: "Well done, thou good and faithful servant. Thou hast been faithful over a few things; I will make thee ruler over many things. Enter thou into the joy of thy Lord" (Matt. 25:21). Compare also Matt. 25:34-36. On Judgment Day the foolish person who sacrificed, fasted, and tortured himself, thinking thereby to earn heaven and relying on these works instead of putting his trust in Jesus, will be condemned to eternal damnation. Such a person neither has had joy here, nor will he have joy hereafter. On the other hand, the believer, even though his faith was only as a bruised reed or a smoking flax, will have his comparatively insignificant works, such as giving a cup of cold water to a thirsty one, richly rewarded for all eternity. Oh, how very important it is that man comes to faith in Jesus Christ! This is also taught by Jesus when He tells His disciples: "Ye are clean through the Word which I have spoken unto you" (John 15:3).

Concerning this matter Luther writes: "Faith is a divine work in us which transforms us, gives us a new birth out of God, John 1:13, slays the old Adam, makes us altogether different men in heart, affection, mind, and all powers, and brings with it the Holy Spirit. Oh, it is a living, energetic, active, mighty thing, this faith! It cannot but do good unceasingly. There is no question asked whether good works are to be done, but before the question is asked, the works have been done, and there is a continuous doing of them. But any person not doing such works is without faith. He is groping in the dark, looking for faith and good works, and knows neither what faith is nor what good works are." (St. Louis, XIV:88.)

Our Confessions teach the same doctrine: "Because, indeed, faith brings the Holy Ghost and produces in hearts a new life, it is necessary that it should produce spiritual movements in hearts. And what these movements are, the Prophet (Jer. 31:33) shows when he says: *I will put My Law into their inward parts and write it in their hearts.* Therefore, when we have been justified by faith and regenerated, we begin to fear and love God, to pray to Him, to expect from Him aid, to give thanks and praise Him, and to obey Him in afflictions. We begin also to love our neighbors, because our hearts have spiritual and holy movements [there is now, through the Spirit of Christ, a new heart, mind, and spirit within]." (Apology, Art. III, par. 4. *Triglot*, p. 157.) We have an example of that in the sacrifices of Cain and Abel. Cain's sacrifice seemed just as good as Abel's, but God did not accept it. Abel's sacrifice was accepted. Why? The Bible tells us: "By faith Abel offered unto God a more excellent sacrifice than Cain" (Heb. 11:4).

Let us therefore keep in mind that we Christians are not to despair because of the imperfections of our good works, aye, we are not to despair because, of the old Adam, sin still clings to us and troubles us. We are not only to pray to God for help and strength, we are all the more to seek God's Word, to receive the Sacrament, in order that God Himself may strengthen the new man in us daily to rise and to live before God in righteousness and purity. Even though a Christian has committed a grievous sin, let him not think that on this account he must withdraw from God or God's Word and the Sacrament until he has improved in his sinful life. No, let him all the more earnestly and prayerfully use the Word of God and seek God's help through confession, absolution, and the Sacrament. Thus the Holy Spirit will carry on His work in his heart and enable him to crucify the old Adam and move him to produce the fruits of the Spirit.

In addition to what has been said, it must also be pointed out that after conversion, after regeneration, the believer becomes a willing co-worker with the Holy Spirit in the work of sanctification. Thus St. Paul teaches: "We, then, as workers together with Him, beseech you also that ye receive not the grace of God in vain" (II Cor. 6:1). The Confessions of the Lutheran Church call attention to the fact that here St. Paul calls himself and other Christians co-workers with the Holy Spirit. True, in order to become Christians the Corinthians could do nothing, but now that they are Christians, they are admonished to co-operate. They are now to make the most of the gifts they have received. Therefore also St. Peter writes: "Grow in grace and in the knowledge of our Lord and Savior Jesus Christ" (II Pet. 3:18). St. Paul writes to the Corinthians: "Having therefore these promises, dearly beloved, let us cleanse ourselves from all filthiness of the flesh and spirit, perfecting holiness in the fear of God" (II Cor. 7:1). This is addressed to Christians. They have received new spiritual powers; they should make use of them. In this sense is to be understood also that passage which has troubled so many persons: "Work out your own salvation with fear and trembling" (Phil. 2:12). "Work out" does not mean that we are to earn our salvation. Paul wrote these words to those who had salvation, who had spiritual gifts. This word means that they should make the most of the spiritual gifts which God has bestowed upon them. Just as a father may turn over a farm to a son, or his business to his heir, and say to him: "Now it is all yours. What wonderful opportunities you have here! Now make the most of them. You have powers, you have means, you have the capital, you have the opportunity. Now use them. Do not lose what I have turned over to you; do not ruin it or waste it." And in order to encourage him in this joyous, fruitful, blessed working together with the Holy Spirit, who produces the fruits of the Spirit, Paul adds these comforting words: "For it is God that worketh in you both to will and to do" (Phil. 2:13). The Christian is to remember that he has been given precious seed, precious powers, and he is now told: "He which soweth sparingly shall reap sparingly; and he which soweth bountifully shall reap also bountifully" (II Cor. 9:6). "Neglect not the gift that is in thee" (I Tim. 4:14). Cp. Formula of Concord, Thorough Declaration, II, par. 65—66, *Triglot*, p. 907.

In addition to what has been said, we must point out that the very purpose of Jesus' work of redemption is the sanctification of man. There can be no question that some have spoken as if the final purpose of Jesus' work were the justification of man, the forgiveness of sin, and nothing more. That is not true. Jesus came, suffered, and died, wrought redemption, not simply that we should be forgiven, but for the purpose of making us holy, holy and righteous, not only by imputation of His righteousness, but holy and righteous in ourselves. The Christian is not only to have the righteousness of Christ by which he covers himself and by which he is accepted before God, but the Christian is also to have his own righteousness, his own innocence, and to enjoy the blessedness of doing good works. The Bible expressly teaches this. Zacharias, speaking by inspiration of the Holy Spirit, declared: "Blessed be the Lord God of Israel; for He hath visited and redeemed His people and hath raised up a Horn of Salvation for us in the house of His servant David . . . that He would grant unto us that we, being delivered out of the hand of our enemies, might serve Him without fear, in holiness and righteousness before Him, all the days of our life" (Luke 1: 68-69, 74-75). St. Paul writes: "He died for all that they which live should not henceforth live unto themselves, but unto Him which died for them and rose again" (II Cor. 5:15). And Jesus told His disciples: "I am the Vine, ye are the branches. He that abideth in Me, and I in him, the same bringeth forth much fruit. . . . Herein is My Father glorified, that ye bear much fruit. So shall ye be My disciples" (John 15:5, 8). And again Jesus said to His disciples: "Ye have not chosen Me, but I have chosen you, and ordained you, that ye should go and bring forth fruit" (v. 16). St. Paul also writes: "For we are His workmanship, created in Christ Jesus unto good works, which God hath before ordained that we should walk in them" (Eph. 2:10). And Peter writes: "Who His own self bare our sins in His own body on the tree, that we, being dead to sins, should live unto righteousness; by whose stripes ye were healed" (I Pet. 2:24). We are not only saved *from* something, but also *for* something!

Jesus excludes from His people everyone who does not show fruits, that is, good works as fruits of the Holy Spirit in his heart, saying: "Not everyone that saith unto Me, Lord, Lord, shall enter into the kingdom of heaven; but he that doeth the will of My Father, which is in heaven" (Matt. 7:21).

This is also taught by the Confessions of the Lutheran Church. In the Small Catechism of Luther we confess that Jesus redeemed us, "not with gold or silver, but with His holy, precious blood." And then the purpose of all this is given: "That I may be His own and live under Him in His kingdom and serve Him in everlasting righteousness, innocence, and blessedness." These words are not to be understood of imputed righteousness, imputed blessedness, imputed innocence, but of the daily life of a Christian in holiness and good works.

Luther himself also emphasized this fact again and again in his writings. He writes: "Our sin is not forgiven in order that we may continue to live in sin, *but in order that we may cease from sinning.* Otherwise it would not be forgiveness, but license to sin" (St. Louis, XII:786). But Luther has written of this matter so frequently that it would take too much time to quote all the passages. Other reliable teachers of the Church called attention to this. It has also been the constant teaching of Synod. We read, for instance, the following: "Holy Scripture teaches very clearly that the last final purpose of the redemptive work of Jesus is sanctification. Our forgiveness, our atonement, our justification, is not the final goal and purpose, but only the means and way by which our sanctification is attained. God forgives our sins that we may leave them. Christ did not become our Redeemer simply in order that we might be rid of our guilt and punishment, but chiefly that we might be perfectly free from sin. As we shall see, perfect sanctification is not attained until we enter heaven." (Western District, 1875, p. 46.)

IV. IN THIS LIFE SANCTIFICATION REMAINS IMPERFECT AND VARIES IN DIFFERENT CHRISTIANS AND IN THE SAME CHRISTIAN AT DIFFERENT TIMES

First of all, then, let us note that in this life sanctification remains imperfect. In this also it differs from justification. Justification is either perfect or null and void. There are no degrees of justification. God does not forgive sins by inches, yards, pints, or quarts. If you have forgiveness, all your sins are forgiven; if you have not full forgiveness, none of your sins are forgiven. Justification is a forensic act. When upon completion of a trial the jury's verdict is brought in and the judge pronounces sentence, the defendant is either guilty or not guilty. And just so, when the perfect forgiveness which Jesus purchased and earned is offered to the sinner and he, repentant, by faith accepts it, he is perfectly forgiven. But that does not mean that he is perfectly sanctified.

By this faith in the forgiveness of sins the Holy Spirit enters the heart, and the work of sanctification begins. Sanctification is a matter of growth. Therefore St. Paul writes to the Ephesians: "But, speaking the truth in love, may grow up into Him in all things which is the Head, even Christ" (Eph. 4:15). Whatever is growing is changed, is increasing. St. Paul tells the Philippians that God, who has begun a good work in them, will perform it, will finish it. He pictures the work of sanctification as begun in them, but not finished. It requires continued work. Therefore also he writes: "Ye are God's building" (I Cor. 3:9). God is still building them inwardly, increasing their faith, their love, their hope, all of which is imperfect. Dr. Graebner (*Doctrinal Theology*, p. 153) calls this "progressive sanctification," "an increasing sanctification of the appetites and affections toward their primeval purity." That is why St. Paul, a very good Christian, confesses: "Not as though I had already attained, either were already perfect; but I follow after, if that I may apprehend that for which also I am apprehended of Christ Jesus" (Phil. 3:12). Just so he also writes, "Know ye not that they which run in a race run all, but one receiveth the prize? So run that ye may obtain" (I Cor. 9:24). They are still running in the race, they are fighting. It is a continued activity; it is not yet completed or finished.

The Bible also illustrates this truth by showing us the imperfections of the greatest of saints. Everyone of us will remember at once the sins, imperfections, weaknesses of such great men of God as Abraham, Hezekiah, Elijah, Peter, Paul, Sarah, Mary, the mother of Jesus, and many others. Therefore also the Scriptures expressly teach: "If we say that we have no sin, we deceive ourselves, and the truth is not in us" (I John 1:8). This is said by a Christian to Christians.

Sanctification differs also in the same Christian at different times, just as a tree or a plant may be more lively or vigorous at one time than another. Job was stronger in his faith when he confessed his faith in the resurrection of the body than when he cursed the day of his birth. Peter was stronger in his sanctification when he made the bold confession of the Lord Jesus on Pentecost Day than he was when Paul had to "withstand him to the face" — "because Peter was to be blamed" (Gal. 2:11).

The Bible teaches this truth at every turn. Thus Paul writes: "For the flesh lusteth against the spirit, and the spirit against the flesh; and these are contrary the one to the other, so that ye cannot do the things that ye would" (Gal. 5:17). Indeed, Paul pictures the Christian's life, not as the life of one who has reached the goal and the perfect victory and has arrived at the pinnacle of his striving, but as of one who is still in the race, is still pressing forward. In the same vein he writes: "For we know that the Law is spiritual; but I am carnal, sold under sin. For that which I do I allow not; for what I would, that do I not; but what I hate, that do I. If then I do that which I would not, I consent unto the Law that it is good. Now, then, it is no more I that do it, but sin that dwelleth in me. For I know that in me (that is, in my flesh) dwelleth no good thing; for to will is present with me, but how to perform that which is good I find not. For the good that I would I do not; but the evil which I would not, that I do" (Rom. 7:14-19). John writes: "If we say that we have no sin, we deceive ourselves, and the truth is not in us" (I John 1:8). The Confessions of our Church teach this. In the Small Catechism, in the explanation of the Fifth Petition, all Lutherans confess: "We daily sin much and indeed deserve nothing but punishment." And in the Formula of Concord we read: "For since we receive in this life only the first fruits of the Spirit, and the new birth is not complete, but only begun in us, the combat and struggle of the flesh against the spirit remains even in the elect and truly regenerate men; for there is a great difference perceptible among Christians not only in this, that one is weak and another strong in the spirit, but each Christian, moreover, experiences in himself that at one time he is joyful in spirit and at another fearful and alarmed: at one time ardent in love, strong in faith and hope, and at another cold and weak." (Formula of Concord, Thorough Declaration, II, par. 68. *Triglot*, p. 907.)

This truth is important for us Christians, for it serves us first of all as a comfort when we are troubled because of our weakness. The sins of Christians are not painted sins; they are real sins. The Christian flees them, he fights against them, he hates them, but they are there. Therefore the Christian daily asks God for forgiveness, and he is comforted by the fact that the saints of old were also troubled by their sinful flesh. The Christian must remember that the ungodly are not troubled because of their sins, but they delight in these sins. They often consider the very sins themselves as the joys which are coming to them. In fact, at times some of these sins are considered virtues, as, for instance, greed, sharp practices, lies, deceit, revenge. We Christians indeed suffer from these temptations and these fruits of the flesh, but we are fighting against them daily. And the very fact that we hate them and fight against them is a sign that we are true children of God and that God's Spirit lives in us.

In the second place, this truth is also to warn us against condemning one in whom we still see weaknesses, defects, although he is a member of the Church, partakes of Holy Communion, is counted among Christians. The Bible tells us that we are to bear with the weak: "Him that is weak in the faith receive ye, but not to doubtful disputations" (Rom. 14:1). Therefore also the Lord Jesus admonishes that even when a Christian brother sins seriously against us, we should not at once condemn him, but speak to him personally, admonish him, and aid him to overcome his sin. (Matt. 18:15-16.) St. Paul writes: "Brethren, if a man be overtaken in a fault, ye which are spiritual, restore such an one in the spirit of meekness; considering thyself, lest thou also be tempted. Bear ye one another's burdens and so fulfill the law of Christ" (Gal. 6:1-2). Again he writes: "We, then, that are strong ought to bear the infirmities of the weak and not to please ourselves. Let every one of us please his neighbor for his good to edification" (Rom. 15:1-2).

This truth is also to preserve in us the proper humility, lest we become proud and self-righteous. We are therefore not to forget that important statement of Luther that the Christian is in process of becoming someone but has not reached perfection.

Again, this truth is to admonish us that we should not be satisfied with our present condition, that it is our duty to go forward, to strive, to fight. Here to stand still means to go backward. Sanctification in every Christian is to increase. There is to be progress. A fighter who ceases to fight is conquered. A fish which no longer swims against the stream is drifting downward. The weak Christian therefore is not to be satisfied to remain in his weakness, but he is to pray for strength; he is to ask God for gifts of the Holy Spirit.

V. THE ONLY MEANS THROUGH WHICH GOD PERFORMS HIS WORK OF SANCTIFICATION IS THE GOSPEL IN WORD AND SACRAMENT

The Bible is very explicit in telling us exactly through what means God sanctifies us.

In His very impressive sacerdotal prayer Jesus prays the Father for His Christians, saying: "Sanctify them through Thy truth; Thy Word is truth" (John 17:17). The Old Testament and the New are replete with positive statements which teach this truth: "The Law of the Lord is perfect, converting the soul; the testimony of the Lord is sure, making wise the simple; the statutes of the Lord are right, rejoicing the heart; the commandment of the Lord is pure, enlightening the eyes" (Ps. 19:7-8). The 119th Psalm again and again reminds us of this truth. We read, for instance (v. 9): "Wherewithal shall a young man cleanse his way? By taking heed thereto according to Thy Word"; v. 72: "The Law of Thy mouth is better unto me than thousands of gold and silver"; vv. 88, 99, 100: "Thou through Thy commandments hast made me wiser than mine enemies, for they are ever with me. I have more understanding than all my teachers, for Thy testimonies are my meditation. I understand more than the ancients, because I keep Thy precepts"; v. 105: "Thy Word is a lamp unto my feet and a light unto my path"; v. 130: "The entrance of Thy words giveth light; it giveth understanding unto the simple." And in the New Testament we read: "As newborn babes, desire the sincere milk of the Word that ye may grow thereby" (I Pet. 2:2). "All Scripture is given by inspiration of God and is profitable for doctrine, for reproof, for correction, for instruction in righteousness, that the man of God may be perfect, thoroughly furnished unto all good works" (II Tim. 3:16-17).

The very fact that our Church admonishes us continually to hear God's Word, to meditate upon it, to read it in our homes, to study the Bible, shows that the Church teaches the efficacy of the Word of God in sanctifying Christians. To hear God's Word, to read it, study it, is not merely our duty, but we need to do it that God may have opportunity to work in us, work out our sanctification, through His Word. The spiritual life of the Christian originates in the Word of God, and it is nurtured by the Word of God. In our Confessions that is taught, for instance, in the explanation of the Third Article, where we read: "The Holy Ghost has called me *by the Gospel*, enlightened me with His gifts, sanctified and kept me in the true faith." Here the Gospel is mentioned as the means through which the Holy Ghost has done all this. Certainly, Christians also need the preaching of the Law, for they still have the old Adam in them. They must be instructed that this old Adam is sinful, is wicked, and his very nature and fruits are like those of the unbeliever (Gal. 5:19-21). Indeed, by the Law we Christians are always again and again reminded of our imperfection. True, we are told (I Tim. 1:9): "The Law is not made for a righteous man, but for the lawless and disobedient, for the ungodly and for sinners, for unholy and profane, for murderers of fathers and murderers of mothers, for manslayers," and that is also true of our new man. As far as we are Christians, believers, and the work of the Holy Spirit is active in us and we co-operate with it, we do not need the urging of the Law. According to our new man we are very willing to do God's will. However, our sinful old Adam is lawless, is a sinner, is disobedient and unwilling to do God's will. He must be threatened also with the curse of the Law. St. Paul himself calls attention to the fact that through the Law we learn what God desires of us, what works we are to do.

However, the Law will never create true godliness, will never sanctify man. In order to produce true faith, true love of God, true love also of our neighbor, the Gospel must be preached. Paul teaches this, inquiring: "This only would I learn of you, Received ye the Spirit by the works of the Law or by the hearing of faith?" (Gal. 3:2). St. Paul here tells these Galatians: You are mistaken if you think that through the Law you become obedient children of God, willing to obey His will. It was the Gospel through which you became Christians, and this work, which only the Gospel has begun, cannot be finished by the Law, but only by the Gospel. That is also definitely stated in the Confessions of the Church. Under "Baptism" we read in the Catechism: "How can water do such great things?" Answer: "It is not the water indeed that does them, but the word of God, which is in and with the water, and faith, which trusts such word of God in the water. For without the word of God the water is simple water and no Baptism. But with the word of God it is a Baptism, that is, a gracious water of life and a washing of regeneration . . . and renewing of the Holy Ghost, which He shed on us abundantly through Jesus Christ, our Savior, that, being justified by His grace, we should be made heirs according to the hope of eternal life. This is a faithful saying." Under the heading "The Sacrament of the Altar" we read: "How can bodily eating and drinking do such great things?" Answer: "It is not the eating and drinking indeed that does them, but the words here written, 'Given and shed for you for the remission of sins'; which words, besides the bodily eating and drinking, are the chief thing in the Sacrament; and he that believes these words has what they say and express, namely, the forgiveness of sins." Even in the Sacraments, it is the Word of God, it is the Gospel, which produces the fruits of the Spirit. Therefore Peter admonished the Christians: "As newborn babes, desire the sincere milk of the Word *that ye may grow thereby*" (I Pet. 2:2.)

A question which arises in this connection is whether tribulation, strange experiences, chastisements, punishments, are to be considered a means of grace. Here again we must call to mind that suffering in itself never has made a Christian. True, many a person turns to God's Word again moved through sad experiences, the punishment of sin, sickness, the fear of death. But remember that when these things happen to a heathen who has never heard the Gospel, they will never produce regeneration or conversion. They may even move him to the most ridiculous, foolish, wicked, sinful practices. Misery, suffering, distress, pain, and the fear of death never make a Christian. Yet it is true that to one who knows the Bible such times of tribulation, sorrow, chastisement, or punishment may arouse remembrances. A person so aroused may remember some truths that he has learned in his youth; or some friend, relative, a Christian pastor and missionary, may point out the right road to him. However, this tribulation is something like pain in physical sickness. Pain never heals the sick, but it may move one to seek a remedy and a physician. The crowing of the cock did not convert Peter (Peter was converted through the word which Jesus had spoken to him), but the crowing of the cock reminded Peter of that word. So, tribulation, sorrow, distress, and pain may be the means through which one is reminded of the Gospel, of the church, of the pastor. We should therefore not call church bells, or the organ, or the cockcrowing, or sickness, or the fear of death a means of grace.

VI. THE IMPORTANCE OF SANCTIFICATION

We have now arrived at that division of our treatment of sanctification which answers the question: *What is the importance of sanctification?* First of all, we must reiterate: The importance of sanctification does not consist in this, that by our sanctification we are saved or that by our sanctification we earn heaven.

We must again refer to what has gone before. Our sanctification on this earth, even the sanctification of the best of us, is very defective, imperfect, and soiled with sin. By sanctification we do not earn heaven; in fact, as far as the intrinsic merit is concerned, even when we do good works, we really deserve nothing but punishment because of the imperfect, defective, soiled condition of our best works. Even the Christian's prayers when they are sincere, even his attendance upon the house of God, even his reading, study, hearing of God's Word, even his good works at home, the love of husband or wife, of children and parents, even his honesty in dealing with money, or whatever good works a Christian performs — none of these works are perfectly pure and sinless. Sin is mingled with all of them and spoils all of them. Every Christian must confess, "Behold I was shapen in iniquity and in sin did my mother conceive me" (Ps. 51:5). And this defiles our best works. Therefore in our Confessions we say, "We daily sin much and indeed deserve nothing but punishment." Scripture also expressly teaches: "For by grace are ye saved, through faith, and that not of yourselves; it is the gift of God, not of works, lest any man should boast" (Eph. 2:8-9).

But, even so, sanctification is of great importance, for, in the first place, by our sanctification *we glorify God*. Jesus calls attention to this by saying in the Sermon on the Mount: "Let your light so shine before men that they may see your good works *and glorify your Father* which is in heaven" (Matt. 5:16). Again Jesus teaches this when He compares the Christians to branches in the Vine, in Himself, and states: "Herein is My Father glorified, that ye bear much fruit; so shall ye be My disciples" (John 15:8).

In our Confessions this is brought out when the First Petition "Hallowed be Thy name" is explained to mean that the name of God be glorified and honored in this world by our believing His holy Word and leading a godly life according to it. Moreover, everyone knows that if church members, those who profess to be children of God, become guilty of sins which even the world despises, such as gossip, hateful behavior, unloving judging of others, intense selfishness, and the like, they profane the name of God. Therefore also St. Paul writes to the Jews that the name of God is blasphemed among the Gentiles because of the wicked lives of those who know the Law and want to teach and preach the Law to others (Rom. 2:17-24). Wherefore we say to one who talks glibly about the duty of a Christian and grows eloquent in condemning sin and wickedness but at the same time shows no fruits of true godliness in his own life, "What you do speaks so loud that I cannot hear what you say." Everyone of us knows what offense is given to weak Christians and to the world by the ungodly life, the lack of Christian virtues, in some who profess faith in Christ. On the other hand, the godly life of the Christians, through which they show the fruits of the Spirit, brings honor upon the Church of Jesus Christ and brings honor therefore upon the Word of God and the Bible. St. Paul was thinking of this when he wrote to the Christians at Rome: "First, I thank God through Jesus Christ for you all *that your faith is spoken of throughout the whole world*" (Rom. 1:8). St. Peter tells the Christians who were maligned and slandered that they should lead godly lives, because by this welldoing they would put to silence the ignorance of foolish men. He says: "Having your conversation honest among the Gentiles that whereas they speak against you as evildoers, they may by your good works, which they shall behold, glorify God in the day of visitation. . . . For so is the will of God that with welldoing ye may put to silence the ignorance of foolish men" (I Pet. 2:12, 15).

Should not all this move us to let our light shine? We have this light in God's Word. We have this light in the Savior, Jesus Christ. Christ indeed is in us, the Hope of glory. Let us beware of bringing shame and contempt upon the name of Christ and His

Church. Let us rather by our good works so impress the children of the world about us that they glorify God in the day of visitation.

In the second place, the godly life of the Christian is *a help in mission work*. St. Peter therefore writes: "Likewise, ye wives, be in subjection to your husbands, that if any obey not the Word, they also may without the Word be won by the conversation of the wives" (I Pet. 3:1). Patricius, the father of St. Augustine, was so impressed with the godliness and virtue of his wife that he gave earnest attention to God's Word and through this Word became a Christian (*Concordia Cyclopedia, s. v. Monica*). Augustine himself was impressed with the godliness not only of his mother, but of many other Christians, so that at one time he said to some of his friends: "Behold these plain, simple Christians, how happy they are in their faith, and we, who consider ourselves educated and superior to them, are miserable in our unbelief!" (*Confessiones*, Bk. VIII, ch. 8.) Tertullian and other early converts to Christianity were first of all impressed by the godliness and the decent lives of the early Christians. Some of the heathen therefore said: "Behold how these Christians love each other! They would die for one another, whereas we heathen wish to kill each other" (*Apologeticum*, ch. 39). We do not on this account make the life of a Christian a means of grace. But the true godly lives of Christians call attention to the means of grace. Therefore the Bible points out the importance of sanctification in the work of missions and in the work of winning souls for Christ.

In the third place, the fruits of the Spirit in the life of each Christian are to assure this Christian of the genuineness of his conversion and regeneration. God wants us to examine ourselves whether our godliness is genuine, whether it is a matter of the heart and not merely of the mouth and hand. Therefore St. Paul writes: "Examine yourselves whether ye be in the faith; prove your own selves. Know ye not your own selves how that Jesus Christ is in you, except ye be reprobates?" (II Cor. 13:5). The Christian is to examine himself according to the Ten Commandments and ask himself whether his sanctification is producing the fruits of the Spirit. And when he sees the fruits of the Spirit in himself and others, he is to rejoice and be comforted. If he is a lover of God's Word, then Jesus tells him: "Blessed are they which do hunger and thirst after righteousness, for they shall be filled"

(Matt. 5:6). If he is forgiving, then Jesus tells him: "Blessed are the merciful, for they shall obtain mercy" (Matt. 5:7). The Christian should ask himself whether he is "hail-fellow-well-met" with all ungodly people or whether he is ridiculed by the world. Then he is to remember what Jesus declares: "Blessed are ye when men shall hate you, and when they shall separate you from their company, and shall reproach you, and cast out your name as evil, for the Son of Man's sake. Rejoice ye in that day, and leap for joy; for, behold, your reward is great in heaven; for in the like manner did their fathers unto the prophets" (Luke 6:22-23). We Christians are to remember that though we must ask for forgiveness for our sins of weakness, must ask forgiveness also for the sins which pollute our good works, nevertheless these good works, imperfect though they are, should prove to others and to us that our faith is genuine, that our faith is not merely a matter of the mouth and head, but works by love: "For in Jesus Christ neither circumcision availeth anything nor uncircumcision, but faith which worketh by love." (Gal. 5:6.)

In the fourth place, the good works of the Christians, which are fruits of their sanctification, are to be rewarded richly, for God has solemnly and earnestly promised that. While it is true that even the good works of the Christians do not in themselves deserve these rewards, God has graciously promised to reward them nevertheless. These rewards are not rewards of merit, but rewards of grace. Therefore our sanctification is of utmost importance, because every good work which we perform is to be richly rewarded. The Bible is full of promises assuring the Christian that everything he does according to the will of God and as a fruit of his faith is to receive a rich reward. When Peter asked the Lord: "Behold, we have forsaken all and followed Thee, what shall we have therefore?" Jesus answered: "Verily I say unto you that ye which have followed Me, in the regeneration, when the Son of Man shall sit on the throne of His glory, ye also shall sit upon twelve thrones, judging the twelve tribes of Israel. And everyone that hath forsaken houses, or brethren, or sisters, or father, or mother, or wife, or children, or lands, for My name's sake, shall receive a hundredfold and shall inherit everlasting life." (Matt. 19:28-29.) In describing Judgment Day, Jesus tells us that the Lord will say to the faithful Christian: "Well done, thou good and faithful servant. Thou hast been faithful over a few things; I will make thee ruler over many things. Enter thou into the joy of thy Lord." (Matt. 25:21.) The promise of Jesus is well known: "And whosoever shall give to drink unto one of these little ones a cup of cold water only in the name of a disciple, verily I say unto you, he shall in no wise lose his reward" (Matt. 10:42). Again He promises rich reward to those who will receive little children, saying: "And whoso shall receive one such little child in My name receiveth Me" (Matt. 18:5). We Christians may therefore rest assured that nothing will pay such rich dividends as true godliness, true Christian good works, for God has promised: "Godliness is profitable unto all things, having promise of the life that now is and of that which is to come" (I Tim. 4:8).

Should not all these promises cheer us? Should they not encourage us not to be weary in welldoing, but to sow abundantly so that we may reap abundantly? How good it will be to hear the Lord say to us: "Come, ye blessed of My Father, inherit the kingdom prepared for you from the foundation of the world. For I was an hungred, and ye gave Me meat; I was thirsty, and ye gave Me drink; I was a stranger, and ye took Me in; naked, and ye clothed Me; I was sick, and ye visited Me; I was in prison, and ye came unto Me." (Matt. 25:34-36.)

VII. SANCTIFICATION WILL BE PERFECTED IN HEAVEN

The most comforting part of this doctrine is that which speaks of *the completion of sanctification in heaven*. The Bible tells us that if we expect to reap all the benfits of the Christian religion in this life, "we are of all men most miserable" (I Cor. 15:19). The highest fruits of our faith, the most blessed accomplishments of Christ's work, will be bestowed upon us in the heavenly home. "Here we know in part, but then we shall know even as we are known. Now we see through a glass, darkly, but then face to face." (I Cor. 13:12.) When that which is imperfect is done away, then perfection will be granted us. Here is the vale of tears, but there God will wipe away all tears from their eyes (Rev. 21:4). Here we must pray daily for forgiveness, there each one of us can say, "I shall be satisfied when I awake with Thy likeness" (Ps. 17:15).

"In Thy presence is fullness of joy; at Thy right hand there are pleasures forevermore" (Ps. 16:11). Here all our righteousnesses are as filthy rags, there we shall be saints made perfect in light, clothed with white robes and palms in our hands, before the throne of the Lamb in heaven (Rev. 7:9-14). No wonder St. Paul could say, anticipating this completed sanctification, "I have a desire to depart and to be with Christ, which is far better" (Phil. 1:23). We cannot better describe this completed sanctification in heaven than by using the words of the Apostle Peter: "Blessed be the God and Father of our Lord Jesus Christ, which according to His abundant mercy hath begotten us again unto a lively hope by the resurrection of Jesus Christ from the dead; to an inheritance incorruptible and undefiled and that fadeth not away, reserved in heaven for you, who are kept by the power of God through faith unto salvation, ready to be revealed in the last time" (I Pet. 1:3-5).

Synergism

I. INTRODUCTORY

CHRISTIANITY is a practical religion. Its doctrines have a direct bearing on human life. Whatever is taught in the great Source Book of Christian theology, the Holy Bible, is there revealed because it has something to contribute toward making human life and character what God wants them to be. If a man's religion is not functional, it is not Christian, whatever else it may be; for Christianity does not propose a mass of religious thought to man in order to satisfy his religious curiosity and to give him an opportunity to exercise his powers of synthesis or analysis. The Christian religion and Christian theology are neither the mother nor the daughter, neither the cause nor the effect, of mere speculation. The Greek philosopher Plato once remarked that it is difficult to discover the truth and when discovered by a few select minds — such as Plato's own — it is equally difficult to transmit it to others. But the Greek sage was apparently not very disconsolate because of this supposed state of affairs. To him the truth consisted in the apprehension of facts comparatively disassociated from daily life. The average man might live a successful and happy life without them. Their discovery was reserved for the privileged few, the intellectual aristocracy. Christianity views the matter differently. Its message is practical. It is to satisfy a need common to all men. Therefore it cannot be esoteric and eclectic. The doctrines of Christianity are there for all to ponder upon; for their truths are to be converted by all into the gold coin of good, God-pleasing lives.

Especially the Lutheran Church has always recognized this great and universal importance of doctrine. She has, in consequence, become the "church of the theologians." Her sons have delved deeply into the depths of the divine mysteries. Her Chemnitzes and Gerhards, her Walthers and Piepers — to say nothing of her "Father Luther" — have echoed the voice of the Spirit that speaks in Scripture with a clarity and fidelity that have excited the holy envy of many and ought to be the admiration of all. And for *all* they and other Lutheran divines wrote. They addressed themselves not merely to professional theologians, but to Christians as such; for the doctrines of Christianity are intended for all men, because they are needed by all men. This emphasis on the study of Christian doctrine by *all* is very appropriately seen at work also in the District conventions of our Synod. Preacher and teacher and layman there meditate upon the revelation of God's saving truth and together admire the stately structure of Christian doctrine.

And they find it to be marvelously joined together. We often speak of the "body of Christian doctrine." The expression itself is not found in Scripture, but what it expresses certainly is. The human body is an organism. It consists of different members animated by a common life. Though the members and organs have differing functions, all minister to the common life. None exist alone and by themselves. They are very largely dependent upon one another. If one is injured, all more or less suffer, for the life they have in common is endangered or deformed. It is just so with Christian doctrine. Its truths are like the members of the body. They perform different functions in God's plan of salvation and in its realization in the spiritual life of man, but all are to minister to that spiritual life. If, then, a doctrine is perverted and falsified, the entire body of Christian truth is endangered, and man's spiritual life suffers. The damage done may, of course, be different in degree. A man will find it more difficult to live without a leg than without a finger; and he will find it impossible to live without a heart. Similarly, spiritual life is more gravely endangered by certain false doctrines than by others; while all spiritual life is impossible without the heart of Christian doctrine, justification by faith. Heart diseases are, therefore, among the most dangerous of sicknesses. Such is the heresy we are to examine these days. It is a disease that weakens the very heart of Christian doctrine.

A superficial diagnosis may not reveal this fact. The heresy of synergism has its immediate roots in the doctrine of the spiritual condition of natural man, but, like a malignant tumor, it sends out roots into other doctrines, notably into the doctrines of conversion and justification. At the same time, it must be confessed that the propounders of this false teaching professed to stand squarely on the doctrine of justification by faith alone. From the sixteenth to the twentieth century they indignantly denounced as a calumny the charge that they were perverting that central doctrine of Christian theology. It is not for us to determine the degree of their sincerity or insincerity, though, to say the least, it is surprising to hear *Lutheran* theologians contend that synergism does not vitiate that treasure of their Church, the *sola fide*. Surely, these men must know that Christian doctrine is not atomistic, that its teachings do not lie aside of one another like so many unconnected pieces of wood, but that, as the branches on a tree, they are parts of a living organism. The interrelation and interdependence of Christian doctrine are such that an error in one doctrine is not without its vitiating effect upon others. In order to misspell a word it is not necessary to misplace all of its letters. The word will be wrong if *one* of its letters is out of place.

But apparently this doctrinal interdependence is often not fully realized even by theologians. There may be various reasons for this lack of discernment. Perhaps a man's study of theology has not been sufficiently comprehensive; or perhaps he is the victim of a prejudice which blinds his eyes to the most convincing evidence. Thus Zwingli was so prejudiced against the real presence of Christ's body and blood in the Sacrament that "is" no longer meant "is" to him. At times one meets people who tenaciously cling to a false doctrine which, if consistently carried out, would make saving faith practically impossible. But with a happy inconsistency the good people do not accept the doctrinal corollaries and implications of their false views. Gustav Kawerau says of Melanchthon: "To the doctrines of the natural corruption of man and of justification by faith alone he immovably adhered; every meritorious work of man is excluded" (*Realencyklopaedie* 19, 230, 56 f.). Nay, not infrequently theologians deny in practice what they assert in theory. Of such people Luther told Erasmus: "When they are engaged in words and disputations, they are one thing; but another when they come to experience and practice" (Luther, *Bondage*, 89), and

Dr. Pieper calls attention to the same "happy inconsistency" on the part of synergists, saying: "Before God and in their private prayers (*in ihrem Gebetkaemmerlein*) they do not believe their own doctrine" (Pieper, *Dogmatik* I, p. 31).

In the following essay on the heresy of synergism we shall have to refer to individuals and to church bodies by name. We desire it to be clearly understood that we pass our judgments on their doctrines rather than on their personal spiritual state and condition. We can only hope that they were better than the creed they professed. We must fault them as theologians, but we may not denounce them as apostates. How consistently and persistently they personally held to the error into which they had lapsed it is both impossible and unnecessary for us to judge. Only God knows that. "Who art thou that judgest another man's servant? To his own Master he standeth or falleth" (Rom. 14:4).

II. THE QUESTION BEFORE US

The false doctrine we are to examine developed out of an attempt to solve an apparent contradiction.

Holy Writ was found to teach the native corruption of man. The tragic fall of man into sin had not had a merely negative effect upon him. It had not only deprived man's nature of its concreated perfect knowledge of its Maker and its complete conformity to His will, but it had also thoroughly perverted its powers and capacities, leaving to him only the power to do evil, sin, iniquity. Henceforth human nature was like a tilted pencil. If left to itself, it could proceed only in one direction; it would inevitably fall into sin, for it was born with a natural inclination to evil only and to all that is evil. And since all men are the descendants of the first human sinners, it would seem to follow, aside even from Scripture pronouncements on this head, that the degree of this natural corruption would be alike in all men. And so it is. Scripture says: "That which is born of the flesh is flesh" (John 3:6). These words of Jesus posit the same spiritual impotence and corruption for all men. Therefore our Formula of Concord correctly says: "The horrible, dreadful hereditary malady by which the entire nature is corrupted should above all things be regarded and recognized as sin indeed, yea, as the chief sin — (Human nature is) thoroughly and utterly infected and corrupted before God by original sin, as by a spiritual leprosy" (*Triglot*, 861).

But Holy Writ teaches with equal clarity that God's love perfected a redemption from the penalty of eternal death which His holiness and justice had to pronounce over the world of sinners: "For God so loved the world that He gave His only-begotten Son, that whosoever believeth in Him should not perish but have everlasting life" (John 3:16). Redemption is as extensive as sin. It is all-inclusive. No one is lost because God has not loved him, Christ has not saved him, and the Spirit has not desired to convert him; for "(God) will have all men to be saved and to come unto the knowledge of the truth" (I Tim. 2:4). "As I live, saith the Lord God, I have no pleasure in the death of the wicked" (Ezek. 33:11); by My shame and sorrow, by My thorny crown and cruel Cross, — as I die, says Jesus, I have no pleasure in the death of the wicked. God's saving grace is universal; for "God was in Christ, reconciling the world unto Himself, not imputing their trespasses unto them" (II Cor. 5:19). Salvation *has* been fully prepared for all men. It is a settled historical fact, like the discovery of America. And facts exist irrespective of man's knowledge of them or his acceptance of them. Just so God has issued a blanket forgiveness to the entire world of sinners. This is frequently called "objective justification" in theological parlance.

But its precious comfort will accrue to the individual only if and when he personalizes it by faith. The Amen of personal assent to, and acceptance of, the blessed state of affairs revealed in "objective justification" makes this justification subjectively effective. Faith is simply the hand that accepts the gift of God's pardon, the arm that clings to Christ, the Rock of Ages, and saves us from the angry storms of guilt and sin. "The just shall live by faith," Paul assured the Galatians (3:11). "He that believeth . . . shall be saved," Jesus told His disciples (Mark 16:16). This is known as "subjective justification." It is not essentially different from "objective justification." It is the personalizing of its benefits.

However, the question now arises: how is this "personalizing" effected, that is, just how and why does a man come to faith? Theoretically, three possibilities exist. Either God alone brings a man to faith, or man works faith within himself, or he is converted by the co-operative effort of God and himself. Let us state these alternatives a little more fully. According to the first of these views, God alone is active in bringing man to faith. He is the Converter who makes man the converted. The human soul comes to recognize Christ as its Savior by powers that are brought to bear upon it entirely from *without*. According to the second view, man, as it were, weighs the evidence for and against acceptance of God's overture of love and thereupon decides by the strength of spiritual powers that are natural to him to become a Christian. He has, in the strictest sense of the word, converted himself. According to the third view of the matter, a man's conversion is to be credited neither entirely to God nor entirely to himself. It is held that either God begins the conversion and man completes it, or that man, however feeble, begins it and God completes it.

Now, on the basis of the doctrinal presuppositions posited above, the total depravity of natural man and the universal grace of God, it would seem to follow that either all men are saved by the grace of God or that all are lost because of their depravity, sin and guilt. But Scripture teaches that some are saved by the grace of God, while others are lost by their own fault. Whence the differing result from the same premises? It ought to be observed that no difficulty whatever exists when the saved and the lost are considered by themselves. Concerning these two classes the teaching of Holy Writ is very clear. On the one hand, we are told that the sinner who is converted and ultimately enters heaven has no one to thank for his salvation but God. The sinner himself, we are emphatically assured, contributed absolutely nothing toward this blessed consummation. On the other hand, God's Word teaches that the sinner who is not converted and therefore ultimately goes to hell has no one to blame for his damnation but himself, his unbelief, his resistance to the converting operations of the Holy Spirit. But now, when these two classes, the saved and the lost, are compared with each other, we are placed squarely before a baffling mystery. If all are equally impotent, and God wants all to be saved, and only He can save all, why are some saved and not all, or, why are some lost and not all? The mystery would be solved if the universal grace of God could be proved to be specific and restricted after all. This is the heresy of Calvinism. Or the difference would be accounted for if it could be proved that men are not by nature altogether spiritually dead, and that, in consequence, the reaction of men to the offer of God's grace is different, some less stubbornly and violently resisting the converting efforts of the Spirit than others. This is, generally speaking, the heresy of synergism. Both of these attempted solutions no doubt dispel the mystery, but they do it at the expense of Scripture. However, that is a price no Christian ought to be willing to pay. But a man can have his "solution" for nothing less. We shall now point out that the synergistic answer of reason to the question before us is, indeed, a patent violation of Scripture.

III. THE ANSWER OF REASON

The heresy of synergism may no doubt be found in every age of the Christian Church. It is as old as sin itself. Its principle is the prolific mother of all sin: exaltation of man, his worth and his capacities at the expense of God. The popularity of synergism, so to speak, and its constant recurrence within the Church are to be looked for in the appeal of this error to the vanity of man. Sin is essentially selfishness, and synergism is a form of selfishness, self-aggrandizement.

Pelagianism is often bracketed with synergism, but in reality it goes beyond synergism. Pelagius (*Realencyklopaedie*, 15, p. 748 f.) was a British monk who lived in the opening years of the fifth century. He was a fair scholar but a shallow thinker with little spiritual depth and experience. This man taught that human nature is morally indifferent or neutral at birth. According to Pelagius, a man needed merely to develop his moral nature in order to be worthy of heaven. This bold religious naturalism needed neither conversion nor Christ. It went beyond synergism, which means co-operation, and recognized man as the sole source and author of his salvation. Various synods condemned this brazen heresy but did not succeed in eliminating its virus from Christendom.

In a modified form the principles of Pelagius continued to disturb the Church by what became known as Semi-Pelagianism. According to this doctrinal aberration, man's spiritual powers are, indeed, no longer what they were before the fall into sin, but they are only partially weakened. If and when assisted by the grace of God, the sinner can work out his own salvation. The Semi-Pelagians clearly made conversion and salvation matters of co-operation. One of them bluntly said that man's free will and God's grace co-operate as the divine and human natures do in the person of Christ. But the Church condemned also this heresy in a number of synods, about the last quarter of the fifth century. However, Semi-Pelagianism continued to trouble and endanger the spiritual life of Christendom throughout the succeeding centuries.

At the time of the Reformation, when the entire field of Christian doctrine was carefully re-examined, the question before us, the presence of residuary spiritual powers in natural man, was also thoroughly ventilated. Some again contended for the presence of such powers, however feeble they professed them to be. These people became known as synergists. Dr. P. Schaff says the error of these men was "a refined evangelical modification of Semi-Pelagianism," and adds: "The defect of the synergistic theory is the idea of a partnership between God and man, and a corresponding division of work and merit" (Schaff, *Creeds*, I, 271). Frequently the only difference discoverable between a Semi-Pelagianist and a synergist is the following: the former holds that man may begin and God must complete the work of conversion; the latter holds that God must begin and man can complete it (Pieper, *Dogmatik*, II, 547). Both are opposed to what is known as monergism, the teaching that God alone can bring a man to faith.

How does the synergist attempt to prove his position to be the correct one? He likes to operate with reason and logic, and to appeal to psychology and kindred sciences. Now, this is not the place to treat at length of the use and the abuse of reason in religion nor to illustrate that, entirely aside from Scripture testimony concerning its own sole and supreme authority, an appeal to reason is not at all an approved way to arrive at certainty and unanimity. Suffice it to say that nothing but a clear passage of Scripture can decide a theological question for us. At the same time we do not hesitate to examine the "proofs" drawn from reason by synergists and others, since experience has taught us that they frequently are not reasonable at all but specious and sophistical. At times they becloud the issue by slightly changing the subject. Thus, we never had a quarrel with those who say that man is capable of conversion if they merely mean to assert that man can be converted. Luther bluntly told quibbling Erasmus: "This power, that is, fitness, or (as the Sophists term it) 'disposition-quality,' and 'passive aptitude' (of man for conversion), this I also confess. And who does not know that this is not in trees or beasts? For, (as they say) Heaven was not made for geese" (Luther, *Bondage*, 76; cp. *Triglot*, 891).

Again, synergists have contended: if man can do nothing to bring about his conversion, he is certain to become careless and fatalistic about the entire matter, telling himself, as it were, "What difference will my attitude and actions make? If I am to be converted, *God* must do it; and if I am to be saved, God *will* do it." To this specious argument Luther replied: "We do all resist God, but the Holy Spirit draws us when He wills, at His own time, through the office of the ministry; therefore one ought always highly to esteem the preached Word and to hear it; the people who despise the preached Word soon become heretics" (Luther, XXII:386). If a man is really sincere, the solemn fact that he can contribute nothing whatever toward his conversion will persuade him diligently and prayerfully to use all the means of grace.

But let us proceed to look at the so-called proofs taken from Scripture by the synergists. Explicitly, we are told, the sinner is called upon to repent in both the Old and the New Testament, by the Prophets, by Christ Himself, and by His Apostles. Mark 1:15 the Savior cries: "Repent and believe the Gospel." In his Pentecostal sermon, Peter exclaims: "Repent!" (Acts 2:38). It were cruel mockery, we are assured, to command a person to do what one is convinced he is not able to do. This call to repentance, it is said, certainly implies that man has the powers to heed it. We reply: Is this implication not more than the synergists themselves are willing to allow to natural man? If the command to repent implies any such powers as the synergist indicates, it can fairly be understood only in the Pelagian sense, and man must be conceded the ability to perform the entire work of his conversion. No! It is evident that the command to repent merely reveals the earnest desire of God for man's salvation and the urgent necessity of repentance to bring this about. And as to the imperative form, — long ago Luther pointed out that it does not necessarily imply anything whatever that is synergistical. Were it so, the Reformer said, God could not command a man to keep His holy Law; for the Lord knows man is not able to do so. (Walch 18, 1787 f.; cp. *Lehre und Wehre* 43, 134 f., Stoeckhardt.) The case is satisfactorily covered by the Latin axiom: *A debito non valet consequentia ad posse,* which may be freely rendered: One may not draw a valid deduction as to what a man *can* do from what he *ought* to do.

Bereft of this "proof", the synergist turns in a different direction and says: But if a man is entirely passive in the moment of his conversion, then that great change is a purely mechanical one, non-moral in its nature. We reply: According to Scripture, conversion is an act of which a man is not only conscious, but in which his soul is very active. Conversion is brought about neither against the will of man nor without it. It neither destroys nor abolishes the functions of the human will. On the contrary, the call to repentance is addressed to man's will. The commonest New Testament term for conversion is *metanoein*. This means, etymologically, "to change one's mind." There is nothing mechanical about that. But a man's mind may be changed either by himself or by some outside influence, some persuasion brought to bear upon him by a friend or a stranger. In order to be a personal, ethical, conscious change, conversion need not be self-originated. Adam's creation out of dust, man's physical conception and birth, the resurrection of dead bodies unto life, — all are acts towards which he has contributed nothing nor can contribute anything whatever. Are these acts, therefore, to be considered unethical and unworthy of a man? Nor let anyone object to this comparison of the bestowal of physical life on the one hand and of spiritual life on the other hand. Holy Writ itself parallelizes the two in such passages as Eph. 1:19-20; 2:10; II Cor. 4:6; John 1:12-13. (See Pieper, *Dogmatik*, II, 572.)

But, the synergist argues, it ought at least be granted that it is man who makes his own conversion *a reality*, though God must be said to make it a possibility. The argument, more fully stated, runs like this: God restores in man, spiritually dead by nature, the power to choose between faith and unbelief; and in and by this God-created power man converts himself. Synergists seem to en-

Synergism 309

vision this restored freedom of choice something like the freedom of the will possessed by Adam and Eve before the Fall. But theirs is untenable ground. Of natural man Scripture says, I Cor. 2:14: "(He) receiveth not the things of the Spirit of God; . . . neither *can* he know them (as the saving truth)." Consequently, the man who *can* accept the Gospel *has* accepted it; he is no longer natural man, but is converted. Paul tells the Philippians: "It is God which worketh in you both to will and to do of His good pleasure," (2:3). Besides, this entire argument is sophistical. If God merely works the ability to choose Christ, but man must make this choice an actuality, the credit for this fact, that some do make this choice while others do not, must be given to man and not to God. In consequence, the really determining factor must lie in *man* irrespective of any gifts of powers conferred on him by God. This fact would, in principle, make man the author of his own salvation. When the monergism of grace is denied, one inevitably arrives at the heretical dualism of *nature* and *grace*.

However, the synergists offer further "proof" in an attempt to make good their position. Their adducing a passage like Luke 7:30 and their manner of handling it are typical. The resultant incongruous mixture of rationalization and Scripture is also characteristic. Luke 7:30 we are told: "But the Pharisees and lawyers rejected the counsel of God against themselves, being not baptized of him (John)." The synergistic syllogism some profess to find in these words is the following: The persons named could refuse the call of John to repentance; therefore they might also have at least ceased to refuse it. We reply, to begin with, if a syllogism of opposites is at all permissible at Luke 7:30, it must, consistently carried out, run like this: Since the "Pharisees and lawyers" could prevent their conversion, they must also have been able to bring about their conversion. Not synergism but the monergism of man results from such syllogistic manipulation of Luke 7:30. (*Lehre und Wehre*, 45, 168, Stoeckhardt.) But that is again more than synergists are willing to concede. The entire procedure of arriving at new and additional truths by drawing deductions from Scriptural doctrines according to the rules of logic and the canons of human reason is, to say the very least, a most hazardous undertaking. Such an undertaking is, as a matter of fact, a gross violation of a fundamental principle of sound Bible interpretation. Doctrines are to be based on the words of Scripture and on nothing besides. At Luke 7:30 we are merely told the reason for the continued unbelief of the "Pharisees and lawyers." Why and how others heeded the call of John to repentance and Baptism is to be learned from passages of Scripture which treat of the origin of faith.

A passage similarly misinterpreted by synergists is Matt. 23:37: "O Jerusalem, Jerusalem, thou that killest the Prophets and stonest them which are sent unto thee, how often would I have gathered thy children together, even as a hen gathereth her chickens under her wings, and ye would not!" Those who hold that natural man can, at least feebly, co-operate with the Spirit in bringing about his conversion find, or rather constitute, a false contrast in this passage. Jesus does not fault the people of Jerusalem for not willing what they might of themselves have willed. The contrast is plainly between Christ's attitude and their attitude. "How often would *I*" — "and (but) *ye* would not." The grim fact that they *could* not of themselves have willed their conversion does not make the words of Jesus a cruel mockery, though it *does* bring a note of sadness into them. Man's spiritual impotence does not remove his responsibility and guilt. But the synergists profess to find at least the desire of man for his conversion implied in Matt. 23:37. They argue thus: If the Jerusalemites remained in unbelief because they refused to accept Christ, those who have come to faith must have done so because they were willing to accept Christ. This argument loses sight of two facts. First, they who show themselves "willing to accept Christ" *are* already converted, for to natural men the acceptance of Christ for personal salvation is foolishness and nonsense (I Cor. 2:14), and impossible (Eph. 2:1, 5). Secondly, the question *why* they declared themselves willing to receive Christ still remains unanswered. Scripture answers *this* question elsewhere and, as we shall see, *not* in the synergistic manner. The natural antagonism of man to the Gospel of Christ is never removed by man himself.

But, we are asked, may one not at least hold that natural man has the ability to *cease* his resistance against the offer of God's pardoning grace in Christ? In this connection our attention is called to Acts 7:51. Stephen there told the Jerusalemites: "Ye stiffnecked and uncircumcised in heart and ears, ye do always resist the Holy

Ghost." Does it not plainly appear from these words, we are asked, that, at least, man can cease his stubborn resistance to the converting grace of God? It is true, some synergists add, that by nature *all* men resist the Spirit's operations, but so long as they do not harden themselves and *stubbornly,* consciously, and voluntarily (*mutwillig*) refuse to accept Christ, their conversion will be brought about. After all, we are assured, this is little enough to expect of man. In fact, it is something purely negative, nothing positively good, practically a mere nothing (*Lehre und Wehre,* 58, 394 ff.).

We reply, this is, indeed, an odd state of affairs! The weighty question before us is: Since God wants *all* men to be saved, and all are *equally* corrupt by nature, and *only faith* in Christ can save them, why do *some* believe, while *others* remain in unbelief? And now we are expected to believe that the decisive factor is "something purely negative, practically a mere nothing." We are assured that this "something" is not meritorious in the eyes of God, and yet we are expected to consider it the indispensable prerequisite in man for his conversion, something necessary in addition to the converting grace of God. It is evident that this something, by whatever name it may be called, whether "proper attitude of submissiveness" or "the ability to appropriate the grace of God" (*facultas se applicandi ad gratiam*) or "the cessation of stubborn resistance," it is evident that we are dealing with theological vagaries that would properly be considered absurd and ridiculous if they were not such a travesty of Holy Scripture and such a danger to the spiritual life of Christians.

To make matters worse, the synergist does not really answer the question before us. He merely pushes the mystery back a little farther. He exchanges a theological problem for a psychological one (*Lehre und Wehre,* 58, 398 f.). When the synergist is asked why one sinner ceases his stubborn resistance to the offer of God's grace while another continues it, he sagely replies: "That is a hitherto unexplained psychological mystery." We reply: A mystery it certainly is, particularly also in view of the fact that, *according to synergistic theories,* men, all of whom instinctively desire to be happy and blessed, are made aware of the fact, when the Gospel is preached to them, that their eternal salvation depends upon their proper deportment (*rechtes Verhalten*) toward it. Thus the attempt of a rationalizing synergism to solve the problem before us leads us into a dead-end street. Synergism answers the question and satisfies the restless curiosity of man as little as Scripture does.

Why, then, do succeeding generations of theologians continue the attempt to solve the unsolvable? One reason, no doubt, is the fact that every new generation of religious thinkers is as curious as the preceding one and flatters itself with the hope that it may succeed where others have failed. For some people the unknowable is irresistibly attractive. Its problems seem like a personal challenge to them. Thus Melanchthon confessed to be troubled by the question "why Saul was rejected, David accepted" (Pieper, *Dogmatik*, II, p. 583). Since Scripture nowhere answers the question, man sets out in quest of his own answer and, upon his return to Scripture, strives to bring his answer into harmony with the Word. The sad result is that in his effort to find out more than God has revealed, man believes less than God has disclosed in His Word.

Nor ought another factor be lost sight of. It is shamefully natural for man to think of his return to his Father's house in terms of human efforts. Since his very conscience tells him that he has forfeited favor and fellowship with God by his evil works, he draws the natural conclusion that his return to God must, at least in part, be the reward of efforts of his own. But what does Scripture teach on this point?

IV. THE ANSWER OF SCRIPTURE

Scripture teaches that natural man is spiritually dead. Jesus told the Jews that the man who has come to faith in Him "is passed from death unto life" (John 5:24). Nowhere does the Bible speak of the condition of the soul of natural man as mere spiritual weakness or merely lying in a spiritual coma. It teaches the entire absence of every spark of spiritual life. Holy Writ pictures natural men as spiritual corpses. Since the fall of man all human souls are stillborn. Therefore Paul tells the Ephesians (2:1): "You . . . were dead in (through) trespasses and sins" before your conversion.

We are certainly not "eisegetically" importing anything into such passages if we find total spiritual impotence expressed in them. Only that can be the point of comparison. Natural man is as utterly bereft of spiritual life as a corpse is of physical life. You

Synergism 313

may call to a corpse, threaten it and beat it or speak kindly to it and caress it, but there will be no response, not the slightest sign of recognition and reaction. Such is natural man in spiritual things. He can do nothing, say nothing, be nothing spiritually good, because he is a spiritual corpse, so to speak. Paul complains: "I know that in me (that is, in my flesh,) dwelleth no good thing" (Rom. 7:18).

But Holy Writ has still more humiliating things to say of natural man. Man's soul is not only dead to everything spiritually good, but it is alive and sympathetic to matters and relations of the opposite nature. Man is not merely indifferent to spiritual things; he is antagonistic to them by nature. In consequence, he is even worse than a corpse in this respect that by nature he stubbornly resists every effort to give life to his dead soul. The Gospel not only makes no sense to him, it seems nonsense to him, it is "foolishness unto him," as Paul puts it. (I Cor. 2:14; see *Triglot*, pp. 887, 905.) The same Apostle tells the Romans that the unconverted mind of man, or, as he expresses it, "the carnal mind, is enmity against God" (Rom. 8:7). It is absurd to expect a soul so conditioned to cooperate with God in its conversion. Nothing such people do has God's approval, or, to use the words of Paul again: "They that are in the flesh cannot please God" (Rom. 8:8).

In view of this utter spiritual impotence of man, we are not surprised to find Scripture very emphatically teaching that the working of God's grace is activity in the act of conversion. Whatever "synergism" there is *follows* upon conversion and is itself the effect of God's monergism. So far as causative energy in conversion is concerned, man is never the actor but merely the acted-upon. Faith is not partly his achievement. It is in every instance a pure gift of God. The Ephesians are reminded (2:8-10): "By grace are ye saved, through faith, and that not of yourselves; it is the gift of God; not of works, lest any man should boast. For we are *His* workmanship, created in Christ Jesus." The Philippians are told: "Unto you it is given ... to believe on Him (Christ)." The Greek word literally says, "The grace was bestowed upon you" to believe; and at the very base of the concept "grace" lies the idea of undeservedness. There is nothing here of synergism.

Again, Jesus, describing the cause and origin of faith, assures the Jews: "No man can come to Me, except the Father ... draw him" (John 6:44). What our Lord meant by this "drawing" is plain from verses 64 and 65. There Jesus is introduced as saying: "There are some of you that believe not. . . . Therefore said I unto you that no man can come unto Me, except it (such "coming-believing") were given unto him of (by) My Father." These words also picture faith as the gift of God, not the self-originated decision of man. (*Lehre und Wehre*, 43, 331 ff.) To prevent any misinterpretation of this passage, it is, we trust, almost unnecessary to call attention to a remark Luther somewhere makes to the effect that God does not draw man by the hair of his head or the back of his neck, but by his heart and his will. "He makes the unwilling willing," Augustine says. The comparison of conversion to a being drawn to Christ calls to mind a passage of Paul in which both the ability and the desire to believe in Christ are said to be lacking in natural man. We refer to Romans 9:16: "So, then, it is not of him that willeth, nor of him that runneth, but of God that showeth mercy." This verse may be paraphrased thus: "From this self-determining principle of God's actions it follows that it is neither the will nor the efforts of a man which determine his conversion, but solely the converting grace which it pleases God to bestow upon him."

This same great truth is driven home by other expressions of Scripture. The Spirit of God makes it difficult for man to believe in synergism; for the point of comparison is ever the complete spiritual powerlessness of natural man. A notable passage is II Cor. 4:6: "God, who commanded the light to shine out of darkness, hath shined in our hearts to give the light of the knowledge of the glory of God in the face of Jesus Christ." The act of conversion is compared at this place to the turning from darkness, the Scriptural symbol of ignorance and sin, to light, the symbol of truth and holiness. Similarly, Paul says to the Colossians (1:13): God "hath delivered us from the power of darkness and hath translated us (transferred, carried us over) into the kingdom of His dear Son." In the passage from II Corinthians the origin of faith is illustrated by a parallelization with the creation of light as recorded in Genesis 1. Just as there certainly was no human co-operation in the creation of light for the physical world, so the creation of faith, spiritual light in the midnight — not twilight — of human ignorance and unbelief, is entirely the work of God Almighty alone.

This appears also from passages such as Eph. 4:24 and II Cor. 5:17. At the former place the Ephesians are assured that the new spiritual life of Christians is a creation. It it said: "Put on the new man, which after God is created in righteousness and true holiness." Now, creation is admittedly the prerogative of God alone. To make something out of nothing is an attribute of divinity; and that is what God is said to do when He converts man. He finds nothing in man with which to work, the repair or development of which would make the sinner a new man. God must create the Christian in the sinner out of nothing. That is the reason Paul says: "If any man be in Christ, he is a new creature. . . . Behold, all things are become new" (II Cor. 5:17). That in the face of such passages anyone can still believe in a residue, however small, of spiritual powers in natural man, powers with which he may engage in synergistic activities, constitutes one of the sad chapters in the history of doctrine.

To conclude this section of our essay, it may be pointed out that every standing ground for synergistic notions is cut away also by passages in which believers and unbelievers are compared and contrasted. One such passage is II Thess. 2:10-14. In this Scripture we are told that the victims of Antichrist will be those who "believed not the truth, but had pleasure in unrighteousness." Thereupon the Apostle turns to address the Christians. But he significantly does *not* continue thus: But you have believed the truth. They had, indeed, done so. But Paul's specific intention is to call attention to the *source* of their love of saving truth, to the origin of their faith. He therefore carries forward the thought like this: "But we are bound to give thanks alway to God for you, brethren beloved of the Lord, because God hath from the beginning chosen you to salvation through sanctification of the Spirit and belief of the truth: whereunto He called you by our Gospel." Soli *Deo* gloria! The Apostle thanks God for the conversion of the Thessalonian Christians; he recognizes *His* to be the "kingdom and the power and the glory forever and ever." Human reason may flatter itself with the notion that man may share the power and glory of his conversion, but the Apostle knows nothing of such synergistic filching of divine prerogatives. In common with all inspired penmen of Holy Writ he teaches: If a man comes to faith, it is because God's creative activity has attained its spiritual end in him; if a man continues in unbelief, it is because he has refused to accept the offer of God's pardoning love. *Soli Deo gloria!*

V. "BY THEIR FRUITS YE SHALL KNOW THEM"

The mystery remains, a gap, as it were, in the structure of Christian doctrine, but the foundation and the pillars of Christian truth stay intact and secure, whereas the synergist, in an effort to explain all and to systematize all, weakens the entire structure of Christian doctrine and undermines its very foundation. This is the price he pays for refusing to "bring into captivity every thought to the obedience of Christ." He is "penny-wise and pound-foolish." The consistent synergist finds that the spirit of rationalization which he conjured up to help him in his systematizing stays on to plague him. It demands consistency; and this consistency works havoc with Scripture doctrine. (*Lehre und Wehre*, 58, 401.)

Synergism cannot consistently retain the Biblical doctrine of original sin, according to which man is spiritually worthless by nature. We have seen that its effort to find neutral ground, on which the soul of man makes its choice of faith or continued unbelief by the use of powers conferred on it by God's Spirit, is futile. No such theological no-man's-land, no such neutral zone, exists; and if the *unconverted* can of himself not merely reject, but also *accept*, the offer of God's grace, then he cannot be totally corrupt by nature as Scripture pictures him to be. In that event there must be something spiritually good in man; and he who diligently uses this remnant of good within him comes to faith and is saved.

But does the synergist not see what he has done to the central doctrine of Scripture, the justification of a man before his God? According to Holy Writ, a man is justified by grace through faith for Christ's sake. This precious revelation is the very heart and soul of the Christian religion. It is, therefore, attested by scores of passages, among them John 3:16; Rom. 3:23-25, 28; Eph. 2:8, 9; II Cor. 5:19, and many others. Almost all other doctrines of

Scripture are related to justification as either its antecedents or its consequents and cannot be corrupted without spreading to it their infection. Look at the case in hand! If natural men possess dormant germs of spiritual good, they do not need a Savior who tells them: "Without Me ye can do nothing" (John 15:5). The gospel for the synergist is the gospel of the Pharisee who thanked God that he was not as other men are. However, it will be remembered that the Pharisee returned to his house unjustified. The sort of gospel the consistent synergist relies upon is *not* the Gospel of Scripture. It is true, he does not stress merit so bluntly and brazenly as the Pharisee, the Romanist, and the Pelagian. In fact, he professes to eliminate all merit from the "better conduct of man, his cessation of stubborn resistance, and his greater submissiveness to the call of God's grace." But his protestations do not impress us. He is juggling words. If the enumerated attitudes spell the difference between faith and unbelief, heaven and hell, if their presence or absence in a man determine the efficaciousness of the call, they *must* have merit, or God's choice possesses that very supposed arbitrariness from which the synergists profess to be so anxious to save it.

From what has been said, it follows that also faith, in the sense of the New Testament, is impossible for the consistent synergist. According to Scripture, saving faith is not merely a general trust in the mercy of God. Justifying faith is something very specific. It is the conviction that one's sins have been forgiven by God because of the atonement wrought by Jesus Christ, and that one has done nothing, can and need do nothing whatever, to merit this forgiveness. The Holy Spirit works only *this* sort of faith in man. Every other faith, no matter how sincere and firm the conviction may be, is utterly worthless as a means of salvation. It is man-made. To it the solemn words of Jesus apply: "Every plant which My heavenly Father hath not planted shall be rooted up" (Matt. 15:13). Now, the faith of the consistent synergist is such a plant. It does not rest upon the grace of Christ alone. However, as the German text of the Apology puts it: "Sooft die Schrift vom Glauben redet, meint sie den Glauben, der auf lauter Gnade baut" (*Triglot*, 136), that is, "Whenever Scripture speaks of faith, it means the faith that bases itself on grace alone." But this is not the faith of the sincere synergist. He believes saving faith to be something for which he must condition himself or *has* fitted himself by proper deportment. He fancies that it rests, at least in part, upon something within him. To the degree in which it does this, it is a *caricature* of Christian faith.

The same stricture applies to the sanctification of the synergist. According to Scripture, genuine sanctification is the fruit of faith; it is the result of justification by reliance upon Christ alone. But a fruit is as good as the tree on which it grows. Strangely enough, however, there have been synergists who have bluntly expressed the fear that the sinner would inevitably be indifferent to personal sanctification if he were taught that of himself he is spiritually impotent. Such a doctrine, it was contended, would paralyze all initiative. However, Scripture assures us, and experience teaches, that it is just the other way around. The penitent sinner who realizes his utter corruption and his entire spiritual helplessness will, in despair of himself, flee for help to the Lord Jesus. Nothing in his hands he'll bring, simply to the Cross he'll cling. But that is the very nature of the faith that inevitably sanctifies because it justifies; it is "the faith which worketh (expresses its vital power) by love," as Paul says (Gal. 5:6). The same Apostle assures the Philippians that truly good works or, as he calls them, "the fruits of righteousness, are by Jesus Christ" (Phil. 1:11). In a series of articles that appeared in *Lehre und Wehre* in 1882, Dr. W. Sihler contended that, strictly speaking, the "sanctification" of the consistent synergist is no better than that of the respectable unbeliever. This may seem to be a severe judgment, but we have yet to come upon a successful refutation of Dr. Sihler's articles.

Finally, no synergist as such can be certain of his ultimate salvation. Some have even cautioned against such certainty. The caution is quite unnecessary from the standpoint of synergism; for no man who hopes to be saved by looking to Christ *and himself,* his better deportment," his "cessation of stubborn resistance," or by whatever name he chooses to call his synergistic efforts, *can* ever be certain of his salvation. The consistent synergist may as well ask the sinner to be certain of his ultimate damnation; for the man who professedly and personally rejects the *sola fide* (salvation by faith alone) is not living in a state of grace; he is no Christian.

In this manner the virus of synergism poisons the blood stream of Christian doctrine. It must be evident to all that the error of synergism is not peripheral to the body of Scripture truth. It is true, all heresy, every departure from Holy Writ, is to be scored and rejected, but those false doctrines in particular are to call forth our energetic protest and arouse our constant watchfulness which strike at the heart of our holy Faith, at the doctrine of justification by faith alone. The heresy of synergism does that very thing. It is therefore not to be lightly esteemed. It is no curious theological museum piece, of interest only to the student of the history of dogma. Dr. E. Schmauck is unfortunately correct when he calls synergism "a heresy which is always with the Church," and when he says, "Man's will is able to decide for salvation through new powers bestowed by God. This is the subtle Synergism which has infected nearly the whole of modern Evangelical Protestantism, and which is or has been taught in the institutions bearing the name of our own (Lutheran) Church" (Schmauck, *Confessional Principle,* pp. 600, 752). These words were written in 1911 and corroborated the statement Dr. G. Stoeckhardt had made in 1897: "The contradiction that arises against pure doctrine from this quarter will never become silent. Polemics against synergistic errors will be tied up with Lutheran theology until all controversy will give way to the peace and the triumph of eternity" (*Lehre und Wehre,* 43, 129). As late as 1912 Dr. F. Bente could quote a theologian who professed to be Lutheran to this effect: "According to the revealed order of salvation, the actual final result of the means of grace depends not on the sufficiency and efficacy of the means themselves, but also upon the conduct of man in regard to the necessary condition of passiveness and submissiveness under the Gospel call" (*Lehre und Wehre,* 58, 390). Synergism is so stubborn an error because it finds such ready response in the Pharisaism of natural man.

The German theologian Schleiermacher once said: "Man is born Catholic." He meant that the so-called gospel of Catholicism, that the sinner must in part earn his own salvation, strikes a responsive chord in the heart of every natural man. Schleiermacher is right. By nature all of us are Catholics and synergists. In consequence, as Dr. Stoeckhardt remarked above, much of the doctrinal controversy of the Lutheran Church has consisted and will continue to consist in polemics against the synergistic leaven.

VI. ANTISCRIPTURAL SYNERGISM IS UN-LUTHERAN

What is Lutheranism? If Dr. F. Bente is correct — and we sincerely believe he is — Lutheranism is "simply consistent Christianity" (Bente, *American Lutheranism*, I, V), it is accepting Scripture at face value, it is taking God at His word. If this is genuine Lutheranism, synergism is not Lutheran doctrine, because it is not Scripture doctrine.

Nor is synergism Lutheran in the historical sense; for Luther never held synergistic views. Perhaps there was no doctrinal error he more emphatically rejected than synergism in all its forms. As early as 1517 he wrote: "If God's mercy is to be praised, then all (human) merits and worthiness must come to naught" (Weimar I, 161). Naturally he recognized the mystery before which the *sola fide* placed a thinking man. But he was too good a theologian to attempt to solve it either in the Calvinistic way, by denying universal grace, or in the synergistic way, by denying the monergism of that grace. In 1524 he wrote against Erasmus, the synergist: "WHY that Majesty does not take away or change this fault of the will IN ALL, seeing that it is not in the power of man to do it; or why He lays that to the charge of the will, which the man cannot avoid, it becomes us not to inquire, and though you should inquire much, yet you will never find out: as Paul saith (Rom.9:20), 'Who art thou that repliest against God!'" (Luther, *Bondage*, 173.) In his pithy, colorful way the Reformer told the great humanist: "'Free will' is a downright lie; and, like the woman in the Gospel, the more it is taken in hand by physicians, the worse it is made" (Luther, *Bondage*, 17). To the very end of his life Luther preached the monergism of grace with an emphasis and incisiveness that have made him famous.

But after the death of the great man of God many did not remain true to this Scriptural and historic position of the Lutheran Church. The so-called Synergistic Controversy is notorious in church history. The fact that no one less than Luther's former co-worker Melanchthon was the father of synergistic leaven in Lutheran circles adds to the sadness of this chapter of the history of our Church. Luther had observed the errors into which Melanchthon's philosophizing and rationalizing were misleading him, but had never succeeded in curing him of them. Melanchthon recognized three concurring causes of conversion, the Holy Spirit, the Word, and the consenting will of man. In the controversy which broke out ten years after Luther's death, Matthias Flacius brilliantly and successfully defended the scripturalness of the Lutheran view. This man deserves more attention and credit than is usually given him. (See Preger, *Flacius*, 2 v.) In the final statement of Lutheran doctrine, the Formula of Concord, synergism is rejected in a thoroughgoing manner. "Our doctrine, faith, and confession are as follows: namely, that in spiritual and divine things the intellect, heart, and will of the unregenerate man are utterly unable, by their own natural powers, to understand, believe, accept, think, will, begin, effect, do, work, or concur in working anything, but they are entirely dead to what is good, and corrupt, so that in man's nature since the Fall, before regeneration, there is not the least spark of spiritual power remaining, nor present, by which, of himself, he can prepare himself for God's grace, or accept the offered grace, nor be capable of it for and of himself, or apply or accommodate himself thereto, or by his own powers be able of himself, as of himself, to aid, do, work, or concur in working anything towards his conversion, either wholly, or half, or in any, even the least or most inconsiderable, part; but that he is the servant (and slave) of sin, John 8:34, and a captive of the devil, by whom he is moved, Eph. 2:2; II Tim. 2:26. Hence the natural free will according to its perverted disposition and nature is strong and active only with respect to what is displeasing and contrary to God" (*Triglot*, 883). These words ought to convince the most prejudiced that synergism is, indeed, un-Lutheran. Whosoever teaches that man contributes one iota to his conversion and salvation is both un-Lutheran and unscriptural. To put it more accurately: he is un-Lutheran because he is unscriptural.

God grant that "un-Lutheran" and "unscriptural" ever remain interchangeable terms. *Soli Deo gloria!*

The Means of Grace

I

The Lutheran Church, the true visible Church on earth, faces the contemporary world to bring it to Christ with the means of grace as its only equipment. The Lutheran Church has the one philosophy of effective action of the Church in relation to the world. It knows that it must use the means of grace to bring men to God. It has them purely and fully.

THE LUTHERAN CHURCH FACES THE WORLD BY CLINGING TO THE MEANS OF GRACE

The doctrine of the means of grace is truly a most timely subject. For just in these last times, according to divine revelation, there will be at work many spiritual brigands who will perpetrate the grossest kind of deception. Christ has warned His Church again and again concerning the false prophets and the deceivers who would deceive the very elect if it were possible. We are living in these last times, when we behold on every hand the abomination of desolation spoken of by the Prophet Daniel. The world today is a world of change and revolution. We have reached an end of an era in the history of the race and are entering upon another whose outlines are still hazy and uncertain.

The world of today is not only involved in revolution and political and social turmoil, it is also a world of religious and moral revolution and change, a world definitely characterized by secularism and moral decay. The evil from which the Church needs to be protected today is something far more insidious and dangerous than the persecution of the Jews or the idolatry of the pagan Roman world to which the disciples and early Christians were exposed. The danger today is the materialistic habit of thought and the almost complete secularization of every institution in society and in life in general. By secularization we mean the divorcement of life from spiritual principles, religious principles, or from God Himself.

Doctor Frey, in his book *The United States Looks at Its Churches*, finds that only 49 per cent of the population of the United States is in some way connected with one of the Christian church bodies, which means that about 70 million people in our country profess no religion and are wholly secular in their way of life. A few years ago the English poet Alfred Noyes visited America, and on his arrival here he was reported as having expressed himself about America as follows: "There isn't any religion any more, there isn't any common belief in anything, and when the test comes, how can a civilization conquer anything when it does not believe in anything? Marriage is going, the home is almost gone. The idea in the increasing hordes of books seems to be repudiation of every uplifting principle that has come to civilization during its history and a reversion to the animal." (*Concordia Theological Monthly*, March 13, 1933.)

A few years ago G. H. Betts of Northwestern University made an investigation regarding the attitude of the Protestant clergy of today over against the fundamental doctrines of the Christian religion. From an analysis of the replies received it is evident that there is a great confusion regarding most of the doctrines considered fundamental in the Christian religion. "All the ministers to whom the questionnaire was sent believe in the existence of God, but only 87 per cent of them believe that He is omnipotent. Only 48 per cent of the Congregational ministers believe that God is unchanging. Sixty-four per cent of the Congregational, 28 per cent of the Methodist, and 14 per cent of the Baptist ministers refused to accept the doctrine of the Trinity. Only one out of four Congregational preachers believes in the Virgin Birth." No wonder that the author comes to the following conclusion: "From this showing within denominations one conclusion can be reached: no denomination, except perhaps the Lutheran, has any right to demand that a fixed creed shall be taught the young; for the clergy of many denominations themselves do not subscribe to a common creed beyond the belief in the existence of God" (*The Beliefs of 700 Ministers*, G. H. Betts, p. 48).

According to this investigation it appears that a very large per cent of the Protestant churches are in a bad way so far as fundamental teachings of the Christian religion are concerned, for they are already spiritually bankrupt. The religion that remains in some of these churches is a secularized type of religion dealing with this world, with improving the life and conditions here, unconcerned about a man's relationship to God, or indifferent about the life beyond.

WHAT ABOUT THE CATHOLIC CHURCH IN AMERICA?

Side by side with Protestantism in facing America's culture stands Roman Catholicism. Both cherish the hope of winning America, each to its own faith. The Catholic Church sees the drift into secularism in nearly all Protestant Churches. The Catholic Church is striking out boldly with all its resources to win America to its faith. It has introduced new features. Always content to produce priests and administrators, she is now sending forth laymen and preachers who address the American public with winsome and persuasive arguments in expounding Catholic doctrine and tradition.

For a long time the Catholic Church has been a potent factor on the American political scene. For some reason or another it always seems to be given special consideration in its requests and given special prominence wherever it appears. Myron Taylor still continues to represent the White House at the Vatican. Mr. Truman issued the following statement (*Washington Star*): "I have asked Mr. Myron C. Taylor to return to Italy as my personal representative to His Holiness the Pope with the rank of Ambassador."

Rome entered the public school system by way of getting Catholic teachers placed in the public schools and Catholic personnel on the school boards. Protestant pastors must begin to put as much thought and energy into Protestant education as Catholic priests put into Catholic education — or we shall be compelled to yield religious primacy in America.

The growth of Catholic power is manifested in its intelligent approach to two large populational blocs — organized labor and the Negroes. It has its own Association of Catholic Trades Unionists — its main objective is to spread the teaching of the Catholic Church. Whether Catholicism can win America depends in part on whether it can win the American Negro. "The Church has kept the doors to the priesthood almost closed to Negroes. Nearly a hundred Catholic institutions of higher learning admit Negroes." (From "Catholicism and the Negro" by Harold E. Fey in *Lutheran Standard* for Feb. 2, 1946.)

WHAT ABOUT THE PROTESTANT CHURCH IN EUROPE?

The Lutheran Church in Europe today is no doubt the greatest casualty of World War II. Let us examine the future of the Lutheran Church in Germany as seen through the eyes of Dr. J. W. Behnken and Dr. L. Meyer.

Lutheranism vs. Calvinism

"There is a definite consciousness of a need for a resuscitation of Lutheranism, led by men like Bishop Meiser of Bavaria and Dr. Sasse of Erlangen, and others. On the other hand there is a movement for *union* for all churches, led by Niemoeller, Dibelius, Wurm, and others. Pastor Niemoeller is sincere and honest in his convictions, but thoroughly inoculated with the spirit of unionism and ecumenicity. These two movements are gaining momentum. Within the next year a decision will be made either for an *Evangelische Kirche in Deutschland,* which will mean the end of confessional Lutheranism in the greater part of Europe, or for an *Evangelische Lutherische Kirche in Deutschland.* Eighty per cent of the congregations in Germany are Lutheran, 15 per cent Reformed, and 5 per cent 'Uniert.' *If the larger part of nominal Lutheranism in the world is to be saved, then it shall be our obligation to strengthen the Lutheranism of Europe 'which remains and which is ready to die.'*" (From Minutes of Emergency Planning Council, Dec. 28, 1945.)

The Lutheran Church Has the Means of Grace Purely and Fully

The Lutheran Church is the true visible Church on earth. Dr. Walther contended for this fact at the general meeting of our Synod held in St. Louis in 1866. It is significant that after a lapse of almost 80 years the same thing can be said to a convention here in Hickory in 1946. Tremendous changes have occurred; several generations have come and gone. The world has advanced on a number of fronts; the North Pole has been reached and the stratosphere invaded, gigantic wars have rocked the foundations of the civilized peoples; the A-bomb has been invented, men have become weaker and wiser in various ways; in the schools theories have been propounded, believed, defended, declared enthroned once and for all among the grand truths of the ages, and then unceremoniously put on the scrap heap of outworn notions; but here is the Missouri Synod of the Lutheran Church in this year of grace 1946 considering, uttering, and confessing the same challenging declaration which the fathers voiced a century ago. That is certainly a striking phenomenon in this unstable, restless, constantly shifting modern world, a special mark, let us say it with genuine gratitude, of divine mercy and goodness.

What precisely did our fathers mean when they spoke of the Lutheran Church as the true visible Church of God on earth? Certainly not that it is the only saving Church, outside of which there is no help for poor sinners. Dr. Walther never made such extravagant claims. And apart from Scriptural considerations, how could a consistent Lutheran declare our Church to be the only saving Church when Dr. Luther himself repeatedly and emphatically stated that in the Middle Ages, when the Gospel was perverted, still there were people living who were children of God in spite of their outward connection with the Roman Church and the Pope. That there are true believers in other Christian denominations in which the Word is preached and the Sacraments administered the fathers cheerfully and gratefully acknowledged. Neither did they wish to say that the Lutheran Church is an infallible Church in the sense that its synodical resolutions and decrees are inspired and hence must be obeyed by Christians. What they did mean to assert is tersely stated by Walther in the treatise to which I have referred repeatedly: "A true visible church is that one only in which the Word of God is taught in its purity, the Sacraments are administered according to the Gospel." And then, in a later paragraph, he states: "If the Evangelical Lutheran Church possesses the characteristics of the preaching of the pure Word of God and of the administration of the Sacraments according to the Gospel, it is the true visible Church of God on earth."

The teachings of the Lutheran Church are Scriptural, and its administration of the Sacraments conforms to the divine institution.

What a tragedy if we, entrusted with the eternal Gospel of Jesus Christ, which saves the soul for this life and for that which is to come, and makes people new creatures serving God and their neighbor in gratitude and joy — what tragedy, I say, if we should forego the proclamation of this Gospel and change our Church into a club for social experimentation. An honored leader of our Church said years ago: "We few ministers shall by faithfully preaching the Word not be able to stay the deluge of sin and wickedness sweeping over the earth in these latter days, but woe to us if we do not shout as loudly as we can into the din and roar of the murky waters the message of repentance and faith in Jesus Christ." (C. F. W. Walther, *Pastoral Theology*, p. 170.)

The Lutheran Church can stand the test that she is the only true Church in the world which gives all glory and honor to God alone. The Lutheran Church does not only teach that we are saved alone by grace, not only that this grace was dearly bought by Christ, the Son of God and Redeemer of the World, not only that this grace is appropriated through faith alone by the power of the Holy Spirit, but also this: that God instituted special means into which He has placed this grace and through which He offers us this grace.

Wherever the means of grace are present, there the Lord Himself is present, and where the Lord rules there is victory. The true doctrine of justification is intimately bound up with the true doctrine of the means of grace. In order to keep the doctrine of justification in all its purity, one must ever maintain that the forgiveness of sins which Christ earned for mankind can never be appropriated by man through any other means than the Word and the Sacrament. Therefore, Walther said, the correct doctrine on justification stands or falls with the correct doctrine concerning the means of grace. The doctrine of the means of grace is a peculiar glory of the Lutheran theology. To this central teaching it owes its sanity and strong appeal, its freedom from sectarian tendencies and morbid fanaticism, its coherence and practicalness and its adaptation to men of every race and every degree of culture, and with these means of grace the Lutheran Church faces the contemporary world.

II

The means of grace are the Gospel and the Sacraments: Baptism and the Lord's Supper. By these means God imparts to man the grace merited by Christ.

A. THE SCRIPTURAL DOCTRINE OF THE MEANS OF GRACE

1. THE DEFINITION OF THE TERM

In speaking of the means of grace it may be necessary to define the term, particularly the word *grace*. Grace is sometimes spoken of as a quality or attribute of man. We say of one who commands ease and eloquence of speech: "He speaks with much grace." In the matter before us grace is always understood as something in God, some quality, or attribute, of God. Grace has been called the benign favor of God; the love which God bestows upon us in spite of the fact that we are unable to repay Him in any way; the love toward sinners for Jesus' sake: *"die Suenderliebe Gottes"*; in this restricted sense, grace cannot be separated from God.

The Definition of the Term by Romanism and by Lutheranism

In the definition of the word *grace* there is a wide difference between us and the Church of Rome. Rome defines saving grace as a quality that has been infused, instilled, imbued into man, a virtue that is now inherent in him, by which he loves God and walks in His ways. To this the Lutheran Church answers, God's grace and man's work exclude each other, as St. Paul so forcefully declares: *"And if by grace,* then is it no more of works; otherwise grace is no more grace. But if it be of works, then is it no more grace; otherwise work is no more work." (Rom. 11:6.) Let us note here, too, that divine grace is universal. "The grace of God that bringeth salvation hath appeared to all men" (Tit. 2:11). God's love has for its object the world, and God's desire is the salvation of men. It is not amiss that we emphasize the universality of grace in this connection, for he who does not understand the word *grace* cannot have a correct knowledge of the Scriptural doctrine of the means of grace.

The Lutheran Definition Is the Scriptural Definition

In order to offer and convey to men the merits which Christ has secured for the world by His death on the Cross (II Cor. 5:21: "For He hath made Him to be sin for us who knew no sin, that we might be made the righteousness of God in Him"; Rom. 5:18: "Therefore as by the offense of one judgment came upon all men to condemnation, even so by the righteousness of One the free gift came upon all men unto justification of life"), God employs certain external, visible means through which the Holy Spirit works and preserves faith and thus accomplishes the sinner's salvation.

The Teaching of Our Confessions

That is the clear teaching of our Confessions. The Formula of Concord, XI, 76, thus writes: "The Father will not do this (draw anyone to Himself) without means, but has ordained for this purpose His Word and the Sacraments as ordinary means and instruments." Smalcald Articles, Part III, Art. VIII, 3: "In those things which concern the spoken, outward Word we must firmly hold that God grants His Spirit or grace to no one except through or with the preceding outward Word." The Augsburg Confession, Art. V, 2: "They (our churches) condemn the Anabaptists and others who think that the Holy Ghost comes to men without the external Word, through their own preparations and works."

2. THE NECESSITY OF THE MEANS OF GRACE

The life and death of Jesus are historic facts, witnessed by Jews and Gentiles of His day. But the meaning thereof no man could know if it were not revealed to us by God (I Cor. 2:9-12): "But as it is written, Eye hath not seen, nor ear heard, neither have entered into the heart of man, the things which God hath prepared for them that love Him. But God hath revealed them unto us by His Spirit; for the Spirit searcheth all things, yea, the deep things of God. For what man knoweth the things of man save the spirit of man which is in Him? Even so the things of God knoweth no man, but the Spirit of God. Now we have received, not the spirit of the world, but the spirit which is of God, that we might know the things that are freely given to us of God."

The Merits of Christ's Redemption Must be Imparted

If ever sinners are to profit by the merits of Christ's redemption, these must be offered and imparted to them; hence the necessity of the means of grace. God determined the means by which salvation was procured for the world, namely, by the life and the death of His Son. He also is the only One who can determine by which means this salvation is to be revealed and transmitted to us. It is exceedingly foolish for man to say how and by what means God should impart to us His grace. "God was in Christ, reconciling the world unto Himself, not imputing their trespasses unto them; and hath committed unto us the Word of Reconciliation" (II Cor. 5:19).

How God Imparts the Redemption of Christ

God desires to bestow His grace in Christ upon sinners through specific means ordained by God as the vehicles and instruments for such transmission. This *is basic,* because it reminds us first of all of *what* is being offered by God to sinners, namely, God's grace in Christ Jesus. Whoever has no knowledge of this grace of God in Christ will never be able to comprehend the doctrine of Scripture concerning the means of grace, and neither will he be able to speak of the same intelligently. The correct doctrine of the means of grace is based upon the correct doctrine concerning grace. That there is so much confusion and error in the visible Church as pertains to the means of grace is due to this, that not always is the grace of God in Christ Jesus fully recognized. But our God has not left us in the dark concerning this matter. Through the heroic services of His witness-bearer Doctor Luther, God once again opened unto us the Scripture. We know the grace of God.

We believe "God was in Christ, reconciling the world unto Himself." God has prepared for the lost world, purely out of His love and mercy, an effective salvation. He did not merely prepare for us an example in Christ Jesus and recommend that by imitating Him we could possibly attain to salvation. But He placed the total sum of our sins and guilt on Christ, His own Son, who atoned for the same and took away the curse. Christ has made full atonement for our sins with His suffering and death. What we should have accomplished, namely, the fulfillment of the whole Law, Christ has done for us. He has fulfilled the Law for us. What we should have suffered, namely, the punishment for our sins, and God's wrath in time and in eternity, that Christ has suffered for us when He gave His back to the smiters and when His side was pierced on Golgotha. What we lost through Eden, namely, Paradise, salvation — that was gained for us again through Christ and gained for all sinners. Thus Scripture says: "Christ is the end of the Law for righteousness to everyone that believeth" (Rom. 10:4). "For the wages of sin is death, but the gift of God is eternal life through Jesus Christ our Lord" (Rom. 6:23). "Think not that I am come to destroy the Law or the Prophets; I am not come to destroy, but to fulfill. For verily I say unto you: Till heaven and earth pass, one jot or one tittle shall in no wise pass from the Law till all be fulfilled. Whosoever therefore shall break one of these least commandments, and shall teach men so, he shall be called the least in the kingdom of heaven; but whosoever shall do and teach them, the same shall be called great in the kingdom of heaven" (Matt. 5:17-19). "Surely, He hath borne our griefs and carried our sorrows; yet we did esteem Him stricken, smitten of God, and afflicted. But He was wounded for our transgressions, He was bruised for our iniquities; the chastisement of our peace was upon Him; and with His stripes we are healed" (Is. 53:4-5). That is the doctrine of God's grace as revealed in Scripture.

3. God's Relation to the Means of Grace

Although God in His spiritual activity is not absolutely bound by the means of grace, still He has Himself instituted these means, through which He works in the Kingdom of Grace, just as He has established the laws of nature, through which, as a rule, He reigns in the kingdom of nature. The Fifth Article of the Augsburg Confession says of the relationship of God to the means of grace: "The Holy Ghost, who works faith wherever and whenever it pleases God, is given through the Word and the Sacraments as through instruments and means." Luther has well said: "If a man deal with God and receive of Him, this must come about, not by man's making a beginning and laying the first stone; but God, without man's request and desire, must come first and give him a promise. Such a word of God is the foundation, the rock upon which all works, words, and thoughts of man will thereafter be established. This word man must gratefully receive, firmly believing the divine promise and in no wise doubting that as He has promised, so it shall be and come to pass. This faith and confidence is the beginning, middle, and end of all works and righteousness. It is impossible that man of his own reason and ability should with his works ascend into heaven and, preceding God, move Him to grace; but God must precede all his works and thoughts."

God has Given Us the Ministry of Reconciliation Through Means

Though God is able to sustain our physical life without material food, yet he who would persistently abstain from taking nourishment would violate the Commandment which says: "Thou shalt not kill." So God has ordained that the spiritual man should live and grow on the Bread of Life, stored in the Scriptures and dispensed by the stewards in the household of God, and by the Sacraments, instituted for our salvation. We have no divine promise that our spiritual life shall be sustained without the means of grace.

Without God man knows nothing of Christ, and without God's Spirit he cannot make his knowledge a knowledge unto salvation. Therefore God has given to His Christians the ministry of reconciliation. God has also created a special office, the duty of which it is to make known to men the reconciliation wrought by Christ and to endeavor to induce men to believe in and accept such reconciliation (II Cor. 5:18-20). To this ministry He has given the public administration of the means or instruments by which the duties of this office are to be executed. These means are commonly called the means of grace. They comprise the Gospel of Jesus Christ and the Sacraments: Baptism and the Lord's Supper.

4. THE MEANS OF GRACE ARE DIVINE AND PERMANENT MEANS, UNCHANGEABLE

Only God can create and establish means of grace, for only God can present to us His grace. In bestowing His gifts to men God often makes use of means. Among others, he used words, blood, water, figs, branches, and leaves. Jesus Christ used means: He healed by a word, a truth, a mixture of spittle and clay, the hem of His garment. He fed five thousand with a few loaves and fishes. He can do Godlike things through simple means. In like manner, God ordained the Word and the Sacraments to be the means, the channels, the vehicles, through which His Holy Spirit should convey redeeming and renewing grace to man.

The Lutheran Church Gives All Glory to God When It Holds the Means of Grace Are Unchangeable

In its teaching on the immutability, unchangeableness, and permanency of the means of grace, the Lutheran Church gives all glory to God alone because it teaches that no one, not even a minister of the Word, can change the means of grace from that which God instituted. It is self-evident that when God ordains something, no creature can change it, for if the creature changes it, then it is no more of God and the creature has put himself above God. Yet popery attempts such a thing. The Roman Catholic Church recognizes seven sacraments as means of grace and declares that not only Baptism and the Eucharist, but also Confirmation, Extreme Unction, Ordination, Penance, and Marriage have been established by Christ as means of grace. *Conc. Trid.*, Sessio VII, De Sacramentis in Genere, Canon I. Popery also has changed the Lord's Supper by refusing the cup to the laity. This is the reason: When the wine is distributed, a small portion of it could be spilled, and thus there would fall upon the ground the blood of Christ; and one could not pick it up again, for instance, as you could pick up a wafer, and therefore the blood of Christ would be trodden under foot. Because of this extreme danger one ought not to give the wine to the laity. In view of this, the Council of Trent decreed, and took it upon itself, to change one of the most sacred ordinances.

Luther writes: "Over against such mockery we inject this thunderbolt where Christ said: 'This do in remembrance of Me.' These words Christ spoke to the Church, and He said, 'This do' and not 'this change or this annul.' In the last chapter of Matthew He said: 'Go and teach all nations . . . teaching them to observe all things whatsoever I have commanded you.'" Surely, these and similar passages declare that the Church has no power to change or to annul the word of Christ or to add to the institutions of Christ but that rather they put the Church under the word of Christ and demand of her that she carry out literally these words as a solemn commandment of God.

Prayer Not a Means of Grace

The Methodists believe that prayer is a means of grace. Yet how is it possible that grace could abide in something that we do? Prayer is a fruit, a product of the means of grace. Without the grace given to me in the means of grace I cannot even pray acceptably. In prayer God does not approach us, but we approach Him. It is part of the Christian's spiritual life, which has been engendered in him by the means of grace.

5. THE TWOFOLD POWER AND FUNCTION OF THE MEANS OF GRACE

1. They exhibit, offer, and grant the objective reconciliation effected by Christ, that is, the grace of God consisting in the forgiveness of sin (*vis exhibitiva, dativa vel collativa*).

2. Through the bestowal of this grace they also forgive sins, produce and sustain faith (*vis effectiva vel operativa*).

This power of the means of grace is clearly taught in such passages as, e. g., Luke 24:47:"And that repentance and remission of sins should be preached in His name among all nations, beginning at Jerusalem"; John 20:23: "Whosesoever sins ye remit, they are remitted unto them, and whosesoever sins ye retain, they are retained"; Rom. 1:16: "For I am not ashamed of the Gospel of Christ, for it is the power of God unto salvation to everyone that believeth"; I Thess. 1:5: "For our Gospel came not unto you in word only, but also in power and in the Holy Ghost and in much assurance, as ye know what manner of men we were among you for your sake."

The Power of God is Inseparably Connected with the Means of Grace

It is God alone who may speak the word of pardon, who can produce faith, but it is God who is speaking in the Gospel and the Sacraments (Luke 24:47: "in His name") and creating faith through them (Acts 16:14 — Lydia; James 1:18; I Thess. 2:13). The word of the Gospel is therefore not a dead letter, nor are the Sacraments empty symbols, but they are the power of God. The power of God is inseparably connected with, is inherent in, the means of grace.

6. THE RELATION OF FAITH TO THE MEANS OF GRACE

Faith is not an essential part of the means of grace, nor does their efficacy depend on faith. Their promise stands and their power remains unimpaired in spite of man's unbelief. But the Sacraments do not profit without faith. The promise is useless unless it is received by faith. Luther says the means of grace and faith are correlatives.

Thus the Gospel is not merely a hand which holds out to us the blessings of salvation that thereby we might be induced to accept them, but it is the power of God. Through it the Holy Ghost operates, bringing such influence to bear on the heart of man that it turns to Christ in faith and accepts the promised gifts. "Through the same Word and forgiveness the Holy Ghost bestows, increases, and strengthens faith" (Large Catechism, Art. III, 62, *Triglot*, p. 695).

The Sacraments Do Not Profit Without Faith

If God offered His grace and worked faith in the hearts of men independently of the means of grace, we could dispense entirely with the Gospel and the Sacraments, as the Quakers do. If, as Calvin maintains, the "external invitation" does not carry with it the "internal efficacy of grace," there is no purpose in reading the Bible or hearing the Gospel.

B. THE ERRONEOUS DOCTRINES REGARDING THE MEANS OF GRACE

The Scriptural doctrine of the means of grace has been grossly perverted by Romanists, Calvinists, and synergists.

1. THE ERROR OF ROMANISM: *Gratia Infusa*

The doctrine of the means of grace is perverted by the Roman Catholic Church in the interest of work righteousness. According to the papistic doctrine, Christ died for the sins of the world in order that God could infuse into the sinner (with his own constant co-operation) so much grace (*gratia infusa*) that he is enabled truly to merit justification and salvation (Council of Trent, Sess. VI, Canons 4, 32) either *de congruo* (co-operating by desiring, or striving after, the good) or *de condigno*, (by making oneself worthy, by actually accomplishing meritorious works). In other words, according to Roman Catholic doctrine, Christ has secured for sinners so much grace that they, by divine gracious assistance (infusion of divine powers), can earn salvation themselves.

Why the Roman Church Rarely Preaches the Word

The Roman Church does not believe in the efficacy of the Word of God. It is not a means of grace to the poor deluded follower of Rome. Rome denies that God offers in the Word the grace which Christ merited. She does not believe that the Spirit of God operates in and through the Word, leading the sinner to Christ and renewing his heart and giving him power to persevere in faith. Therefore the preaching of the Word of God has rarely found a place in the service of the Catholic Church. We hear the priest mumbling Latin prayers, chanting Latin liturgies, we see him swinging incense before the altar, we hear him reading Mass, but we strain our ears in vain to hear him preach the Gospel.

Why Rome Suppresses the Written Word

The Pope suppresses the Gospel not only in its spoken, but also in its written form. If the Bible contained only the Law of God, the Pope and his henchmen would not be so eager to suppress it. But the Bible contains also the Gospel, and that is what makes it so dangerous to Rome. Never was the Bible in greater danger than during the Dark Ages, when Romanism reigned supreme. At the present time, in most Romish countries, Italy, Spain, Mexico, Central and South America, one can readily see the effects of suppressing the Gospel. The attitude of the Roman Church to the Scriptures has not been at all consistent at all times and in all places. It has varied from toleration to destruction of the sacred books. No modern Catholic would venture to repeat the judgment of English Catholic Bishops upon Tyndale's translation, "A certain heretical and damnable book called the 'New Testament.'" The condition in America today is that Romanism is compelled to be somewhat "Protestantized" as far as its nature allows. But even here Romanism gives abundant proof of the fact that it is the enemy of the open Bible. Through the influence of Protestantism the Roman Catholic Church is not forbidding the reading of the Bible, and even stimulates it, but always under the condition that the Bible used is one sanctioned by the Church of Rome and containing the footnotes offering the interpretation of that Church.

Proof of the Catholic Suppression of the Word

Quotations: *"Rome and the Bible."* — The fourth rule of the Congregation of the Index of Prohibited Books, approved by Pius IV and still in force, runs as follows: "Since it is manifest by experience that, if the Holy Bible in the vulgar tongue be suffered to be read everywhere without distinction, more evil than good arises, let the judgment of the bishop or inquisitor be abided by in this respect, so that, after consulting with the parish priest or the confessor, they may grant permission to read translations of the Scriptures, made by Catholic writers, to those whom they understand to be able to receive no harm, but an increase of faith and piety from such reading (which faculty [permit] let them have in writing). But whosoever shall presume to read these Bibles or have them in possession without such faculty shall not be capable of receiving absolution for their sins, unless they have first given up their Bibles to the ordinary [the bishop]."

"The common doctrine of the Church is well expressed in the saying of Cardinal Manning, in his *Temporal Mission of the Holy Ghost.* 'We neither derive our religion from the Scriptures, nor does it depend upon them,' p. 176; and by the editor of a leading English Roman Catholic journal: 'It is strange that any reasonable man in the present day can imagine for a moment that Almighty God intended the Bible as a text-book of Christian doctrine.' *The Month,* Dec., 1888."

" 'The Catholic Church existed before the Bible; it is possible for the Catholic Church to exist without the Bible, for the Catholic Church is altogether independent of the Bible. The Bible does not give any systematic, complete, and exhaustive treatment of the doctrines of Christ. In many respects it is, like a stenographer's notebook, partial and fragmentary, to be supplemented later on in more elaborate detail by other agencies. Christ never wrote a word of the Bible. One might naturally expect Him to have set the example by writing at least some portions of the Bible if He intended His followers to take their entire religion from it. Christ never ordered His apostles to write any part of the Bible. We might well expect such a command from Him if He desired the members of His Church to have recourse to the Bible for their religion. Christ could not have intended that the world should take its religion from the Bible, since so many millions of the human race to-day, to say nothing of past ages, cannot read or write.' *Inside Facts About the Catholic Church*, Thomas F. Coakley (Catholic Truth Society pamphlet), p. 21 f."

The Romanist's doctrine of the Sacraments is a radical perversion of the Scriptural doctrine of the means of grace. The Mass finds its analog not in the Upper Room, but in the Temple at Jerusalem.

2. The Error of Calvinism: Grace Is Particular, or Limited

"Since Calvinism denies the *gratia universalis* and insists that the grace of God in Christ Jesus is particular (*gratia particularis*), that is, designed for and confined to a limited number of men (the elect), it is obligated to teach that there are no real means of grace for the non-elect." Calvin distinctly advises the believer not to judge his election and salvation according to the universal Gospel call which is extended through the external Word, but only according to the special call, which consists in *"inward illumination"* by the Holy Ghost.

"It is true, Calvinism speaks of the Word and the Sacraments also as 'signs,' 'symbols,' etc., of divine grace. But as long as it holds that divine grace is particular and that the same signs may be 'signs of salvation' and 'signs of condemnation,' the believer must forever remain in doubt regarding his state of grace, since he cannot determine whether in his case the sign means salvation or damnation. However, the case is still more serious. The Calvinistic denial of universal grace and of the Scriptural doctrine of the means of grace destroys also the Scriptural doctrine of saving faith and saving grace. A faith that does not rely solely on the gracious promises of the Gospel is not a true faith in the sense of the Scripture. A faith that does not trust exclusively in the grace of God for Christ's sake is not true faith in the sense of Scripture." (*Christian Dogmatics*, J. T. Mueller.) Compare also *Popular Symbolics*, Engelder, Arndt, Graebner, pp. 210–219, on the error of Calvinism.

3. THE ERROR OF SYNERGISM: MAN CAN DECIDE FOR GRACE

Synergism also perverts the doctrine of the means of grace by its denial of the *sola gratia*. It ascribes salvation in part to the virtuous efforts of man to apply himself to, or to decide for, grace. It looks upon the means of grace as an incentive by which the sinner is induced to convert himself through the divine powers communicated to him.

The Error of Synergism Leads to Modernism

It is almost superfluous to mention the fact that all errorists who deny the vicarious satisfaction of Christ cannot teach the Scriptural doctrine of the means of grace. Since they refuse to accept the reconciliation secured by Christ's substitutionary death, they are obliged to reconcile God by "trying to keep the commandments of God," and this leaves no room for any divine means of grace. Modernism is paganism, veiled by, and decked with, Christian terminology, which destroys the very heart of the Christian religion, namely, justification by grace through faith in the atoning blood of Christ.

WHICH ARE *Not* THE MEANS OF GRACE?

The Law is not a means of grace. "By the Law is the knowledge of sin" (Rom. 3:20). It proclaims the curse of God (Gal. 3:10): "For as many as are of the works of the Law are under the curse; for it is written: Cursed is everyone that continueth not in all things which are written in the Book of the Law to do them."

Prayer is not a means of grace. A means of grace is that by, and through, which grace and forgiveness is offered and conveyed to man; in prayer, however, we ask for grace and blessings. The grace we ask for in prayer, God offers and bestows on us through His Word and the Sacraments. In prayer we deal with God; through the means of grace God deals with us.

Self-imposed works and exercises are no means of grace. Through them God does not convey grace and blessings to man; but man erroneously often hopes thereby to earn favor with God.

Which *Are* the Means of Grace?

The means of grace are the Gospel and the Sacraments. The Sacraments are such only because of the Gospel promise connected therewith. Therefore we may say that there is but one means by which the knowledge of grace and salvation, and grace and salvation itself, are imparted to us, namely, *the Gospel,* which is the glad tidings of the grace of God in Christ Jesus. It is for this reason that it is called *"the Gospel of Grace"* (Acts 20:24); "the Gospel of Peace" (Rom. 10:15); "the Word of Reconciliation" (II Cor. 5:19); "the Gospel of our Salvation" (Eph. 1:13). The Gospel is a means of grace. It not only instructs the sinner concerning the forgiveness of sins, but offers and imparts to him the forgiveness of sins gained for him by Christ, and it creates faith (Rom. 10:17): "So, then, faith cometh by hearing and hearing by the Word of God."

C. THE WORD AS THE MEANS OF GRACE

The Gospel is the primary means of grace, "the chief thing in the Sacrament." It is the means of grace in every form in which it reaches man, whether it be preached, or printed, or pictured, or meditated upon. In writing, in speech, in the sign language of the deaf and dumb, in being broadcast over the radio, etc., it may be copied or repeated any number of times without losing or diminishing in its saving power.

The Gospel a "Universal Absolution"

The Gospel is not merely a reliable biography of Christ, it also reveals to us the meaning and the achievements of His life and death. It tells us of the love of God, who sent His Son into the world (John 3:16). It tells us that Christ made full atonement for our sins and reconciled us to God. "When we were enemies, we were reconciled to God by the death of His Son" (Rom. 5:10). Yes, the Gospel does even more than this. Every time we read or hear the Gospel, God really and actually pronounces forgiveness of sins upon us. Therefore Luther calls the Gospel a "universal absolution." It actually imparts to man all the blessings whereof it tells him. "Saving grace is not proclaimed in the tantalizing manner which a cruel man would adopt who comes to a people famished with hunger and shows them an abundance of food which is suspended in the air and which they can never reach, but there is in this Gospel (*vis collativa*) the power to confer on the hearers the very things which it announces to them" (W. H. T. Dau).

THE GOSPEL DELIVERS FROM SIN AND CONFERS SALVATION

Therefore the Lutheran Church believes that the Word of God is more than a Book of information. It not only tells about sin and salvation, but it *delivers* from sin and *confers* salvation. It not only points out the way of life, but it leads, it carries us into and along that way. It not only instructs concerning the need of the Holy Spirit, but it conveys that Spirit to the very mind and heart. It is indeed a precious truth, that this Word not only tells me what I must do to be saved, but it also *enables me* to do it. It is indeed the principal means of grace. It is the vehicle and instrument of the Holy Spirit. Through it the Holy Spirit works repentance and faith. Through it He regenerates, converts, and sanctifies. Wherever the divine Word is, there is also the divine Spirit; and whenever a person uses the Word of God in any form, God is divinely operative in it (I Cor. 2:4).

THE OPERATIVE POWER OF THE GOSPEL

To insure a correct understanding of the operative power of the Gospel, we may add that the very act of accepting the gracious gift of God is an achievement of the Gospel. St. Paul, in a very pointed question, emphasizes the fact that the Galatians had received the Spirit "by the hearing of faith." The blessings of the Gospel, the Spirit with all His gifts, the forgiveness of sins, the assurance of the mercy of God, their adoption as His children, had come to them through the preaching concerning faith. (Galatians 3.)

Not only is man moved to the initial act of faith by means of the Gospel, but faith which has been engendered in him is kept alive and maintained by the same means. "Ye are saved by the Gospel"

(I Cor. 15:2). "The Gospel is the power of God unto salvation" (Rom. 1:16). "The engrafted Word, which is able to save your souls" (James 1:21). In these texts the ultimate purpose of the Gospel is held up before the eyes of the readers. The ultimate end and aim in every instance is the salvation of the soul. This, however, is not only the aim and purpose of the Gospel, but the actual accomplishment. In other words, we are saved by the faith which is wrought and maintained in us by the Gospel.

D. THE SACRAMENTS AS A MEANS OF GRACE

(Compare *The Abiding Word*, II, pp. 385—393.)

E. THE VALIDITY AND EFFICACY OF THE MEANS OF GRACE

The validity or the efficacy of the means of grace does not depend on the personal or the official character of the minister. *Their validity rests on their divine institution, and they have their efficacy in themselves.* The evil works of the scribes did not deprive the Word of God they preached of its authority (Matt. 23:2-3): "Then spake Jesus to the multitude and to His disciples, saying, The scribes and the Pharisees sit in Moses' seat. All therefore whatsoever they bid you observe, that observe and do; but do not ye after their works, for they say, and do not." The insincerity of the preachers characterized in Phil. 1:16-19 did not affect the truth of their message. The personal or the official character of the minister affects the truth, authority, and efficacy of the Word of God he preaches as little as the grade of paper does on which it is printed in our Bibles.

It Is the Message That Counts, Not the Messenger

The minister is only a steward, an ambassador, a messenger of God, and it is the message that counts, and not the messenger. If the character of the person who administers the Sacrament could invalidate the Sacrament, then God Himself would be dependent upon human beings. If a minister deals with us according to the Word of God, his personal impiety cannot invalidate the message he brings or render the divine power inherent in the Word and the Sacraments inefficacious. "Both the Sacraments and the Word are effectual by reason of the institution and commandment of Christ, notwithstanding they be administered by evil men." (Augsburg Confession, Art. VIII. *Triglot,* p. 47; Apology, Art. VII, VIII, 28, *Triglot,* p. 237.)

Neither does the fact that a man is ordained to the ministry contribute anything towards the validity and efficacy of the means of grace. A promise of God, when quoted by a layman, is as valid and certain as it is when pronounced by an ordained clergyman. The Word and the Sacraments are valid because God Himself ordained them (Matt. 28:19). When administered in His name (Luke 24:47), they are efficacious (Heb. 4:12).

Luther says: "Our faith and Sacrament must not rest on the person, be he godly or wicked, ordained or unordained, called or sneaking in, the devil or his mother, but on Christ, His Word, His office, His command and ordinance" (St. Louis, XIX:1272). Neither does the ministry avail on account of the authority of any person, but on account of the Word given by Christ.

The Error of the Religious Enthusiasts

A denial of the efficacy and sufficiency of the means of grace is contained in the theological systems of all religious enthusiasts. By their erroneous doctrine that the Holy Spirit works without the means of grace and entirely independent of them the means of grace have become unnecessary. Quakers, Shakers, Holy Rollers, Christadelphians, and the Salvation Army belong to this class. In seeking to defend their unscriptural position they point out that God is almighty and therefore does not need the Word and Sacraments to convert the sinner, but can do so directly by His Spirit. We do not deny the almighty power of God. The point at issue, however, is not what God can do, but what He does and wills to do according to His Word.

The Gospel is always efficacious, always able to produce an effect, and to turn the hearts of men to God. It is powerful and quick to turn the heart (Heb. 4:12; Jer. 23:29); able to convert the soul and to comfort the distressed (Ps. 19:7-8; James 1:21).

The Resistibility of the Means of Grace

The reason why not all to whom the Gospel invitation is extended are converted is not to be found in the supposed inefficacy or insufficiency of the means of grace, but in man's natural hostility toward the Gospel and in his power to resist the means of grace. The fact that natural man assumes a hostile attitude towards the Gospel is clearly taught by St. Paul, who says: "The natural man receiveth not the things of the Spirit of God, for they are foolishness unto him; neither can he know them, because they are spiritually discerned" (I Cor. 2:14). "The preaching of the Cross is to them that perish foolishness" (I Cor. 1:18). The power operating through the Gospel can be resisted by men. "Ye do always resist the Holy Ghost; as your fathers did, so do ye" (Acts 7:51). The fault lies not with God, nor with the Gospel, but with the perverse will of man, which, dominated by other considerations, will not yield to the persuasive influence of the Holy Ghost. The seed we put into the ground has inherent power to germinate, grow, and bring fruit; but adverse weather conditions may prevent it from doing so. Thus the seed of the Gospel has power to affect the heart and to work faith, but inhibitions such as love of sin, self-righteousness, etc., often prevent it from taking root.

Why does man resist the Gospel call? Is it the overwhelming honesty of his conviction that will not suffer him to embrace a religion which he cannot bring into harmony with his enlightened reason and understanding? Certainly not. Christ offers this commentary: "And this is the condemnation, that light is come into the world and men loved darkness rather than light because their deeds were evil. For everyone that doeth evil hateth the light, neither cometh to the light, lest his deeds should be reproved" (John 3: 19-20). Men will either love the Gospel and hate sin, or they will love sin and hate the Gospel.

III

The correct understanding of the doctrine of the Means of Grace will have a salutary influence on pastors and hearers; without the proper use of the Means of Grace no sinner can expect to be saved and no Church can hope to grow.

THE IMPORTANCE OF THE CORRECT DOCTRINE REGARDING THE MEANS OF GRACE

"Scripture itself stresses the doctrine of the means of grace as one of fundamental importance. In the first place, it teaches expressly that regeneration, or conversion, occurs solely through the means of grace, that is, through the Word (I Cor. 2:4-5; I Pet. 1:23; Rom. 10:17) and the Sacraments (Acts 2:38; Matt. 28:19-20; I Pet. 3:21, etc.). In the second place, it affirms most definitely that all who reject the means of grace forfeit salvation (Luke 7:30; John 8:47; I Cor. 10:21-22; 11:26-29). In the third place, it shows clearly and emphatically that contempt for the means of grace is not a little sin, which God readily condones, but rebellion against the Lord of mercy and grace (I Cor. 1:22-23), which He punishes with eternal damnation (I Cor. 1:18-21, 26-29; Mark 16:15-16)." (*Christian Dogmatics,* J. T. Mueller, p. 458.)

Thus God builds His Church here on earth. As we turn the pages of the history of God's Church and examine the records of the Apostles, our verdict must be: Their labors have not been in vain. The Lord abundantly blessed the preaching of His Word. The Gospel seed brought forth thirty, sixty, and a hundredfold. Millions of souls were saved from heathen vices and superstitions and brought to Christ. Thus congregation after congregation of believing Christians was established through the Gospel which the Apostles preached.

What makes that part of the Lutheran Church to which we belong the spiritual backbone of the Christian Church of our country? It is the adherence to the Gospel and the Sacraments. A Church is a power in the Kingdom of God in the same measure in which it clings to the Gospel of the Son of God; for it is by the Gospel and by the Sacraments, and by them alone, that God leads men to Christ, preserves men in Christ, and builds His Church here on earth.

"The principal duty of the pastor is the public preaching of the Word of God. He preaches to his congregation and to himself. A correct understanding of the doctrine of the means of grace ought to induce the pastor to be the most diligent student of the Word of God in his parish for the sake of his own soul, lest he preach to others and himself become a castaway.

"The hearers of the Word of God who understand the doctrine of the means of grace will be diligent hearers of it. While God has commanded the pastor to preach the Gospel, He has commanded the congregation to hear it. The Gospel is the means not only of converting the sinner, but also of strengthening the faith of those who already are converted. Christians having this knowledge will be faithful and diligent in the use of the means of grace." (Central District, 1925, No. 11.)

May God awaken us to a true knowledge and genuine thankfulness for the means of grace and the hope of glory they give us and preserve His Gospel and Sacraments unadulterated and unmutilated to us and our children to the end of time, unto the salvation of immortal souls and the glory of His holy name.

The Gospel

INTRODUCTION

Dr. Martin Luther, in the sixty-second of the Ninety-five Theses, says, "The true treasure of the Church is the holy Gospel of the glory and grace of God." In this judgment we agree. Without the Gospel there would be no reason for the existence of the Church, for the proclamation of the Gospel is the Church's business; without the Gospel there would be no Church, for the Gospel is the means whereby the Church is built.

Realizing all this, we know that the Gospel of the glory and the grace of God is the real treasure of the Church. It is the only thing that can give meaning to life and victory in death. For the Gospel, men have undergone the greatest labors and sufferings; for it they have stood on the scaffold; for it they have laid their heads on the block; for it they have been bound to the stake and burned alive. They knew what a treasure it was. May the Lord of the Church grant us His Holy Spirit that we, too, may realize its great value and be ready to live for it, and even to die for it if it becomes necessary in these last troubled days of the world.

I. DEFINITION

Our Catechism defines the Gospel as the glad tidings of the grace of God in Christ Jesus. The word *gospel* literally means "good news." And the Gospel is truly news, for it is something entirely new to man. No one knows it by nature and it cannot be discovered by human reason. The Bible speaks of it as a mystery, as something unknown to men (Eph. 6:19; I Tim. 3:9; Rev. 10:7; cp. also Mark 4:11; Rom. 11:25; 16:25; I Cor. 15:51; Eph. 1:9; 3:3, 4, 9; 5:32; Col. 1:26, 27; 4:3; 2:2; II Thess. 2:7; I Tim. 3:16).

In His loving-kindness and mercy, God has not left us in darkness and ignorance, but He has revealed this news which is hid from natural man (II Cor. 4:3, 4). If men were to know this news set forth in the Gospel, it was necessary that God Himself should reveal it. Our Gospel is not man-made. It comes from God, and because of that it is good and right and true and has the highest value and the deepest meaning for our life. We are dealing here not with empty theories or a beautiful dream, but with a work of God Himself (California and Oregon District, 1895, p. 15). It could come from no one else (Gal. 1:11, 12, 16; I Cor. 2:10; Rom. 16:25, 26). Because of this characteristic of the Gospel, that it is new and unknown to men, it was necessary that the Bible should be written by inspiration by the holy Apostles, Evangelists, and Prophets to whom it was revealed by the Spirit (Eph. 3:5).

But the Gospel is not only news, it is good news, glad tidings. When the message of the Gospel is brought to men, the meek are exalted; the broken and contrite heart is filled with joy; the captives of the devil are delivered into the glorious liberty of the children of God; they who sit in the prison house of death see the gates of a new and perfect life opening before them; they who have lost their birthright have it restored to them; they who have been feeding on the dry husks which the world offers them are received back into their Father's house; and the hearts which have been heavy with grief are moved to rejoice and praise the Lord for His marvelous mercy to the children of men. Beauty for ashes, indeed! (Is. 61:1-3).

And the Gospel is such good news because it brings us tidings of the grace of God. It does not only bring us the news that there is a God, but it reveals that God is gracious. This is the news that man needs. The cry of every awakened conscience is the cry of Martin Luther in the monastery, "How can I find a gracious God?" Such a gracious God is to be found nowhere but in the Gospel. It is true, as Paul says, that God has not left Himself without witness in nature (Acts 14:17; 17:23-29; Rom. 1:20). The heavens declare His glory and our own conscience testifies to His holiness, but without the Gospel there is no comfort in this, and it leaves us only with a certain fearful looking unto Judgment. Because of

The Gospel

this testimony of God in nature and in our own hearts, there is not a single people which is not forced to acknowledge God. God has created man for fellowship with Him, and man continually seeks in his own way to re-establish this fellowship. He is conscious of the fact that it has been lost, as Augustine says, "Thou hast created us for Thyself, and restless is our heart until it rests in Thee" (*Confessions*, I, 1.). Luther says, "No people has ever been so reprobate as not to institute and observe some divine worship" (*Triglot*, p. 585).

In spite of all this, natural man, who has lost his original relationship with God by sin, is, for all his worship, truly without God in the world (Eph. 2:12. Nebraska, 1898, pp. 9–12). But the Gospel reveals how man can find a gracious God, how man is brought once more into the right relationship with God. It speaks comfortably to Jerusalem and cries unto her that her warfare is accomplished, that her iniquity is pardoned, that she has received of the Lord's hand double for all her sins (Is. 40:2). Therefore it is called the Gospel of the grace of God (Acts 20:24).

This grace of God is found only in Christ. Outside of the Lord Jesus, God is a consuming fire. Only in Christ does God forgive our sins and accept us as His children. It is only vain, empty prattling to speak of God as good and gracious outside of Christ, if men seek to find in such goodness and grace comfort in respect to their sins (California and Oregon, 1895, p. 15). Only through Christ has the fellowship between God and man been re-established (II Cor. 5:19). Only through Christ can we come to God (John 14:6).

The Gospel therefore centers in, begins, and ends with Christ. Because Christ is the entire content of the Gospel, therefore Paul wrote to the Corinthians, "I determined not to know anything among you save Jesus Christ, and Him crucified" (I Cor. 2:2). For this reason it is again and again called the Gospel of Christ (Mark 1:1; Gal. 1:6; II Cor. 2:12). Without Christ there is no Gospel, for only Christ has done and could do what the Gospel proclaims to us (California and Oregon, 1895, p. 15). To preach the Gospel and to preach Christ is one and the same thing (Rom. 16:25).

A gospel which does not proclaim Christ or which sets up Christ as another lawgiver, or only as a great teacher, even the greatest teacher who ever lived, or only as a perfect man, or as an example whom we are to follow, that is no gospel at all (Gal. 1:6-8). Only that which presents Jesus Christ as He is set forth in the Scriptures, as the Son of God, who died for our sins, in whom we have redemption through His blood, only that is Gospel.

The Gospel, then, is the good news of the grace of God in Christ. In this definition lie tremendous implications for our Christian life. We who are ignorant of it by nature and who without it would be sitting in darkness and the shadow of death should be moved to gratitude because it has been revealed to us. Gospel preachers should preach Christ. Christian laymen should never be satisfied with any other kind of preaching.

The fact that the Gospel is news also makes mission work necessary. Without the Gospel, men are without hope, without comfort, and without God in the world (Rom. 10:14). For the sake of the proclamation of the Gospel alone, the world is still spared from the fire of the Last Judgment (Matt. 24:14). Because the Gospel is news, we are assured of a hearing. God has created all men with a measure of curiosity, and they differ from the Athenians only in degree (Acts 17:21).

And people not only like to hear news, they like to tell it. It is a surprising thing that this news set forth in the Gospel is not spread more rapidly. We ought to make use of every facility at our command to tell this news. Our reaction to the Gospel ought to be that of Jeremiah when he was not preaching it. He said, "His Word was in mine heart as a burning fire shut up in my bones, and I was weary with forbearing, and I could not stay" (Jer. 20:9). Oh, if we would only listen more to the call of the Prophet, "O Zion, that bringest good tidings, get thee up into the high mountain; O Jerusalem, that bringest good tidings, lift up thy voice with strength; lift it up, be not afraid; say unto the cities of Judah, Behold your God!" (Is. 40:9). To be able to bring this news to a bewildered, dying, and hopeless world is a glorious privilege. "How beautiful upon the mountains are the feet of him that bringeth good tidings, that publisheth peace, that bringeth good tidings of good, that publisheth salvation, that saith unto Zion, Thy God reigneth!" (Is. 52:7.)

II. THE GOSPEL AND THE LAW

Christ sent out His disciples to preach the Gospel, and yet if the preaching of the Gospel is to have its proper effect, then the Law must also be preached, for the Gospel can be understood correctly only in relation to the Law. In our day, when so much emphasis is placed on the goodness and grace of God at the expense of His holiness and justice, there is great need of sin-conscious preaching. We are often told that God is too good and too gracious to punish anyone eternally in hell. This may seem to some to be real Gospel preaching, but actually it not only destroys the Law, but it makes the Gospel of none effect. It is not long before those who do not preach the Law also begin to call the Gospel an old-fashioned blood religion. God is not jesting when He speaks to us in the Law. It is a serious matter with which men must reckon if they are to find hope and comfort in the Gospel. The Law must therefore be preached not as a set of fine moral rules, whereby this world can be made a better place, but instead, its condemning testimony against sin must be given full weight.

The Gospel is given to deliver us from sin, but the strength of sin is the Law (I Cor. 15:56). The very nature of the case therefore demands that a Gospel preacher will preach the Law, not for its own sake but for the sake of the Gospel. The kind of preaching which makes of God an indulgent old father, like Eli, who does not enforce his commands, the kind of preaching which speaks of God as loving and good, indulgent over against the sinner, and not seriously concerned with sin, and which promises men salvation by ignoring the Law, that is not Gospel preaching. It can only lull men into spiritual sleep and carnal security. In the interest of the Gospel a Christian should always and ever more fully test his life by the touchstone of the divine Law. In the interest of the Gospel, a true preacher of the Word should always expound the Law in all earnestness and severity. If this is done, the Gospel will never lose its power, and our people will never say, "Our soul loatheth this light bread."

Men must learn over and over again that they are wretched and miserable and poor and blind and naked; and then they will also learn to appreciate the happiness and the blessedness and the riches which they have in the Gospel. Only where Law and Gospel stand side by side will men learn to sing with their whole heart,

Not the labors of my hands	Nothing in my hand I bring,
Can fulfill Thy Law's demands;	Simply to Thy Cross I cling;
Could my zeal no respite know,	Naked, come to Thee for dress;
Could my tears forever flow,	Helpless, look to Thee for grace;
All for sin could not atone;	Foul, I to the fountain fly, —
Thou must save and Thou alone.	Wash me, Savior, or I die.

The Gospel therefore does not annul the Law. St. Paul says, "Do we then make void the Law through faith? God forbid; yea, we establish the Law" (Rom. 3:21). And Christ Himself said, "Think not that I am come to destroy the Law" (Matt. 5:17). And if we examine the preaching of the Lord, we find that He by no means set aside the Law, nor did He diminish its severity in any way. The Sermon on the Mount is an example of this. This sermon is often looked upon as being the high point in the Savior's preaching, but it is merely Christ's exposition of God's moral Law as laid down in the Decalog, and it testifies conclusively to the fact that Christ preached a God who was just as holy, just as strict, as the God whom Moses preached. The Gospel does not detract one bit from the severity and the authority of the Law. The Law has its origin in the holiness and justice of God, and if the Gospel set aside the Law or ignored it, the Gospel could not be a divine revelation, for it would mean that God, who is unchangeable, has altered His holy, immutable will. Since God cannot abdicate His rule over all things, since God cannot change His nature, therefore the Law, which is the expression of the holiness and justice of God, cannot be abolished.

Rather, the Gospel establishes the Law and testifies to its authority. The Cross which once stood on Calvary and the blood of Christ which was shed there bear eloquent testimony to the fact that God is in dead earnest in the demands of the Law. The Gospel proclaims, not that the Law has lost its authority, but rather that the debt, owed under the Law, has been paid. The Gospel is our receipt which assures us that the demands of the Law have been completely and finally fulfilled. On a blank piece of paper the words "Paid in full" are meaningless; they have force only on the face of a bill or note of indebtedness. Thus the Gospel acknowledges God's perfect right to require payment of the sinner, and it bears unmistakable testimony that God does require such payment.

Christ paid our debt by meeting every demand of the Law. As our Substitute, He fulfilled the Law for us (Gal. 4:4, 5). And His inexpressible suffering and shameful death was nothing else than the payment of the penalty of our guilt (Col. 2:14). At the Cross of Christ all men may read that our account has been paid in full, but the canceled handwriting also testifies to the fact that the debt was once owed. Christ's Cross and blood therefore reveal to us not only the goodness and the mercy and the grace and the love of God, but they give us a deeper insight into His complete and unchangeable holiness and justice. The suffering of our Savior cannot be viewed as being a kind of bribe offered to God whereby He is moved to relax some of the sternness of the Law. Nor should we look upon it merely as a means of awakening the mercy of God, as though God became merciful to us when He saw the suffering of His Son, just as Pilate sought to arouse the pity of the Jews by placing the scourged and thorn-crowned Savior before them. The Lord Jesus actually suffered everything we had deserved.

This is shown also by the manner in which He died. His death was not a death of glory and honor, like a death on the battlefield, but to the people of His time it was a criminal's death, a shameful, inglorious end. He was numbered among the transgressors. We often fail to realize this because to us the Cross has become a symbol of peace and hope and comfort and victory. It was not that when Jesus died on it. It was so disgraceful to die on a cross that Cicero, in defense of one of his clients, said, "The very word *cross* should be absent not only from the body of Roman citizens, but even from their thoughts, their eyes, and their ears." Christ did not only die, but He died as a condemned sinner, because that is the kind of death we had merited. And He died not only as a criminal condemned by an earthly judge, but He felt the verdict of divine judgment in body and soul when He cried out of the depths of anguish and despair, out of hell itself, "My God, My God, why hast Thou forsaken Me?" His death was not the death of a man dying for his ideals, as it is so often pictured by the modernistic pulpit, but it is this that puts His death beyond all powers of understanding, that He who knew no sin actually experienced all the fearful torments of the damned.

And because Christ has paid such a perfect price, such a complete ransom for our deliverance, therefore salvation is ours by right of purchase. It actually belongs to us because Christ bought it for us with His holy, precious blood. The Law, though it has the right to exact payment from the sinner, has no right to require it of us who trust in the Lord Jesus (Rom. 8:1). It is this that makes us so very certain of our salvation.

Every promise of salvation without Christ is therefore a lie, every hope of heaven without Christ is a vain hope, every comfort in respect to sin without Christ is empty consolation. All such teaching offends against the holiness and justice of God. It implies that God is a liar when He says, "Cursed is everyone that continueth not in all the things that are written in the Book of the Law to do them" (Gal. 3:10).

The Gospel therefore does not set aside, ignore, or annul the Law, but rather it is God's own testimony and assurance that the wages of sin have been paid to the very last farthing. A Gospel which violates the holiness of God could not ever create the proper respect and reverence for the Lord. Where this relation between Law and Gospel is properly observed, there will be no danger of abuse of the Gospel.

III. THE GOSPEL AND THE CEREMONIAL LAW

Everything that has been said about the relation of the Gospel to the Moral Law applies also to the Ceremonial Law. However, the Ceremonial Law partakes also of the nature of the Gospel. The purpose of the various ceremonial regulations was to set Israel apart as the people from whom the Savior was to come (Deut. 14:2. Michigan, 1889, p. 30). And more than that, these various ceremonies and regulations were themselves types of the coming Savior, given to Israel to make plain to them the nature and work of the promised Redeemer (Col. 2:17, 18; Heb. 9:1—10:18). If the Jews in spirit saw the meaning of the ceremonies, they were able to glean from them a saving knowledge of Christ, and these regulations were, so to speak, a living portrait of the Savior.

The Gospel

This will become increasingly clear if we study the Ceremonial Law from this angle. The festivals of the Jews had their spiritual significance. The festival of the new moon spoke to the Jews of the coming of the true Light of the world. The Sabbath prefigured the rest which was to come to men through Christ. The year of jubilee was a type of the New Testament times, when we have been freed from the bondage of the devil, when our debt to God has been paid by Christ, and when our heavenly home is restored to us for Christ's sake (Luke 4:19, 21; cp. Lev. 25:8-17). Pentecost foreshadowed the harvest of souls redeemed by Christ. The Feast of Tabernacles was to remind the Jews that they were strangers and pilgrims and to teach them to look to that city which hath foundations, whose Maker and Builder is God.

The many sacrifices were types of the sacrifice of our Savior, the Lamb of God which taketh away the sins of the world. The Passover lamb, without spot and blemish, of whose body not one bone was to be broken and whose blood was painted on the doorposts of the houses of the children of Israel, was a prefiguration of the sinless Son of God and His saving blood (I Cor. 5:7). The sacrifices taught the Jews that without shedding of blood there is no remission (Heb. 9:22), and the fact that these animal sacrifices had to be repeated again and again made it clear to them that the blood of bulls and of goats could not really take away sin (Heb. 10:4), and that a better sacrifice would have to be brought (Heb. 9:23). The mercy seat itself was a type of Christ and His cross (Rom. 3:25).

The priests also foretokened Christ and His work. In the Book of Hebrews we are told that the priests "serve unto the example and shadow of heavenly things" (Heb. 8:5). Their mediation continued until the coming of the Great High Priest, holy and higher than the heavens (Heb. 7:26), who brought one offering by which He perfected forever them that are sanctified (Heb. 10:14), through whom we have been made a royal priesthood (I Pet. 2:9), who have free access through Him unto the Father (Rom. 5:2). Thus Christ fulfilled the Ceremonial Law not only in the sense that He perfectly obeyed its provisions, but also in this, that He did those things in His life and death of which these regulations and ceremonies were a shadow. Because this relationship existed between the Gospel and the Ceremonial Law, therefore it came to an end when the veil in the Temple was rent at the death of our Lord, so that no man may judge us today in meat, or in drink, or in respect of the holy days, or of the new moon, or of the Sabbath days, so that the Old Testament priesthood, and the Temple, and the sacrifices are no more (Col. 2:17, 18; Jer. 3:16). We in the New Testament see the great facts of the Gospel no longer in shadows, but in all their glorious fullness. For that may God be praised.

IV. THE GOSPEL AS A MEANS OF GRACE

(California and Oregon, 1895, pp. 28—33)

The Gospel and the Sacraments are the means of grace, that is, they are the means whereby the grace of God is offered and given to men. The world needs to be assured of the grace of God, and it must be assured of this by God Himself. No man has a right to believe that God is gracious to him unless he can point to some definite promise of God on which he can base his faith. We must remember that all sins are committed against God, and that therefore only God can forgive sins, and the assurance of forgiveness can come only from God. We must bear in mind that God is the Lord of heaven and that He alone determines who shall enter it. And in the Gospel and the Sacraments we have the means whereby we are assured of the grace of God, in which God Himself testifies to us that our iniquity is pardoned and our sin is covered.

The preaching of the Gospel is therefore not only a preaching about the grace of God. Jesus did not tell His disciples that they should preach about the forgiveness of sins, but He said that "repentance and remission of sins should be preached in His name among all nations." The preaching of the Gospel actually gives the forgiveness of sins. Pastors are not only teachers of religion. Their highest duty is not to preach morality nor to see that everything is done decently and in order; they are not only to enlighten men as to their duty toward God, but they are actually messengers from God, who in God's name and by God's command are to announce to men their reconciliation with God (II Cor. 5:19-21). The assurance of the pastor therefore is the assurance of God Himself (Luke 10:16; Matt. 18:18; John 20:23). Through the Word

God Himself testifies to me that my sins are forgiven, that for Jesus' sake He accounts me righteous and fit for everlasting life.

Because of this, we should believe that when we receive forgiveness from the pastor in the absolution, this is as valid and certain as if Christ, our dear Lord, dealt with us Himself, and by it our sins are forgiven before God in heaven. The absolution rests on the nature of the Gospel. Because it is true that God loved the world, because it is true that Christ died for all, because God has reconciled the world unto Himself, because Christ is the Savior of all men, because He has commanded us to preach the Gospel to every creature and has promised that "whosoever believeth in Him should not perish but have everlasting life," therefore the pastor can go to the individual and say, "I forgive thee all thy sins in the name of the Father and of the Son and of the Holy Ghost."

Calvinism vitiates the means of grace because it denies the doctrine that Christ has redeemed all men. Romanism vitiates the means of grace because it makes forgiveness dependent not on the Word, but on the satisfaction rendered by the sinner. Because the Gospel is what it is, namely, God's own declaration that He is reconciled to the world, therefore the pastor can say, "Son, be of good cheer, thy sins are forgiven thee." It is this that makes the office of the ministry such a high and holy office.

Where the doctrine of the means of grace is not followed, people are directed to other things outside the Word for the assurance of salvation. They are directed to their religious experiences, or to their feelings and emotions, or even to their religious acts, the fact that they attend church, go to the Lord's Supper regularly, are baptized, perform penances, and pray. The sectarian churches say that the means of grace are not necessary because faith must rest on Christ. It is true that faith must rest on Christ, but faith in Christ is faith in His Word (John 8:31, 51; Rom. 10:6-8).

The doctrine of the means of grace is closely connected with the doctrine of justification. Those who in any way look upon justification as something done in us and not simply as the act of God whereby He declares the ungodly righteous, not imputing their sins to them, must also look for the assurance of salvation in themselves and not in the Gospel.

To the means of grace belong also the Sacraments, Baptism and the Lord's Supper. They are the visible Gospel. Sectarians may ask, "How can water do such great things?" but in Baptism we again have the Word of God. It is His command that we should baptize, and it carries His promise (I Pet. 3:21). The water of Baptism might be compared to the waters of Bikini atoll, where the atomic bomb exploded. For days ships could not enter the lagoon. To pour some of that water over your hand meant certain death. The water of Baptism is connected with a power far greater that atomic fission. It is connected with the almighty Word of our God, and this water brings us spiritual and eternal life. The power of Baptism is the power of the Word. And as it is with Baptism, so it is also with the Lord's Supper. They are not simply ordinances which we follow, but they are means of grace through which we receive the forgiveness of sins. The Gospel and the Sacraments therefore are rightly called God's hand, which He reaches down from heaven, filled with all the treasures of His grace. They do not tell us what God has to give us in some other mysterious way, but they actually offer, convey, and seal to us the forgiveness which Christ has earned for us by His death on Calvary's Cross (Nebraska, 12, 1898, p. 51).

V. THE GOSPEL AND FAITH

The relation between the Gospel and faith really belongs under the discussion of the Gospel as a means of grace, but because the effect of the Gospel as a means of grace is a twofold one, namely, that on the one hand it gives the grace of God, and on the other, that it works that faith whereby the forgiveness is received, we have chosen to discuss this matter in a separate chapter. In the first part of our essay we made the point that the Gospel is unknown. Without the help of the Holy Spirit it is unknowable (I Cor. 2:14). If we are to receive God's forgiveness, it is not only necessary that God should reach out His hand, filled with the treasures of grace, but also that man should take the grace offered and given to him. But no man can do this by his own power. Natural man is spiritually blind, dead, and an enemy of God (Rom. 8:7; Eph. 2:1).

Modernism is not ashamed to boast of its hatred against the true God. Bishop Oxnam, Methodist, president of the Federal Council of Churches, wrote in his *Preaching in a Revolutionary Age*: "Hugh Walpole, in *Wintersmoon*, tells of a father and a son in church. The aged rector read from the Old Testament, and the boy learned of the terrible God who sent plagues upon the people and created fiery serpents to assail them. That night, when the father passed the boy's room, the boy called him, . . . and said, 'Father, you hate Jehovah. So do I. I loathe Him, dirty bully.' We have long since rejected a conception of reconciliation associated historically with an ideal of a Deity that is loathsome. God, for us, cannot be thought of as an angry, awful, avenging Being, who because of Adam's sin must have His Shylockian pound of flesh. No wonder the honest boy, in justifiable repugnance, could say, 'Dirty bully'" (*Concordia Theological Monthly*, XVII, 1946, p. 542 f.). Blasphemy such as one would expect from Voltaire or Ingersoll uttered by one who is honored as a bishop by what still calls itself a Christian church!

But how shall man, who is spiritually blind and dead and an enemy of God, reach out and take the gifts offered by the God whom he hates? Not by his own power or will. Being dead, he is without strength to assist in his conversion. But the Gospel comes to his rescue. Luther has expressed this in his usual clear and simple way in the Third Article. This truth is already taught by the name which the Savior gave to the process whereby a sinner comes to faith, whereby the unwilling is made willing. He calls it "being born again." Just as little as a man has to do with his own birth, so little he has to do with being born again as a child of God. It is the Holy Ghost who converts the enemies of God, who causes the spiritually dead to be born again, and who enlightens the spiritually blind, and He does this through the Gospel. The Scriptures give us ample proof of this fact (Rom. 10:17; Eph. 1:13; I Thess. 1:5; II Thess. 2:13, 14; I Pet. 1:22:23; John 17:17, 20).

The Reformed churches may vilify this doctrine that faith is worked through the Word, and say, "The Holy Spirit needs no wagon," but we know that our Lutheran doctrine is Bible doctrine. The Gospel is the vehicle by which the Holy Spirit comes to us, and the work of the Holy Spirit is part of the Gospel. The promise of the Spirit is a very important part of the Gospel promise (John 16:14). And because this is true, we should emphasize in our preaching not only the part which Christ has in our redemption, but also the work of the Holy Spirit.

But the Gospel is not only the means whereby faith is created. It is also the only means by which it is preserved and strengthened. What food and drink is to the body, the Gospel is to the soul (I Pet. 1:5; Rom. 16:25). That is the reason why in our churches we emphasize the preaching of the Gospel Sunday after Sunday, not only for the sake of those who may never have heard it before, but also for the sake of the Christians, who need to be strengthened and edified in their faith. The Apostle Paul was not ashamed to preach over and over again the same old Gospel, for he knew that it is the power of God unto salvation (I Cor. 15:1, 2; Rom. 1:16).

And the faith which is worked by means of the Gospel is itself the means whereby the treasures of the Gospel are appropriated. If I am to benefit by a gift, it is not only necessary that there should be a giver and a gift, that it should actually be offered to me, but it is just as necessary that I should take it. And the hand that takes God's gift offered in the Gospel is faith.

And faith is all that is necessary. There is nothing else that a man needs to do to receive God's grace except to take it. The Gospel is an unconditional promise of pardon. This doctrine is an offense to natural man, and we ourselves are often afraid that it will make men carnally secure. We invent some work for a tramp to do before we feed him. Men think that God must deal with us in the same way. They say that He is indeed merciful and wants to save us, that the gift is ready for us, but that there is something that we must do before God will bestow His gifts upon us. Such doctrine of necessity destroys the very nature of faith. If the blood of Christ actually cleanses us from sin, if salvation is truly a free gift, if our redemption and justification is complete, then certainly nothing more is necessary than that I take it as a free gift. Any other doctrine can only make us uncertain of our salvation. And this is Bible doctrine. "Every one that thirsteth, come ye to the waters, and he that hath no money; come ye, buy, and eat; yea, come, buy wine and milk without money and without price. Wherefore do ye spend money for that which is not bread? and your labor for that which satisfieth not? hearken diligently unto Me, and eat ye that which is good, and let your soul delight itself in fatness. Incline your ear, and come unto Me; hear, and your soul shall live" (Is. 55:1, 2, 3a; cp. Rom. 11:6).

It is true that we must confess that we are all as an unclean thing and that all our righteousnesses are as filthy rags (Is. 64:6; Jer. 3:12, 13). Yet even our repentant confession does not make God merciful, but He is merciful, was merciful from eternity, and all that is necessary is that men recognize that they need His mercy and take it by faith. Even my faith, however, does not make God gracious. Whether I believe it or not, Christ died for me, and faith is necessary not as a condition of salvation, but only as the means of accepting that salvation. From this it follows that we must never base our hope for salvation on our own faith. Faith is necessary only as the receiving means. In this sense a vital, personal faith is indispensable for salvation.

On the other hand, we must guard against attaching all sorts of conditions to faith itself. The circumstances under which a man comes to faith and the religious experiences which go with it differ. Because many do not realize this, they live in doubt all their lives as to whether they truly have faith. They say, "Oh, how I wish that I could firmly believe that the Lord died for me so that I too could go to heaven." Such expressions arise from a false view of faith. When that desire is in a man's heart, the Holy Spirit has already done His blessed work in him, for the Bible says, "It is God who worketh in us both to will and to do of His good pleasure" (Phil. 2:13). Such faith may be weak faith, but faith does not justify because of what it is in itself, but because it lays hold on Christ. Therefore weak faith saves just as surely as strong faith. A diamond does not change in value according to whether the hand that wears it is weak or strong. So also the salvation of Christ does not take its value from the faith which grasps it. The promise of the Gospel is unconditional. "Come," says our God, "for all things are now ready."

VI. THE GOSPEL AS THE BASIS OF THE TRUE MORALITY

The Gospel promises us that we are saved without good works, and yet the Gospel alone can create good works in us. The very nature of the Gospel, which proclaims pure grace, excludes all good works from the very beginning. Grace is for those who have sinned. He who denies that he is a sinner cannot include himself in the Gospel promise. Faith does not justify because it makes us godly, because it is a good work, but only because it trusts in Him who justifies the ungodly. When God justifies, He has in view not our good works, but our sins, not our merit, but our unworthiness (Matt. 9:13; I Tim. 1:15; Rom. 4:5; Eph. 2:8, 9; Titus 3:5; Gal. 5:4).

Even after we are Christians, we can do nothing for our own preservation in faith. From the fact that faith can be lost by our own fault, many draw the wrong conclusion that by our good works, done after conversion, we at least help to keep ourselves in the faith. Yet from the fact that I can prevent a tree from growing by chopping it down, it does not follow that I have power to make that tree grow. So also in the preservation of faith all good works are excluded (I Pet. 1:5). Even the best works of the Christian are still marred and spoiled by sin. All our righteousnesses, our good works, are still filthy rags in God's sight, which are acceptable to God only because their blemishes and imperfections are covered by the blood of our Savior (Is. 64:6; I Pet. 2:5; Ps. 143:2). From beginning to end, therefore, the only thing that saves us is the grace of God in Christ.

Because our Lutheran Church teaches this, we are often accused of thereby making men carnally secure and of giving them the impression that good works are not necessary or even to be despised. The Apostle knew that some people would draw the wrong conclusion that a Christian may live in sin, since Christ has died to save us and since we are saved without good works. To forestall any such reasoning he wrote, "What shall we say then? Shall we continue in sin that grace may abound? God forbid!" (Rom. 6:1-2.)

Actually the Gospel is the only cause of truly good works. The Gospel brings us freedom, not only from the guilt and punishment, but also from the dominion of the Law. A Christian no longer serves under the compulsion of the Law, but that does not mean that he does not do good works. I am dead to the Law, for this very purpose that I might live unto God (Gal. 2:19; Rom. 7:6). There is no law for the righteous man, not in the sense that he may be lawless, but rather in the sense that he needs no legal compulsion. We need no law telling the sun to shine or water to run downhill, for that is their very nature. Likewise, good works are not demanded of the Christian by the Gospel, for it belongs to the nature of a Christian, who has come to faith by the Gospel, that he does good works. The attitude of men toward the Law is changed by the Gospel (Jer. 31:33, 34; Michigan, 1889, p. 82). In so far as he still has the old Adam, the Christian needs the Law, but in so far as he is a Christian, he does not need it, for he serves God willingly.

Faith, which is worked by the Holy Spirit, must sanctify our lives. Faith makes me a child of God, and here, too, the proverb holds good, "Like father, like son" (Eph. 5:1). Faith can exist only where sin is repented of, but repentance views sin with hatred and horror. He who has faith has come to Christ to be free from sin. Where there is a desire to be free from sin, there will be no more pleasure in sin. Faith knows what sin cost the Savior. He who by faith stands in spirit beneath Calvary's Cross, how can he ever think lightly of sin again? Where that faith is which knows that Jesus loved us unto the end, there will also be a fervent love for the Lord. And if we love Him, we shall desire to please Him by a holy life. In the heart of every Christian there will be an echo, however faint, of the words of the Apostle who wrote so eloquently of salvation by faith without the deeds of the Law, "The life which I now live in the flesh I live by the faith of the Son of God, who loved me and gave Himself for me" (Gal. 2:20).

St. Paul urged the Philippians to live a life which becomes the Gospel of Christ (Phil. 1:27). He found the basis of true morality not in the Law, but in the Gospel. Good works are a necessary fruit of faith (John 15:5). That is why St. James could write, "Faith without works is dead" (James 2:20), not because good works add anything to faith and make it alive, but because faith must of necessity lead to good works. Immediately after Paul wrote that we are saved without works, he added, "We are His workmanship, created in Christ Jesus unto good works" (Eph. 2:10). The thief on the cross and the jailer of Philippi, saved by grace, did good works in which they expressed their faith. When Paul became a Christian on the Damascus road, the first question on his lips was, "Lord, what wilt Thou have me to do?" Luther is right when he says, "Oh, it is a living, active, working thing, this faith, so that it is impossible that it should not constantly be doing good." Since the Gospel works faith, it alone is the basis of a truly Christian life.

And the Gospel is the only thing that can really make us able to do good works. Men may lead outwardly moral lives, but those works of theirs are not good in God's sight. There are several reasons for this. First, their heart is not right with God, and their works are not done from true love of God. Secondly, even the good works of the Christian still need the blood of Christ to make them acceptable to God (I Pet. 2:5). Therefore, without faith it is impossible to please God (Heb. 11:6). But once a man has this faith, then good works will follow as a matter of course. The Law is no longer the Christian's taskmaster, but simply the rule whereby he orders his life. The Law has a place in the life of the Christian, not as the cause, but only as the norm of his good works.

Though the Christian is motivated by the Gospel to live according to God's law, yet it must be emphasized that his life never becomes perfect. Those who teach that a Christian no longer sins contradict God's Word (John 1:8), and they destroy all certainty of salvation. A Christian therefore should never be satisfied with himself. Repenting daily of his many sins, he will constantly turn to the Gospel for the assurance of forgiveness. As he grows in knowledge and faith and in his understanding of the Gospel, he will also increase in sanctification and good works.

VII. THE GOSPEL THE TRUE TREASURE OF THE CHURCH

Luther says, "The true treasure of the Church is the holy Gospel of the glory and grace of God." Without the Gospel there is no comfort for men. Sometimes even people who want to be Christians say, "Why should we send missionaries to the heathen? They have a religion." They have a religion, but they do not have the Gospel, and their religion will not bring them to heaven. A mere belief in the existence of God can provide no comfort for men, for there is nothing more terrifying than to know that there is a God and not to know that He can and does forgive sins.

To such men without hope the Gospel comes with the glorious message of the Good Shepherd who seeks the lost sheep, of the gracious Father who welcomes the lost son with open arms and

The Gospel

clothes him in the garments of salvation and the robe of righteousness, the precious blood of Jesus. Though he is oppressed by sorrow and afflicted with tribulation, the Gospel assures him, "Son, be of good cheer, thy sins are forgiven thee." And when death comes, the Gospel again gives us our only hope, and makes it possible to say, "Though I walk through the valley of the shadow of death, I will fear no evil, for Thou art with me." Through the Gospel the grave that shuts us in will but prove the gate to heaven.

All these treasures of the Gospel are ours here and now. He that believeth on the Son hath everlasting life. The assurance that God loves us, that He is merciful and gracious, that we have peace with God and rest for our souls, — can there be anything more delightful than this? The joy of heaven will not be different in kind but only in degree. There we will have these things in fuller measure. There we shall have the substance of those things for which we have here and now the title deed in our faith.

The glory of God is nowhere manifested as fully as it is in the Gospel. We may survey the marvels of nature and stand in awe of the majesty and the wisdom of God, for the heavens declare His glory and the firmament showeth His handiwork. But even these fade into insignificance when we stand beneath the Cross of our Lord. There we begin to probe into the depths of God's love and into all the marvels of His mercy. There are no words in human language which can express the glory of these wondrous works of which the Gospel tells us, and only when we stand with palms in our hands among that great host arrayed in white, like thousand snowclad mountains bright, only then shall we praise Him as we ought.

And the simple preaching of the Gospel is the only thing which can make the world better. In our day we hear much about how the Church must become a leaven and improve conditions in the world. It is true that the Church will act as a leaven. Civilization and freedom follow in the wake of the Gospel. But the Church did not bring these blessings to the world by preaching on political and social problems, nor by agitating for all sorts of political and social changes. When the Church preaches the Gospel of the love and mercy and grace of Christ, then it goes beneath all the outward evils in the world and strikes at the root of every evil, sin. The Church which seeks to improve conditions by agitating for all kinds of regulations and ordinances is operating with the Law. By a fearless, faithful devotion to the business of the Church, the preaching of the Gospel, we shall accomplish what all the laws and treaties in the world cannot accomplish. We shall by the working of the Holy Spirit give men a new heart.

The Gospel may seem to be a still small voice which can barely be discerned amidst all the confused noise of the wind and earthquake and fire of political policy, but, brethren, the power of God is in it. Let us thank God that our Synod still has the Gospel. With it we shall accomplish the purpose for which God put the Church into the world, we shall save souls to the glory of God. The more faithful we are in this, the more we shall accomplish for the social and political betterment of the world. We have had the Gospel now for a hundred years. The signs of decay are all around us, we are becoming lukewarm, let us confess it with a penitent heart. Oh, may God in His mercy grant that we as a Church may always say with the Apostle, "I am not ashamed of the Gospel of Christ."

And in these last evil days, may the Holy Spirit for Jesus' sake give us hearts rededicated to the great unfinished task of bringing lost souls to their Savior and ours by the preaching of the comforting, life-giving Gospel. To do this work well, we shall have to appreciate what the Gospel means to us, we shall have to realize that the Gospel is the true treasure of the Church.

The Sacraments

The Term "Sacrament"

Concerning the term *Sacrament* a great deal has been said and written, and very heated, sometimes bitter, arguments have been conducted. Lutheran theologians in general, and the teachers of our Synod in particular, have been careful in this matter not to permit the argument to degenerate into "a strife about words."

It must be noted that the term does not occur in the Scriptures. *Sacrament* is a Latin word which had its origin in profane literature. Classical writers have used it to designate a thing dedicated, solemnly set apart, as, for example, a sum of money laid down as a pledge in court and given as bond or paid as forfeit or fine. Hence they also employ it to indicate a solemn pledge, specifically, in military usage, the pledge of loyalty, the oath of allegiance of a soldier to the flag of his country, and then, in general, any formal oath.

Early Christian teachers, among them Ambrose and Augustine, adopted the word into ecclesiastical language and employed it in the meaning of "a holy thing, a secret, an inscrutable mystery." And thus Jerome employed it in his Latin Bible, the Vulgate. We find it there, for example, in Daniel 2:18, where Daniel asks his friends to "desire mercies of the God of heaven concerning this *secret*." Again we find the word used in the Vulgate in I Tim. 3:16: "Without controversy great is the *mystery* of godliness." And the widespread use of the word in the Church in its looser meaning is undoubtedly owing to the fact that Jerome employed it in his translation of I Cor. 4:1, where St. Paul calls himself and his colaborers "stewards of the *mysteries* of God."

Jerome himself designated a variety of things as "sacraments," such as preaching, blessing, confirming, visiting the sick, and praying. As a result the term was employed in a loose sense in the language of the Church for many years to designate a variety of Christian signs, symbols, rites, and activities. The Apology of the Augsburg Confession (Art. XIII, 3.4) defines a Sacrament, saying: "If we call Sacraments *rites which have the command of God, and to which the promise of grace has been added,* it is easy to decide what are properly Sacraments. For rites instituted by men will not in this way be Sacraments properly so called. For it does not belong to human authority to promise grace. Therefore signs instituted without God's command are not sure signs of grace, even though they perhaps instruct the rude (children or the uncultivated), or admonish as to something (as a painted cross). Therefore *Baptism, the Lord's Supper, and Absolution,* which is the Sacrament of Repentance, are truly Sacraments. For these rites have God's command and the promise of grace, which is peculiar to the New Testament." (*Triglot,* p. 309.) But, again (Art. XIII, 14), it speaks in a stricter sense only of the two, Baptism and the Lord's Supper, as being properly "signs of the New Testament and testimonies of grace and the remission of sins" (*Triglot,* p. 311). And it arrives at the conclusion which our Church has always endorsed: "No prudent man will strive greatly concerning the number or the term if only those objects still be retained which have God's command and promise" (*Triglot,* p. 313).

Accordingly, our synodical Catechism does not ask the blunt question: What is a Sacrament? but rather formulates the question in this way: "What do we mean by a Sacrament?" Our concern is not to give a fixed definition to a word and to deny the right of any other definition. We will not quarrel about the number of Sacraments. But we object to the placing of other things, be they what they may, on the same level with Baptism and the Lord's Supper, as in every way equal to them.

The tendency to multiply Sacraments beyond the number of two is usually due to a desire to lift human ordinances and rites to the level of Baptism and the Lord's Supper, or to a denial of some of the precious, distinctive, divinely declared characteristics of Baptism and the Lord's Supper, or to an attempt to detract from their importance and benefits. Accordingly, our method of establishing our definition of the word *Sacrament* by studying what Scripture says of Baptism and the Holy Eucharist and listing the combination of features which these two institutions have in common is not "arguing in a circle," but it is rather our way of setting these institutions strictly in a category by themselves, because Scripture teaches that they are absolutely unique and stand in a classification by themselves among all institutions, even among divine institutions. Thus we arrive at a thoroughly Scriptural definition.

Dr. A. L. Graebner gives the following clear definition: "The Sacraments are sacred acts of divine institution, by which, wherever they are properly performed by the prescribed use of the prescribed external elements in conjunction with the divine words of institution, God, being present with the word and elements in a manner peculiar to each Sacrament, earnestly offers to all who partake of such Sacraments forgiveness of sins, life, and salvation and operates toward the acceptance of such blessings or toward greater assurance of their possession. This definition, though not found in the Scriptures in the same terms, is Scriptural inasmuch as it states the *notae* common to two peculiar institutions, described in Holy Writ, which in the Christian Church are designated as Sacraments, Baptism and the Lord's Supper." (*Theological Quarterly*, IV, p. 406.) Our present Catechism gives the gist when it says:

"By a Sacrament we mean *a sacred act* —

"A. Instituted *by God Himself*;

"B. In which there are *certain visible means connected with His Word*; and

"C. By which God *offers, gives,* and *seals* unto us *the forgiveness of sins* which Christ has earned for us."

In these Lutheran definitions we have stated the features in which Baptism and the Lord's Supper agree and by the combination of which they stand forth in a class by themselves as unique institutions.

I. A SACRAMENT IS A SACRED ACT ORDAINED BY GOD

The Sacraments are sacred acts. Christ, our Lord, says in the last chapter of Matthew: "Go ye, therefore, and teach [make disciples of] all nations, baptizing them in the name of the Father and of the Son and of the Holy Ghost; teaching them. . . ."

Here He clearly distinguishes baptizing as an action differing from teaching. Action is clearly indicated in the stories of the Baptism of Jesus (Matt. 3:13-17), the Baptism of the Ethiopian eunuch (Acts 8:36-38), and the Baptism of St. Paul (Acts 22:16).

Also in the Lord's Supper we have action. Our Lord did not only pray and speak, but He took bread and gave it to His disciples, and He took the cup and gave it to them. He told His disciples: "Take, eat." "Drink ye all of it." It is self-evident that they ate the bread. And we are expressly told (Mark 14:23) that "they all drank" of the cup. These are actions, and of these actions Christ says: "This do!"

The Sacraments are not things that can be carried about by clergymen, set upon an altar, enshrined in a tabernacle, or carried in procession and worshiped, but acts in which living persons participate. The action is of the nature and essence of Baptism and the Lord's Supper, and without it they simply are not. This eliminates from the list of real and true Sacraments matrimony and penance, which are so regarded by the Roman Church.

Not every act, even though a sacred rite, is a Sacrament. The Sacraments are furthermore defined as being sacred acts of *divine institution, ordained of God*. In the case of Baptism and the Lord's Supper we rightly speak of "words of institution," which are passages of the Scriptures that show these sacred acts to be instituted by Christ Himself while engaged in visible conversation with His disciples on earth, charging them to perform these sacred acts after His departure, even to the end of time.

In the case of Baptism we are given these "words of institution" in Matthew 28:19, where we have the command: "Go ye, therefore, and teach [make disciples of] all nations, baptizing them." And the promise "I am with you alway, even unto the end of the world" indicates how long the command is to remain in force, namely, to the end of days. (Also Mark 16:15-16.) Hence the Apostles proclaimed Baptism as a divine ordinance and required its administration (Acts 2:38-39; 10:47-48; 16:15, 33).

In the case of the Lord's Supper we have these words of institution recorded four times, namely, Matt. 26:26-28; Mark 14: 22-24; Luke 22:19-20; and I Cor. 11:23-25. These words describe the occasion in the Upper Room when our Lord, on the night of His betrayal and arrest, replaced the Old Testament Passover with the Sacrament of His own body and blood. They tell us what He said and what He did, and they report His twofold solemn charge: *"This do."* Such command, too, is in force to the end of time. This fact our teachers have emphasized over against Quakers, Unitarians, and others, who declare that the Sacraments were not instituted for all Christians of all times and that the Lord's Supper was meant only for that evening in the Upper Room. The disciples of Jesus made most frequent use of the Sacrament in the days that followed, for they "continued steadfastly in the Apostles' doctrine and fellowship and in *breaking of bread"* (Acts 2:42). And to his record of the institution of the Lord's Supper St. Paul expressly adds the statement: "As *often as* ye eat this bread and drink this cup, ye do show the Lord's death *till He come*" (I Cor. 11:26). This means that it is understood that Christians will celebrate the Lord's Supper frequently until Judgment Day.

This again eliminates from the classification into which we place Baptism and the Lord's Supper all other things which are by some called Sacraments. It eliminates from the Romish list Ordination, Confirmation, Penance, and Extreme Unction. It also eliminates the so-called "ordinances" which certain sects would add to the list, such as the footwashing, the laying on of hands, the anointing of the sick with oil, etc. (Mennonites, Irvingites, Mormons, Primitive Baptists, Universalists). For in the case of all these the divine command is missing.

II. IN A SACRAMENT PRESCRIBED VISIBLE MEANS ARE USED ACCORDING TO DIVINE INSTRUCTION IN CONNECTION WITH PRESCRIBED DIVINE WORDS

A. A SACRAMENT MUST HAVE A DIVINELY PRESCRIBED VISIBLE ELEMENT

The prescribed visible element in Holy Baptism is water. Though in the words of institution no mention is made of water, yet the very command to "baptize" implies the use of water. In the common usage of the people the word *baptize* was employed to designate the cleansing of the human body (Mark 7:4; Luke 11:38; Heb. 9:10) and of household utensils (Mark 7:4, 8), which certainly presupposes washing with water. And, therefore, if the act of "baptizing" is to be done with something other than water, then this element is expressly mentioned (Matt. 3:11 b; Acts 1:5). But water is expressly referred to as the external means in baptizing when St. Paul tells us that the Israelites of the Exodus "were all baptized unto Moses in the *cloud* and in the *sea*" (I Cor. 10:2).

However, there is, in addition, clear instruction on the use of water in the Sacrament of Holy Baptism. John the Baptist used water in his Baptism (Matt. 3:11; Mark 1:8; Luke 3:16; John 1:26; Matt. 3:16; Mark 1:10; John 3:23; Acts 1:5; 11:16). Jesus speaks of this Sacrament when He says (John 3:5) that those who enter into the kingdom of heaven must be "born of *water* and of the Spirit." St. Peter asks in the home of Cornelius: "Can any man forbid *water*, that these should not be baptized?" (Acts 10:47; see also Acts 8:35-39; Eph. 5:26; I Pet. 3:20-22.) To substitute another fluid for water is meddling with a divine institution and thoroughly reprehensible. Any person so "baptized" is to be validly baptized with water, for water is essential to the Sacrament.*

In the Sacrament of the Holy Eucharist the Lord has prescribed not one, but two visible elements. These are bread and wine. The Scriptures clearly state, in all four passages where the words of institution are recorded, that the Lord took *bread* and gave it to His disciples (Matt. 26:26; Mark 14:22; Luke 22:19; I Cor. 11:23). So also St. Paul refers again and again to the bread of the Sacrament (I Cor. 10:16; 11:26-28). Bread is an article prepared by the baking of grain flour. Further than this the nature of this element is not defined. We are not told of what kind of grain the flour in the bread is to be milled, nor what is to be the form and shape and size of the baked product, nor whether it is to be salted or unsalted. We do know that the bread our Lord used must have been unleavened, because the Lord's Supper was instituted at the Passover Festival, the Feast of Unleavened Bread

---

* NOTE: As long as water is used, it does not matter what kind of water it may be, whether river, lake, well, rain, dew water, whether standing or flowing water. For in regard to these matters there is no prescription.

(Ex. 12:8). Our churches have therefore consistently used the unleavened wafer, or host, without, however, demanding the use of unleavened bread as necessary, since no such requirement is made in Scripture. Yet the fathers of our Synod have warned not to change to the use of leavened bread for the sake of satisfying the criticism of sectarian groups, but to maintain the right of Christian liberty over against such pressure.

The other visible element in the Sacrament is "the cup." The words of institution say of Jesus: "He took *the cup*." (Matt. 26:27; Mark 14:23; Luke 22:20; I Cor. 11:25.) They also state that Jesus said: "This *cup* is the New Testament in My blood" (I Cor. 11:25; Luke 22:20). The term *cup* is here used, of course, for the contents of the cup, for Jesus asks His disciples to drink of the cup. St. Paul also speaks of drinking the cup (I Cor. 11:26-27), explaining in the same connection that he means drinking "out of the cup" (v. 28). What was in the cup? We know from Jewish tradition that it had become customary to have on the Passover table a cup filled with wine mingled with water. But we are not left to human authority in this matter. For it is clearly indicated that this Jewish custom was observed also by our Lord and His disciples at the last Passover. For in the verse following the words of institution in Matthew's Gospel (26:29) we have these words of Jesus Himself: "I say unto you, I will not drink henceforth of this (note the "this") fruit of the vine, until the day when I drink it new with you in My Father's kingdom." What was in the cup was the "fruit of the vine." The Greek word "ampelos," *vine*, is used exclusively of the grape vine. The content of the cup was a product yielded by grapes. More the words do not say. But in saying so much they make "the fruit of the vine" essential to the Sacrament.

There can be no doubt that the content of the cup was nothing else than grape *wine*. And this is indicated also I Cor. 11:20-21. The early Church used grape *wine* mingled with water in the celebration of the Lord's Supper according to statements by Justin Martyr, Irenaeus, Cyprian, and others. The Roman Church has always used grape *wine*. So has also the Lutheran Church consistently used the same element. Throughout the history of our Church the Sacrament has been celebrated with grape *wine* upon its altars, and the fathers of our Synod have warned specifically against the use of grape juice, lest any uncertainty arise as to the validity of the Sacrament.

The essential, indispensable visible elements in the Sacrament of the Holy Eucharist, then, are "bread, prepared of grain flour, and wine, the fruit of the vine." Without these prescribed elements there can be no Lord's Supper. And in this the Sacraments agree, that both of them have expressly prescribed visible elements for which no substitutions dare be made.

B. IN A SACRAMENT THE PRESCRIBED USE IS ESSENTIAL

The water in Baptism and the bread and wine in the Eucharist are essential, and so is their prescribed use. The baptismal water is not to be drunk or preserved in superstitious veneration. The water is to be applied externally to the person receiving the Sacrament in the manner prescribed by the word *baptize* and familiar to the Jews from their ritual baptisms (Heb. 9:10). That means that while the prescribed use of the water calls for external application to the applicant, the manner of such application is entirely an indifferent matter, whether it be by washing, pouring, sprinkling, or immersing, for the word *baptize* covers every such form of application of water (Heb. 9:10; Luke 11:38; Mark 7:3-4; Rom. 6:3-4; Titus 3:5-6; Acts 22:16; I Cor. 10:2). And nowhere in the Scriptures, which record a large number of Baptisms, is any indication given how in any single case the water was applied. Hence, while the external application of the water is prescribed, we have no prescribed method of the application of it in Holy Baptism.

The prescribed use of the elements in the Lord's Supper consists in their being given and eaten and drunk. Such is the requirement of the words of institution. Of the bread it is said: "Take, *eat*" (Matt. 22:26). And of the cup, that is, the wine, it is said that Jesus "*gave* it to them, saying, *Drink* ye all of it" (Matt. 26:27). The distribution and the eating and drinking of the elements in the Eucharist are therefore essential to the Sacrament. For of these things Jesus emphatically says: "*This* do." Where such essential prescribed use is neglected or set aside, either altogether or in part, there is no Sacrament, no Lord's Supper. When Roman Catholics

The Sacraments

refuse the cup, the wine, to the communicants, do not distribute it to them so that they may drink of it (since the 12th century, confirmed by the Council of Trent), they destroy the sacramental nature of the observance and reduce what is supposed to be a Sacrament to a mere valueless human ordinance. This is the more apparent and certain since Jesus expressly stated of the cup: "Drink ye *all* of it" and since Mark particularly records the fact that "they *all drank* of it" (Mark 14:23).

Again since no other use except the distributing and the eating and drinking of the visible elements is prescribed, no other use is valid and warranted. When therefore either of the elements is carried in solemn procession, set apart for veneration in an altar tabernacle, elevated before a congregation for adoration, or supposedly sacrificed for the sins of the dead and the living, this is contrary to the divine prescription. Such use has nothing in common with the Eucharist, is no Sacrament, and constitutes a blasphemous tampering with a holy and unalterable divine institution.

The question has been debated whether or not certain other actions are not also part of the prescribed use of the elements in the Lord's Supper, as, for example, the *breaking* of the bread and the *taking* of the elements into the hands of the communicants. Our teachers have rightly classed these matters as *not* belonging to the essence of the Sacrament and therefore as optional. Since the eating and drinking are essential, the taking with the mouth is essential and constitutes a sufficient "taking" (John 19:36). The *breaking* of the bread constituted a part of the necessary distributive *giving*, but it is the giving, the distribution, that is essential. So "breaking of bread" is an expression often synonymous with distributing (Mark 8:6, 19; Is. 58:7; Lam. 4:4).

C. In a Sacrament the Prescribed Element Is to be Used in Connection with the Prescribed Divine Word

To be a Sacrament, however, a divinely ordained act must be performed by the prescribed use of the prescribed external means in conjunction with the prescribed divine words. Which are these divine words? Not just any of the statements of Scripture, but the words of institution, given us by Christ Himself. These words are to be used not only in a preliminary consecration of the elements, but in close conjunction with the prescribed use of the prescribed elements.

Baptism is called by St. Paul (Eph. 5:26) "the washing of water *by the Word*." This statement clearly sets forth that Baptism is a washing in which water and the Word are together, are used simultaneously. So Luther properly declares: "Baptism is not simple water only, but it is the water comprehended in God's command and *connected with God's word*." What word? None other than that word which Christ spoke when He charged His Church to baptize "in the name of the Father and of the Son and of the Holy Ghost" (Matt. 28:19).

In the institution of the Lord's Supper Christ did not silently distribute bread and wine, but spoke words as He distributed them. He gave the bread, saying: "Take, eat, this is My body." He gave the cup, saying: "Drink ye all of it; for this is My blood of the New Testament, which is shed for many for the remission of sins." (Matt. 26:26-27.) And when He charged His disciples, saying: "*This* do," such command comprised the speaking of the words as well as the distributing and the taking of the visible elements.

Thus these divinely ordained acts of Baptism and the Lord's Supper distinguish themselves from all other sacred acts by the fact that in them a prescribed use of prescribed elements is connected with prescribed words to be spoken. Therefore we apply to these sacred acts exclusively the term *Sacraments*, in order to distinguish them from other sacred acts which we do not so designate.

D. No Qualities in the Administering Person Affect the Validity of the Sacraments

The completeness and the validity of the Sacraments depend solely and altogether upon Him who has instituted them. Whenever and wherever they are administered according to the divine command by the prescribed use of the prescribed elements, together with the prescribed words, they are complete and valid. Therefore the worthiness or unworthiness of the celebrant neither add anything to them nor take away anything from them. Therefore any quality or characteristic of the person who administers it is not of the essence of the Sacrament.

The Roman Catholic Church, the Greek Catholic Church, and the Episcopal Church insist that only such as have been properly ordained by a bishop who can trace his own ordination back to the Apostles (Apostolic Succession) is able to administer a Sacrament, that only by virtue of the administration by such a one does an act become a valid Sacrament. Also some Romanizing Lutherans (Grabau and his adherents) have taught that no act, even though it fulfill all requirements of the divine institution, is a valid Sacrament unless administered by a properly ordained minister, that therefore the call and ordination belong to the essence of the Sacraments. This our Missouri Synod fathers have consistently denied. They have pointed out that in the administration of the Sacraments, as well as in the preaching of the Word, ministers are only God's instruments (I Cor. 3:5-7; I Cor. 4:1).

Scripture knows nothing of an Apostolic Succession; and while Scripture mentions ordination through the laying on of hands and prayer, it yet nowhere commands it as an ordinance of the Church. How, then, can such a qualification as Apostolic Succession, or even simple ordination of the celebrant of the Sacraments, be made a requirement for a true Sacrament?

Rome insists that in the preparation for, and in the administration of, the Sacraments the priest must have the *intention* to do what the Church requires. Pietists and various sects insist that unbelief and ungodliness in the celebrant vitiates the Sacraments. This is a dangerous doctrine, which would necessarily cast doubt on every administration of the Sacraments. The very purpose of the institution of the Sacraments, to give to the individual a positive assurance of the grace of God, would therewith be defeated.

Scripture assures us that the Word of God does not lose its power even if it is preached by hypocritical scribes and Pharisees (Matt. 23:2-3), or from impure motives (Phil. 1:15-18), or by wicked Balaam (Num. 24:1-25), or by ungodly Caiaphas (John 11:49-52).

Hence a Sacrament is a Sacrament regardless of the intention, belief or unbelief, piety or ungodliness, of the one by whom it is administered.

E. The Public Doctrine of the Church in Which the Sacraments are Administered Does Affect the Validity of the Sacraments

On the other hand, whenever churches by their public confession and teaching empty the words of institution of their intended meaning, then such churches have robbed the Sacraments of something which is absolutely essential to them, and their sacramental observances are no longer the true Sacraments. They have robbed the words of institution of that which makes them the word of God, the divine sense and meaning. And so the rite which they observe is minus the word of God and no Sacrament.

If Unitarians, and all others who deny the doctrine of the Holy Trinity, baptize, even though in doing so they use the correct Scriptural formula, this is no valid Baptism, because their formula, though it sounds exactly the same to the ear, has a different meaning from that of Scripture and such different meaning is publicly confessed, preached, and taught. (F. Pieper, *Christliche Dogmatik*, III, pp. 307—308; Walther, *Pastorale*, p. 121.)

The Roman Mass is definitely not the Sacrament of the Lord's Supper, because Rome claims that the Mass is essentially a sacrifice. That claim contradicts the clear words of institution and denies the completeness and the sufficiency of the sacrifice of Christ on Calvary for the sins of the world (Heb. 10:10, 14). Hence it denies the central doctrine of Christianity, which is also the very heart of the Sacrament of the Lord's Supper, as set forth so plainly in the words of institution. "This is My body, which is given for you" (Luke 22:19), "This is My blood of the New Testament, which is shed for many for the remission of sins" (Matt. 26:28).

Professed Modernistic churches, which in their public teaching deny the Atonement, have no Sacraments, since by such teaching they deny the true meaning of the words of institution and thus take from them that which makes them the words of God.

The "conservative" Reformed churches also do not have the Sacrament of the Lord's Supper. For with the denial of the real presence of the body and blood of Christ in the Sacrament they publicly declare themselves at variance with the clear words of institution, though they may use them exactly as they are recorded in the Scriptures. Thus they have in their supper no word of God, and hence it is no *Lord's* Supper. For a supper in which bread and wine are distributed and received as mere symbols of the absent body and blood of Christ — such a supper the Lord did not institute.

Thus the public doctrine of a church does affect the validity of the Sacraments. Where such public teaching is at variance with the words of divine institution, there these words are emptied of their God-intended meaning, are made to say something that the Lord never meant them to say, and therefore are no more God's word, but human phrases. A Sacrament requires that it be instituted by Christ and that it be what Christ instituted it to be.

F. THE VALIDITY OF A SACRAMENT DOES NOT DEPEND UPON THE PERSON OR CHARACTER OF THE RECIPIENT

Also the faith and piety of the person receiving a Sacrament does not belong to the nature and essence of a Sacrament. Though an unbeliever be baptized, the Baptism is a true Baptism. Though all who at a given time and place participate in the Lord's Supper should be unbelievers, yea, vicious and hardened murderers, thieves, and adulterers, it would yet be the Lord's Supper. And though a true and sincere believer should participate in the observance of what is claimed to be the Lord's Supper in a Reformed church, yet all his believing will not make a Sacrament of such observance.

Calvin and his Reformed followers indeed insisted that "it is faith which determines the contents of the Sacraments!" The argument of such is often taken from the words in Mark 16:16: "He that believeth and is baptized shall be saved; but he that believeth not shall be damned." But in these very words Christ distinguishes between "believing" and being "baptized," between the faith of the recipient and the Sacrament, and states that unbelief, and not the lack of the Sacrament, damns. He implies that an unbeliever who is eventually eternally damned may have received Baptism, a true Baptism. In the institution of the Holy Supper Jesus did not say: "If you believe, then this is My body, given for you; if you believe, then this is My blood, shed for you for the remission of sins." The Gospel is the Gospel whether anyone believes it or not; and the Sacraments are valid Sacraments regardless of the faith or unbelief of the recipients.

III. IN A SACRAMENT GOD EARNESTLY OFFERS TO ALL WHO PARTAKE OF IT THE FORGIVENESS OF SINS AND OPERATES EARNESTLY AND EFFICACIOUSLY TOWARD THE ACCEPTANCE OF THIS BLESSING OR TOWARD GREATER ASSURANCE OF ITS POSSESSION

A. A Sacrament Offers All the Blessings of the Gospel

To the nature of a true Sacrament belongs also this very important fact that it contains the promise of God's grace in Christ, that it earnestly offers to all who receive such Sacrament the forgiveness of sins and eternal salvation. Since the Word of God, specifically that word of God which is the word of institution, is essential to the Sacrament, therefore both Sacraments have the same purpose and effect as the Word of God. Since the word of God in the Sacraments is not Law, but pure Gospel, the Sacraments have no other purpose and aim and benefit than the purpose and aim and benefit of the Word of the Gospel. The blessings offered and promised in the Sacraments are not something in addition to, or beyond, the promises of the Gospel, or part of them, but the identical blessings. Hence the spiritual blessings promised in the Sacraments are all the benefits of Christ's vicarious satisfaction, the forgiveness of sins, the salvation which Christ, the Mediator, has merited for all mankind. Such forgiveness therefore includes life and salvation and every divine, spiritual gift and effect which is imparted to the Christian as a result: the state of grace, the indwelling of the Holy Ghost, the mystical union, sanctification, the love of God and the neighbor, membership in the invisible Church and all privileges connected therewith, the hope of heaven.

Thus the whole counsel of God for man's spiritual welfare, all that He has prepared in Christ Jesus for man's salvation, is earnestly offered by Baptism and rejected by those who refuse to be baptized. So the words of institution clearly declare. Our Lord commanded His disciples in the last chapter of Matthew: "Go ye, therefore, and teach [make disciples of] all nations, baptizing them in the name of the Father and of the Son and of the Holy Ghost, teaching them to observe all things whatsoever I have commanded you." According to these words, disciples of Christ are made by "baptizing" and "teaching." Only such a person is a disciple of Christ as has received the forgiveness of his sins and has thus become a child of God. This means that through "baptizing" and through "teaching" the forgiveness of sins is brought to people in order that they may become Christ's disciples. And as the forgiveness is not brought in part, say, 50 or 90 per cent of it, by "teaching," by the Word, but completely and altogether, so also the entire forgiveness is brought by Baptism to him who receives the Sacrament. The word of promise Mark 16:16 is even more direct and explicit: "He that believeth and is baptized shall be *saved.*" In Luke 7:30 we read that "the Pharisees and lawyers rejected the counsel of God against themselves, being not baptized of him," that is, of John the Baptist. This passage states that in rejecting Baptism one rejects the sum total of all the blessings of the divine plan of salvation. St. Peter says: "Repent, and be baptized, every one of you, in the name of Jesus Christ *for the remission of sins, and ye shall receive the gift of the Holy Ghost*" (Acts 2:38). Compare also Luke 3:3; Acts 22:16; Tit. 3:5-7; I Pet. 3:21.

Likewise in the Eucharist, Christ assures us of the forgiveness of sins, giving us the selfsame body which was sacrificed for us and the selfsame blood which was paid as a ransom for us, *for the remission of sins.* The words of institution admit of no other meaning or interpretation. Jesus clearly says: "This is My body, which is *given for you*" (Luke 22:19). "This is My blood of the New Testament, which is *shed for many for the remission of sins*" (Matt. 26:28). Also in this Sacrament we have God's loving offer of pardon for the sake of Him who died and shed His blood as a ransom for sinners.

Since the offer in the Sacraments is a divine offer, it is an offer which conveys and brings, gives and bestows, the divine gift of forgiveness. It is, moreover, such an earnest bestowing of the merits of Christ the Savior that the Sacraments are seals of God's favor in Christ to the individual who receives them. To His word God has added the visible element to make the offer, the bestowal, all the more noticeable to the individual recipient. The Apology of the Augsburg Confession (XIII [VII], 6) declares: "Just as the Word enters the ear in order to strike our heart, so the rite itself strikes the eye in order to move the heart. The effect of the Word and of the rite is the same, as it has well been said by Augustine that a Sacrament is a *visible Word*, because the rite is received by the eyes and is, as it were, a picture of the Word, signifying the same thing as the Word" (*Triglot*, p. 3,090). In the Sacrament, God, as it were, takes the individual apart from the throng to assure him most intimately and personally that Christ's merits were won also particularly for him and are in God's loving heart intended for him, to bring him all their peace and joy here and hereafter.

This is denied by both Reformed and Romanist theology. Reformed theology in general denies that the Sacraments are mediums which convey the forgiveness of sins and insists that they are only symbols, reminders of the merits of Christ, and Calvin's teaching, by its denial of universal grace and its teaching of particular grace, removes every assurance which the individual might seek in the Sacraments that the forgiveness of sins is intended also personally for him.

Roman theology indeed speaks of the Sacraments, notably of Baptism, as mediums which convey grace. With the term *grace*, however, it means not the grace of God in Christ Jesus, the forgiveness of sins. As the Council of Trent curses the doctrine of the justification of a sinner before God by grace alone through faith in Christ, so it also (Sess. XIII, Can. 6) anathematizes all who set forth the gracious forgiveness of sins as the chief purpose of the Sacraments. The grace which the Sacraments convey according to the Romanist view is infused grace, a sanctifying grace, which God is supposed to give, "pour into," man to enable him to earn for himself justification and salvation. With such teaching, again, no Sacrament can be an assurance of personal forgiveness and right relations with God.

B. The Sacraments Require Faith in Christ

Since the Sacraments offer, convey, and seal the forgiveness of sins which Christ has merited, they require faith on the part of the person who receives them. For this Gospel assurance can be received only by faith. According to the emphatic teaching of Scripture the sinner is saved, justified, by faith alone (Rom. 3:21-24, 27-28; 4:5). And therefore, according to the general teaching of

The Sacraments

the Word of God, the blessings the Sacraments offer, convey, and seal can be appropriated only by faith.

This fact must be emphasized over against Romanists, who teach that the Sacraments impart an infused grace to the participants in a mechanical, magical way, that simply by the mechanical submission to the act of Baptism or participation in the Mass, without faith on his part, a person receives and possesses this infused grace.

The Apology of the Augsburg Confession states over against this error: "This is absolutely a Jewish opinion, to hold that we are justified by a ceremony, without a good disposition of the heart, i. e., without faith. And yet this impious and pernicious opinion is taught with great authority throughout the entire realm of the Pope. Paul contradicts this, and denies (Rom. 4:9) that Abraham was justified by circumcision, but asserts that circumcision was a sign presented for exercising faith. Thus we teach that in the use of the Sacraments *faith* ought to be added, which should believe these promises and receive the promised things there offered in the Sacrament. And the reason is plain and thoroughly grounded. This is a certain and true use of the Holy Sacrament, on which the Christian hearts and consciences may risk to rely. The promise is useless unless it is received by faith. But the Sacraments are the signs and seals of the promises." (Art. XIII [VII], 18—20, *Triglot*, p. 313.)

This pernicious doctrine has also afflicted Protestantism. Yes, even some so-called Lutherans have ascribed to the Sacraments magical and medicinal qualities, by which a mere partaking of them has been said to confer various benefits, all the way from an indelible character to a better state of physical health. And how many a Lutheran comforts himself with the mere physical reception of the Sacraments, without inquiring into his heart to see if he have faith! One goes his way in neglect of the Word and in unbelief and sin, falsely comforting himself that he is a baptized Lutheran. Another goes to the Lord's Table thus to retain his church membership, to fulfill one of its requirements, or because he believes that it will do him good in some indefinite way if he goes through the act, or because he hopes to "feel better" if he will once again participate in this rite. This is nothing but papistic work-righteousness, which believes that because of compliance with a divine command it merits divine favor and blessings.

It is therefore well to note that the Sacraments require faith on the part of the recipient. In speaking of Baptism, Jesus emphasizes the absolute importance of faith for salvation. He says in the last chapter of Mark: "He that *believeth* and is baptized shall be saved; but he that *believeth not shall be damned*." Clearly enough these words of the Savior state that Baptism without faith will profit nothing, will not confer salvation. Luther therefore speaks with good reason of the "*faith*, which *trusts* such word of God in the water," and says correctly that Baptism "gives eternal salvation to all who *believe* this, as the words and promises of God declare." And our synodical Catechism is right in saying that "through faith, which trusts this word of promise, we accept the forgiveness, life, and salvation in Baptism and make these blessings our own." (Acts 8:12-13, 36-37.)

Likewise in the Lord's Supper the very words of institution insist on the necessity of faith. When Jesus says in the Sacrament: "This is My body, which is *given for you*," "This cup is the New Testament in My blood, which is *shed for you*" (Luke 22:19-20), these words certainly require faith of the communicant, the faith that forgiveness of sins is established in the substitutionary death of Christ. And just as in regard to Baptism we are told that "he that *believeth* not shall be damned," so also we are told that the unworthy, that is, the unbelieving communicant, "eats and drinks damnation to himself" (I Cor. 11:29).

So, again, in speaking of the words "given and shed for you for the remission of sins," Luther says correctly: "He that believes these words has what they say and express, namely, the forgiveness of sins." He points out that the Lord's Supper does require faith when he states: "He is truly worthy and well prepared who has faith in these words"; and, again: "The words 'for you' require all hearts to believe." (Cp. also "The Lord's Supper," F. Zucker page 440.)

From this Sacrament also appears very plainly what is to be the specific object of such faith. Indeed, at the Lord's Table the communicant must believe that Jesus Christ gives him His true body and His true blood to eat and to drink. This is a necessary prerequisite to the salutary use of the Sacrament of the Altar (I Cor.

11:29). But not faith inasmuch as it believes the real presence of Christ's body and blood makes the use of the Sacrament beneficial, but rather faith inasmuch as it believes the words "given for you" and "shed for you" and "for the remission of sins." The faith which the Sacrament requires is faith in the forgiveness of sins. That is to say: If anyone is to receive the benefits of the Sacrament, he must believe that he personally receives forgiveness of sin, life, and salvation in the Sacrament, the very forgiveness which most surely was won for him by Jesus Christ in His substitutional life, suffering, and death. In other words, the Sacrament requires faith in what the Scriptures say concerning both the essence and the object (purpose) of the Sacrament.

Let it be said here, by way of repetition, that such faith does not belong to the essence of the Sacrament. Its presence or absence does not affect the validity of the Sacrament. Let it be said also that such faith is in no way meritorious, a work which man does in order to make the Sacraments personally effective to him. This would militate against the Scriptural doctrine that we are saved by grace alone (Eph. 2:8).

C. The Sacraments Are Means of Grace

The Sacraments serve the purpose of creating, sustaining, and strengthening faith. The requirements, demands, admonitions, exhortations of the Sacraments are not commands of the Law, but Gospel invitations, which in their very nature, through the divine power that is operative in them, themselves produce what they require. In the Sacraments God not only offers, conveys, and seals to men the forgiveness of sins, life, and salvation, but in them He also "operates earnestly and efficaciously toward the acceptance of such blessings, or toward greater assurance of their possession."

The Sacraments are means of grace, through the instrumentality of which God appropriates His blessings to the individual, that is, they create faith in the promises they make, faith in the Gospel of the forgiveness of sins in Christ. Through them the Holy Spirit works regeneration and conversion. And where faith already exists, there the Holy Spirit through the Sacraments strengthens and preserves such faith.

Since it belongs to the essence of the Sacraments that in them the prescribed use of prescribed earthly elements be combined with the prescribed word of God, and that they have the Gospel promise, *the power of the Word is in the Sacraments,* and all passages of the Bible which treat of the power of the Word are pertinent here. For where the divine Word is, there is also the divine Spirit; and wherever a person uses the Word of God in any form, God is divinely operative in it (I Cor. 2:4).

The Scripture declares over and over again the power and efficacy of the Word of God, specifically the Word of the Gospel, to create, increase, sustain, and strengthen faith. Let us hear just one significant passage: "As God is true, our word toward you was not yea and nay. For the Son of God, Jesus Christ, who was preached among you by us, even by me and Silvanus and Timotheus, was not yea and nay, but in Him was yea. For all the promises of God in Him are yea and in Him Amen, unto the glory of God by us. Now He which establisheth us with you in Christ, and hath anointed us, is God; who also hath sealed us and given us the earnest of the Spirit in our hearts" (II Cor. 1:18-22).

What Paul here emphasizes concerning *all* the promises of God certainly applies also to the promises of God in the Sacraments. Since God has connected His most gracious promise of forgiveness with Baptism and the Lord's Supper, these also are true and efficacious means of grace. And they are that by virtue of the divine promises attached to them.

Accordingly, the Scriptures describe the Sacraments to us as means of grace, through the instrumentality of which the Holy Ghost imparts to us the merits of the Redeemer, working in us, preserving in us, and strengthening in us the saving faith.

For Baptism the Bible claims the power to work regeneration, renewing, cleansing, faith in the forgiveness of sins, and the assurance of salvation.

Jesus tells Nicodemus: "Except a man be born of water and of the Spirit, he cannot enter into the Kingdom of God" (John 3:5).

St. Paul declares: "Ye are all the children of God by faith in Christ Jesus. For as many of you as have been baptized into Christ have put on Christ." (Gal. 3:26-27.)

St. Paul tells Titus that Baptism is "the washing of regeneration," that by it the Holy Ghost renews us, that by it God saves us, that this is done by virtue of the abundant merits of Christ, our Savior, that Baptism bestows upon us Christ's justifying grace, that by Baptism we are made heirs, that is, God's children, that by Baptism we are blessed with the hope of heaven (Titus 3:5-7).

In I Cor. 6:11 we are told: "But ye are washed, but ye are sanctified, but ye are justified in the name of the Lord Jesus and by the Spirit of our God."

To the Romans St. Paul writes that those who are baptized are by Baptism made sharers of the death and resurrection of Christ (Rom. 6:3-5). Cp. also Luke 3:3; Acts 2:38; 22:16; Eph. 5:25-27; I Pet. 3:21.

What does Baptism give or profit? Christ, our Lord, says in the last chapter of Mark: "He that believeth and is baptized shall be saved." And these words of Jesus alone are sufficient for Luther to answer in his Small Catechism: "It works forgiveness of sins, delivers from death and the devil, and gives eternal salvation to all who believe this, as the words and promises of God declare."

"Baptism is expressly said to *save us* (I Pet. 3:21), not as a first cause, which is God, our Savior; not as the prompting cause, which is the grace of God; not *ex opere operato*, as by a meritorious work, for the *causa meritoria* of our salvation is Christ and His sacrifice; but as a means whereby we are made partakers of Christ and His righteousness and salvation (Gal. 3:27)." (*Theological Quarterly*, IV, p. 410.)

Baptism is also of such benefit to adults who have already been regenerated by the Word of the Gospel. Our dogmaticians have asserted that in such adults the Sacrament operates toward perseverance and greater assurance of the possession of the divine spiritual blessings. The Bible records a number of instances showing that also such as already possess the assurance of the forgiveness of their sins are to be baptized. There is the case of St. Paul, of Lydia, and of the Philippian jailer. There is the case of the Samaritans who "believed Philip, preaching the things concerning the Kingdom of God and the name of Jesus Christ," but who were nevertheless baptized (Acts 8:12; cf. also v. 13). There is the case of the Ethiopian eunuch, who confessed his faith in Christ before he was baptized. Nevertheless Philip baptized him. "And he went on his way rejoicing." Such joyful faith was the product of both the spoken Word of the Gospel (Is. 53) and the Sacrament of Holy Baptism (Acts 8:35-39).

Moreover, Baptism is a means of grace not only at conversion or at the time of its administration, but continuously. Through the baptismal confirmation of the promises of the Gospel it works toward keeping and strengthening the baptized member of Christ in the faith. Peter speaks to baptized Christians of the continuing present effect of their Baptism when he writes: "Baptism doth also now save us (not the putting away of the filth of the flesh, but the answer of a good conscience toward God)" (I Pet. 3:21). It is implied in many of the passages which treat of Baptism that it is our Baptism which enables us to keep our baptismal vow (Eph. 5:25-27; Rom. 6:3-4; Gal. 3:26-27).

Luther writes in the Large Catechism: "If you live in repentance, you walk in Baptism, which not only signifies such a new life, but also produces, begins, and exercises it. For therein are given grace, the Spirit, and power to suppress the old man, so that the new man may come forth and become strong.

"Therefore our Baptism abides forever; and even though someone should fall from it and sin, nevertheless we always have access thereto, that we may again subdue the old man" (*Triglot,* p. 751).

In the Sacrament of the Altar the precious Gospel promises of the words of institution preach the atoning death of Christ with such force and clarity that no doubt should ever have arisen concerning the truth that this Sacrament possesses the Gospel's power and is a means of grace, efficaciously operating toward the acceptance of the greater assurance of the forgiveness of sins. Here the Lord speaks of His given body and His shed blood and thus declares the historic fact of His voluntary death. But here He also explains the meaning and the purpose of that death when He says: "This is My body, *given for you.*" "This cup is the New Testament in My blood, which is *shed for you.*" According to St. Matthew He added the words: "*For the remission of sins.*" This clear Gospel can here have no other and no less a purpose than it has in the read or preached Word, namely, to create, strengthen, and sustain faith. And the giving of His body and His blood to be eaten and drunk can have no other purpose than to bless the communicant with the firm personal assurance that he has and possesses and enjoys in Christ the forgiveness of his sins.

Particularly noteworthy are the words of Christ as recorded by two of the inspired writers (Luke 22:20; I Cor. 11:25): "This cup is the New Testament in My blood." The New Testament is the Covenant of grace established on the forgiveness of sins. The very essence of this Testament, or Covenant, is the forgiveness of sins. These words therefore mean: "With this cup I give you the New Testament, or the forgiveness of sins." The particular gift of the Lord's Supper is therefore the same blessing which the Gospel conveys generally and Baptism individually, the forgiveness of sins.

How logically correct and Scripturally sound, then, is Luther's reply to the question as to the benefits of the Lord's Supper! "That is shown us by these words, 'Given and shed for you for the remission of sins'; namely, that in the Sacrament forgiveness of sins, life, and salvation are given us through these words. For where there is forgiveness of sins, there is also life and salvation."

Also here it must be remembered that the Lord's Supper has such effect not only at the moment of its celebration, but continuously thereafter. Being a continuing assurance of the grace of God, it continues to be operative as a means of grace.

As means of grace the Sacraments do not operate irresistibly. By persistent unbelief man can thwart their purpose and effect. By receiving the Sacraments in unbelief man can reject and cast away from himself their blessings. By turning to unbelief, after having accepted and received their blessings in faith, man can nullify these.

"The full pardon thus freely and unconditionally offered and extended to the sinner can be and often is rejected, its acceptance refused. The Sacrament is not a charm, a magic lotion or potion, but a means of grace. Being but another form of the Gospel, it, too, is the power of God unto salvation to every one that believeth. But by the Sacrament, too, the power of God operates by mediate action. *As many of us as have been baptized into Christ have put on Christ.* (Gal. 3:27.) But in this, also, *we are all the children of God by faith in Christ Jesus.* Faith is the receiving hand by which we receive and accept what by the giving hand of God is offered in the Sacrament. The giving hand is God's, the Sacrament being God's own means of saving grace. What that hand contains and offers is also God's gift, a good and perfect gift, which cannot be augmented or diminished by the will or power of man, neither of the officiating minister nor of the recipient. Faith, likewise, is the gift of God, engendered by the power of God through the means of grace. But unbelief is in the power of man, who can by persistent unbelief reject the precious gift of God and refuse to accept what is truly and earnestly offered in the Sacraments to all to whom they are administered. And thus it is that the unbeliever *eateth and drinketh damnation to himself* (I Cor. 11:29.) For this reason, lest he become guilty of receiving the grace of God in vain (II Cor. 6:1), the eunuch, upon his inquiry, *What doth hinder me to be baptized?* is told, *If thou believest with all thine heart, thou mayest* (Acts 8:36-37; cf. v. 12). (A. L. Graebner, *Theological Quarterly,* IV, 410—411.)

Imparting of the forgiveness of sins, with life and salvation, is the one great gift and benefit of the Sacraments. All other blessings offered and imparted by them are only concomitants and results of the impartation of forgiveness. Among these we may mention strengthening of faith, union with Christ, implanting into the spiritual body of Christ (the Church) (I Cor. 12:13), fellowship in the Church (I Cor. 10:17), sanctification and growth in sanctification (Rom. 6:2-5), love to God and the neighbor and furtherance therein, increase in patience, greater joy in confessing Christ (I Cor. 11:26), heavenly-mindedness, the crucifying of the old man and the revival of the new man (Rom. 6:3-6), and increase in the hope of eternal life (Titus 3:5). All of these effects, which both Sacraments have because the Holy Spirit is operative in them, rest, not only in part, but altogether, upon the fact that the Sacraments are the means which effectually impart the forgiveness of sins.

To ascribe to the Sacraments, in distinction from the Word, a physical effect, such as the planting of the resurrection body in the Lord's Supper, goes beyond the clear statements of the Scriptures (I Cor. 11:30 notwithstanding) and is idle speculation. Moreover, it leads into the Roman error which teaches that the Sacraments work magically and mechanically without faith on the part of the recipient and that they bestow infused grace. Such errors set aside the supreme importance of the forgiveness of sins and faith, the doctrine of justification by faith, and hence strike at the very heart of Christianity. (I Cor. 15:44, 53 is spoken of believers who have received the Sacraments, and therefore these words contradict the teaching of the implanting of the resurrection body in the Lord's Supper.) (See *Lehre und Wehre,* III, 12—13.)

It must be maintained that it is the Word of God which gives the power to the Sacraments. St. Paul says that Baptism is "the washing of water *by the Word*" (Eph. 5:26). And the Eucharist imparts forgiveness of sin only because Christ so declares in the words of institution, and by virtue of these words. The Sacraments indeed distinguish themselves from the Word in that in them the Word is connected with visible means and visible action. For this reason they are often called the "visible Word." But Word and Sacraments have the identical power and purpose, the power and purpose of the Word.

Differences Between Baptism and the Lord's Supper

We might point briefly to the relationship between Baptism and the Lord's Supper. Baptism has been called the Sacrament of Initiation; and the Eucharist has been called the Sacrament of Confirmation. Reception of Baptism precedes the use of the Lord's Supper. On Pentecost Day the 3,000 were exhorted to be baptized, not to participate in the Lord's Supper. This same procedure is found in many other cases, e. g., the jailer of Philippi, the Ethiopian eunuch, Cornelius and his kinsmen and friends (Acts 10:44-48). This does not constitute an essential difference either in the nature or in the effect of the Sacraments.

Again, Baptism is to be administered but once in an individual's lifetime. The Scriptures nowhere exhort to repetition of Baptism. But it repeatedly reminds the Christians of the one Baptism they have received (I Cor. 1:13; 6:11; 12:13; Rom. 6:3 ff.; Eph. 4:5; Col. 2:12; Titus 3:5-6; I Pet. 3:21; Gal. 3:26-27). But the Lord's Supper should be used frequently by the believer (I Cor. 11:26; Acts 2:42; I Cor. 11:20).

Furthermore, while Baptism is expressly described as the "washing of regeneration" and has as its purpose the generation of the faith it requires, the Lord's Supper is not so described, and its purpose is specifically to strengthen and preserve the faith already existing before the Sacrament is received. Therefore, while Baptism is administered also to children and such as are unable to confess a conscious faith, the Lord's Supper is to be given only to those who by word and deed confess a conscious faith in the Triune God, in Christ, in the doctrine of justification by faith, and in the truth that in the Sacrament they receive Christ's body and blood in, with, and under the bread and wine for the gracious remission of their sins.

No Absolute Necessity of the Sacraments

The Sacraments are indeed not indifferent matters, but divine institutions and ordinances, and it is the gracious will of God that Christians use them faithfully for the benefit of their faith, comfort, life, and hope. Nevertheless, we are not to ascribe to them an *absolute* necessity by teaching that no one can obtain forgiveness of sins and attain to eternal life who does not receive them. A person living in ignorance of Baptism is not excluded from the spiritual blessings of the state of grace by the lack of Baptism if he is a believer in the Gospel of Christ. And children to whom the Lord's Supper is not as yet given, because they are unable to examine themselves (I Cor. 11:28), or because, though already able to examine themselves, they have not yet been received into communicant membership, are not thereby excluded from any part of the blessings of God's children.

However, while we refrain from teaching an absolute necessity in the case of the Sacraments, this is by no means the same as saying that the Sacraments are unnecessary (Quakers, Unitarians, *et al.*). It is the gracious and good will of God that Christians use the Sacraments for their souls' salvation. Those who think little of Baptism and even refuse to be baptized, those who neglect the Sacrament of the Altar, despise the gracious will of God and refuse to obey a command of God. They thereby manifest an unchristian spirit. For when the Lord says: "Be baptized!" or "This do!" of the Sacraments, it is the nature of the Christian heart to comply with such command and invitation. Therefore Luther says in the Large Catechism: "It must be known that such people as deprive themselves of, and withdraw from, the Sacrament so long a time are not to be considered Christians" (*Triglot*, p. 763).

Jesus commends the people that heard John the Baptist and says that they "justified God," i. e., they acknowledged God's counsel of salvation by "being baptized with the Baptism of John." But He pronounces a solemn doom upon the Pharisees and lawyers and says of them that they "rejected the counsel of God against themselves" by not receiving the Baptism the Baptist offered them and urged upon them (Luke 7:29-30). It is of such that Jesus speaks when He declares to Nicodemus, a Pharisee: "Except a man be born of water and of the Spirit, he cannot enter into the Kingdom of God" (John 3:5). To reject and despise the Sacraments means to shut the door of grace and of heaven into one's own face. St. Luke records it as something very commendatory and salutary that the members of the church in Jerusalem after Pentecost regularly used the Sacrament of the Eucharist, for he writes: "They continued steadfastly in the Apostles' doctrine and fellowship and in *breaking of bread* and in prayers" (Acts 2:42). And Paul warns against the unworthy reception of the Lord's Supper when he chides the Corinthians (I Cor. 11:20-22). Our teachers have therefore summed the matter of the necessity of the Sacraments up in the dictum of St. Augustine: "Not the privation, but the contempt of the Sacrament damns."

The Sacraments are therefore to be held in high regard by all Christians as never-failing fountains of God's grace. The question: "Why did God ordain these additional means of grace when already the Word suffices to confer and appropriate to the sinner His grace and the forgiveness of sins?" should never have been raised. Scripture and experience teach that nothing is more difficult for one who has recognized his sinful state and condition than to believe that God is gracious and forgiving. The repeated and manifold assurance of grace and forgiveness through Word *and Sacraments* corresponds to the great need of sinful man. It emphasizes that Christianity is the one practical religion which cares with a divine efficiency for all the requirements of man's salvation. The great and terrifying need of sinful men is met in such a superabundant way because God is superabundantly "rich in mercy" (Eph. 2:4; Ex. 34:6; Titus 3:6; I Pet. 1:3; II Pet. 1:11).

Such superabundant riches of the grace of God fills every true Christian with grateful marvel and should induce all of us most thankfully to consider, painstakingly to study, and most zealously to guard against adulteration and perversion of the truths which God in His Holy Word teaches us concerning the blessed Sacraments and to use these glorious, God-given means of grace for our present comfort and strength and for our eternal salvation. In them shines the glory of God in the face of Jesus Christ. In them is revealed God's deep love, His great wisdom, and His glorious saving power.

Holy Baptism

As we study the doctrine of Holy Baptism set forth by our fathers, we find that they proclaimed and inculcated it in a most simple manner without any Barthian or Modernistic veiling of the truth by means of complex and ambiguous terms. Nor did they rationalize the doctrine, so as to accommodate it to the so-called enlightened reason of man, but they taught it in its whole Scriptural truth and purity. God grant that this reverent spirit of our fathers may continue in our midst so that we neither tire of and neglect God's Word nor misrepresent, misinterpret, and pervert it by making it conform to the perverse and conceited reason of unbelieving men. We are living in critical and perilous times. May God endow us with grace to remain faithful to His Word.

As we study the writings of our fathers on the doctrine of Holy Baptism, we find that, in the main, they set forth and defended it in its three essentials, namely, (I) *the essence of Holy Baptism, or what Baptism really is*; (II) *the benefit, or blessing, of Holy Baptism*; and (III) *the relation of Holy Baptism to our Christian life*. In connection with these three essentials they defended Infant Baptism, which, as we know, is being rejected by the various Baptist sects, and they repudiated all errors of the Roman Catholics, the Reformed, and other enthusiasts on the doctrine.

I. THE ESSENCE OF BAPTISM, OR WHAT BAPTISM REALLY IS

It is only natural that we should consider this point first, for upon this it depends whether we should highly esteem Holy Baptism or whether we may despise it; whether we should use it diligently or whether we may neglect it; whether we should regard it as a means of grace or as a mere ceremony.

Now, when we question our fathers concerning the essence of Holy Baptism, or what Baptism really is, we find that they entertain no doubt on this point, but answer in a most definite and decisive manner: "Baptism is that sacred act, ordained by God, in which, in the name of the Father and the Son and the Holy Ghost, water is applied to a living person by sprinkling or pouring or immersing."

This brief and simple definition of Holy Baptism sets forth a number of very important truths which must be considered in greater detail. In the first place, *Holy Baptism is a sacred act.* As a sacred act it must be treated with becoming respect, so that when, for example, children or adults are being baptized in our public services, we should diligently listen to the holy words spoken or read by the pastor, unite in intercession with our fellow Christians in behalf of the baptized, and gratefully recall to our minds the meaning and importance of our own Baptism.

In the second place, we confess, on the basis of God's Word, that Holy Baptism is a sacred act, *ordained by God.* We are sure that no believing Christian who knows the Small Catechism requires any lengthy Scripture proof for the statement that Holy Baptism has been instituted by our Lord and Savior Jesus Christ. He knows this from such simple passages as Matt. 28:19, Mark 16:15-16, and many others. When, for instance, our Lord says: "Go and teach all nations, *baptizing them,*" or: "Preach the Gospel to every creature. He that believeth and *is baptized* shall be saved," this means to every believing Christian that Holy Baptism is a divine institution which must be observed by the Christian Church till the end of time. Despite the clear and emphatic command of our Lord that Holy Baptism should be observed by the Church as a divine institution, rationalizing errorists have denied this for such vain and frivolous reasons as: "There is no divine command for Baptism"; or: "The Trinitarian formula in Matthew's Gospel is not genuine"; or: "The Holy Trinity was not known to the early Christians"; or: Matthew's account is not historical"; or: St. Paul did not highly regard Baptism"; or: "A commanded Baptism forces upon the New Testament a legalistic element"; or: "Holy Baptism was instituted only for the early Christian Church"; or: "The Church does not need Holy Baptism";

or: "Holy Baptism was a mere Jewish ceremony"; and the like. We see from this how eager the devil is to rob us of the divine blessings of Holy Baptism, and we are amazed at the temerity of such heretics whose minds manifestly Satan has blinded.

In the third place, in our definition we say that water must be applied to a living person *in the name of the Father and of the Son and of the Holy Ghost.* This is so clearly taught in Scripture that really we need not waste any words to defend this manifest Bible truth. Still, there have been rationalizing errorists who taught that the New Testament knows only of a Holy Baptism administered *in the name of Jesus.* They claim, for example, that when St. Peter in his Pentecostal address exhorted the alarmed Jews: "Repent, and be baptized every one of you in the name of Jesus Christ for the remission of sins" (Acts 2:38), he did not teach Baptism in the name of the Triune God, but Baptism merely in the name of Christ. Now, St. Peter, of course, admonished the penitent Jews to be baptized in the name of Jesus, for Jesus Christ, as the Head and the Lord of the Church, has instituted Holy Baptism. But this does not mean that St. Peter did not baptize these believing Jews in the name of the Triune God. Whoever baptizes in the name of Jesus baptizes also in the name of the Triune God. Again, when in Gal. 3:27 St. Paul writes: "As many of you as have been baptized into Christ, have put on Christ," he thereby does not mean to exclude the thought that these Galatian Christians were baptized also in the name of the Father and the Son and the Holy Ghost, for (to say it again) whoever is baptized in the name of the Triune God is thereby also baptized into Christ, that is, into communion with Him, receiving by faith the merits which He procured for all men by His vicarious obedience. It is understood, of course, that unbelieving, anti-Christian churches, which do not believe in the Holy Trinity and the deity of Christ, do not baptize rightly and validly even if at their sham baptisms they use the Trinitarian formula. Their Baptism is only deceit and blasphemy and therefore offensive to God and no true Baptism.

In the fourth place, we say in our definition that Holy Baptism is that sacred act, ordained by God, in which, in the name of the Father and the Son and the Holy Ghost, *water* is applied to a living person. Very emphatically we here state that *water* must be applied to a living person in Holy Baptism, not (let us say) sand or any other substitute. Holy Baptism, as described to us in Scripture, was always performed with water as the earthly element, and we have no right to depart from this earthly element, as did some sects and enthusiasts already in the early history of the Christian Church. When St. Augustine says that the right word must come to the right element in order that there may be a Sacrament (for this is the meaning of his famous axiom), he pronounced a truth which in every way is Scriptural.

Again, in our definition we say that in Holy Baptism water must be applied to a *person*, and that means to human beings only, not to inanimate objects, such as bells, ships, vessels, and the like. The unscriptural practice of christening inanimate objects was originated by the papists just because of their false doctrine that the Sacraments work mechanically or merely by the act performed (*ex opere operato*), conferring divine grace, power, and blessing upon the objects thus christened. The christening of bells, ships, and other inanimate objects is an abuse of Holy Baptism, which is displeasing to God, contrary to His Word, and offensive to all true and enlightened Christians.

We say, moreover, that in Holy Baptism water is to be applied to a *living* person as Christ clearly tells us in Matt. 28:19 and Mark 16:15-16. We assert this Scripture truth against such sects as, for example, the Mormons, who affirm that a dead person may be baptized for salvation by proxy, that is, a living person may be baptized in the place of the dead. They thus (as the writer has been told) have baptized Washington, Lincoln, and many other great men, in order that these might have a chance to enter into their Mormon heaven on Judgment Day. But this unbiblical practice is not only opposed to Mark 16:15-16, which passage implies that the person baptized must believe personally, or for himself, for the words read: "He that believeth and is baptized shall be saved," but also against Hab. 2:4: "The just shall live by *his* faith." When a person has died, he is either in heaven or in hell, just as he has either believed or rejected the divine Word (II Cor. 5:10). This thought should induce parents "to hasten with their infants to Holy Baptism," lest through their negligence their little ones might be deprived of the blessing of Baptism by a sudden, unexpected death; for while, in the case of stillborn children, Christian parents may comfort themselves with the abundant grace of God, which makes all things work together for good to them that love God (Rom. 8:28) and so commend their dead infants to the never-failing mercy of Him who can work regeneration also without means (Luke 1:15), their conscience may not easily be quieted if they must blame themselves for having neglected the means of grace and sinfully delayed the Baptism of their children.

Furthermore, when stressing in our definition that water must be applied to a living person, we include in this expression also *little children* or *infants,* which, as the Baptist sects teach, need not, indeed, *should* not, be baptized. The reason for their antagonism to Infant Baptism lies in their false conception of this Sacrament; for, contrary to Scripture, they do not regard Holy Baptism as a means of grace, but merely as an outward symbol of the inward washing which the Holy Ghost performs without means. In agreement with other Calvinistic Reformed bodies they hold that Holy Baptism merely has the significance of an act of obedience, or also an act of confession, so that in reality their Baptism, being performed only in the case of adults, has, in a general way, the significance which our ecclesiastical rite of Confirmation has.

Contrary to this false doctrine, we maintain, on the basis of Scripture, that also little children should be baptized. The doctrine of Infant Baptism we base on the following proof and evidence: (1) Christ's general command, Matt. 28:19: "Teach all nations, baptizing them," which certainly includes children; (2) The fact that in the New Testament, Baptism has taken the place of circumcision, which, as we know, was performed in the Old Testament on all male children on the eighth day after their birth (cf. Col. 2:12: "In whom also ye are circumcised with the circumcision made without hands . . . buried with Him [Christ] in Baptism"); (3) The general practice of the Apostles, as mentioned in Scripture, of baptizing whole families (I Cor. 1:16: "The household of Stephanas"; Acts 16:15: "She [Lydia] was baptized and her household"; Acts 16:33: The jailer at Philippi "was baptized, he and all his"). If anyone denies that in all these households there were no children, he must furnish the proof. The words

Holy Baptism

themselves ordinarily suggest children; (4) The children's need of Holy Baptism, for they are flesh born of flesh (John 3:6) and so must be born again of water and of Spirit (John 3:5), before they can enter into the Kingdom of God, Holy Baptism being the washing of regeneration and renewing of the Holy Ghost, by which they are born again (Tit. 3:5). The Baptist sects, which reject Infant Baptism, deny both that Holy Baptism is a means of grace and that the children of believers by their natural birth are totally corrupted; but on these points they err; (5) The desire of Christ to bless little children and have them saved (Mark 10: 13-16; (6) The testimony of the Christian Church, which witnesses to the fact that also children were baptized and that this was an Apostolic institution (cf. the testimony of the Apostolic Fathers and Church Fathers, Clement of Rome, d. 101; Justin Martyr, d. 165; Irenaeus, d. 202; Tertullian, d. ca. 240, though himself an opponent of Infant Baptism; Origen, d. 254: "The Church has received from the Apostles the tradition (command) to baptize also little children"; cf. *Lehre und Wehre*, 1909—1911) *;

---

* *Additional Testimony for Infant Baptism:* Augustine (d. 430): "The Pelagians have never dared deny Infant Baptism, because they know that if they had denied it, they would have to fight quite manifestly with the whole Church" (cf. *Lib.* I: 26). Again he says concerning Infant Baptism that "the whole Church is making use of it" and that the custom of baptizing infants "stems from the holy Apostles." In his *Tenth Sermon* he admonishes his hearers: "Let no one mislead you by false doctrine. The Baptism of children the Church has practiced at all times . . . and has guarded it to this day continuously." (Quoted in *Rambachs Erlaeuterungen*, p. 681; for the entire quotation cf. Canada, 1888, p. 45.) The same report quotes also a decree of the Council of Carthage (418): "Whosoever denies that newly born children are to be baptized, let him be accursed" (*ibid.*, p. 46). The report, moreover, quotes Tertullian's argument against Infant Baptism (Tertullian, d. ca. 220): "For the nature and disposition, indeed, also the age of each person, the delay of Baptism is much more useful, and this applies especially to little children. . . . Let them, then, come as they grow up; let them come as they learn [that is], as they are taught to what they come. Why should the innocent age hasten to forgiveness of sins? In earthly matters people certainly act much more cautiously; they entrust to those divine things to whom they do not entrust earthly goods. Let the children first learn to ask for salvation, so that it is clear that we give to those who ask for it. For the same strong reason also the unmarried also are to delay [Baptism]. If anyone recognizes the importance of Baptism, he will be more afraid to obtain it than to delay it." *Ibid.*, p. 48.) The report quotes Luther as saying that "Tertullian was among the church fathers a real Carlstadt" (p. 47). — Cyprian, Bishop of Carthage (d. A. D. 258) was a friend, but not a follower of Tertullian. This Cyprian

(7) The fact that little children can believe (Matt. 18:6: "Whoso shall offend one of these little ones which believe in Me"). The Baptist sects, which reject Infant Baptism, claim the inability of children to believe as one of the chief reasons why they should not be baptized; (8) The silence in the New Testament regarding Infant Baptism, which the Baptist sects quote as a proof why children should not be baptized, but which in reality speaks for Infant Baptism. No doubt Infant Baptism is not especially mentioned in Scripture because it was considered as a matter of course (Col. 2:11-12; Acts 11:14: "Then all thy house shall be saved"; Cornelius was baptized with all his house; Acts 10:48 Peter "commanded *them* to be baptized"). In short, the Baptist sects have no valid Scripture proof for rejecting Infant Baptism; they repudiate it on grounds of reason and not on grounds of Scripture and thus sin grievously by rejecting Infant Baptism.

Finally, in our definition we say that Holy Baptism is a sacred act in which water *is applied* to a living person *by sprinkling,*

---

rebuked a presbyter in Numidia, by the name of Fidus, because he taught that little children should not be baptized before the eighth day, because in the Old Testament male children were circumcised on the eighth day. He writes: "And so, dearest brother, this was the final verdict at our Council [at Carthage] that no one should be kept by us from Baptism and from the grace of God, who is merciful, good, and faithful to all. Since, then, this [gracious divine] purpose should be referred to and maintained with regard to all, we hold that this purpose pertains all the more to young children, as also the newly born." (*Ep.* LIX. *Ad Fidum. Ibid.*, 49.) Irenaeus, a student of Polycarp, who himself was a student of St. John the Apostle, was Bishop in Gaul (France) since A. D. 177. In his well-known writing "Against the Heretics" he says (II:22): "Christ is come to save all through Himself, I say, all, who are born again through Him unto God, the infants (*infantes*) and the little children (*parvulos*) no less than those who are boys or young men or old men." Here Irenaeus does not mention Baptism expressly, but, as the report shows, he always writes of the regeneration and salvation of little children in such a way that Infant Baptism must be presupposed (*ibid.*, 49). Again the report shows that Justin Martyr (b. A. D. 89; d. A. D. 166) in his *Dialog with Trypho, the Jew*, states that Baptism is the circumcision of the New Testament, and in his *Apology addressed to Antoninus Pius* (A. D. 81–166), he writes: "Very many people of the age of sixty or seventy, both men and women, who *from a child* were made disciples of Christ [he here uses the same verb, *matheteuein*, which Christ uses in Matt. 28:19], remained spotless and unmarried." Very clearly Polycarp here refers to Holy Baptism. But that means that Infant Baptism was practiced not only during his life (ca. A. D. 100), but even while some of the Apostles (*e. g.*, St. John) were still living (*ibid.*, p. 50).

pouring or immersing. We assert this over against the Baptist sects which teach that Baptism is valid only if the baptized person is immersed. Now, we do accept immersion as a right mode of Baptism, among others, but we reject it as unbearable legalism for anyone to try to force us to use this mode exclusively, since the Greek word *baptizein,* to *baptize,* denotes not only immersing, but also sprinkling and pouring, and since Holy Baptism signifies not merely the drowning of the old Adam, but also the washing or cleansing of the baptized person from sin (Eph. 5:26). So also sprinkling, pouring, and washing symbolize what Holy Baptism works or does. In Baptism, for example, we are sprinkled with Christ's blood and thus cleansed from all sin. So also in Baptism our sins are washed away, and in Baptism the Holy Ghost with His manifold gifts is poured out upon us. The matter has been fully treated in our periodicals and reports. But let us quote just two passages to show that the verb to *baptize* in Greek does not always mean to immerse.

St. Mark tells us: "And when they [the Pharisees] come from the market, unless they *baptize themselves* (literal translation), they do not eat; and many other things there are which they have received to hold: the *baptizings* of cups and vessels and of brazen utensils and of couches" (Mark 7:4). The Authorized Version translates the verse freely as follows: "And when they come from the market, except they *wash,* they eat not. And many other things there be which they have received to hold, as the *washing* of cups, and pots, brasen vessels, and of tables." This translation is correct, for the verb *baptize* in this connection simply means *to wash* and does not necessarily denote a cleansing by immersion of the objects into water, but rather a washing in general. In v. 3 it is said of the Pharisees that they do not eat except they wash (*nipsontai*) their hands with the fist, which suggests a washing of the hands by sprinkling or pouring water upon them and then rubbing them, a usual way of washing in the Orient.

In Matt. 3:11 John the Baptist said of Christ: "He shall baptize you with the Holy Ghost and with fire." How this baptizing with the Holy Ghost was accomplished we are told in Acts 2, which relates to us the *outpouring* of the Holy Ghost upon the disciples on Pentecost. The word *to baptize* therefore has also the meaning of *pouring*, a mode of Baptism to which we and most other historical churches are accustomed. This is also the Christian tradition, for the *Didache* commands, among other things: "Pour water three times on the head," namely, of the person to be baptized (ch. VII). The *Didache*, or *Teaching of the Twelve Apostles*, was written ca. A. D. 110 (so Zahn; Harnack, between A. D. 120—165) and thus dates from the early history of the Church. It therefore attests the Church practice of pouring in Baptism at a very early time. Ancient pictures, too, show how at that time Baptism was performed on persons sitting or standing in water and having water poured upon their heads. It is certainly very probable that the three thousand persons who on Pentecost were added to the Church by Holy Baptism were not immersed. Nor does Acts 8:38-39 prove that the eunuch who was baptized by Philip was immersed, for the "certain water unto which they came" (v. 36) was certainly not a deep lake, but no doubt little more than a small reservoir of water intended for travelers and their horses, the entire road to Egypt being sandy and without water. The Baptist sects, who urge Baptism by immersion, insist upon the shell, but have given up the kernel, that is, they cling to the outward form, but have yielded the real essence, significance, and comfort of Holy Baptism.

In his large Catechism Dr. Luther writes of Holy Baptism: "Baptism is no human trifle, but instituted by God Himself, moreover . . . it is most solemnly and strictly commanded that we must be baptized, or we cannot be saved, lest any one regard it as a trifling matter, like putting on a new red coat. For it is of the greatest importance that we esteem Baptism excellent, glorious, and exalted, for which we contend and fight chiefly, because the world is now so full of sects clamoring that Baptism is an external thing and that external things are of no benefit. But let it be ever so much an external thing; here stands God's Word and command which institute, establish, and confirm Baptism. But what God institutes and commands cannot be a vain, but must be a precious thing, though in appearance it were of less value than a straw. . . . For to be baptized in the name of God is to be baptized not by men, but by God Himself. Therefore, although it is performed by human hands, it is, nevertheless, truly God's own work." (Cf. Large Catechism, Of Baptism, par. 6 f.; *Triglot*, p. 734 f.)

II. THE BENEFIT, OR BLESSING, OF HOLY BAPTISM

We cannot define the benefit, or blessing, of Holy Baptism better than Luther has done in his Small Catechism, in which he says: "It [Holy Baptism] works forgiveness of sins, delivers from death and the devil, and gives eternal salvation to all who believe this, as the words and promises of God declare."

Perverse and conceited human reason is constantly inclined to stray away from God's Word and either to add to God's Word or to take away from it. The Reformed sects also here take away from God's Word, for they do not give Baptism its Scriptural due. They say that Holy Baptism is a mere symbol or outward sign, while some erring Lutherans have added to it by saying that without Baptism the divine Word does not place us into full communion with Christ or God (so Sommerlath). Reformed rationalists declare that Holy Baptism does not profit us at all. Lutheran rationalists, by the definition just given, in the last analysis, declare that all who die without Baptism cannot be saved, for without Baptism they are not in complete communion with Christ, and that certainly means lost. Luther's Small Catechism is both directive and corrective: it teaches of Holy Baptism exactly what Scripture says of Holy Baptism and refutes the erroneous doctrine; and that is the reason why we should highly esteem and diligently use it. Luther not only says: Holy Baptism "works forgiveness of sins, delivers from death and the devil, and gives eternal salvation to all who believe this," but also points us to Holy Scripture and says: "The words and promises of God declare this." Luther's doctrine of the benefit of Holy Baptism therefore is based upon God's Word, is taken from God's Word, is anchored in God's Word.

But which are (so we ask) the words and the promises of God which declare these great benefits and blessings of Holy Baptism? Luther directs us to Mark 16:16 and says: "Christ, our Lord, says in the last chapter of Mark: He that believeth and is baptized *shall be saved;* but he that believeth not shall be damned." Here, then, is God's gracious promise: "He that believeth and is baptized *shall be saved.*" That means: All baptized believers (so far as God is concerned) shall be saved, and this one word *salvation* includes all the benefits which Luther enumerates: forgiveness of sins, deliverance from death and the devil, and the granting by grace of eternal life.

Now, by pointing us to Mark 16:16, Luther answers a very important question, a question about which many modern rationalizing theologians are in doubt. The question is: "Does Holy Baptism belong into the Law or into the Gospel? Or, more briefly expressed, is Holy Baptism essentially Law or Gospel?" Christ's promise in Mark 16:16 is pure Gospel, a gracious offer of life and salvation; and so Luther rightly places Holy Baptism where, according to Scripture, it really belongs, namely, into the sphere of the Gospel. Yes, indeed, Holy Baptism is pure Gospel; and just because it is Gospel, it is a means of grace. Of course, Holy Baptism also has been commanded; that is true. But so also the preaching of the Gospel has been commanded. Yet the fact that the preaching of the Gospel has been commanded does not make it Law. It remains pure, sweet, saving, comforting Gospel, the glad and blessed tidings of God's grace in Christ Jesus. Holy Baptism, being pure Gospel, is therefore not a meritorious act which *we* perform to earn salvation. That is the erroneous doctrine of many errorists. No, Holy Baptism is God's gracious, loving, beneficent work which He does "in us" (Luther's expression: *Gottes Werk in uns*) to offer, convey, and seal unto us the grace of God, which Christ has merited by His vicarious obedience. So, then, Holy Baptism is Gospel, not Law. In this blessed truth we rejoice, for in this lies the whole comfort of Holy Baptism.

Here, however, arises a new question: "If Holy Baptism is nothing else than the application of the Gospel, why has Christ, in addition to the preaching of the Gospel, instituted this Sacrament? Why should we have this special means of grace?" We might extend the question and say: "Why should we have Absolution, which, too, is Gospel? Or, why should we have Holy Communion, which likewise is Gospel?" Luther answers this question very well in the Smalcald Articles, where he writes in Art. IV: "We will now return to the Gospel, which not merely in one way gives us counsel and aid against sin; for God is superabundantly rich (and liberal) in His grace and goodness. First, through the spoken Word by which the forgiveness of sins is preached . . .

in the whole world, which is the peculiar office of the Gospel. Secondly, through Baptism. Thirdly, through the Holy Sacrament of the Altar. Fourthly, through the power of the keys, and also through the mutual conversation and consolation of brethren, Matt. 28:20. . . ." (Cf. Smalcald Articles, IV: *Triglot*, p. 491.)

In these words Luther teaches a most weighty truth, namely, the comforting truth: God is so superabundantly rich in His grace that He gives us counsel and aid against sin not merely in one way, but in many, by the Gospel which is preached; by Baptism, or the visible Word, in which, as it were, we see the Gospel in action; by the Lord's Supper; by the Office of the Keys or Absolution; by special consolation of Christian brethren. Let us always bear this in mind, so that we may not despise Holy Baptism, but rejoice and find true comfort in it. Holy Baptism is not useless, but very necessary. In the first place, it individualizes God's promise of grace in Christ Jesus; for when a person is baptized, then God deals with him personally and assures him of the gracious remission of his sins, while, when the Gospel is proclaimed, it is, as Luther says, "preached into the crowd" (*"in den Haufen hinein gepredigt"*). In the second place, as the Lord's Supper, so also Holy Baptism is God's seal, by which He certifies to us His gracious pardon and love. This truth we learn from Rom. 4:11, where St. Paul writes: "He [Abraham] received the sign of circumcision, a seal of the righteousness of the faith," etc. As circumcision, so also Holy Baptism is a seal of God's grace in Christ Jesus. The sealing of a promise does not merely offer and convey, but it makes the person who receives the sealed promise absolutely sure and certain of what the promise offers and gives. (Cf. the seal attached to a deed.)

But while this is true, our Confession is right when it says: "The effect of the Word [Gospel] and of the rite [Sacrament] is the same" (Apology, Art. XIII, *Triglot*, p. 309). Holy Baptism does exactly what the preached or read or symbolized (crucifix, John 3:14) Gospel does: it offers us forgiveness of sins, life, and salvation, and it works faith in us to accept the forgiveness which it offers. In other words, it has an offering power, and it has an operative power. When, for instance, God's Word says: "Be baptized . . . for the remission of sins" (Acts 2:38), then it is clear to every believing Christian that Holy Baptism is not a mere outward ceremony, but a divine means of grace, which seriously offers us forgiveness of sins. Again, when God's Word says: Holy Baptism is a "washing of regeneration and renewing of the Holy Ghost" (Tit. 3:5), then it is clear to every believing Christian that Holy Baptism is a divine means of grace which works the very faith that accepts the forgiveness of sins, and through this faith, regeneration, conversion, justification, sanctification, the implanting into the body of Christ (I Cor. 12:13), and so forth. Holy Baptism thus is operative toward faith and salvation, because there is connected with this divine washing the Gospel of Christ, which is a power of God unto salvation to everyone that believeth (Rom. 1:16).

When we bear in mind that "Baptism is not simple water only, but it is the water comprehended in God's command and connected with God's Word" [the Gospel], then we readily understand why Scripture ascribes to Holy Baptism such great and glorious things as the granting of forgiveness, the deliverance from death and the devil, and the bestowal of eternal salvation. Then we readily understand also such words as: "As many of you as have been baptized into Christ have put on Christ" (Gal. 3:27), that is, have by faith received His merits; or: "Baptism doth *save* us" (I Pet. 3:21); or: "A man *is born* of water and of the Spirit" (John 3:5); or: "Christ sanctifies and cleanses [His Church] with the washing of water by the Word" (Eph. 5:26); or: "Be baptized, and wash away thy sins" (Acts 22:16); or: "We are buried with Him [Christ] by Baptism into death" (Rom. 6:4), and so forth. The precious divine washing of Holy Baptism, which seems so simple and insignificant to human reason is connected with Christ's mighty, converting Gospel, and so it regenerates, sanctifies, and makes us children of God. It is the divine Word, the precious Gospel, which does all these great things (Eph. 5:26), of course, through the operation of the Holy Ghost.

Luther was confronted with the problem that, on the one hand, the Romanists declared that water saves mechanically by a sort of magical power, and, on the other, the Reformed said that water could not do the great things which are described so beautifully in the Small Catechism. But Luther answers in his Small Catechism: "It is not the water indeed that does them, but the Word of God which is in and with the water." By "the Word of God" Luther here means the Gospel, for he continues: "For without the Word of God the water is simple water, and no Baptism. But with the Word of God it is a Baptism, that is, a gracious water of life and a washing of regeneration in the Holy Ghost, as St. Paul says, Titus, chapter third [Tit. 3:5]: By the washing of regeneration and renewing of the Holy Ghost," etc. Luther's reference is therefore to the Gospel; and the Gospel does such great things, since it is "a power of God unto salvation to everyone that believeth" (Rom. 1:16).

In this beautiful explanation Luther also uses the words: "And faith which trusts such Word of God in the water." Luther directed these words against the Romanist error of the mechanical operation of Holy Baptism, which is contrary to God's Word. But how (we ask) can little children have faith which trusts such Word of God in the water? Believing adults, of course, by faith trust the baptismal Gospel promise. But how can infants have faith? Here, again, the fact that Baptism is essentially Gospel helps us understand the problem. The Gospel, on the one hand, is the object of faith; that is, the foundation upon which our faith rests. Our faith thus rests upon the precious Gospel fact that Christ died for our sins (Rom. 4:25). But, on the other hand, the Gospel is also the means by which faith is engendered in the hearts of men (Rom. 10:17), since the Holy Ghost is always and efficaciously connected with the Gospel (I Cor. 2:4-5). And so through the Gospel, connected with Holy Baptism, the Holy Spirit works and preserves an active, direct faith in the little children that are baptized, while He strengthens the faith of believing adults that are baptized. We cannot, of course, understand this divine operation of the Holy Spirit in little children, just as little as we can understand how sleeping adults, or adults in a coma, are kept by the Holy Ghost in saving faith. However, we are not to understand the mysteries of faith, but only to believe them (John 20:29). In the realm of the spiritual, reason must forever remain silent, as Luther affirms time and again.

At this point also some modern Lutheran theologians err who permit their perverse reason to gain the ascendancy over God's

Word and teach doctrines contrary to the clear words of Scripture. Some say that Holy Baptism works in a physical way, so that a person, in Baptism, even though faith be absent, is nevertheless united with Christ and regenerated. This is, in the final analysis, the Roman Catholic doctrine of the mechanical operation of the Sacrament (*ex opere operato*), and it is opposed to the clear Scripture doctrine that by faith we are saved (Eph. 2:8-9; Rom. 3:28). Some of these errorists go still farther, for they say that even if a baptized person should lose his faith, he nevertheless remains a member of Christ's body. They thus misrepresent I Cor. 12:13. Scripture knows of no membership in Christ's body, that is, the Church, without faith. Faith is the necessary hand which by God's grace and operation we reach out to receive the blessings offered to us in the Gospel as the conferring means. Other errorists of this sort teach that a baptized person is first implanted into the Church or, as they call it, into "the new humanity," and then through membership in the Church he obtains forgiveness of sins. This, too, is a papistic error, for in reality it bases justification and reconciliation on sanctification. The person baptized (according to this view) obtains reconciliation because, as a member of the Church, he leads a holy life; but this is altogether anti-Scriptural. Any teaching which denies that forgiveness of sins is the chief gift of Holy Baptism, and which rejects faith in the precious Gospel promise as the receiving means of forgiveness, is not Scriptural, is not Lutheran, but Roman Catholic. In Holy Baptism we receive by faith the precious divine gifts which are offered to us in the Gospel promises that are connected with this glorious Sacrament.

This, however, does not mean that our faith makes Holy Baptism an effective means of grace. In the language of the theologians this thought has been expressed thus: Faith does not belong to the essence of Holy Baptism. By this statement we mean to say that Holy Baptism is an effective means of grace by virtue of Christ's institution, and not through the piety of the administrant or the worthiness of the person baptized. No, indeed, the divine command is there, and the divine promise is there, and because of the divine command and the divine promise Holy Baptism is a means of grace and not merely an outward symbol or an empty washing. But my faith must *receive* the gifts of Holy Baptism, as said before. Faith is indeed necessary to obtain the divine blessings, though faith does not make the Sacrament a means of grace. We stress this point so much because it is one of great importance and because it is being constantly denied by errorists of all kinds.

The Romanists boast that they are the Church which preserves the Christian faith and the Sacraments. And indeed, they do preserve the essence of Holy Baptism, for they baptize children and adults in the name of the Father and the Son and the Holy Ghost, and they use the name of the Triune God in the Christian sense. But they have perverted the doctrine of Holy Baptism so greatly that it is only by the grace of God and contrary to Rome's teaching if a baptized Romanist finds comfort in his Baptism. In the first place, as said before, the papists deny that the faith of the baptized receives the benefits of Holy Baptism; instead, they teach that the Sacrament works *ex opere operato,* or by the mere act performed. They thus eliminate the doctrine of salvation by faith also in the doctrine of Holy Baptism. In the second place, the Romanists teach that Holy Baptism wipes out or utterly destroys all original sin, so that the evil lusts and desires which remain in the baptized after Holy Baptism are no longer sin. This false doctrine tends to carnal security, misleading the baptized person to regard himself as perfectly pure and holy so far as his hereditary corruption is concerned. In the last place, the Romanists teach that when a baptized person commits a mortal sin, the covenant of Holy Baptism is broken, so that he must look for salvation to the "second plank," namely, to Rome's sacrament of penance, and thus by the good works of contrition, confession, and actual satisfaction make amends for his sins. But this doctrine of work-righteousness destroys all hope of salvation, as God's Word testifies (Gal. 3:10; 5:4). In reality the "ship never breaks," as Luther says in his Large Catechism (cf. Large Catechism, Infant Baptism, par. 82; *Triglot,* p. 751), and as Holy Scripture emphatically testifies (Is. 54:10).

The Reformed or Calvinists also retain the essence of Holy Baptism, but teach erroneously regarding its purpose or effect. The extreme Baptist sects go so far as to reject Infant Baptism. However, while other Calvinists retain Infant Baptism, they do not regard it as an effective means of grace, but merely as an outward symbol or sign. All Reformed sects teach that Holy Baptism has only the necessity of the divine *precept,* which means that persons must be baptized merely because God has commanded this. But they deny its necessity as a means of grace. To them Holy Baptism signifies only the inner washing which the Holy Ghost performs, without means, in the heart of God's elect. On the part of man it signifies the Christian's engagement to God or a duty the performance of which he owes to God. They thus change Holy Baptism from Gospel into Law and make it a good work of man, whereas in reality Holy Baptism is God's gracious work which He does to save us. So also the Reformed, because of their false doctrine regarding the means of grace, are forced to rely for salvation on work-righteousness, just as the Romanists do.

The objections of the Reformed to Holy Baptism as a means of grace are all based on grounds of reason and are easily refuted from Scripture. When they say that water cannot do such great things (Boehl), they purposely ignore the fact that Holy "Baptism is not simple water only, but water comprehended in God's command and connected with God's Word," and that the Gospel is a power of God unto salvation also in Holy Baptism. When they say that many baptized persons do not remain Christians, so that Holy Baptism cannot be a means of grace, they ignore the Scriptural truth that there are indeed temporary believers (Luke 8:13) and that God, working by the means of grace, can be resisted. When they say that we are saved not by Holy Baptism, but by faith alone, they ignore the distinction between the conferring and the receiving means (Matt. 23:37). Holy Baptism indeed offers, conveys, and seals to us God's grace, but faith is the means by which we receive the gracious forgiveness of our sins. When they say that a person can be saved by believing the Gospel, without his being baptized, that indeed, is true. But when a person despises Holy Baptism and perverts the doctrine of Holy Scripture concerning it, he endangers his salvation; for as the ancient church fathers said: Lack of Baptism indeed does not condemn (that is, provided one is brought to faith by the preaching of the Gospel), but

Holy Baptism 411

contempt for Holy Baptism does condemn (Luke 7:29-30). The Reformed therefore do not follow Scripture when they oppose the efficacy or benefit of Holy Baptism, but they reject the clear Scripture passages which do teach that Holy Baptism is an effective means of grace.

A few examples may illustrate the pernicious perversion of Holy Scripture on the part of the Reformed in order to "prove" that Holy Baptism is not a means of grace. In Acts 22:16 we are told: "Be baptized and wash away thy sins," which passage clearly declares that Holy Baptism washes away sins. But the Reformed say: "If Baptism saves, it saves as an act or manifestation of faith," thus making it a work of man, whereas Holy Baptism saves as a work of God. In Acts 2:38 the Word of God says: "Be baptized, every one of you, . . . for the remission of sins." But the Reformed say: "Rest not in the sign (Holy Baptism), but in the thing signified," that is, in the inward washing of the Holy Ghost without means. God's Word says: "By the washing of regeneration and renewing of the Holy Ghost" (Tit. 3:5); but the Reformed say: "This does not treat at all of Holy Baptism, but what the passage says is: 'The Holy Spirit's inward cleansing, or His regeneration and renewing, performed without means, is like a washing with water.'" God's Word says: "Except a man be born of water and of the Spirit, he cannot enter into the Kingdom of God" (John 3:5). But the Reformed say: "A man is born directly of the Holy Spirit, and his new birth is only illustrated by this washing of the body with water." In short, God's Word may say what it will, the Reformed always have some answer to force upon the sacred text their own false and misleading teaching. They thus show that they have a different spirit from us Lutherans who believe the Word of God, no matter whether we understand it or not. They rationalize the doctrine and therefore err with regard to it; in other words, their false teachings regarding Holy Baptism spring from their perverse and conceited reason.

In spite of the fact that the Reformed teach that Holy Baptism is not a means of grace, they often speak of it as a "sign," "seal," or "pledge" of God's grace toward us. But these are only so many empty words; for if Holy Baptism is not a means of grace, by which the Holy Ghost regenerates and sanctifies us, it can not be a "sign," "seal," or "pledge" on God's part assuring us of our salvation. The Augsburg Confession also speaks of the Sacraments as signs and seals of God's grace toward us. But the Augsburg Confession describes the Sacraments as "signs and testimonies of the will of God toward us, instituted *to awaken and confirm faith*" in us. To the Reformed, Holy Baptism is an empty sign, a meaningless seal, but to us Lutherans, who believe the Bible, it is a true sign and seal, by which God, in His infinite mercy not only offers and bestows but also seals to us the gracious forgiveness of sins which Christ has obtained for us by His vicarious obedience. When we Lutherans speak of Holy Baptism as a sign or seal, we mean by that expression a true or real sign or seal which puts us into a sure possession of God's grace, while the Reformed at best can think of it only as a sham sign and a sham seal that has nothing to offer and give.

Concerning the benefit, or blessing, of Holy Baptism Luther writes in his Large Catechism: "We must also learn why and for what purpose it [Holy Baptism] is instituted; that is, what it profits, gives, and works. And this also we can not discern better than from the words of Christ above quoted: He that believeth and is baptized shall be saved. Therefore state it most simply thus, that the power, work, profit, fruit, and end of Baptism is this, namely, *to save*. For no one is baptized in order that he may become a prince, but, as the words declare, that he be saved. But to be saved, we know, is nothing else than to be delivered from sin, death, and the devil, and to enter into the kingdom of Christ, and to live with Him forever.

"Here you see again how highly and precious we should esteem Baptism, because in it we obtain such unspeakable treasure, which also indicates sufficiently that it can not be ordinary, mere water. For mere water could not do such a thing, but the Word does it, and . . . the fact that the name of God is comprehended therein. But where the name of God is, there must also be life and salvation, that it may indeed be called a divine, blessed, fruitful, and gracious water; for by the Word such power is imparted to Baptism that it is a laver of regeneration, as St. Paul also calls it, Titus 3:5." (Cf. Large Catechism, par. 23 ff.; *Triglot*, p. 737 f.)

III. THE RELATION OF HOLY BAPTISM TO OUR CHRISTIAN LIFE

There remains yet one important point to be considered, namely, *the relation of Holy Baptism to our Christian life.*

This point has been rightly stressed not only by Luther and our dogmaticians, that is, the great teachers of our Church, such as Gerhard, Quenstedt, and others, but also by our fathers in their synodical reports and the periodicals of our Synod. The reason for this is not hard to find; for while Scripture commands us to receive the Lord's Supper frequently, it never commands us to be baptized over and over. Baptism is to be received only once. But while this is true, Christians are to make constant use of it. Scripture nowhere calls for a repetition of Holy Baptism, yet it persistently urges the baptized believer daily to use Holy Baptism for consolation and sanctification, that is, for his comfort in the troubles of sin and his growth in piety and godliness.

In his Small Catechism, Dr. Martin Luther calls attention to the relation of Holy Baptism to our Christian life when he says: "It [Holy Baptism] signifies that the old Adam in us should, by daily contrition and repentance, be drowned and die with all sins and evil lusts and, again, a new man daily come forth and arise, who shall live before God in righteousness and purity forever."

Luther supports this statement by quoting Rom. 6:4: "We are buried with Christ by Baptism into death, that, like as He was raised up from the dead by the glory of the Father, even so we also should walk in newness of life."

The verb *signify* in this connection has been frequently misunderstood or purposely misinterpreted, just as if Holy Baptism were in itself an unimportant rite or a mere sign or symbol. In reality, however, the verb here has quite another meaning. When Dr. Luther says that Holy Baptism signifies this or that, he means to say that it has a deep significance, a most important meaning, for us who are baptized. This important meaning is that our old Adam, that is, our entire sinful depravity or corruption, which has come upon us by the fall of Adam and is ours by our natural birth, should be drowned by daily contrition and repentance, by which we withstand all evil desires and suppress them. That is the negative side of Christian sanctification. The positive side of Christian sanctification is that the new man, or our new spiritual being and life, created in us by the work of the Holy Spirit in Holy Baptism, should from day to day be strengthened before God in true faith and good works. In short, we baptized Christians should daily, through the power given us in Holy Baptism, suppress our lusts and sins, and walk in holiness of life, doing that which is pleasing to God. That is what Holy Baptism signifies, and for that Holy Baptism also gives us the necessary power. Dr. Engelder well puts it thus: "In daily repentance the Christian appropriates the forgiveness of sins and the strength needed to lead a godly life, granted him in Baptism."

Just that is what Luther means when he speaks of the meaning, or significance, of Holy Baptism. In his Large Catechism he says: "Baptism must be practiced without ceasing" (cf. Large Catechism, Infant Baptism, par. 65; *Triglot*, p. 749). Again, in the same place: "The Christian life is nothing else than a daily Baptism, once begun and ever to be continued." Regarding this point Luther in his writings on Holy Baptism is very serious. He stresses it again and again. There are some who think that Holy Baptism must be supplemented by confirmation, just as if confirmation were a sort of additional sacrament (as indeed the Romanists teach), making Baptism truly effective. But confirmation is only a church rite, and its chief purpose is to instruct the confirmands regarding the essence and the meaning of Holy Baptism and to inculcate upon them its glory. This definitely means instruction in the chief parts of the Christian faith. After having been thus instructed, they will, of course, solemnly make the very confession before the congregation which they made in Holy Baptism when they were infants. But confirmation is not a supplement of Holy Baptism; not something that gives value to Holy Baptism or that renders Baptism valid.

That Luther was right in emphasizing the important meaning of Holy Baptism for Christian sanctification is clear from the many Scripture passages which speak of Holy Baptism in its relation to the Christian life. Let us examine a few of them.

In I Cor. 6:11, St. Paul writes: "And such were some of you, but ye are washed, but ye are sanctified, but ye are justified in the name of the Lord Jesus and by the Spirit of our God." The expression: "Ye are washed" here manifestly refers to Holy Baptism. This Sacrament the Apostle regards as an effective means of grace, for he adds: "Ye are sanctified, but ye are justified." Holy Baptism is a washing, a sanctifying, a regeneration, in which the person baptized is declared righteous. But why does the Apostle say all this? Because the Corinthians permitted fornication and other scandalous sins to continue in their church. This must not be! So the Apostle warns the Christians at Corinth. You must not tolerate sin in your midst; for you were baptized, and thereby you were made holy and declared righteous. St. Paul thus uses the doctrine of Holy Baptism for reproof, correction, and instruction in righteousness.

Again, in I Cor. 12:13, St. Paul writes: "For by one Spirit are we all baptized into one body, whether we be Jews or Gentiles, whether we be bond or free." Holy Baptism is an effective, saving means of grace, by which we are implanted into the one body of Christ, the Church Invisible. But why does St. Paul here refer to Holy Baptism? Why does he tell the Corinthians that through the Holy Ghost believing Christians of all nations are baptized into one body? Well, they were divided into parties, and so envied and opposed one another, so that the Church at Corinth was indeed in a bad situation. Now, their Baptism was to remind them of their spiritual unity, effected by His holy Sacrament. So here again St. Paul uses the doctrine of Holy Baptism for reproof, correction, and instruction in righteousness.

Or, let us take Gal. 3:26-27, where St. Paul writes: "For ye are all the children of God by faith in Christ Jesus. For as many of you as have been baptized into Christ have put on Christ." Here the Apostle stresses the doctrine of salvation by grace through faith in Christ. And the blessed state of the believers as children of God through faith in Christ Jesus he traces back to Holy Baptism; for, as he says, when they were baptized into Christ, they put on Christ, that is, they by faith, worked or strengthened through Holy Baptism (according as they were baptized as children or adults), received all the merits of Christ, offered in the holy Sacrament. The doctrine of Holy Baptism is therefore used here, on the one hand, as a warning against the false teachers who taught salvation by good works, and, on the other, for the consolation of those who believed in Christ Jesus. St. Paul tells them: "By faith in Christ Jesus, through Holy Baptism, you have everything you need for salvation, and so you need not, indeed, you must not, go back to the so-called good works which the Judaizers or false prophets are trying to teach you."

Another passage to be considered in this connection is Rom. 6: 3-4, where St. Paul writes: "Know ye not that so many of us as were baptized into Jesus Christ, were baptized into His death? Therefore we are buried with Him by Baptism into death, that like as Christ was raised up from the dead by the glory of the Father, even so we also should walk in newness of life." Why, we ask, does St. Paul here refer to Holy Baptism? In chapters 3 to 5 he had set forth the comforting doctrine of justification by grace through faith in Christ, who died for all sinners. Now, there was danger that some persons might abuse this doctrine, saying, as St. Paul writes, chapter 6:1: "Shall we continue in sin that grace may abound?" The meaning of the words is: "Well, since we are saved by grace, let us sin all the more in order that God's grace may be magnified by our very sinning." But these despisers of the grace of God St. Paul here warns, reminding them, on the one hand (v. 3), of the great blessings which Holy Baptism gives and seals, and, on the other, of the high demand which Holy Baptism makes of all baptized believers. They must not sin against grace, but walk in newness of life, that is, in purity and holiness before God. The doctrine of Holy Baptism is therefore used here for very earnest admonition.

In Eph. 4:5, St. Paul writes: "One Lord, one faith, one Baptism," that is to say: "We Christians have but one Lord, one faith, one Baptism." But why does the Apostle say this? In v. 3 of this chapter he had admonished the Ephesians "to keep the unity of the Spirit in the bond of peace." This means that they were to try with all their might to be united in love and to live in peace, just as the Holy Spirit had granted to them the blessing of love and peace through the Gospel in Holy Baptism. That, of course, presupposes unity in doctrine. The Ephesians were to believe one and the same doctrine and to be at peace among themselves; and as a reason for this exhortation the Apostle mentions, among

Holy Baptism

other things, *Holy Baptism*. They all were baptized with one and the same Holy Baptism, by which they were born again and so became children of God. St. Paul therefore also here uses the doctrine of Holy Baptism for instruction and admonition.

In Eph. 5:25-26 St. Paul uses the doctrine of Holy Baptism to admonish husbands to love their wives, an admonition which indeed is very necessary. He writes: "Husbands, love your wives, even as Christ also loved the Church and gave Himself for it, that He might sanctify and cleanse it with the washing of water by the Word." This passage incidentally shows us very clearly what Baptism is, namely, a divine washing of water by the Word, that is, the Gospel. It tells us just what Luther says in his Small Catechism: "Baptism is not simple water only, but it is the water comprehended in God's command and connected with God's Word." But why does the Apostle here refer to Holy Baptism? The answer is: To make Christian homes really Christian, to fill them with love and peace and good will. If Christ has so greatly loved us that He has given Himself for us, and if He loved us so dearly that He has sanctified and cleansed us with the washing of water by the Word, then surely we who are Christ's disciples, must love one another and help one another in the home as co-heirs of everlasting life. So here again St. Paul uses the doctrine of Holy Baptism for admonition.

In Col. 2:11-12, St. Paul clearly refers to Holy Baptism, for he writes: "In whom [Christ] also ye are circumcised with the circumcision made without hands, in putting off the body of the sins of the flesh by the circumcision of Christ; buried with Him in Baptism, wherein also ye are risen with Him through the faith of the operation of God, who hath raised Him from the dead." Why, we ask, does he here refer to Holy Baptism? As we read the verses preceding the text, we find that they contain very earnest warnings against false prophets who tried to lead the Colossian believers away from Christ and His instituted means of grace. St. Paul writes, for example: "Beware, lest any man spoil you through philosophy and vain deceit" (v. 8). The Apostle thus, by way of admonition, reminds the Christians at Colossae that if they give up Christ and His divinely ordained means of grace, they imperil their salvation, for in that case they reject the only means by which sinners can be saved. So here also the doctrine of Holy Baptism is used for admonition.

In Tit. 3:5-7, St. Paul writes the well-known words: "But after that the kindness and love of God, our Savior, toward man appeared, not by works of righteousness which we have done, but according to His mercy He saved us, by the washing of regeneration and renewing of the Holy Ghost, which He shed on us abundantly through Jesus Christ, our Savior, that, being justified by His grace, we should be made heirs according to the hope of eternal life." Why (so we ask again) does the Apostle write these glorious words, in which he speaks so emphatically and consolingly of Holy Baptism as the washing of regeneration and renewing of the Holy Ghost? As we know, he addressed these words to Titus, one of his fellow workers in spreading the Gospel and establishing the Christian Church. He had left young Titus in Crete, whose people were notorious because of their ungodliness, untruthfulness, (v.12), philosophical and other speculations, and their lack of religious stability. The small church in Crete, no doubt, had to face many false prophets, many deceitful hypocrites, proclaiming another Gospel than that which St. Paul had preached. So, in the words quoted, St. Paul reminds his beloved fellow minister Titus of the foundation doctrines of the Christian faith, which by all means must be preserved, namely, salvation by grace through faith, the means of grace, especially Holy Baptism, sanctification, and the assurance of eternal life. These words therefore emphasize the importance of the doctrine of Holy Baptism, which indeed is not secondary in our Christian faith, but fundamental, and so must be maintained in its Biblical purity by all means. Here, then, the doctrine of Holy Baptism is used for consolation and admonition.

Let us consider, as a last passage setting forth the doctrine of Holy Baptism, I Pet. 3:21, in which there occur the very clear and emphatic words: "Baptism doth also now save us." In these words St. Peter tells us that Holy Baptism saves us, not indeed as a putting away of the filth of the flesh, or as an outward washing of the body, but as the answer of a good conscience toward God. The Greek word which our Authorized Version translates with *answer*, may also be translated with *demand*, or still better, I personally believe, with *covenant*, as Luther has translated it, *der Bund eines guten Gewissens mit Gott;* for just that is what Holy Baptism is, a covenant which God makes with us, and we again, as His regenerated and sanctified children, with Him. At any rate, the passage clearly says: "Baptism saves us"; and: "It saves us by giving us a good conscience." But a good conscience we can have only when by faith in Christ our sins are forgiven and we have peace with God through our Lord Jesus Christ. The passage thus extols the great value of Holy Baptism as a means of grace that saves us, giving us a good conscience before God.

But (for the last time) we ask: What meaning has this clear and emphatic reference to Holy Baptism in this connection? In the preceding words the Apostle has spoken of the sufferings of Christians in this life. They must suffer even as Christ, their Savior, has suffered, who indeed humbled Himself and became obedient unto death (I Pet. 3:18; Phil. 2:8), but who afterwards was highly exalted (I Pet. 3:19; Col. 2:15; Phil. 2:9 ff.). Now, the Apostle continues, so also the believers in the Old Testament suffered, but they were nevertheless saved by the Lord, as, for example, Noah (I Pet. 3:20), who, with his family, was saved by water. Just so, St. Peter then continues, Holy Baptism, as the antitype of the water that saved Noah, now saves us. In other words, St. Peter comforts the readers of his Epistle with the sure hope that since they have been saved by Holy Baptism, Christ will not forsake them in their suffering, but will preserve them unto eternal life; for He is now on the right hand of God, and all creatures are subject to Him (I Pet. 3:22). The Apostle therefore in this passage uses the doctrine of Holy Baptism to comfort his believing fellow sufferers as they passed through the fiery furnace of affliction.

Thus we see that Holy Scripture constantly applies the doctrine of Holy Baptism to admonish and to comfort us who are God's dear children, regenerated or born again by Holy Baptism. And who would doubt that we need the admonition and the comfort which Holy Baptism gives to us?

In the first place, we need such admonition, for we are still burdened with our old Adam, who is so utterly unwilling to do God's will and who so greatly loves sin and every evil thing. Again, our old Adam is very much attached to this world and loves its deceitful pleasures and treasures, so that we are constantly tempted to forget our Savior and become like the prodigal son, who left his father's house to spend his life in wickedness. Lastly, our old Adam also is only too greatly inclined to yield to the temptations of Satan, who "walketh about as a roaring lion seeking whom he may devour" (I Pet. 5:8). Hence we are in constant danger of losing our salvation. Satan desires to sift us as wheat (Luke 22:31), and so we must daily remember the covenant of Holy Baptism, in which we have renounced the devil and all his works and have promised to be faithful to our precious Savior, who has redeemed us from sin, death, and the devil. Our entire daily repentance is nothing else than that we deeply deplore the many sins that still cleave to us, but which we have renounced and put away in Holy Baptism, and that we comfort ourselves with its blessed promise of forgiveness. Oh, let us often think of Holy Baptism and use it for daily earnest admonition in order that we may live as true children of God in Christ Jesus on our way through this world to eternal glory.

But let us use it also for consolation, which, too, we greatly need. The report of the 22d Convention of the Central District (1879) offers an excellent essay on "Holy Baptism in Its Relation to the Christian Life," in which the essayist shows, on the basis of Scripture, that the Christian life owes to Holy Baptism (1) its beginning, (2) its continuation, and (3) its blessed end. The entire essay really is nothing else than an excellent exposition of Tit. 3: 4-7. To Holy Baptism we owe our regeneration; to Holy Baptism we owe our renewal or sanctification; to Holy Baptism we owe the assurance of our eternal salvation, or as the Apostle puts it: "That, being justified by His grace, we should be made heirs according to the hope of eternal life" (Tit. 3:7). Oh, how exceedingly rich is the comfort which we find in the Scripture doctrine of Holy Baptism!

In the report of the 8th Convention of the Southern District (1892) the same subject is treated from a slightly different viewpoint: "The Pure Doctrine of Holy Baptism in Its Significance and Importance for the Faith and Life of Christians." We recommend both these essays for special devotional reading, since in our own epitome we could present only a mere digest of what our fathers have written on this important doctrine. We shall offer here, by way of conclusion, a summary of the second thesis of the excellent essay mentioned last. We Christians, alas, remain sinners until our death; and since we are sinners, there come to us at times very severe trials, especially when we wrestle with the temptations of the devil, the world, and our flesh, the anxious thought that after all we are not true Christians and heirs of salvation. These trials are increased by the fact that "we must through much tribulation enter into the Kingdom of God" (Acts 14:23), the daily cross which often becomes so very heavy. And lastly, we face death, the greatest of all foes, death, which is constantly threatening us, death, of which we, too, according to our old Adam, are very much afraid. I need not expatiate on this subject, for the trials and tribulations of the Christian life are well known to you all, who are fellow believers with me in Christ Jesus.

What, then, shall comfort us in the trials and troubles of our life on earth? Scripture points us again and again to Holy Baptism as the source of all consolation, since Holy Baptism is nothing else than the application of the Gospel of God's grace in Christ Jesus, or we may say, since it is God's gracious covenant which can never be removed from us, even though mountains should depart and hills should be removed; for so the Lord says: "But My kindness shall not depart from thee, neither shall the covenant of My peace be removed, saith the Lord that hath mercy on thee" (Is. 54:10). We may fail God, but God will never fail us. We may sin, but God's covenant, which He established with us in Holy Baptism, will never be broken on His part. We may always return to God's baptismal covenant of grace in Christ Jesus. God will always receive us, just as the loving father received his penitent prodigal son. "There is joy in the presence of the angels of God over one sinner that repenteth" (Luke 15:10).

In his Large Catechism, Dr. Martin Luther speaks very consolingly about this point. He writes: "Thus it appears what a great, excellent thing Baptism is, which delivers us from the jaws of the devil and makes us God's own, suppresses and takes away sin, and then daily strengthens the new man; and (it) is and remains ever efficacious until we pass from this estate of misery to eternal glory.

"For this reason let everyone esteem his Baptism as a daily dress in which he is to walk constantly, that he may ever be found in the faith and its fruits, that he suppress the old man and grow up in the new. For if we would be Christians, we must practice the work whereby we are Christians. But if any one fall away from it, let him again come into it. For just as Christ, the Mercy Seat, does not recede from us or forbid us to come to Him again, even though we sin, so all His treasures and gifts also remain. If therefore we have once in Baptism obtained forgiveness of sin, it will remain every day, as long as we live, that is, as long as we carry the old man about our neck." (Cf. Large Catechism, Infant Baptism, par. 83 ff.; *Triglot,* p. 751 f.)

May God grant us His grace that we may constantly adhere to the pure doctrine of Holy Baptism as it is taught in Holy Scripture and set forth in the writings of our fathers. Dear Lord, preserve unto us Thy Word, for Thy Word is unto us the joy and rejoicing of our hearts. Amen.

The Lord's Supper

THERE are three great treasures that we should learn to appreciate ever more highly as we make progress in our Christian life: the Word of God, Holy Baptism, and Holy Communion. These three are the means of grace, the only means of grace, the channels through which God's grace comes into our personal lives, the medicines through which God gives and restores spiritual life and health to us, the documents through which God proves the full reality and validity of our status as citizens in His kingdom and as children in His family.

WE ARE IMMEASURABLY RICH

We have the Word of God; we have it in its truth and purity; the Word shines like a bright morning star in a dark night, foretelling the coming of a bright dawn and the full light of day, when we shall know God even as He knows us and praise Him as He deserves. Others around us may still be in semidarkness or in complete darkness, but we have a good light to see the road ahead. Surely, we want to help light up the way for others.

We are immeasurably rich. For we have Holy Baptism; you and I have been baptized. Though Baptism does not give us any other blessings than the Word gives, it gives them in another manner, that is, with an outward sign connected with the Word. The Lord comes to the rescue of our weak faith; we often wish so much that we might be permitted to see and feel. So the Lord deals with us as Christ dealt with doubting Thomas; He gives us something visible for our weak faith, and with that He combines the invisible and spiritual blessings. Through Holy Baptism He richly blessed us when we were not yet able to receive the message of the Word; and that great gift of sonship given to us in our

Baptism He is able to preserve unto us until that great Day. For He has in Baptism given us not only the right to speak to Him as His dear children, but also the inheritance preserved for us in heaven.

We are immeasurably rich. For we have Holy Communion. In Holy Communion the body and the blood of Christ, our Lord, are given to us together with the bread and the wine. Our hearts may tremble as we think on these words; can we really believe them? Our emotions may resemble those of the women at the tomb of the risen Lord: we are filled with fear and great joy. But we dare not doubt the Lord's word. With great assurance and rejoicing we believe what Christ, our Lord, has said: "Take and eat; this is My body; drink ye all of it; this is My blood." Indeed, the Lord gives us His body and His blood; and we receive it with our mouths. And yet His body and His blood is only, as it were, the jeweled case in which the precious jewel lies enshrined. And what is that jewel? Christ says: "For the remission of sins." In these words He has named what can make us truly happy and blessed, for where there is forgiveness of sins, there is also life and salvation. Christ offers you riches more precious than all the kingdoms of this world and their glory, for He says, as it were: All this, grace, forgiveness, sonship, and the eternal inheritance will I give you; only believe, and it is all yours.

And because these treasures are so precious, we must be prepared to fight for them. We are surrounded on all sides by enemies that try to take away from us our most valuable possessions, the Word, Holy Baptism, and Holy Communion. We must defend the true teaching of the Lord's Supper at all costs and to our dying day maintain the word of the Lord: "This is My body; this is My blood."

Luther observed that if we were not already certain of the great importance of the Lord's Supper in the Christian Church, then the very fact that it has been so persistently attacked, and from so many angles, should teach us the great value of the Sacrament; for, says he, the devil fights most against the most precious parts of Christian doctrine. Indeed, few points of doctrine have been so often attacked as the Sacrament of the Altar. People who are not well grounded in Scriptural teaching might consider this one of the weak sides of Christian teaching. But the truth has no weak sides. It is just the chief parts of Christian doctrine that have been most bitterly attacked. And that the Lord's Supper is indeed one of the chief parts is not difficult to see; for the Lord instituted this Supper as His testament; and the Apostle Paul glories in the fact that it was especially revealed to him. (Central District, 1888, pp. 14–15.)

Luther saw from the beginning that in these controversies on the Lord's Supper there were involved also other important points of Christian teaching, as, for example, the authority of the Scriptures (the formal principle of Christian doctrine) and the grace of God (the material principle); for whosoever attacks one of the means of grace is violating them all; and with the means of grace set aside, the working of God's grace itself is hindered or made altogether impossible. Hence the very facts of the frequency and the bitterness of the enemy attacks against the Lord's Supper should move us to appreciate its great value anew and to thank the Lord for this important part of our Lutheran heritage and of clear Scriptural teaching. (Central, 1889, pp. 13–14.)

This essay is arranged in four parts: I. *The Essence of the Lord's Supper;* II. *The Benefits connected with Holy Communion;* III. *The Power of Holy Communion;* IV. *The Proper Use of the Lord's Supper.*

I. THE ESSENCE OF THE LORD'S SUPPER

What our Lord Jesus Christ and His Apostles said about the Lord's Supper nineteen hundred years ago was summarized by Luther four hundred years ago and has been maintained at all times by the loyal Lutheran Church through the last one hundred years. Luther's masterful summary is this: "The Sacrament of the Altar is the true body and blood of our Lord Jesus Christ, under the bread and wine, for us Christians to eat and to drink, instituted by Christ Himself."

This summary of essentials is based on another summarized statement combining the accounts of four inspired writers who told the story of the institution of this Sacrament, the Evangelists Matthew, Mark, and Luke, and the Apostle Paul. These four accounts are found in the Bible in Matt. 26:26-28; Mark 14:22-24;

Luke 22:19-20; and I Cor. 11:23-25. Every one of these four writers has in his account some words and phrases not occurring in any of the other three accounts; but these differences, as can be clearly seen, are in non-essentials; none of these differences is a contradiction, and none would yield a different sense. Hence these very differences are a powerful proof of the truthfulness of the witnesses and the absence of any collusion. Apart from the minor differences, all four accounts agree completely in their statements on essentials. Hence these four accounts constitute an overpowering proof that the words must be taken in their original, natural sense, not in any part as figures of speech. The summarized account of the institution follows: "Our Lord Jesus Christ, the same night in which He was betrayed, took bread; and when He had given thanks, He brake it and gave it to His disciples, saying: Take, eat; this is My body, which is given for you. This do in remembrance of Me. After the same manner also He took the cup when He had supped, and when He had given thanks, He gave it to them, saying: Drink ye all of it; this cup is the new testament in My blood, which is shed for you for the remission of sins. This do, as oft as ye drink it, in remembrance of Me."

These words of Holy Scripture must be the basis of our teaching and of our faith with regard to the Lord's Supper. Attempts have been made to prove false teachings concerning this Sacrament from Bible passages which do not speak at all of the Lord's Supper. Such attempts violate one of the basic rules of interpretation: a passage which does not at all speak of the matter at issue may not be used to prove one's views or statements.

The Reformed churches hold that the words "This is My Body" must not be taken in their proper, but in a figurative sense. While they are by no means agreed as to the interpretation, there being in their camp more than twenty different ways of interpreting them (cf. Krauth, *Conservative Reformation*, p. 607), they are all persuaded that the words must not be taken to mean that Christ's true body and blood are actually present and orally received by the communicants. Zwingli says, revealing his own position and at the same time grossly misrepresenting the position of the Lutherans: "That Christ's body according to its essence and in reality, that is, the natural body itself, is present in the Lord's Supper or that is is chewed with the mouth and our teeth, as the papists teach and all those who are looking back to the fleshpots of Egypt, this we not only deny, but we maintain consistently that it is an error contradicting the Word of God." *Confession* ed. Niemeyer, p. 26. The Reformed think that the Real Presence is ruled out by the ascension of Christ to heaven, which they explain as involving His being shut up in heaven in such a way that His body and blood cannot be present in the Lord's Supper. The Heidelberg Catechism says: "What does it mean to eat the crucified body of Christ and to drink the blood that He shed? It means not only to receive with a believing heart the whole Passion and death of Christ and thereby lay hold on forgiveness of sins and life eternal, but besides, through the Holy Spirit, who lives at the same time in Christ and in us, to be united more and more with His blessed body in such a way that, although He is in heaven and we are on earth, we are nevertheless flesh of His flesh and bone of His bones and live and are governed eternally through one Spirit just as the members of the body live and are governed through one soul." When the Reformed churches do say that Christ's body and blood are present in the Lord's Supper, they have in mind merely His spiritual influence, as the foregoing quotation shows. Very vehemently do they assert that Christ's body and blood are not received orally, but spiritually, by faith. Chap. XXIX, 7, of the Westminster Confession declares of the body and blood of Christ that they are not "corporally or carnally in, with, or under the bread and wine, yet as really, but spiritually, present to the faith of believers in that ordinance as the elements themselves are to their outward senses." (*Popular Symbolics,* p. 219.) Article XXIX, 8, of the Westminister Confession declares: "Although ignorant and wicked men receive the outward elements in this Sacrament, yet they receive not the thing signified thereby." In this point all the Reformed are agreed.

Over against this figurative interpretation of the words of institution Luther, and with him the loyal Lutheran Church, has steadfastly maintained that the words of Christ "This is My body," "This is My blood" must be accepted as they stand, in their literal sense. We have done that and shall continue to do that for the following reasons.

1. Christ Himself calls His Holy Supper His testament. In the words that St. Paul has preserved He says: "This cup is the New Testament in My blood," and in the phrase that Matthew and Mark report He said: "This is My blood of the New Testament." When any man writes his last will or testament, he will use the clearest, most unmistakable words that he can find, to avoid every chance of ambiguity; and when such a testament is later opened and read, the words are taken in their usual sense. Neither the writer nor the heirs will attempt figurative flights and flourishes. Should not the words of Christ command at least that much respect? Let us not forget whose testament this is. It is the testament of our Lord Jesus Christ, the God-Man, who is the Truth, who is all-wise and almighty. Truly, "The Word of the Lord is right, and all His works are done in truth," and He "is able to do exceeding abundantly above all that we ask or think."

2. Holy Communion is a Sacrament of the New Testament, as Christ says: "This cup is the New Testament in My blood." If we were to set aside, reject, the proper sense of the words and teach that bread and wine only signify the body and blood of the Lord, that they are only symbols and types, we should be going back into Old Testament times and manners of speaking; of the Old Testament the Bible says (Heb. 10:1) that it has "a shadow of good things to come" and "which are a shadow of things to come, but the body is of Christ." The Old Testament has figurative language, symbolic actions and happenings, signs and types, prophecies of better things to come in the future; but the New Testament records the actual, the fulfillment of types and prophecies. The Passover supper was typical, the supper which the Lord had just celebrated with His disciples for the last time. In place of that supper, which foreshadowed Him, He now instituted something new, which was not another shadow. Christ really gave His flesh and blood. He said: "This cup is the New Testament in My blood." If bread and wine were to be only symbols, He would be giving less in the New Testament than they had in the Old. The Paschal lamb with its actual flesh and blood, really slain, would have been a much clearer and more impressive symbol than a symbol of bread and wine. Humanly speaking, Chirst would then have left us no more than the Passover supper of the Jews.

3. The words of institution should be taken in their proper sense, because Scripture nowhere indicates that we should set aside the proper sense or that we should take them in a figurative sense. They are the words of an article of faith, of a divine institution. Now, there is nowhere in the whole Bible any article of faith that is not somewhere revealed and stated in proper, clear, and nonmetaphorical words. If these words of a divine institution were to be taken in a figurative sense, then Scripture itself must indicate that and explain what the figurative words are meant to express. Would four men of God, writing by inspiration of God, narrating the institution of a Sacrament to be observed throughout the New Testament times, describe the very essence of the Sacrament in figurative language and use such language without the slightest hint as to its correct understanding? Perish the thought. It is clear that no figurative meaning was intended.

4. Scripture confirms the literal understanding of these words in other clear passages that also treat of the Lord's Supper. St. Paul writes: "The cup of blessing which we bless, is it not the communion of the blood of Christ? The bread which we break, is it not the communion of the body of Christ?" (I Cor. 10:16.) The Apostle says clearly that the blessed cup is not merely a sign or symbol of something, but that it is the communion of the blood of Christ; and he also states clearly that the bread is not merely a sign of the body of Christ, but that it is the communion of this body. One thing alone can never have union or communion; but when one thing is united with another, then there is a union or communion. As surely, then, as there is bread and wine in the Supper, so surely is the body and blood of Christ present together with these elements in communion with them. (See also I Cor. 11:27, 29.)

Let us now learn from Scripture just what are the essential things in the Lord's Supper. They are five, summarized as follows: 1. In the Lord's Supper there is really present the true body and the true blood of Jesus Christ. 2. This presence takes place in, with, and under the blessed bread and wine. 3. The body and the blood of Christ should be taken by eating and drinking. 4. This eating and drinking is oral, is done with the mouth, by all communicants. 5. All this takes place by virtue of the words Christ spoke in instituting this Sacrament.

1. In the Lord's Supper the true body and the true blood of the Lord Jesus Christ are really present. We say, "the true body and the true blood of the Lord Jesus Christ"; what do we mean by these words? We mean "the true, natural, human body of Jesus Christ that was born of the Virgin Mary, received into the person of the Son of God and given into death for us; and the true, natural blood shed for the forgiveness of our sins on the altar of the Cross"; for Christ's words say plainly and clearly: "This is My body, which is given for you; this is My blood, shed for you for the remission of sins." Hence it is not a "figurative body," as Zwingli maintained, nor "a certain power proceeding from His body and His blood," as Calvin taught; for no figurative body was given into death for us, and no metaphorical blood was shed for the remission of our sins; nor was it some power proceeding from Christ's body, but His true body and His true blood.

The true body and the true blood of Jesus Christ are really present in the Lord's Supper. So we learn from the words of institution, taking them in their simple meaning, just as they read. That understanding is further confirmed by the passages I Cor. 10: 16 and 11:27, 29. By saying this, however, we do not by any means intend to teach a visible presence, as Reformed theologians insinuate. For they do not seem to know of any other presence than one predicable of a mere man; and they think that also Jesus Christ could not be present in any other manner than as a mere man, that is, in a local and visible manner. So they bring forth against the doctrine of the real presence "various alleged reasons and futile counterarguments pertaining to the natural qualities of a human body." Our Formula of Concord quotes Luther on this point as follows: "My reasons are these: First, this article of faith that Jesus Christ is essential, natural, true and complete God and man in one undivided person; second, that the right hand of God is everywhere; third, that the Word of God does not deceive or lie; fourth, that God has various ways of being anywhere, and not only the one that the philosophers call 'local' or 'spatial.' — Christ's one body has three different ways of being anywhere; first, the bodily manner that is open to sense perception, in which He occupied space according to His height. This manner of being anywhere He can still use, as He did after His resurrection and will on the Last Day. — Second, the spiritual manner of being anywhere, in which He does not occupy space, a manner that is not subject to the perception of human senses; in this manner He goes through creation wherever it is His will to go, as my eyesight (if I may use a crude comparison) goes through air, light, or water, without occupying any space; or as a sound or a musical tone goes through air, water, a board or a wall, without occupying space when it comes or relinquishing space when it goes; or as light and heat go through air, water, glass, without occupying or relinquishing space. This manner of being Christ used when He came out of the closed and sealed grave and when He came through the locked door, in the bread and wine in Holy Communion and, as many believe, when He was born of His mother. — The third is the divine, heavenly manner, because He is one person with God, according to which all creatures are far more permeable and present to Him than they are according to the second manner. For if according to that second manner He can be in and with the creatures in such a manner that they do not feel, touch, measure, nor grasp Him, then how much more will He, in this third manner, be in all creatures in a wonderful way, so that they do not measure or sense Him, but that He can have them present and measure and know them. For you must remember that, being one person with God, He is so far, far above all creatures as God is above, but, on the other hand, so deeply inside and near all creatures as God is near. But who can fully explain or think that through? Since this is unfathomable to us, and yet true, we should not undertake to deny His word, until we are able to prove convincingly that it is utterly impossible for the body of Christ to be where God is. That is what the Reformed theologians would have to prove. But I do not think that they will furnish such proof. Whether God may have still other manners of being anywhere, I am not undertaking to deny; but merely want to indicate what a gross error it is to maintain that the body of Christ has only that first manner of being that would be subject to our sense perception; although they cannot prove even that as being contrary to our reason. For I certainly do not want to say that the power of God would not be able to make a body present in different places, also in a bodily manner and open to sense perception. For who will prove that God is unable to do that? Who will define just how far God's power goes? Those who reject God's revelation and make reason their sole guide say it is impossible for God to do this. But who wants to believe their thoughts? How would they convince us that their thinking is the truth? Our faith is based on the truthfulness and the almighty power of God." (Formula of Concord, Thorough Declaration, VII, pars. 92 to 103. *Triglot*, p. 1005 ff.)

2. This real presence takes place in, with, and under the blessed bread and wine. The Lord used bread and wine in instituting the Holy Supper; and He commanded us to do the same. Therefore bread and wine are essential. That Christ broke the bread was merely for the purpose of distribution; and His command to "take" does not make it necessary to take with our hands; the taking can be done with the mouth (cf. John 19:30). It is essential that bread and wine be blessed. The Apostle says: "The cup of blessing which we bless" (I Cor. 10:16). It means simply that by speaking the words of institution and prayer we declare that the Holy Supper is being celebrated in accordance with Christ's command; that bread and wine are being set apart from their ordinary use and that what has been promised in this Sacrament is truly being done.

The words "in, with, and under" are used to safeguard ourselves and our church against three false teachings that have been imputed to us, those of transubstantiation, impanation, and consubstantiation. We do not teach that the bread and wine are changed into the body and blood of Christ. (Example: "Here is a drink of water for you" does not mean that the glass has been changed into water.) We do not teach that the body of Christ is locally inside the bread, as a loaf of bread would be in a basket. We do not teach that the body of Christ and the bread, or the blood of Christ and the wine, are so mixed as to form a third substance. We merely teach that the body and the blood of Christ are really present in the Sacrament, without explaining the "how." "With our eyes we see the bread, and with our ears we hear that the body of Christ is there," says Luther.

3. The body and the blood of Christ should be taken by eating and drinking. So the Lord directed us; therefore the eating and the drinking are essential. It follows that the bread and wine, when

not eaten and drunk, do not constitute the Lord's Supper and are no Sacrament. In contradiction the Pope maintains that the elements remain a sacrament, also outside any use as sacrament; therefore the Roman Catholic Church has its consecrated hosts and its Corpus Christi Day processions. (Thursday after Trinity Sunday; instituted in 1264, on the basis of a dream of a nun; promises of indulgences for 40 to 100 days. Gross and crude idolatry.)

What a blasphemous perversion of the blessed Sacrament is the Roman Catholic Mass! Christ instituted His Supper for the living to eat and drink, the Pope changes this Supper into a sacrifice for the living and the dead. That is one of the horrible abominations of Popery, slandering and dishonoring, as it does, the perfect sacrifice of our Savior on the Cross. Of all human idolatry this is undoubtedly the one that is celebrated with the greatest pomp; one for which effects manifestly beyond human power are blasphemously claimed: that the work of reading Mass delivers men from their sins, both in this life and in purgatory. How shamelessly contrary to the words of Christ, "This do in remembrance of Me"! "To eat *and to drink*" this Sacrament was established. Another abomination of Popery is the refusal of the cup to the laity. The Pope pretends that this was necessary by reason of what the sophists called "concomitance," the alleged logical principle that one of any two things that are really united must always be where the other one is. Now, they say, in any living body flesh and blood are indissolubly united, that wherever the body of Christ is, there His blood must be; hence, when laymen receive the body, it is not necessary to give anything more. Surely, such sophistry cannot be allowed to change Christ's command.

"*Drink ye all* of it," said Christ; but the Pope says: "No, not all; only the priest." St. Paul also says: "Let a man examine himself, and so let him eat of that bread *and drink of that cup.*" Depriving the laity of the cup was made a law of the Roman Catholic Church only in 1415 (by the Council of Constance), and in outspoken disregard of the command of Christ. The resolution of the Council of Trent contains these words, that although Christ instituted Communion in both kinds, "tamen, hoc non obstante" (that is, "nevertheless, in spite of that"), only the bread was to be distributed to the laity. What Christ has commanded and what the Church had observed for fourteen centuries does not seem to trouble these people; for "nevertheless, in spite of it," the Pope has his own way. Who cannot see that the Pope is truly the Antichrist, "who opposeth and exalteth himself above all that is called God, or that is worshiped"?

4. This eating and drinking is an oral one, is done with the mouth, by all communicants. Reformed church leaders speak of "eating and drinking the body and the blood of the Lord," but they mean a spiritual eating and drinking. That would be a figurative use of the words eating and drinking; the words would be a metaphorical description of faith, in this sense that faith receives and makes its own what Christ has earned for us by giving His body into death and shedding His blood on the Cross. The Bible does speak of a spiritual eating and drinking in John 6:53-56. That is faith. This passage is wrongly applied to the Lord's Supper by the Reformed, since it speaks of an eating and drinking without which no one can have eternal life.

In the Lord's Supper the Lord speaks of an eating and drinking that is done with the mouth, eating and drinking in the proper sense. Luther calls it "bodily eating and drinking." No other kind of eating and drinking could be meant. Or should the bread and the cup be received through faith?

Do we, then, teach a natural eating and drinking of the body and blood of Christ? That charge has been made against us, but it is untrue. We say that the eating and drinking is done in a manner that is beyond human understanding, for which reason we also do not attempt to explain it. It is enough that we believe the Word of Christ, that there is an eating of Christ's body and a drinking of His blood in the Sacrament, even if we do not understand its exact manner.

Because this eating and drinking is oral, therefore all communicants take part in it. St. Paul, in I Cor. 11:27, 29, speaks of unworthy eating and drinking and continues: "For he that eateth and drinketh unworthily, eateth and drinketh damnation to himself, not discerning the Lord's body." From these words it is clear that also unworthy communicants receive the body and the blood of the Lord, though not to their salvation, but to their damnation.

5. In the Holy Supper the true body and the true blood of Jesus Christ are really present and are received through eating and drinking by all communicants because of Christ's words. Because Christ, our Lord, has instituted this Sacrament, therefore what He said really takes place. No man's faith, piety, or works, not to say words, can make the Lord's Supper. And no man's unbelief or wickedness can unmake it. For the words of Christ were true and powerful not only in the first celebration, but continue to be true and powerful in all places wherever this sacred act is celebrated according to Christ's institution, where His words are used, because of the divine authority that lies in His words. Compare Formula of Concord, Thorough Declaration, VII, par. 75; *Triglot*, p. 999.

But it is necessary that the whole institution of Christ be followed. And that brings up the question whether the Reformed sects really have the Lord's Supper. Luther denied this, and we cannot but agree with him; they do not have the words and the order instituted by the Lord, but they have changed God's word and order; hence they have nothing but bread and wine, as they themselves say. Even though they keep the sound of the words of institution, they take away their sense; Christ said: "This is My body"; they say: "This is not His body." They change the thing to the very opposite and take away the essence of the Holy Supper. (Kansas, 1895, pp. 24—42; *Lehre und Wehre*, 1904, pp. 145 ff.)

II. THE BENEFITS CONNECTED WITH HOLY COMMUNION

The benefits of the Lord's Supper consist in this, that all the blessed fruits of Christ's atoning work are offered, given, and sealed to the communicant. Hence it serves to strengthen us 1) in faith; 2) in our union with Christ; 3) in our hope of the resurrection to eternal life; 4) in our love toward God; and 5) in our love toward our neighbor.

1. Jesus Christ, true God and true Man, has redeemed us from all sins, from death, and from the power of the devil, that we might be His own and live under Him in His kingdom and serve Him in everlasting righteousness, innocence, and blessedness. These are the great blessings that Christ has earned for us; and it

is God's will to impart these blessings to us. How can that be done? There is only one way: through the means of grace. Although redemption has been completed, it cannot come to us except through the Word. Says St. Paul: "Christ gave Himself as a ransom for all, to be testified in due time" (I Tim. 2:6); "God was in Christ reconciling the world unto Himself . . . and hath committed unto us the Word of reconciliation" (II Cor. 5:19). Here St. Paul shows the three links in the anchor chain that makes us sure that we are eternally saved: God's grace, Christ's work of redemption, and the Gospel message. Through the glad tidings in the Word of God all the blessings that God's love has willed for us and that Christ's redemption has wrought for us are brought to us personally and made our own.

But God has from the beginning dealt with man, not only through the Word, but also through signs connected with His Word for the purpose of begetting and strengthening saving faith. "If you were only a spirit without a body, God would give you only spiritual gifts, but since your soul is united with your body, God gives you spiritual things in material things" (Chrysostom). In the Old Testament God had instituted the sacrament of circumcision (Gen. 17:9-14; cp. Rom. 4:11) and the Passover Supper; and in the New Testament, Baptism and the Lord's Supper. All these were visible signs of the invisible grace. Our hearts should be moved through the Word and through outward signs to believe that God is gracious to us, as St. Paul has said: "Faith cometh by hearing"; for as the Word goes through the ears, so the signs go through the eyes, to move our hearts to faith. St. Augustine has aptly said: "The Sacrament is a visible Word."

The outward sign must indeed be "comprehended in God's command and connected with God's Word"; there must be God's command and His promise of grace. Where is the promise regarding the Lord's Supper? In the words "My body, which is given for you" and "My blood, shed for you for the remission of sins." If you ask: "What is the benefit of such eating and drinking?" the Small Catechism instructs you: "That is shown us by these words, Given and shed for you for the remission of sins; namely, that in the Sacrament forgiveness of sins, life, and salvation are given us through these words. For where there is forgiveness of sins, there is also life and salvation."

Someone may ask: If the Lord's Supper gives us only the same blessings as the Gospel, why was the Sacrament added? We answer: For two reasons: The fact that the Lord so richly forgives our sins, in more ways than one, should be a source of great joy and comfort to us, for we daily sin much and deserve nothing but punishment. And God does something special for us personally, when the grace that has been proclaimed to all in general is now in the Sacrament brought to us personally, offered, given, and sealed to each communicant in particular.

In addition to this personal assurance in the words of the Sacrament, there is a second assurance in the fact that the very body and blood of Christ are given us as a pledge and seal of the forgiveness of our sins. If you are asked: "How do you know that Christ died for you and shed His blood for the forgiveness of your sins?" you answer: "From the holy Gospel and from the words of the Sacrament, and by His body and blood given me as a pledge in the Sacrament."

Thus through the Lord's Supper we are *strengthened,* first, *in faith.* We certainly need such strengthening; for there is still in us, as long as we live in this world, the sinful flesh; and there are round about us the devil and the world. There are so many hindrances to our doing the good works that we ought to do, or have even planned to do. These hindrances make us weak and weary so that we lose interest and are almost ready to give up. The Holy Supper is given us for our nourishment and refreshing, that our faith may grow, that we may go from strength to strength.

The faith that makes a Christian is faith in a gracious God, in forgiveness of sins, and in an inheritance in heaven. Yet it is often difficult for a Christian to believe that he personally has part in the general salvation; for he cannot find his name in the Bible, and he does read that many are not saved, although they were redeemed. A Christian does not always feel God's grace working in his heart. He does feel the working of sin in his life, and he does hear the threats of the Law. What more comforting and more strengthening help could there be to restore his sinking courage, to fill his heart with life and peace and joy, than these words of Christ's command: "Take, eat and drink; this is My body and My blood, given and shed for you for the forgiveness of your sins," for your reconciliation and salvation! Here all doubt is silenced.

2. The Lord's Supper *strengthens us in our communion with Christ*. Through faith we are intimately united with Christ. This is that spiritual union which Christ describes when He says that He is the Head and we are the members, He, the Vine and we, the branches, He, the Bridegroom and His Church, the bride. The marvelously close intimacy of this communion with Christ is described by St. Paul, who tells us: "We are members of His body, of His flesh, and of His bones" (Eph. 5:30). This intimate communion with our Savior is strengthened through the Lord's Supper, since it strengthens our faith.

3. The Lord's Supper also is *a means of strengthening our hope of the resurrection to eternal life*. In the Sacrament of the Altar we receive the body of our Lord, which was given into death for us. This body did not remain in death, it was raised again and entered into eternal life a glorified body. This body is given to us in the Lord's Supper to eat and is a pledge and seal for our confidence that our bodies, though they die, will rise again, be glorified, and enter into eternal life.

4. Through the Lord's Supper we are also *strengthened in our love toward God*. If our faith is strengthened in the Lord's Supper, then our love must also be increased, for love is the necessary fruit of faith. God proved His love toward us by sending His Son into the world, who loved us and gave Himself for us; "greater love hath no man than this that a man lay down his life for his friends" (John 15:13). In His Holy Supper the Lord manifests His great love to us by giving us His body and blood as a means of uniting Himself to us and us to Himself, and of enabling us to put into practice the words of the Apostle of Love: "We love Him, because He first loved us" (I John 4:19).

5. The Holy Supper *strengthens us in our love toward our neighbor*. The Apostle Paul says of fellow communicants (I Cor. 10:17): "For we, being many, are one bread and body; for we are all partakers of that one bread." The Lord's Supper is a banquet of the most intimate friendship and fellowship; a love feast of the highest order, that both demands and promotes most ardent love. There we assemble, without any distinction of rank,

as children at the family table of our heavenly Father, all to receive the same heavenly food, the body and blood of our Savior. Whatever distinctions there may be otherwise between communicants, as those of wealth, education, color, or social status — all these distinctions disappear at the Lord's Table. Surely, communing at the Lord's Table will make a community of people that are united in heartfelt brotherly love. The early Christians, threatened by deep cleavages in their outward life, but deeply realizing this result, after each Communion embraced and kissed each other. In the post-Communion collect we pray that the almighty God would strengthen us in faith toward Him and in fervent love toward one another. (Kansas, 1895, pp. 43—56.)

III. THE POWER OF HOLY COMMUNION

The question arises: In what manner does Holy Communion bring about the blessings of which we have just heard? Where does it get the power to accomplish such great things?

Certainly the Lord's Supper does not bestow its blessings in a mechanical, automatic manner, so that every one who attends the Table of the Lord will also receive all the gifts offered to all who receive the body and the blood of Christ. The mere attendance at Holy Communion does not guarantee to anyone the forgiveness of sins, life, and salvation.

The power of Holy Communion lies in the words "Given and shed for you for the remission of sins." These words, besides the bodily eating and drinking, are the chief thing in the Sacrament; for in the Sacrament forgiveness of sins, life, and salvation are given us through these words. Luther writes: "We teach that bread and wine alone will not help, yes, that body and blood in the bread and wine alone will not help; and I will go beyond that, Christ on the Cross with His suffering and death will not help, no matter how fervently you know it and consider it; there must be one thing more. What is that? The Word, the Word, the W-O-R-D, do you hear me? The WORD will do it. If Christ had been crucified for us a thousand times, it would be all in vain, unless the Word would come and distribute it and bring it to you and say: 'Take it, it's yours.' Let me speak plainly: In treating of the forgiveness of sins we must speak on two points: how it was procured and how it is to be distributed. It was procured by Christ on the Cross, but He did not distribute it on the Cross. In the Sacrament He did not procure it, but there it is distributed, as also wherever the Gospel is preached. When I need forgiveness of sins, I must not go to the Cross, for there it is not distributed; also I must not go to the memory or the knowledge of the suffering Christ, because there I do not find it. But I must go to the Sacrament or the Gospel; there I find it; for here is the Word that gives to me the forgiveness procured on the Cross. Everything depends on the Word." (St. L., X:273 ff.)

And because everything depends on the Word, only he who believes the words has what they say and express. Because the treasure is brought to us in words, it cannot be received in any other way than through faith in these words. Christ's words are not a magic formula, automatically, irresistibly effecting their purpose. Nor are they like a powerful medicine which works irrespective of the attitude of the person to whom it is administered. The words of Christ call for faith. The Gospel is the power of God unto salvation to everyone that believeth (Rom. 1:16). The Letter to the Hebrews speaks of such as had the Gospel preached to them, "but the Word preached did not profit them, not being mixed with faith in them that heard it" (Heb. 4:2). This truth applies also to Christ's words in the Sacrament. Only he who believes these words has what they say and express, namely, forgiveness of sins.

Hence only one who has faith in the words of Christ, "Given and shed for you for the remission of sins," is a worthy guest at the Lord's Table and will receive the full intended blessing of Holy Communion.

Anyone that does not believe these words of precious promise is an unworthy communicant. He will not receive any of the blessings offered so graciously in the Lord's Supper to all who come in true faith. On the contrary, the Apostle says, "He that eateth and drinketh unworthily, eateth and drinketh damnation (judgment) to himself, not discerning the Lord's body" (I Cor. 11:29). He, too, as we have heard, receives the true body and blood of the Lord, but because of his unbelief it will do him no good.

Here we cannot apply the common saying: "If it does no good, neither will it do any harm." No, in this case it harms; it harms horribly! The unbeliever brings God's wrath upon himself. Besides, the unbeliever, as a despiser of God's grace, was not invited; yet he has presumed to come into the Lord's house, into the Lord's sanctuary, he has even dared to take and eat the body and drink the blood of the Lord. He sins against the Holy of Holies. What in the Savior's love was meant as a seal of his salvation becomes to him a seal of his damnation. (Kansas, 1895, pp. 56—64.)

IV. THE PROPER USE OF THE LORD'S SUPPER

Unlike Baptism, which is the Sacrament of reception into the Christian Church, the Holy Supper should be used often, because it is the Sacrament of confirmation in the Christian faith. Being a supper, it is meant for our nourishing and strengthening. A frequent or at least a repeated use is implied in the words of the Lord: "This do, as oft as ye drink it, in remembrance of Me," and the words of the Apostle Paul: "As often as ye eat this bread and drink this cup, ye do show the Lord's death till He come." But the words of Acts 2:42 imply much more than repeated or occasional Communion, undoubtedly weekly and daily Communion: "They continued steadfastly in the Apostles' doctrine and fellowship, and in breaking of bread, and in prayers." We know from history that the early Christians had daily Communion; also in post-Apostolic days for several centuries the daily, or almost daily, use of the Sacrament is often mentioned. During the fifth century it became customary to attend Holy Communion only rarely, perhaps at great festivals, or annually. The Pope made a law (Council of Trent) for all church members to commune once annually. While Luther objected to all legalistic methods, he emphasized that Christians should be diligently taught and admonished to come to the Lord's Supper frequently; and he warned earnestly against the great danger of neglecting or despising the Holy Supper. He stressed three reasons for frequent Communion: first, the Lord's command, "This do"; second, the Lord's promise, "Given and shed for you"; and third, the troubles, difficulties, and sins that we have. But as to those who do not feel the need, Luther says that the patient who does not realize his illness is, for that reason, in so much greater danger; he recommends this: "To such a person no better advice can be given than that, in the first place, he put his hand into his bosom and feel whether he still have flesh and blood, and that he by all means believe what the Scriptures say of it in Gal. 5 and Rom. 7. Secondly, that he look around to see whether he is still in the world, and keep in mind that there will be no lack of sin and trouble, as the Scriptures say in John 15 and 16, I John 2 and 5. Thirdly, he will certainly have the devil also about him, who, with his lying and murdering, day and night, will let him have no peace within or without, as the Scriptures picture him in John 8 and 16; I Pet. 5; Eph. 6; II Tim. 2."

The Holy Supper was instituted when the disciples were assembled as a group; and in the early Christian Church it was in the assembly of the church that the Supper was celebrated. According to Christ's command this sacred act was a public confession of faith, a visible acknowledgment of a common faith and unity of Christians; partaking of the same bread, they had become one body.

It follows that orthodox Christians should not commune in heterodox churches; the confession of faith would become a contradiction and confusion. A Lutheran communing in a Reformed church would not receive Holy Communion at all, because the Reformed have discarded the essential part of the Holy Supper.

However, when we say that the Sacrament should ordinarily be celebrated in the public service, we do not mean to forbid giving the Sacrament to an individual in cases of illness or other trouble that makes it impossible or inadvisable for the person to attend public worship, because often in these cases the need for strengthening is great. But it should be the pastor who administers the Sacrament. True, emergency Baptism is administered by laymen; but administration of the Lord's Supper presupposes pastoral care. Nor is a deathbed Communion necessary for salvation. And in rare cases, when a Christian facing death has a very great desire for the Sacrament and no pastor can be found, but there is a pious laymen present who is qualified, our Church does not absolutely forbid administration of Holy Communion by a layman. Walther, *Pastorale*, p. 180: Fritz, *Pastoral Theology*, 2d Edition, p. 126.

Holy Communion should not be given to: 1) those not yet baptized; 2) the manifestly wicked and impenitent; 3) the heterodox; 4) those who have given offense and not yet removed it; 5) those unable to examine themselves.

From the Bible we learn that the Lord's Supper is not to be given indiscriminately to all, and also who those people are to whom it should not be administered. It is a practice both wrong and harmful that in some sectarian churches the minister will invite all those present in the public service to take part in the Lord's Supper. Pastors are called not simply as distributors, but to be faithful stewards of the mysteries of God; and since this is the *Lord's* Supper, it must be administered according to the Lord's directions. — Our Church has stated its position in the 25th Article of the Augsburg Confession: "We observe the custom of giving the Sacrament only to those who have been previously examined and absolved." It is customary in our congregations that all those who wish to come to Holy Communion previously register with the pastor. Luther said that just as in the case of Baptism it is right that the pastor should be previously informed as to who the persons are that are to be baptized, so those who desire Holy Communion should ask the pastor, so that he knows their names and what sort of life they lead. After that he should not admit them unless they can give such answers as will prove their faith, especially to such questions as, whether they understand what the Sacrament is and what blessings it brings us and why they want to come to the Sacrament (Luther, St. Louis, X:2247.) And we continue this old custom of our Church, because we want to do all we can to prevent the great harm that unworthy and unprepared communicants would bring upon themselves, and to help all communicants to become worthy and well prepared, so that they may receive the rich blessings of this heavenly feast.

Those to whom the Holy Supper must not be given are —

1. Such as have not been baptized. Through Baptism people are received into the Kingdom of God; but the Lord's Supper is given for the confirmation and strengthening of faith. Unbaptized adults need first of all instruction and Baptism.

2. Manifestly wicked and impenitent people. By "wicked" we mean people who live in the works of the flesh as described in

Gal. 5:19-21. Those who live after the flesh will die. (Rom. 8:13.) And it is the preacher's duty to tell them so. (Ezek. 3:17-18.) But when the pastor admits people to Holy Communion, he says to them: Thou shalt live. Both the unworthy communicant and the negligent pastor would be under God's judgment. Luther said that the Lord's Supper would be twice profaned, by those who receive it unworthily and by those who negligently give it to unworthy communicants.

Those who are wicked and have no desire to give up their evil ways should not be admitted to the Lord's Supper. (Matt. 7:6 and I Cor. 5:11.) — We said "wicked and impenitent people"; for those who have been wicked, but have repented and have confessed their sins and promised to amend, should be admitted to the Sacrament. (Prov. 28:13.) — And we said "manifestly"; if the pastor suspects or feels that a person asking to be admitted is wicked or impenitent, he has no right to refuse Holy Communion so long as he has no real proof of that person's wickedness or impenitence.

3. The heterodox. Partaking of the Lord's Supper not only implies, but is a confession and a bond of faith. Therefore only those may commune together who really have the same faith. — As to those heterodox who deny the real presence of Christ's body and blood in the Holy Supper, we dare not admit them to our Communion table because they would be unworthy communicants, "not discerning the Lord's body." And as to all other heterodox Christians, church fellowship with them is forbidden, and Communion fellowship is church fellowship. (See I Cor. 10:17, 18, 21; Rom. 16:17.) To admit heterodox people to our Communion would also be contrary to the admonition in Eph. 4:3-6, to "endeavor to keep the unity of the Spirit in the bond of peace." Altar fellowship with the heterodox proclaims that the truth and the unity in the truth are both unimportant; it denies the truth and grants error equal rights with the truth.

4. Those who have given offense and not yet removed it. (Matt. 5:23-24.) This shows clearly that all who seek reconciliation with God must also be reconciled with men whom they have wronged.

5. Such as are not able to examine themselves. In accordance with I Cor. 11:28-29 we cannot administer the Lord's Supper to children not yet sufficiently instructed or not of sufficient intellectual

The Lord's Supper 445

maturity; nor to those who are insane (unless it be in lucid intervals); nor to those who are unconscious.

As to the salutary use of the Lord's Supper, we stress the need of self-examination for every communicant; for that is what the Lord commands through the Apostle Paul: "Let a man examine himself." We dare not come to the Lord's Supper in a careless or frivolous mood, but we must in all seriousness examine ourselves whether we are worthy communicants. Our Small Catechism says: "Fasting and bodily preparation are indeed a fine outward training; but he is truly worthy and well prepared who has faith in these words, Given and shed for you for the remission of sins. But he that does not believe these words, or doubts, is unworthy and unprepared, for the words 'for you' require all hearts to believe." Worthiness consists in faith in these words: "Given and shed for you for the remission of sins." If a communicant does not believe these words, how can his partaking of Communion be of any value? But he that believes the Lord's words has the blessings of the Sacrament: forgiveness of sins and strengthening of faith. For details, see Article XIII of the Augsburg Confession. Just because strengthening of faith is the blessing that we are to receive from the Lord's Supper, therefore faith is the prerequisite.

Not in the slightest measure can our own works of preparation make us worthy communicants. For it is Christ who has cleansed us of our sins; we have not contributed anything. And we cannot now contribute anything to our redemption. But does not the Catechism speak of "fasting and bodily preparation"? It does, but not as a means toward acquiring worthiness; as such, bodily preparation is ruled out. It is fitting, but not meritorious.

Luther gives good advice for proper self-examination. He says: "You must prepare yourself so that these words fit you. That will be the case when you have epxerienced the attacks of sin and temptation. At one time you may be angry or impatient; at another miserly or worried; sometimes you fall into a cruder sin. Are you not then a miserable and weak sinner, afraid of death, depressed and unable to rise to joyful faith? You have more than enough cause to go and confess your troubles to the Lord and say: 'Lord, Thou hast instituted the Sacrament of Thy body and blood for the forgiveness of sins; I deeply feel my need, for I have fallen into sin and am filled with fear and despair; I do not have the necessary courage to witness boldly to Thy Word; I have so many other faults. Therefore I come to Thy Table for healing, comfort, and strength.'" (St. Louis, XI:594 f.)

And then you should believe without a doubt that your sins are forgiven for Christ's sake, as He Himself assures you in the Gospel and in the words of the Sacrament and for which purpose He has given you His body and His blood as a pledge. Take the pledge, and be comforted and strengthened in your faith.

As repentance precedes, so amendment must follow upon faith, for faith can exist only where there is an earnest purpose of amending our sinful lives. Faith is active through love; but so-called "faith" without works would be dead. Christ has earned forgiveness for us, not that we should live in intentional sin without fear of punishment, but that we should be His own, and live under Him in His kingdom and serve Him in everlasting righteousness, innocence, and blessedness. Where sin has abounded, there grace should much more abound. (Rom. 5:20-21; 6:1-11; Tit. 2:11-14.) Luther says: "Faith is God's work in us; it changes us into new creatures, gives us a new mind and new powers. Oh, faith is a living, busy, active, and powerful thing, so that it is impossible that it should not be constantly doing good works."

The Lutheran Congregation

I. DEFINITION

An intelligent and fruitful discussion of our theme demands a definition of terms. Dr. Walther in his preliminary remarks to his great work, "The Proper Form of a Local Ev. Lutheran Congregation," published in 1863, offers a precise and thoroughly Scriptural description of a Christian congregation, organized and established according to God's Word and our Lutheran Confessions. He writes (Thesis 1): *"An Evangelical Lutheran local congregation is a gathering of believing Christians at a definite place, among whom the Word of God is preached in its purity according to the Confessions of the Evangelical Lutheran Church and the holy Sacraments are administered according to Christ's institution as recorded in the Gospel, in whose society, however, false Christians and hypocrites will always, and manifest sinners may sometimes, be found."*

By *congregation* we have in mind a body, or an assembly, or a gathering, of believers at a certain place. Yet not any accidental gathering of believers at a certain place constitutes a Christian congregation in the Biblical and Lutheran sense in which this term is here used. This convention, for example, although it is composed of Christian believers who are assembled for the Lord's service, is not a local Christian or Lutheran congregation. A Christian congregation is a gathering of Christians who have united for the purpose of having the Word of God preached and the Sacraments administered to them by a pastor whom they have called. Such a congregation is commonly spoken of as a church, as when Paul writes "unto the church of God which is at Corinth" (I Cor. 1:2). In Acts 19:39 the *Church* (*ekklesia*) retains its original classical usage, meaning an assembly of citizens. The common usage of "ekklesia" in the New Testament, however, refers either to the invisible Church, consisting of all believers in Christ, "the communion of saints," as the Creed says (Eph. 1:22-23; 5:23-27; Heb. 12:23; Matt. 16:18), or in the majority of cases, to the visible local church (*Ortsgmeinde*) (Matt. 18:17; Acts 2:47; 8:1; 11:26; 13:1; 14:23, 27; 15:2, 22, 41; 18:22; Rom. 16:5; I Cor. 4:17; 14:34; 16:1; Gal. 1:22; Col. 4:16; Philem. 2, 3; John 9; Rev. 1:4). In the English New Testament the word for "congregation" (*synagog*) occurs only in Acts 13:43.

The word *Lutheran* eliminates from this discussion heretical communions and schismatic, or separatistic, communions. That which makes a congregation distinctively Lutheran in a confessional sense is the fact that God's Word is preached in its truth and purity and His holy Sacraments are administered in agreement with the Lutheran Confessions. While therefore not every Christian congregation is a Lutheran congregation, every Lutheran congregation is a Christian congregation.

Such a gathering of Christians is not "a communion of saints" in the sense of the invisible Church, in which every member is a true child of God; but local or visible churches include in their external membership also hypocrites and, in places where church discipline is neglected, even manifest sinners. Nevertheless these hypocrites, or nominal Christians, are, properly speaking, neither members of the invisible nor of the visible Church. They are only outward adherents of the Church.

II. ITS ORIGIN AND CHARACTER

1. Its Origin

When the Church of the New Testament was formally founded, on Pentecost Day, the Lord, as indicated in His own words (Matt. 18:15-20), arranged to have the believers form individual groups or local congregations, whose outward organization was modeled, in part, after that of the Jewish synagog and, in part, after that of the town meetings of the Greek cities. The story of how the first Christian congregation, in the city of Jerusalem, came into being is told in Acts 2—4. Here we learn that God has directed that the Christian Church should exercise its God-given rights through the local church, or congregation. That the 3,000 who were converted on the day of Pentecost were added to the church at Jerusalem and that they "continued in fellowship" with that church was not merely a matter of expediency, or a mere arrangement of the Apostles, but in accordance with God's will. For we read: "The Lord added to the church daily such as should be saved" (Acts 2:41-42, 47). To "the church that was at Antioch" the Holy Ghost said: "Separate Me Barnabas and Saul for the work whereunto I have called them. And when they had fasted and prayed and laid their hands on them, they sent them away" (Acts 13:2-3). After one who has given offense has been fruitlessly admonished, the Lord says: "Tell it unto the church" (the local church, of course, for it would be impossible either to tell all believers in the world or to get any action from them), "but if he neglect to hear the church, let him be unto thee as a heathen man and a publican. Verily I say unto you: Whatsoever ye shall bind on earth shall be bound in heaven, and whatsoever ye shall loose on earth shall be loosed in heaven" (Matt. 18:17-18; I Cor. 5:13). Also the divine arrangement that a congregation shall have its own pastor or pastors (Acts 20:17, 28; Titus 1:5) goes to prove that the local church is a divine institution.

2. Its Character

The local congregation is a body of people differing from all human organizations by its unique spiritual character divinely granted to it. Speaking to the local congregation at Corinth, Paul accosts its members as the church of God, as them that are sanctified in Christ Jesus, called to be saints. The same Apostle, addressing the local congregation at Ephesus, calls them saints and the faithful in Christ Jesus (Eph. 1:1), and he assures them that God has chosen them in Christ before the foundation of the world, that they should be holy and without blame before Him in love, having predestinated them unto the adoption of children by Jesus Christ (Eph. 1:3-5. Compare also Eph. 2:19-22). Peter tells the congregations of Asia Minor: "Ye are a chosen generation, a royal priesthood, an holy nation, a peculiar people, that ye should shew forth the praises of Him who hath called you out of darkness into His marvelous light" (I Pet. 2:9). The local congregation stands supreme, unequaled in splendor, power, and influence among the organizations of the world and surpasses in importance all other institutions.

III. ITS RIGHTS AND POWERS

Dr. Walther in Thesis 4 of *Proper Form, etc.*, points out these rights when he says: "All the rights which an Evangelical Lutheran local congregation possesses are included in the keys of the kingdom of heaven, which the Lord has originally and immediately given to His entire Church, and in such manner that they belong to each congregation, the smallest as well as the largest, in like measure. Matt. 18:18-20 (Tell it unto the church. . . . Whatsoever ye shall loose on earth shall be loosed in heaven); Matt. 16:19; John 20:22, 23."

In explaining this thesis Dr. Walther points out several important truths.

1. The Office of the Keys indeed embraces all the rights of Christian congregations, since it is the power to preach the Gospel, to administer the Sacraments, and especially the power to remit and to retain sins. Since the local congregation is the working unit of the Church, Christ has delegated the authority to represent Him and to act for Him to the local congregation. This is seen very clearly from Matt. 18:17, where the final disposition of a case of church discipline is put into the hands of the local congregation. Melanchthon writes: "Scripture clearly identifies the ecclesiastical power and the keys" (*Corpus Reformatorum* XII, 494, quoted from *Walther and the Church*, p. 90).

2. These rights have been bestowed by Christ upon the entire Church, not mediately through ordained ministers, as the Romanists teach, but originally and directly, so that each believer as a member or the congregation should claim and use them (Matt. 18:19-20; I Cor. 3:22). The Romanists claim that the Pope is the supreme head and ruler of the Church on earth. Other denominations believe that the bishop, or the board of elders or ministers, or the synod, is the highest authority. The Bible teaches that the local congregation possesses the highest spiritual authority and church power on earth. Our Confessions therefore declare: "These keys belong not to the person of one particular man, but to the Church. Christ grants the keys principally and immediately to the Church and not merely to certain persons (Matt. 18:20). 'Where two or three are gathered together in My name, etc.'" (Smalcald Articles: "Of the Power, etc.," pars. 24, 29. *Triglot*, pp. 511 and 523.)

The Lutheran Congregation

3. It is not necessary for any Christian congregation to be joined with others into some larger executive or judiciary church body in order that it may exercise its divinely bestowed rights, but it may and should exercise these just because it is a local congregation. The congregation does not get its power from the ministry, but the ministry from the congregation. Nor does the local church derive its authority and right from the church at large. It is not dependent on any superchurch, any larger church body, any other congregation.

4. The fact that there may be hypocrites among the members of a Christian congregation does not limit or destroy the rights belonging to it, nor nullify the actions performed by it. For whatever a Christian congregation resolves and does in obedience to God's Word, is recognized and is fully valid even in heaven, because to the Christian congregation Christ has given all the rights of the Office of the Keys. (Matt. 16:15-19; 18:15-18.)

That the Christian congregation truly possesses the Office of the Keys and with it the entire spiritual power and authority to ordain and execute all things required for its government, Dr. Walther proves from the fact that Scripture calls all true church members "priests and kings before God," or "the royal priesthood" (I Pet. 2: 5, 9; Rev. 1:6). He quotes Luther, who says: "The Holy Ghost was careful not to use the term 'priest' for the Apostles or any other offices. It is the name reserved for the baptized, the Christians. For none of us is born in Holy Baptism an Apostle, preacher, teacher, pastor, but we are all born priests. Out of the number of these born priests some are then chosen and elected to the offices, which they administer in the name of all of us." (St. Louis, XIX:1260.)

Such then, is the proper sphere and dignity which the local Lutheran congregation possesses by the direct promise of God's Word. If God thus highly exalts the true members of the congregation, then their rights as Christian church members must not be curtailed or even removed by tyrannical church lords or overbearing church councils. Thus Dr. Walther, and our Synod throughout the past century, exalts the Christian congregation and upholds the Scriptural and Lutheran principle of true church democracy.

IV. ITS DUTIES AND PRIVILEGES

The possession of extraordinary treasures brings with it solemn responsibilities. Jesus says: "For unto whomsoever much is given, of him shall be much required" (Luke 12:48). The truly Lutheran congregation has a mission in the world. Its business is twofold: it must keep pure the doctrine committed to its care, and it must give this doctrine to the world.

1. Preach the Word

Speaking of the duties of a local Lutheran congregation, Dr. Walther mentions as the first and foremost that of *preaching God's Word*, so that it "may richly dwell and have full and free scope in its midst" (Col. 3:16). Basically God wants one thing to be done. The Gospel is to be preached in the world, and thereby the Kingdom of God is to be built. Souls are to be saved for time and for eternity. (I Tim. 2:4.) The redemptive work of the Savior is to be brought unto the children of men. Jesus commands (Matt. 28:18-20): "All power is given unto Me in heaven and in earth. Go ye, therefore, and teach all nations, baptizing them in the name of the Father and of the Son and of the Holy Ghost, teaching them to observe all things whatsoever I have commanded you, and, lo, I am with you alway, even unto the end of the world." Acts 1:8: "Ye shall be witnesses unto Me, etc." Especially in our day we must guard against giving undue prominence to social work, charitable endeavors, organizations, etc. Our great task is, and must ever remain, the *preaching* of the whole pure Word of God, the divine source and foundation of faith. Luther says: "God's Word cannot be without God's people. On the other hand, God's people cannot be without God's Word" (St. Louis, XVI:2276). Dr. F. Pfotenhauer, in his Foreword to the book *Walther and the Church*, pp. X and XI, aptly remarks: "The treasure of the pure Gospel, committed to the Lutheran Church, was esteemed by our fathers above all else in the world, and it was their ardent wish and prayer to transmit this treasure intact to their posterity. How appropriate therefore that in our centennial year we should give ear to the voice of Walther as he unfolds the glories of our Church! Grateful appreciation of our treasures will safeguard us against the temptation to surrender aught of our inheritance; it will cause us to shun the unionistic movements, so popular in our day, which seek to build the Church through external fellowship amid internal discord; it will serve to increase our eagerness to apprehend and our zeal in the pursuit of our great task, that of carrying the pure Gospel to the nations."

2. Administer the Sacraments

The obligation of preaching the Word embraces also that of *administering the Sacraments* according to Christ's institution (Matt. 28:20; I Cor. 11:24 f.). In order that the Sacraments may be administered, the Lord has established the Church. "The true adornment of the churches is godly, useful, and clear doctrine, the devout use of the Sacraments, ardent prayer, and the like" (Apology, XXIV, 51. *Triglot*, p. 401).

3. Care of Purity of Doctrine and Life

Moreover, "it is the duty of the congregation to care for the purity of doctrine and life in its midst and to exercise church discipline in these matters. Matt. 18:15-18; Rom. 16:17; I Cor. 5: 1-13; 6:1-8; II Cor. 2:6-11; Gal. 6:1; I Thess. 5:14; II Thess. 3: 6, 14, 15; II John 10—11" (Walther, Thesis 7, *Proper Form, etc.*). Smalcald Articles: "Of the Power," etc., *Triglot*, p. 519: "When the true judgment of the Church is removed, godless dogmas and godless services cannot be removed, and for many ages they destroy innumerable souls." That by the Church all Christians are meant, is made clear in the following paragraph (56): "And as the rest of the Christians must censure all other errors of the Pope, so they must also rebuke the Pope when he evades and impedes the true investigation and true decision of the Church" (*Triglot*, p. 521). Luther: "The right to judge and pronounce on matters of doctrine belongs to each and every Christian, so much so that he is doing an accursed thing who impairs this right by a hair's breadth. Christ gives them this right. Moreover, He commands them to judge the doctrine." (St. Louis, XIX:341.) Dr. Walther once remarked: "Rob the congregation of the right to judge doctrine, and you give them over into slavery." "I bow to the humblest member coming with Scripture." (Quoted in *Walther and the Church*, p. 45.)

4. Practice Christian Charity

Furthermore, "it is the duty of the congregation to concern itself also with the temporal *welfare of all its members*, that they may not suffer want of the necessities of life nor be forsaken in any need. Gal. 6:10: 'Let us do good unto all men, especially unto them who are of the household of faith.' Deut. 15:4; Rom. 12:13: 'Distributing to the necessity of saints.' Gal. 2:9-10; James 1:27; I Thess. 4:11-12." (Walther, Thesis 8, *Proper Form, etc.*) Dr. Walther quotes from Luther: "After the preaching of the Gospel the office and charge of a true and faithful pastor is to be mindful of the poor so that they suffer no need" (on Gal. 2:10, quoted in *Walther and the Church*, p. 93.) Compare also Luther, St. Louis, XI:2065).

5. Do all Things Decently and in Order

"It is the duty of the congregation to see that in its midst 'all things be done *decently and in order*,' I Cor. 14:33, 40, and to 'provide for honest things, not only in the sight of the Lord, but also in the sight of men,' II Cor. 8:21; Col. 2:5" (Walther, Thesis 9, *Proper Form, etc.*). Since the congregation represents Christ and His true religion in this world, this duty is obvious, lest offense be given within and without. The Augsburg Confession (Article XXVIII, par. 53, *Triglot*, p. 91): "It is lawful for bishops, or pastors, to make ordinances that things be done orderly in the Church." The pastors are acting, of course, only "as servants and stewards, not as masters, of the Church" (Luther, St. Louis, XVI:1014). The power to make such ordinances "as may be most useful and edifying" lies with "the congregation of God of every place" (Formula of Concord, Epitome, X, par. 4, *Triglot*, p. 829. Compare *Concordia Theological Monthly*, 1941, p. 737).

6. Keep the Unity of the Spirit

Because God is a God of peace, the Christian congregation must *"endeavor to keep the unity of the Spirit in the bond of peace"* also with all parts of the orthodox Church (Eph. 4:3; I Thess. 4:9-10). The tie which binds them to all the other Christians is the unity of the Spirit, the unity which the Holy Spirit created by giving them the grace of faith. He bids them to *keep* this unity of the Spirit. He who teaches a different doctrine violates the unity of faith. When a congregation is given to a different doctrine or tolerates a doctrine other than that taught by the Word of God, it is to be admonished by the Church like all other people in the church. This implies, then, that the individual groups have contact with one another, guard and watch over one another. Further expression is to be given to this unity of the Spirit by working together at the common task. So much needs to be done by the Christian people in the extension of the Kingdom of God that no one Christian congregation can possibly do justice to the work. So it is only natural for the individual congregations to form some sort of a brotherhood through which they give expression to the unity of faith and through which they would co-operate in the common task.

7. Promote the Welfare of the Church at Large

Dr. Walther, in the last thesis (11), under this heading points out the duties of the congregation toward its brethren outside of its own limits and toward the world at large, pointing out that the upbuilding of the Church and the establishing of missions must be a matter of deep concern to it. He writes: "It is incumbent upon the congregation to do its part in *building up and promoting the welfare of the Church at large.* Amos 6:6; Acts 11:21-23; 15:1 f." In substantiation of this thesis he quotes Luther, who, writing on Mark 16:16, says: "It will not do for each one hearing the Gospel to go his own way, to believe for himself and not to confess his faith before others. . . . For that purpose Christ brings us together and holds us together through this divine sign of Baptism. Otherwise, if we remained apart and separate without such an external bond and sign, Christendom could not be extended and preserved. Therefore Christ binds us together in this divine community in order that the Gospel be spread farther and farther and others be brought into the fold through our confession." (St. Louis, XI:982 f.)

"The whole Christian Church constitutes the body of Christ, the individual Christians and congregations being members of this body. To each Christian and to every congregation God has given certain gifts, and these gifts are to be used not only for the welfare and edification of the individual member or congregation. As in the human body all the members put their own peculiar gifts into the service of the whole body, so every Christian and every congregation must, according to the will of God, co-operate with those of like faith in the great work of bringing the Gospel in its truth and purity to all mankind. In this business, commanded to the Church by its Lord Supreme, all congregations are to unite and work together in harmony and peace. That is a matter not of their own choice; that is their God-appointed obligation" (*Concordia Theological Monthly*, 1941, p. 736).

Thus a congregation will find it difficult to give a good reason for not being a member of Synod. The duties that we have now discussed are things that God wants to have done. Until a better method of doing them can be found, every congregation had better become a member of Synod and not insist on standing aloof and remaining separate from those with whom it professes a common faith.

"Briefly expressed, the congregation must glorify God by keeping and preaching His Word and exercising Christian love both temporally and spiritually, so that, as far as it is concerned, all men may be abundantly blessed by God through the means of grace with all spiritual and heavenly benedictions" (*Concordia Theological Monthly*, 1939, p. 335).

V. ITS PERFORMANCE OF ITS PREROGATIVES AND OBLIGATIONS

In order to function as a group, two things are essential: the group must know what is to be done, and, secondly, it must know how to do the things that must be done.

The essayist of the Central District Convention of 1898 remarks: "The performance of the duties of a local congregation is frequently neglected because we are not conscious of its rights. . . . No pastor can lead his congregation to the proper knowledge and performance of its duties if he does not know its rights and privileges and seek to make his congregation conscious of them. The more fully conscious a congregation is of its rights, honors, and glories, the more diligently and cheerfully it will seek to perform its duties." (Central District, 1898, p. 10.)

1. Indoctrination In God's Word

In order that God's Word may abundantly dwell and have free course among men, Christian congregations must establish and maintain the office of the public ministry (Titus 1:5; Eph. 4:11, 14). The Christian pastor is the divinely appointed teacher of the congregation which by divine command has called him. He is the steward of the mysteries of God, of the divinely revealed Word and of the divinely instituted Sacraments (I Cor. 4:1).

In teaching his congregation the pastor will make use of every available means for such indoctrination. There is above all the divine institution of public worship. In the public church services, as the church has arranged them in Christian liberty, everything is arranged to help us think of God, and to make us realize that we are in His presence. The liturgy adds to the beauty and the devotional spirit of the services (Ps. 96:1-9). The Lutheran Church is a singing Church; her members love to sing the great hymns of the Church (Ps. 33:1-3). The services direct particular attention to the church year and its changing festival seasons. The church building, its furnishings, its music, and its art help to make the worship inspiring and uplifting. Its symbols remind us of the great truths and facts of our religion (Phil. 4:8). Whenever a child or an adult is baptized in public service, all the members assembled are reminded of their own Baptism, its blessings and its obligations. In Holy Communion the faith of the communicants, as well as their love to God and their fellow men, is strengthened and increased. But the most important part of the service is the sermon. "There is no better way whereby people may be held to the Church than by good preaching" (Apology, Art., XXIV, par. 24. *Triglot*, p. 401). Good preaching requires that the whole counsel of God unto salvation be clearly set forth to the congregation. What a sad mistake we should make if we made our churches and schools lecture halls in which to hand out dubious opinions on debated and debatable projects of our day! What a tragedy if we entrusted with the eternal saving Gospel of Jesus Christ, should forego the proclamation of this Gospel, which saves the soul for this life and for that which is to come, and change our congregations into clubs for social experimentation! Let the pastor never forget the charge of His Lord to teach the members of his congregation to observe all things whatsoever Christ has commanded (Matt. 28:20).

In order that the Word of God may dwell richly in a congregation, it is furthermore incumbent upon the congregation to insist upon the proper Christian education of the young by means of home instruction, Christian day school, Sunday school, catechumen instruction, Saturday schools, vacation Bible schools, etc., in order that souls may not be lost through the fault of those who are responsible to God for them.

Ours is indeed a doctrinal Church. That means that we not only insist on acceptance of certain doctrines, but that we teach doctrine. Looking back over the past century, and seeking to visualize the work done by our Lutheran congregations, doctrinal instruction in church, home, and school stands out very prominently. It is here where the emphasis has to lie in the future also if we and our congregations are to measure up to the sacred obligations resting upon us. "The sermons of our pastors must continue to be doctrinal sermons in the best sense of the word, spreading out before the congregation members as a rich repast the divine truths given us in the Word. The children of the Church have to be carefully indoctrinated. That marvelous instrument of religious instruction which has played such an important role in our past history, the Christian day school, must be lovingly fostered, the teachers encouraged and assisted, and the whole institution placed on as high a plane as possible. The instruction classes of catechumens must in the future as well as in the past be taken very seriously, so that those who are being taught will receive more than a mere coat of varnish consisting in the name Lutheran. In the Sunday schools, with careful planning and supervision, indoctrination must ever be the chief goal. What a sad situation does not obtain in a congregation if the sermons are nothing but a series of paragraphs exhorting and admonishing the hearers to support this or that movement; if in the Sunday school the pupils do not advance far beyond the First Commandment and 'Now I Lay Me Down to Sleep,' and if in the catechetical classes instruction is mainly centered on hints of what to wear on the day of confirmation and with what decorum to approach the Lord's Table. . . . What I have been presenting just now is a caricature; but I hope that it will remind all of us of our sacred duty with respect to thorough indoctrination of the souls entrusted to us. . . . Let us here at this convention encourage one another lest we become lukewarm, indolent, slothful in carrying on that work of careful, painstaking indoctrination with respect to the members of our congregations, the adults and the children, in which our fathers excelled." (*Concordia Theological Monthly*, 1935, p. 815 f.)

2. Maintaining Purity of Doctrine and Life

We have seen that the entire life of Lutheran Christian church members should be sanctified and blessed by the Word of God and prayer. All members of the congregation should seek to grow in the blessed knowledge of God's Word (II Pet. 3:18; I Cor. 1:5), so "that they may not remain children tossed to and fro and carried about with every wind of doctrine (Eph. 4:14; Heb. 5:12), but try and judge by the Word of God the doctrine preached to them. Acts 17:11; Matt. 7:15 f.; I John 4:1; I Cor. 10:15." (Walther, Thesis 26, *Proper Form, etc.*). To this end, "The congregation must see that none but pure church- and schoolbooks, recognized by the orthodox Church, be introduced and tolerated in its midst (I Thess. 5:21; II Tim. 1:13) and that the confessional ceremonies be retained (Gal. 2:4, 5)." (Walther, Thesis 28, *Proper Form, etc.*) Church members who refuse obedience to God's Word either in profession or life should be properly dealt with and disciplined according to God's Word, to the end that they may see the error of their way and repent. (Compare "Church Discipline," p. 542 ff.)

3. Care of the Needy

"In the first place, it is the duty of the congregation to provide according to its ability for the maintenance of the pastor that he may have food, clothing, and a dwelling for himself and his family (the dwelling to contain a room for study and for meeting his people in undisturbed privacy), Matt. 10:9-10; that he may have the means of practicing hospitality, I Tim. 3:2; Titus 1:8; that he may be able to live of the Gospel exclusively, I Cor. 9:14; that he be not compelled to neglect his studies, to forego social and fraternal intercourse, or to entangle himself with the affairs of this life, I Tim. 4:13; II Tim. 2:3-4; (Eccles. 38:26, 27). This applies also in due measure to the teachers of the young." (Walther,

Thesis 33, *Proper Form, etc.*) Deliberate refusal to obey God's Word in this respect will call down upon such members and congregations God's wrath and punishment (Gal. 6:6-7).

Secondly, the congregation must also provide for the needy in its midst, such as the widows, the orphans, the sick, the aged, and the infirm — all those who are unable to support themselves and cannot be cared for properly by their own relatives and friends (II Thess. 3:11-12; I Tim. 5:16; cp. I John 3:17; Matt. 25:35-36, 40, 45; James 1:27). In case of special calamities such as pestilence, fire, drought, floods, etc., the congregation "should relieve the need and distress, so that no brother or sister may be tempted to appeal to the mercy of them that are without, to the dishonor of the Gospel, or even to join secret societies for the sake of the aid promised, II Cor. 8:13-14; Rom. 12:15; I Cor. 12:26; I Thess. 4:11-12"; (Walther, Thesis 34, *Proper Form, etc.*).

Finally, the Bible shows that the congregation must see to it that the sick receive the necessary help and are made comfortable (Matt. 25:36; I Tim. 5:10); and that it should make provision for the decent, honorable, and Christian burial of each, even the poorest, of its deceased members (Matt. 14:12; Acts 8:2; Jer. 22: 18 f.; Tob. 1:20).

4. Proper Management of All Church Matters

A. *The Voters' Meeting*

If the congregation is to function and fully exercise its divinely imposed rights and duties in a conscientious, profitable, and God-pleasing manner, it must, in the first place, hold public church assemblies in which it considers and determines all things that are necessary for its special church management. Such public executive church assemblies Christ presupposes when He commands Matt. 18:17-18: "Tell it unto the church." Such executive assemblies were generally maintained in the first Christian congregations, as the Book of Acts records, 1:15, 23-25 (election of Matthias); Acts 15:5, 23 (matter of circumcision).

We call these assemblies *voters' meetings,* for we admit to them as authorized to vote only the adult male members of the church. Since the final authority in all matters is vested in the congregation and not in a few members of the congregation, it would seem evident that *all* of the members of the congregation are responsible for what the congregation does. But God Himself has made certain restrictions. The *children* of the congregation are truly members of the congregation. Yet on account of their youth they are of necessity excluded from some of the privileges of membership. So, for example, they are excluded from the Sacrament of the Altar, not because they are not Christians, nor because they are not in every sense of the word members of the congregation, but because they cannot examine themselves. Just so the children of the congregation are of necessity excluded from taking part in the business of the congregation. They lack certain qualifications. The Fourth Commandment indicates that they are to be in subjection and not sit in places of authority. Just when the young can be classified among the elders is nowhere indicated in the Scriptures. That is a matter which is left entirely to the discretion of the elders in the congregation. Since the age of 21 is commonly fixed as the border-line in our country, most congregations have accepted that borderline. (I Cor. 10:15; I Pet. 5:5.)

The *women* of the congregation are in every respect members of the congregation. They share in all the duties and all the privileges and all the responsibilities of every member of the congregation. Yet they also are excluded from taking part in the ruling of the congregation. They are excluded not because of an inferiority so far as knowledge and understanding is concerned, but because of the position which God has fixed for them. St. Paul says: "Let the women learn in silence with all subjection. But I suffer not a woman to teach, nor to usurp authority over the man, but to be in silence. For Adam was first formed, then Eve. And Adam was not deceived, but the woman, being deceived, was in the transgression." (I Tim. 2:11-15; cp. I Cor. 14:34-35.) Paul's argument is not based on social conditions, nor on the custom of his time, but rather on natural spheres assigned to the sexes by the Creator. So his argument holds good for all times. Our voting-membership arrangement, by which the right to suffrage is limited to a group of men, is a representative form of church management. Acting for the congregation, the voters must take into consideration the entire congregation. When it comes to the building of a new church, inaugurating new church customs, fixing the hours of worship, the calling of a pastor, etc., the voters would act very unwisely if they did not give all the members of the congregation an opportunity to express themselves.

In order that all things may be done decently and in order, each congregation should have an approved *constitution,* in which all rules and regulations are laid down in clear and unmistakable language. Whenever the congregation becomes a corporate body, recognized as an entity by the State, articles of incorporation will be prepared under the guidance of an attorney who knows the laws of the particular State governing such religious corporations. In the constitution proper the congregation will set forth its aims, the condition of membership, the regulations governing the pastoral office, etc. The by-laws will set forth in detail the working rules and regulations by which the congregation is governed in the joint effort. A model constitution has been prepared by our Synodical Committee on Constitutional Matters and may be had from our Publishing House. Dr. Schwan is credited with giving this advice: "An ideal congregation should need but two brief paragraphs in the regulations governing its existence and its activities: (1) All matters decided by God in His Word shall be held and done as the Bible directs. (2) All other affairs shall be regulated in peaceable agreement under the law of Christian charity." Dr. Walther advises: "If the congregation adopts a written constitution, the latter should contain only what is most necessary and has already stood the test of congregational life, and no provision therein embodied concerning things neither enjoined nor prohibited in the Word of God should be unalterable, but all such provisions should be subject to alteration or repeal at any time, in due order, and by a considerable majority (Thesis 50). Luther says: "Go slow, and after this wise: 'Kurz und gut, wenig und wohl, sachte und immer an!' Let these regulations first take root; you can always add what is found to be necessary." (St. Louis, XXI a:915.)

The executive church assemblies are to be *conducted* according to God's Word and the principle of brotherly love under the leadership of those whom the congregation has chosen for this purpose. "In order that all things be done decently and in order, with due regard for the rights of all, every voters' meeting must be duly announced in advance and be held at a suitable time. Those who fail to appear thereby waive their right to vote. For the sake of love and peace and needful prudence it is advisable that important resolutions concerning matters which admit of postponement should be considered valid only when they have been confirmed in a subsequent meeting." (Walther, *Proper Form, etc.,* Thesis 17.) We have found it expedient to announce all our regular and special voters' meetings by mail. A penny government card is sent by the secretary to every member.

"The time of opening for all the meetings should be definitely fixed and strictly observed" (Thesis 43). "In the meetings no important matter should be put to vote at once, without previous discussion, explanation, and deliberation" (Thesis 44). "While the meetings are in progress, the chairman of the assembly must enforce the rule that but one speaker may speak at a time (I Cor. 14:27-31), and only after the previous speaker has finished, so that every one has an opportunity to express his opinion and the discussion does not turn into a brawl, I Cor. 14:23, 33 (Thesis 46). The elections should be so conducted that all members know who the candidates are and be free to vote for whomever they will; "absent voters being permitted to vote by ballot only" (Thesis 47). "All citations to appear in the meeting of the congregation should be in writing and be delivered by a responsible person" (Thesis 48). "An exact record of the important transactions should be made by the secretary, read to the meeting at the close for necessary corrections or at the beginning of the subsequent meeting" (Thesis 18). "All papers and documents which concern the congregation or have been directed to it or go out from it should, together with the minutes, be preserved, in the originals, if possible, by the stated secretary" (Thesis 38). "The pastor should keep and have in his custody two books, a register containing the names of all the members of the congregation, voting and non-voting members, and the church record, in which he should enter the ministerial acts, Baptisms, confirmations, marriages, burials, and Communions, stating names, dates, places, and other important circumstances. Both books should be furnished by, and remain the property of, the congregation." (Thesis 37.) "The congregation should, if it has the means, acquire realty suiting the needs of the congregation, such as a well-equipped church of sufficient size, a schoolhouse, parsonage, burial ground, etc., and choose men who shall not only represent the congregation as trustees in its dealing with the State in matters of property, but also have the supervision of such property and see that it may not be damaged but kept in good condition and that the necessary improvements be made" (Thesis 41). "It should also procure all the requisites for public service, such as a church Bible, hymnbook, agenda, baptismal and Communion vessels, official vestments, etc., and appoint a sexton, who is to have them in custody, keep the church clean and in proper order. ..." (Thesis 42.)

Subjects, or topics, for discussion, deliberation, and action in voters' meetings are: (1) Matters of doctrine and life (Acts 15); (2) The establishment and administration of all offices in the church (Acts 1:15-26; 6:1-6; II Cor. 8:19); (3) Questions of church discipline and polity (Matt. 18:17-20; I Cor. 5:1-5; II Cor. 2:6-11; I Tim. 5:20); (4) Removal of public offenses (Acts 21: 20-22); (5) The adjustment of quarrels and disputes among members (I Cor. 6:1-8); (6) Matters of good order and ceremonial (I Cor. 14:26-40; 16:1-2). It goes without saying that each meeting should begin and close with a suitable prayer by the pastor. Since God's Word is the basis, source, and norm of our whole Church's faith and life, there ought to be some doctrinal discussion at every meeting.

"In matters of doctrine and conscience there must be unanimity, all giving assent to the teaching of God's Word (Is. 8:20) and to the Confessions of the Church. Adiaphora (*Mitteldinge*), matters neither commanded nor prohibited by God's Word, are ordered according to the principles of love and equity; after the matter has been fully and orderly discussed, it is decided by majority vote (I Cor. 16:14; 14:40)." (Thesis 16.) By signing the congregation's constitution everyone pledges himself to accept and follow the decisions of the majority in all matters not settled by Scriptures (Eph. 5:21: "Subjecting yourselves one to another in the fear of God"). The congregation has the right to ask all its members to observe its rules and the decisions of the majority, not indeed for conscience' sake, but for the sake of love and peace and united service (I Thess. 5:21). All Christians should be willing "to follow after the things which make for peace and things wherewith one may edify another" (Rom. 14:19).

B. Church Officers

To carry out the decisions of the congregation and to see that everything is done properly and to the best advantage, the congregation elects capable men who serve as the *officers* of the congregation. The various church offices stem from the one office instituted by God, the ministry. All such special officers are to assist the pastor in the work of the church. So it is quite proper that in the installation service for such auxiliary officers it is said: "You are to be associated with me, the appointed minister of the Word, in the work of upbuilding the kingdom of God among us." So we have in the church other officers besides the pastor. Special men are selected who have been especially trained to teach the children in church schools. There will be other things that need to be done. As in the church at Jerusalem seven men were chosen to look after the poor, so today there will be many things to be taken care of. Our congregations do well to select special men who, again under the supervision of the pastor, will look after these things. In some of our congregations these officers form a *church council* (vestry), which meets frequently to discuss important details of church work, to take care of certain matters assigned to them, or to study important problems and make recommendations to the congregation.

The main officers of a congregation are usually a Board of *Elders*, who assist the pastor with the spiritual work of the congregation, visit the sick, the lax members, the unchurched, admonish those who are not living as Christians, etc. The *trustees* are in charge of the church property, buildings, repairs, maintenance, fuel, etc. The *treasurer* takes care of all money collected and disposes of it as he has been instructed by the congregation. He may be assisted by a *finance committee*, a *financial secretary*, or others who help secure the needed money. (Cp. Walther, *Proper Form, etc.,* Theses 39—40.) The *secretary* keeps record of all transactions and resolutions of the meetings. The *chairman*, or president, presides at the meetings and performs other duties assigned to him. According to its needs the congregation elects various committees, such as finance, education, building, almoners, ushers, delegates to Synod, and engages sextons (janitors) and organists.

C. Church Societies

With the approval of the congregation, groups of church members may unite and organize *societies*. In many churches we find choirs, young people's societies, ladies' aids, men's clubs, altar guilds, missionary societies, which aim to help the church in some special way. These exist only for the purpose of serving the common welfare of the congregation and the Church. The congregation, let it be noted, is *the* society. Under ideal conditions no other society ought to be necessary. Societies within the congregation are of themselves not an indication of great strength, but may be evidence of great weakness. There is nothing which forbids societies in the congregation. There is some real danger, however, that a congregation may have so many societies that the strength of the congregation will be dissipated. In any case, congregations must be careful that societies do not develop into a hindrance when the pastor must spend so much time in arranging for, and managing and supervising, the many societies, that there is little or no time left for him to do his real work — preaching, teaching, and all that this implies. Societies in the congregation ought to give the individual groups for whom they are organized an opportunity to work in the interest of saving souls. They ought to be a department of congregational activities and should serve the best interest of the congregation. Societies become a nuisance when they degenerate into mere money-raising agencies or into social clubs.

This entire matter is something which needs a great deal more attention and study than is usually given to it. Aptly Dr. F. Pfotenhauer, in his Foreword to the book *Walther and the Church*, pp. IX—X, remarks: "The modern multiplication of church societies is attended by the danger that the activities belonging to the congregation are made the business of societies and that congregation members gradually show more interest in, and zeal for, the work of the society than for that of the congregation, with the result that the congregation steadily loses in importance and prestige. In this book Walther makes mention of not a single congregational society, showing his conviction that societies are not essential to a congregation established in proper form. It is true, Walther was

The Lutheran Congregation

not opposed to societies within the Church. He himself founded and fostered such in his own congregation, for example, a young people's society and a ladies' aid. But he saw to it that these societies remained under the control of the congregation and that they did not encroach upon the congregation's business. Walther teaches us that the Christian congregation is the society founded by God within and through which Christians are to function conjointly as kings and priests of God in performing the work of the Church. From early youth our Christians must be trained to become congregation-minded, so that membership in the congregation means more to them than membership in a church society."

5. Maintaining the Unity of the Spirit (Relation to Sister Congregations)

A Lutheran congregation should seek not merely its own interests, but should keep in mind its sister churches, joined to it by the unity of faith. This implies: (1) that the congregation pray for all saints (Eph. 6:8); (2) since they have the same public confessions of faith, they should give all diligence to be one with the entire Evangelical Lutheran Church in point of life and to "speak the same thing, in the same mind, and in the same judgment" (I Cor. 1:10); (3) that neighboring congregations come to a clear understanding with regard to members and other matters, so that disputes may not arise and injure the extension of God's kingdom (Titus 1:5; Gal. 2:9; I Pet. 4:15; 5:2; Heb. 10:25); (4) that members seeking release are given transfers and that without such transfers no persons be received as members by sister congregations (Acts 18:27; III John 8—10); (5) that no congregation receive into membership such as have been rightfully excommunicated (I Tim. 1:20; II Tim. 4:14-15); (6) that the congregation should receive as brethren such as have been exiled or have been wrongfully excommunicated or come as guests from other congregations and care for them as for their own members (I Pet. 4:9; Rom. 16:1-2; I Cor. 16:10-11; John 16:2; Matt. 25:35); (7) when calling a pastor of a sister congregation, or when a call is extended to its own pastor by a sister congregation, they should endeavor to bring about a mutual agreement as to its being a divine call;

(8) that they assist one another with mutual advice, assistance, and financial support as the case may require (Acts 15:1 f.; I Cor. 16: 1, 2; II Cor. 8:1-14; 9:1-15); (9) that congregations permit their pastor, if at all possible, to serve as an affiliated charge a neighboring congregation which cannot by itself establish the ministry in its midst or be merged with the main congregation. (Walther, *Proper Form, etc.*, Theses 52—61.)

6. Serving the Church at Large (Synod)

In order that the Church may be established throughout the world, it is the privilege and the duty of the congregation to work jointly with others in carrying out those measures by which Christ's kingdom may be brought to men. It is the duty of the congregation: (1) to provide for the education of gifted young men (and girls) for the service of the Church as pastors and teachers; (2) to make provision that the Bread of Life be broken to such of its brethren in the faith as suffer spiritual want; (3) to engage in the work of Bible distribution (I Thess. 1:8; 3:27); (4) to engage in mission work at home and abroad; **(5) that** it should be ready to unite with other orthodox churches in establishing a large church body by which the work of the Lord may be accomplished all the more effectively (Eph. 4:3-6; I Cor. 12:7).

It is difficult to see how these and the many other common objectives can be carried out unless the congregations form some sort of a brotherhood through which they give expression to the unity of faith and through which they would co-operate in the common task. While it is true that in the Apostolic churches we do not find an organization like our Synod, yet it is also true that we find evidences of the congregations' giving expression to their common faith (Acts 15; II Cor. 8:9). Our Synod is merely an organization of a number of congregations that have banded together to carry on the Lord's work more efficiently. Synod is not an organization which lords it over the congregation, but Synod is the handmaiden of the congregations through which the congregations jointly do that which no individual congregation could do singlehanded, things that are essential for the growth of the Church. Our congregations should not only become members of Synod, but

The Lutheran Congregation

they must keep themselves informed on the work which it is doing through Synod. In the meetings of the congregations regular reports on the work being done through Synod must be received and discussed. Reports on the conventions of Synod must be presented. The official periodicals ought to be read diligently. While Synod as such is not a divine but a human institution and therefore a congregation and its pastor are not *for conscience' sake* bound to affiliate with it, yet "it is not God's intention that a Christian congregation should be an isolated unit, unconcerned about other Christians and other Christian congregations in this world and the great work of the Lord which God has commissioned His Christians everywhere to do." Lutheran congregations "should not only foster the brotherly relation that exists among Christians, but, persuaded by their love to Christ and to the souls for which He died, should cheerfully join their forces against the hosts of evil and for the promotion of Christ's kingdom in this world." (Fritz, *Pastoral Theology*, p. 321.)

VI. ITS MEMBERS

We have considered the work and the functions of a Lutheran congregation. These fix the duty of every believer to become a member of a Christian congregation. Every believer has the duty to carry out the Savior's command as outlined above. It is impossible for any one believer to carry out these commands without joining himself to a group, a congregation. Any believer who refuses to join a congregation and take an active part in the work of the congregation makes it impossible on his part for the congregation to function. Such a person is blocking the way. If all believers would do what such an individual insists on doing, the congregation and the church at large could not possibly do the work which the Lord would have it do. Would God have instituted a church, and commanded church organizations, if it were not His earnest desire that all who profess to be His children should join such an organization? Dr. Walther in his instructive monograph: "Von der Pflicht der Christen, sich an eine rechtglaeubige Ortsgemeinde gliedlich anzuschliessen" (Thesis 5, p. 50), writes: "Whoever does not affiliate with a local congregation of his faith, although he has the opportunity, or who severs his connection, although he still remains within its parish, or who simply refuses to become a full-fledged member, although by his Baptism or by the membership of his parents when he was still a minor he already became a member, such a person deals in a manner unbecoming to a Christian, walks disorderly, and should, if he despises and rejects all admonition, no longer be regarded and treated as a Christian brother (I John 2:19; II Thess. 3:16)."

How, then, do we become members of a Lutheran congregation? Dr. Walther, in the monograph just mentioned, says that there are three ways: (1) By receiving Baptism in a congregation we become its member (Acts 2:41-47: "were baptized . . . added to them"); (2) By one's parents, becoming members or being members, so long as one is a minor, and still under parental authority (Acts 2:39; cp. Gen. 17:7, 12-14; Mark 10:14; Eph. 6:1-3); (3) By requested reception into its membership (III John 9—10) or by a letter of transfer.

1. Qualifications for Church Membership

A Lutheran congregation which makes it its duty to care for purity of doctrine and life will certainly use circumspection in the matter of admitting others to church membership. "Such only are to be admitted to membership by the congregation as (1) are baptized in the name of the Triune God (Eph. 5:25 ff.; I Cor. 12:13); (2) if adults, make profession of their faith that the Holy Scriptures of the Old and the New Testament are the Word of God and that the doctrine contained in the Confessions of the Evangelical Lutheran Church, especially in Luther's Small Catechism and the Unaltered Augsburg Confession, is the pure Christian doctrine (Gal. 2:4; II Cor. 6:14-15, 17; II John 10—11; Eph. 4:3-6); and (3) lead an unoffensive Christian life (I Cor. 5:9-13)." (Walther, *Proper Form, etc.*, Thesis 29.) Church members who refuse obedience to God's Word either in profession or in life should be properly dealt with and disciplined according to God's Word, to the end that they may see the error of their way and repent (Matt. 18:15 f.; I Tim. 5:20). In case they refuse to heed God's Word, they must be excommunicated after due brotherly admonition, as the Bible declares (Matt. 18:17-20; I Cor. 5:13).

2. PRIVILEGES OF CHURCH MEMBERSHIP

In an address to the members of his congregation, Dr. Walther summarizes these privileges: "Church membership makes us stockholders in a firm that possesses and distributes vast treasures. A Christian congregation is a court that is supreme in its particular sphere of jurisdiction, and each one who joins it is a fellow judge. The Christian congregation is a prayer league, and the church member shares every one of its prayers. A Christian congregation is Christ's spouse here on earth, whose powers and privileges every member shares." (Prange, *Church Membership*, p. 10.)

"But, alas! also many members of a Lutheran congregation do not prize their membership properly; they regret that so great a sacrifice of time and money is required. Theirs is the privilege to attend worship and to partake of the Lord's Supper, but they rarely make use of it. Theirs is the privilege to take part in the meetings of the congregation, to join in the discussions and to cast their vote, but hardly ever do they make use of it. They look upon their membership as a burden rather than as an honor. Such people betray their spiritual blindness.

"There was a time when Roman citizenship was regarded as a great honor. Even so it is considered a great honor today when a city which enjoys rare privileges extends honorary citizenship to some famous person. Yet, dear brother, such citizenship cannot be compared with the privileges which membership in a Christian congregation carries with it.

"A citizen is assured human protection; a member of a congregation, heavenly privileges. A citizen enjoys earthly privileges; a member of a congregation, heavenly privileges. A citizen is part of a temporal kingdom; a member of a congregation, of an eternal kingdom. A citizen at best elects earthly rulers; a member of a congregation, stewards of the mysteries of God. The greatest benefit accruing to a citizen is that under a good government he may lead a quiet and peaceable life in all godliness and honesty; church membership, however, offers something greater — forgiveness of sins, peace of conscience, the comfort of the Holy Spirit, and finally eternal life. A citizen is the subject of a government composed of mortal men like himself; a member of a congregation is the subject of the Son of God, but at the same time a king, a priest, and a prophet. A citizen may gain honor before men; a member of a congregation is privileged to look forward to eternal glory, to a state of everlasting bliss in the presence of God." (Prange, *Church Membership*, p. 33 f.)

3. Duties and Obligations

A. *As Part of the Congregation*

Every individual Christian is a *part of his congregation.* The whole work and various duties of the entire body therefore are placed upon the shoulders of every individual member. As every citizen is expected to be and show himself loyal to his country, so every Christian should be *loyal* to his church. For their own spiritual welfare and to encourage others, loyal Lutheran church members will be regular and punctual in their *church attendance* (Jer. 31:6-7; Pss. 92:13; 122:1; Luke 2:37,46). They will "not forsake the assembling of ourselves together" (Heb. 10:25), but they will follow the example of the early Christians, "who continued *steadfastly* in the Apostles' doctrine and fellowship and in breaking of bread and in prayers." They will partake regularly of Holy Communion. They will establish a family altar in their home, so that "the Word of Christ may dwell in you richly in all wisdom" (Col. 3:16). They will rear their family in the nurture and admonition of the Lord, sending them to the schools provided by their congregation, and will do their utmost for the support of such schools. They will also pray regularly for their congregation, their pastor, teacher, fellow members, and for the whole Christian Church. They stand ready to defend the doctrine of their Church.

B. *As a Worker in the Congregation*

As we need the Church, so the Church also needs us. There is much work for every one of us to do in and through the congregation. "We are laborers together with God" (I Cor. 3:9) — not shirkers, loiterers. The ideal congregation is the one where every member is active and does all he can for the welfare of the church. A loyal, faithful, sincere Lutheran loves his congregation and strives to promote her welfare. A love which is genuine is willing to make sacrifices. A loyal Lutheran gladly gives and cheerfully supports his church as God hath prospered him. He cheerfully contributes his money for the work of the church both at home and abroad. He also supports his church with his service, giving time and energy willingly. He attends congregational meetings and takes a hearty interest in the reports and discussions. He supports with voice and vote the plans which he deems wise and prudent, but should some measure which he has advocated be defeated, he is sufficiently fair-minded to submit to the majority. He never sulks. When some task is assigned to him in keeping with his talents, he is always dependable and trustworthy (I Pet. 4:10).

C. *As an Example in Daily Life*

It is not enough to *join* a Lutheran congregation. To share its blessings, we must become *living* members through faith. A loyal Lutheran therefore lives in harmony with the teachings and doctrines of his Church. He lives as a Christian not only on Sunday, but every day of his life. He endeavors "to walk worthy of the vocation (call of faith) wherewith he is called" (Eph. 4:10). As a loyal Lutheran he strives to live to the glory of God (I Cor. 10:31), seeking in his daily life to give proof of his faith by living as it becomes a child of God. By the grace of God he strives to surrender his life completely to God's will. He does this so that he will not give offense to those that are without. He knows that if he fails to live as a Christian, he dishonors God and brings disgrace upon his church. A loyal Lutheran will not, by any act of his, place before the door of his church a bar which tends to keep souls out. On the contrary, he works for the winning of souls, witnessing for Jesus, his Savior.

"In short, a loyal Lutheran church member is one who consecrates himself body and soul to the service of God and the Church. What God reveals, that he believes. What God forbids, that he shuns. What God commands, that he does. The loyal Lutheran has his eye fixed upon an ideal, toward which he is constantly pressing with all that in him is. Not an imaginary ideal, but the ideal Man — the God-Man. He who fixes his eyes upon the God-Man, heeding and believing His words, following in His steps, is a loyal Lutheran." (Schramm, *A Loyal Lutheran.*)

The Office of the Public Ministry

The doctrine which we are about to review has claimed the special attention of our Synod for nearly a hundred years. What we hold and confess concerning the Office of the Public Ministry was a very live issue at the time when our Synod was born, and it has continued to be of great interest ever since. It was born out of a theological turmoil that threatened to scatter to the four winds the early efforts of our synodical forefathers to build a Church of the pure Word and Sacraments. It was fiercely attacked both here and in Europe as soon as it became known beyond our circles. In some quarters it was denounced as a subtle introduction of the old Roman Catholic heresy of hierarchical tyranny. Others laughed at this doctrine as a certain cause of every kind of disorder wherever it would be practiced. No wonder that the very first article in the first issue of *Lehre und Wehre*, January, 1855, by O. Fuerbringer, is a strong defense of the doctrine we hold. He opens his discussion with the observation that the question of the Church and the Office of the Public Ministry is indisputably a question of the day. It agitates not only the Lutheran Church, but also others.

For our Synod the long and sometimes bitter controversies over the doctrine concerning the Office of the Public Ministry were productive of much good. They were for us a refining fire. In the end the truth of our Confessions stood out firm and clear, and many an opponent was won over. In 1883 Dr. Stoeckhardt expressed the judgment that our Synod is indebted to the doctrine of the royal priesthood of all believers and its related doctrine concerning the Church and the Office of the Public Ministry for its growth and flourishing condition. (Iowa District, 1883, p. 11.)

The Office of the Public Ministry

Thesis I

The Office of the Public Ministry is a position of trust conferred by a Christian congregation for the purpose of preaching the Gospel of Jesus Christ publicly.

We approach our study of the doctrine of the Office of the Public Ministry with the question: What is this Office? Our first thesis answers that it is a position of trust. So Paul conceives of it in his Letter to Titus, to whom he writes that the preaching of the Christ is committed or entrusted to him (Titus 1:3). He is not the owner, but a trustee, an agent, a minister, a steward. Luther, borrowing an analogy from the city government of his time, likens the Office of the Public Ministry to that of a mayor. He uses such terms as *Geschaeftstraeger der Gemeinde* (business manager of the congregation) and *Vollstrecker der Gemeindegewalt* (executive of the congregation's power), who can do only as much as the congregation itself can do. (*Lehre und Wehre*, 1861, p. 144.) The dependence upon the will and instructions of another, inherent in every position of trust, is emphasized again and again by Luther as applicable to the nature of the Office of the Public Ministry. And with him the theologians of Synod have, without exception, found themselves in complete agreement. There is no deviation from the view that the rights and powers of the Office of the Public Ministry are and remain in the possession of the congregation that has acted. (*The Abiding Word*, Vol. I, p. 369 ff.) From among the many pertinent Biblical passages adduced by the fathers as a basis for the particular point to which we are restricting our attention at the moment, we shall select the following one: "Let a man so account of us as of the ministers of Christ and stewards of the mysteries of God. Moreover it is required in stewards that a man be found faithful" (I Cor. 4:1-2). The idea of being entrusted with something is basic also in the other terms used by the Scriptures to name the incumbents of the Office of the Public Ministry, such as "shepherd," "bishop" (overseer) and its German equivalent *Pfarrherr*, and "minister." Basing his definition on II Cor. 5:18, Dr. A. Graebner explains: "A minister is one who labors in the service of another, performing the task committed to him who would otherwise have to perform it himself. One who gives a ministry to another makes him his agent to do the work for his principal." It should be noted here that Paul includes among the persons concerned also such men as Apollos and Tychicus (I Cor. 3:5 and Col. 4:7), who were not Apostles. (*Theological Quarterly*, 1902, p. 19.)

Helpful for clarifying the idea of the Office of the Public Ministry as a position of trust is the study of two aberrations which from time to time have appeared in some quarters of the Lutheran Church. The first magnified the clergy into a means of grace and made the efficacy of their ministrations depend upon their personal faith and worthiness. Taking account of it in his day, Paul wrote to the Corinthians: "Who, then, is Paul, and who is Apollos, but ministers by whom ye believed, even as the Lord gave to every man?" (I Cor. 3:5). And about ten years later he encouraged Timothy thus: "Take heed unto thyself and unto the doctrine; continue in them; for in doing this thou shalt both save thyself and them that hear thee" (I Tim. 4:16). Hence, it has been pointedly remarked: "Neither is a common Christian, because he is a royal priest, a bishop, nor a bishop or pastor, because he is an incumbent of the Office of the Public Ministry, a royal priest." Again: "The Gospel is effective also when the clergy are unbelievers." (*Lehre und Wehre*, 1889, p. 221; Central Illinois, 1916, pp. 27 and 28.)

The second aberration struck away from the truth in the opposite direction. It changed the position of trust into a job. According to it, the bishop or pastor is not a trustee or manager, but a common employee, who can be hired and fired, engaged and dismissed as is done in any secular business. This view rested upon a misconception of the term *servant*, often used by the Scriptures to name a minister of the Gospel. It has caused much harm in the Church. In obedience to it, congregations have sometimes stooped to haggling over the salary to be paid their pastors and teachers and, as is the practice in business, sought to pay their servants of the Lord just as little as possible or in accordance with the special gifts and powers which, in their judgment, they possessed. Long ago the Apostle Paul wrote to the Corinthians: "Be not ye the servants of men"; that is, slaves, employees, hirelings (I Cor. 7:23). (Minnesota, 1916, pp. 19—20; Wisconsin, 1892, p. 22.)

The Office of the Public Ministry

Proceeding with our answer to the question: What is the Office of the Public Ministry? we shall observe next that it is a position of trust conferred by a Christian congregation. We note first that the office under discussion is conferred, or, to use the traditional German term, *uebertragen*. When we consider the fact that this expression is used in the connection with *position of trust*, it would appear that the meaning intended is at once clear and simple. But, strange as it may seem, this particular aspect of the doctrine of the Office of the Public Ministry caused the most violent attacks to be made upon it. As one early writer of our Synod puts it, this doctrine was made to stink throughout the Lutheran Church, so that some who were not otherwise inimically disposed, because of the odium fastened upon it, shied away. (*Lehre und Wehre*, 1862, p. 97.) Some of those to whom the Missouri Synod view was unacceptable insisted that one cannot confer or commit anything without at the same time giving it away and losing it. Others interpreted the doctrine to mean that the acting congregation thereby is reduced to a mere messenger boy or notifying agent. As a result every effort was made by the Missouri Synod theologians to show that in no way the congregation conferring the Office was giving up or even limiting any of her possessions and powers. The act of conferring was explained as indicating the giving of a mandate or the placing into the hands of another the Office of the Public Ministry. (*Lehre und Wehre*, 1862, p. 101; 1877, p. 295, pp. 360—361; Central, 1880, pp. 50, 84.) In order to disavow every trace of Roman Catholic theology, laid to the charge of our fathers by some of their opponents, it was brought out that it is specifically Lutheran to say that the Church speaks absolution; that, in principle, it is the Church that forgives sin; it is specifically Roman Catholic to say that only the clergy do so, by virtue of a mandate, call, or priesthood given only to them. (*Lehre und Wehre*, 1861, p. 179.)

We turn our attention now to the body which does the conferring of the Office of the Public Ministry. This is the Christian congregation. By *congregation* is meant a group of confessing Christians, large or small, wherever located, organized for the preaching of the Gospel. An early example of such a congregation in action is the one in Jerusalem, which conferred some of the work connected with the Office of the Ministry, specifically, that which had to do with the "daily ministration" for the physically undernourished, upon seven "men of honest report . . ." (Acts 6:3-6). (*Lehre und Wehre*, 1855, p. 7.) The earliest evidence, perhaps, for the fact that the local congregation is the acting body in the conferring of the Office of the Public Ministry is the action taken by the disciples of Jesus — "the number of names together were about an hundred and twenty" — who, meeting shortly after Christ's ascension in an upper room somewhere in Jerusalem, conferred upon Matthias the position left vacant by the defection and death of Judas Iscariot (Acts 1:12-26). The congregation at Antioch by divine command sent out Paul and Barnabas as missionaries (Acts 13:1-3.)

Who precisely is the congregation which is conferring the position? It is the local church, but in a metaphorical sense, for since it is visible, being made up of a number of persons, it may have within it not only believers, but also unbelievers. And unbelievers can not rightfully act in this matter; they are separated from Christ and do not possess any of the powers and rights conferred. Strictly speaking, it is only the true believers who do the conferring, for they really possess all the treasures procured by the Lord Jesus Christ. They are the children and heirs of God. They are royal priests. They are priests in that they are in immediate association with God. They are of royal stock in that they are sovereign; they are subordinated to no one human. This the Apostle Peter makes clear in his First General Epistle: "Ye are . . . a royal priesthood" (I Pet. 2:2-10). (Central, 1880, p. 24.) It is impossible to overstress this great truth, since the Scriptures set it out before us in both the Old and the New Testament repeatedly and clearly. Peter's great words are, in fact, a kind of reiteration of Moses' announcement made at the order of God, and at Sinai at that: "And ye shall be unto Me a kingdom of priests and an holy nation" (Ex. 19:6). To be sure, during the Old Testament dispensation God placed a certain limitation upon the exercise of the general priesthood of all believers in that He set apart the tribe of Levi as a special priestly tribe, but even then God again and again set aside the boundaries He had fixed. The prophets, for example, prophesied of Christ as the true Priest, as we note from Isaiah (chapter 53) and David's Twenty-Second Psalm. What can be more specific than Isaiah's pronouncement made in connection with his praise of the Church and the office of Christ: "But ye shall be named the priests of the Lord; men shall call you the ministers of our God" (Is. 61:6). Very emphatically the royal priesthood of all believers is asserted by St. John the Divine, who in his opening chapter of the Book of Revelation names as the real objective of our Lord's suffering and death His fashioning us into kings and priests. These are the words: "Unto Him that loved us and washed us from our sins in His own blood and hath made us kings and priests unto God and His Father; to Him be glory and dominion forever and ever. Amen" (Rev. 1:5-6). (Iowa, 1883, pp. 13—15.)

The question may now well be asked: If the validity of the conferring of the Office of the Public Ministry depends upon the fact that true believers have acted, for they alone are royal priests, how can we be certain that a given local congregation, when it acts to confer the Office is actually doing so in the sight of God? In answer it can be safely declared that as surely as the Gospel is being preached in the local congregation, so surely there are in it true believers (Is. 55:10-11), who have the Office of the Keys. (*Lehre und Wehre*, 1855, p. 48; 1862, p. 137.)

In spite of the fact that the Scriptures establish the status of the individual Christian as that of a sovereign priest and with it his right to join with other Christians to confer the Office of the Public Ministry on whomsoever they will, there arise ever and anon voices in the Church to assert that the conferring is done only indirectly. The Office, it is contended, belongs originally to individuals, say, the clergy, and only after a clergyman has been called and installed in his congregation, does it, too, have the keys. (*Lehre und Wehre*, 1861, p. 179.) That such a view refuses to accept the universal priesthood of all believers at face value is obvious. It, no doubt, is based on the misconception that there are in the Church various orders, some holier, or more privileged, than others. In correction of this erroneous idea, it may be said further that after the Apostles had organized churches in the various localities, they referred to them not by the pastors in charge, but rather by houses, towns, and provinces. (Wisconsin, 1892, p. 29.)

While it is true that the individual Christian, since he is a royal priest of Christ, is the original human authority behind the conferring of the Office of the Public Ministry, the ultimate or absolute Author of this Office is God. And He, too, remains forever active in it. He will not suffer it ever to be taken out of His hands. This truth the Apostles make very plain. Paul, for example, tells the Corinthians: "Let a man so account of us as of the ministers of Christ and stewards of the mysteries of God" (I Cor. 4:1). It is, then, only "by His will, appointment, and commission that a man can truly be a minister to perform his work" (*Theological Quarterly*, 1902, p. 21). And God the Holy Ghost, likewise, is active, as Paul explains to the elders of Ephesus: "Take heed, therefore, unto yourselves and to all the flock, over the which the Holy Ghost hath made you overseers to feed the church of God, which He hath purchased with His own blood" (Acts 20:28). (*Lehre und Wehre*, 1855, p. 7.)

We find, then, that the Office of the Public Ministry is doubly sanctioned and that the clergy are responsible not only to the congregations which they serve, but also to God. Hence, Paul will say to the Colossians concerning the Church: "whereof I am made a minister" (Col. 1:24-25), and tell the Corinthians that their pastors are "your servants" (II Cor. 4:5). And on the other hand, we will say to the same congregation that he is a minister of Christ, and so are their pastors (I Cor. 4:1). (Michigan, 1907, p. 15; Central, 1897, p. 16.)

Continuing our answer to the question: What is the Office of the Public Ministry? we observe next that it has as its purpose the preaching of the Gospel of Jesus Christ. So Paul puts it in his Second Letter to the Corinthians: "And all things are of God, who hath reconciled us to Himself by Jesus Christ and hath given to us the ministry of reconciliation. . . . Now, then, we are ambassadors for Christ, as though God did beseech you by us; we pray you in Christ's stead, be ye reconciled to God" (II Cor. 5: 18-20). (*Theological Quarterly*, 1902, p. 19). This preaching of the Gospel is in reality not only the chief purpose of the Office of the Ministry, but, in fact, the only purpose. The preaching of the Law merely serves and should merely serve the Gospel. (Michigan, 1907, p. 17; *Lehre und Wehre*, 1889, pp. 233 ff.; F. Pieper,

The Office of the Public Ministry 481

Christliche Dogmatik, III, p. 501; Central Illinois, 1916, p. 15.) As such it is necessary that it be preached, but it must always, without exception, be only a kind of prolog and epilog to the Gospel. Convincing man of his sin, it sets the stage, as it were, for the preaching of the Gospel. Showing man how to perform really good works, it spreads out before him a field of activity for his living faith, generated by the Gospel.

In order to achieve the purpose of preaching the Gospel, the Office of the Public Ministry has a variety of duties to perform, dictated by the needs of the congregation. First among these is teaching, for man knows nothing by nature of the Gospel and also after his conversion is prone to lose his knowledge of the Gospel and to fall prey to all manner of error. Hence, the Scriptures enjoin the incumbents of the Office of the Public Ministry to give their first and best attention to teaching. To the teaching they will link comforting, for which there is available the Gospel in double strength through Word and Sacrament. There is, in addition, the duty to watch both doctrine and life, as Paul points out to Timothy (I Tim. 4:16), and, closely related to it, warning as temptations appear. Of it Paul spoke feelingly to the elders of Ephesus: "Therefore watch, and remember that by the space of three years I ceased not to warn everyone night and day with tears" (Acts 20:31). Finally there remains the duty of exhorting to good works, lest the faith of the believers lack them and thus die of dry rot. Commenting on this phase of preaching the Gospel, Luther once remarked: "A preacher must be not only a good Easter preacher, but also a good Pentecost preacher." (Michigan, 1907, pp. 20—24.)

The functions which have been listed above may be said to describe in general the scope of the Office of the Public Ministry and to fix its limits. It will, then, consider anything which either directly or indirectly has to do with the preaching of the Gospel as its business; it will, on the other hand, studiously avoid anything which has no connection with the ministry of reconciliation. In matters for which there are not divine mandates it will not attempt to legislate, but only advise and execute in accordance with the will of the congregation. It will always recognize the existence of an area of *adiaphora*; that is, of things not definitely determined by the Scriptures, but rather relegated to the free choice and judgment of the congregation. (*Lehre und Wehre*, 1870, pp. 184–186.)

Another limit set for the Office of the Public Ministry touches the act of excommunication. Though a matter of such gravity and importance certainly belongs to the business of the Office, it must always remain also the business of the congregation as a whole. This is evident from Christ's words recorded in the eighteenth chapter of the Gospel according to St. Matthew: "And if he shall neglect to hear them, tell it unto the church; but if he neglect to hear the church, let him be unto thee as an heathen man and a publican" (Matt. 18:17). We have here a situation in which the Office and the congregation act conjointly. Similarly, the clergy and the laity participate together in the judgment of doctrine. For this reason it has been the practice of our Synod to accord to both the clergy and the representatives of congregations equal voice and vote. (*Lehre und Wehre*, 1878, p. 267; 1889, pp. 233 ff.)

To complete the answer to the question: What is the Office of the Public Ministry? we observe finally that through it the Gospel of Jesus Christ is preached publicly. Hence it is named a Public Ministry. The preaching is intended for the entire congregation, not a part of it only. Comparing the preaching of the Public Ministry with that of the individual Christian, we note that the difference between the two consists in the manner in which the duties, which are essentially the same for each, are carried out. Through the Office of the Public Ministry the preaching ministrations are carried out publicly; that is, the pastor acts as the authorized representative of the congregation; through the priestly office of the individual Christian, privately, in his own home, by virtue of his being a royal priest. Well stated is this difference by Dr. A. L. Graebner in these words: "All Christians are priests, and therefore every Christian has a right to and the duty to bring the sacrifices of his heart and lips and hands before his God. But his spiritual priesthood does not empower him to offer up his neighbor's sacrifices or the sacrifices of an entire community of such as are like himself priests before God. The police power of the state is shared by all the members of the state. But not every citizen is empowered to exercise this power by restraining his neighbor's private rights or punishing him for a disregard of his restraint. Thus even on general principles it would appear that the exercise of the powers of the church is not at the arbitrary disposal of every member of the church." (*Theological Quarterly*, 1902, pp. 18—19. See also *Lehre und Wehre*, 1870, p. 173.)

THESIS II

The Office of the Public Ministry was instituted by God, and the believers in Christ are obligated to establish and to maintain it.

In the October issue of *Lehre und Wehre*, 1861, there appeared an article on the Office of the Public Ministry, in which the unnamed author declared that he did not know of any Scriptural statement saying in direct words that this office is instituted by God. He was ready, nevertheless, to accept it as divinely ordered because the official Confessions of the Lutheran Church so teach of it. Walther and Lange, the editors of *Lehre und Wehre*, in a footnote, hastened to correct the assertion made. They stated that it is an error to say that the express command from God is lacking. It is given, they continued, in the command which the Apostles received and in their call to go out to preach, as recorded in Matt. 10, and of the Seventy, as reported in Luke 10. The Office of the Public Ministry is only a continuation of the ministerial office of the Apostles, which was to remain to the end of the world according to Matt. 28:19-20. Hence, the Apostles named also those who were called indirectly (*mittelbar*) their "fellow servants and fellow soldiers," etc., as is seen Col. 4:7 and Phil. 2:25, and themselves "fellow elders," as in I Pet. 5:1. Therefore, then, our Confessions (*Symbole*) state: "We have the certain doctrine that "the Office of the Ministry proceeds from the general call of the Apostles." (*Lehre und Wehre*, 1861, p. 303.) For the differences between the office of the Apostles and that of the public ministry, see *Theological Quarterly*, 1903, pp. 18—20.

Lest we gain the impression that within our Synod there was current considerable uncertainty as to whether or not it is true that the Office of the Public Ministry was instituted by God, it should be pointed out here that such is not the case. The evidence to the contrary is at hand everywhere in the writings of the fathers. It is interesting to note that the very first page of the first article in the first issue of *Lehre und Wehre* contains the statement:

"The public ministry in the church of God until Judgment Day is a divine establishment (*Stiftung*) and not essentially different from the holy office of the Apostles." (*Lehre und Wehre*, 1855, p. 1.) Scriptural proof for his belief Fuerbringer finds first in St. Paul's words to the Corinthians: "Therefore let no man glory in men. For all things are yours; whether Paul, or Apollos, or Cephas, or the world, or life, or death, or things present, or things to come; all are yours; and ye are Christ's; and Christ is God's" (I Cor. 3: 21-23). To this declaration he adds Eph. 4:11, pointing out that according to the original Greek (*autos*) He Himself, the Christ, gave some, apostles; and some, prophets; and some, evangelists; and some, pastors and teachers." The most important Biblical source for the doctrine that the Office of the Public Ministry is of divine origin is for him John 20:21-23, for here Jesus, says he, gave the Office of the Keys to the Apostles assembled there, first and foremost, as believers, since no one except a Christian can qualify as an apostle or prophet or bishop. (*Lehre und Wehre*, 1855, pp. 3, 7—9.)

In later writings this doctrine is further fortified with such Biblical passages as I Cor. 12:28: "And God hath set some in the Church, first Apostles, secondarily prophets, thirdly teachers"; Acts 20:28: "Take heed therefore . . . to all the flock, over the which the Holy Ghost hath made you overseers." (Central, 1880, pp. 42—44.) Noteworthy is the fact that all three persons of the Trinity are named as Creators of the Office: the Father in I Corinthians; the Son, in Ephesians; the Holy Ghost, in the Acts. (Iowa, 1883, pp. 29—30.) And it is striking, indeed, that as our Synod continued to express itself regarding this doctrine from time to time, the passages quoted were adduced over and over again as sound proofs with unbroken unanimity. (*Lehre und Wehre*, 1889, p. 221; Wisconsin, 1892, p. 15 f.; Kansas, 1900, p. 44; Central Illinois, 1916, pp. 17—22.)

Since the Office of the Public Ministry was created by the will and ordinance of God, the Church is obligated to establish and maintain it. To that end it is necessary that all those who are being served by the Office render it obedience. This is enjoined Heb. 13:17: "Obey them that have the rule over you, and submit yourselves: for they watch for your souls as they that must give account, that they may do it with joy and not with grief." The obedience is unqualified, for it has to do not with any human directives and decrees, but with such as are of divine origin. If such obedience is refused, the Office ceases to exist for all practical purposes in the congregation involved. The area in which obedience is demanded is fixed by the Word of God. Obedience cannot be demanded therefore to anything not stipulated by the Word of God. (Eastern, 1862, p. 29; *Lehre und Wehre*, 1870, p. 183; 1889, pp. 231—232; Wisconsin, 1892, pp. 29—31; Michigan, 1907, pp. 55—73.)

Coupled with obedience should be honor and esteem. These, too, are strongly recommended to the Christian congregations. Paul writes to Timothy: "Let the elders that rule well be counted worthy of double honor, especially they that labor in the Word and doctrine" (I Tim. 5:17), and Jesus tells the Seventy as He sends them out: "He that heareth you heareth Me; and he that despiseth you despiseth Me" (Luke 10:16). (Eastern, 1862, p. 29.) And Paul, lest some deny him honor because he lacked prestige as a person, asked for it indirectly in declaring to the Romans: "Inasmuch as I am the Apostle of the Gentiles, I magnify mine office" (Rom. 11:13). (Kansas, 1900, p. 46.) Paul's case calls for the observation that Christian congregations sometimes forget that they are to honor the clergy for the sake of the Office. As a result they are tempted to yield to the temptation to terminate the services of their pastors when they do not command worldly honor and glory. Walther once protested against the practice in America to call pastors temporarily in order that the congregations would be able conveniently to rid themselves of pastors who failed to gather the prestige which through him the congregations desired to enjoy. (*Lehre und Wehre*, 1889, p. 230.) Needless to say that a pastor must prove himself worthy of the honor granted to his office (Central, 1897, p. 37).

Where there is honor, there is also love. This is the golden band that ties both pastor and people into a social unit that reflects the love of God which brought them into being. Of it Paul reminds the Thessalonians in these words: "And we beseech you, brethren, to know them which labor among you and are over you in the Lord and admonish you, and to esteem them very highly in love for their work's sake" (I Thess. 5:12-13). An outstanding example of love for their pastor is the congregation in Galatia. So genuine and fervent was that love that the Christians there were not irritated at the physical infirmities with which Paul was afflicted, but accepted him as a messenger from God. And so deeply is Paul moved by their forbearance that he must express his appreciation of it in these words: "Ye know how through infirmity of the flesh I preached the Gospel unto you at the first. And my temptation which was in my flesh ye despised not, nor rejected; but received me as an angel of God, even as Christ Jesus" (Gal. 4: 13-14). (Kansas, 1900, pp. 50—51; *Concordia Theological Monthly*, 1941, p. 733.)

Furthermore, where the love is true and intelligent, congregations will not proceed rigorously and harshly whenever certain professional weaknesses and deficiencies show themselves, or when mistakes, even bad mistakes, are made and wrongs have been committed. The sins will be pointed out, and rebuke will be administered, but always in love, as was done with Peter, whom Paul had to take to task for dissembling. However, it was done in such a manner that Paul and Peter remained friends and continued to respect each other. (Kansas, 1900, p. 47.)

In order that the Office of the Public Ministry be properly maintained, it is further imperative that the congregation provide for its servants in the Word a livelihood that is decent and adequate. When Jesus sent out the Seventy, He told them: "And in the same house remain, eating and drinking such things as they give, for the laborer is worthy of his hire. Go not from house to house. And into whatsoever city ye enter, and they receive you, eat such things as are set before you" (Luke 10:7-8). And Paul lays down this rule to the Galatians: "Let him that is taught in the Word communicate unto him that teacheth in all good things. Be not deceived; God is not mocked; for whatsoever a man soweth that shall he also reap" (Gal. 6:6-7). Reiterating that physical sustenance of the ministers of the Gospel is not a matter left to the free choice of the congregation, but an express command of God, Paul lays down this principle: "Even so hath the Lord ordained that they which preach the Gospel should live of the Gospel" (I Cor. 9:14). (Eastern, 1862, p. 29; Iowa, 1883, pp. 39—40; Wisconsin, 1892, pp. 29—31; Michigan, 1907, pp. 55—73.)

The supplying of the physical sustenance for the clergy has been a constant problem in the Church, sometimes a rather vexing one. Luther called attention to it in his day, bemoaning the fact that when the congregations were under the tyranny of the Pope, they saw to it that the priests and bishops were well nourished; but now, when they were made free, they did not support the Gospel ministry adequately. (Kansas, 1900, pp. 53—54; Luther, The Large Catechism, *Triglot*, p. 626; also Luther, III:413 and 618; V:369; XII:1222.)

To this we add a pertinent remark by Dr. A. L. Graebner: "The support extended to the ministers was not to be looked upon as alms given to the poor, but as the merited reward of their labor, and to make ample provision for their support was to be part of the honor to which they were entitled." (*Theological Quarterly*, 1903, pp. 25—26.)

Finally, the Office of the Public Ministry is to be maintained by training servants of the Word. If this is not done, the congregations will soon find it exceedingly difficult to fill the Office with the kind of servants whom the Lord desires. In the primitive Church the Apostles immediately began to train pastors and teachers and deacons. (*Theological Quarterly*, 1903, pp. 28—29; Luther, St. Louis, IV:1118; VII:1058; X:437; XI:1378.) It is certain that the Gospel could not have been brought to the entire civilized world of Paul's day so rapidly as was done if there had been no training of competent preachers of the Word. It is certain also that our Synod was hampered for a number of decades in its great program of missions because the number of trained men available was too small. Hence, congregations must continue to send to their training stations of servants of the Word an adequate number of students and provide for them the most thorough education at their command.

Thesis III

The Christian congregation fills the Office of the Public Ministry by electing and calling into it men adjudged worthy.

We come now to consider the question: How does the Christian congregation go about filling the Office of the Public Ministry? Let us approach it by inquiring into the method used by the first congregations. In the first chapter of the Acts of the Apostles we are told that a congregation of about 120 believers met to fill the apostolic office then vacant because of the death of Judas Iscariot. The disciples present set up a list of two candidates and by giving forth their lots chose Matthias. Clearly, the method here used was the elective. In the sixth chapter of the Acts we read that the congregation at Jerusalem chose, that is, elected (*exelexanto*) Stephen and six others as deacons. And in Acts 14:23 we note that an election by the congregation accompanied Paul's and Barnabas' ordaining acts, for the Greek word *cheirotonesantes*, translated with *ordained*, denotes the lifting up of hands to vote. This word we find also in II Cor. 8:18-19, again denoting *electing*: "And we have sent . . . the brother . . . who was also chosen of the churches to travel with us." (Central, 1880, pp. 62—65; Wisconsin, 1892, pp. 17—18; *Theological Quarterly*, 1902, pp. 23—25.)

This method of filling the Office of the Public Ministry was continued by the congregations for at least several centuries, as is seen from Cyprian's letter to Cornelius, which Martin Luther included in the Smalcald Articles, 1537, in refutation of the Pope's claim to the sole right to fill the Office. (Central, 1880, pp. 52—53; Smalcald Articles, Of the Power etc., *Triglot*, pp. 507—508.)

And this is the method which from its inception our Synod has used. Whenever a congregation of our Synod proceeds to fill the Office of the Public Ministry, it will, first of all, set up a list of candidates. In doing so, it will avail itself of the services of the President of the District to which it belongs, for it is one of the duties of his office to assist vacant congregations in finding men who possess the general and the specific gifts of which the congregation in question is in need. The congregation, through its voting members, will elect one of the group accepted by it as candidates. (Kansas, 1900, p. 45.)

The election having been made, the congregation next issues a solemn call or divine call to the pastor-elect. If he accepts it, the Office is filled. (Iowa, 1883, pp. 33—34; *Lehre und Wehre*, 1877, p. 305.)

Is there any other method by which the Office of the Public Ministry can be filled? None at all. Nowhere do the Scriptures suggest another method. Hence, our Synod, in agreement with the Augsburg Confession, has stressed the truth that no one can enter the Office of the Public Ministry without a regular call; that is,

The Office of the Public Ministry

a call issued by a Christian congregation. (Central, 1880, pp. 35 to 42; Augsburg Confession, Article XIV, *Triglot*, p. 49.)

Here and there in the Lutheran Church some have held that the method of electing and calling by the congregation is not the correct one; they advanced the theory that the Office is actually filled by the clergy. In support of their claim they point to Titus 1:5, where Paul says: "For this cause left I thee in Crete, that thou shouldest . . . ordain elders in every city, as I had appointed thee." But, as Luther points out, this passage must be interpreted in the light of Titus 1:7 and I Tim. 3:2 and Acts 6:3, 6, showing that the congregations called and the Apostles ordained. Prominent among those opposing the doctrine that the Office is filled by the congregation through the call issued by it was Loehe, who put his conception of the proper method thus: "The Office transplants itself. . . . Only he who has the Office can transfer it to another." (Central, 1880, pp. 48—49, 66; Kansas, 1900, p. 44.) We have here evidently a survival of the Old Testament dispensation regarding the transplanting of the office of the Levitical priesthood, practiced today by the Roman Catholic Church.

This error expresses itself very impressively in the sacrament of ordination, so-called. And since the Lutheran Church, too, practices ordination, it is perhaps not superfluous to state that our Synod has never considered it to be a divine ordinance nor a sacrament in the true sense, but rather a rite or ceremony that has come down to us from the days of the Apostles. It is an ecclesiastical form denoting the public and solemn confirmation of the call. (*Lehre und Wehre*, 1870, p. 179; 1878, p. 267.)

C. C. Schmidt calls attention to the fact that sometimes our Confessional Writings use the word *ordain* in a double sense, occasionally for the word *call* by the congregation; again for the public confirmation of the call through the servants of the Church. Both usages, however, indicate that always the congregation is the body or authority that makes the act valid. The ordination, therefore, is dependent upon the election and call. What the marriage rite is to the engagement, the ordination is to the call. (Central, 1880, pp. 71–72.) In his illuminating essay on Walther as a theologian, Dr. Pieper declares that the ordination ceremony is an apostolic, ecclesiastical rite (*Ordnung*), but not instituted by God, for the Scriptures do not speak of it as so ordered. It has nothing to do with the creation of the Office of the Public Ministry. Grabau contended that ordination has and that it is instituted by God. On the other hand, the rite of ordination is not an empty ceremony, but as it is connected with prayer and glorious promises, through which spiritual gifts are outpoured, it is a good ecclesiastical ordinance and should be retained. (*Lehre und Wehre*, 1889, pp. 226—227.)

THESIS IV

The Office of the Public Ministry is, strictly speaking, the only divinely instituted office in the Church.

The functions of the Office of the Public Ministry are many and varied. To indicate and distinguish them from one another the Scriptures employ a number of terms. They speak, for example, of apostles, evangelists, teachers, bishops, pastors, elders, deacons. We today have pastors, assistant pastors, associate pastors, vicars, teachers, elders, deacons, professors, presidents, executive secretaries, superintendents, visitors, and various other synodical officials. How are all the offices, filled by these servants of the Church, related to each other? Are they all divinely instituted?

As we undertake to answer these questions, we begin by recalling that God gave us Christians the command to preach the Gospel as individuals and as congregations. In order to carry out this command as congregations, we have received from God the Office of the Public Ministry. This Office of the Word is the only one instituted by God for the building of His kingdom. The Scriptures mention no other. (Wisconsin, 1892, p. 16.)

What shall we say, then, of the various offices listed above? Which are divinely instituted? Which not? Inasmuch as through all of them the Gospel is preached and through them the congregation acts, each one has divine sanction. However, the particular form which distinguishes one from the other is not divinely fixed. Wherefore our synodical writings liken the Office of the Public Ministry to a tree with many branches. The preaching of the Word as it is performed by the pastor of the congregation is the trunk of the tree. The preaching as it is carried out by the various auxiliary or ancillary offices constitutes the branches. So O. Fuerbringer pictured it in the following words: "Therefore the bishops, superintendents . . . and others assisting the pastors have, without question, a divine call; their offices are, however, only branches of the one divine ministry as the center, out of which, in Christian liberty and in accordance with the example set by the apostolic Church, they are organized and distributed up and down." Using another image, Dr. Pieper declared that all other offices flow from the Office of the Public Ministry and are consequently auxiliary offices, such as that of elders (I Tim. 5:17), church government (Rom. 12:8), diaconate or any other which may be created. (*Lehre und Wehre*, 1855, p. 6; p. 229.)

The oneness of the Office of the Public Ministry and the diversity within it are described by Dr. A. L. Graebner in these words: "These deacons were subsidiary or assistant officers in the churches. Their office was not properly a second ministry with different duties and functions, as the functions of a secretary differ from those of a treasurer. The duties assigned to these assistants had previously been performed by the Apostles as pastors of the congregations, until these pastoral labors exceeded their united energies and the church began to suffer in consequence, Acts 6:1 ff." (*Theological Quarterly*, 1903, p. 22.)

Dr. Walther, in the eighth thesis of his classic exposition of the doctrine regarding the Office of the Public Ministry, calls it the highest office in the Church. From his development of this thesis it is clear, however, that he does not mean to indicate that God instituted various offices, some higher, some lower in authority and efficacy. He has in mind rather the pastorate of a congregation, large or small, and contends that it occupies the center of the Office of the Public Ministry. He expresses himself as strongly as he does to voice his opposition to the Roman Catholic form of church government with its gradations of offices of varying powers. Commenting on our own form of church government, Walther stresses that synods and other ecclesiastical forms of government can have for the individual congregations only an advisory status. On the other hand, congregations should be encouraged to join with other congregations to form synods for the purpose of extending the kingdom of Jesus Christ and preserving the unity of faith. (*Lehre und Wehre*, 1870, p. 182; 1878, p. 273; 1889, pp. 330—332; Walther, *Die Stimme, etc.*, p. XVL 1870, p. 182.)

The principle of equality has received much emphasis within our Synod. The existence of holy orders by divine right or institution has been consistently denied. All the incumbents of the ministerial office, either in one congregation or in different congregations, are held to be equal in rank and station among themselves, since no degrees in the ministry have been established by the Head of the Church. Whatever superiority of station there may be among the officers of any church or confederation of churches is, like the form of church polity, which may involve or condition such gradations, merely of human origin and dignity. By divine right Peter was the "fellow elder" of all the elders of all the churches (I Pet. 5:1). (*Theological Quarterly*, 1902, p. 36; Michigan, 1907, pp. 15—16; Central Illinois, 1916, p. 18; *Concordia Theological Monthly*, 1941, p. 726.)

By the same right, all incumbents of the Office of the Public Ministry today are fellows and brethren, with only one Master above them, the Lord Jesus Christ.

We conclude our review of the Office of the Public Ministry with an expression of deep thanks to the God of our salvation for having given us the great and good ministry of reconciliation. Through it all of us have been assured of an orderly continuation of the preaching of the Gospel according to our needs. We pray that God would preserve this precious office for us, that He would always grant us servants of the Word who are mindful of their high and holy calling and are endowed with knowledge, wisdom, and power from the Holy Spirit. May He increase in all Christian congregations everywhere intelligent appreciation of the rights and obligations of their royal priesthood, by virtue of which they have been directed by God to set up, establish, and maintain among themselves the Office of the Public Ministry. Thus they will never deprecate or degrade it, but rather consider it a choice spiritual possession and feel themselves divinely bound by all means to keep it pure and strong.

Doctrine, True and False

DOCTRINAL indifference and religious unionism are two prominent traits of the Church of our day. Pure doctrine is viewed by many as a matter of small importance, while error in doctrine is deemed an innocent trifle. We are told that the Christian who differs with us in doctrine merely sees truth from a different point of view and that we should not deny him fellowship because he does not agree with us regarding the teachings of Scripture. This sentiment threatens to deluge the Church. It is preached from thousands of pulpits, published in numberless papers, and proclaimed in many radio broadcasts. Pastors of different denominations form ministerial associations, exchange pulpits, officiate at church functions, and unite in joint religious endeavors. Such practice is praised as proof of true Christian charity and is held to be characteristic of American Christianity. Those Christians, however, who insist on pure doctrine and who warn against error and errorists are unpopular. They are reproached, derided, and sometimes persecuted. They are called sticklers for orthodoxy and narrow sectarians. They are told that their conduct is inconsistent with the spirit of the meek and gentle Galilean who said: "Judge not; condemn not." Thus the champions of doctrinal indifferentism would make it appear that our Master was tolerant toward error, as if He who said: "The Scripture cannot be broken," and: "If ye continue in My Word, then are ye My disciples indeed," could have countenanced or condoned even the least error!

The Lutheran Church with its motto "Sola Scriptura" takes a unique position with reference to doctrine. It insists on purity of doctrine. That its position is in full accord with Holy Scripture we shall see by considering the topic

DOCTRINE, TRUE AND FALSE

I

*The Source and Norm of All True Doctrine
Is the Inspired Word of God*

The Christian religion is not a man-made religion. Natural man knows of the existence of God by the visible world which God has created. (Rom. 1:19-20.) Man's conscience tells him that he is accountable to this God. (Rom. 2:14-15.) But this natural knowledge of God does not reveal to man God's will or the way to salvation. "Eye hath not seen nor ear heard, neither have entered into the heart of man the things which God hath prepared for them that love Him; but God hath revealed them unto us by His Spirit" (I Cor. 2:9-10). The Spirit of God spoke through Moses and the Prophets in the Old Testament and through the Evangelists and Apostles in the New Testament. "No prophecy of the Scripture is of any private interpretation; for the prophecy came not in old time by the will of man, but holy men of God spake as they were moved by the Holy Ghost" (II Pet. 1:20-21). The writers of the Scriptures wrote what the Spirit of God put into their minds, for "all Scripture is given by inspiration of God" (II Tim. 3:16). These words, originally referring to the Old Testament, are equally true of the New Testament, for Paul says: "Which things also we speak, not in the words which man's wisdom teacheth, but which the Holy Ghost teacheth" (I Cor. 2:13). Thus Holy Scripture is the verbally inspired Word of God.

There are no degrees of inspiration, as though God revealed by inspiration His nature, His will, and His plan of salvation, while all statements pertaining to history and science reflected merely the views of the writers of the respective books. Everything in the Old and in the New Testament is given by the same inspiration of God. We believe and teach the verbal and the plenary inspiration of the Scriptures.

The inspired Word of God embraces only the canonical books of the Old and the New Testament and excludes the Apocrypha. These books were not given by inspiration. They contain errors (Tobit 6:7 ff; II Macc. 12:43 ff; 14:41 ff.), were never included in

Doctrine, True and False

the sacred volume which Jesus names Luke 24:44, and are, therefore, not a part of Holy Scripture.

With the revelations of Jesus and the Apostles the Scriptural canon is complete, and the Christian Church is to look for no further revelations from God. (John 17:20; Eph. 2:20; Heb. 1:1-3.) Thus there can be no "development of doctrine" or doctrines other than those of the Scriptures we now possess.

The Scriptures set forth all doctrines of Christian faith and life in terms which are clear, in words which can be understood by the simple no less than by the learned. "Thy Word is a Lamp unto my feet and a Light unto my path" (Ps. 119:105). "From a child thou hast known the Holy Scriptures" (II Tim. 3:15). To understand Scripture, therefore, we must let it speak for itself. We must "receive the words as they read, in their proper and plain sense" (*Triglot*, 987). Scripture interprets itself and is not waiting for any human interpreter, for a church council, or for reason to determine its true sense. We must abide by the plain statements of Scripture and rule out everything that conflicts with the analogy of faith, that is, with the clear passages of Scripture that set forth the doctrine.

The Scriptures are so plain and clear that every Christian can judge as to the truth of a promulgated doctrine. Christ placed the Scriptures into the hands of all. (Luke 16:29-31; Acts 17:11; John 5:39.) The Apostles ask the entire congregation, not merely the elders, to read the Epistles. (Rom. 1:1, 7; I Thess. 5:27; Col. 4:16.) And so the Lutheran Church insists that we "must daily use it" (*Triglot*, 571) and must not "be idle and remiss in reading, hearing, and meditating upon God's Word" (*Triglot*, 887).

The inspired Word of God, the canonical books of the Old and the New Testament, are the source from which all doctrine must be drawn and the norm by which doctrine must be judged. This is fundamental. This principle of Scripture, or the fact that the Holy Scriptures are the only source and norm of faith, has been abrogated by the substitution of something else for God's Word. Thus the Roman Catholic Church recognizes besides the inspired Scriptures the apocryphal books, the traditions of the Church, the decrees of councils, and the dicta of the Popes as authorities in matters of doctrine. Some sects, e. g., the Swedenborgians, the

Pentecostals, etc., add new revelations. The Reformed Churches accept Scripture and reason as its *principium cognoscendi*. The Lutheran Church, however, recognizes no other source and norm for doctrine than the inspired Word of God. Says the Formula of Concord: "We receive and embrace with our whole heart the Prophetic and Apostolic Scriptures of the Old and New Testaments as the pure, clear fountain of Israel, . . . which is the only true standard by which all teachers and doctrines are to be judged" (*Triglot*, 851). Therefore our Church rejects all human authority in matters of doctrine. "We concede neither to the Pope nor to the Church the power to make decrees against this consensus of the Prophets" (*Triglot*, 271). She refuses to put reason in judgment over Scripture. "We are certainly in duty bound to receive the words as they read and allow ourselves to be diverted therefrom by no objections or human contradictions spun from human reason" (*Triglot*, 987).

And that is the teaching of the Scriptures. "If any man speak, let him speak as the oracles of God" (I Pet. 4:11). "If ye continue in My Word, then are ye My disciples indeed, and ye shall know the truth" (John 8:31-32). "To the Law and to the Testimony; if they speak not according to this Word, it is because there is no light in them" (Is. 8:20).

II

Doctrine and the Christian Life

The Lutheran Church is a doctrinal Church. She attaches supreme importance to pure doctrine. The preaching and teaching of God's pure Word is her central activity. Say the Confessions: "The true adornment of the churches is godly, useful, and clear doctrine" (*Triglot*, 401).

Our Church has often been criticized for her emphasis on doctrine. She has been accused of teaching creeds but not deeds and of being so much concerned with orthodoxy that she produces dead orthodoxists.

The Lutheran Church does not underrate the Christian life. We endeavor to heed the Savior's words: "Let your light so shine before men that they may see your good works" (Matt. 5:16). We try to follow Paul's instruction: "This is a faithful saying, and these things I will that thou affirm constantly, that they which have believed in God might be careful to maintain good works" (Titus 3:8). We are mindful of the Master's threats against everyone who does not produce fruits of righteousness, when He taught: "I am the true Vine, and My Father is the Husbandman. Every branch in Me that beareth not fruit He taketh away" (John 15:1-2.) And we are not ignorant of the Lord's command to exclude from our congregations such as refuse to amend their sinful life. (Matt. 18:15-17; I Cor. 5.) Knowing the nature of saving faith in Christ Jesus, we teach that faith without works is dead, (James 2:17), and therefore exhort our members to yield themselves unto God as those that are alive from the dead and their members as instruments of righteousness unto God. (Rom. 6:13.) We exercise church discipline in our congregations. In short, the doctrine of the Lutheran Church with reference to doctrine and life is stated succinctly in Article VI of the Augsburg Confession: "Also they teach that this faith is bound to bring forth good fruits and that it is necessary to do good works commanded by God, because of God's will, but that we should not rely on these works to merit justification before God" (*Triglot*, 45).

However, while we do not ignore the injunctions of the Scriptures pertaining to our sanctification, and while we exhort our people to become rich in good works, we do emphasize doctrine, pure doctrine. And we do this for several reasons. In the first place the doctrine is not ours but God's, and we are bound by the Savior's words: "Teaching them to observe all things whatsoever I have commanded you" (Matt. 28:20). Again, it is not the Christian life, but the doctrine that constitutes the mark of the Church of God. "If ye continue in My Word, then are ye My disciples indeed" (John 8:31). Says the Apology: "Which fellowship nevertheless has outward marks, so that it can be recognized, namely, the pure Gospel and the administration of the Sacraments in accordance with the Gospel of Christ" (*Triglot*, 227). Furthermore, pure doctrine alone teaches correct Christian living. "Thy Word is a Lamp unto my feet and a Light unto my path" (Ps. 119:105). "Wherewithal shall a young man cleanse his way? By taking heed thereto according to Thy Word" (Ps. 119:9). "We beseech you, brethren, and exhort you by the Lord Jesus, that as ye have received of us how ye ought to walk and to please God, so ye would abound more and more" (I Thess. 4:1). The true norm of the Christian life is not man's will (Col. 2:23), nor man-made regulations (Col. 2:16), nor decrees of the churches (Matt. 15:9), nor the good intentions of men (I Sam. 15:22; John 16:2), but only the revealed Word of God. (Deut. 5:32.) To ignore the Word of God as the rule and guide for Christian living is not only apostasy, but idolatry. Says the Large Catechism: "Therefore I constantly say that all our life and work must be ordered according to God's Word, if it is to be God-pleasing or holy. Where this is done, this commandment (the Third Commandment) is in force and is being fulfilled. On the contrary, any observance or work that is practiced without God's Word is unholy before God, no matter how brilliantly it may shine, even though it be covered with relics, such as the fictitious spiritual orders, which know nothing of God's Word and seek holiness in their own works." (*Triglot*, 607, 92.)

And finally, true doctrine alone works true sanctification. "I will run the way of Thy commandments, when Thou shalt enlarge my heart" (Ps. 119:32). The Word of God is a power which quickens and strengthens us to every good work. (Titus 3:8.) Wherever the doctrine remains pure, sinful life can be changed and improved, but if the doctrine be not pure, Christian life will not be perfect. Not that we would teach perfectionism. We know the words of Paul: "Not as though I had already attained either were already perfect" (Phil. 3:12). Says the Formula of Concord: "We reject also the error that man, after he has been born again, can perfectly observe and completely fulfill God's Law" (*Triglot*, 789). But having the pure doctrine, we follow after, if that we may apprehend that for which also we are apprehended of Christ Jesus, (Phil. 3:12.) Thus we hold that the teaching of the Word of God in its truth and purity produces not only saving knowledge, but also Christlike deeds, and that the cry for deeds, rather than creeds, has its origin in the dogma of salvation through works.

III

Pure Doctrine, God's Greatest Gift to Man

Pure doctrine is a gift of the Lord. Man with his own reason or strength can never obtain it. It must be given to man by God. The Savior tells His disciples: "It is given unto you to know the mysteries of the kingdom of heaven, but to them (namely, the Pharisees) it is not given" (Matt. 13:11). Likewise church bodies have the full Gospel solely by the grace of God. The Missouri Synod owes its purity of doctrine not to any superior wisdom of a Walther or a Pieper, nor to any inherent qualities or merits of its members. It is the gift of God's pure, unmerited grace. We say very humbly with the Smalcald Articles: "Through God's grace our churches are now enlightened and equipped with the pure Word and right use of the Sacraments" (*Triglot*, 457).

Pure doctrine is the greatest blessing man can receive. Whosoever has the full truth of the Gospel is rich in all spiritual gifts and has lack of nothing. In the truth of the Gospel he has the power of salvation and the power of sanctification. The Lutheran Church is the Church of the pure Word and unadulterated Sacraments. Not the number of her adherents, not her organizations, not her charitable and other institutions, not her beautiful customs and liturgical forms, but the precious truths entrusted to her constitute her true beauty and richest treasure.

God has given us the pure doctrine of His Word as a sacred trust. We, the church at large, and the world need the Gospel as it is proclaimed by the Lutheran Church. We must preserve the truths we have received for our own spiritual well-being and for the salvation of our children and children's children. The church at large is torn and divided into many denominations. A God-pleasing union of the churches can be effected only through an inner unity of the spirit, and this can be accomplished solely by subscribing to the full truth of the Gospel. The testimony of the Lutheran Church and her insistence on loyal adherence to the full truth alone will achieve that measure of a godly union of the churches of Christendom which the gracious providence of God has in store for them. It is for our Church to spread its truth of the Gospel throughout the world, preaching it with a loud voice and adorning it with a godly life. The sin-cursed world needs the salvation wrought by the Gospel, and God has entrusted His testimony of the Savior to us that we might bring many to the knowledge of the truth. If we as a Church no longer witness to our doctrine, we as a Church shall be of no use in the world; we shall no longer be the salt of the earth; we shall be fit only for the dunghill. In short, the fact that God has given us the truth of the Gospel implies that we use it, preserve it, and spread it. "Unto whomsoever much is given, of him shall be much required" (Luke 12:48).

We must faithfully guard our doctrine, for although God is the Giver of the truth, man has the dreadful power to lose it. Whenever a Christian ceases to watch and to pray, when he begins to despise preaching and the Word, when he no longer trembles at the Word of the Lord, when he does the will of his flesh and follows the allurements of the world, he will fall from grace and eventually lose the truth entirely. And although he still confess the truth outwardly and read it and hear it, his heart has become estranged from the truth; he has become indifferent to doctrine, and finally surrenders entirely to unbelief.

What is true of the individual, is true also of church bodies. When the members of our congregations begin to despise preaching and the Sacraments, when they are remiss in the exercise of church discipline, when they become indifferent to doctrinal purity, when they fail to appreciate the spiritual gifts they have received, when they bury the treasures entrusted to them instead of using them for the benefit of God's kingdom, in short, when they do not use the Gospel, they are in grave danger of losing it. God in his divine and just judgment takes from an ungrateful church the gifts He has given to it. The prophecy of Amos is fulfilled, who said: "Behold, the days come, saith the Lord God, that I will send a famine in the land, not a famine of bread nor a thirst for water, but of hearing the words of the Lord. And they shall wander from sea to sea and from the north even to the east, they shall run to and fro to seek the Word of the Lord and shall not find it" (Amos 8:11-12). Says the Formula of Concord: "Moreover even as God has ordained in His eternal counsel that the Holy Ghost should call, enlighten and convert the elect through His word and that He will justify and save all those who by true faith receive Christ, so He also determined in His counsel that He will harden, reprobate, and condemn those who are called through the Word, if they reject the Word and resist the Holy Ghost, who wishes to be efficacious and to work in them through the Word, and persevere therein" (*Triglot*, 1077). Church history gives proof to the truth of this statement. The apostolic churches in Palestine and

Asia Minor and in Greece did not continue long. They put from themselves the truth of the Gospel and judged themselves unworthy of everlasting life. (Acts 13:46.)

Hence, to preserve the purity of the Gospel which God has given us, we must use the agencies the Lord has provided for its preservation. We must be diligent and faithful in the use of the means of grace, strive to increase our knowledge of the doctrines of Scripture by faithful study of the Scriptures and the literature of our Church, and be on guard against indifference to doctrinal purity. We must let the Word of God live and rule in our homes and provide for thorough indoctrination of our children. We must be ready to testify of the hope within us and support the program of our Church in her missionary endeavors. And last but not least, we must adorn the confession of our faith with a God-pleasing life, which, of course, will also include a life of prayer to the effect that God's Word be taught in its truth and purity.

IV

False Doctrine, the Most Baneful Evil

Just as true doctrine is the greatest gift we can enjoy, so false doctrine is the most baneful evil that can beset us. False doctrine is sin, it is the invention of Satan, and it imperils and destroys salvation.

False doctrine is every teaching contrary to the Word of God. Scripture enjoins upon us to proclaim only the truth. "Whatsoever I command thee thou shalt speak" (Jer. 1:7). "He that hath My Word, let him speak My Word faithfully" (Jer. 23:28). "The priest's lips should keep knowledge, and they should seek the Law at his mouth; for he is the messenger of the Lord of Hosts." (Mal. 2:7.) Christ Himself instructed His disciples: "Teaching them to observe all things whatsoever I have commanded you" (Matt. 28:20). Again, Scripture enjoins upon us to avoid error. "Be not carried about with divers and strange doctrines" (Heb. 13:9). "If any man teach otherwise and consent not to wholesome words, even the words of our Lord Jesus Christ, and to the doctrine which is according to godliness, he is proud, knowing nothing, but doting about questions and strifes of words, whereof cometh envy, strife, railings, evil surmisings, perverse disputings of men of corrupt minds, and destitute of the truth, supposing that gain is godliness; from such withdraw thyself" (I Tim. 6:3-5).

False doctrine is definitely a sin, not only because it is contrary to Scripture's commands to preach the truth and avoid error, but also because it transgresses God's holy Law. Every errorist transgresses the Second Commandment, for he lies and deceives by God's name, which, as our Catechism informs us, is done by teaching false doctrine and saying that it is God's word or revelation. The errorist sins against the First Commandment, for either he is trusting his own reason in matters of religion or he is following someone who is erring and whom he is holding in greater esteem than God. In either case he is committing idolatry. Hence John writes: "Whosoever transgresseth and abideth not in the doctrine of Christ hath not God" (II John 9). False doctrine is a sin against the Third Commandment, which demands that we hold the Word of God sacred, in other words, that we tremble at God's Word in holy awe. Changing this Word either by adding thereto or by taking away therefrom is despising the holy Word of God. To commit murder is generally considered a heinous crime. But worse than destroying the body is the destroying of a soul. But just that is done when the pure Word of God, which is able to save souls (James 1:21), is taken from someone and he through error is led on the path that leads to destruction. The Lord says: "But if they had stood in My counsel and had caused My people to hear My words, then they should have turned them from their evil way and from the evil of their doings" (Jer. 23:22). Hence, false doctrine is a transgression of God's holy Law. God threatens to punish not only the errorist (Jer. 23:25-32; Is. 8:20; Gal. 1:9; Rev. 22:18-19), but also the adherents to error (Ezek. 20:21-22; II Thess. 2:8-12).

The Scriptures call false doctrine a strong delusion (II Thess. 2:11), really, the power of delusion. Its power originates from Satan, the inventor of all false doctrine, who through error endeavors to keep men from the Kingdom. (II Cor. 11:3.) Truth is not in him; when he speaketh, he speaketh lies. (John 8:44.) He is the "old serpent, called the devil and Satan, which deceiveth the whole world" (Rev. 12:9). He is the prince of darkness, holding his subjects enslaved in error until their eyes are opened and they are turned from darkness to light and from the power of Satan unto God. (Acts 26:18.) Compare also I John 3:8; John 8:44; II Thess. 2:9.

The baneful evil of false doctrine is shown by its results. In Matt. 16:6-12 and in Gal. 5:7-9 Scripture likens false doctrine to leaven. This figure implies that false doctrine is a corrupt and corrupting thing. Leaven is a piece of sour dough which is in a state of putrefaction. It is therefore a sign of impurity and corruption. (I Cor. 5:7-8; Lev. 2:11.) By comparing false doctrine to leaven, Christ characterizes it as a dinstinctly impure and corrupt thing. But this does not exhaust His meaning. Leaven is also a corrupting substance. It comes out of corruption and corrupts that with which it is mingled. "A little leaven leaveneth the whole lump" (Gal. 5:9). The microscopic yeast plants in the piece of dough are in continual motion. Under favorable conditions they multiply with extraordinary rapidity, and quickly pervade the whole lump, changing it into their nature. Even so the leaven of error grows and develops most rapidly. It propagates itself with amazing rapidity. It penetrates and pierces through till it pervades and so corrupts the holy bread of Scripture truth on which our souls are fed. Moreover, false doctrine spreads with corrupting effect through the heart that admits it. Look at the Pharisees. The leaven of their error caused their heart to swell and become inflated with spiritual pride. It led them to trust in themselves as being righteous and to despise others. It blinded them to the deep depravity of their whole nature and to their need of a Redeemer and of regeneration. It led them to reject and to persecute Christ, the only Redeemer, and to die in their sins. That was the effect, the fearful and fatal effect of their leavenous teaching. Indeed, erroneous teaching is not the harmless thing so many imagine. It is a most dangerous, pernicious, and ruinous thing. It injures and ruins the soul that admits it.

In II Tim. 2:17-18 St. Paul compares false doctrine to a cancer, or gangrene. Just as cancer, or gangrene, attacks a weak spot in the body, one which in some manner has been prepared for such an attack, so false doctrine is most apt to find lodging in a heart that is not firm in the doctrine of the Bible. With terrible quickness the disease will spread if once it has gained a hold in a Christian congregation. The sound flesh of the body of Christ, the church, is then attacked and ruined and eventually completely destroyed. Certainly, false doctrine is the most baneful evil, and the knowledge of this causes us to pray daily: From this preserve us, heavenly Father.

V

Christ, the Prophets, and the Apostles, Opposed False Doctrine

People given to doctrinal indifference and religious unionism misquote Scripture for their position. They refer to Gal. 5:14-15: "For all the Law is fulfilled in one word, even in this: Thou shalt love thy neighbor as thyself. But if ye bite and devour one another, take heed that ye be not consumed one of another." Or Phil. 1:18: "What then? Notwithstanding every way, whether in pretense or in truth, Christ is preached, and I therein do rejoice, yea, and will rejoice." Again, they use the dictum of the Master: "Judge not; condemn not."

The Savior's attitude toward error and errorists is plainly set forth in the Gospels. There is His general statement (Matt. 7:15): "Beware of false prophets which come to you in sheep's clothing, but inwardly they are ravening wolves." Again, He says (Matt. 24:23-26): "Then if any man shall say unto you: 'Lo, here is Christ, or there,' believe it not. For there shall arise false Christs and false prophets and shall show great signs and wonders, insomuch that, if it were possible, they shall deceive the very elect. Behold, I have told you before. Wherefore if they shall say unto you: 'Behold, he is in the desert,' go not forth; 'behold, he is in the secret chambers,' believe it not."

But besides these general statements we have the record of His encounters with the errorists in the Jewish Church of His day, the Pharisees and the Sadducees. The Sadducees denied, among other doctrines, the resurrection of the dead. The Lord rebuked them (Matt. 22:29), saying: "Ye do err, not knowing the Scriptures." The errors of the Sadducees were strongly opposed by the Pharisees, who were the patriotic party of the people. While they clung to the doctrine of the resurrection, they falsified a number of Scriptural truths. They added to the Word of God by their traditions and took away from it by their restricted interpretation.

One of their most highly prized traditions referred to the observance of the Sabbath. They claimed that it was unlawful to heal or to carry any kind of burden, to pluck corn, for this would be reaping, to rub the ears of corn in the hands, for this would be threshing. They had their traditions regarding washing their hands before meals and other religious ablutions, besides other commandments of men, which they had received to hold. (Matt. 7:4-8.) Not only did they teach that these human additions to the divine Law were binding upon all; they even placed them above the divine Law, inasmuch as they taught that, whenever their oral traditions came into conflict with a written commandment, the former had to be obeyed and the latter set aside. (Matt. 15; Mark 7.) And so, since they corrupted the Word of God, they went astray in the doctrine of salvation by teaching that they were able to keep the Commandments and thus merit everlasting life by their own righteousness.

The Savior did not ignore the errors of the religious parties of His day. True, He did not go out of His way to begin a controversy with the opponents of the truth, but He boldly faced and denounced error wherever He found it. In the Sermon on the Mount He exposed the false interpretations of the Pharisees of the divine Law and their idea of righteousness. He publicly declared that the traditions of the elders were the commandments of men, that the observance of these man-made commandments is vain worship of God, often involving a direct and gross violation of God's holy will. When He said, with reference to the teachings of the Pharisees: "Every plant which My heavenly Father hath not planted shall be rooted up" (Matt. 15:13), He manifested His position towards every false doctrine. He regarded error as a weed which His heavenly Father has not planted. Hence, it has no right of existence. He deemed it His duty to pluck it up by the roots, to destroy it completely and utterly. He spoke of the leaven of the Pharisees and Sadducees, thereby mentioning the errorists by name and designating error as a most dangerous, pernicious, and ruinous thing, because it injures and ruins the soul. No wonder, therefore, that our blessed Savior, who died to atone for sin, also the sins of the errorists, opposed all error in doctrine and earnestly cautions us to take heed and beware of the leaven of false doctrine.

What Christ did was done before His day by His Prophets in the Old Testament. There comes to mind immediately the zeal of the prophet Elijah on behalf of true religion and his constant and persistent opposition to the prophets of Baal. Jeremiah exclaimed: "Behold, I am against the prophets, saith the Lord, that use their tongues and say: He saith" (chap. 23:31). Ezekiel by command of the Lord had to proclaim: "Her priests have violated My Law and have profaned Mine holy things; . . . they have put no difference between the unclean and the clean and have hid their eyes from My sabbaths, and I am profaned among them" (chap. 22:26). Again Jeremiah laments: "A wonderful and horrible thing is committed in the land; the prophets prophecy falsely, and the priests bear rule by their means, and My people love to have it so. And what will ye do in the end thereof?" (Chap. 5: 30-31.)

The Apostles followed in the footsteps of their Master in their attitude towards false doctrine. At the convention of the Apostles (Acts 15) Peter says: "Now, therefore, why tempt ye God to put a yoke upon the neck of the disciples, which neither our fathers nor we were able to bear? But we believe that through the grace of the Lord Jesus Christ we shall be saved, even as they" (vv. 10-11). In very determined and scathing language Paul speaks against the errorists in Gal. 1:8-9, and against those who denied the resurrection in I Cor. 15. How carefully he avoided any commerce whatsoever with errorists is shown by his words in Gal. 2: "And that because of false brethren unawares brought in, who came privily to spy out our liberty which we have in Christ Jesus, that they might bring us into bondage; to whom we gave place by subjection, no, not for an hour, that the truth of the Gospel might continue with you" (vv. 4-5).

And if we read the Epistles of James or Jude or John or the Letter to the Hebrews, we find the same testimony against error and errorists. There never is a compromise of truth and error in Scripture. The Prophets testify against error, the Savior witnessed against it, and the Apostles condemned it, for they knew that the Word which they preached was the Word revealed by God and that, accordingly, the doctrine was not theirs, but God's, who had sent them.

Doctrine, True and False

VI

It Is the Duty of the Teachers of the Church Not Only to Proclaim the Truth, but Also to Denounce Error

The first and foremost duty of the teachers of the Church is to bring their people to a knowledge of divine truth. Hence the command to "preach the Word" (II Tim. 4:2). "Preach the Gospel" (Mark 16:15). "Teach them to observe all things whatsoever I have commanded you" (Matt. 28:20). That is the Lord's command. The purpose of such preaching is to engender and to strengthen faith and to encourage the doing of good works. All this can be done only by means of the full and complete truth. False doctrine cannot save, nor can it promote the interests of the Kingdom, for, says Jeremiah: "Truly in vain is salvation hoped for from the hills and from the multitude of mountains; truly in the Lord our God is the salvation of Israel" (chap. 3:23). Again he says: "He that hath My Word, let him speak My Word faithfully" (chap. 23:28). Hence Luther says: "After his sermon a preacher shall not pray the Lord's Prayer or ask for forgiveness of sins, if he at all be the right kind of preacher, but he should rather be able to say boastfully with Jeremiah: 'That which came out of my lips was right before Thee' (Jer. 17:16)."

But while strengthening the faith of the people in the truth is the primary purpose of the teacher of the Church, he must also use the Word of God to refute error. When the walls of Jerusalem were being rebuilt, "the builders every one had his sword girded by his side and so builded. Every one with one of his hands wrought in the work and with the other hand held a weapon" (Neh. 4:17-18). Even so the builders of the walls of the Lord's spiritual Zion must use the Word of God not only to teach the true doctrine, but also to refute false doctrine. Error, false doctrine, must be refuted; not only gross error, as Paul does in the 15th chapter of First Corinthians, where he refutes those who deny the power of Christ's resurrection, but also error of a finer sort, as Paul mentions in Gal. 5, when he writes: "A little leaven leaveneth the whole lump" (v. 9). Such refuting of error should be done not only in a most friendly manner, as Paul does in the fourth chapter of Galatians, when he says: "Ye observe days and months and times and years. I am afraid of you lest I have bestowed upon you labor in vain" (vv. 10-11), but also very positively and even vehemently, as the same Apostle does in the first chapter of Galatians, when he states: "As we said before, so say I now again: If any man preach any other gospel unto you than that ye have received, let him be accursed" (v. 9). Or we think of Phil. 3:2: "Beware of dogs, beware of evil workers, beware of the concision." If necessary, the name of the sect as well as the name of the false teacher must be mentioned, as Christ did when He said: "Take heed and beware of the leaven of the Pharisees and of the Sadducees" (Matt. 16:6), and as Paul did II Tim. 2:17-18: "And their word will eat as doth a canker, of whom is Hymenaeus and Philetus, who concerning the truth have erred, saying that the resurrection is passed already and overthrow the faith of some."

To Titus Paul writes, and this applies to every teacher of the Church, that he should "hold fast the faithful Word as he hath been taught, that he may be able by sound doctrine both to exhort and to convince the gainsayers. For there are many unruly and vain talkers and deceivers, specially they of the circumcision, whose mouths must be stopped, who subvert whole houses, teaching things which they ought not, for filthy lucre's sake" (Titus 1:9-11). Whoever teaches the true doctrine, but does not warn against false doctrine and against wolves in sheep's clothing (Matt. 7:15), is not a faithful steward of the mysteries of God, not a faithful shepherd of the sheep entrusted to his care, not a trusty watchman on the walls of Zion, but, as the Word of God says, a wicked servant, a dumb dog, a traitor. It is evident that many souls are lost, because they are not warned against false doctrine, which is poison to the soul. Moreover, the true doctrine is better understood when the false doctrine is placed in juxtaposition. Hence the Formula of Concord says: "Every simple Christian can perceive what is right or wrong, when not only the pure doctrine has been stated, but also the erroneous, contrary doctrine has been repudiated and rejected" (*Triglot*, 837). False teachers transforming themselves into apostles of Christ (II Cor. 11:13-14), present their false doctrines in such terms that even those who love the truth are easily deceived, if they have not been warned. To be forewarned is to be forearmed.

When error is refuted, it should be done in a very thorough manner. A cold and indifferent refutation of error is really a strong confirmation of it. Hence, the teacher of the Church should carefully, if possible from original sources, study the false doctrine which he wishes to refute, make sure that he presents it just as those who teach it, and quote Scripture passages which clearly condemn it. In order to be better prepared to refute error, the teacher of the Church must be thoroughly at home in the doctrines of the Scripture and in the Confessions of his Church. He should "give attendance to reading" (I Tim. 4:13), and our congregations should see to it that their pastors and teachers have ample time for study.

The members of our congregations must not take it amiss when their pastor refutes error. He is doing this in obedience to the Word of God and is following the example set by the Prophets, by Jesus, and by the Apostles. After all, our congregations have called their pastors and are paying their pastors to proclaim to them the truth as it is found in the Scriptures in accordance with the Confessions of the Lutheran Church. And when their pastors faithfully do this, the congregations, realizing that error is poison to the soul, will be grateful to the Lord for having given them faithful shepherds, and not hirelings who flee when the wolf approaches.

VII

It Is the Duty of Every Christian to Avoid Error and Fellowship with Errorists

False doctrine is a sin against God's holy Commandments. It jeopardizes the salvation of every person who comes in contact with it. Hence, it is evident that every Christian is to avoid false doctrine and all fellowship with errorists.

That we are to avoid false doctrine is stated in Scripture in all those passages that exhort us to abide in the truth. We are to observe all things whatsoever Jesus has commanded us. (Matt. 28:20.) Paul writes to Timothy: "As I besought thee to abide still at Ephesus, when I went into Macedonia, that thou mightest charge some that they teach no other doctrine" (I Tim. 1:3). Again: "Hold fast the form of sound words, which thou hast heard of me" (II Tim. 1:13), and: "Continue thou in the things which thou hast learned and hast been assured of" (II Tim. 3:14). Paul exhorts the Thessalonians: "Therefore, brethren, stand fast, and hold the traditions which ye have been taught, whether by word or by our epistle" (II Thess. 2:15). We should not be "children, tossed to and fro, and carried about with every wind of doctrine" (Eph. 4:14). We should "hold fast our profession" (Heb. 4:14) and not be "carried about with divers and strange doctrines" (Heb. 13:9).

We are to continue in purity of doctrine also in view of those passages in which the Lord denounces those who deviate from the truth. "Behold, I am against the prophets, saith the Lord, that use their tongues and say: He saith" (Jer. 23:31). "Whosoever therefore shall break one of these least commandments and shall teach men so, he shall be called the least in the kingdom of heaven" (Matt. 5:19).

In view of these passages, truth and error cannot fellowship with each other. "Can two walk together except they be agreed?" (Amos 3:3.) How can I recognize him as a brother in the faith, worship with him, and do joint spiritual work with him whom I must condemn as an errorist? For me to give countenance and sanction to false doctrine, as I would do by fellowshiping with one who teaches otherwise, would mean to share in the responsibility for all the harm false doctrine does. I would thereby become the partaker of the errorist's evil deeds. (II John 11.)

But the Scriptures actually forbid spiritual association with those who depart from the truth. Rom. 16:17 we read: "Now I beseech you, brethren, mark them which cause divisions and offenses contrary to the doctrine which ye have learned; and avoid them." II John 10—11: "If there come any unto you and bring not this doctrine, receive him not into your house, neither bid him Godspeed; for he that biddeth him Godspeed is partaker of his evil deeds." II Thess. 3:6: "Now we command you, brethren, in the name of our Lord Jesus Christ, that ye withdraw yourselves from every brother that walketh disorderly and not after the tradition which he received of us." Alexander, the coppersmith, withstood the words, marginal reading, the preachings, of Paul, hence Paul writes Timothy: "Of whom be thou ware also" (II Tim. 4:15). To Titus Paul states: "A man that is an heretic after the first and second admonition reject" (Titus 3:10). And finally there are the words of the Savior: "Beware of false prophets which come to you in sheep's clothing, but inwardly they are ravening wolves" (Matt. 7:15). Now these terms: "avoid them," "shun," "receive not," "greet not," "withdraw," reduced to terms of our day, mean that we are to refuse church fellowship with those who depart from the truth and continue not in the wholesome words of the Savior.

And let us note furthermore, that these passages make no difference between so-called fundamental and non-fundamental errors. We are to observe all things whatsoever the Lord has commanded us, whether they be classified by us as fundamental or non-fundamental. Says Dr. Luther: "The Holy Ghost (who speaks in all words of the Scriptures) does no permit Himself to be parted or divided that He should permit one point to be taught or be believed as true and the other as false." Our own Synod at its Fort Wayne convention in 1941 declared "that it be understood that the term non-fundamental doctrine which has been used should not be made to convey the idea that anything clearly revealed in Scripture, although not absolutely necessary for salvation, may be denied." Again Luther said: "We are bound to keep all articles of the Christian doctrine, great and small ones (we do not consider any one of them small), pure and certain. We consider this of great importance, and it is necessary."

To fellowship with such as do not agree with us in doctrine is called unionism. And we repudiate unionism, that is, joint church work or worship with adherents of unorthodox church bodies, because thereby the truth is either denied or the appearance of denial or at least of indifferentism is given in disobedience to God's command, as causing divisions in the Church (Rom. 16:17; II John 9:10) and as involving the constant danger of losing the Word of God entirely. (II Tim. 2:17-18; Gal. 5:9.)

The only fellowship which we can recognize is that which springs from the unity of faith and doctrine. Church fellowship without the fellowship of faith and confession is not expressive of the unity of the one holy Christian Church (Eph. 4:3-6), but is merely a sham unity, which confines the errorist in his delusion and breeds indifference to the truth. Unionism is wicked and pernicious and utterly condemned by Scripture.

VIII

In Her Attitude Towards Truth and Error the Lutheran Church from Her Very Beginning Has Been Obedient to Scripture

The Scriptural injunction to uphold divine truth and to denounce error has been characteristic of the Lutheran Church since her very beginning. This becomes evident when we study the origin of the Reformation, the Confessions of the Lutheran Church, Luther's polemics, the discipline of the early Lutheran Church, and the controversies within the Lutheran Church after Luther's death until the writing of the Formula of Concord.

The Reformation was brought about by preaching the truths of Scripture. Luther did not attack the life of the prelates and Popes of the Roman Catholic Church, but his attacks were directed against its false doctrine. Luther said: "Every Reformation which is to be undertaken will prove to be useless unless the doctrine is purified." In his work of reforming the Church, Luther emphasized and restored the great principles of the supreme authority of the Scriptures in all matters of faith and life, justification by faith, and the universal priesthood of all believers, and by this teaching wrought his wonderful work.

Likewise the Confessions of our Church underscore true doctrine and reject all error. The Lutheran Confessions were born of controversies and therefore state the truth and refute aberration from the truth. In the Augsburg Confession ten articles specifically reject error, and in the last seven articles such errors are reviewed as have been corrected by the Protestants. The Formula of Concord in its eleven articles consistently states first the principal question in the controversy, next the doctrine of the Christian Church concerning the controversy, and finally the false, contrary doctrine. In the 12th, and last, article, the Formula of Concord treats the errors of other factions and sects which never embraced the Augsburg Confession. And it concludes with the words: "These and like articles, one and all, with what pertains to them and follows from them, we reject and condemn as wrong, false, heretical, contrary to the Word of God, the three Creeds, the Augsburg Confession and Apology, the Smalcald Articles and Luther's Catechisms. Of these articles all godly Christians should and ought to beware, as much as the welfare and salvation of their souls is dear to them"

(*Triglot*, 1103). Our confessions, indeed, are outspoken in presenting the truth of Scripture and in denouncing error.

The discipline of the early Lutheran Church likewise was in accord with its confession and practice with reference to error. Says the Formula of Concord: "And so far as it depends on our service, we will not connive at or be silent lest anything contrary to the same [the genuine and sacred sense of the Augsburg Confession] is introduced into our churches and schools, in which the almighty God and Father of our Lord Jesus Christ has appointed us teachers and pastors" (*Triglot*, 1097). To quote just one case. John Saliger, pastor in Rostock, was removed from office because he stated and adhered to his statement that as soon as the words of institution are read, before the distribution and apart from the use of the consecrated bread and wine in Holy Communion, the bread and wine has become the body and blood of Christ.

The Scriptural attitude toward truth and error was shown furthermore in the polemics of the early Lutheran Church. Luther not only exposed the errors of the Papacy, he also attacked the wrong doctrines of the enthusiasts and of the Reformed Zwingli. Naturally Luther has been and still is being charged with having been unduly vicious in his controversies, of having disturbed the peace, and of fighting about insignificant matters. But to Luther every teaching against the Word of God, be it ever so slight, was an error which threatened to destroy the entire doctrine. Said he: "In philosophy a small error in the beginning is a very serious error in the end. So also in theology a slight error will destroy the whole doctrine. For the doctrine is like a mathematical point; it cannot be divided, that is, it cannot brook either subtraction or addition. Hence, the doctrine must be one certain, perpetual, and round golden ring, in which there is no break. If even the least break occurs, the ring is no longer perfect." St. Louis, IX:644.

After Luther's death the Lutheran Church was torn by strife and dissention. There were chiefly seven controversies which caused much heartache and bitterness: the Adiaphoristic, the Osiandrian, the Majoristic, the Synergistic, the Antinomian, the Flacian, and the Crypto-Calvinistic. It would have been, humanly speaking, perhaps more expedient if the Lutheran theologians had overlooked the differences in question and joined hands in the critical days in which they were living. But the genuine Lutherans of the day would not yield for a moment, that the truth of the Gospel might be upheld. They loved the truth and would not enter upon relations of church fellowship with those who espoused the untruth. Although many thought that only minor errors were involved, the genuine Lutherans stated that "the controversies which have occurred are not, as some would regard them, mere misunderstandings or disputes concerning words" (*Triglot*, 849).

Therefore the Formula of Concord, which settled the controversies, states: "From this our explanation, friends and enemies, and therefore everyone, may clearly infer that we have no intention of yielding aught of the eternal, immutable truth of God for the sake of temporal peace, tranquillity, and unity (which moreover, is not in our power to do). Nor would such peace and unity, since it is devised against the truth and for its suppression, have any permanency. Still less are we inclined to adorn and conceal a corruption of the pure doctrine and manifest condemned errors. But we entertain heartfelt pleasure and love for, and on our part are sincerely inclined and anxious to advance, that unity according to our utmost power, by which His glory remains to God uninjured, nothing of the divine truth of the holy Gospel is surrendered, no room is given to the least error, poor sinners are brought to true, genuine repentance, raised up by faith, confirmed in obedience, and thus justified and eternally saved alone through the sole merit of Christ." (*Triglot*, 1095.)

IX

The Missouri Synod Since the Day of Its Organization Has Followed the Confessional Lutheran Church in Its Attitude Towards Truth and Error

The fathers and founders of our Synod have by the grace of God followed in the footsteps of the genuine Lutherans of the 16th century with reference to the Scriptural injunctions regarding truth and error. Already before the organization of the Missouri Synod, the component groups, the Saxons and the Loehe men, had striven valiantly for the faith delivered to the fathers. The Saxons had fought against and freed themselves from the hierarchical dogmas foisted upon them by Stephan, notably in the well-known Altenburg Debate of 1841. The Loehe men under the leadership of Sihler contended against the unionism of the Ohio Synod and the Michigan Synod and severed their connection with these bodies when they refused to submit to the teachings of Scripture and the Confessions of our Church. Wyneken acted in accordance with the principles of confessional Lutheranism when he left the General Synod in 1845, because it refused to reject the teachings and practices of those who were advocating a so-called American Lutheranism.

After its organization the Missouri Synod became involved in a number of controversies, and although, humanly speaking, it might have been more advantageous to compromise with error, our Synod remained steadfastly confessional in its Lutheranism, which means to say, it remained Scriptural. The early members of our Synod were not separatistic, nor were they fond of polemics. They did not love controversy, but they did love God's Word more than a sham peace and friendship of men, and so they simply had to expose error and defend the truth. They contended with the Buffalo Synod about the doctrines of the Church and the office of the ministry, excommunication, and ordination. They testified against the Iowa Synod with reference to the doctrine of Sunday and Chiliasm. They stood up for the truth against their former brethren, the Ohio Synod, in the controversy on election and conversion.

Throughout all these controversies our Synod by the grace of God remained true to its Confessions, and therefore, true to Scripture. It fought the good fight of faith without any respect of person.

And its fidelity to Scripture and to the Confessions has been acknowledged as the source of the vitality and strength of our Synod. Wrote Dr. Lenski of the Ohio Synod in the *Kirchenzeitung* of May 20, 1922: "If there ever was a strictly conservative body, it surely is the Missouri Synod. Nevertheless, this growth! Here is a historical fact that refutes all talk trying to persuade us that we must be liberal, accommodate ourselves to the spirit of the time, etc., in order to win men and grow externally. The very opposite is seen in the Missouri Synod. Missouri has at all times been unyielding; it is so still. In this body the Scriptures and the Confessions have been, and still are, valued to their full import. There was no disposition to surrender any part of them. With this asset Missouri has been working in free America, abounding in sects and religious confusion, and now exhibits its enormous achievements. What so many regard as Missouri's weakness has in reality been her strength. This fact we might write down for our own remembrance. It is a mark of the pastors and leaders of the Missouri Synod that they never, aye, never, tire of discussing doctrine on the basis of Scripture and the Confessions. That is one trait that may be called the spirit of Missouri. People who thus cling to doctrine and contend for its purity are of an entirely different nature from the superficial unionists who in the critical moment will declare five to be an even number. God will bless all who value His Word so highly. Gratitude towards God, who has granted this division of American Lutheranism so much glorious blessing, and through Missouri has communicated this blessing also to other parts of the Lutheran Church, will be the basic note of this festival celebration. May God keep Missouri and us and all Lutheran Christians faithful in the doctrine and confession of His Word and grant us His blessing for our external growth and prosperity."

We are the heirs of the labors of the fathers. We are what we are by the grace of God. "Who maketh thee to differ from another? And what hast thou that thou didst not receive? Now, if thou didst receive it, why dost thou glory as if thou hadst not received it?" (I Cor. 4:7. Cf. also Rev. 3:7-10.)

Let us, therefore, watch and pray so that we lose not the doctrine entrusted to us. Luther writes: "It is not my doctrine, not the product of my mind, but God's gift. Good Lord, I have not spun it out of my head; it did not grow in my garden; it did not flow from my spring; it was not born of men. It is God's gift, not any invention of man." "We are nothing; Christ alone is all. If He turn away His face, we must perish, and Satan will triumph, even though we were as holy as Peter and Paul. Let us, therefore, humble ourselves under the mighty hand of God, that He may exalt us in due time, for God resisteth the proud and giveth grace to the humble." I Pet. 5:6, 5. (VIII:27; XIV:455.)

Church Fellowship

THE service had come to an end. The plain little church building had been dedicated to the service of the Triune God. It was such a simple little building, unfinished, unplastered on the inside, with homemade wooden benches without backs; and yet the service had been heart-warming. One middle-aged woman, who spoke to the pastor at the door with tears on her cheeks, put it into words. "Pastor," she said, "when I left home with my family three years ago to come to this prairie, I did not really appreciate what it meant to have a church and to belong to a congregation. We just took those things for granted. You'll never know what it has meant to me after three years without a church to worship once more in company with fellow Christians. I felt so at home here in this little church today." That woman was experiencing the joy of true church fellowship.

This joyful appreciation of true church fellowship is the keynote of three essays on this subject. Two of them were read at gatherings of the Synodical Conference, one in 1873 by Dr. W. Sihler, the other in 1880 by Dr. F. Pieper; and the third was read by Pastor J. M. Buehler to the small group of pastors and delegates who had met in 1888 to organize the first District of our Church on the Pacific Coast. These men knew what a blessing true church fellowship is, what a precious, joyful possession it can be. They prized it highly and wanted their brethren in faith to realize its great value, to seek such fellowship, to be ever alert to preserve it, and to bring its blessings to as many people as they could reach. This joyful appreciation must be ours today. With this emphasis in mind, we take up, on the basis of the three essays mentioned, our study of Church Fellowship.

I

The basis of true church fellowship is personal fellowship with Christ by faith. This saving faith, begotten by the Holy Ghost through the Word, and this faith alone, is the inward, invisible bond of fellowship truly uniting all believers into one spiritual body.

Fellowship is a communion, an association, of like-minded people, a sharing together by people that have a community of interest. Church fellowship is such an associating and communion on the spiritual level. That which binds folks together in true church fellowship is something inward and invisible. It is saving faith in Christ Jesus. The Apostle said: "Ye are all the children of God by faith in Christ Jesus . . . ye are all one in Christ Jesus" (Gal. 3:26-28). The basis of true church fellowship is personal fellowship with Christ by faith. Unless we have that, there is no church fellowship, no matter what else we have. Jesus recognizes a oneness with Himself on the basis of faith alone, and this oneness with God makes for oneness of the believers with each other. He declares: "Neither pray I for these alone, but for them also *which shall believe on Me through their word,* that they may be one, as Thou, Father, art in Me, and I in Thee; *that they also may be one in Us*" (John 17:20-21).

We must be careful to put and keep first things first in this whole matter of church fellowship. It seems of the utmost importance to some that they have a complete church organization, highly developed, that they have the good old church customs and forms, that they have what makes for a Lutheran church outwardly. It is for this they work without ceasing. The danger in such efforts is that the one great effort is neglected, to win souls for Christ and to bring them into fellowship with Christ and to keep them there. Lutheran forms and usages have their place, and good organization has its purpose, but you can have all these outward things and not have true church fellowship. You might lack some of these forms, and still, having fellowship with Christ through faith, you would have true church fellowship.

That is Rome's great error. It avers that the Church is "a gathering of men so visible and palpable as is that of the Roman people or the kingdom of Gaul or the republic of Venice." "Where a priest is celebrating the Mass, there is the Church, even if there is no one present who is in fellowship with Christ by faith." (Bellarmine, quoted in Mueller, *Christian Dogmatics*, p. 548.)

We must never put our Lutheran Church as an organization first and faith in Christ, which it preaches, second or last if we wish to maintain and preserve the precious treasure of true church fellowship. There may be men and women who confess the same faith and participate with us in the same forms outwardly, but they may be outside the true fellowship, for they may lack fellowship with Christ by faith. Without that faith they lack the inward, invisible bond which alone unites all believers into one spiritual body.

In this inward, invisible fellowship are included all believers, all children of God. There may be differences in age, sex, calling, and culture. There may be differences in race and color, for there are white and black, brown and yellow and red Christians. There may be differences in conditions, some living as free people, others as slaves, some toiling as common laborers, others surrounded by wealth. They may even be separated outwardly by the fact that they belong to different church denominations; yet in their common faith they have something that ties them together in a marvelous manner into one body, of which Christ is the one Head.

What is this faith? It is faith in Christ, the Savior. It is justifying faith, saving faith, begotten by the Holy Ghost through the Gospel of Christ. It is not a mere conviction that there is a God. It is not a faith in a man-made Christ, fashioned after man's reason into a superman whose great goodness shines as a beacon light for others to follow. It is not the faith that trusts, at least in some measure, in its own merits. Such a faith cannot save men or bring them into fellowship with Christ. The Apostle declares: "Knowing that a man is not justified by the works of the Law, but by the faith of Jesus Christ, even we have believed in Jesus Christ, that we might be justified by the faith of Christ and not by the works of the Law" (Gal. 2:16).

Saving faith is the "faith of the Son of God, who loved me and gave Himself for me" (Gal. 2.20). This faith the Galatians received by the working of God's Spirit, and the Spirit came to them and worked in them not by the works of the Law, but by the hearing of faith, by the Gospel (Gal. 3:2). Through this faith they had become children of God (Gal. 3:26). Through this faith they had peace with God and hope of eternal life (Rom. 5:1-2).

Of those that have this faith St. Paul says: "There is neither Jew nor Greek, there is neither bond nor free, there is neither male nor female; for ye are all one in Christ" (Gal. 3:28).

Through that fellowship with Christ in faith all Christians do have a unity of spirit. If a man or woman in the Roman Catholic camp has saving faith, it is not because of the official teaching of Rome that man is saved by faith and works, but despite that teaching. It is because the Spirit through the Gospel still found in the Roman Church, has brought that man or woman to trust wholly in Jesus as the Savior and in nothing else, that he or she is of one spirit with all other believers. The inward bond that binds believers is saving faith in Christ. Of course, where there is no Gospel, there can be no saving faith; for the Gospel alone is "the power of God unto salvation." In church bodies that have lost the message of the crucified Christ and Savior, there is no true Christian fellowship. They lack God's means for begetting saving faith in the hearts of men. Yes, saving faith in Christ is the only inward bond that binds together.

There is one body of Christ, and there is only one faith that binds together in the unity of the Spirit. And this is the faith of every child of God, wherever he may be. A child of God in another Church than the Lutheran has truly no other saving faith in his heart than a believing Lutheran has. Let us not forget that there may be a hypocritical Lutheran with whom we seem to be very closely united in all doctrines of God's Word, and yet, because he has not saving faith in his heart, we are really not united in Spirit. That is why we speak of the bond of saving faith in Christ as the only inward and invisible bond that truly binds all children of God into one spiritual body. The Apology says: "The Church is not only the fellowship of outward objects and rites, as other governments, but it is originally a fellowship of faith and of the Holy Ghost in hearts" (Art. VII, *Triglot*, 227). Luther declares: "Christendom means an assembly or congregation of all believers in Christ on earth, as we pray in the Creed: I believe in the Holy

Ghost, a communion of saints. This congregation or assembly consists of all those who live in true faith, love, and hope, so that the essence, nature, and life of Christendom is not an outward assembly, but a gathering of hearts in one faith, as St. Paul says (Eph. 4:5): one Baptism, one faith, one Lord. Therefore though they be separated bodily thousands of miles, they are nevertheless called a congregation in the Spirit, because each one preaches, believes, hopes, loves, and lives as does the other. . . . Without this spiritual unity, no unity, whether it be of place, time, person, or work, constitutes *one* Christendom." (St. Louis, XVIII:1013 f.)

II

This inward, invisible fellowship should manifest itself according to God's will in outward, visible fellowship of believers in the local congregation and beyond the local congregation. We recognize fellow believers by their confession of a faith based on God's Word and expressed in the Confessions of the Lutheran Church. This confession of faith constitutes the outward bond of fellowship.

Dr. Pieper tells the story of a prominent heathen who had been converted to the Christian faith, who, however, refused to have any outward fellowship with other Christians. He refused to attend their meetings and services. When he was reminded that this was his Christian duty, he asked mockingly: "Does Christianity cling to the church walls?" There are people that say: "If the basis of true church fellowship is saving faith and nothing else, then I see no need of joining a local congregation and practicing outward fellowship. I have that which is essential, why demand more?" Such a person shows a remarkable lack of understanding of what church fellowship means and implies. His attitude shows that he does not know and realize that by faith in Christ he has entered into an intimate fellowship with Christ and through Christ, the Head, with His body, the Church. "We, being many, are one body" (I Cor. 10:17). Close fellowship with believers in Christ is not something that is real to him, or he would be eager to practice it. It is nothing precious to him, or he would prize it. Such an attitude, persisted in, can and does quickly lead to loss of fellowship with Christ.

Scripture considers the practice of church fellowship of such importance that it repeatedly speaks of it as a matter of course on the part of every believer. Saving faith can never be inactive. It is bound openly to confess the Savior. Faith and confession go together. "With the heart man believeth unto righteousness, and with the mouth confession is made unto salvation" (Rom. 10:10). Righteousness and salvation, which belong together, are ascribed to the man that believes and confesses, so that it is clearly shown that these two acts of the child of God belong together. In practice you cannot separate the one from the other. Now, it is true, a man can stand all alone and confess his Lord, but how can he continue to stand alone if he finds others that are confessing Him, too? Shall we be ashamed of them and their confession? Hearken to what Christ says: "Whosoever shall be ashamed of *Me and of My words* in this adulterous and sinful generation, of him also shall the Son of Man be ashamed when He cometh in the glory of His Father with the holy angels" (Mark 8:38). There were men in the days of Jesus who heard His Word and believed on Him. But because they were ashamed to come out openly, step to the side of Christ and His disciples and confess Him with them, they were censured severely: "they loved the praise of man more than the praise of God" (John 12:42-43). There is something wrong with a faith that will refuse to seek the company of fellow confessors and openly declare for Jesus.

It is true, a Christian should sing with grace *in his heart* to the Lord and should let the Word of Christ dwell *in him* richly with all wisdom (Col. 3:16); but the same Apostle declares he should also do that in fellowship with those of the same faith, "teaching and admonishing *one another* in psalms and hymns and spiritual songs." It is true, a Christian should search the Scripture privately and find Christ in it for himself (John 5:39); but the same Christian should get busy to do his part with fellow Christians in setting up and maintaining the ministry in their midst so that they can and will hear the Word and use the Sacraments in fellowship with one another. We read in Holy Scripture again and again that the Apostles gathered such groups of people, preached to them, formed them into congregations of confessing believers, and "ordained them elders in every church" (Acts 14:23), which means, they had them elect and choose pastors by the raising of hands. To Titus, Paul writes: "For this cause left I thee in Crete, that thou shouldest set in order the things that are wanting and ordain elders in every city, as I had appointed thee" (Titus 1:5).

In short, that believers in Christ should gather together in local congregations, establish the public ministry in their midst, and jointly use the means of grace is not a matter that lies in the discretion of the child of God; it is something that his Lord wants him to do and expects him to do without fail. Christians are to continue steadfastly "in fellowship" (Acts 2:42). Nor are we to forsake "the assembling of ourselves together, as the manner of some is," (Heb. 10:25). That is our blessed privilege, that is God's will, that all believers be joined to local congregations in true church fellowship.

God has nowhere expressed it as His will that Christian congregations must organize in the form of synods and larger church bodies. There are examples in Scripture showing us that it is a good and wise and commendable and God-pleasing thing when Christians far beyond the limits of the local congregation counsel together and work together to carry forward the work of the Lord. When the question of the place of the ceremonial laws in the lives of the Christians had become a burning issue, the Apostles did not counsel that the churches at Antioch and at Jerusalem do as they pleased in this matter, but they called a meeting in Jerusalem, at which both were represented and all interested brethren were given the floor. The joint decision reached as brethren was then published. If church fellowship means anything to us, it is self-evident that we will seek such fellowship beyond the local congregation and joyfully and diligently practice it.

Joining together in a synod is not commanded of God as the form of fellowship we must set up beyond the local congregation, but it is God's will that we acknowledge fellow believers beyond our local congregation as brethren confessing the same faith with us. The Apostle Paul says to Timothy: "Be not thou therefore ashamed of the testimony of our Lord nor of me, His prisoner" (II Tim. 1:8). Accordingly Timothy *must* acknowledge Paul as his fellow confessor and brother in faith. If he is ashamed of Paul because of his confession, he will be ashamed of Christ. Hear what Luther says about confessing His name: "I observe that a good admonition must be administered to those whom Satan now begins to persecute. There are some among them who would escape danger, when being attacked, by saying, 'I am not siding with Luther nor with anybody, but with the holy Gospel and with the Church, or with the Roman Church.' By such tactics they secure their personal peace, and yet in their heart they regard my doctrine as evangelical and adhere to it. Verily, such a profession does not help them; it is the same as if they had denied Christ. Hence I pray these people to have care. True, you must not on your life and soul say: 'I am a Lutheran or papist'; for neither Luther nor the Pope has died for you, nor is he your master, but Christ alone, and to Him you must profess allegiance. But if you hold that Luther's teaching is evangelical, and the Pope's unevangelical, *you must not utterly cast Luther aside*, or you will cast his teaching aside, which you regard as the teaching of Christ." (St. Louis, XX:90 f.) Here Luther clearly states the principle that true fellowship must manifest itself even beyond the local congregation, wherever we find fellow believers, and he also shows how we can recognize such fellow believers. "If you hold that Luther's teaching is evangelical," then, says Luther, "you must not utterly cast Luther aside." Men who confess with us the same faith based on God's Word are men whom we will and must fellowship.

The reason for this is clear. It is a deplorable, yet undeniable fact that there are many that appeal to Scripture, but wrest its meaning and therefore bring doctrines that are strange and unscriptural. It becomes necessary, therefore, that Christians declare in clear and unmistakable words what they hold to be the true meaning of God's Word. This the Lutheran Church has done in its public Confessions. There it has clearly expressed what every true Lutheran believes on the basis of God's Word, and there it has clearly shown that what it confesses is the clear teaching of God's Word. This is in full keeping with Christ's Word. Christ did not say: "He that says he believes the Bible but then proceeds to teach any other doctrine than the Bible teaches is My disciple." Christ declared: "If ye continue in My Word, then are ye My disciples indeed; and ye shall know the truth, and the truth shall make you free" (John 8:31-32). He wants a clear-cut confession, so that everyone may know where we stand, with or against Him.

All that confess Him thus are His disciples. They belong together, and they also practice church fellowship by continuing at all times in this clear confession of the Apostles' doctrine (Acts 2:42).

Therefore our Church has always demanded that men whom we fellowship must accept the three Ecumenical Creeds, the Apostles' Creed, the Nicene Creed, and the Athanasian Creed, for they clearly answer the question: What think ye of Christ and His work? What think ye of God? They clearly express what God's Word says about these important articles of faith in antithesis to the many false, misleading, and soul-destroying teachings of men prominent in the counsels of many denominations. We cannot fellowship men that will not accept these Confessions as their very own in the exact sense in which they are written, for such men refuse to continue in Christ's Word and in the Apostles' doctrines, they will not confess Christ as He wants to be confessed. Therefore our Church has also always recognized those who subscribe to the particular Confessions of the Lutheran Church, the Augsburg Confession and Luther's Small Catechism in particular, as fellow believers and fellow Lutherans whom we can acknowledge as such, for they are in agreement of faith with us. With such we joyfully enter into visible and outward fellowship, for this confession of faith is the outward bond of such fellowship.

III

It is God's will that the believers should always be intent to keep the outward bond of fellowship intact so that God's Word is purely taught and the practice of the Church is in harmony with that teaching. Believers who because of lack of knowledge do not comply with God's command to continue in His Word and as a result have fellowship with errorists, separate themselves from fellow believers that continue in all of God's Word and thus destroy the outward bond of fellowship.

When Christ declared: "Whosoever, therefore, shall confess Me before men, him will I confess also before My Father which is in heaven" (Matt. 10:32), He wanted a confession of Himself, as He is identified in His Word. His disciples are not to say: Christ is Elias, Christ is John the Baptist, Christ is another of the Prophets. They must confess Him as He is: Christ, the Son of the living

God. In their confession they are also to keep the unity of faith and confess one Lord, one faith, one Baptism. They are to teach all things whatsoever He has commanded (Matt. 28:10). They are to mark and avoid those that are the causers of divisions and offenses contrary to the doctrine they have learned (Rom. 16:17), for these disrupt the bond of fellowship. They are not to become guilty of divisions among themselves. They must confess all of Christ, the Christ that rose from the dead, the Christ that taught, let us say, Infant Baptism, or whatever else He has taught us in His Word. That is the way in which to keep the outward bond of fellowship intact. What untold damage men did in the past to the cause of Christ when they rent asunder the bond of fellowship that joined them with fellow believers by setting up teachings that were not Christ's! At Trent it was Rome that made the rift in the Church greater with its denial of justification by faith alone and its insistence upon salvation by infused grace, by which man was said to be made capable of saving himself. At Marburg it was Zwingli with his rationalizing spirit that refused to accept the Real Presence in the Lord's Supper. Later it was Wittenberg under Melanchthon that advocated synergism by finding in man a faculty to apply himself to grace. God does not want this to happen in His Church. He wants His children to keep the outward bond of fellowship intact so that His Word is purely taught and confessed by them.

He also wants the practice of the Church to be in harmony with His teaching. There are some who have said: Why be so insistent upon practice? Article VII of the Augsburg Confession states: "The Church is the congregation of the saints, in which *the Gospel is rightly taught* and the Sacraments are rightly administered. And to the true unity of the Church *it is enough to agree concerning the Gospel* and the administration of the Sacraments." (*Triglot*, p. 47.) We must, however, never forget that confession is not only a matter of words, but it also must show itself in deeds. The Apostle Paul declares that in Jesus Christ the faith that availeth anything is the faith that worketh by love (Gal. 5:6).

Jesus declares: "Not everyone that saith unto Me, Lord, Lord, shall enter into the kingdom of heaven; but he that doeth the will of My Father which is in heaven" (Matt. 7:21). Paul writes to Titus (1:16): "They profess that they know God, but in works they deny Him." Luther, speaking of the truly Christian and holy people of God, states that this people can be recognized by the Word of God that it has and possesses and confesses. He put it this way: "Wherever you hear such a Word or see it being preached, believed, confessed and *people doing according to it*, doubt not but that there assuredly must be a true *ecclesia sancta catholica*, a Christian, holy people, I Peter 2:9, though their number be but small." (*Von den Conciliis und Kirchen*, vom Jahr 1539. Hall. A. XVI, 2785 ss. — Synodical Conference, 1875, p. 8.)

Now, it is true, when it comes to our "doing according to the Word," we will often fall short of the mark. Nor would we want to say that a church whose practice is not always in perfect harmony with the Word of God thereby destroys the bond of fellowship between it and other fellow confessors. Again and again our practice, even as a church group, does not keep up with our profession. We must ever be conscious of the fact that we come short and daily need the pardoning grace of God because of these failings and weaknesses. What dare not occur, if our confession is to be an honest one, is that we tolerate, justify, and defend false practice, though this practice can be shown from God's Word to be out of harmony with that Word. We dare not justify and promote altar and pulpit fellowship with errorists, ignoring their errors and treating their departure from the Word of Christ as unimportant and inconsequential. We dare not ignore the fact that those Lutherans who assume the obligations of the Masonic order or other similar lodges with rituals which demand joint worship and prayer that ignore Christ Crucified and all He stands for are unequally yoked together with unbelievers. To refuse to recognize this fact, to defend this yoking together, and not to point such Lutherans to the Apostle's call "Come out from among them" (II Cor. 6:17) is certainly not confessing Christ.

Again and again wickedness and ungodliness will manifest itself in Christian congregations. That in itself does not mark those congregations as ungodly or anti-Christian bodies. When, however, congregations tolerate such gross sins and harbor such sinners in their midst without admonition, that is not confessing Christ and His Word. Such persistent indifference to, and toleration of, evil despite all admonition of fellow believers in other congregations will eventually destroy the bond of fellowship once uniting these congregations with others, for such a course, persisted in, will eventually lead to the denial of the need of repentance and the need of the saving Christ. If we prize the active fellowship of faith that is ours, we must hold to purity of doctrine and to a practice in harmony with the teachings of God's Word.

Men have sometimes set up standards for outward fellowship different from those we have just mentioned. Forms of church government, whether by elders or by bishops; orders of service and rituals, whether there be only Psalms sung or other hymns permitted, whether a prayer be chanted or spoken, whether certain pictures and statues be permitted in the church or not — all these and many other church rites and forms have been declared so important that fellowship was refused on the ground of difference at this point. We do well to recall what our Augsburg Confession states in Article VII: "Nor is it necessary that human traditions, that is rites or ceremonies, instituted by men, should be everywhere alike." (*Triglot*, p. 47.)

Uniformity in these things may be very desirable. To move from place to place and to find the same hymnbook in use in the church services, to have the children use the same Catechism, to be greeted with familiar hymns and a familiar order of church service, is certainly helpful and desirable, but God has not demanded such uniformity for conscience' sake; neither must we. Ceremonies, church customs, like sponsors at Baptisms, midweek Lenten services, and many more arrangements may well serve the congregation in bringing children and adults to their Savior and keeping them with Him. Yet we must remember, God has not commanded them; therefore we dare not refuse to enter into fellowship with anyone because he has not accepted all of our church customs as we practice them.

What about the believers in churches with which we are not in outward fellowship because these churches uphold teachings that are contrary to God's Word? We know there are believers in these churches, for the Gospel of the redeeming love of God in Christ is still being preached there. Despite the error that is mixed with the truth in such churches, the Gospel manifests itself as the power of God unto salvation in such groups also. We know that the Word of God never returns void; it accomplishes that which God pleases; it prospers in the thing whereunto God sends it (Is. 55:11).

We have an example of that in II Sam. 15. There we are told that Absalom stole the hearts of the men of Israel by leading them to believe that his father, King David, was a very unjust and unfair judge and that he, Absalom, would give them a very fair deal. And now we read: "And with Absalom went two hundred men out of Jerusalem that were called; and they went in their simplicity, and they knew not anything" (II Sam. 15:11). It would seem that Absalom's purpose must have been evident to all. Yet God's Spirit tells us that it was not apparent to these two hundred men. Does it seem impossible to you that sincere believers in Christ in churches where error is mixed with truth do not know that this error is taught and held in their midst? It is not impossible. Perhaps they have been born into that church body, brought up in its teachings from early youth. Perhaps they have been led by persistent appeals to reason and the Scripture to believe that God teaches, for instance, that infants are not to be baptized, that God's Word and the Sacraments are not the means of grace whereby God's Spirit creates and preserves faith in men's hearts. Yet the Cross of Christ has taken hold of their hearts and lives, and they have been led by the Holy Spirit, through the message of the Cross, to cast all their sins on Jesus. They trust Him for all things in life and in death. They are truly fellow believers.

However, you and I do not know this. God alone knows them that are His. All we can tell is that they have fellowship with those who teach and uphold the word of men as equal in authority with, or as taking the place of, God's Word. They have set up a wall between themselves and us, not intentionally perhaps, but nevertheless a wall. We cannot fellowship with those who are not loyal to Christ in all that He has commanded to be observed and taught. Christ would not have us do that. These believers, whom we are unable to recognize as such, have joined themselves with errorists. They may have done it in the simplicity of their heart, yet done it they have. They have closed the door to active fellowship with themselves on our part. This is not a happy situation.

It is one that fills our hearts with sadness. Why should Satan have such a power to separate those who belong together in this world and in eternity? For they are truly one because of the saving faith that is theirs in Christ Jesus, their Head.

We cannot solve the situation by saying: Let's be tolerant and overlook this disloyalty. We cannot tolerate any other teaching, for Christ has said: "If ye continue in My Word, then are ye My disciples indeed; and ye shall know the truth, and *the truth shall make you free*" (John 8:31-32). For this same reason He has commanded His Church: "Teach them to observe all things whatsoever I have commanded you" (Matt. 28:20).

Luther felt the gravity of a position that forced him to be separated from so many with whom he had once been united in outward fellowship. He knew there were believers in the Roman Church, as he himself repeatedly stated. Yet there was no other choice if God's Word and will was to be done. He writes: "To dissent from the agreement of so many nations and to be called schismatics is a grave matter. But *divine authority commands all not to be allies* and defenders of impiety and unjust cruelty." (Smalcald Articles. *Triglot*, p. 517.) Luther had in mind, when he spoke these words, the many abuses practiced in the Roman Church with its man-made laws about scapulars and fasts, relics and saints, and with its demand of subjection to the Pope in all things. But the principle he sets forth applies to all doctrines that are the commandments of men. We cannot be allies of such teachings and defenders of them. Whoever defends them separates himself by this act from those who in their confession seek to be loyal to Christ.

Men have sought to confuse the issue. They have blamed the proponents of the truth for the many divisions in Christendom. They have said repeatedly that these are the people that are setting up the walls of separation. Let us keep the issue clear. Christ Himself has asked us to be loyal to Him in all things He has taught. He has asked us to refuse to tolerate error side by side with His Word. He has warned us through His Apostle that a little leaven leaveneth the whole lump (I Cor. 5:6). He wants us to heed this warning and as good stewards to be faithful to His truth. His is the voice that counts. His sheep are to hear that voice and to follow it.

It is unnatural that Christians should follow false teachers instead of Christ, for One is their Master. If they do it outwardly because of ignorance, and if by the grace of God they are preserved from following them in their heart, let us praise God for His mighty grace. But let us not minimize the danger these believers are in. How easily may the error of men lead them from Christ! They are in a position where they might in ignorance mistake the voice of men for the voice of their Lord. Their standard is not the one established by God. We have the true standard. It is the one Jesus has given us: "Continue in My Word!" It is the standard that our Confession set up when it defined the Church as "the congregation of saints, *in which the Gospel is taught and the Sacraments are rightly administered.*" That state of the Church, and none other, must always be our goal.

IV

The purpose of Christian fellowship is the mutual strengthening in faith, the preservation and promotion of the unity of faith, and the joint extension of God's kingdom throughout the world. The end purpose is the glory of God and the eternal welfare of men. Therefore we should diligently strive to preserve the true fellowship of faith that exists among us, avoid everything that hinders it, and strive to help remove all errors and difficulties that separate fellow believers from one another.

The purpose of the outward fellowship is the mutual strengthening in faith. When members of a family or of a large relationship gather for a reunion, when they meet someone from their home town in a faraway place, they feel drawn together by a certain bond of fellowship that makes them one and impels them to join forces for mutual encouragement. Children of God should be drawn into an even closer fellowship because of the bond of faith that binds them together in Christ. They are strangers together in a strange land. They are children together of the same heavenly Father, called out of darkness into the kingdom of His dear Son. In their hearts dwells the one Spirit, the whole Trinity. They have *one* Lord and Savior, *one* faith, *one* common hope. They have the same interests, the same work, the same objectives, to serve the Lord Jesus Christ. It is therefore a matter of course that such children of God will find themselves drawn together for mutual encouragement and fellowship.

They greet each other joyously. The Apostle Paul sent greetings to the Corinthians: "Unto the church of God which is in Corinth, to them that are sanctified in Christ Jesus, called to be saints, *with all that in every place call upon the name of Jesus Christ, our Lord, both theirs and ours*: Grace be unto you, etc." (I Cor. 1:2-3). There are many such greetings in Holy Writ. Perhaps, when reading your daily devotions, you have skipped over them quickly. These greetings seemed unimportant to you. You may have become well acquainted with Rom. 16:17-18, which treats of avoiding those who cause divisions and offenses contrary to the doctrine you have learned. It is important for you as a child of God to know it well. But what does the whole section of Rom. 16:3-16 mean to you? That, too, should mean much to you. It is a glorious example of the fostering of fellowship in faith. It demonstrates concretely that such fellowship is a thing that God wants us to foster. The congregation in Rome had not been founded by the Apostle Paul. Rome was not his particular field of labor. Yet these fellow believers were near and dear to Paul. He writes: "I long to see you" (Rom. 1:11), and he devotes half a chapter to the writing of greetings to individuals and to the group. What Paul has in mind is to draw the bond of fellowship closer for mutual encouragement.

Christians like to visit together and talk things over. They have much to tell one another. In the Church of our Savior events are continually occurring that are of intense interest to its members. The Church is daily winning victories. New souls are added to the Church daily, and new territories are being occupied. That a church had been founded in Rome and that this church was making good progress was a matter of conversation among Christians all over the world. Paul writes: "Your faith is spoken of throughout the whole world" (Rom. 1:8). In a similar manner today children of God look forward to meeting with their fellow believers and discussing the forward march of the Gospel here at home and on all the continents of our world and on the isles of the seas. The Church continually has problems to overcome. Often it is beset by foes from without and disturbances within. Christians meet to discuss these problems and to prepare themselves with the help of God's Word and His Spirit to

Church Fellowship

meet the foes and to quiet the troubled waters. They encourage one another, and they come away from such meetings and discussions refreshed in spirit, even as the first Christians returned from the conference in Jerusalem with new courage to carry on the Lord's work, because a problem that had vexed and hindered the work had been solved in this meeting of fellow believers.

There is real spiritual strengthening in Christian fellowship. When Paul says he longs to see the Christians in Rome, he gives the reason for such longing: "that I may impart unto you some spiritual gift, to the end that ye may be established; that is, that *I may be comforted together with you by the mutual faith* both of you and me" (Rom. 1:11-12). When Paul was led captive to Rome and arrived in the neighborhood of Rome at Puteoli, the brethren from the capital city came to meet him as far as Appii Forum and The Three Taverns. In Acts 28:15 we are told what effect this manifestation of fellowship had upon this great Apostle of Christ: "Whom when Paul saw, he thanked God and *took courage.*" How often have we been refreshed and strengthened in a similar manner in joint worship with fellow believers, in smaller gatherings, at conventions, conferences, and circuit meetings, whenever or wherever we have been privileged to discuss the Lord's victories and our needs with those who are of the household of faith!

Another purpose of Christian fellowship is the promotion of the unity of faith. There is no more effective way of doing that than having those who confess the same Christ and Lord band together to maintain and preserve this precious unity. That was done in Jerusalem in the days of the Apostles. As a result they were one heart and one mind, and they did continue "steadfastly in the Apostles' doctrine and fellowship and in breaking of bread and in prayers." So our people today not only follow God's command to band together in congregations to promote and foster the unity of faith. They also band together in synods and larger church groups for the same purpose, because the history of the Church has shown the need and advisability of such co-operation.

Separated from each other, fellow confessors can easily drift apart even in their confession. Questionable expressions may be used to confess a certain article of faith. If there are no fellow believers in close fellowship to help correct these expressions, it may happen that those who should have continued in outward fellowship have become completely separated. Walls have gone up between them that might never have been raised had they practiced real fellowship of faith. Error has been permitted to creep in to darken the souls of men where at first there may never have been the least intention to foster error. It is for this reason that our own Synod, organized almost 100 years ago, seeking to foster a closer fellowship of faith, placed this object first in its constitution:

1. "The conservation and promotion of the unity of the true faith (Eph. 4:3-6; I Cor. 1:10) and a united defense against schism and sectarianism (Rom. 16:17)."

Still another purpose of outward Christian fellowship is the extension of God's kingdom throughout the world.

God does not want His children to lock the mystery of their faith in their hearts and to walk alone as solitary pilgrims in the world, until God takes them to their heavenly home. Christ gives these instructions: "What I tell you in darkness, that speak ye in light; and what ye hear in the ear, that preach ye upon the housetops" (Matt. 10:27). Christians should confess their faith openly, so that all can hear. God wants this done in an orderly manner. Christians should organize local congregations, call pastors, have the ministry in their midst. To what end? The Prophet Isaiah addresses the Church of the New Testament on this subject in these words: "O Zion, that bringest good tidings, get thee up into the high mountain; O Jerusalem, that bringest good tidings, lift up thy voice with strength; lift it up, and be not afraid; say unto the cities of Judah, Behold your God" (Is. 40:9). Above everything else it is the business of the Church to bring the Gospel of the saving Christ to the knowledge of men. It is to be an association which with united forces and with great courage proclaims this Gospel. It is to get up on a high mountain and to lift up its voice with strength and not be afraid. From the very beginning of the history of the Christian Church we find that the preaching of the Gospel in all the world was the business of the Church as a Church. Of the church in Antioch we read: "The Holy Ghost said: Separate Me Barnabas and Saul for the work whereunto I have called them.

And when they had fasted and prayed and laid their hands on them, they sent them away." (Acts 13:2-3.)

The Church of Christ, to which has been entrusted this Gospel, is to become the spiritual mother of many children, as Paul indicates: "But Jerusalem which is above is free, *which is the mother of us all.* For it is written: Rejoice, thou barren that bearest not; break forth and cry, thou that travailest not; for the desolate hath many more children than she which hath an husband." (Gal. 4: 26-27.) We, who have been privileged to work together in unity of faith with our Synod and with others with whom we are in fellowship, we know what it has meant for the spreading of the Kingdom to have such a large group working together at this task, training men for the ministry and sending them out into the world to bring men to Christ. Many millions will praise God for this fellowship, which has made it possible to reach them with the pardon and the power and the hope that only Christ can bring.

The end and object of such outward fellowship must always be the glory of God and the welfare of men. Gathering together an ever-growing number of people must never be an end in itself. Our goal must never be that we can boast of great numbers and strut before the world with our great achievements, simply because they seem great in the eyes of the world. We dare not boast of our orthodoxy and look with disdain upon others that have not the pure doctrine, forgetting that it is only by the grace of God that we are what we are. Daily we must with the help of God's Spirit cleanse our hearts of such evil motives and goals in all our fellowship strivings. We must and, God helping us, will always keep in mind that the ultimate purpose of our fellowship of faith is none other than that the name of God may be hallowed, that His kingdom may come, and that His will may be done. When God's Word is taught in its truth and purity among us, then His name is made great, not ours; when we carry that Word to the nations, then sons are born to him as dew from the Lord, children of God that know His grace and love Him and walk His way.

Let us make no mistake about it, it does make a powerful impression upon the world, and it should make such an impression, when Christians in unity of Spirit and of life witness unto the salvation of God which is in Christ Jesus.

In His high-priestly prayer, Jesus prays for His Church "that they all may be one, as Thou, Father, art in Me and I in Thee, that they may also be one in Us; *that the world may believe that Thou hast sent Me*" (John 17:21). In the Acts of the Apostles we are told how this has worked out. "And the multitude of them that believed were of *one heart* and of *one soul.* . . . And *with great power* gave the Apostles witness of the resurrection of the Lord Jesus, and great grace was upon them all" (Acts 4:32-33). "And they were all *with one accord* in Solomon's porch. And of the rest durst no man join himself to them, but *the people magnified them.* And believers were the more added to the Lord, multitudes both of men and women." (Acts 5:12-14.)

If, however, the world notes disunity among the children of God who are by their confession one in faith; if it notes how they disagree and refuse to work together, how readily do unbelieving men find excuse for continuing in their unbelief! And those who have permitted error to creep into their church will say: "Behold, it is impossible to insist upon complete unity of confession and faith. We shall not need to worry too much about such unity. It is impossible to attain!"

We must strive to preserve the true fellowship of faith among us. We must preserve to ourselves all the great blessings of this fellowship, and we must avoid doing harm to the cause of our Lord. God helping us, we will avoid everything that hinders this fellowship.

If error rears its head in our midst, we will deal with that error in a brotherly, kindly way, speaking the truth in love. Patiently but firmly we will seek to drive out the error and help one another return to the truth of God. We will be humble and always concede the possibility of being misled ourselves. If we find error elsewhere that separates us from fellow believers in other church groups, we will always be eager and ready to do what we can to remove that error and to bring these fellow believers into closer fellowship with us here and now.

In our daily life and in our relation with fellow Christians everywhere we will be watchful, seeking to keep the unity of the Spirit in the bond of peace.

In our congregations we will be intent upon attending church services faithfully, taking a deep interest in the Word as it is taught and preached. Nothing can be more harmful and dangerous to the maintenance of true church fellowship than neglect of Word and Sacraments. We will seek the daily fellowship of those who are of the household of faith, so that we may truly walk hand in hand upon the narrow way that leadeth unto eternal life. We will take a lively interest in the weal and woe of fellow believers in other churches affiliated with us, will pray for them, and work with them in unity and in love.

In our relation with one another and in our relation of congregation with sister congregation, we will seek to "be clothed with humility." It is so easy to insist upon "our rights," so that persons and congregations who are one in faith become embittered and the bond of fellowship is rent asunder. "If ye bite and devour one another, take heed that ye be not consumed one of another" (Gal. 5:15).

To sum it up: If true unity, with all its blessings, is to be maintained among us at all times, we must watch ourselves, see that we do not ever let pride rule our hearts. We must strive to become ever more firmly rooted in the Word, use the means of grace diligently, grow in grace and love and walk in the Spirit, admonish one another in love, and be ready to receive such admonition with a willing heart. (Eph. 4:1-6.)

Church Discipline

THE essence of the Gospel is God's gracious and unmerited love as manifested particularly in His work of redemption and sanctification. As soon as man has through faith in Christ, his Savior, come to a realization of this unspeakable love of God, he will begin to love Him who loved us first (I John 4:19) and will prove the sincerity of his love to God by loving his neighbor, particularly those who are his brethren in faith (I John 4:11, 20, 21).

This love of the Christian toward his fellow Christians will manifest itself in various ways. One special phase of the love which Christians must practice at all times is repeatedly emphasized throughout the Holy Scriptures, and is known as the doctrine of church discipline. Wherever this doctrine is taught in the Bible, the Lord God specifically commands His children that they prove their faith by evidences of love, solicitude, and assistance toward their fellow Christians.

As earnestly as God requires of us to love our brother, so earnestly does he also demand of each one of us that we accept the duty and responsibility of practicing church discipline.

This essay is intended to summarize those fundamental truths and approved practices which must govern a Biblical and orthodox procedure in church discipline.

For purposes of convenience and clarity we shall consider the various aspects, and more especially the basic essentials, of this doctrine under fifteen separate theses.

Thesis I

Church discipline comprises certain essential duties which are enjoined upon every Christian and every Christian congregation by a clear and direct command of God.

Our Savior's own words recorded in Matthew 18 present a clear and direct command to practice church discipline. **The Lord**

Church Discipline 539

there instructs the individual Christian, employing the singular number and saying: "If *thy* brother shall trespass against *thee,* go and tell him his fault between *thee* and *him* alone." He is issuing a mandate to the one fellow member who personally knows about the brother's trespasses and spiritual dangers, and requires of him that he exercise the necessary measure of Christian love to admonish that erring brother, to befriend him, and to rescue him from the grave consequences of mortal sin.

Assuming that the brother might not always repent after private admonitions, our Lord continues His precise commands to include the earnest efforts of one or two witnesses and finally the special love, prayers, and admonitions of the entire congregation.

The book of Leviticus records the Lord's command "Thou shalt in any wise rebuke thy neighbor" (Lev. 19:17), and makes it directly obligatory upon the Israelite to manifest a proper love toward his brother by admonishing him and saving him from the dire results of his iniquity and impenitence. He adds also the significant words "and not suffer sin upon him," which have been consistently interpreted to mean not to become personally guilty of the brother's offenses by failing to reprimand him, or to help free him from the weight of his transgressions. P. E. Kretzmann, *Popular Commentary. Old Testament,* I, p. 219.

A rather striking parallel to this Old Testament injunction of God is found in the Savior's express command recorded in the 17th chapter of St. Luke, "If thy brother trespass against thee, rebuke him; and if he repent, forgive him" (Luke 17:3).

Under divine inspiration the Apostle Paul commanded the Christians to give spiritual counsel, comfort, and admonition to the person overtaken in a fault, and thus to assist him in returning to the path of virtue and of righteousness (Gal. 6:1). His fervent appeal to their Christian love and patience was fittingly expressed in these words: "Bear ye one another's burdens and so fulfill the law of Christ." That well-known law of Christ was obviously the law of love toward one another as Christian brethren, revealing itself in words of spiritual admonition, instruction, and encouragement.

This same Apostle urges the Thessalonians to consider their erring fellow member as a friend and commands them, saying: "Admonish him as a brother" (II Thess. 3:14, 15).

In his Epistle to the Corinthians he reprimanded the congregation for neglecting church discipline; he charged its members with the glaring sin of pride and haughtiness for having set themselves above the commandments of the Holy Word of God. Finally, in referring to the incestuous person and his public offense, the Apostle instructed the congregation to take at once the third and last step in the process of church discipline, saying: "Put away from among yourselves that wicked person" (I Cor. 5:13).

That no one be inclined to regard the matter of brotherly admonition or the first steps in church discipline as being of minor or secondary importance, the Lord in the Old Testament emphasized His impending judgment upon the person who failed earnestly to warn the manifest sinner. In His divine righteousness the Lord declared that in such instances of monitory negligence or indifference the guilt of the offender would be charged to the person who failed in his duties and responsibilities.

The words of direct command addressed to Ezekiel by God Himself with respect to the duty of warning and admonishing the evildoer were followed by grave threats of dire judgment reading thus: "When I say unto the wicked, Thou shalt surely die; and thou givest him not warning, nor speakest to warn the wicked from his wicked way, to save his life: the same wicked man shall die in his iniquity; but his blood will I require at thine hand" (Ezek. 3:18).

In commenting on the grave importance of church discipline, Dr. Fritz concurs in the opinions earlier expressed on the same subject by Dr. Walther and affirms with unmistakable emphasis that "God has commanded church discipline, Matthew 18:15-17, and therefore we must exercise it." (J. H. C. Fritz, *Pastoral Theology*, p. 233.)

This imperative nature of the Bible passages urging church discipline is perhaps most forcefully indicated by Luther himself when he says: "This command to admonish the brother is just as necessary as 'thou shalt not kill; thou shalt not steal,' for if out of fear or for any other reason you neglect the duty to admonish, then not his body, not his property, but the salvation of his soul is endangered." (St. Louis, VI:1633.)

The Scriptural records leave no doubt in the Christian's heart that church discipline is enjoined upon every Christian and every Christian congregation by a clear and direct command of God.

Thesis II

All the communicant members of a given church come under the disciplinary authority of that church, or congregation, and its individual members.

Obligations to practice church discipline extend only to those people who are mutually joined together with one another in the same Christian faith. Our Savior does not require us to admonish everyone who trespasses against us, but He very specifically states: "If *thy brother* shall trespass against thee. . . ."

Christians should indeed concern themselves about the spiritual welfare and salvation of the unbelievers and unconverted in their community and in the world, and strive to bring them the Gospel of salvation, but until they have accepted the Christian faith, they and all the heathen and all the heterodox, whoever they may be, are outside the pale of spiritual brothers and sisters and do not come within the sphere of their church's disciplinary authority.

As effectually, however, as the term "brother" excludes all unchurched people, just so effectually it includes all fellow members, whether they be the prominent or the lowly, whether they be the young or the old, whether they be pastor, teacher, or elder.

Sometimes it has been assumed that the person to be admonished must be a voting member of the congregation or that he must be experienced in life and mature in years. Such conception of a brotherly or sisterly status is plainly an erroneous one, for it is the Christian's duty to admonish every communicant member who is inclined to follow the broad path to perdition and is therefore in personal need of another's counsel of love and solicitude.

In conformity to this Biblical principle, Nathan admonished King David, and John the Baptist publicly rebuked King Herod. Similarly the churches at Corinth, Pergamus, and Thyatira were severely censured because they failed to exercise their churchly authority and neglected to ban the persistent and impenitent evildoers.

One of the truly exemplary instances of brotherly admonition in the New Testament occurred between the two most prominent of all the Apostles. It was Peter who erred in his conduct with respect to the Ceremonial Law, and Paul admonished him. It was with a becoming Christian humility and a spirit of true repentance that Peter accepted the admonition of his fellow Apostle and made due amends.

This brotherly procedure serves as a notable pattern for a pastor and a teacher to negotiate with one another if there be a fault or a trespass on the part of the one or the other. They must be governed in their relations by the kindly, patient, and gentle nature suggested by our Lord, and His discourse on church discipline.

Similarly the children of our parish schools, the youth at our colleges, and the students at our seminaries should be duly trained to admonish or correct their brothers and sisters according to the disciplinary yet loving and helpful methods prescribed in Matthew 18.

Finally it should be remembered that changing conditions give rise to new and distinctly current problems. Modern conveniences afford Christians an opportunity to meet members of other congregations at different places and on different occasions. In the event that one Christian trespasses against another of a sister congregation, the brother who has personal knowledge of the offense must admonish his fellow Christian just as earnestly as if they were members of the same local church. Should the second step become necessary, it is recommended that he choose his witnesses from the local church of the offender, and in the event of the third step, the local church of the offending or impenitent wrongdoer must act to the point of ultimate exclusion from membership if that step becomes necessary.

Thesis III

A brother's manifest sins relating to doctrinal error or an ungodly life require disciplinary action.

Upon referring to the Lord's explicit instructions of Matthew 18 we learn that the offense requiring disciplinary attention is designated as a "trespass against thee." Christ has in mind a willful and flagrant violation of some specific command of God. The trespass itself is described as being of such a nature that the offender is in actual jeopardy of his soul's salvation, that he must be regained for the Kingdom of Grace, and that unless he hears and repents, he will remain under the curse of God and be lost forever. (Vv. 15 b-17.)

Church Discipline

It might, then, be summarily stated that the term "trespass" denotes a gross wickedness or a mortal sin which has the power and effect of destroying the offender's faith and leaving him remorseless and impenitent.

In a synodical essay read before the Wisconsin District convention of 1886, G. Kuechle stated: "Whoever is not guilty of mortal sins or soul-destroying error must not be subjected to church discipline." (Wisconsin, 1886, p. 35.)

Much the same opinion was expressed in the sixteenth century by Dr. Martin Luther. In commenting on the nature of the transgressions which require disciplinary treatment, he contended that church discipline must be resorted to when the forfeiture or loss of the grace of God or spiritual life itself is entailed. (Oestlicher, 1879, p. 63.)

Whatever specific designation may be employed, whether it be "loss of grace" or "loss of spiritual life," the terms include trespasses of a twofold nature: (1) persistent adherence to false doctrine and (2) manifest sins of the flesh.

(1) Believing or teaching false doctrine is not a light matter. It is a transgression of God's commandment which tells us not to add to His Word nor to diminish from it (Deut. 4:2; 12:32) lest one be found a liar (Prov. 30:6), a sin upon which God has pronounced His curse (Jer. 23:25-32; Gal. 1:8, 9). When a professed church member follows his own perverted religious views or philosophical speculations rather than the clear and fundamental tenets of the Holy Scriptures, he must be admonished with patience and forbearance, yet with uncompromising firmness. A brother's adherence to false doctrine indicates not only the presence of a spirit of pride and insubordination, but a defiance of God and refusal to accept even the infallible Word of divine truth as the final authority in matters of Christian faith.

Youthful Titus met with such persons in his Gospel ministry, and the Apostle instructed him in the procedure to be followed in such cases, saying: "A man that is an heretic after the first and second admonition reject: Knowing that he that is such, is subverted and sinneth, being condemned of himself" (Titus 3:10, 11).

In the congregations served by Timothy, men appeared who similarly clung to certain grave religious errors. In counseling this young colaborer, the Apostle Paul implied that after due admonition and instruction these errorists be left to go their own way, as such from whom the congregation has withdrawn its hand of brotherly unity and Christian fellowship. (I Tim. 6:3-5.)

Much the same situation is treated by the Apostle in his Epistle to the Romans where he commands those to be avoided who make divisions within the Church by propagating errors contrary to the pure doctrines of the grace of God in Christ Jesus. (Rom. 16:17.)

In a case of obdurate adherence to heresy and false doctrine, the process of successive admonitions must be carried to the third stage of admonition and ultimate excommunication. This occurred when Paul dealt thus with two unorthodox brethren of his time concerning whom he writes: "Which some having put away, concerning faith have made shipwreck; of whom is Hymenaeus and Alexander; whom I have delivered unto Satan, that they may learn not to blaspheme" (I Tim. 1:19, 20).

Describing the glaring errors of others who had evidently been influenced by an earlier heretic, he warns against the spreading dangers of false doctrine and urges the need of constant vigilance with recourse to church discipline, saying: "But shun profane and vain babblings, for they will increase unto more ungodliness, and their word will eat as doth a canker; of whom is Hymenaeus and Philetus, who concerning the truth have erred, saying that the resurrection is past already, and overthrow the faith of some" (II Tim. 2:16-18).

(2) Manifest sins of the flesh committed in a flagrant and willful manner against better knowledge and therefore in conscious disregard of God's Holy Law are known in theology as mortal sins.

Such sins are desertion of family (I Tim. 5:8) and "adultery, fornication, uncleanness, lasciviousness, idolatry, witchcraft, hatred, variance, emulations, wrath, strife, seditions, heresies, envyings, murders, drunkenness, revellings and such like" (Gal. 5:19-21).

Once more naming the works of the flesh as leading to certain damnation, and requiring prompt and solicitous admonition and warning, should a brother become guilty of such transgression, the Apostle states: "Neither fornicators, nor idolaters, nor adulterers, nor effeminate, nor abusers of themselves with mankind, nor thieves, nor covetous, nor drunkards, nor revilers, nor extortioners shall inherit the Kingdom of God" (I Cor. 6:9).

From these passages it becomes plain and evident that both adherence to false doctrine and manifest sins of the flesh require prompt and ready recourse to church discipline in the proper attitude and in the best interests of the offending brother.

It should be noted further that mere rumors of hearsay remarks about a brother, as well as all common sins of human weakness, do not fall into the category of offenses requiring disciplinary procedure.

Thesis IV

The purpose of church discipline is to gain the brother, to further the glory of God, and to purify and strengthen the congregation.

To comprehend fully the serious objectives of disciplinary procedure, we must first become aware of the true spiritual status of the offender. Our Lord Jesus Christ clearly implies that the brother is in danger of abandoning the narrow path to heaven and joining the ungodly multitudes on the way to spiritual ruin and eternal perdition. For this reason the Savior speaks of gaining him when He says: "If he will hear thee, thou hast gained thy brother."

Even when the third step of excommunicating the offender becomes necessary, it is not an act of retribution, but a final attempt to bring the sinner to repentance. That one benevolent purpose was distinctly named by the Apostle Paul when he recommended that the incestuous person at Corinth be excommunicated. He urged the congregation therefore "to deliver such an one unto Satan for the destruction of the flesh, that the spirit may be saved in the day of the Lord Jesus" (I Cor. 5:5).

Church discipline with its patient and kindly progress through the three stages of earnest and prayerful admonition can be correctly regarded only as being a deed of love and compassion in which unselfish brothers, and finally the entire congregation, strives to win the offender from the powers of evil and the clutches of Satan.

Since Christ Himself has commanded church discipline and has defined its purpose as being one of helpfulness and service toward the brother, we are assured that its practice even to the point of excommunication will be a source of blessings to us and often to the erring brother. Says Luther: "The congregation should exclude the persistently impenitent as heathen, so that they may come to a realization of their sins and repent and that others may take warning from such example and guard against sin" (St. Louis, XIII:190).

To further the glory of God is the second major objective of proper church discipline. Whenever a wayward brother is regained, there is gratitude in many hearts that humbly pause to acknowledge the effectual grace of God toward the sinner. There is also special praise and glory in heaven, for there is gladness and "joy among the angels of God over one sinner that repenteth." And even the excommunication of manifest, impenitent sinners proves to the world that our God is indeed not a God that hath pleasure in wickedness, neither shall evil dwell with Him who has told His Christians, "Put away from among yourselves that wicked person" (I Cor. 5:13).

Furthermore, church discipline contributes toward the proper conduct among its members; it promotes Christian love and brotherly relationships; it fosters unity and co-operation; it raises the church to an honored and respected position and exerts a wholesome influence throughout the entire community. Church discipline in its divinely intended form prepares the congregation to let its light shine before men and glorify the Father who is in heaven.

Finally, church discipline serves to purify and strengthen the congregation. It was the evil example of the incestuous person at Corinth which threatened to demoralize its entire membership. Recognizing the dangers involved, the Apostle warned the members: "Know ye not that a little leaven leaveneth the whole lump? Purge out therefore the old leaven that ye may be a new lump, as ye are unleavened" (I Cor. 5:6, 7). Even as leaven permeates the entire bread dough, so flagrant sin permeates the entire membership of a congregation and contaminates it with the savor of ungodliness, laxity, indifference, and immorality. It was for the purpose of cleansing and purifying the congregation that the Apostle entreated his members: "Therefore put away from among yourselves that wicked person" (I Cor. 5:13).

Accepting the Apostle's precept without qualification and speaking from personal experience, Dr. Stoeckhardt rightly contends that by tolerating evildoers the entire congregation becomes accessory to the offense and is in danger of being corrupted by its influence and example. (Minnesota, 1918, p. 53.)

It would be impossible to estimate correctly what irreparable harm can be done in a congregation when manifestly impenitent and shamelessly flagrant sinners are regularly admitted to the Holy Sacrament. The entire constituency becomes bewildered and confused; the ideals and standards of virtue and integrity are perceptibly lowered; and the danger that the name of Christ will be blasphemed among the heathen is daily increased.

Gentleness and kindness combined with uncompromising insistence upon God's will in disciplinary action will not only cleanse and purify the congregation, but will restore confidence, resolution, and good will among its members and give strength to its entire constituency. Church discipline strives toward the highest and holiest objectives.

Thesis V

Church discipline must be practiced in an evangelical manner.

The friendly and sympathetic attitude which should govern a member's approach to the offender's heart is strikingly indicated in the Savior's kindly appellation "thy brother." This brotherly relationship begets an unselfish interest in the offender; it presupposes common ground between the one and the other; it assumes a spirit of meekness, humility, and patience; it avoids every semblance of pride and superiority; it reveals a generous desire on the part of the one to be of help and service to the other.

A God-fearing monitor will seek the Holy Spirit's guidance and the Lord's bestowal of a special measure of wisdom and understanding. Realizing his own weaknesses and human limitations, he will come prayerfully and humbly to stand by the erring brother and to aid him in overcoming Satan, sin, and temptation.

Not every visit with the brother, however, may be a timely or convenient occasion to tell him his faults. Indeed it should not be attempted in his place of business, neither should it be undertaken when he is in the midst of his family or his friends. Under no circumstances should it be made a harrowing or embarrassing experience.

Examples which demonstrate the proper evangelical practice are found in the methods employed by Nathan in his admonitions to David, and by Christ our Lord in His kindly demeanor and His appropriate words to Peter and to the woman who was a great sinner. (II Sam. 12:1 ff.; John 21:15-19; Luke 7:36 ff.)

In presenting his reasons for employing the evangelical method in church discipline, Dr. Walther says: "As always, so here, too, love is the highest law. If love to the offender demands first of all a private admonition, even though the offense be public, the practice of acting in a public manner would constitute a grave injustice" (C. F. W. Walther, *Pastorale*, p. 326).

Particular care must be exercised also in presenting the sin of the offender in its proper aspect. Never should the gravity of the transgression be underestimated or minimized. The brother has grieved God and his Savior, and he can receive grace and pardon only when he recognizes the weight of his guilt, accepts pardon through the atonement made for his sin by the Son of God on Calvary, and resolves to mend his ways and errors.

It should be remembered, too, that a truly evangelical manner in the process of church discipline does not exclude a proper use of the Law. Under circumstances it may even become imperative to employ the Law with all its exacting demands and dire threats before the Gospel can effect its desired purpose. The evangelical manner will apply the Word of God in its entirety as the needs dictate, but it will avoid every human tendency which might create a feeling of suspicion or hostility on the part of the erring brother.

Thesis VI

The procedure employed in a disciplinary action must conform to the instructions of our Lord set forth in Matthew 18.

Every Christian is presumably familiar with the three successive steps prescribed by our Savior in exercising church discipline and therefore only the most important aspects will be presented in this thesis.

The words "If thy brother trespass against thee" do not mean "in the event that he personally insult or offend thee." They do mean that, if he commit an act of wickedness or a grave sin of which you have personal knowledge, then it becomes your duty as

Church Discipline 549

a brother to go to him "and tell him his fault between thee and him alone." First of all this entire matter must be kept in strictest privacy between the witness to the evil-doing and the perpetrator of the sin. Then, at the earliest opportunity and at a time convenient to the brother, the member must personally go to him and in a modest, confidential manner inform him of his transgression and urge him to repent.

Should the first effort fail in its desired results, it might be advisable to make a second or even a third attempt to gain him, for Christ our Lord does not say that each step may not be repeated, but that each step must be performed at least once. If the words of admonition do move the guilty brother to acknowledge his transgression and he repents of his sin, then a soul has been gained, and the words of James apply with peculiar force: "Let him know that he which converteth the sinner from the error of his way shall save a soul from death and shall hide a multitude of sins" (James 5:20).

The second step in the course of disciplinary progression becomes necessary if the brother responds in any one of five possible ways: (a) If he refuses the private admonition, (b) If he denies his guilt and persists in that denial, (c) If he refuses to repent or make amends after admitting his sin, (d) If he admits his alleged behavior but denies that this is actually a sin, or (e) If after promising to amend, he continues in his wickedness.

Luther advises at this point as follows: "If he will not accept your counsel, then you must bear with him in patience and take with you one or two witnesses who can verify your contentions or bear witness that you have admonished and instructed him and told him" (St. Louis, VIII:920).

This second step in admonishing the brother must be taken at least once, but may be repeated as often as charity and wisdom dictate or as often as the hope of ultimate success remains in prospect. Our Lord's instructions now oblige the member to take with him one or two more. These should be sober-minded men or even friends of the impenitent brother, for they are to counsel and guide him in decisions of great moment. Their purpose, as that of the original monitor, must be to lead the brother back to his Savior. Fortunate and grateful indeed are these members and their brother if this second step leads to blessed repentance. In that event the entire matter must be kept a close secret within their small circle and never again be mentioned in the future, unless the sin has become public.

Disappointing indeed is the outcome if the brother persists in his obstinacy and sinfulness. However, it next becomes the duty of the admonishing member to "tell it to the church." At this point the entire membership is expected to pray for the offender and with meekness and forbearance to persuade him to make due amends. The fellow members who assisted in the second step now become witnesses. It devolves upon them to testify, not only that the brother under admonition has committed a sinful act, but that he has been earnestly exhorted to desist from sin, to acknowledge his guilt before God, to accept pardon through Christ, and to practice virtue through the power of the Holy Spirit; and, finally, that despite these private efforts, he has remained adamant and unmoved.

Having fully satisfied itself that the charges of wickedness committed are true, having recognized the gravity of the offense, and having found that adequate private admonition has been applied, the congregation must accept its solemn duty as the supreme earthly monitor and strive with tact and long-suffering to induce the wayward brother to return in the fear of God to his fold and its divine Shepherd.

In the event that these united efforts of the entire membership fail in attaining their purpose, the congregation is constrained to excommunicate the persistently impenitent individual and deny him the right hand of Christian fellowship.

Occasionally a brother's offense is made public through the newspapers, or it becomes widely known from the nature of the deed itself. Under such circumstances it is obviously not necessary to employ the first two steps prescribed in Matthew 18, since the matter is no longer private. In discussing the subject of public sins the Apostle asserted without further qualification: "Them that sin rebuke before all, that others may also fear" (I Tim. 5:20). That he himself followed this practice is evident from his admonition to Peter, as described in Galatians, chapter two, where he states: "I said unto Peter before them all" (Gal. 2:14).

That the private sin of a brother must be treated as such with utmost strictness has been emphasized under the first step of Matthew 18. Another aspect of this divine command needs to be remembered, however, when another comes to us with the intention of divulging or enumerating the private sins or offenses of a brother. Perhaps the most concise and effective counsel that can be applied in such a situation is expressed by Dr. Luther in his Large Catechism, where he states: "If someone report to you what this or that one has done, teach him, too, to go and admonish him personally if he have seen it himself; but if not, that he hold his tongue" (Eighth Commandment, *Triglot*, p. 659).

THESIS VII

In cases of church discipline where evidence must be submitted to establish the guilt of a person charged with an offense, the congregation should be familiar with the rules and principles which govern the validity of testimony and the qualifications of the witnesses.

A church member may be charged with some serious offense supposedly committed in the presence of one or more of his brethren. When the person so accused denies his guilt, he cannot be convicted or excommunicated except upon the testimony of two or three reliable and qualified witnesses.

In the Old Testament the Lord God ordained that "at the mouth of two witnesses or three witnesses shall he that is worthy of death be put to death" (Deut. 17:6).

Neither was this Old Testament rule or principle restricted only to major crimes or capital punishment, for the general rule in the law of Moses reads thus: "One witness shall not rise up against a man for any iniquity or for any sin that he sinneth: at the mouth of two witnesses or at the mouth of three witnesses shall the matter be established" (Deut. 19:15).

Our Savior's own words with reference to confirming the second admonition in the process of church discipline demand the presence of one or two witnesses that, as He explicitly declares: "In the mouth of two or three witnesses every word may be established."

This same rule has been embodied in the laws of evidence recognized by the civil and criminal courts throughout the entire world, but, although this basic rule is perhaps universally accepted, it has not always been correctly applied. Records of a church's procedure in a disciplinary action show that a member was excommunicated because one individual witnessed certain words spoken at a specified time and place and another testified to having heard the same words spoken at another time and place. Even in the face of the member's denial it was held that two witnesses had established his guilt. Upon the later investigation of this case it was correctly held that there was but one witness to each alleged instance of wrongdoing in view of the denial of the charge on the part of the accused. Witnesses qualified under the Scriptural rule must submit concurrent testimony to the same act. If they fail in this, their evidence "agreeth not together" as in the trial of Christ before Caiaphas.

Dr. A. L. Graebner clarifies this point when he says: "Thus if the same person had committed theft three times and one witness had seen the first theft, another the second theft, and still another the third theft, each being the only witness present in each instance, the testimony of the three witnesses would be of no avail if the accused denied the charge of theft" (J. H. C. Fritz, *Pastoral Theology*, pp. 252, 253).

Certain other very important comments on the rules governing the validity of testimony and of witnesses, as well as a keen analysis of circumstantial, written, and parol evidence is presented by Dr. A. L. Graebner in Vol. VI of the *Theological Quarterly*, pages 216–231. Dr. J. H. C. Fritz plainly regards this dissertation on "The Evidence in Church Discipline" of such far-reaching importance that he has quoted it in its entirety in his *Pastoral Theology*.

Thesis VIII

The act of excommunication includes the exercise of the power of the keys and must be invoked as a last resort when dealing with an impenitent sinner.

When church discipline leads a congregation to the necessity of excommunicating a member, it pronounces him persistently impenitent, adjudges him to be a heathen and an unbeliever, and dissolves the bonds of Christian brotherhood. This action closes heaven to him and leaves him under the burden and the curse of his own sins. Not only does it deny him admission to the Holy Sacrament, but it denies him church fellowship in sister congregations as well as his own. Those properly excommunicated are not merely severed from an external and earthly organization but from the Kingdom of Grace and the body of Christ. Paul calls this solemn step "to deliver such an one unto Satan" (I Cor. 5:5). Concerning Hymenaeus and Alexander he reports: "Whom I have delivered unto Satan" (I Tim. 1:20).

In stressing the force and power of the ban, Pastor H. J. Bouman states: "The banned person forfeits all rights, titles, and blessings of the Christian Church as long as he does not repent" (Minnesota, 1918, p. 40 ff.).

This power of excommunication is in reality the power of the keys. After stating that the incorrigible and impenitent offender is to be regarded as a heathen man and a publican, Christ our Lord affirms the universal and effectual power of such an act of excommunication when He declares in the very next sentence: "Verily I say unto you, whatsoever ye shall bind on earth shall be bound in heaven, and whatsoever ye shall loose on earth shall be loosed in heaven."

Luther interprets this passage as indicating that God has so intimately identified Himself with the Church that where she proceeds according to His Word, her action is as valid in heaven as on earth, saying: "Here God binds Himself by the judgment of the Holy Christian Church, when she uses her authority properly, so that the Church's judgment becomes God's own judgment" (St. Louis, VIII:926).

This brief summary of the force and significance of excommunication plainly reveals its serious nature. Before invoking this power a congregation should be certain that it has exhausted every possible religious influence to move the obdurate sinner to repentance. The entire process of disciplinary action dictates caution on every hand and a conscientious procedure. However, when the need to excommunicate a member becomes clear and obvious, the congregation should act with unwavering confidence.

Thesis IX

The custom of seeking counsel and guidance from orthodox and learned Christians of the circuit or District in difficult cases of church discipline is commendable.

Pastors and congregations have always received invaluable counsel and much-needed encouragement from brethren in the Church whom the Lord has given a special measure of wisdom and practical experience. This has been true throughout the entire history of our own Lutheran Church, even as it was true in the Christian Church of the first century.

Timothy and his members evidently sought the counsel and guidance of the Apostle Paul. In the Epistles addressed to his young colleague the Apostle presented much valuable and practical advice on pastoral duties and church life. He offered special instructions as to how he might proceed in admonishing both the weak and the willful.

To Titus this same Apostle directed his kindly interest and offered the young missionary guidance and valuable information relating to his ministerial duties.

When Peter was unable to visit the churches of Asia Minor, he wrote them two Epistles, not about personal matters, but to dispense instruction and advice designed to enhance their Christian welfare.

In his First Epistle to the Corinthians, Paul not merely recommended, but urged the immediate excommunication of an impenitent flagrant sinner, and in the Second Epistle, after the offender had proved himself remorseful and penitent, he encouraged special consideration toward this same sorrowing brother.

As the early Christians, and even as our fathers in the past, so throughout the future, our own congregations and pastors will profit from the recommendations and the counsel of their spiritually more mature brethren. In very difficult cases of church discipline, the congregation and the pastor may avoid much bitter heartache and many unhappy regrets by consulting with devout and experienced church leaders.

Furthermore, if these recognized leaders are personally still strangers to the local membership and their existing problems, or the peculiarly unsettled affairs of the church, they will be less inclined to show partiality. For such reasons Dr. Fritz advocates:

"If a case of church discipline presents unusual difficulties or if a pastor is convinced that a person should be excommunicated, but cannot persuade his congregation, which is not at all unwilling to submit to the Word of God, to pass a resolution to that effect, the congregation ought to call in and ask the advice of one or more experienced pastors of good judgment. Of course, finally the congregation itself must decide the case" (*Pastoral Theology*, p. 241).

Above all else, the riper judgment of a devout and discerning brother may prevent the congregation from excommunicating an innocent member.

Thesis X

The excommunication of a member from the church must be unanimous.

When Christ our Lord says: "Tell it to the church," He confers upon the local congregation the final and supreme authority to excommunicate a former brother when that becomes necessary. The pastor can therefore not order the congregation to exclude a certain person who might be undesirable to him personally, neither may he prohibit the excommunication of an impenitent sinner for reasons of intimate friendship.

Luther reminds us that although Saint Paul was an Apostle, he would not presume upon his own right to ban the incestuous person at Corinth. He required the congregation to act in the matter. (C. F. W. Walther, *Pastorale*, p. 324.)

Excommunication as an official church act is valid only upon the unanimous vote of the congregation. Should there be members in the church who are unwilling to support the resolution to exclude a given member, so that the vote cannot be made unanimous, when the guilt of the accused has been established, they must state the reasons for their opposition. If they have valid reasons to justify their negative vote, they are indeed serving the ends of justice, but they should have spoken before the ballot was taken. In the event, however, that they have no justifiable grounds for their minority vote and are unwilling to change their stand, they must be admonished and disciplined, and, if necessary, excommunicated before the original case is brought to its final conclusion.

Furthermore, not all members of the congregation need necessarily be present when the excommunication is decreed by unanimous vote; however, the entire congregation must be previously informed of the matter under consideration.

Finally, it has always been deemed a wise policy that, when the excommunication has been decided in one congregation meeting, it be ratified in the succeeding meeting before it is published.

Thesis XI

Anyone who severs his connection with the church while disciplinary proceedings are in progress excludes himself from the congregation.

A brother who is summoned to appear before the congregation should be made to understand that his fellow Christians are genuinely interested in his spiritual welfare. He must be informed of the sincere good will and the high objectives motivating the entire procedure. The special meeting has been expressly called for the primary purpose of regaining him and assisting him on his pilgrimage to heaven.

He should preferably be informed of the scheduled meeting in writing. The summons itself should be delivered by several officers of the congregation, and they should await and bring with them the reply of the offending brother as to whether he will attend the meeting. Should the wayward member persistently refuse repeated requests to appear, he cannot of course be excommunicated because the congregation has been prevented from admonishing him as prescribed in Matthew 18. The church must, however, declare that he has sinfully severed his connection with the congregation.

Such a case evidently occurred in one of the early churches and was reported thus by the Apostle John in his First Epistle: "They went out from us, but they were not of us; for if they had been of us, they would no doubt have continued with us: but they went out that they might be made manifest that they were not all of us" (I John 2:19).

When a member persists in his unwillingness to appear before the congregation, it remains for the pastor only to make public declaration of his status as one who has withdrawn himself from the church's ministrations as a Christian brother.

Experience has taught that an offender may agree to be present at a stated meeting but fail to appear as promised. Under such circumstances the congregation must continue to exercise Christian charity, for it is better to suffer a wrong than to commit a wrong. Not until the reason for the absence has been ascertained, should the church pass judgment. Dr. Fritz states very succinctly: "If an offender has promised to be present at a meeting of the congregation to which he had been summoned, but fails to do so, he should first again be heard before his name is stricken from the list. This should be done even if rumor has it that he had remained away intentionally and without good excuse." (*Pastoral Theology*, p. 242.)

Thesis XII

The person excommunicated by a congregation may appeal from the church's judgment and demand a review of the proceedings before another congregation or some qualified board or committee.

A valid appeal from a church's unanimous resolution to excommunicate a certain person must be based upon proof from God's Word that an error has been made in the disciplinary proceedings. Obviously the burden of proof in such appeals rests entirely upon the person preferring charges of error against the excommunicating congregation.

Since every Christian here upon earth is still weak and sinful and all too fallible, it is indeed possible for him and for the others associated with him in a Christian congregation to err in their judgment. "Human beings may err," says Dr. Dau, "even the members of the communion of saints may err; a Christian congregation may err and erroneously decree to ban a fellow man" (Central, 1904, p. 72).

Realizing therefore that it would be a gross violation of God's purpose to declare a former brother a heathen man and a publican upon false grounds, no congregation can regard herself as being above the requirement of justifying her procedure before the appellant or other Christian congregations when that procedure has been seriously challenged. Among the causes which have been admitted as a basis for challenging a congregation's action in excommunicating a member are: (a) when a false or unjustifiable cause was named as the basis for excommunication, (b) when the impenitence of the excommunicated person was not proved beyond all reasonable doubt, or (c) when the procedure has been so irregular as to be confusing to the appellant.

Under such circumstances a congregation must be held to review its process step by step. Only if she refuses to do this, shall a neighboring congregation or a duly authorized commission act with respect to, or in defense of, the appellant. In commenting on this particular question, Dr. Dau contends that: "The banning congregation owes it to other Christian congregations to establish the validity of its ban, and if this cannot be done, she must correct her error or lift the ban" (Central, 1904, p. 70).

If a congregation proves herself obstinate and uncharitable toward the appellant or toward another congregation or commission, then again the considered opinion of Dr. Dau must prevail when he says in substance: Should a congregation fail in this important matter of correcting her error in the process of decreeing a ban, fraternal bonds with her must be finally and permanently severed. (Central, p. 72.)

Thesis XIII

The attitude and relationship toward an excommunicated person must be one of civil courtesy, but not of religious fellowship.

Severance of the bonds of Christian faith and Christian brotherhood dissolves the most intimate of all earthly relationships. It leaves the unbelieving offender isolated and apart from the body of Christ. He has forfeited the privileges of sonship in the family of God. The Church and its members cannot take him into their confidence in matters of Christian faith or any problem of a religious nature. Nothing should be said or done which might give him cause to think otherwise than that his former brethren consider him a heathen man and a publican. He naturally loses the comfort, the blessings, the counsel, the encouragement, and the brotherly assistance which Christians are expected to lend one another on their way to eternal life. Serving as a sponsor at Holy Baptism must be denied him; admission to the Sacrament of the Altar is utterly impossible under his status; and Christian burial must be definitely refused him. The spiritual plight of an ex-

Church Discipline 559

communicated person is a desperate one, and fortunate indeed will he be if he recognizes it as such.

Pronouncement of excommunication does not, however, dissolve his marriage status or family relationships. If he has children of his own, he will exercise the parental authority of a father over them. Neither need a business partnership be dissolved solely because one of its members has been placed under a ban.

An excommunicated person may well lay claim to the neighborly love and good will of church members. The same considerate and courteous conduct expected of Christians toward their common associates in life must be maintained toward the banned person. (Minnesota, 1918, p. 40.)

Neither do Christians refuse the excommunicated person attendance at church services; they rejoice to see him under the influence of God's Word; indeed, they pray for him as for any heathen man and publican. Luther expressly states that such a person is not "deprived of the church's love, intercession, and good deeds" (St. Louis, XIX:887).

Such passages as Rom. 16:17; I Cor. 5:11; II Thess. 3:14, and II John 10, which prohibit "to eat with" or enjoin "to avoid" or "have no company with" or "receive him not into your house," refer only to brotherly relationships, but do not forbid normal civil intercourse or polite and civil manners. St. Paul very definitely teaches that a Christian should not sever his marriage with a spouse who is or has become an unbeliever, a heathen (I Cor. 7:12-14); and just as definitely he states that only the brotherly relations of Christian and Christian have been severed, not the social and generally human relations, "for then must ye needs go out of the world" (I Cor. 5:9-13).

After duly considering his own sad and unfortunate situation, an excommunicated person may long again for spiritual ministrations and the privileges of a blessed child of God. In truth, excommunication is designed to arouse the offender to sense the gravity of his sins and move him to remorse, contrition, confession, and a ready acceptance of the Gospel of Christ. When such a person sincerely repents in the manner indicated and gives his church the unqualified assurance that he will mend his ways, then he must be received again as a brother into the communion of saints. Special thoughtfulness and consideration should be accorded him as the Apostle recommends, II Cor. 2:7-9.

Dr. Stoeckhardt therefore encourages the congregation to act promptly and gratefully in taking the necessary steps to restore the penitent sinner to full membership. (Minnesota, 1918, p. 48 ff.)

Under like circumstances it behooves every Christian to remember that "Christ came to seek and to save that which was lost" and also to reflect again upon the fact that "there is joy among the angels in heaven over one sinner that repenteth."

Thesis XIV

A church or congregation that has never exercised the right and duty of employing the successive steps of church discipline must not for that reason be adjudged unorthodox or unchristian.

Since the practice of church discipline is not the essence of the Christian religion, it cannot be made a condition of true orthodoxy. This becomes quite evident from clear instances of New Testament history.

The congregation at Corinth had definitely been remiss in its duty to exercise church discipline, as indicated in the Apostle's rebuke of the entire membership (I Cor. 5:1-6). Yet he does not for that reason denominate them as being unorthodox or unchristian; rather he greets them as "the church of God which is at Corinth. . . . sanctified in Christ Jesus, called to be saints with all that in every place call upon the name of Jesus Christ our Lord" (I Cor. 1:2).

The church at Pergamus was praised and commended by the Apostle John for its faith and devotion to the Gospel and as such was accepted as Christian in character; yet it had the one distinct failing of having neglected church discipline. It was rebuked for this sin in the words: "I have a few things against thee" (Rev. 2:14). Naturally it was to repent of this act of disobedience and mend its faults.

Thyatira was credited with charity, service, faith, patience, and good works and as such was fundamentally Christian and orthodox, but it failed in its obligation to exercise church discipline, and the Lord stated warningly: "I have a few things against thee" (Rev. 2:20).

Our Formula of Concord condemns the Schwenkfeldians because they insisted that "it is not a true Christian congregation in which no public excommunication or no regular process of the ban is observed" (Epitome XII, par. 7, *Triglot*, p. 843).

In a newly organized mission congregation, where the members do not yet have a full understanding of their responsibilities, it may not be possible to proceed to the final steps of church discipline until the members have increased their religious knowledge and progressed in their personal sanctification. This situation, however, does not prevent the pastor himself from suspending a manifest sinner from attendance at the Holy Sacrament. And he must exercise that duty as a spiritual shepherd entrusted with immortal souls because an impenitent guest at the Lord's Table would "eat and drink to himself damnation."

It should be clear from the foregoing that the congregation is not identified as a Christian congregation merely through the act of church discipline nor through failure in excommunicating a fellow member, but also that evident neglect in employing church discipline in instances of persistent impenitence is a flagrant disobedience of God's command and, as such, a serious sin.

Our Synod must ever be alert to its duties and responsibilities, and while church discipline involves many difficult tasks, we dare not shrink from obeying the Lord's express commands.

Church and State

OUR topic is not "The Church," nor "The State"; it is the relation between the two. When we speak of the relation between Church and State, the term *Church* does not designate the invisible Church of Christ; nor does it mean any particular denomination, nor a local congregation. It refers to the visible organization of the Christian Church in its activity on earth. *State*, again, designates the government, whatever form it may take, in its activity, its official acts as a government.

Our topic is not one of the basic doctrines of Scripture, one on which hangs our eternal salvation, with which the Church or Christianity stands or falls. Yet our Confessions correctly state that the topic concerning the distinction between the Kingdom of Christ and a political kingdom is a most important and necessary one and declare that it is most necessary that we know it (*Apology*, XVI, 54. *Triglot*, p. 330, German text).

I

Church and State are two separate, distinct, and different realms.

Church and State have one thing in common, that is, their Founder. There are on earth two realms ordained by God: The Kingdom of God, in which Christ alone rules, and the secular State, in which the government, ordained by God, rules. Jesus plainly speaks of these two realms when He says to Pilate: "My kingdom is not of this world" (John 18:36). He refers, of course, not to His Kingdom of Power, but to His Kingdom of Grace, His Church on earth; and He wants that distinguished from the other realm, the world.

The Church was founded by God just as soon as there was a need for a Church. When man had fallen into sin, a way had to

Church and State 563

be found to restore his disturbed relation with God. And God said: "I will put enmity between thee (Satan) and the woman and between thy seed and her Seed. It shall bruise thy head, and thou shalt bruise His heel" (Gen. 3:15). There was instituted the Church of Jesus Christ.

Throughout Old Testament times this Church was active. God elected one nation, Israel, to be the carrier of the Church's message to man. They worked in hope, trusting in the promises of God's Messiah. In the fullness of time He came and wrought out the redemption in which the Church of the Old Testament had trusted and on which the Church of the New Testament is built; for God's will was not only that the world should be redeemed, but that all the redeemed should form one great, glorious realm, a spiritual State. That is not the choice of Christian free will; that is God's eternal counsel. Of the unintentional prophecy of Caiphas, that "it is expedient for us that one man should die for the people," the inspired Apostle says: "This spake he not of himself; but being high priest that year, he prophesied that Jesus should die for that nation; and not for that nation only, but that also He should gather together in one the children of God that were scattered abroad" (John 11:51-52). So the Apostles speak of the Church as a corporate body distinguished from others. I Pet. 2:9-10: "Ye are a chosen generation, a royal priesthood, an holy nation, a peculiar people, that ye should show forth the praises of Him who hath called you out of darkness into His marvelous light; which in time past were not a people, but are now the people of God." And St. Paul speaks of the Church as the body of Christ, of which Christ is the Head (Eph. 1:22-23), which Christ loved, and for which Christ "gave Himself" (Eph. 5:25-27).

Unlike the Church, the State is not an immediate, direct ordinance of God; it gradually developed from the family. The first father was king, and so government in his family, and that by divine right. Again, this order came as soon as there was a need of it, after the Fall, when because of sin man's relation to his fellow men was disrupted, and a power to settle differences had to be established. God made man the head of the family, made him a father, and stationed him over the son. We may even conclude that God gave him the power of the sword, the power over life and death. Gen. 9:6: "Whoso sheddeth man's blood, by man shall his blood be shed," was said to Noah when he was the sole family head on earth. So Abraham was ruler in his household and even exercised a protective rule over Lot.

Then men multiplied. Families became tribes, and tribes, nations. Man has a natural impulse to unite with others to form a community — hermits live an unnatural life. This gregarious impulse in man is as natural and as universal as the sex instinct. It is implanted in man in creation. In these communities the rule by the head of the household was transferred to the leader of tribes and nations for the purpose of mutually protecting each individual's rights, the rights which every man recognizes as the individual's natural rights. So developed government. But now note: This was not a previously planned, humanly pre-calculated development; behind it is God. Rightly the Apology says: "A natural right is truly a divine right, because it is an ordinance divinely impressed upon nature" (Apology, XXIII, 12. *Triglot*, p. 367). Rousseau, in his *Social Contract*, recognized in people the common urge of uniting and forming some government, some authority, to control community affairs. But he should have gone a step farther; even the evolutionary materialist cannot escape the final argument that evidently, since this urge is natural in all men, it must have been implanted by the Creator. Because of this urge men combine into communities, these into States, in order that the power and authority of their combined interests may protect the rights of individuals. And that is civil government — and its Author is the Creator, God.

More than that. God has not only planted the knowledge of these natural rights in man's heart, He has directly given each individual these rights in His inspired Word, in the second Table of the Law; He has protected them by His Commandments. He wants these Commandments enforced, their transgression punished; and He wants it punished by men. Gen. 9:5-6: "Surely your blood of your lives will I require; at the hand of every beast will I require it and at the hand of man; at the hand of every man's brother will I require the life of man. Whoso sheddeth man's blood, *by man* shall his blood be shed." Luther says: "In this word civil government is established, and the sword is given to it" (Erlanger, 22, 64). Hence government exists by God's will.

Moreover, wherever government is established, God acknowledges it in His Word and stamps it as His ordinance. There is no divine command as to the form the government it to assume; but whatever form it takes, God wants us to regard government not as a human, but as a divine institution. The chief text that applies here is Rom. 13:1-7: "Let every soul be subject unto the higher powers. For there is no power but of God; the powers that be are ordained of God. Whosoever therefore resisteth the power, resisteth the ordinance of God; and they that resist shall receive to themselves damnation" (vv. 1-2). Wherever government exists, if it is the power in the land, if it has the power to maintain its governmental authority, to exercise governmental duties, it is the ordinance of God, and we must be subject to it, obey it; if we do not, we resist the ordinance, the will and command of God, aye, God Himself. "Wherefore ye must needs be subject, not only for wrath, but also for conscience' sake" (v. 5); not only because disobedience will be punished, but because we know it is God's will that we obey. That holds true whether the government is good or bad, Christian or pagan, just or unjust. When Paul wrote his Letter to the Romans, the "higher power" was Nero; surely, a more pagan, a more wicked and unjust government, is hardly on record. And to Pilate, the Son of God said: "Thou couldest have no power at all against me, except it were given thee from above" (John 19:11). The government is God's ordinance whether it has received its power by means right or wrong. The Romans had obtained power in Jewish lands by wholly unjust means; yet Christ acknowledged the government of Caesar. When a foreign power attacks our land, we have the right to resist while it is conquering; but when it has become the established government, it is the power ordained by God — perhaps as a rod of judgment, a chastisement for the people's wickedness. I Pet. 2:13-17: "Submit yourselves to every ordinance of man (that is, ordinance regulating the affairs of men) for the Lord's sake, whether it be to the king, as supreme; or unto governors, as unto them that are sent by him for the punishment of evildoers and for the praise of them that do well. . . . Honor the king." (Large Catechism, Com. IV, par. 141 f. *Triglot*, p. 621.)

That establishes the principle of government. In passing, it should be noted that St. Paul calls the government "the minister of God to thee for good"; "the minister of God, a revenger to execute wrath upon him that doeth evil"; "rulers are not a terror to good works, but to the evil" (Rom. 13). There is the case of governments becoming the ministers of Satan, commanding subjects to act contrary to God's will and Law; that absolves Christians from obedience. There may come a time when a government violates all principles of right and justice, so that they cease to be revengers to execute wrath upon him that doeth evil and become a terror to good works and not to evil. Governments have not only rights, but duties and responsibilities; when they totally fail to meet these, there may come a time when Christians may join with their fellow citizens to call the government to account and bring about reform. When that time comes is a question which must be considered and decided in every individual instance.

Within the State exists the Church. Christians live in both realms; they are citizens of the Kingdom of God and of the State. They have their rights in each, God-given rights; they have their duties in each, God-imposed duties. It is vital that we know the difference between the two realms and the implications of this distinction for our life.

There is, in the first place, a difference in the nature of the two realms. The State is external, visible; "the Kingdom of God cometh not with observation; neither shall they say, Lo, here! or, Lo, there!" (Luke 17:20.) You cannot find it on the map; it is not limited to a certain country or nation; it knows no boundaries; it extends over all the earth. The State is temporal; the Kingdom of Christ is eternal (Luke 1:33), not doomed to decay and death like all the kingdoms of the world. The State is physical, earthly, secular; the Church is spiritual; it is in the world, but not of the world, (John 18:36). The Church is the habitation of God through the Spirit (Eph. 2:22; I Pet. 2:5). (Apology, VII, VIII, 11—13. *Triglot*, p. 229 f.)

Next there is a difference in membership. Subjects of the State are all who live within its borders. Members of the Church are those only who accept Jesus Christ as their Savior. Men are born into the State; they must be regenerated into the Church; they become members by a living faith in Christ.

The membership of the State is composed of two classes: rulers and subjects. The government of the State takes different forms, the officials bear different names: emperors, kings, princes, presidents, parliaments, cabinets, congresses, etc. Always there are a number of officials necessary to maintain law and order. They rule; they make the laws and enforce them. And under them are the subjects who obey the laws — or suffer for transgressions. — Nothing like that in the Church. "One is your Master, even Christ; and all ye are brethren" (Matt. 23:8). No man, no organization of men, has the least right to command, to make laws in the Church; they are all followers of God as dear children, and of Christ, who has loved them (Eph. 5:1-2); and in their relation toward each other, "submitting yourselves one to another in the fear of God" (Eph. 5:21). Neither the whole Church, nor a single person, nor any number of men, may assume the right of ruling, or enacting laws for the individual conscience. One is Master, and no one may share that place with Him. — No Pope, no bishop, no pastor, no council, consistory, or synod, has a right to rule in the Church. When the two sons of Zebedee came to Jesus and asked Him to make them cardinals, princes of the Church, the Lord called His disciples together and said: "Ye know that the princes of the Gentiles exercise dominion over them, and they that are great exercise authority upon them. But it shall not be so among you; but whosoever will be great among you, let him be your minister; and whosoever will be chief among you, let him be your servant" (Matt. 20:25-27). Church princes, Church authorities, Church governments with legislative, judicial, and executive powers, have no place in the Church. Pastors have the duty to feed the flock of God, not of being lords over God's heritage (I Pet. 5:2-3). An interesting example for this is 2 Cor. 8. In passing, St. Paul recommended a collection for the needy brethren in Jerusalem; but he says: "I speak not by commandment." He does not think of ordering it. He only appeals to their love. God has commanded love, but not the way in which it must be shown. — Our Confessions condemn especially the arrogant claims of the Roman hierarchy (Apology, Art. XXVIII. *Triglot,* p. 443 ff.; Smalcald Articles, Part II, Art. IV. *Triglot,* p. 471 ff.). But the temptation to follow that same trend is present everywhere, and it is characteristic of the Calvinistic sects to give way to it in ordinances that go beyond the Word of God: Methodists, with their ordinances against tobacco and liquor; Baptists, with their compulsory immersion; there was a time when Baptists prohibited all ornaments, even forbade Baptists to have their pictures taken (1889).

The object and purpose of civil government is altogether different from that of the Church. Both objects are briefly stated in the old sentence: The object of the State is world peace; the object of the Church is eternal peace. The State is to guard and promote the temporal welfare of all its citizens; the Church works for the spiritual and eternal welfare of all men. Jesus Himself states the object of His State on earth when He says to Paul (Acts 26:18): I send thee to the Gentiles "to open their eyes and to turn them from darkness to light and from the power of Satan unto God, that they may receive forgiveness of sins and inheritance among them which are sanctified by faith that is in Me." Cp. Eph. 4:11-16. The purpose of the Church is to bring sinners to heaven. As the Church we are not here to make men outwardly pious — that will follow of itself — we are here to save them. The State, on the contrary, is concerned only with the temporal welfare of its citizens — of all its citizens; hence it must sometimes sacrifice the welfare of individuals for the sake of the community, as in the case of war, the condemnation of individual property for the building of a street, a railroad, etc. The State must punish wickedness when thereby others are harmed. It must prevent such wickedness, and so employ watchmen, police, FBI men, etc. The State must have an army and a navy to protect citizens from outside enemies. The State must make regulations concerning commerce, trade, and industry, adopt and enforce health ordinances; it must provide for the care and support of the poor, not because of pity and mercy, but because of its duty to protect and promote the welfare of all citizens, those who are directly involved and their neighbors and fellow citizens — starvation makes criminals. To do all this, the State must have funds. It therefore has the right to levy taxes; and the duty of citizens is to pay such taxes fully and honestly (Rom. 13:6-7).

The domain of Church and State in their activity is altogether different. Both deal with the same men, but in different ways. They deal perhaps with the same sinners, the same criminals; but the State looks at the crimes, the actual works of the flesh, curbs them with laws, punishes them with fines, prison, perhaps even with death. The Church has not only the purpose of keeping men from committing such crimes, but of providing that the sinners are not damned eternally. The domain of the State, then, includes only purely civil, earthly matters, earthly welfare of citizens, government, protection, defense; its control extends only over the body. The domain of the Church is the spiritual welfare of men; all that pertains to the service of God, all that concerns the soul and the salvation of men; her jurisdiction is the relation of man to God. The State "beareth the sword" (Rom. 13:4); no one else but the State; to the government it is said: "Whoso sheddeth man's blood, by man shall his blood be shed" Gen. 9:6); to it the sword is given; to all others Jesus says: "All they that take the sword shall perish with the sword" (Matt. 26:52). The government is to "execute wrath upon him that doeth evil," to praise those who do that which is good (Rom. 13:3-4). Morals and habits of men concern the State only in so far as they affect the life of others or the safety of the State. For that reason it prohibits exhibition of lewd pictures, mailing of obscene literature, lotteries, etc., not because such things may send souls to hell, but because they may produce criminals.

The State therefore aims only at outward discipline and obedience. Only wicked actions fall under the jurisdiction of civil government. But the Church aims at the thoughts and desires of the heart. The Church condemns anger, hatred, envy, etc. Luther says: "These two orders must be strictly distinguished, and both remain; one that makes pious; the other that creates outward peace and hinders evil work; neither of the two without the other is sufficient in the world." (Erlanger, 22, 70.)

As State and Church have different domains, different aims and purposes, so they follow different principles and have different standards. The State's laws follow the dictates of reason. All ordinances are given on the basis of prompting the temporal welfare of its citizens in the best way possible. Laws may therefore be changed as conditions change. While perfection is aimed at, the State must often compromise and be satisfied with less than perfection, since that is the best that can be attained. The State is not governed by Christian principles, based on the divine Word. In that case it would have to require all citizens to go to church, to read the Bible, to forgive all injustice, with the result that criminals would run wild. The State knows no brotherly admonition, no excommunication, etc. Hence the State should not base its laws and acts on the Bible. It decrees capital punishment for murderers, not because God has said: "Whoso sheddeth man's blood, by man shall his blood be shed," but on the reasonable assumption that severe and sure punishment will intimidate criminals and keep the land from becoming a den of murderers. Sunday laws may be enacted, but only because rest is necessary for workers and because some citizens want to have opportunity to hold divine services undisturbed. Laws against polygamy have their basis on reasonable grounds; that is one way of protecting the rights of female citizens. The State has no business to tell people what they owe to God. The State's business is only to see to it that all citizens may lead a quiet and peaceable life in all godliness and honesty (I Tim. 2:2); that all render to all their dues (Rom. 13:7). Since State laws are based on the best application of reason to existing conditions, the State may permit certain things which the Church must prohibit. It permits unscriptural divorces, as Moses did (Matt. 19:8). It may permit marriages in prohibited degrees and prohibit marriages which are permitted in the Bible. A Christian citizen will, of course, not make use of such permission; he is bound by another Law. A Christian judge will in his court permit a divorce which in the congregational meeting he must and will condemn. A legislator may enact or vote for a law, and then advise Christian citizens not to take advantage of the law, but to follow their better principles. — The Church, on the other hand, has only one Law, which is invariable and eternal. The Church teaches people to observe all things whatsoever Christ has commanded them (Matt. 28:20). Nor does the Church use harsh means to enforce that Law. "My sheep hear My voice . . . and they follow Me," Jesus says. That's a mere plain statement of fact. When men become sheep of Jesus Christ, and as far as they are sheep of Christ, they hear His voice and follow Him. That's natural procedure for them. All the Church has to do is to show them what the will of Christ is. On the other hand, the Church has no right to go beyond the Word of Christ, to set up articles of faith, or to change His teachings. In the Roman Church you hear regularly as basis for their teaching and practice: The Church holds; the Pope defines; the Church Fathers teach. Our Confessions answer: "It will not do to frame articles of faith from the works or words of the holy

Church and State 571

Fathers.... The rule is: The Word of God shall establish articles of faith, and no one else, not even an angel" (Smalcald Articles, Part II, 15. *Triglot*, p. 467.) The objection is sometimes raised: Do not you Lutherans do the same thing and "frame articles of faith" in your Confessions? But our Confession itself gives the answer (Formula of Concord, Solida Declaratio, 3. *Triglot*, p. 851): "We confess also the First, Unaltered Augsburg Confession as our symbol for this time, not because it was composed by our theologians, but because it has been taken from God's Word and is founded firmly and well therein."

Finally, the means used to carry out what is deemed right differ in the two realms. The State uses force as a means of executing its business — police, prison, sword. The Church uses only the Word of God. When that is ineffective, the Church can dissolve fellowship (Matt. 18:17), nothing more. The Church cannot use force. Peter is told to sheathe his sword. To Pilate Jesus says that it is not in harmony with the nature of His kingdom to have His servants fight for it. "The weapons of our warfare are not carnal," says St. Paul (II Cor. 10:4). "Not by might, nor by power, but by My Spirit, saith the Lord of Hosts" (Zech. 4:6). The Church can only admonish, warn, plead, point out God's grace and wrath; nothing more. If people will not receive her testimony — for that eventuality, too, the Lord has outlined our procedure: "Whosoever shall not receive you, nor hear your words, when ye depart out of that house or city, shake off the dust of your feet" (Matt. 10:14).

State and Church — two totally different realms; in fact, they are opposites. And yet they should work in complete harmony. Augsburg Confession, XXVIII, 10–11 (*Triglot*, p. 85): "Therefore, since the power of the Church grants eternal things, and is exercised only by the ministry of the Word, it does not interfere with civil government; no more than the art of singing interferes with civil government. For civil government deals with other things than does the Gospel. The civil rulers defend not minds, but bodies and bodily things against manifest injuries, and restrain men with the sword and bodily punishments in order to preserve civil justice and peace." "The kingdom of Christ is spiritual, inasmuch as Christ governs by the Word and by preaching, to wit, beginning in the heart the knowledge of God, the fear of God and faith, eternal righteousness, and eternal life; meanwhile it permits us outwardly to use legitimate political ordinances of every nation in which we live, just as it permits us to use medicine or the art of building, or food, drink, air. Neither does the Gospel bring new laws concerning the civil state, but commands that we obey present laws, whether they have been framed by heathen or by others, and that in this obedience we should exercise love. . . . For the Gospel does not destroy the State or the family, buying, selling, and other civil regulations, but much rather approves them, and bids us obey them as a divine ordinance, not only on account of punishment, but also on account of conscience." (Apology, XVI, 54—57. *Triglot*, p. 331.)

II

It is evidently God's plan that the two realms, Church and State, should exist side by side in the world.

The wording of this thesis is deliberate. Nowhere has God said: The State shall not govern the Church; if it does so, it has forfeited its rights and ceases to be an ordinance of God. Nowhere has God said: The Church must not rule the State; a Church State has no right of existence, and whoever submits to it transgresses a divine commandment and sins. If it were so, if there were such a definite commandment of God in the Bible, the matter would be very clear: We must insist on absolute separation of Church and State, refuse to submit when the State takes the rule over the Church, and rather suffer all, even death, than transgress such a command of God. If there were such a clear commandment, membership in a State Church would be sin. But our fathers left the State Church, not because it was a State Church, but because of false doctrine and practice in that Church. It is, however, an abnormal condition if the State governs the Church, or vice versa. There is sufficient evidence in Scripture to show that it is God's plan that the two should exist side by side in the world.

Matt. 22:21: "Render unto Caesar the things which are Caesar's and unto God the things that are God's." The Pharisees had asked Jesus the trick question: "Is it lawful to give tribute unto Caesar or not?" Jesus led them to acknowledge that Caesar, the Roman Empire, was the de facto government in the land, the actually ruling power; and Jesus tells them that He is not come to release subjects from their duties to government. But when He adds: "and unto God the things that are God's," He evidently puts more into His answer than they had asked for. What it is that we owe to God the Pharisees knew very well: obedience to His commandments. But when Jesus contrasts the two: Caesar and God, He plainly indicates the distinction between the two realms: the State and the Church. There is a line of distinction between that which is due to the government and that which is due to God. It has been held that all Jesus here says is: You owe to the government one thing, to God another thing; see to it that you give to each what you owe; that's all this passage teaches. — This passage teaches more. According to it, there are things that do not belong to Caesar, that we must render to God. There is a limit to the State's right; if it oversteps that, it is out of bounds, and we must not render to the State what God has reserved for Himself. What these things are we must learn from Scripture. There is, for example, the rule in the Church. Jesus said that in His Church "One is your Master, even Christ." There is to be no rule in the Church but that of Christ. If Caesar usurps that, he takes what does not belong to him. — On the other hand, by the same word of Christ, there are things which God Himself has given to Caesar: the rule in the State. God gave it; God can take it away again, but no one else. God can limit it, does limit it ("We must obey God rather than man"); but no one else has the right to interfere. Whoever, whether it be Pope, council, or synod, interferes with the rule of the State, usurps the domain which God has assigned exclusively to the civil government. — Clearly this implies separation.

We turn to John 18:36-37. Pilate was examining Jesus. Was He, as the Jews claimed, a rival of Caesar, dangerous to the Roman Empire? Jesus tells him: You need not fear; My kingdom is an altogether different realm and does not interfere with that of Caesar. My kingdom is not of this world; Caesar's is. You use physical force, sword, scourge, cross; My disciples must not even fight for the life of their Master, much less for less causes. Evidently Jesus draws a wall of partition between the two, State and Church; the State has no rival in the Church; the Church has nothing to do with the things of this world, where Caesar has his domain. — Just so Jesus said to overzealous Peter: "Put up again thy sword into his place; for all they that take the sword shall perish with the sword" (Matt. 26:52). Violence has no place in His kingdom; it definitely has in the State; to the government God has given the sword; if the Church uses force, it takes a power which God has given to the State and to which the Church has no right.

Christ acted consistently. He refused to state whether the adulteress should be stoned; that was the court's business. He rebuked the man who wanted help from Him in a division of disputed property; He said: "Man, who made Me a judge or a divider over you?" (Luke 12:14.) That was the court's business, and Jesus refused to hake a hand in it. He acknowledged the Roman government as the power in the land to whom all citizens, including Peter, owed obedience in earthly things. To Pilate He said, "Thou couldest have no power at all against Me except it were given thee from above" (John 19:11). Pilate had power over His life. That was an earthly thing. But His kingdom is not of this same world; and while Pilate need fear no competition from Him in this world, Pilate and his realm of violence had no place in Christ's kingdom. When Peter and the Apostles were called before the Sanhedrin, they obeyed; when they were sent to prison, they raised no rebellion. But when the Sanhedrin told them not to preach the name of Jesus, they said: "We ought to obey God rather than men" (Acts 5:29). That was something which God had not delegated to Caesar, but had reserved for Himself.

That is what we gather from the Word of God. Our Confessions reiterate that plainly and forcibly. Augsburg Confession, Art. XXVIII, 1–4, 12–17 (*Triglot*, p. 83): "There has been great controversy concerning the Power of Bishops, in which some have awkwardly confounded the power of the Church and the power of the sword. And from this confusion very great wars and tumults have resulted, while the Pontiffs, emboldened by the power of the Keys, not only have instituted new services and burdened consciences with reservation of cases and ruthless excommunications, but have also undertaken to transfer the kingdoms of this world and to take the Empire from the Emperor. These wrongs have long since been rebuked in the Church by learned and godly men. Therefore our teachers, for the comforting of men's consciences, were constrained to show the difference between the power of the Church and the power of the sword, and taught that both of them, because of God's commandment, are to be held in reverence and honor, as the chief blessings of God on earth." "Therefore the power of the Church and the civil power must not be confounded. The power of the Church has its own commission, to teach the Gospel and to administer the Sacraments. Let it not break into the office of another; let it not transfer the kingdoms of this world; let it not abrogate the laws of civil rulers; let it not abolish lawful obedience; let it not interfere with judgments concerning civil ordinances or contracts; let it not prescribe laws to civil rulers concerning the form of the Commonwealth. As Christ says, John 18:36: My kingdom is not of this world; also Luke 12:14: Who made me a judge or a divider over you? Paul also says, Phil. 3:20: Our citizenship is in heaven; 2 Cor. 10:4: The weapons of our warfare are not carnal, but mighty through God to the casting down of imaginations." Cp. Apology, Art. XVI, 54—55. *Triglot,* p. 329 f. Luther never tired of setting forth, not only the distinction between Church and State, but also that the two must needs be kept separate (X:395, 403; VII:1789 f.; XIII:207; VII:1741).

In spite of the clear statements of Scripture the principle of separation of Church and State was almost perpetually disregarded in the history of the Church. A glance at this history is therefore indicated.

The Church was born a free Church. Jesus asked neither Caiaphas nor Pilate nor Herod for permission to establish His Church, nor for their assistance in maintaining it. And so later on there was neither a spiritual nor a temporal government in the Church. Christians asked no emperor, no king, no government, for permission to found congregations; what sort of order they should adopt in the Church; whom they should elect and call as their pastors. That was solely their own concern. When it became necessary to elect deacons (Acts 6), the Apostles called the multitude of disciples together, stated the case, and the Church then elected them. Nobody else was asked. Neither Pilate nor Caiaphas was notified. When the Church was persecuted, they did not defend their cause with the sword, as Zwinglians and Calvinists did later on; but, like our Lutheran fathers, they suffered. They left all things to God; they let the storm howl; they were either killed or, according to Christ's instruction, they fled to other lands — and preached the Gospel anew.

All this not because the mixing of Church and State was something unheard of at that time. The Church was born among the Jews in a theocracy; and while they had lost the most of their jurisdiction to the Romans, the old theocracy remained the ideal and its restoration the hope of the Jews. And in the Roman Empire civil government and religion were inextricably mixed. Among the Romans, as before them among the Greeks, religion was a matter of the State. The Roman emperor was pontifex maximus, the high priest. It was a duty of the State to appoint priests for the Roman temples. The gods were national gods. Taking part in the religious cult was the duty of every citizen. Persecution at times resulted because the Christians refused to comply with this custom. Romans did not usually compel conquered nations to give up their religion. Quite commonly they adopted the gods of the conquered people and, sometimes in a formal ceremony, added them to their own menagerie. But the Roman government, in defense of its religion, turned against Christians because they were not unionistic but insisted that the Christian God was the only God. Christians during the first three centuries not only had no alliance with the State, they were persecuted by the State; at best, and for certain times only, they were a permitted religion. But on the side of the Roman Empire the treatment accorded the Christians was in line with common custom: Religion was a part of the State's field of activity, and the control of religion a part of the regular government program.

Quite naturally, then, this kind of religious establishment was foisted on the Christian Church when the head of the State joined the Christian Church. Constantine turned to Christianity — this seems evident — as a prop for his tottering empire. Diocletian had tried to revive and stabilize old Roman paganism for the same purpose, had signally failed, and Constantine, witnessing this, had calmly turned to the new powerful opponent of paganism, to Christianity. And, quite naturally, he assumed that Christianity now would take the same role that paganism had formerly played, that of State religion. And so the Church lost its freedom.

It is true, Constantine's Edict of Milan (313) reads like a perfect toleration edict. The pertinent paragraphs read: "We thought that, among other things which seemed likely to profit men generally, we ought, in the very first place, to set in order the conditions of the reverence paid to the divinity by giving to the Christians and all others full permission to follow whatever worship any man had chosen; whereby whatever Divinity there is in heaven may be benevolent and propitious to us and to all placed under our authority. Therefore we thought we ought, with sound counsel and very right reason, to lay down this law, that we should in no way refuse to any man any legal right who has given up his mind either to the observance of Christianity or to that worship which he personally feels best suited to himself, to the end that the Supreme Divinity, whose worship we freely follow, may continue in all things to grant us his accustomed favor and good will. . . . These things we thought it well to signify in the fullest manner to your carefulness that you might know that we have given free and absolute permission to the said Christians to practice their worship. And when you perceive that we have granted this to the said Christians, your devotion understands that to others also a similarly full and free permission for their own worship and observance is granted, for the quiet of our times, so that every man may have freedom in the practice of whatever worship he has chosen. And these things were done by us that nothing be taken away from any honor or form of worship." (Ayer, *Source Book for Ancient Church History*.)

Constantine, however, at once extended the old control of religion in the State to the Christian Church. He retained the title Pontifex Maximus, which was later changed to Episcopus Universalis. He was the absolute head of the Church and exercised arbitrary authority over the Church. He called the great Council of Nicaea, paid the expenses of all the bishops from State funds; at least part of the time he acted as chairman of the meeting; he decided whether the confession was acceptable or not. He no longer performed the functions of a priest, but he united in himself all ecclesiastical authority: he appointed and disciplined priests; he created laws and rights for the Church by his dictum. The Christian Church became an institution of the State. In a short time it became a compulsory institution. The very persecution which in the name of religion had formerly been directed against Christianity was now employed to uproot heathenism and to put down dissent in the Church; and in the latter endeavor not rarely true witnesses of truth were persecuted. Constantine himself was persuaded by Arians to depose Athanasius for his testimony and to exile him. To be a citizen of the Empire one had to be an orthodox Christian — orthodox in the opinion of the government. Emperor Valentinian II (392) prohibited all heathen worship. Justinian I (550) persecuted paganism. Another phase that had far-reaching results entered with Emperor Arcadius, 398. Constantine, with good intentions, had established ecclesiastical courts; he did not want the affairs of the Christian Church discussed and decided in pagan secular courts. But Arcadius also permitted people to go to the bishop's court with their temporal, secular matters. His brother and successor Honorius instructed his State officials that such decisions of bishops were to be executed by the officers of the State. This was later on repeated in the Codex of Theodosius, and in due time was incorporated in the Canon Law of the Roman Catholic Church. And so it became the beginning of the rivalry between secular and ecclesiastical courts which lasted far beyond the Reformation and made the bishops "two-faced monsters, showing on one side a bishop, on the other a politician."

Under the Christian emperors, then, Church and State were most thoroughly mixed. The Church became a part of the State's machinery. Emperors and others used the bishops as tools to attain their political objects. This system was most consistently developed in the Eastern Empire after its separation from Rome. It reached perhaps its greatest perfection in Russia. There was, indeed, the Holy Directing Synod, since Peter the Great, in nominal control of the Church; but the dictator in that Synod was a lay minister appointed by the Czar. The Czar was, in fact, the only source of authority in the Church. The ecclesiastical organization was used to strengthen the State. Withdrawal from the State Church was not permitted. Not without reason many have held that the close association between Church and State inaugurated by Constantine was the beginning of corruption in the Church. Formalism and worldliness entered, and the Church became thoroughly depraved.

This close alliance between Church and State, with the State at the helm, was not limited to the East. But with the division of the Empire the West entered on a period of chaos. Order in the State returned with Charlemagne. And at once we see him attempt to translate the Old Latin State Church into German. He waged campaigns against the remaining pagan tribes in Western Europe, and the price of peace was Baptism. It was not only politics with

Charlemagne; it was, no doubt, also a conviction of duty that moved him to spread the Church with the sword and to permit the Pope to crown him emperor; he wanted to be the protector of the Church in the West. But there was no free Church under Charlemagne. Christianity was State religion, and Charlemagne would have been the last one to deny that.

The ideal of Charlemagne and of other Christians of that period was an equal and mutually profitable partnership between Church and State. Actually the result was a century-long fight between State and Church for supremacy. In the meantime something had happened in the West: The Papacy had developed. When the Western Empire fell under the onslaughts of the Barbarians, there was one institution that stood firm, unaffected by these attacks: the Western Church, which had already been well centralized under the Bishop of Rome. As the Western Empire decreased in power and prestige, the Church not only remained intact; it increased in power. Most of the Germanic tribes were already at least tinted with Christianity (Arianism), and they looked with some awe at this finished, compact, orderly operating institution, which contrasted beautifully with the decrepit political Empire. When the Lombards attacked Italy and also threatened the Church State, and no one of the Italian princes was strong enough to take the lead in defense, it was Gregory the Great, Bishop of Rome, who united the princes and led the campaign. The Church — now the Roman Catholic Church, under the leadership of the Papacy — had become a power to be reckoned with. Slowly and carefully it extended this power. 800 A. D., on Christmas Day, the Pope more or less surprised Charlemagne by crowning him emperor. During Charlemagne's lifetime the claim was never advanced that this made the emperor a creature of the Pope and therefore subject to him. Rome, with very few exceptions, knows when to talk and when to keep silence. Charlemagne was too strong a character to stand for such an assertion. But Rome never forgets; and Rome is never in a hurry: Wait for the psychological moment to gain advantages. The time came when under Charlemagne's successors the Empire fell apart. In 962, Otto I was crowned by the Pope, who now claimed this as a right. To this day your textbooks tell you that Otto established the Holy Roman Empire of the German Nation, though his father, Henry the Fowler, did much more to establish a German empire; but

Henry was too busy fighting the Huns and too averse to Papal interference to go to Rome to be crowned. Do we see the influence of a fine Italian hand in this? Otto helped the cause of Rome in another way: He made all bishops secular princes, investing them with land and official position and power in the State, largely secularizing their functions.

It was partly due to the increasing worldliness of the hierarchy that the Papacy struck low ebb ca. 1000 A. D. The wealth of the Church drew many unfit men into office in the Church. In 1024 a layman was elected Pope, John XIX. Then a boy was elected, Benedict IX, twelve years old, yet well accomplished in vice, evil-minded. The Romans drove him out and sold the tiara to Silvester III. But Benedict came back and drove out Silvester. When, however, he grew up, he wanted to marry, and his prospective father-in-law would not listen to his advances while he was a priest, so Benedict sold the papal crown to Gratian, who took the name Gregory VI. Gratian was one of the monks of Clugny, a reform party. When the offer of the Papacy was made to him, he asked his associates whether it might be permitted to commit simony, buy the Papacy, with the good intention of reforming it. The common consent was that it was all right, the end justifying the means. So he bought the Papacy with 1,000 lbs. of silver. But Benedict's marriage schemes miscarried; so he came back again and claimed the Papacy. Now the Church had three Popes: Silvester III; Benedict IX; Gregory VI.

Disgusted with this state of affairs, the Synod of Sutri, 1046, called on the emperor, Henry III, to clean house, giving him the power to appoint Popes for all time to come. He appointed Clement II, who started reforms and died within a year; poison was suspected. Then Damasus II, who was Pope for 23 days, died, which ended the ardor of papal candidates. After a two-year deadlock the Emperor persuaded his cousin Bruno of Toul to take the job as Leo IX. With Hildebrand, the later Gregory VII, as power behind the throne, Leo began a program of reform; however, the opportunity came to take a second step which Hildebrand thought necessary: to shake off the dependency on the emperor. Henry III died, 1056, leaving a son and successor only six years old. Promptly a Lateran Synod in 1059 placed the election of Popes into the hands of the cardinals — and the open battle with the Empire had begun.

The next 200 years are the age of absolute papal rule. The principle that the Pope is the vicar of God on earth and therefore lord over all other earthly powers, and subject to none, it not only frankly stated but enforced as far as conditions allowed. Gregory VII still had an uphill fight against men like Henry IV; but his principles are plainly stated in the so-called "Dictatus Papae," composed, under his direction perhaps, by the cardinal Deusdedit. These are the pertinent sentences: "That the Pope has the power to depose emperors; that his decree can be annulled by no one, and that he alone may annul the decrees of any one; that he can be judged by no man; that he has the power to absolve the subjects of unjust rulers from their oath of fidelity." With 1095 came the Crusades, and the Popes used to the fullest extent the opportunity that leadership in a popular movement gave to them, to increase their prestige. Rightly Innocent III (1216) is called the Arbiter of Europe. Hardly a crowned head in Europe who was not forced to bow to his authority. Without the least scruples he wielded the dread weapons of excommunication and interdict to enforce his decrees. The Church ruled the State. Because education was almost entirely for the clergy, a majority of State officials were clergymen; and the clergy had been brought under the ironhanded authority of Rome. And so education, charity, care of the sick, even legislation and administration of justice, were made affairs of the Church. The State, crude, undeveloped, split by dissensions and never-ceasing wars, fed by the feudal system prevalent in all Europe, was no match for the Church; it was practically helpless.

Hundred years after Innocent, Boniface VIII gave the boldest and baldest expression to the political claims of the Papacy. In his bull *Unam Sanctam* (1302) he said: "In this Church and in its power are two swords, to wit, a spiritual and a temporal, and this we are taught by the words of the Gospel; for when the Apostles said, 'Behold, here are two swords' (in the Church, namely, since the Apostles were speaking), the Lord did not reply that it was too many, but enough. And, surely, he who claims that the temporal sword is not in the power of Peter has but ill understood the word of our Lord when he said, 'Put up again thy sword into his place.' Both the spiritual and the material swords, therefore, are in the power of the Church, the latter indeed to be used for the Church, the former by the Church, the one by the priest, the other by the hands of kings and soldiers, but by the will and sufferance of the priest. It is fitting, moreover, that one sword should be under the other, and the temporal authority subject to the spiritual power." "Hence, the truth bearing witness, it is for the spiritual power to establish the earthly power and judge it, if it be not good. Thus in the case of the Church and the power of the Church, the prophecy of Jeremiah is fulfilled: 'See, I have this day set thee over the nations and over the kingdoms,' etc. Therefore, if the earthly power shall err, it shall be judged by the higher. But if the supreme power err, it shall be judged by God alone and not by man, the Apostles bearing witness, saying, The spiritual man judgeth all things, but he himself is judged by no one. Hence this power, although given to man and exercised by man, is not human, but rather a divine power, given by the divine lips to Peter, and founded on a rock for him and his successors in him (Christ) whom he confessed, the Lord saying to Peter himself, 'Whatsoever thou shalt bind,' etc. Whoever, therefore, shall resist this power, ordained by God, resists the ordination of God." (Under political pressure the second successor of Boniface, Clement V, had to rescind this Bull; but centuries later Leo X, in 1516, in his Bull Pastor Aeternus, reinstated it — and it stands today as the official teaching of the Roman Catholic Church.)

There was nothing new in these claims of Boniface. For 200 years Popes had promulgated them; Innocent had enforced them to the utmost and met with relatively weak opposition. But Boniface's Bull called forth revolt. The times were changing. Men of the Renaissance were no longer ready to take dictation from above without questioning its right and binding power. Dante (1321), in his *De Monarchia*, held that both powers, Church and State, are co-ordinate, both ordained by God; the Pope has no temporal powers. Marsilius of Padua (Defensor Pacis, 1324) denied that either of the two, Pope or emperor, functions by divine right; the basis of power lies in the people — the citizens, in the State, the believers, in the Church; officials in both are accountable to the people and may be deposed. Next William of Occam (1350), an Englishman, attacked the temporal power of the Pope: Christ gave to Peter only spiritual power and jurisdiction, and more than that Peter could not confer on his successors. Both were excommunicated and died while under the ban of the Pope. Another Englishman,

John Wycliffe (1384), attacked papal arrogance in his Theory of Dominion: God gives power and authority on terms of service; if this service is not rendered, the right to power is forfeited. He drew the conclusion: The Pope is not rendering useful service, hence has no right to the office he holds. Wycliffe was the first to attack the Papacy on Scriptural grounds and to realize that the Pope is the Antichrist, but he was condemned by the Pope for reviving "the damnable heresies of Marsilius of Padua." Wycliffe died before the Papacy could take vengeance on him. The best they could do was to order his bones exhumed and burned (Council of Constance, 1414–1418), which was done. In spite of these testimonies the Pope still retained his fearful weapons, ban and interdict, with which he could quash any opposition. But under the surface these "heretical" opinions persisted and spread. This was definitely a preparation for the Reformation, a part of which was that Luther maintained that the Pope has no right of existence in the Church; that every Christian is a priest and a king before God; that the two realms should be kept separate: The Church should not interfere in secular things, nor the secular powers in spiritual things. And since Luther had taught the people from the divine Word that the Pope's ban and interdict has no validity, the Pope's excommunication of Luther and threatened interdict on Germany had no effect whatever; Luther's Reformation was successful.

There should be no doubt in our mind as to the fact that Luther, in the first place, held the true Scriptural conception of the relation between Church and State; secondly, that he hoped to organize a Church self-subsisting, self-governing, separate from the State. That Luther in theory held that Church and State should be separate has rarely been contested; testimonies for this are rather numerous in his writings (VII:1780; XIII:1442). But the statement that Luther ever had the plan, or even the hope, of organizing a Church separate from the State is frequently denied. Generally, when Luther is attacked in current literature, one of the allegations is: Luther subjected the Lutheran Church to the State. He is called the Father of the State Church (shades of Constantine the Great!), or at least of the Lutheran State Church, and so the example to other Protestant Churches. Luther himself, so they like to say, asked the government of Saxony to take over the rule of the Church. —

This much is true: Luther did ask his Elector to take the first step toward organizing the new Church. Does that signify that Luther wanted to organize a State Church? that in his opinion that was the ideal? A statement like that is absurd in view of his many emphatic arguments for a free Church. We had better examine how Luther came to make that request of the Elector, and above all, what it was that Luther actually asked when he addressed that request to his Elector.

There was, of course, no thought of a new Church organization before 1521. Luther's own separation from Rome came only with the Leipzig Debate, 1519, his three great epoch-making books of 1520 (*Letter to the Christian Nobility of the German Nation; On the Babylonian Captivity of the Church; On the Liberty of a Christian Man*), and the burning of the Pope's bull *Exsurge Domine*, December, 1520. In January, 1521, he was excommunicated in the bull *Decet Romanum*; and at the Diet of Worms he made his good confession. Then, to save him from papal violence, the Elector had him hidden at the Wartburg, until in 1522 the revolt of the radicals and the threatening disorder among the people drove him back to Wittenberg. In the meantime all over Germany the Reformation was making its influence felt. We must not think of it in this way that here a priest and there a priest stepped before his church and said: "Now I'm leaving the Roman Church and joining the new Church; will you go along?" There was no new Church. But these priests would begin to preach the Gospel as they learned it, and as far as they learned it, from others, piecemeal, often faulty. What Luther in these days thought about the future of the Church, whether he thought of a new organization at all, we do not know; the obvious hope in those days was that the old Church, perhaps by a council, could be reformed effectively and thus the rift healed. But it surely became evident at this time that something had to be done about these churches and preachers who no longer wanted to be under the Pope, to instruct them rightly, to watch that they did not go astray. Then came the Knights' War of 1523, giving evidence that the higher, the educated class of German laity had so little understanding of Luther's Reformation as to put his name on the banners of a purely political revolution. Then, in 1525, the great Peasants' Revolt with an even sadder revelation of misunderstanding and gross ignorance and even unwillingness to listen to instruction on the part of the German people. Now, Luther had an absolutely wonderful trust in the efficacy of the Word of God. Just preach the Gospel, that is his ever repeated argument, and all will turn out right. So he preached and trained others to preach. Beginning with 1523, he cleansed the church service, the Order of Worship. Then in 1526 came his *Deutsche Messe*. In the preface he speaks of three kinds of serivces: first the Latin, which he had already published and did not want abolished altogether; second, the German Mass and Order of Service, which he was now about to publish "for the sake of simple laymen." He knows that a large part of the people who come to church "do not believe and are not yet Christians. The greater part stands around and gapes, hoping to see something new, just as if we were holding a service among the Turks or the heathen in a public square or out in a field. For there is as yet no well-ordered and organized congregation here, in which the Christians could be ruled according to the Gospel. Our Service is a public provocation to faith and to Christianity" — mission work among people who had well-nigh lost all true Christian knowledge.

And he proceeds: "The third kind of service which a truly Evangelical Church Order should have would not be held in a public place for all sorts of people" — in a community church — "but for those who mean to be real Christians and profess the Gospel with hand and mouth. They would record their names on a list and meet by themselves in some house in order to pray, read, baptize, receive the Sacrament, and do other Christian works. In this manner those who do not live Christian lives could be known, reproved, reclaimed, cast out or excommunicated, according to the rule of Christ in Matthew 18. Here one could also establish a common benevolent fund among the Christians, which should be willingly given and distributed among the poor, according to the example of St. Paul (II Cor. 9). The many and elaborate chants would be unnecessary. There would be a short, appropriate Order for Baptism and the Sacrament and everything centered on the Word and prayer and love. There would be need of a good brief catechism on the Creed, the Ten Commandments, and the Our Father. In short, if one had the people and persons who wanted to be Christians in fact, the rules and regulations could easily be supplied. But as yet I neither can nor desire to begin, or to make rules for such a congregation or assembly. I have not yet the persons necessary to accomplish it; nor do I observe many who strongly urge it." (Holman edition, VI, pp. 172–173.)

These words show his conviction, urged upon him by recent experiences, that the people are not yet able to run their own Church. Yet some sort of orderly organization was necessary; the need daily became greater. Hence in November, 1526, Luther wrote a letter to his Elector, asking him to send out a visitation committee to establish what was needed in the Church of the land. He tells about that in the "Preface to the Visitation Articles" (X:1628 ff.). He speaks of the great services a true bishop rendered the Church by visiting the churches and schools; how this office was neglected by the papal bishops, and so the Church suffered general decay; now that the Gospel was restored he would gladly see this true bishop's and visitor's office restored; but none of them (Luther and his co-workers) felt that they had a call or command to do so. Hence they decided to go the sure way and appeal to the duty of love, which is imposed on all Christians, and petitioned Elector John that he in Christian love (for as secular government he was not bound to do so) and for God's sake, to further the Gospel and to the welfare and salvation of poor Christians in the Elector's lands, appoint some able men to such an office. That the Elector did. This led, later on, to the appointment of a consistory; and that, in the development of history, was the first step to State Churchism.

But now note: It is not right to say that Luther asked the government to take a hand in the management of the Church; he asked the most prominent of the members to do the Church that service of love. In 1520, when all efforts to move the Pope, the hierarchy, the priesthood, to reform corruption in the Church had failed, Luther addressed the laity in his *Letter to the Christian Nobility of the German Nation*. Now, when those who should have cared for the Church, the bishops and other Church officials, turned their back and clung to the old corrupt establishment, Luther turned to the members of the reformed Church who were best able to lend a hand in this necessary business. The sinister thing was that these men **were** at the same time the governors of the land, and they later on grasped control of the Church as government. That was not Luther's intention. The consistory in his land was purely an advisory body. It had no jurisdiction over churches and pastors, could not even cite pastors for investigation, much less install or depose them. It had less power than among us the officials of Synod. In ducal Saxony, Duke Maurice appointed a consistory which was to have legislative and judicial power; and Luther very earnestly declared, "We must abrogate that consistory, for we cannot have jurists or the Pope in it. Jurists do not belong into the Church with their profession." (XXII:2210.) Just as definitely he protested when here and there a prince took it upon himself to call or to depose a preacher. In the Smalcald Articles Luther says (*De Potestate*, 54. *Triglot*, p. 519): "But especially the chief members of the Church, kings and princes, ought to guard the interests of the Church." And in a theological opinion of 1536, signed also by Melanchthon, Bugenhagen, Jonas, and Myconius, Luther says: "The calling and election of orthodox ministers of the Church is really and originally not the function of the government, but of the Church. If the government consists of believers and members of the Church, they call, not because they are the government, but because they are members of the Church. For: 'My kingdom is not of this world.'" (*Synodical Report*, Central District, 1874, p. 29, quoting Loescher's *Unschuldige Nachrichten*, 1715.)

That was Luther's stand and conviction. That the Lutheran Church did become so closely linked with the government, even in Luther's day, was a result of emergency. Did not Luther himself call the princes who thus took a hand in the management of the Church "emergency bishops" (*Notbischoefe*)? It was not Luther's will that practically all European governments sooner or later took control of the Church. It was partly due to lust of power, which is the temptation that hardly any government can resist. History teaches us that no government ever of its own free will gives up any power which it has received in an emergency. And particularly autocratic governments are never satisfied with purely secular control; they always strive also for control of that other realm in which man lives, the spiritual. On the other hand, on the part of Church members there is usually no serious objection because of the *vis inertiae*, common laziness, inherent in most men; if the government will do the work of managing the Church, particularly the necessary finances, why should they object!

Two factors entered in the history of the Reformation era which furthered the union between State and Church. Both Zwingli and Calvin favored it. Zwingli from the very beginning of his reformatory work followed the policy of letting the government carry out and enforce his reform measures; co-operation between the two was his principle. And while Calvin in theory emphasized the difference between the two realms, in actual practice they overlapped; and while in Geneva he organized a theocracy, the actual development in Calvinistic lands was the State Church.

The second factor lay in the political compromises which had to be adopted in Reformation days. The Diet of Worms adopted the Edict of Worms, outlawing Luther and his followers. Why was it not enforced and the Reformation rooted out then and there? It would have been so easy. The Pope and his legate insisted on it. In Hapsburg lands, Austria, the Netherlands, persecution at once started; but in Germany nothing was done. The Emperor, of course, was gone on a campaign against France. But the matter was carried to the Diet of Nuernberg, 1522, by the new Pope himself, Adrian VI, the Emperor's old tutor, for whose election to the Papacy the Emperor was responsible. He insisted that the Edict of Worms be carried out. But Germany was a feudal State, many practically independent States loosely federated in the Empire; each little principality chronically jealous and mistrustful of all the others. It became evident at once that any attempt to enforce the Edict of Worms would lead to civil war. Say, e. g., the Diet had instructed Bavaria to force Saxony to deliver Luther to the Pope. Bavaria would gladly have undertaken the job; there was a long-standing rivalry between the princes of the two countries for the hegemony in the Empire. But what would have happened? At once other lands would have lined up with Saxony, not because they loved Luther, but because they feared and mistrusted Bavaria; others would support Bavaria, but because they were opposed to the Saxon Elector. To avoid trouble, the Nuernberg Diet resolved that with regard to the Edict of Worms every prince should do what he felt he could account for to his God and his emperor — despite all the fulminating of the papal legate! That was the beginning of what later on was called the *"cuius regio eius religio"* policy: Territorialism; let each prince decide which religion shall be the Church of his land. This resolution was repeated by the second Diet of Nuernberg, 1524; was made temporary law in Germany ("until a council") by the first Diet of Speier, 1526; rescinded by the second Diet of Speier, 1529; actually made law in the Empire after the fiasco of the Smalcaldic War, in the Religious Peace of Augsburg, 1555; re-enacted in the Peace of Westphalia, 1648, here with the inclusion of the Calvinists, who had not been mentioned in the Peace of Augsburg. It can readily be seen that this policy worked directly toward government control of the Church.

There seems to have been no objection to this policy — except on the part of Catholics, who, of course, fought for the opposite extreme: Church control of the State. Catholics protested against this stipulation in the Religious Peace of Augsburg. The Peace of Westphalia was condemned by Pope Innocent X in a special bull of Nov. 10, 1648, in which he declared it prejudicial to the Catholic religion, to the divine worship, to the Apostolic Roman See, in granting to heretics and their successors, among other things, ecclesiastical goods, in permitting to heretics the free exercise of religion, the right to ecclesiastical offices, dignities, etc. He declared the treaty "perpetually null, void, of no effect, iniquitous, unjust, condemned, reproved, frivolous, without force and effect"; he declared that no one was obligated to observe the treaty, even though he had promised under oath to do so. At the Congress of Vienna, in 1815, Pius VII renewed this condemnation pronounced by Innocent X. In his Syllabus of Errors of 1864, Pope Pius IX condemns these statements as errors: "The Church has not the power of availing herself of force, or any direct or indirect temporal power; the Church ought to be separated from the State, and the State from the Church." On Dec. 9, 1905, France passed a law separating Church and State in that country; Pope Pius X issued a special encyclical, published in the *Osservatore Romano* of Feb. 17, 1906, in which he says: "By virtue of the supreme authority which God has conferred upon us, we reject and condemn the law passed in France for the separation of Church and State as profoundly insulting to God, whom it officially denies by making it a principle that the Republic recognizes no religion." In the same document, very significantly, he admonishes all Catholics to be led by their shepherds and to follow them. — On the other hand, Calvinistic sects have also favored a mixing of Church and State. Presbyterians teach in their basic symbol: The State is in duty bound to root out false doctrine and to establish true service of God.

Luther knew what the right relation between Church and State is. Had he been able, he would have organized a Church like ours, congregations like ours. He could not do so because of existing conditions. In the emergency the princes had to become *Notbischoefe*, since there was no one else who could take the thing in hand. And that pleased the princes; they saw their chance in that; and the Church again had visible heads, now not the Pope, but the princes who became the *summi episcopi*, the supreme bishops. So the freedom of the Church, lost under Constantine, was not even regained in the Reformation. The Church of Germany — and of all Protestant countries of Europe — became, and to this day has remained, a part of the State's machinery. Not until the United States of America was established did the world see a land in which this right and natural and Scriptural relation between Church and State exists — separation.

From the very beginning this separation has carried the evidence that here is a divine organization which is not the work of man. If in the beginning the Church had been founded by high priests and elders with a subsidy from Herod, perhaps (like later on Philo) appealing for the support of Rome, this would be some encouragement for the State Church people. But here was a small band, composed to a great extent of slaves, persecuted by all; yet in a short time it spread over the earth. "Not by might, nor by power, but by My Spirit, saith the Lord of Hosts." And that applies to our times, too. The government has nothing to do with the Church as Church, nor the Church as Church with the State.

Opponents of this separation never tire of citing the example of Israel in the Old Testament. But the example does not apply. That was a unique situation — a people put under the direct control, spiritual and secular, of God. God could, of course, do that again, give us laws for all imaginable contingencies — and the result would no doubt be a fine State and a fine Church. But it simply has not pleased Him to do that; that stopped, and a new principle began to apply when God's Son said: "My kingdom is not of this world."

III

This principle is violated when either Church or State usurps or interferes with the powers, rights, and duties of the other. Since both, however, are institutions established by God for the welfare of mankind, it is evidently God's will that they serve one another.

In this thesis we shall try to apply to practical life the principles which we have outlined before. We shall consider, first, cases in which the separation of Church and State is plainly violated, and then we shall consider that field in which the two realms touch or even overlap.

Lutheran Witness, Vol. 55, p. 50: "The principle of separation of Church and State as laid down in Scripture is violated: (a) when the State uses its powers — the laws, officers of the law, courts of law, fines, imprisonments, and other penalties — to compel adherence to a certain doctrine, a certain form of worship, or observance of certain ceremonies, or to forbid these; (b) when the Church uses its spiritual power to compel adherence of its members to a certain form of government, or absolves them from obedience to a certain state or ruler, or causes the State to use its political or police powers to compel members of the Church to perform their religious duties, or makes use of its power of numbers or influence to bring about civil legislation that will compel citizens to conform to the conceptions of right and wrong held by the Church." Let us look at this a little more in detail.

St. Peter writes to the Church (I Pet. 4:15): "But let none of you suffer as a murderer, or as a thief, or as an evildoer, or as a busybody in other men's matters." St. Peter tells Christians: Let every one tend to that business which the Lord has given him. That applies to the Church. The Lord has given the Church one great work: the saving of men's souls by the preaching of the Gospel; whatever does not pertain to this great object of the Church's existence is not the business of the Church. Earthly, secular affairs are not within the domain of the Church.

Let us cite some examples. The Church should not be active in politics. This does not mean that Christians should not take an active part in the affairs of the State. They are citizens, and they may, they should, work for what they consider best. The pastor of a church is a citizen, and will take note of civic affairs, and for his person will act to the best of his conviction. Sometimes it may not be wise for a pastor to voice his political convictions; it may hinder his work to do so; but he has the same rights as other citizens. But the affairs of the State are not the pastor's business as servant of the Church. St. Paul's advice to Timothy applies here (II Tim. 2:4): "No man that warreth entangleth himself with the affairs of this life, that he may please him who hath chosen him to be a soldier." Political pastors are an anomaly. Politics should not be dragged into the pulpit, the congregation meeting, the Sunday school. Our fathers liked to cite a word of the Old Emperor William I. His court preacher, the noted Stoecker, had worked hard for a new Christian-Social party. The Emperor sent him a telegram: "Politische Pastoren sind ein Unding. Die Herren Pastoren sollen sich nur um die Seelen ihrer Gemeinden kuemmern, die Naechtstenliebe pflegen, aber die Politik aus dem Spiele lassen, dieweil sie das gar nichts angeht. Wilhelm, I. R." — It was, of course, inconsistent on his part, the inconsistency of the State-Church system. He thought it all right that he took a hand in the control of the Church, but he wanted the Church to keep out of the State's affairs. It is the same inconsistency when today pastors, or other representatives of the Church, as such meddle in the affairs of the State. Whether a city or a county has open saloons or "local option" is not the Church's business. Investigations as to whether the laws of the State are being enforced or not is not the Church's business. To solve social questions, promote purely civic reform movements, improve the public school system, that's not the business of the Church or of the pastor. He has no right to meddle with the temporal affairs of his members, especially of the sick, testamentary affairs, etc. The Apostles set up a definite program for the pastor when they asked the church to elect deacons, and said: "We will give ourselves continually to prayer and to the ministry of the Word" (Acts 6:4). There is only one case in which the Church must take an active part in politics: when the State interferes with the business of the Church, when, e. g., it attempts to close our schools, when it forbids the use of wine in the Sacrament, and the like.

The Church must not give laws and ordinances concerning the body, temporal life, or property. The Church has no right to collect fines, to impose penances, to deprive people of the lawful use of their possessions. If the Church gives laws for civil life, it takes a sword that is not given to her. Cf. Augsburg Confession, XXVIII; Apology, XVI. The temptation is always great to make rules and regulations in order to preserve unity in the Church. That was the Pope's method: Preserve unity by confiscating the property of those who voiced divergent opinions or by depriving them of liberty, even of their life. Others say, "We must have a strong church government, Visitors, synods, who not only advise but have legislative and executive power." In proof of this opinion John Wesley cited Heb. 13:17: "Obey them that have the rule over you," i. e., the teachers who guide you. Pastors' commands, he said, may pertain to three classes of things: those which God has forbidden; there we must not obey them; hence the text does not apply. Or they may be things which God has commanded; but there we obey not them, but God: again the text does not apply. Then their orders may concern things which God has neither commanded nor forbidden; those are the only things to which the text can apply; and referring to them the Apostle demands that we obey our pastors. Hence he demanded obedience to his regulations regarding clothing and the like. That's poor exegesis. Luther said: At home Dr. Pomeranus can give his servant orders, and he must obey; but in church, in the congregational meeting, he cannot say to that same servant: You must do what I as pastor of Wittenberg tell you to do.

The Church's business is not to mete out temporal punishment or to see that it is inflicted. The Church is not in the police business, and above all, the pastor is not a sheriff or State attorney. Let us again refer to John 8:5-7: Jesus does not answer the question whether the adulteress is to be stoned; that was the business of the State authorities. It does not concern the congregation or the pastor whether the member who is a thief is punished or not; their concern is that the man's soul is saved; so they are interested in the restitution he must make, but not in the punishment he receives. Yes, teachers in school, and pastors when they teach school, will inflict physical punishment when necessary, but they do that not as ministers of the Church, but as representatives of the parents. Cyprian calls attention to Christ's example in dealing with the adulteress and refusing to be a judge or divider for the people (Luke 12:13-14), and he adds: "But if we are priests of God and

Christ, I do not know whom we should rather follow than God and Christ."

The Church must never strive for temporal power. The Church of the Middle Ages gained much of its prestige and political power through its vast possessions in estates and income. A large proportion of the flagrant corruptions of that time may be traced back more or less directly to the riches of the Church (simony, nepotism). That was recognized, too, so that Wycliffe, e. g., proposed to initiate reform by confiscating all the property of the Church. Today that same Church tries to, and frequently does, exert political and economic influence by controlling and directing the voting power of her membership. Such a practice is evil and unworthy of the Church. Christ said (Matt. 20:25): "Ye know that the princes of the Gentiles exercise dominion over them, and they that are great exercise authority upon them. But it shall not be so among you." And Christ's own example bears that out. When the people wanted to make Him king (John 6:15), He withdrew, and to Pilate He repeatedly stressed the altogether otherworldly character of His kingdom. Therefore our Confessions say: "The power of the Church has its own commission, to teach the Gospel and to administer the Sacraments. Let it not break into the office of another; let it not transfer the kingdoms of this world; let it not abrogate the laws of civil rulers; let it not abolish lawful obedience; let it not interfere with judgments concerning civil ordinances and contracts; let it not prescribe laws to civil rulers concerning the form of the commonwealth." (Augsburg Confession, XXVIII, 12—14. *Triglot*, p. 85.)

Finally the Church must not resort to the use of the sword, of earthly means, to advance or to defend the kingdom of Christ. The Church is the communion of believers; by physical means not a single soul can be added to that communion. No one can be forced to accept the Word of God, and the Church must not try that. Again, the Roman Church is the vicious example of what Christians must not do. The Crusades and the Inquisition are a dark blot on the record of that sect; and the fact that, officially at least, they do not recognize the wrong in such measures and do not condemn them to this day, is a sinister characteristic of that Church which all those of another faith do well to keep in mind. Christ still says to all His Peters: "Put up again thy sword into his place; for all they that take the sword shall perish with the sword" (Matt. 26:52). This again does not mean that the Church may not appeal to the government for that protection which the State owes to all its citizens, both by the courts against civil wrong and by the armed forces against violence.

On the other hand, the domain of the State does not include conscience and religion. Luther said: "Civil government has laws that extend no further than to body and property and external things on earth. For the soul God can and will let no one rule but Himself. Therefore when civil authority dares to give laws to the soul, it interferes with God's order and only seduces and destroys souls." Government, he says, is to "let people believe this or that as they can and will, and not constrain any one with force." (Von weltlicher Obrigkeit, wie weit man ihr Gehorsam schuldig sei," 1523. Repeated in a sermon in 1524, and in 1525 in "Ermahnung zum Frieden.")

Hence, to mention particulars, the State has nothing to do with sin as the transgression of God's Law. The State's business is to protect its citizens, hence it deals with crimes, acts by which others are harmed. It was one of Calvin's great mistakes that he made every sin a crime, punishable by the government; the State's duty was, as he held, to enforce the Ten Commandments, the First Table as well as the Second. So his government in Geneva, with his participation, burned Servetus and thirty-odd others for false teaching. It is not the State's duty to promote true religion and suppress the false. Luther in one of his first writings against the Papacy ("Arguments in Defense Against the Bull Exsurge Domine of 1520") upheld the principle: "The burning of heretics is contrary to the will of the Holy Spirit" (Holman, III, p. 103). And later on, in his "Admonition to Peace," he said: "No ruler ought to prevent anyone from teaching or believing what he pleases, whether Gospel or lies. It is enough if he prevents the teaching of sedition and rebellion." (Holman, IV, p. 224.) Even against the Turk, he wrote in 1529, no force was to be used on account of his religion. "Let the Turk believe and live as he will, just as one lets the Papacy and other false Christians live. The emperor's sword has nothing to do with the faith; it belongs to physical, worldly things, if God is not to become angry with us. If we pervert His order and throw it into confusion, He, too, becomes perverse and throws us into confusion and all misfortune, as it is written, Ps. 18:26: With the perverse Thou art perverse." ("On War Against the Turk," Holman, V, p. 104.) Luther's principle (Small Catechism, Introduction, 21. *Triglot*, p. 537): "We are to force no one to believe," extends also to the government. Even a Christian government must not occupy itself with the religion of the subjects; that is no neglect of duty. Do I neglect my Christian duty if I do not train my neighbor's children? The government has no business in that domain nor the means to accomplish anything; faith cannot be planted by physical force; it can only create hypocrites. Nor should a Christian government suppress false religions. Only in the case of those religious cults being dangerous to the State or the community should the government take issue with them. Hence government action against Anabaptists in Reformation times was justified. While the bulk of them was perhaps harmless, many of their leaders and teachers were anarchists; they began with Chiliasm and ended in anarchy. It was perfectly justified that the Jesuits were banished in the 18th century, that the secular powers exerted such pressure on the Pope that he had to suppress them in 1773. Not in a single instance was the religion of the Jesuits the cause of their troubles, but it became evident that their activities were dangerous to society. Our government's action against the Mormons in Utah comes under this same heading. When the Anabaptists rose in rebellion in Muenster, Luther wrote to the princes of Saxony: If people want to do more than fight with words, when they want to break and hit with the fist, then the prince must take hold, "whether it be we or they," and forbid them the land and tell them: We will gladly permit battling with words and look on, so that the true doctrine may be proved, but you must not use your fist; that's our office (the government's); otherwise leave the land. (St. Louis, XVI:13.)

The government, then, has no right to meddle in Church affairs, in congregational business. It cannot call or depose ministers or take any hand in it. It has no right to appoint consistories which govern the Church wholly or in part; to forbid or in any way to control the religious education of children. Government has the right to make education compulsory; reason, the standard by which government is guided, teaches that a good education of its citizenry works for welfare of the community. It may even urge parents to give children a religious training, since all men who listen to their own conscience, or even sound reason, know that true and effective moral training must be based on religion; and experience corroborates that. But the State has not the right to make laws requiring schools to include religion in their curriculum. Nor has it the right to forbid parents to give their children the spiritual training they deem necessary and for that purpose establish their own schools — provided these schools give the children the secular training which the State deems necessary for its citizens. It must not prescribe books for the Church or for religious schools, nor include religious or anti-religious ideas in textbooks prescribed for the secular schools. It has no right to meddle in cases of church discipline and excommunication (though here again a case may arise where the State is appealed to: when a church member by excommunication loses his share of valuable church property). In short, the State has no right of supervision over the Church beyond that of preventing dangerous practices; it has no rule over the Church; that is God's domain; and even though it is at times assumed with good intentions, it has usually proved poor service to the Church.

It was noted before that the State may allow things which God does not permit, e. g., divorces, etc. But the State may not command things which God has forbidden; if it does, it oversteps its limits and encroaches on God's domain, and we are relieved of all obligation toward the government; we must refuse obedience, and Daniel goes to the lions' den, and his three friends to the fiery furnace, rather than obey such government edicts. The State has no right to dictate in spiritual things, to tell men what they owe to God, to bind consciences, to force men to act against their own conscience. Luther discusses the question of unjust wars in two of his books. In "Secular Authority: To What Extent It Should be Obeyed," he says: "But when a prince is in the wrong, are his people bound to follow him then, too? I answer, No, for it is no one's duty to do wrong; we ought to obey God, who desires the right, rather than men. How is it when the subjects do not know whether the prince is in the right or not? I answer, As long as they cannot know, nor find out by any possible means, they may obey without peril to their souls. For in such a case one must apply the law of Moses, when he writes in Exodus 21 that a person who has unknowingly and involuntarily killed a man shall be delivered by fleeing to a city of refuge and by the judgment of the congregation." (Holman, III, p. 270.) Again, in his treatise on "Whether Soldiers, too, Can be Saved", he says: "A second question: 'Suppose my lord were wrong in going to war.' I reply: If you know for sure that he is wrong, then you should fear God rather than men (Acts 4) and not fight or serve, for you cannot have a good conscience before God. 'Nay,' you say, 'my lord compels me, takes my fief, does not give me my money, pay, and wages; and besides, I am despised and put to shame as a coward, nay as a faithbreaker in the eyes of the world, as one who has deserted his lord in need! I answer: You must take that risk and, with God's help, let go what goes; He can restore it to you a hundredfold, as He promises in the Gospel, 'He that leaveth house, home, wife, goods, for My sake, shall get it back a hundredfold.' In all other works, too, we must expect the danger that the rulers will compel us to do wrong; but since God will have us leave even father and mother for His sake, we must certainly leave lords for His sake. But if you do not know, or cannot find out whether your lord is wrong, you ought not to weaken a certain obedience with an uncertainty of right, but should think the best of your lord, as is the way of love, for 'Love believeth all things; thinketh no evil' (I Cor. 13). Thus you are secure, and walk well before God. If they put you to shame, or call you faithless, it is better that God call you faithful and honorable than that the world call you faithful and honorable. What good would it do you, if the world held you for a Solomon or a Moses, and before God you were counted as bad as Saul or Ahab?" (Holman, V, p. 68 f.)

As Luther indicates, in this matter of conscience a clash between the government and the individual citizen, perhaps even an entire Church body, may occur. The State may deem it necessary for the welfare of the community to put individuals or groups under restrictions. In this the State may be wrong; then it oversteps its rights and is guilty of persecution; the restricted parties suffer persecution. On the other hand, the government may be right, and the other parties misled by an erring conscience; the latter are then in that sorry state in which they would do wrong in acting against their conscience, yet also sin in following their erring conscience. Such clashes will occur as long as man is suffering the results of the fall into sin.

A final conclusion from this principle is this, that the State has no right to establish a State, or national, Church, to designate which church the citizen must attend or that he must practice any religion whatever. Nor has it the right to forbid citizens to join any religious groups or to form new associations, and to practice any rites, ceremonies, etc., prescribed by such religions, as long as they are not harmful to the community. It has no right to order churches to observe certain festivals, to offer prayers for the government of the nation. It may ask or recommend such favors — it is then really a case of the individuals which compose the personnel of the government asking this favor of the Churches — but the State has no right to order and command it. There may also be emergencies, e. g., epidemics, when the State, in the interest of public health, may for a time suspend all public meetings. A government, finally, has no authority to decide doctrinal questions, to settle religious controversies. It may, in the cause of public peace, request the churches to get together and settle the matter; but it has no right to settle it by government dictum. It should recognize that it is not able to do so. When the Jews brought their objections to Paul's preaching before the Roman governor Festus (Acts 25), he said: "I doubted of such manner of questions"; "I was doubtful how to enquire thereof" (margin); i. e., I was not able to decide such questions. A good example! "The natural man receiveth not the things of the Spirit of God; for they are foolishness unto him; neither can he know them, because they are spiritually discerned" (I Cor. 2:14). Again, such cases may come before secular courts when property is involved; they will be asked to decide such purely secular matters. Then the court must do the best possible at the hand of the evidence furnished. Its decision may often be wrong, because matters come under consideration of which the State officials have no conception or a wrong conception. And again Christians must suffer the wrong as a result of human imperfection.

Let me cite some examples applying the principle set down in the previous pages. A matter on which there has been, and still is, much argument is Sunday laws. Are Sunday laws a violation of the principle under consideration? — These laws may have a twofold motivation. If the reason for enacting them is that God, or God's Law, requires the observing of Sunday as a day of worship or a day of rest, it is a violation of this principle. God, of course, has not given such a command; but even if He had, it is not the State's business to enforce God's Law. It is therefore a violation of the principle of the separation of Church and State when sectarians (even some Lutherans) have initiated or favored such legislation with that motivation. But the question has another side. The State may adopt legislation setting aside one day as a day of rest because it deems it advisable, even necessary, that working people have one day of rest in a week. Again, a large number of citizens want one day a week for religious services; the State, moreover, values religion as a powerful factor in building up a morally strong citizenry. To meet both requirements, the State makes provision by law that citizens are given ample opportunity to practice their religion.

An ever-recurring problem is that of religious instruction for children. The oft-discussed question whether the State has the right to take in hand the education of youth can only be touched here. It is now perhaps universally accepted in our land that education of children is the duty of parents, not the State. However, the State has the right to demand that children be educated; the welfare of the community is to a great extent dependent on that. In our land the State provides the schools instead of directing the parents to establish schools. It is a moot question whether the State has the inherent right to do this, or whether it is entitled to do so by common consent of a majority of citizens. It is clear that education must include not only the three R's, but also civic morality. An educated criminal is more dangerous to the community than a savage. The State must strive to train people to obey laws because they want to, and not merely because there is a policeman watching. But — how is a purely secular system of schools to teach morality? All they have to offer as basis is expediency — it pays! — ambition, respect and honor in the community. All men who listen to their own conscience and learn the lessons experience teaches, know that true and effective morality teaching must be based on religion, on the conviction that every man is responsible to a higher Being, to God. The result: Efforts to introduce religious teaching into the public schools. That has usually, and rightly, been prevented. Not touching at all the troublesome question of what kind of religion will be taught by the teachers employed by the State, under the direction and supervision of politicians who may be infidels, the basic consideration is this: The State has no right to teach religion; that's the Church's business. The solution is: Sunday schools, Saturday schools, vacation schools, or best of all, in fact, the only really efficient method: the Christian day school — all of those established by the Church.

But now: The State is, or should be, vitally interested in such endeavors; they have an immense value to the State. Is it mixing of Church and State if the State extends aid to such institutions? It goes without question that the State is in duty bound to protect such institutions and the people who establish and maintain them and to grant them all rights extended to other similar organizations. May it not go farther than that, e. g., urge parents to establish such schools and send their children? There seems to be no cause for objection when the State grants facilities for religious teaching, rooms, free time, as long as all religious organizations are given the same privilege. The State grants are given for value received. Opinions, however, differ particularly on such questions as granting free transportation or financial support to religious schools. — Another question is: Is it advisable for the Church to take such grants? This applies chiefly to money grants. And the answer is: No, it is not advisable. Every help that the State offers to schools beyond that given to all citizens entitles the State to expect a certain measure of participation in the management of the school; it, at least, gives officials, especially such as are not friendly, an opportunity to demand it. It pays to recall the lesson of history that government officials are very often anxious to extend their rights and powers; and even if (this is the usual excuse in such cases) these grants and privileges are safeguarded by all kinds of promises, they can at least cause trouble all out of proportion to the benefit received. Nor should it be forgotten that any election may change the attitude of the government. But there is more. Any grant from tax funds for any Church purpose really gives officials the right of examination how the money is spent and so a voice in the management of the institution, which may at any time have serious results.

A related matter is that of Bible reading in public schools. You may read arguments for and against, in our own literature, too. It is generally admitted that Bible reading in State schools is an inconsistency. Any citizen who is opposed to it would seem to have the right to protest if his children are forced to listen. If, however, the community is satisfied, why should we object? The Bible is God's Word and a power unto salvation, no matter who reads it; it can only do good. But again there are dangers. Teachers, with good and with evil intent, may add their own comment which may do more harm than good. And it is a wedge that may be used to cut a breach into the wall separating Church and State in our land. While therefore we need not oppose it, we should not work for its introduction.

Before leaving this subject, we should note that any legislation aiming at the suppression of religious schools is a violation of the principle of separation. In such a case we rightly go back to the original rights of parents, they have the responsibility for the children and the right to decide where to send them so that they may be trained to be good citizens.

The State has the right to pass liquor laws, even prohibition laws, as well as antinarcotic laws. It is purely a social matter concerning public health. The question is not whether such legislation is good or not, especially when it is passed by a minority because the opposition has not the moral courage to voice their opinion; the question is whether the State oversteps its right in such legislation.

It is a violation of our principle to drag the religion of a candidate for political office into the election campaign. Only when his religion requires him to adhere to un-American principles should it be a matter for consideration.

It is, on the other hand, a violation of this principle when Churches aim to have legislation adopted that makes religion a State affair. This applies as well to endeavors of Catholics to have our government restore the official embassy at the Vatican, as to attempts to adopt a "Christian Amendment" to our Constitution, designating our land officially as a Christian land by putting the name of God or of Christ into the Constitution, requiring the courts to judge by Christian and Biblical principles.

One point remains to complete our consideration of the relation between Church and State: How can the State serve the Church and the Church the State without either's interfering with the business of the other? Let us again consider examples.

The State can serve the Church best by a good administration of its own affairs. If the land is governed justly and efficiently, the community in general, individual citizens, and so such associations of citizens as the Church, will prosper. Under poor government the Church, too, suffers, because her members suffer. Take only the financial side. If the State enacts and enforces good laws to preserve peace and order, Church members can devote means to the support of the Church which otherwise they must use for the protection and preservation of their own lives and property. The Church, too, needs money to build churches and schools, to pay pastors', teachers', missionaries', and other workers' salaries. It depends entirely on the income of Christians whether the work of the Kingdom prospers in this respect or is handicapped and hindered. Now, if the State has a poor industrial, commercial, and labor policy, if there is poor enforcement of laws, poor police protection, etc., Christians, too, must suffer. They become poorer, Church contributions decrease, Church institutions cannot be sufficiently supported. Particularly does the State serve in preserving peace and preventing war. War is the most destructive of God's visitations. War not only destroys property; it destroys character; it destroys souls. Other visitations will to some extent drive men to repentance; war rarely does; on the contrary, it usually leads men into even greater excesses and vices. And the Church, too, has to suffer the effects. Not only members in general, but also her workers, being but human, are affected by the prevalent atmosphere. A State may pay a high price for peace and yet be better off than by waging war; and the Church, apart from all other considerations, for her own welfare will support the peace-preserving efforts of the government. (Walther, *Epistel Postille*, p. 495 f.)

Good government serves the Church by protecting her in her activity, giving police protection, that services are not disturbed by individuals or by mobs; protecting lives and livelihood against persecution for religion's sake and property against destruction. Good government provides and maintains courts which in honesty and justice protect the individual and the Church in their rights from persecution by foes, particularly also from the revenge of those who have been members and have been excluded. Such protection is, of course, no special privilege; all other associations within the State are protected thus if they are legal and law-abiding. It should be extended to all religious associations. If preferences are shown, it is a violation of the principle of separation of Church and State. The State serves the Church by readily granting the protection of the courts to the Church and her workers; and the Church should not hesitate to invoke such protection; that is no violation of our principle. (St. Paul, Acts 25:10-11; Luther against Rome; Walther, *Lutheraner*, XL, p. 109 — an example showing that a pastor has not only the right, but under conditions even a duty to invoke the protection of the courts against slander accusing him of crimes that would disqualify him for his office, or at least greatly hinder him in his work, I Tim. 3:7.) In this same connection may be mentioned that the State extends to religious associations the same rights that others enjoy, e. g., that of incorporation, of holding property, etc.

Without violation of the principle of separation the State may grant the Church certain privileges, because it recognizes the moral value of the Church in the community and so its service to the State. That is the reason why most generally church property is tax-free in our land. Bryce, in his *American Commonwealth* (II, p. 562) says: "The State does that because the Church and her schools serve education, especially in morality, and so promote the peace, prosperity, and welfare of the land; it also helps to raise the value of adjoining property." — Again it is a question whether, considering everything, it would not be better if all such privileges were abrogated. The custom results in many inequalities among the churches, which give rise to much hard feeling. We should not protest if it were altogether abolished.

The Church, too, serves the State best by tending to her own business, and that only. The Church's business is to preach the Gospel. The prime purpose of such preaching is the salvation of souls. The Church is to teach men how to prepare for the life to come, so that when they leave this world, they may enter heaven. But this preparation takes place in this world during the earthly life of her members. Very pertinently William Adams Brown, in his *Church and State in Contemporary America*, asks: "Is it true that this life *is only* a training school for the life beyond the grave; or isn't it rather true that God's purpose for man includes this life as well as the next, and the function of the Church is not only to fit man for a heaven to come by and by, but to point out to him what is the kind of life that it is God's will that he should live here and to fit him to play his part in it worthily?" In other words, God has outlined the kind of life that Christians must live during this time of preparation, and the Church's business is to teach her members how to live. That again is done by the preaching of the Gospel. That changes man. We know that in this life we shall never reach perfection; but wherever the Gospel is accepted, people are on the road to perfection; every earthly relationship is improved, the relation between married people, between parents and children, between employers and employees, between capital and labor. Why, the Church alone knows how all these relationships may be improved. The Church alone knows how married life can become truly happy, how that burning problem of youth delinquency may be solved. The Church alone knows the answer to the labor question. The Church can, and must, point out to her members the fundamental principles on which industrial relationship should rest according to Scripture; that every man is his brother's keeper; that every man is only the steward of the earthly goods entrusted to him — wealth, power, time, ability, opportunity; that every man owes an account and, when the time comes, will have to give an account to Him who is Master and Lord of all. The Church must point out that the laborer is worthy of his hire, that he must receive sufficient to maintain a home, raise a family, and insure security for old age; that on the other hand the laborer must give honest work for his hire and not steal part of what he receives; moreover, that God Himself has sanctioned the right of private property. The Church must work toward spreading God's principles of righteousness, justice, tolerance, and helpfulness — all this not by efforts to control legislation, not by direct administration, but by changing the lives of men to conform to these principles.

So the Church serves the State best by tending to her own business and preaching the Gospel in public services, in Christian day schools, in Bible classes, in young people's work, in home and foreign missions, in bedside ministration, through religious publications, by radio, by any and every means that offers a possibility of bringing the Gospel to more men.

It is surely significant that the Apostle in his general exhortation to pray for all men makes special mention of kings and all who are in authority (I Tim. 2:1). That is a service which only the Church and her members can render to the State and its officials.

But more than this. The Church should do more than stand aloof, let others do the work in the State, and hope for the best. The Church should take an active interest in this, that her members do their duty toward the State and in the State. Such duties have been mentioned before: Obedience to government regulations, paying taxes, etc. But church members have duties not only toward the State, but in the State. It would seem natural that Christians, being citizens of the State, should take part in the business of the State. There have always been some who refused to do that; the *Schwaermer* in Luther's days, the Anabaptists, later the Mennonites, the Society of Friends, or Quakers. Some have denied the State the right of existence, called it idolatry to salute the flag, etc. But these are vagaries of religious eccentrics. The Church holds that her members, as citizens, should take an effective part in public life by doing their full duty as citizens; and Christians, being what they are, will always prove a salt in this, too; they have a wholesome influence. And the Church renders a service to the State by not only permitting this, but urging members to do so. So the Church will urge her members to make use of the right of voting; to vote intelligently, and therefore to inform themselves as to the questions the vote is to decide; to make sure that they vote for the right man. The Church, through her ministers, will enlighten the conscience of members on matters before the public as to what is right and wrong; encourage them to keep informed on what kind of laws are being considered by the legislature; if good, to support them; if not good, to oppose. The Church will not discourage, but rather encourage her members to take office in the various departments of the State. Luther said: If you are able, you should offer yourself for some office and try to get it (Erlanger, 22, 73). And did you ever notice how many public officials are mentioned in Gospels, Acts, and Epistles, who, when they became Christians, did not quit and resign, but kept their office? Our Confessions say (Augsburg Confessions, XVI, 1–2. *Triglot*, p. 51): "Of Civil Affairs they teach that lawful civil ordinances are good works of God, and that it is right for Christians to bear civil office, to sit as judges, to judge matters by the Imperial and other existing laws, to award just punishments, to engage in just wars, to serve as soldiers, to make legal contracts, to hold property, to make oath when required by the magistrates. . . . They condemn the Anabaptists who forbid these civil offices to Christians." Again (Apology, XVI, 53, 65. *Triglot*, pp. 329, 333): "Legitimate civil ordinances are good creatures of God and divine ordinances, which a Christian can use with safety. . . . By the kind of doctrine which we follow, the authority of magistrates and the dignity of all civil ordinances are not undermined, but are all the more strengthened, and that it is only this doctrine which gives true instruction as to how eminently glorious an office, full of good Christian works, the office of rulers is."

These, then, are the principles which God has laid down in His Word for the relation between Church and State. Wherever men have departed from them, the results have been evil. Where God does not join both parts in a union, it is evil. If God had wanted such a union between Church and State in the New Testament, it would have been a blessing; but He Himself has changed the old order and established the principle of separation. When State Church people today are asked to give up that unholy alliance, they sometimes speak of a historic right of the Church in their lands. But Luther wrote to Henry VIII of England on this matter, that in the kingdom of Christ there is no historic right; here God's Word stands. "What was wrong a hundred years ago is never right, at no time. If years made things right, the devil would be the most just on earth, for he is more than five thousand years old."

God has been good to us. He led our fathers to the shores of this land, where, for the first time in history, Church and State were separated. The "experiment" — for so, more or less, it was regarded by many — has proved marvelously successful. For a hundred years God has preserved this blessing to us. Let us remember this and include it in our songs of praise when we celebrate the Centennial. — But this principle, too, has its enemies. The medieval Church is not yet dead, nor has the Calvinistic leopard changed its spots. Eternal vigilance is the price of liberty. — We add to our thanksgiving the plea of the Psalmist: "Lord, preserve unto us Thy Word" — also this principle, laid down in Thy Word!

Luther's Catechism

"IF I get back into a parish," said a returning chaplain to a distinguished Episcopalian rector, "I shall teach and teach. Everything that goes on which does not teach, I shall regard as superfluous. . . ." Correct! The primary purpose of the Christian Church on earth and of the individual Christian, whether he be a special servant or another member of the Church, is — to teach. (Quotation from *News Service*, January, 1945, p. 1.)

The fact was tersely stated in a memorial to Synod twenty-six years ago in these words: "The thorough instruction of all its members in the Word of God, notably the immature, is not a branch of the work of the Church, but its only, all-inclusive commission. Christ has compressed the work of the Church into His command, 'Go ye, therefore, and teach all nations . . . teaching them to observe all things whatsoever I have commanded you.'" (*Proceedings*, 1920, p. 229.)

The source of all our teaching is the Bible. There we have the teaching which Christ has commanded us to observe. St. Paul writes to Timothy: "And that from a child thou hast known the Holy Scriptures, which are able to make thee wise unto salvation through faith which is in Christ Jesus. All Scripture is given by inspiration of God and is profitable for doctrine, for reproof, for correction, for instruction in righteousness, that the man of God may be perfect, thoroughly furnished unto all good works." (II Tim. 3:15-17.)

But the Bible is very much like a large city with its many streets and avenues and boulevards running hither and yon. To find one's way around, it is good to use a guide. The best guide to the treasure house of divine truths contained in the Bible is Luther's Catechism. Dr. Charles Porterfield Krauth, one of the most prominent theologians produced by the American Lutheran Church, once said: "The Catechism is a thread through the labyrinth of divine wonders. Persons often get confused, but if they will hold on to this Catechism, it will lead them through without being lost." (Th. Graebner, *Story of the Catechism*, p. 140.)

Since this is an accepted fact, we ought to

I. Acknowledge the NEED of Luther's Catechism
II. Recognize the IMPORTANCE of Luther's Catechism
III. Make Proper USE of the Catechism

I. FIRST OF ALL, LET US ACKNOWLEDGE THE NEED OF LUTHER'S CATECHISM

A. The need of Luther's Catechism becomes evident from the fact that the *people of God in both Old and New Testament times taught and were taught the fundamental truths of the Bible* (Catechism truths).

Instruction in the basic teachings of the Bible — the Catechism truths — did not have its beginning in Luther's day, but is as old as the Church itself. People of the Old Testament times found it necessary to teach these doctrines.

In Gen. 18:19 we read: "For I know him, that he will command his children and his household after him, and they shall keep the way of the Lord to do justice and judgment; that the Lord may bring upon Abraham that which He hath spoken of him." Here God bore testimony that as a devoted father and house priest Abraham with all diligence would instruct his family in the fundamental teachings of God's Word. Without such instruction his children would have failed to keep the way of the Lord.

Moses records these words in Deut. 6:6-7: "And these words which I command thee this day shall be in thine heart; and thou shalt teach them diligently unto thy children, and shalt talk of them when thou sittest in thine house and when thou walkest by the way and when thou liest down and when thou risest up." From these words and those preceding this particular text one can rightly conclude that already in the days of Moses the instruction in the Ten Commandments, concerning God, faith, and prayer, was to be the order of the day. Children were to be instructed in these things by their parents. They were to teach diligently, i. e., impress upon the minds and hearts of the children the very fundamental truths of God.

From Deuteronomy (chap. 11:2-3, 18-19) we also quote the following, where particularly the history of the Kingdom of God and the teachings drawn therefrom are stressed: "And know ye this day; for I speak not with your children which have not known and which have not seen the chastisement of the Lord, your God, His greatness, His mighty hand, and His stretched-out arm, and His miracles, and His acts which He did in the midst of Egypt unto Pharaoh, the king of Egypt, and unto all his land. . . . Therefore shall ye lay up these My words in your heart and in your soul and bind them for a sign upon your hand, that they may be as frontlets between your eyes. And ye shall teach them your children, speaking of them when thou sittest in thine house and when thou walkest by the way, when thou liest down and when thou risest up."

From the New Testament we take the example of Jesus when, at the age of twelve, He was found in the Temple at Jerusalem, asking and answering questions. "And it came to pass that after three days they found Him in the Temple, sitting in the midst of the doctors, both hearing them and asking them questions. And all that heard Him were astonished at His understanding and answers" (Luke 2:46-47). Jesus is being catechized in the things that pertained to His heavenly Father's business.

We are all familiar with the passage in II Tim. 3:15: "And that from a child thou hast known the Holy Scriptures, which are able to make thee wise unto salvation through faith which is in Christ Jesus." When we link this passage with that of II Tim. 1:5: "When I call to remembrance the unfeigned faith that is in thee, which dwelt first in thy grandmother Lois and thy mother Eunice, and I am persuaded that in thee also," then we readily see that the need for instruction in divine truths was recognized by the Christians of the Apostolic Church.

One more reference will suffice. In Acts 18:25-26 we have this statement: "This man [Apollos] was instructed in the way of the Lord. . . . They took him unto them and expounded the way of God more perfectly." The Greek term *katechemenos* is here used —

catechizing, translated with "instructed." (Other references: Rom. 2:17-18, 21 f.; Acts 5:42; Heb. 6:1-2.)

From these references we see that the saints of both Old and New Testament times took the matter of instruction of both young and old most seriously. This was done because of God's command, but also because they felt a real need for the same.

We must not forget the example of the Christians of the post-Apostolic Church. During the first three hundred years the Church provided with great diligence for the thorough instruction of those who were about to become Christians, also for the adult candidates for Baptism as well as for the children of parents received into the Church. Such instruction was given not only in private homes, but also in the public service, such service having two distinct parts — the *missa catechumenorum* and the *missa fidelium*. (Mueller, *Symbolische Buecher*, Historisch-theologische Einleitung, 2. Abschnitt, V, VI, par. 1.) The ancient Church too recognized the need of thorough instruction.

B. The need for thorough instruction is also apparent when we recall to mind the *days of spiritual darkness and ignorance that preceded Luther's Reformation*.

Dr. Th. Graebner writes in his *Story of the Catechism* (p. 10): "The age before the Catechism was the age of darkness. We call that time the Dark Ages. Not as if human achievement had come to a standstill. There was some splendid building and painting and carving, and there was an interest in literature, ancient as well as contemporary. But the masses of the people were ground between the upper and nether millstones of the nobility and the clergy. Illiteracy like unto that of modern Mexico and Portugal covered most of Europe. The teachings of Christianity had become encrusted with a mass of legends and superstitions. Even the greater part of the aristocracy was ignorant of the art of writing, and the scholarship of the ordinary priest was a mockery upon the word "education."

This is what Luther said about the confusion of Christian knowledge before the Catechism was published: "No one knew what was Gospel, what Christ, Baptism, Confession, Sacrament; what was faith, spirit, flesh; what were good works, the Ten Commandments, the Lord's Prayer; what was praying, what suffering, what comfort;

what was government, matrimony, parents, children, lords, servants, lady, maid; what was devil, what angel, world, life, death, sin; what was righteousness, what forgiveness of sins, God, bishop, clergy, Church; what was a Christian and what the Christian cross. In a word, we knew nothing of what a Christian ought to know." (Written in 1531. As quoted in Th. Graebner's *Story of the Catechism*, p. 9.) Cf. also *Triglot*, Historical Introductions, par. 85, p. 65.

In the preface to his Small Catechism, Luther writes concerning those times: "The deplorable destitution which I recently observed, during a visitation of the churches, has impelled and constrained me to prepare this Catechism or Christian Doctrine in such a small and simple form. Alas, what manifold misery I beheld! The common people, especially in the villages, know nothing at all of Christian doctrine; and many pastors are quite unfit and incompetent to teach. Yet all are called Christians, have been baptized and enjoy the use of the Sacraments, although they know neither the Lord's Prayer nor the Creed nor the Ten Commandments and live like the poor brutes and irrational swine. Still they have, now that the Gospel has come, learned to abuse all liberty in a masterly manner.

"O ye bishops, how will ye ever render account to Christ for having so shamefully neglected the people and having never for a moment exercised your office! May the judgment not overtake you! You command Communion in one kind, and urge your human ordinances; but never ask in the meantime whether the people know the Lord's Prayer, the Creed, the Ten Commandments, or any part of God's Word. Woe, woe unto you everlastingly!"

Luther's words above were not an exaggeration. Erasmus and others (authors of the *Letters of Obscure Men*) describe conditions not so moderately. You can say that Luther's words were an understatement. The ignorance among the people was indescribably deplorable.

With this we do not mean to say that Christianity had vanished from the earth. Baptism was still administered. Sponsors were to have some knowledge of the Creed and the Lord's Prayer. There were cases of priests instructing people in the meaning of the Creed and the Lord's Prayer. Table prayers, the Hail Mary, and a few Psalms were still taught in the Latin schools. The prayer books and Communion books of that day were plentiful but "had the tendency to fasten the shackles of the priest rule upon the people" (Th. Graebner, *Story of the Catechism*, p. 11). Of all this Luther says in the Smalcald Articles: "Here was neither faith nor Christ, and the communicant would not be directed to the strength of Absolution, but rather trained to count his sins and trust in the intensity of his repentance."

Regarding this age Dr. Th. Graebner (*Story of the Catechism*, p. 15) writes: "In the age immediately preceding the Reformation religious instruction, such as it was, had reached a point of lowest efficiency. Parents and sponsors were extremely indifferent and were incapable of attending to the work of instruction. Some of them . . . tried to supply handbooks for instruction. But that which is specifically Christian, the fear and love of God and salvation by the merits of Jesus Christ, at best sounded as diminishing overtones through the lesson material provided by these intellectual leaders. The emphasis remained on works, and the very meaning of faith was as yet like a book sealed with seven seals."

What the Church needed was a textbook that would contain a condensed statement of all that was necessary for the Christian to know, and a Biblical explanation thereof. And this is what Luther gave the Church in his Catechism.

C. And now, when we behold the *great blessings* which the publication of Luther's Catechism brought to the people of his day, we shall acknowledge indeed that such a book was not superfluous, but a real necessity.

For thirteen years Luther had treated the Catechism truths in sermons and otherwise had brought them constantly to the attention of the people. Already there was a marked improvement among the people. The Catechism, therefore, was the fruit of years of preaching and experience. Portions of Catechism truths had already appeared as early as 1517, when a very brief explanation of the Ten Commandments was written and published. From time to time there were other essays and short publications on catechetical truths. In 1520 there appeared "A Short Form of the Ten Commandments"; "A Short Form of the Creed"; "A Short Form of the Lord's Prayer." In 1523 — "Five Questions in Regard to the Holy Supper." In 1525 Luther commissioned Justus Jonas and Agricola to prepare a catechism for children. But when this project failed to be carried out, Luther went to work himself. In 1526 he wrote in his *Deutsche Messe*: "What we need for our church services first of all is a plain, simple, and well-written catechism." The exact time when Luther completed his catechisms cannot be stated. Undoubtedly he worked on both — the Large as well as the Small — throughout the winter of 1528 and '29. It is beyond doubt that the material prepared by him was ready for, and given to, the printer for publication in the spring of 1529.

During the ten years prior to the publishing of the Catechism, Luther had done momentous things for the Church. He had broken the hold of the Papacy upon the Church. He had given the New Testament to his people in the German language. Many of his sermons were published and spread far and wide. The first hymnal had appeared. One thing that was still needed was a book of simple instruction for the people. The Catechism was the book to fill that need. By means of it the light of the Gospel had come in simplest form so that even the smallest child could grasp the fundamental truths of the Bible. With the spreading of Luther's Catechism among the people and into the homes the yoke of the papal Church was thrown off. The wonderful truths of the Bible began to infiltrate into the churches, and the results were nothing less than astounding. There was a real spiritual awakening. John Mathesius wrote (*Concordia Pulpit*, 1936, p. 32): "If Luther had done no more than write the two catechisms and to introduce them into the homes, schools, and churches, the world could never sufficiently pay nor thank him for his work." It is indeed a right Bible for the laity.

D. Again, must we not acknowledge the need of a booklet like Luther's Catechism when we think of *the millions in our day who live in complete ignorance of God's Word?*

Jesus, our Master, tells us in Matt. 7:13: "Enter ye in at the strait gate; for wide is the gate, and broad is the way, that leadeth to destruction, and *many there be* which go in thereat." It is an indisputable Biblical fact that the great multitudes go their way through life *without* Christ or *without* any knowledge of His work of redemption for the souls of men. The wide world over, there are millions of souls that sit in the darkness of sin and despair. They have no hope beyond the grave because they know not of such hope. We look not only at the teeming millions of China, India, Africa, and many sections of other foreign countries, but also at the multitudes here in America. It has been estimated that approximately 70,000,000 people here in America are outside of the pale of Christianity. 17,000,000 children living, moving, and having their being in these United States of America are totally ignorant of even the most simple and elementary knowledge of the saving Word! In a report made to the Home Missions Conference recently held in Detroit, Pastor E. T. Bernthal stated that there are 1,225 communities in America with a population of 2,000 to 5,000 yet without one Lutheran church; 337 communities with a population of 5,000 to 10,000, 85 communities with a population of ten to fifteen thousand, 75 with a population of fifteen to thirty-five thousand — all without one Lutheran church! And we of the Lutheran Church not only possess the Gospel true and pure, but also have the means by which the light of the Gospel can be brought in the simplest form to the adult population of these many cities as well as to the children, namely, Luther's Catechism. What a challenge! Seeing these millions living in either partial or complete ignorance of the Word of God, should we not acknowledge the need of the Catechism? For what these millions need is not a superficial and general knowledge of the Bible, but a knowledge of its doctrines as we have them in the Catechism. Yes, "each one reach one!" — but for the purpose of teaching them and firmly establishing the fundamental truths of the Bible in their hearts.

II. THE IMPORTANCE OF LUTHER'S CATECHISM

A. The importance of this Catechism is determined first and foremost by *its contents.* The very fact that it contains the *chief* parts, the very fundamental truths, of our most holy Christian religion is enough to emphasize its supreme value. Luther himself stated that it is the right Bible for the laity, which holds the entire content of Christian doctrine and everything that a simple Christian must know. He writes in his *Short Form of the Ten Commandments,* etc. (Graebner, *Story of the Catechism,* p. 55), published in 1520: "It did not come to pass without the special providence of God that, with reference to the common Christian, who cannot read the Scriptures, it was commanded to teach and to know the Ten Commandments, the Creed, and the Lord's Prayer, which three parts indeed thoroughly and completely embrace all that is contained in the Scripture and may ever be preached, all that a Christian needs to know, and this, too, in a form so brief and simple that no one can complain or offer the excuse that it is too much, and that it is too hard for him to remember what is essential to his salvation. For in order to be saved, a man must know three things: First, he must know what he is to do and leave undone. Secondly, when he realizes that by his own strength he is unable to do it and leave it undone, he must know where he may take, seek, and find that which will enable him to do and to refrain. Thirdly, he must know how he may seek and obtain it, even as a sick man needs first of all to know what disease he has, what he may or may not do or leave undone. Thereupon he needs to know where the medicine is which will help him use one thing and abstain from another, like a healthy person. Fourthly, he must desire it, seek and get it, or have it brought to him. Accordingly the Commandments teach a man to know his disease and to perceive that he is a sinner and a wicked man. Thereupon the Creed holds before his eyes and teaches him where to find the medicine, the grace which will help him become pious that he may keep the Commandments; and shows him God and His mercy as revealed and offered in Christ. Finally, the Lord's Prayer teaches him how to ask for, get and obtain it, namely by proper, humble, and trusting prayer. These three things comprise the entire Scriptures."

Luther did not only embody the first three of the chief parts, but since he regarded a correct knowledge of Baptism and the Lord's Supper as necessary, he added these two parts.

In the introductory words to Baptism he writes in the Large Catechism (*Triglot*, p. 733, par. 1—2): "We have now finished the three chief parts of the common Christian doctrine. Besides these we have yet to speak of our two Sacraments instituted by Christ, of which also every Christian ought to have at least an ordinary, brief instruction, because without them there can be no Christian; although, alas! hitherto no instruction concerning them has been given."

So, then, the Catechism does not contain unnecessary *Nebensachen* — side issues — but truly the chief parts of Christian doctrine.

It might be added here that "the three questions regarding the Office of the Keys were not formulated by Luther. They are found in the *Nuernberg Textbooklet* of 1531. But as they are in complete agreement with Luther's doctrine of absolution, they were soon recognized as a valuable addition and have since retained their place in the Lutheran Catechism." (Graebner, *Story of the Catechism*, p. 67.)

Since the Office of the Keys was a later addition, Luther had placed the part of Confession between Baptism and the Lord's Supper, thereby actually making this the Fifth and the Lord's Supper the Sixth Chief Part. This part appeared for the first time in the second Wittenberg edition of 1529.

The collection of Bible texts known as the "Table of Duties" first appeared in 1529. Here Luther quotes Scriptures to show how we are to act and live in the station, or position, of life in which God has placed us.

According to the best sources of information the twenty "Questions and Answers in Christian Doctrine" first appeared in 1549. Since 1558 they form an appendix to the Catechism.

In arranging the Ten Commandments as he did, Luther omitted everything which was intended for the Jews only and had no further value for the Christians of the New Testament time, such as particular reference to graven images, the Sabbath day question. He placed at the close of the Commandments the divine threat upon evildoers and the promise of reward, which in the Book of Exodus is appended to the First Commandment. This he did to emphasize the fact that this particular statement applies to all of the Commandments.

The arrangement of the Creed in Luther's Catechism is particularly noteworthy. Originally the Creed was arranged in twelve independent sections. Luther grouped the twelve points around the three works of God — the Creation, the Redemption, the Sanctification. Thus we have the three parts, or articles. The First Article speaks about the creation, the preservation, and the government of the world by God. In the Second Article we have the entire work of Christ, Son of God, Son of Man. In the Third Article is emphasized the work of the Holy Ghost, that He sanctifies and gathers the Christian Church and makes it the partaker of the blessed fruits of Christ's redemption.

Study the contents of the Catechism, and you will realize that it holds all that a simple Christian must know for his salvation.

B. Taking up the next point — the *conservative character of Luther's Catechism* — the importance of this little book becomes apparent.

In the year 1541 Luther wrote (Graebner, *Story of the Catechism*, p. 71): "We have remained with the true ancient Church." Bente has this to say (*Triglot*, Historical Introductions, p. 64, par. 84): "The text of the first three chief parts Luther considered a sacred heirloom from the ancient Church. 'For,' says he in his Large Catechism, 'the holy Fathers or Apostles have thus embraced in a summary the doctrine, life, wisdom, and art of Christians, of which they speak and treat, and with which they are occupied.' Thus Luther, always conservative, did not reject the traditional catechism, both bag and baggage, but carefully distinguished between the good, which he retained, and the worthless, which he discarded. In fact, he no more dreamt of foisting a new doctrine or catechism on the Christian Church than he ever thought of founding a new Church. On the contrary, his sole object was to restore the ancient Apostolic Church; and his catechetical endeavors were bent on bringing to light once more, purifying, explaining, and restoring, the old catechism of the Fathers."

In his Catechism he was merely protecting and guarding an inheritance of the Fathers. He eliminated from the Christian teaching of the Roman Church all that was wrong. He removed the doctrine of salvation by works, the seven sacraments, the celibacy of the priests, penance, the worship of Mary, and the like. But he showed himself truly conservative in retaining everything that could stand under the light of Scriptures.

So, then, there is nothing new in the Catechism. It is simply a return to the Bible. This simple fact makes this book of such tremendous importance to us. Luther was not a religious crackpot, who, dissatisfied with the *status quo*, looked for something new to arouse the excitement of the people. He was not a rabble-rouser. He was not one of those who "*bringen stets was Neues her, zu faelschen deine rechte Lehr'."* His sentiments are expressed in the words of the hymn (*Lutheran Hymnal,* 292, v. 6):

> The haughty spirits, Lord, restrain
> Who o'er Thy Church with might would reign
> And always set forth something new,
> Devised to change Thy doctrine true.

C. To underscore the importance of Luther's Catechism, we must mention that *it excels all other booklets of its kind.* Both Loehe and Graebner tell of a number of characteristics and outstanding merits "which give the Catechism its unchallenged supremacy." We refer to them here.

Loehe says: "It contains the most definite doctrine, resisting every perversion, and still it is not polemical — it exhales the purest air of peace." The absence of polemics is most surprising when we remember the conflicts that Luther had with his adversaries. These conflicts were one of the reasons that compelled Luther to write the Catechism. And since so much of Luther's writings was of a polemical nature, one might expect at least a tinge of it here. But in the Catechism we find only "definite doctrine" and positive statements. There is a constant stress of fundamental truths. Luther considered not only the Church of his day but also that of the future. He was wise in giving the Christians of all times a book of simple instructions telling each one what to believe and how to live. (Loehe's statement in *Triglot,* Historical Introductions, p. 92, par. 117.)

Then we must also remember that the Catechism of Luther is evangelical in spirit throughout. "Justified by faith without the deeds of the Law" — that is the thought that runs through the Catechism like a silken cord. He says in his introduction to Deuteronomy: "Faith in the words and promises of God is everything. For this reason we have said in the Catechism that true worship consists in the fear and love of God." It is only natural that the Three Articles should be permeated with this doctrine. Note also the evangelical tone struck in the Introduction to the Lord's Prayer: "God would by these words tenderly invite us to believe that He is our true Father and that we are His true children. . . ." The same can be said of the two Sacraments. Throughout the Catechism we have nothing negative and barren, but only statements that are edifying, uplifting, and refreshing.

The beauty of Luther's Catechism is also evident from the fact that it speaks in a most pleasing personal tone. "Warm, hearty, childlike, yet it is so manly, so courageous, so free the individual confessor speaks here" (Loehe, *Triglot*, p. 92). Examine the explanation to the Three Articles. "I believe that God has made me . . . given me my body and soul . . . provides me with all that I need . . . defends me . . . guards and protects me . . . for all which it is my duty. . . ." "I believe that Jesus Christ . . . is my Lord . . . redeemed me . . . that I may be His own. . . ." "I believe that I cannot by my own reason or strength . . . but the Holy Ghost has called me. . . ."

We look at Luther's literary style and form employed in the Catechism, and we must say that it is exquisite. He is a master of language. Th. Graebner says (*Story of the Catechism*, p. 81): "What a wonderful feeling for harmony and rhythm is shown in the familiar combinations 'luegen und truegen,' 'reichlich und taeglich,' 'lehret und lebet,' 'mit aller Notdurft und Nahrung des Leibes und Lebens,' etc. . . . Besides these phrases with their artful alliterations, so well adapted to memorizing, we have expressions which gather into striking combinations that which is related in thought, as: 'love and trust,' 'hold in love and esteem,' 'help and befriend,' 'property and business,' 'heaven and earth,' etc. . . ." Here we have indeed a masterful use of the language of the common people.

The Catechism is a veritable little treasure box of God given to the Church. And since "it grew out of the life and experience of a great man of God and was not composed in the meditations of a cloistered cell," it is a very practical book for all those who will use it. Sublime truths are brought in simplest form.

Leopold von Ranke (*Concordia Pulpit*, 1936, p. 32) writes: "The Catechism is as childlike as it is deep-minded, as plain as it is unfathomable, simple and sublime. Happy he that feeds his soul with it, that clings to it! He has an unfailing comfort in every moment, behind a thin shell the kernel of truth, which satisfies the wisest of the wise." The Catechism is not a shallow cistern, but, like a deep-flowing well, it refreshes the soul with the Water of Life.

D. The importance of the Catechism is furthermore stressed by the fact that as *a symbol of the Church it is a powerful bulwark against all error.*

The Catechism of Luther is truly a confession of the Church. Not only has it been incorporated into the confessional writings of the Lutheran Church, but it is actually confessed by more lips than any other. "It is a confession of the Church, and of all, the best known, the most universal, in which God's children most frequently meet in conscious faith." (Loehe, in *Triglot,* Historical Introductions, p. 92, par. 117.)

Every Church and every congregation, yes, every individual Christian must have a confession. Such a confession is the answer of the Church or the individual to the voice of God, which the Church or the individual has heard in the Scriptures and still does hear. Even as the Word of God is always the same, so the confession of the Church must always remain the same. In Luther's Catechism God has given the Church a fine confession for all time to come, showing what the Church is to believe, how it is to speak and confess. Without such a confession the Church would soon become a prey to all sorts of spirits who would not be bound to any confession. The Christians soon would be swayed by every kind of religious opinion afloat. But in the Catechism they have a sure guide. Like the needle of a compass, which always points in the same direction, irrespective of weather conditions or the position of the instrument, the Catechism always points in the same direction — toward the divine truth, regardless of contrary winds of popular opinion and the spirit of the times. Without a confession such as is embodied in the Catechism every preacher and layman would soon make his own, and in the place of unity of doctrine we would lay ourselves open to the attacks of errorists, and there would be nothing but utter confusion. In the home, in the school, in the church, it serves as a strong bulwark against false teaching and ungodly life. The Catechism makes it easy to detect these things. The fact that the Lutheran Church has remained moored to the Gospel teachings true and pure is chiefly due — next to the grace of God — to the fact that the Catechism of Luther is taught and impressed upon the people. (Luther, Walch, edition, XIII, 1796.)

E. For the edification of Christ's holy people the Catechism serves as a *book of prayer and is a source of genuine comfort.*

We have Luther's own word for it that the Catechism is a book of prayer. He said: "But for myself I say this: I am also a doctor and preacher, yea, as learned and experienced as all those may be who have such presumption and security; yet I do as a child who is being taught the Catechism, and every morning, and whenever I have time, I read and say, word for word, the Ten Commandments, the Creed, the Lord's Prayer, the Psalms, etc. And I must still read and study daily, and yet I cannot master it as I wish, but must remain a child and a pupil of the Catechism, and am glad so to remain." On April 18, 1530, Luther said in a sermon: "When I rise in the morning, I pray the Ten Commandments, the Creed, the Lord's Prayer, and also a Psalm with the children."

If a catechism is to be good, one must be able to pray it. In this, too, Luther's Catechism excels all. Every sentence is so constructed that one can use it as a prayer and can come confidently before God with the same. This is especially true of the explanation of the Second Article. It is the work of an artist. Here is gathered together the comfort of the entire Gospel story. The Catechism should be not only a book of instruction — *Lehrbuch* — from which we gain knowledge of the Word of God, but also a book of prayer — *Gebetbuch* — by means of which the soul is truly refreshed and edified.

Because it is a book of prayer, it is also a source of real comfort, particularly so in the days of trial. Each chief part is a powerhouse of divine comfort and consolation also over against the temptations of Satan. Luther himself is proof for this. On one occasion he was sorely distressed. Nothing seemed to brace him up, not even the words of his co-workers and the passages of comfort they adduced. Turning to one of his students, Luther asked him for comfort. Feeling himself not equal to the task, the student offered an excuse. But Luther insisted that he simply speak as the Spirit gave him utterance. Thereupon the student recited the Three Articles of the Creed. At once the spirit of Luther was revived, and he felt strengthened. The Catechism is indeed a source of great comfort for all who will use it and pray it.

F. The Catechism *awakens and stimulates Christian life*. Rightly dividing Law and Gospel, it quickens faith and love.

It is not the purpose of this statement to deny the power and effect of the preaching of the Gospel. But it is certainly true that the Catechism has carried its share in stimulating Christian life.

One reason why the Catechism has been a powerful instrument in the hand of the Church to awaken and to arouse Christian living is the fact that it teaches Law and Gospel and properly divides the same. Before the day of the Catechism, Christian life was at low ebb. Those who attempted to be pious made pilgrimages, fasted, used the rosary in order to produce a large number of prayers, entered a cloister if they wished to be especially pious, and the like. A thousand and one rules and regulations were foisted upon the people. Of all these things the Lord Jesus has said: "In vain they do worship Me, teaching for doctrines the commandments of men" (Matt. 15:9). But when Luther's Catechism made its appearance and gained entry into the many homes as well as the churches, Christian faith, sincere love, and a God-pleasing life were developed. The Catechism was simply a tool of the Holy Spirit, and the works of the Spirit manifested themselves. Works, good works, that have their source in Christian faith, were produced. Only such works can please God, as stated in Rom. 14:23: "Whatsoever is not of faith is sin." Like a silken cord Law and Gospel run through the whole of the Catechism, and so faith and love are bound up with and in each other intimately. Graebner says: (*Story of the Catechism*, p. 74): "He [Luther] vivified the concept 'Christian instruction of youth' and placed the emphasis on Christian. Not any kind of religious instruction, not any kind of catechism would serve; only the true Biblical doctrine, the recovery of which was the essence of the Reformation, was hereafter to be given domicile in the Christian schools and homes. It was not sufficient to tell the children that the Ten Commandments must be kept, that God must be confessed as the Triune God and Jesus as the Son of God, but above all, that our salvation depends not on efforts of our own, but on grace, based upon the merits of Christ and accepted by faith; that the truly Christian life will grow forth from such faith as naturally as fruit grows upon a tree in the summertime. To bring the newly rediscovered Gospel into the hearts of men and thus make them happy in this life and the next, that, in simple words, was the purpose of Luther's catechisms and is their keynote."

We do well to note the following examples in this connection. In the First Commandment we read: "We should fear, love, and trust in God above all things." Faith and trust is basic. From that only can flow a Christian life demanded in the Ten Commandments. Also in the Creed, Luther adds to the doctrine of faith instruction in righteousness. In the First Article he says: ". . . for all which it is my duty to thank and praise, to serve and obey. . . ." In the Second Article we have: ". . . that I may be His own and live under Him in His kingdom and serve Him. . . ." In the Third Article we read: ". . . sanctified and kept me in the true faith." In the Petitions we have expressions such as these: ". . . lead a holy life according to it . . . to receive our daily bread with thanksgiving." There is a combination of Christian faith and life in Baptism: Faith — "Baptism works forgiveness of sins . . ."; life — "it signifies that the Old Adam in us should, by daily contrition and repentance, etc." In the Sacrament of the Altar we have the same.

In all this we see how Luther moves from the Law, serving as a mirror, to the Gospel and from the Gospel back to the Law, serving as a rule and guide. "Vom Sollen durch den Glauben zum heiligen Wollen und Tun" (Eastern District Synodical Report, 1879, p. 47). The Catechism is a healthy leaven which should permeate the home and society and thus help to produce a strong and vigorous people, healthy in body and soul.

III. THE PROPER USE OF THE CATECHISM

Luther said in his *German Mass*: "For the paramount thing is to teach and to lead people" (Walch, 19, 97). Dr. Bente in his Historical Introductions (*Triglot*, pp. 80 and 81, par. 102) writes: "Above all, Luther endeavored to acquaint the 'dear youth' with the saving truths, not merely for their own sakes, but in the interest of future generations as well. He desired to make them mature Christians, able to confess their faith and to impart instruction to their children later on. . . . Accordingly, both catechisms, though in various respects, are intended for all: people, youth, parents, preachers and teachers. . . . He desired to instruct all and, at the same time, enable parents and pastors to teach. According to Luther it is the duty of every Christian to learn constantly in order also to be able to teach others in turn."

A. From this we gather that we must put the Catechism to *proper use. We begin in the home.* The Catechism was intended for this very purpose, as we see from the superscription to each of the six chief parts: "As the head of the family should teach it in all simplicity to his household." Though written for all, it was to be placed into the hands of the children, who were to use it and memorize it at home and then bring it with them for instruction in the church. In his sermon of March 25, 1529, Luther says: "This exhortation ought not only to move us older ones, but also the young and the children. Therefore you parents ought to instruct and educate them in the doctrine of the Lord: the Decalog, the Creed, the Lord's Prayer, and the Sacraments."

Hence parents of today should be urged to teach most diligently the Catechism truths to their children. Parents ought to familiarize themselves with the Catechism and study the material presented there. Thereupon they should endeavor to do more teaching at home. The family devotions afford ample opportunity to "run through," to recite, to memorize, to explain, to teach in all simplicity, those fundamental, essential, beautiful truths of the Bible as they are incorporated in the Catechism. If there were more insistence upon this, we should be able the better to cope with the problems of our present-day youth and effectively to counteract such negative influences as may come from radio programs, the reading of comic strips, movies, and the like. Perhaps there would be less complaining about youthful delinquency if parents had given more attention to inculcating the simple teachings of the Catechism. And who can measure the good that will flow from such indoctrination in the home! Well taught and firmly rooted in the Word, what a blessing such children will be in life to the nation as well as to the Church in years to come!

B. *The Catechism is also a book for the schools.* Certainly, when planning and writing the Catechism, Luther did not overlook the schools and schoolteachers. Bente writes (*Triglot,* Historical Introductions, p. 83, par. 106): "In the 'Instruction for the Visitors' we read: 'A certain day, either Saturday or Wednesday, shall be set aside for imparting to the children Christian instruction. . . . Hereupon the schoolteacher shall simply and correctly expound at one time the Lord's Prayer, at another the Creed, at another the Ten Commandments, etc.'" In the schools referred to, Luther's Small Catechism served as the textbook.

Down to the present day no other book has become and remained a schoolbook for religious instruction to such an extent as Luther's Catechism. Since Luther called the Catechism the "Laymen's Bible" — *der Laien Biblia* — since it contains the essential facts of salvation, since the Catechism is the frame for the picture which is Christ, this book ought to have its proper place in our schools. The first hour of the day ought to be devoted to it.

"The hearts of young and inexperienced children are like a bottle with a narrow neck. If you pour buckets of water over it, very little will enter the bottle; but if you pour the water into it gradually, by drops, the bottle will soon be filled. Thus it is necessary to offer God's Word to little children piecemeal, as is done in catechetical instruction. Then it will be retained by them, and their hearts will be filled by an abundance of divine wisdom." (Scriver, *Concordia Pulpit,* 1936, p. 31.)

Teachers ought to prepare themselves most conscientiously for the teaching of the Catechism. It should be for them not merely another lesson or subject. Making a most thorough study of the secular branches of learning, bringing these up to date, employing modern methods, attending higher schools of learning in order to become better equipped and better able to teach, is certainly praiseworthy and should be encouraged. However, all this should not be done at the expense of proper inculcation of the Catechism, but rather enhance it. Here too every conscientious teacher will strive to improve himself, remembering the words of Luther *"Ich muss ein Schueler des Katechismus bleiben und bleib's auch gerne"* ("I must remain a pupil of the Catechism and am glad so to remain").

Again, what blessings will flow from such a school into the lives of those children entrusted to the care of conscientious teachers!

C. Certainly, if in the home and in the school, then *also in the church must the teaching of the Catechism find a prominent place.*

That Luther intended his Small Catechism as a help also for pastors was, in so many words, stated on the title page of the first book edition. The Preface of the Catechism also is addressed "to all faithful, pious pastors and preachers" and shows in detail how they are to make use of it. There we read (third paragraph): "Therefore I entreat you all, for God's sake, my dear brethren who are pastors and preachers, to devote yourselves heartily to your office, and have pity upon the people who are committed to your charge. Help us to inculcate the Catechism upon them, especially upon the young." In following paragraphs we read: "First, the minister should above all things avoid the use of different texts and forms of the Ten Commandments, the Creed, the Sacraments, etc. . . . Secondly, when they have well learned the text, teach them the sense also, that they may know what it means. . . . Thirdly, after you have taught them this short Catechism, take up the Large Catechism, and impart to them a richer and fuller knowledge."

Bente writes (Historical Introductions, *Triglot*, p. 82, par. 105): "Luther's intention was to make the Small Catechism the basis of instruction in the church as well as in the home; for uniform instruction was required to insure results. Having, therefore, placed the Catechism into the hands of the parents, Luther could but urge that it be introduced in the churches too. He also showed them how to use it. On June 11, 1529, for instance, he expounded the First Article after he had read the text and the explanation of the Small Catechism. This pastors were to imitate, a plan which was also carried out."

The Catechism, therefore, should have and does have a rightful place in our churches. It is one of the main tools of the pastor and his helpers. While the work in our Sunday schools is based on selected stories from the Bible, yet the Catechism application should always be made. The very backbone of our instruction in confirmation classes is Luther's Small Catechism. Even in our adult membership groups no better course of instruction can be found than that which is built around the Catechism text. Luther once said: "The Catechism is a fine instruction of conscience, so that one may know how to lead a Christian life, how to know Christ." In a day when that type of instruction is more necessary than ever, when to "know Christ" and to "have instruction for conscience" is vital for the very future of mankind, it might be well to make good use of the Catechism even in young people's groups, such as our Walther League societies. Combine Christian knowledge and Christian service with the study of this little book, and you will undoubtedly move many to keep it next to their Bibles and hymnbooks as a real aid to Christian living.

The pastor will certainly not neglect to preach on the Catechism truths. Luther preached the Catechism for many years before he published it. In fact, the Catechism was the outgrowth of these many sermons. In order to have a well-indoctrinated congregation, a pastor must in his sermons present the teachings of the Catechism again and again.

D. Luther's Catechism should also find room in our Church literature. The simple text can be printed in pamphlet form and spread far and wide for missionary purposes. Devotional books and booklets can be based upon the Catechism (Pasche's *Daily Bread*). Many catechetical helps have been published. Of these we mention the following: The new synodical Catechism, Mezger's *Lessons in the Small Catechism of Dr. Martin Luther*, Kurth's *Catechetical Helps*, Koehler's *Annotated Catechism*, Fehner's *Outlines for Catecheses*. Our official church papers have done much to bring to the attention of our people the truths of the Catechism. The Catechism has also been the basis for many literary efforts, such as synodical essays, sermon books, poetry, and church hymns.

IV. CONCLUSION

Luther's Catechism is the gem of the Reformation. It is held in high esteem. Only thirty-seven years after the first publication of Luther's Catechism, Mathesius was able to say: "There now have been printed of the Catechism — praise be to God! — more than a hundred thousand copies in this and other countries and are being used in all academies and public schools!" (Graebner, *Story of the Catechism*, p. 93.) The supreme worth of Luther's Catechism was recognized by his contemporaries. Justus Jonas said: "The Catechism is only a small book, which may be purchased for six pennies, but which six thousand worlds do not outweigh in value. I am convinced that the Holy Spirit has indited it to our sainted Luther." (Graebner, *Story of the Catechism*, p. 134.)

"Blessed are the hands that have written this book," exclaimed a Catholic cleric in Venice, not knowing it was Luther's Catechism he was reading. (*Concordia Pulpit*, 1936, p. 31.)

A more modern estimate is that of Loehe: "If a deluge would be caused by writing thousands of expositions of Luther's Small Catechism, yet Luther's Catechism would remain the ark which soars over the waters of them all." (*Concordia Pulpit*, 1936, p. 31.)

Dr. Charles Porterfield Krauth, referred to above, said: "The Catechism is a thread through the labyrinth of divine wonders. Persons often get confused, but if they will hold on to this Catechism, it will lead them through without being lost. It is often called the 'Little Bible' and the 'Bible of the Laity,' because it presents the plain and simple doctrines of the Holy Book in its own words. Pearls strung are easily carried, unstrung they are easily lost. The Catechism is a string of Bible pearls. The order of the arrangement is the historical, the Law, Faith, Prayer, Sacrament of Baptism, and all crowned with the Lord's Supper—just as God worked them out and fixed them in history."

Many other fine tributes have been paid this booklet. Let these suffice. It now behooves us, the children of the Reformation, who have seen this book in use for more than four hundred years, to thank God for this unspeakable gift to His Church on earth. If the blessings of the Catechism are to remain ours in the future, then by all means let us make diligent and constant use of it in the home, in the school, in the church. May our good and great God preserve it unto the end of time.

> Like a beacon that rears its lofty head,
>   Disdaining the test of the surge's prod,
> Unmoved and unmoving because its bed
>   Is the granite rock of the Word of God,
> Are you, little book. Your light has shone
> On the lost at sea, has guided them home.
> Through fogs of the night and mists of the day
> You have marked out the reefs and guided the way.
>
> (*Concordia Pulpit*, 1936, p. 31)

Christian Training of Youth

WHEN the Church focuses her attention on youth, she proves herself mindful of the future. For us present-day workers in the Church the future of the Church lies not so much in the things that are ahead as in the youth which shall follow us. For both reasons, then, for the salvation of youth and for the salvation of the Church, the present Church must devote herself to the cultivation, development, and training of youth. This is the subject of our present study: *Christian Training of Youth*.

I. THE NEED

Youth needs Christian training because of the nature of youth and the nature of the influences, many of them quite unreligious, under which youth grows up.

A child is born. A child is different from a chick. A little chick has hardly popped out of its shell when it itself starts pecking around for food. A child, however, needs constant care and provision. It must be carried around from place to place. It must be fed. It must be bathed. Things need to be done for a child for a number of years. The kind of care and attention the child gets in these first few years of life will influence the child's whole life. Foundations for character are laid even in these first years. A slovenly, careless, inefficient mother without a program and schedule of tasks and duties will hardly rear children who will be prompt and neat. Like parents, like child.

As we look at the nature of a child, we find more of the parent in it than a certain similarity resulting from an emulation of example. The very nature of the child is determined by the nature of the parents. "That which is born of the flesh is flesh" (John

3:6). The child, "shapen in iniquity" (Ps. 51:5), is bound to be iniquitous. The prayer "Create in me a clean heart" (Ps. 51:11), which must be prayed continuously through life, even in old age, must also be prayed over youth and the newborn infant because of the taint with which man comes into being, the imperfection and corruption of inherited, original sin. The moot question of the determinative influence of heredity and environment is really answered in the Biblical doctrine so annoying and repulsive to the natural man, the doctrine that all mankind, born of sinful seed, must of necessity be sinful. When the nature of youth and of children is under consideration, this fact of original sin, taught in the Bible and observed in dealing with children, may not be overlooked.

It is an old experience of parents that their children do not turn out according to their hopes. Eve had given birth to her first son. She exclaimed, "I have gotten a man from the Lord." Luther translated, "I have gotten the man, the Lord" (Gen. 4:1). She thought this was the Seed of the Woman, who was to crush the head of the serpent. How terribly guilty Eve must have felt when she realized that this son of hers had inherited her image rather than the image of the Lord! How Adam and Eve must have worked in order that their children might come into the possession of the salvation, the dawn of which they perceived in the promise of the Seed of the Woman.

Effect of Original Sin

The Psalmist, speaking of the effect of original sin, says: "The wicked are estranged from the womb, they go astray as soon as they are born, speaking lies" (Ps. 58:3). We see the extremes in the case of spoiled children. Spoiled children are those in whom the corrupted natural tendencies are allowed to develop and grow. By the indulgence of parents, who laugh at the precocious naughtiness of their infant children, these easily grow up into little discourteous, proud, boastful, demanding tyrants, disobedient, saucy, willful, disrespectful, selfish, disdainful brats.

Think of the disappointment experienced in Cain, in the descendants of Cain, in Esau, in the wicked sons of Eli, in the sons of Jacob, of Samuel (I Sam. 8:5), of David, of Hezekiah

(II Kings 21:1-16), in the youth in the days of the Prophets Elisha (II Kings 2); Jeremiah (Jer. 6:10-11), and Ezekiel (Ezekiel 9).

Youth is sinful and does sinful things. Youth outside the Christian Church must first be won to faith, and youth inside the Church needs to be trained. To allow a child to grow without directive training indicates either disinterest or lack of understanding and conviction. If a decadent generation has no positive constructive design for life, it really has nothing to say to youth. Inactivity and silence give eloquent expression to intellectual and spiritual bankruptcy and ignorance. Where there is Christian knowledge and where there is conviction of Christian faith, there will also be found intelligent and active training of youth into Christian ideas and ideals.

What happens when children are left to grow up by themselves is too well known to need a long dissertation here. *Juvenile delinquency* is a phrase which has been in the daily news of our time all too frequently. This delinquency has been traced to a lack of religious instruction and training. Paul's warning "Flee youthful lusts" (II Tim. 2:22) is not an idle word. The agitation on the part of the sectarian Protestant churches for the introduction of religious instruction in the public schools is occasioned by the realization of the need.

A Mobile World Situation

Consider some of the influences under which our youth grows up. Strange though it may seem, yet it is possible and has happened. We who have a half century of life behind us often fail to consider the complete upheaval of life's course which has taken place in our time. When we were in our childhood years, we could play on the streets with little need for caution on account of traffic. Perhaps the only time we had to hurry was when the three-horse fire engine would come thundering down the dusty street. At night there was no reading in bed, nor did the neighbor's blaring radio keep us awake. By ten o'clock the house was silent. It remained so till six in the morning. All that is changed. Call to mind just a few other marks of identification of changed times. Calico wrappers and crocheted fascinators have given way to modish housecoats and colorful babushkas. The children's music lesson has been turned into listening absent-mindedly to

Red Seal records and sometimes to records just luridly red. The once peaceful and quietly restful tranquillity of the home is gone — not only from the living room. The ubiquitous radio has taken over. The latest song hits, both the nice and the nasty ones, drone through the house. In the morning we are admonished, "Come on now, Lazybones, hit the deck." Hot bands, interspersed with nonsensical but amusing chatter, see us through our ablutions and breakfast, with a fifteen minute interruption to hear what is happening not only on Main Street, but also on the Champs Elysees as well as in Honolulu and Piccadilly Square and in the White House and the Kremlin and 10 Downing Street and Java and Siam and Bikini Atoll.

Indeed, times have changed. We older people sometimes forget that our children lack the anchorage of our own quieter youth days. The youth of today has never known any other kind of days than the kind we call abnormal. Children are growing up unaccustomed to quieter peace times. Their economy is a wartime economy with bloodshed and bombing and hatred propaganda and strikes and industrial conflict and high taxes and high wages and military uniforms and brothers and sisters in Asia and the South Pacific and in Europe.

This is a picture of the mobile situation which confronts the present-day Christian, the Christian home, and the Christian Church. It is startling.

INFLUENCE OF THE TIMES

When we look away from the outside world and take a survey of the situation within the churches, what do we find? Where do we find great numbers of people flocking to the house of God? Here and there, where unusually gifted preachers are in the pulpit, larger congregations are attracted. Let that preacher depart and a man of less color come to that pulpit, and the discovery will be made that the people did not come out of love for the Word of God, but because of the personal magnetism of the preacher. In desperation, it seems, churches are tempted to introduce special features in order to attract the people. These special features must of necessity grow constantly more spectacular to continue in their drawing power. By way of illustration, we point to our Synod's adoption of special days in spite of the church year with its spiritual arrangement of a presentation of the great works of God in a logical and chronological sequence of Christian doctrine. Thus the church year is disturbed in the post-Easter-Pentecost season by the insertion of Mother's Day. Has it come to this that Lutheran churches celebrate Mother's Day but let Ascension Day pass by unobserved? It has!

Thus being influenced by the pressure of the times, the Church loses the function of influencing the times as powerfully as it should. Church attendance is looked upon popularly, not as an opportunity for communion with God, but as a polite paying of respect, a courtesy shown to a hang-over idea from the days of our fathers, who lacked the advantages of our advanced civilization. Preachers are treated with a sort of amused toleration. In the movies the exceptions are so rare that one anticipates the rule of placing a minister on the same level with a "dumb" movie detective.

The churches should be filled in this postwar era with penitent sinners, grateful, saved children of God. Instead they are empty except for the few faithful who bear the heat and burden of the day (Matt. 20:12). And even these sometimes grumble! How many a pastor labors under the terrific handicap of discouragement because his own flock does not respond to the Word of Life he ministers to them. Christmas and Easter, yes! But Pentecost, no! With Pentecost almost supplanted by Mother's Day, the Holy Spirit has been lost by many. Have the days of Noah returned? "My Spirit shall not always strive with man, for that he also is flesh" (Gen. 6:3). Luther: "The people will no longer bow to the correction of My Spirit, for they are flesh." One third of the congregation constitutes the ordinary Sunday attendance in the preaching service. 25 per cent of a congregation carries 75 per cent of the financial load of a congregation. How strong an influence can a congregation so constituted and so operating exert on the upcoming youth?

The religionless instruction in the nation's school system is a vital factor in the shaping of the outlook of the younger citizens of our country. The young people of our congregations who have received their primary education in the religionless schools naturally also have an outlook on life in which religion plays a decidedly minor part. When you follow through into colleges and universities, you will notice that higher education is no longer in the hands of church-controlled, or even church-influenced schools, but in schools thoroughly secularized. Small wonder that our educated youth often bids the Church farewell with a pitying look, if not with a look even of scorn.

So many cultural influences of our day are unreligious. God and man's relation to God simply do not receive any consideration, as though God no longer existed. Literature, both the good and the cheap, is quite evolutionistic. Art and music are sensual, quite definitely so in their more popular forms.

Is Not This the Time?

Not to recognize the need of Christian training for youth marks a man as being entirely out of touch with the entire tone of our time. This is not a time in which to say comfortably, "Oh, well, everything will eventually turn out all right." Is not this the time in which perils are upon us, when men are selfish, boastful, proud, blasphemers, disobedient to parents, unthankful, unholy, without natural affection, trucebreakers, false accusers, incontinent, fierce, despisers of those that are good, traitors, heady, high-minded, lovers of pleasures more than lovers of God, having a form of godliness but denying the power thereof? (II Tim. 3:1-5.)

II. THE SCOPE

Christian training includes imparting definite Christian truth and instruction and guidance in applying Christian principles of living.

Once the need of Christian training is recognized, our thoughts turn to a consideration of its nature and scope. Without becoming involved in a technical discussion on the meaning of terms, let us agree that for the purpose of our present study these two things shall be considered as an adequate definition of Christian training, first, imparting definite knowledge of Christian truth, and, second, instructing and guiding in applying Christian principles to living.

Christian Knowledge Not Inherent

Christian truth must be imparted. Christian knowledge is the foundation of Christian culture. It is true, of course, that any and all knowledge can be used to serve Christian training. The Christian is not a person who shuts himself off from the world. The more a Christian asserts himself in the world, the more will the world be profited. The Christian is to be in the world, but not of the world (John 17:14-15). General cultural knowledge of the arts and sciences is not identical with Christian knowledge, nor can it alone produce Christian training, fitting a man for living. Here definite knowledge of Christian truth is needed. This knowledge is not obtainable from within. There is a definite body of truth which must be acquired from outside oneself.

Learning Process Needed

The learning process must be used by which God's revealed truth becomes the possession of the individual. This learning process has been summarized as *education*, "drawing out," and *instruction*, "building in." The human mind is endowed with gifts and abilities. These must be aroused and put to use. Natural ideas, however, may be in error. Nor does the human mind inherently contain complete knowledge which is developable from within. Facts and truths outside our human ken must be brought to the human mind and received by the human mind. From the Christian point of view the learning process goes a step farther. Natural knowledge and ability is corrupt by the effect of original sin. Hence the learning process must continually introduce the elements of reproof and correction, in addition to doctrine and instruction in righteousness. This short outline for Christian training is stated in II Tim. 3:16.

Christian doctrines and principles are quite different from the natural ideas of man. The basic difference is that natural man harbors the notion that he can work out his own satisfactory life principles. He argues that if his life principles are satisfactory to himself, they ought also to be satisfactory to God. Christian doctrine, however, teaches something entirely different. All men are sinners. Therefore all men are doomed. All are under the sentence of death. As the sinners' Substitute, Christ Jesus lived and suffered and died and rose again. Having thus taken the sinners' place and dealt with God as the sinners' Representative, Jesus effected the sinners' liberation, their full justification before God (Rom. 5:18). Through faith in Christ the sinner enters into this state of justification. God regards all who come to Him through Jesus as re-established sons and daughters of His. They are free. Their sins are covered and so forgiven. They have life, eternal life (John 3:36; Mark 16:16).

This doctrine is not a humanly devised philosophy, but a revelation of God. If mankind today is to learn this fact, man must be told. He cannot find this in his own mind or in the test tube or in nature. This way is so contrary to man's natural ideas that both the cultured and the uncultured find it easy to reject God's whole plan as unworthy. Indeed, this revelation of God must be brought to the human mind, and the natural resistance of the human mind to this idea must be broken down (I Cor. 2:14). So it can readily be understood why special training in these new supernatural life principles becomes necessary in making the practical application to daily living. The experienced must guide the new learner.

Integrated Learning

It is at this point where much instruction has failed in the past and is failing today. The funnel system of instruction has not entirely disappeared. It is gratifying to note that integration of instruction into life situations has become more general in religious instruction material in our own new publications. Is it not true that much instruction has been given without relating it to the immediately present life of the pupil? If, however, religious instruction is given in this unrelated fashion in its major portions, need the teacher be astonished if his pupils retain little or nothing of the subject matter? The teacher of religion, in the major portion of his instruction, must present his material in such fashion that it is transferable into action and life then and there.

An illustration will help at this point. The teacher has been talking about missions. He has told interesting stories about the experiences of men and women who have gone into dangerous places. He has described the hostility of the natives of a foreign island. Then he described the slow but definite conquest of the hearts of the people by his unfailing kindness and love. Having gained the confidence of the people, the missionary then finds and uses his opportunity to tell the people about Jesus. He tells what Jesus has done and how Jesus changes a man's whole way of thinking and acting. If the lesson ends there, the whole matter is left suspended. The learners must now be led to arrive at certain decisions and to engage in certain action. The decision must be that the world in darkness must have the light of the Gospel. The action can take different routes of expression. A silent or a spoken prayer by members of the class may be an immediate result. The class may decide to gather money to give for the work of Christianizing the world. Personal invitation of some acquaintance to attend religious instruction would be a great achievement. If this sort of outcome could be accomplished in class after class of children, Mission Sundays would produce marvelous results all through the life of these learners. Religious instruction must be integrated into life. Why is religious instruction considered dull by pupils? Because they fail to see that the memory material and the Catechism lessons have any bearing on their life.

Home Laboratory

How parents can introduce a similar type of instruction in the family life is not difficult to demonstrate. A child will be taught obedience and respect for the rights of others in a practical manner in the home as a laboratory of living. This instruction will be given in all the home relations between parents and children and between sisters and brothers.

Parents will teach their children honesty by such an expedient as giving them money occasionally or by giving a regular allowance, with directions as to its use. Parents will then check to see that the child has used its allowance wisely and in accordance with instructions. The wise use of money, it seems necessary to instruct, is to spend less, not more, than one has. Mr. Micawber advised David Copperfield: "If a man had twenty pounds a year for his income and spent nineteen pounds, nineteen shillings, and sixpence, he would be happy; but if he spent twenty pounds one, he would be miserable." The amount not spent should be saved. From this lesson the next step is easy. Save first an amount of the allowance. The danger of foolish spending is thus precluded. Having come along this far with a child, the parent will not find it difficult to lead him into another and greater lesson in the proper use of money: As God must come first in all things, so God must come first in our use of money. Now, God is represented to us by our Church. The church building is God's house. In God's house we hear God's Word. In His Word, God comes to us. I can put God first in the use of my money by first of all, even before my savings, putting some of my allowance aside for God. If the church and Sunday school use the envelope system of gathering contributions, Christian stewardship principles and practices can easily be taught, and the children of the family can be guided into the habitual exercise of this Christian virtue.

THE OLDER GENERATION MUST LEAD

Guidance of youth is no haphazard business. Every pastor, teacher, elder, deacon, every officer in the congregation, must be alert to this duty of translating into daily living the truth learned from the Word of God. At this point let us put emphasis on this *personal, individual,* responsibility. Organized congregational efforts in this direction will be dealt with in following sections of this presentation.

No one can guide another person, least of all alert youth, into a way which the guiding person does not follow in his own life. The personal example counts for very much in guidance. The pastor who is not prompt will have a congregation of stragglers. The Sunday school superintendent who does not show reverence in his own conduct will not have a reverent Sunday school. The day school teacher who has no orderly schedule will not produce orderliness in his pupils. The elder who is not in his place in church every Sunday can do little by way of encouraging, and certainly nothing by way of admonishing, the absentee. The deacon and church officer and all the other adult members of a congregation who are themselves not faithful and loyal in the performance of every Christian duty are remiss in not setting before youth a proper pattern of life.

Why should young people try if the older members show in their life that Christian living is not essential and practical? Why should children study their Sunday school lesson if Father and Mother never or seldom read their Bible? Why, indeed, should children attend Sunday school if Father finds the garden, or the lawn, or the Sunday papers, or golf, or fishing, or almost anything else more important than Bible-class attendance or teaching a class or even attending the formal church service? And to what kind of life is Mother training her sons and daughters if she finds the preparation of the week's *pièce de resistance* the one thing needful?

III. THE RESPONSIBILITY

The God-appointed agencies for Christian training are the home and the Church.

Two agencies have been appointed by God for the work of Christian training. The first is the home, the second is the Church.

THE HOME FIRST

It is necessary in our day to emphasize that the home stands first in this task. It is true, the Church also stands in a primary position in the matter of Christian training. However, in responsibility the home comes first. The Church stands first in the duty to teach and train the home. The instructions "Take heed . . . to all the flock" (Acts 20:28) and "Feed My lambs" (John 21:15) do not take precedence over the instruction to parents, specifically to fathers, to "bring them [your children] up in the nurture and admonition of the Lord" (Eph. 6:4).

This duty of fathers needs to be stressed again and again. To point out the fact that home life in America has suffered greatly in the past several decades is not necessary, since it is generally acknowledged.

"Ye fathers!" the Apostle cries out rather sharply. Fathers, notice — and mothers, the fathers' helpmates, listen — "Bring up your children in the nurture and admonition of the Lord." Bringing up of children is part of the responsibility of parenthood.

CHILDREN GOD'S GIFTS

Children are a precious gift of God (Ps. 127). They are not the property of parents. They are a sacred trust of God. Parents are accountable to God for how they bring up their children. Parents who regard their children as servants, as income producers, not as individuals redeemed by the blood of Christ, "provoke their children to wrath" (Eph. 6:4).

To bring up children is a task that requires faith and intelligence. One of our synodical fathers remarked sagely, "To rear children as Christians, the parents must themselves be Christians." One of the first fruits of faith on the part of parents is that with their entire household, they believe. To fulfill the task of bringing up children requires knowledge, understanding, wisdom, plan and program, and a continued good example. It is a lifetime job. No person is sufficient to this task of himself. Prayer before a child is born, yes, even conceived, prayer after birth, prayer during the process of rearing the child, is necessary. God wants to give the necessary spiritual, intellectual, and physical equipment for the parents' work. God wants to be trusted for it. God wants to be asked for it. "Ask . . . seek . . . knock . . ." applies here as in every sphere in life (Matt. 7:7-8). When God gives children, He also wants those children to have their chance to live.

BALANCED PROVISION

Properly providing the physical needs of our children is quite general in our country at this time. They are being prepared for their economic and social existence. Their intellectual needs are being met in the secular sphere. When we turn to the spiritual needs, the provision is not so good. Where are the family prayers? The little devotional booklets are good. They are helping to revive the family altar. While they are a step in the right direction, are they not, however, taking the place of Bible reading in many homes? How often does a father hear his child's recitation of Bible verses or go over his Sunday school lesson with him? How many fathers, parents, could correct inexact Catechism recitations of their children? The family Bible has disappeared. Half of our homes do not even subscribe to our church papers. Where the congregational blanket subscription plan is in vogue, are the papers read? Many of our people do not even know what the Book of Concord is! Ye fathers, your task is to bring up your children.

Luther writes in his Large Catechism (*Triglot*, p. 629): "God does not wish to have in this office and government (*viz.*, of father and mother) knaves and tyrants; nor does He assign to them this honor, that is, power and authority to govern, that they should have themselves worshiped; but they should consider that they are under obligations of obedience to God; and that, first of all, they should earnestly and faithfully discharge their office, not only to support and provide for the bodily necessities of their children, servants, subjects, etc., but most of all, to train them to the honor and praise of God. Therefore do not think that this is left to your pleasure and arbitrary will, but rather, that it is a strict command and injunction of God, to whom also you must give account for it."

There are two essentials in the nurture of children in the admonition of the Lord. One is instruction by word. The other, and perhaps the more impressive and influential, the quite incidental instruction by the parents' example. What we fathers *are* is far more influential with our children than what we *say*. While we must say the right things to our children, it is equally important that we are sincerely and faithfully and considerately Christian in all our conduct. The character of the home, the type of leisure and relaxation and conversation, the company brought into the home, these and kindred things are the determining factors in child nurture. Ye fathers, measure up! The breakdown of the home or the building of a real Christian family life is your responsibility. God will require your children from your hand. Father and mother must work together. Luther points out the desirability of starting the training of the children in the cradle: "No one should become a father unless he is able to instruct his children in the Ten Commandments and in the Gospel, so that he may bring up true Christians. But many enter the state of holy matrimony who cannot say the Lord's Prayer, and knowing nothing themselves, they are utterly incompetent to instruct their children. Children should be brought up in the fear of God. If the Kingdom of God is to come in power, we must begin with children and teach them from the cradle." (Painter, *Luther on Education*, p. 119. C. P. H.)

THE CHURCH ALSO

Since God gives the children to the parents, theirs is the first stewardship and accountability. The Church has also been given its assignment in the work of Christian training of youth. This is twofold. There is the assignment to Christianize all nations. Then follows the other assignment of seeing to it that parents do their duty by their children. Jesus said: "Teaching them to observe all things whatsoever I have commanded you" (Matt. 28:20). This teaching is to go on to the end of time. Teaching is not confined to any one age group. All nations, every creature, all the flock, designate the field of the Church (Matt. 28:19; Mark 16:15; Acts 20:28).

Where anyone fails in his duty, the Church must admonish, correct, instruct, so that the Christian may be properly equipped for life's tasks (II Tim. 3:16-17). When fathers and mothers fail to provide for their children, the Church must step in to see to it not only that care is taken for the children's needs, but that the parents are taken to task for their neglect.

Parents' classes would certainly not be amiss. Adult education is not only possible but, educators insist, easier of accomplishment than the teaching of children. Classes for parents teaching proper ways of home instruction and home management will both meet the Church's duty and be found to be popular. Churches have conducted parent-teacher meetings successfully. Where these have not been mere social evenings, they have certainly had the character of adult schools, even though they may not have been thus named. Discussion groups in which parents can be mutually helpful by exchanging opinions and experiences can be real schools. The pastor of a congregation will certainly use the sermon for parent training. In addition, the pastor will avail himself of the opportunities in adult societies to speak on the subject of Christian training. The congregation and the pastor and the teacher who bemoan the fact that parents do so little in training their children, yet themselves do nothing to correct this state of affairs, are guilty of neglect and sin. A blowup will surely come in such a situation. The time to go to work on this immediate problem is not at some future date, but as soon as the problem is recognized.

IV. THE MACHINERY

The God-appointed agencies may arrange subagencies for Christian training. Included in these subagencies are schools on the various levels.

God has laid upon the home and the Church the duty of training youth. We have considered the scope of the work to some extent and the difficulties confronting the workers. Home and Church will need *aid*. Wise parents and wise pastors and church officers will devise ways and means for supplying help.

In its teaching and training program the Church has set up schools. These schools have proved themselves to be of great value. Schools on the different levels of age and interest have been established also by the State for its training program. The Church has pioneered in the establishment and development of schools. Luther has been given credit by historians for laying the foundation for a free educational system, from primary schools all the way through to the university.

Considerable adjustment is necessary for the child when starting in school. For this reason the kindergarten has been introduced, so that the child might be ready for the first grade. More recently nursery schools have been added.

THE CHRISTIAN DAY SCHOOL

The school which has rendered the greatest service to the lay members of our congregations and exerted the greatest influence in the first century of Synod's life and work is the Christian day school. In an earlier convention of the Eastern District (34th, 1897) this definition of a Christian day school was given: "A Christian day school (*Gemeindeschule*), in the sense in which we use the term, is an institution established by a congregation in which the children of the parish, and others outside the congregation, who are entrusted to it, are faithfully instructed, in obedience to the Word of God, in the saving truth of the Evangelical Lutheran Church by regularly called teachers and educated and trained to be useful members of the congregation." The value of such a school is quite generally conceded within the membership of Synod.

Christian Training of Youth 645

OBJECTIONS TO CHRISTIAN DAY SCHOOLS

However, objections like the following were raised against these schools:

1. We pay taxes — we want our money's worth in the public school.

2. We cannot afford a Christian day school.

3. Our people live scattered over too large an area.

4. The language of the land will be learned better in the public school than in a bilingual church school.

5. We have gotten along without a school thus far — why change now?

6. Our congregation need not be the first to call a teacher. Let others make the start.

7. Will not offense be given by withdrawing our children from the public school?

8. Do not some children go astray who attended a Christian school?

9. Could we not arrange to have one of our teachers appointed to teach in a public school, and then have this teacher instruct our children in religion after school hours?

OBJECTIONS ANSWERED

These objections were answered in this manner:

1. We do not insist on personal occupancy though we support many public institutions like orphanages and jails.

2. We can afford schools because we spend money for less beneficial things. Our teachers, as a rule, give much more extensive service to a congregation than the small salary they receive would ordinarily lead one to anticipate.

3. Even if some children live at too great a distance to attend a Christian school, why deprive the others who could attend? Besides, boarding arrangements can usually be made.

4. Language is important, but Jesus said (Matt. 6:33) "Seek ye first the Kingdom."

5. We have gotten along without a school — but how? Great losses have been sustained among the youth.

6. To put off opening a school because others do so is no valid reason. If a congregation leads in establishing a school, it sets a good example and has earned a high honor.

7. Christians are within their civil rights to place their children in private Christian schools. Even if offense is taken, the welfare of the child and the doing of God's will are the more important considerations.

8. If some Christian school products go astray, merely pointing them out acknowledges that these are the exceptions.

9. A Christian teacher in a public school could not apply the Word of God as the determinative element in discipline and training.

A reason for the loss of the Christian day school in many areas was the overemphasis on the German language, evidenced by reference to the Christian day school as *die deutsche Gemeindeschule*. Also failure to evaluate the Word of God as God's precious gift and the need for the children to learn that Word as well as the lack of pulpit emphasis on the necessity of parental nurture of their children in the fear of the Lord, loses schools.

Other Types of Schools

Of course there are other subagencies. The Bible does not command that a Christian congregation must establish a Christian day school. There is the Sunday school, the Saturday school, the vacation school, the summer school. There is released time religious instruction. There is confirmation instruction. An increasing number of summer camps is serving our churches. All of these agencies can serve the purpose of teaching and to some extent of training. No informed observer, however, will put any of these agencies on the same level with a Christian day school under the direction of an able Christian teacher or group of teachers. Criticisms may be offered in some cases against the personnel manning these schools. There weaknesses are bound to occur, as they do in the Church otherwise. Until, however, some more effective way of teaching and training our children is devised, the Christian day school stands as the ideal teaching and training agency of a Christian congregation.

Lutheran High Schools

In recent years there has been in evidence a growing appreciation of the need for Christian instruction and training on the high school level. If the young people of our congregations can be held to the Church and to the exercise of their Christian faith into their adult years through the unstable years of adolescence, they will, quite likely, remain faithful through life. Congregations act wisely to supply opportunities for their young people to continue their study of the Word of God. Great benefit to the youth and to the present and future Church will result from the establishment of Christian high schools, especially in such centers where several congregations undertake such a venture jointly. While it is true that a strong faith will be strengthened when it successfully withstands a test, it likewise is true that much damage is done the weak faith of young Christians when they come under the influence of unbelieving instructors in secondary schools.

Lutheran Higher Education

To be consistent, the Church that truly wants to train youth in proper Christian thinking and living must reach into the fields of higher education — college, university, and graduate studies. These must prepare for the Church the educators and the leaders in the various professions, in industry, and in business. Our Church will not rise to a place of influence on world thought without trained men, in the indicated fields, in positions of prominence. Luther, speaking in the Large Catechism of the duty of parents toward their children, says (*Trigl.*, p. 631): "If they are talented, have them learn and study something, that they may be employed for whatever need there is [to have them instructed and trained in a liberal education, that men may be able to have their aid in government and in whatever is necessary]." When our Church expects these leaders to be trained in other schools than our own and then, later, to return to our own denominational church work, it puts a terrific strain on synodical loyalty. Indeed, schools on all the levels of instruction may be instituted and maintained by the home and the Church. In our day, with education so general through high school and not uncommon through college, our families and congregations must provide the best in Christian education, or Synod will die.

Valparaiso University needs and deserves the active support of the congregations of Synod. The direction of Valparaiso is Lutheran. Its purpose is to provide the Church with informed and trained men, soundly Christian, who will be ready and equipped to step into the positions of influence, intellectually equal to other educated men, but with a sound Christian outlook on life. Luther said: "Any fatal wound to his (the devil's) cause must come through the young, who, brought up in the knowledge of God, spread abroad the truth and instruct others" (*Address to the Christian Nobility*). Synod's Student Service Commission is active in serving students at non-Lutheran schools in spiritual things.

Where schools are lacking, a greater responsibility rests on the homes. Where schools are in operation, the parents dare not think that their own responsibility has ceased. Fathers cannot transfer the responsibility which God has laid upon them. Pastors and churches cannot escape their duty in the matter of Christian training. Teachers are not to carry the load alone. Together the great task must be performed. God will bless it.

V. YOUTH PROGRAM

While the Church is not responsible for providing a program of entertainment for youth, it may well plan activities for purposes of training and prevention. An organized plan and program is essential for achievement and necessary for attracting youth to, and enlisting youth in, so-called young people's work.

Preach the Gospel

The Church has one task — to preach the Gospel. Anybody who thinks this is a simple matter shows that he has no comprehension of the implications of Christ's command. Some carry these implications too far, demanding complete church control of the whole life of the community and of the whole world. Others hide their inactivity behind the phrase "We stick to preaching the Gospel."

The Church has a responsibility for the spiritual well-being of all its members. It is not outside the sphere of the Church's work, then, to adapt its work of preaching and teaching to the age and to the interest of its members. This, of course, does not mean to satisfy itching ears (II Tim. 4:3), but to be all things to all men (I Cor. 9:22).

Church Societies

The Church has no command to organize societies. This thesis has been set forth with considerable insistence and criticism of such churches as have societies. We will all grant that God has not commanded the organization of societies. In the same breath, however, we want to remind any critic of church societies that God has nowhere commanded the organization of a school. Experience has taught the Church that the establishment and operation of Christian schools is practical and accomplishes excellent results in Christian training. So the Church urges the establishment of more and better schools. Why not follow the same reasoning in the matter of church societies? Youth organizations have proved to be of value in teaching and training young people. Yes, youth societies sometimes are a bother, and problems are multiplied because of their existence. If we were to avoid every organization which poses problems, we should have no congregations! Societies can be good and useful.

To those who object to a society of young people it may readily be granted that the name *society* is not essential. What else would such a group of people be by any other name? Again, this society or group need not join the Walther League, but it misses much if it does not affiliate with the synodically authorized youth-work movement. Without a society, or at least an organized program for young people, the Church will accomplish little with its young people.

No thoughtful churchman will argue against the thesis that "entertainment is not the Church's business." Of course it is not. If, however, the young people of a congregation organize and then plan and program proper forms and opportunities of entertainment, this is only a natural expression of a natural interest of young people. Luther said, "The young must leap and jump or have something to do, because they have a natural desire for it, which should not be restrained (for it is not well to check them in everything)." (Painter, *op. cit.*, p. 198.)

It is quite a different matter when a church or a church society goes into the field of entertainment and "sociables" on a commercial basis. It is then going into business. It is entering into competition with commercial business establishments and seriously endangering the practice of a true Christian spirit of stewardship if entertainment and "sociable" revenue is to supply the church treasury with funds. Not all entertainments, however, are thus sweepingly to be condemned. Where the principles of Christian stewardship are not violated, where other activities, not directly religious, are employed as aids in the work of the Church, as points of contact, or, if you insist, as "bait," let none raise the accusation that the Church is departing from her actual duty and dissipating her energies by giving attention to non-essentials and foreign subjects. Jesus, on one occasion at least, asked for a drink of water for this one purpose, to establish a contact with a person to whom He wished to open the way of life (John 4:7).

Shall Youth Talent Be Buried?

Youth is full of life. Youth demands action and bodily movement. If proper outlets are not found for this natural urge, then youth will be tempted to sinful and improper activities. The Church will do well to plan for, and to provide youth with, opportunities for self-expression. Such activities will serve the double purpose of training in Christian life and work and of preventing the misdirection of interests. If youth is kept busy in the Church and in church circles, it will be less apt to seek its occupation and diversion, in leisure time, outside the influence and fellowship of the Church. What youth does determines what age will be and do. Why do we lose so many young people from our congregations? Can it be the fault of the Church and the program or lack of program for youth?

How often has the Church been guilty of burying the talents of youth, its own youth, by denying young people the opportunity of activity and self-expression in the work of the congregation! What will the Lord say when He calls us to account for the use we made of the youth talent which He entrusted to our congregations?

Where do our young people spend their time? Does the congregation know? Does it care? Can it be that mixed marriages between Romanists and Lutherans result from the dances that Roman Catholic parishes arrange? We will not be combating an evil by introducing the same evil into our churches. Everyone will admit that an ounce of prevention is better than a pound of cure and that as the twig is bent, so will be the tree. Church entertainments are not the cure. The solution lies in a different direction.

Appeals to the delights of the flesh will not be conquered by the church's offering something similar under church auspices. The church must make its appeal to youth in spiritual things. For example, many young people have found that spiritual dramatizations attract the young people. Practically every church has some experience in successful youth activity in mission canvasses. With the present mission expansion program no church will be without suggestions for youth activity.

Understanding Leadership

In dealing with young people responsible leaders must avoid the danger of attempting regimentation. Young America resents it as much as does older America. Youth should not have a program crammed down its throat. Even a good program, like that of the Walther League, must not be given to the young people as *the* thing and nothing else. The better way to use such a program is as a pattern and as source material for self-construction of a program adapted to the particular group and the peculiar situation of the particular church. Here wise assistance and guidance of the pastor, teacher, church officers, and, especially in our Eastern District setup, the congregational Committee on Christian Education, formerly known as the School Board, come into play.

There is an art in suggesting. How much more readily suggestions in the "do" category are received than those in the "don't" category! Some parents "don't" their children into desperation. Some churches "don't" their young people out of the congregation. Pastors, teachers, church officers, committees on Christian education will become very unpopular and consequently accomplish very little beyond their own indignation, which they will erroneously consider righteous, if they persist in guiding only in a negative fashion, vetoing every youth-suggested activity. The better and the only workable way is to be in on the original planning and to be a step ahead of the young people. Leaders must have ideas of purposeful and interesting activities for youth. As Lochner says, this requires work. It requires research. It requires thought. It requires guidance from above for the adult leaders. It requires prayer. It requires a spirit of humility begging for worthiness to lead youth, the

Church's hope. When adult leaders have no ideas and no plans and no projects to suggest, they cannot blame youth if it goes off at a tangent now and again.

An organized program and a plan is essential for achievement. Drifting youth groups will as soon be wrecked as drifting individuals. The Church has a purpose: to preach the Word to save souls. With this idea as basis for planning, the congregation must consider how well it has taught Christian doctrine to its youth in the pre-confirmation age. How can this instruction be continued? Among Lutherans the chief teaching function of the Church is the sermon. The sermon should therefore be planned with the young people also in mind. Special youth services will help to develop and hold the interest of young people. If the congregation has no Christian day school, the need for post-confirmation instruction becomes more urgent. Different devices have been invented. A few may be mentioned. Lectures, Bible history presentation in chronological order and tie-up, Bible *reading* groups, the reading of Luther's Small Catechism, talks and topic discussions by the young people themselves, debates on current questions and on life situations — all these and more prove helpful, especially if used with variation. Courtship and marriage are always interesting and pertinent topics. Visual aids developed for educational purposes can be used to advantage in youth groups. Showing a moving picture, then following with a critical discussion as to its moral and religious values, can teach a lesson. Anent discussion it should be remembered that nothing has been gained if the discussion is not completely summed up at the end to crystallize the conclusions at which the group has arrived.

Youth Appreciates Responsibility

Parish work of various kinds could be employed to interest youth and hold it in the congregation. Taking pictures of church activities, preparing materials for the instruction classes, making slides which could be used for presentation of the church budget to the annual meeting of the congregation, beautifying the church property, decorating for church festivals, supplying office help, bringing cheer to the sick — the field is limitless. Once a committee sets itself honestly to work at aiding youth, the work will grow and ideas will multiply almost as miraculously in the committee's hands as did the bread in the hands of the disciples at the feeding of the 5,000 (John 6:11). The most difficult thing is to start. Once started, keep going. When you have a plan and a program, you set a goal, and then you set out to reach that goal. God's blessing will attend such purposeful youth work. Youth will be attracted by purposeful activity.

VI. THE COST

Liberal allowances of time and money should be invested by home and Church in the training of youth. It must be remembered, however, that only the Spirit of God can make and keep Christian. He works through the Word, which is the power of God.

Christian training of youth pays big dividends in time and in eternity. Dividends don't just happen. There must be investments. Home and Church must make liberal investments. Child and youth training requires expenditures all through life. These expenditures begin when the home is preparing to receive a child as God's gift. After the child is born, there can be no vacation from making investments for several years. The time spent with an infant during the first two or three years of his life will pay dividends according to the investment made. Parents would not be perplexed about what has gotten into their five-year-old if they had made the proper investments in the first years. A mother cannot, as a regular practice, fondle and coddle her infant and then expect that child to grow up into a well-balanced adult able to meet the world's competition. A pampered child produces a pampered and pouty adult.

If parents do not teach their children to know and love God, it will be much more difficult to have these children, when they grow into the adult years, to accept God and to worship Him. It is the kind of home and family life which the parents by a considered plan project that will eventuate by the constant daily adherence to their plan. A home in which there is strife, in which parents argue over money matters, in which love is not exercised, in which the Word of God is not heard, in which Christian ideals and principles are not translated into family life, will hardly be attractive to young people. They will leave that home as soon as possible. A home that is not orderly and clean will prove to be repulsive to young people when they visit other homes which are neatly kept.

Family finances play into the training of children and young people. Furniture and fitting beyond the means of the family income are not a good investment. Cash purchases are to be advised, even though the Joneses have more and finer furniture. They likely also have more debts. Good and clean beds, wholesome well-prepared food, an orderly household, clean rooms, a sensible family time schedule, the Word of God dwelling richly in the home (Col. 3:16), love and sympathetic understanding, love of family members rather than family pride, camaraderies, good music, good books — home investments of this type will pay big dividends.

What investment ought the Church to make in its children and youth? So much of the Church's thought and activity is planned and conducted with the adult in mind! Certainly the present congregation in its administration is adult. The own personal interest naturally receives first consideration. Very often after this consideration has been satisfied, there is no time, and surely no money, left for the interests of children and young people. Why are there so few Christian day schools? The first answer today still is, "We cannot afford a school." The congregation that does not have a school is living for the present and is making no investment, or only a minor one, for the future. It demonstrates an adult mental complex and comes suspiciously close to adult selfishness. Such a congregation is something like the married people who want no children. Having been given children in spite of themselves, they continue to live selfishly. If poor, such people neglect their children. If they are people of means, they turn their children over to maids and nurses.

A right-minded congregation will always think of its children and young people in present work and future plans. A spiritually wise congregation will, for example, in a contemplated building program make *first provision for its school.* Some churches are in flourishing condition financially today because of just such wise planning. When new buildings become imperative, the first unit of the new church plant had better be a building which will adequately house the Christian day school and provide a temporary meeting place for worship in a school auditorium rather than a church building with no provision for the training of the congregation's children and youth, but with financial encumbrances which tie a whole generation to nothing but debt payment.

If we indulge in a brief congregational self-examination, we may make a number of wholesome discoveries. Does our congregation have a well-indoctrinated membership? Are we making the best possible investment of time and money for the purpose of producing a well-indoctrinated membership? Are we investing money — even allowing for the lack of a Christian day school — are we investing money in our Sunday school and other classes of religious instruction, or do we expect the Sunday school to help support the church for operating its adult program? Is youth investing in the Christian training of adults, or is the adult congregation investing in youth training? (II Cor. 12:14.) Self-analysis usually produces amazing, disconcerting, but wholesome revelations. Let our congregational committees on Christian education make such an honest and fact-finding and revealing analysis within the home parish, not for the District Board for Christian Education, but for the next voters' meeting. Progressive steps in the right direction will result.

Let us pastors, teachers, and laymen see to it that our congregation's Committee on Christian Education is properly manned. Men well-indoctrinated, soul-loving, courageous Christian men, are needed for this work. Having secured such men, let us support them.

Educational Reconversion

What steps can a congregation take when it discovers to its shame that it has been neglectful of its duty toward its own youth? Surely, when we see that we have not been as aggressive in our work as we thought, corrective measures will be intelligently undertaken. Say, a congregation realizes that it has made too small an investment or has neglected to make any investment in its children and young people. How can it get started on the road back to the desirable ideal of operating a Christian day school? The simplest and most practical procedure is to start with a kindergarten or first grade. If the kindergarten is chosen as the starting point, have a look at the present kindergarten or primary Sunday schoolroom. Is it a room well lighted? Is it well ventilated? Is it attractively furnished and decorated and properly equipped? Visit the kindergarten rooms in the neighborhood. Your church's kindergarten room ought to be (shall we say, must be) just as good.

When the kindergarten is in operation, preparation for the first grade must be made. Following through each year, in nine years a congregation would have a well-equipped going school, in good condition, and smooth production of a group of young people that would be an invaluable asset to the congregation. A modern Psalmist would say, "Happy is that congregation that hath its quiver full of such well-trained Christian young people." Such a church has both a living present and an assured future.

There remains the teacher problem. As an emergency measure, members of the congregation might serve as teachers. The proper personnel in a well-established school, it will be agreed, consists of regularly called synodically trained and graduated teachers. Here again congregational investment must be made. Proper boys and girls of promise should be encouraged to prepare for the office of teaching. They should be given financial aid if necessary. The congregation's teachers must be properly paid. Nor should the pastor be expected by a reduced or low salary to pay more toward the teacher's salary than the rest of the congregation's membership. Investment of adequate salaries of teachers and pastors will pay the congregation good dividends.

We cannot expect that we shall be able to set up good and efficient schools overnight. Here long-range planning is needed. For this reason the turnover in the congregational Committee on Christian Education should not be too rapid. It may be found wise to add new members, yet enough of the originators of the new movement for proper Christian training of youth must be retained to keep the movement in motion. It must not be forgotten that even a long-range program must get into motion! Long-range planning is essential for continuous and for lasting results. Immediate action is also imperative. Our Croydon school will tell you: "The way to start is to start!"

While this long-range planning is going on, no congregation dare neglect the present confirmed youth. Here, too, investments of time and money will pay dividends. Should the congregation's Committee on Christian Education find itself so completely occupied with the development of work among and for the children, a subcommittee for the care of youth could be set up. This committee could include a representative of the official church board, some of the young people, some of the women of the congregation, and some non-officeholding voting members. With such a representative committee the interests of youth within a congregation would receive proper consideration, attention, and action.

This committee would make itself responsible for adequate coverage of youth's needs in the annual church budget. The young people would thus be spared the humiliation of having to ask. The church that makes no provision for its youth aids the outside agencies and commercial establishments which reach out also for our Lutheran youth.

Christian training of youth is work. God expects parents to work at it. Christ, the Head of the Church, instructed the Church to work at it. The home and the Church must put forth real efforts and make real investments. The One who has the greatest interest in this work and is most concerned about its success is God. God has also made the greatest investment in this work. As may be expected, God does not make an investment and then sit back idly, hoping for dividends. Look at God's investment. "It is He that hath made us" (Psalm 100). Mankind is God's creation. In the interest of mankind, God gave His only Son. The Son devoted His whole life to just this work of making worth-while children of God out of God's creatures. With Christ's redemptive work completed and our Redeemer's withdrawal from earth to heaven accomplished, man is not left without guidance and assistance. The Holy Spirit, the Comforter, the directing and implementing Force, is active now in the world, and especially in the Church. If God invests so much, we have the assurance and guarantee that the investment is sound. We ought to make liberal investments.

The Christian home and the Christian Church are Christ's working force. These must bring people to the Word and the Word to the people. The Holy Spirit, however, alone can produce the desired result of making and keeping a person Christian (John 17:19; Rom. 1:16; II Thess. 2:13; I Pet. 1:2; Eph. 5:26; Tit. 3:4-7).

Knowing that home and church are doing the Lord's work as His agents, mindful of the high honor of being God's co-workers (I Cor. 3:9), remembering to teach every age all things (Matt. 28:20), assured of the Holy Spirit's guidance and blessing (John 14:28), how can we do otherwise than with renewed determination and energy, with Christian humility and confidence, individually and congregationally, set ourselves anew to work at this God-given task of *The Christian Training of Youth!*

The Lutheran Parochial School

WHEN Synod organized in 1847, one of the conditions of membership set up by the Constitution was that congregations provide Christian "Schulunterricht" for their children (*Lutheraner* III, p. 3). At the same time one of the duties outlined for Synod was the establishment of schools for the training of teachers (*op. cit.*, p. 4). The President of Synod was also given explicit instructions regarding schools. On his official visits he was expected to inquire about the conditions in the local congregations with reference to surveillance of this agency, to look into the course of study, particularly the religious subjects, and to discuss the general discipline of the school. With such recognition given to it, it is natural that the parochial school enjoyed a dominant position in the Missouri Synod from its very beginning and was regarded as the crown and hope of the Church. That Synod meant business can be seen in the establishment of a separate teachers' department at Fort Wayne in 1857, which department was subsequently transferred to Addison, Illinois, in 1864, as a regular normal school. This is significant, because teacher training schools in the United States at that time were few in number.

It was natural, however, that in the phenomenal growth of our Synod the planting of churches and the establishment of schools could not keep step. The many openings for new preaching stations prevented pastors, who for the most part had to teach school, from giving adequate time to teaching. Since these congregations were much too weak to support a teacher even if the supply had been adequate, they were forced to be satisfied with parochial schools on a part-time basis. Under such conditions the school system suffered, and in many instances parochial schools were such in name only. With the turn of the century, after the flow of immigration decreased considerably, opportunity offered itself to take up the slack, but congregations frequently failed to make use of it. In time this neglect took a terrific toll in the number of schools, especially where the essential purpose in the establishment of such schools had been lost sight of. The slump appeared during and soon after World War I when there was a change in the method of computing statistics. Accuracy required many of the so-called parochial schools to be dropped from the records. In addition, the sudden change in language needs sounded the death knell of scores of schools. One essayist observed, "It doesn't require unusual powers of observation to note the indications of a growing indifference . . . toward the Christian day schools . . ." (Iowa District, 1919, p. 136). It was commonly accepted by all but a few that the parochial school was a lost cause.

Today, as we are about to enter the second century of our history, an entirely different future confronts us. It is unmistakably evident that we are gradually regaining our balance as we witness a gradual rebirth in interest. A healthy enthusiasm exists in many sections of Synod in behalf of our schools, particularly in the pioneering sections. There is great joy as we begin to recapture some of the original spirit of the place and importance of the Lutheran school. That this will bring corresponding problems should not discourage us, for every opportunity is accompanied by a challenge. There will be questions related to teacher supply, to school administration and supervision, to State aid. Many other problems will surely vex us, but we cannot expect blessings without a corresponding obligation.

In approaching our theme, let us consider in the first place:

I. THE BASIC PRINCIPLES UNDERLYING A LUTHERAN PAROCHIAL SCHOOL

If we are to appreciate and evaluate the significance of our schools, it is most important that we know the principles which underlie them. In the past we have not always been conscious of them. We have taken our schools too much for granted. As in the case of every other blessing, this led to indifference and the loss of much valuable ground. The maintenance of parochial schools in a church body such as ours is dependent, next to God, on the general understanding of the individual members. Where this understanding is lacking, schools will either not be established, or will be maintained for only a short while (Central, 1919, p. 48 f.). The particular need for proper understanding arises from the costs which such schools require, costs not only in terms of dollars and cents, but in labor and prayers. For when this labor on the part of teachers and pastors is not appreciated, it takes a firm conviction of the heart based on sound knowledge to withstand the dampening chill of indifference.

One of the reasons why many schools have collapsed has grown out of the wrong conception of their purpose. This highly prized institution had degenerated in the minds of many Lutherans merely as an instrument to keep a foreign language alive (Nebraska, 1906, p. 17). When this need lessened, congregations surrendered their schools, seeing very little reason for continuing to make sacrifices for an institution that had outlived its usefulness. This was the price we have paid for failing to impress upon our Church the underlying principle of our schools.

On the other hand, a large number of congregations have never seriously looked the situation in the face, have never taken the time to evaluate the need of a parochial school or to think seriously of the meaning of Christian education. They have been "satisfied to run along as best they can, in the meantime joining the loud chorus of the faultfinders and wondering what is the trouble with the Lutheran Church in general and the Missouri Synod in particular" (Atlantic, 1930, p. 31).

The principles of a Lutheran parochial school are determined by a Christian's goal in life. Since this is changeless, the principles underlying our schools will ever remain the same, unaffected fundamentally by transient problems or current philosophies. What is the Christian's goal in life? The answer will determine our definition of Christian education. Our goal is a life with God and in God. The purpose of a Christian's being is not only the here, though this is important, but also the hereafter, which is the most important. Christian education must reach the individual from the cradle to the grave, but fit him for a life that does not end with the grave, but comes to its complete fruition in eternity. Anything less is decidedly inadequate.

The Lutheran Parochial School

To prepare himself for such a life with God, man is totally unprepared. Scripture describes the natural man as spiritually bankrupt, yea, dead. Here we part company with the majority of educators, who find something basically good in man. The Christian, however, knows that by virtue of sin man's inherent powers have been cut off and his iniquities have separated him from his God. He also knows that his life here on earth is his one opportunity to prepare himself for a life in the hereafter with God. Therefore his chief goal is that he knows his Savior, who has won this eternal union with God. Having arrived at that saving knowledge, his chief goal has been reached (John 17:3).

This goal is not an end in itself, for God has made us His own that we might serve Him in all eternity, which service begins here in time. "For we are His workmanship, created in Christ Jesus unto good works, which God hath before ordained that we should walk in them" (Eph. 2:10; 2 Cor. 5:15; Luke 1:74-75). To live a life in harmony with God is consequently included in the Christian's goal in life.

But once having become citizens in God's kingdom is no assurance that we shall remain therein. We know that there are foes who would defraud us and God. To offset the onslaughts of the Evil One, the Christian must also grow in knowledge. He must not merely know something about his salvation, but he must become thoroughly grounded so that the Word planted in his heart is not snatched by the Evil One. Hence, with the help of the Holy Spirit he must grow in sanctification in order that his goal may be achieved.

This, then, is the goal of a Christian and to this end Christian education must serve. This, in turn, determines the basic principles of the parochial school.

From this we observe that Christian education means more than imparting certain facts and making impressions on the intellect. Some would limit education to the mere accumulation of Biblical data and knowledge of doctrine. But unless the heart, the conscience, the emotions, and the will are touched, that is to say, unless there is Christian living, Christian knowledge is of little value, and education has not achieved its purpose. "Let us get this firmly fixed in our mind, true education implies the discipline and the regulation of the heart even more than the furnishing of information to the head. Where there is not this forming and developing of character, there education is not really educating" (Southeastern, 1942, p. 10).

But Christian education is not only otherworldly, concerning itself merely with the soul. While man is more than body, he is also more than soul. Hence the Lutheran school offers an education for "the total man." Because of its otherworldly view it would be wrong to assume that our schools overlook the needs for life here on earth. The Bible is not the only textbook. Christian education in the proper sense cannot neglect the "3 R's." But these "3 R's" must be linked up with Christianity so that they become a blessing and not a curse. Because our schools reach the total man, body and soul, they prepare for this life as no other agency can. In fact, because they subordinate this life to a life which has an eternal span, they offer education which properly coordinates and integrates body and soul for time and eternity.

Actually an education for the body and the soul cannot be separated, for what affects the one must affect the other. In the real sense there can be no secular education, *i. e.*, an education which affects only the body. There may be secular subjects, but no secular education. When we teach such subjects as history, geography, mathematics, and spelling, we affect the soul as well as the body. When education is divorced from the Christian philosophy of life, we are exposing pupils to an education based on principles contrary to divine truth. The moment we leave God out of the picture, we distort it, failing to offer a true education and to reach in a positive manner the total man. For example, we cannot teach geography and speak of the topography of the earth, the resources of the nations, the climate, and the physical life and not mention their origin. By simply ignoring God as the Creator, we give the impression that God either had nothing to do with the creation of the world, or that we deny His supremacy. This is true of all subjects, even in seemingly remote subjects, such as arithmetic. The name of the subject may appear the same whether it is taught in a Christian school or from a "neutral viewpoint." But everything depends upon the spirit in which that instruction is given. There is, for example, a tremendous difference in the simple sentence $2 \times 2 = 4$ if used by a Christian or a non-Christian. For the non-Christian, this sentence is absolute according to all the laws of logic so that God Himself would be subject to it, but for the Christian this sentence expresses a condition which God has given to us here on earth in conformity with situations under which God Himself is not bound. God is the Lord also over the rules of logic. While the doctrines of the Trinity and the union of the natures of Christ seem to violate all the laws of arithmetic and logic, the Christian knows that God is not bound by such rules (Synodical Conference, 1920, p. 8). Only the full balance of a Christian education creates the correct attitude and life-motive acceptable to a child of God. This is another basic principle underlying a Lutheran parochial school.

Together with an education for the whole man is the principle that the process of education must be unified. There must be a unity among educators. This is of prime importance with children. This means there must be a unity between parents, between the church and the home, between the school and the home, and between church, home, and school. The child which is put under divergent influences will be bewildered. A child taught under a non-Scriptural influence in one agency part of the time and in a Christian agency at another time will be frightfully handicapped, whether that non-Christian influence is the home, the church, or the school. The parochial school gives the child from a Christian home and church an education which is an integral part of the same unit.

Consider the negative influence of an education from which religion is barred. The child will either consider religion of minor importance, or when exposed to negative influences, find his mind in a turmoil. In either case some adjustment must be made by other influences, since the unity is lacking. What is true of the subject itself is even more true of the part the teacher plays in maintaining or destroying the unity. "If the goal of Christian teaching is the Christian life, the Christian teaching ought to be the experiences of the teacher's own life with God, and it must be his steadfast purpose to guide his pupils into such a life. If the teacher himself does not live the Christian life, it is difficult to imagine that he will be a very good teacher of a subject which is foreign to his own experience. We must guard against the danger that our children receive the impression that Christianity consists in knowing a given amount of Scripture truths. 'Christianity is a living fact, resting in a living Savior and in receiving from Him a daily measure of spiritual power.' How much, then, depends upon the teacher! 'You cannot put an interrogation point into the teacher's chair and put an exclamation mark in the pupil's desk.' The question therefore forces itself upon us, Ought Christian parents to put their children under the daily influence of an educational system in which they have no voice in the selection of the teachers, a system in which the spiritual side of the teacher's life is never inquired into?" (Atlantic, 1930, p. 29 f.). In the Lutheran school the teacher is responsible not only to the church and the parent, but above all to his God. His school, whose principles are determined by a Christian point of view of life, reaching in a positive manner "the total man," enjoys the distinction of being an integral part of the necessary unity in the education of the child.

II. THE PLACE OF THE LUTHERAN PAROCHIAL SCHOOL IN THE COMPLETE FRAMEWORK OF OUR EDUCATIONAL TASK

The Lutheran parochial school is not an end in itself. It is not a divinely ordained institution, and it must, therefore, be kept within the framework of the Christian's educational task. Its specific task is to serve as a tool for such divinely ordained institutions as the Church, the home, and the State. It has a specific place in the complete framework of Christian education. What is this place?

a. *The Christian Home.* That the home has a divine responsibility toward the child goes without saying. The Christian regards the child differently than does the unbeliever. He knows with the Psalmist that children are an heritage of the Lord. They have been loaned to him by an act of grace and actually belong to God by the triple tie of creation, redemption, and sanctification. A Christian parent looks upon himself merely as a steward entrusted with a precious ward. This is stressed in the Fourth Commandment, which bids children to honor their parents, because they are representatives of God. As Luther has so aptly emphasized in his explanation in the Large Catechism: "We must, therefore, impress it upon the young that they should regard their parents as in God's stead and remember that however lowly, poor, frail, and queer they may be, nevertheless they are father and mother given them by God." (*Triglot*, p. 611, par. 108.) Hence Christian parents know that children are to be brought up as God wants them to be. His Word is to be their guide.

God requires two things of parents concerning their children. First, they are to teach them diligently in the Word; and secondly, they are to bring them up in the nurture and admonition of the Lord.

God has given parents definite instructions that they are to teach their children. "And these words, which I command thee this day, shall be in thine heart; and thou shalt teach them diligently unto thy children, and shalt talk of them when thou sittest in thine house, and when thou walkest by the way, and when thou liest down, and when thou risest up. And thou shalt bind them for a sign upon thine hand, and they shall be as frontlets between thine eyes. And thou shalt write them upon the posts of thy house, and on thy gates" (Deut. 6:6-9). We know that this does not only include the formal instruction. God specifically emphasized the instruction which takes place in Christian living — "when thou walkest," "when thou sittest," "when thou liest down." This teaching on the part of parents is further emphasized in Ps. 78:1-8.

The obligation on the part of the parents is more than mere instruction. It isn't enough for parents to tell their children what God teaches, what they should do and what they should not do. The devil would be happy if we would remain with mere instruction. Children are to be trained to live as Christians. The instruction which they receive must be functional in their lives. "Ye fathers, provoke not your children to wrath; but bring them up in the nurture and admonition of the Lord" (Eph. 6:4). This includes that parents set a good example in their lives lest they offend children by denying what they have taught with their actual conversation (Iowa, 1882, p. 30 f.).

This equal Christian instruction and training must begin in the home so that it can be said of our children as Paul was able to say of Timothy, "From a child thou hast known the Holy Scriptures." This responsibility has been given to the home by God, and neither the church nor the school nor the state can in any way take this responsibility away. The church must not permit the false notion to gain foothold that it can take over the responsibility merely by establishing a parochial school or any other educational agency. Nor may the church countenance the idea that religion is such a private matter between the individual and his God that parents ought not to force their religious convictions upon children, but leave the choice of any religion or no religion to the good judgment of their children (Atlantic, 1930, p. 22).

Where the basic and correct understanding of the responsibility of the parent toward his child is wanting, the home is in a serious plight. The spiritual life, begun in Baptism, is given no opportunity to grow and fails for lack of nourishment. Where this Scriptural concept is lacking entirely, there can be no Christian education in the family, and even the best influences outside, the church and the parochial school, cannot continue long, because they are working at tremendous odds. The focal point of Christian education must ever remain with the Christian home.

If parents could give their children the thorough instruction which they should have, there would be no need for parochial schools. But we know life as it is, and we must view it realistically. It gives us ample evidence that Christian parents cannot meet the high standards set by God without additional help. It is with us as it was already in Luther's time. Most parents do not have the time, some not even the desire, and many frequently lack the necessary knowledge, and to them the words of the author of the Epistle to the Hebrew Christians apply: "We have many things to say and hard to be uttered, seeing ye are dull of hearing. For when for the time ye ought to be teachers, ye have need that one teach you again which be the first principles of the oracles of God, and are become such as have need of milk, and not of strong meat" (Heb. 5:11-12).

Christian parents who know their responsibility and have the earnest desire to conform to the will of God look elsewhere for assistance. They know that to the Church has been given the responsibility to train the youth, and so look to it for assistance. They, together with other Christian parents, yes, with the entire congregation, are anxious to seek the welfare of their children and therefore to establish a Lutheran parochial school. Where the correct understanding of Christian education exists, there parochial schools are established even against the greatest odds. Parents will be willing to send their children in spite of the obstacles which may beset their paths, for the parochial school to them is a prize held in highest esteem.

Unfortunately there are many cases where such assistance cannot be given to the parents because no school has been established. Perhaps the congregation is too weak or lacks a sufficient number of Christian parents who have a proper understanding, or faces other circumstances which prevent the establishment of a school. What shall parents then do? Such circumstances cannot take the responsibility away from parents, and they must, therefore, make a double effort to see to it that their own children are trained in a proper way. Where children, by force of circumstances, must attend a public school, parents will be mindful of the educational cross currents and will in some measure seek to offset the handicap. The church, too, cannot shift its responsibility under such circumstances and must make every effort to fill in the gap through its part-time agencies, ever nourishing the hope that some day opportunities will be given it to establish a school of its own.

b. *The Christian Congregation.* Together with the home, the congregation has been given the command to teach. One of the last injunctions of our Lord to His disciples was that they teach all nations to observe whatsoever He had commanded them. This command included children no less than adults. The church has been enjoined to feed the lambs and has been warned specifically not to despise the little ones. The Christian congregation regards children, in spite of their youth, as important, not merely because they are future members, but even if they would always remain children. A congregation which forgets its youth and does not provide it with spiritual food as circumstances allow it, offering only a superficial instruction in the Word of God and an inadequate training, will find a grave judgment against itself. Children are not only to be baptized by the church, they must be kept in that faith, and that is done only by the Word (Central, 1918, p. 61 f.).

The duty to instruct children is a specific responsibility of ministers. They have been charged to take heed unto themselves and to all the flock over which the Holy Ghost has made them overseers and to feed the church of God, which He has purchased with His own blood (Acts 20:28). Without exception, pastors have been instructed to feed the flock of God which is among them (I Pet. 5:2). Concerning the unfaithful pastor who neglects any or part of his flock the Lord warns: "Behold, I am against the shepherds; and I will require My flock at their hand and cause them to cease from feeding the flock; neither shall the shepherds feed themselves any more; for I will deliver My flock from their mouth that they may not be meat for them" (Ezek. 34:10).

We recognize, of course, that this feeding is done in various ways. The youth of the Church is reached through the divine services, the confirmation instruction, the Sunday school, the vacation Bible school, and through other educational agencies of the Church. The Church, of course, will want to use every means of education at its command. It cannot afford to overlook any opportunity, but it must at the same time give most serious consideration to the best and most effective tool. In no other agency of the Church can children learn to know their heavenly Father more intimately and recognize Him more clearly as their Creator and Preserver; learn to know God's Son so well as the Savior, who earned for them and all men the remission of sins; learn to know the Holy Spirit, who in Holy Baptism richly poured out His heavenly grace upon them.

Christian education in the broadest sense is the one task of the Church. Not only is the Church extended thereby, but through it, it is preserved. "The church that teaches will live; the church that does not will die. It is not easy for most Protestant churches to fulfill their teaching function, both because they are not sure of a stable content and are not agreed as to what constitutes the best way of teaching religion," is the comment of Irvin L. Shaver, a Modernist (*Information Service,* May 29, 1943). We of the Lutheran Church, who have the Scriptures as the stable content upon which we can base our education and have the parochial school as the best medium for teaching, may well agree that if we are to live as a Church of the future, it will depend upon the way in which we educate today.

In our day we are witnessing a tremendous growth in interest for world-wide missions, and there isn't one of us here who would gainsay this. But in our ardor for missions, let us not lose our balance. Let us not lose what we have in our effort to get what we have not. If the Church as a whole had been more faithful in its program of Christian education in the past, there would not be as many mission prospects as we have today. We cannot afford to win souls one by one through missions and lose them by the scores because we fail to educate. We must do the one, but we cannot dare to fail in the other. Education and missions must ever go hand in hand. In the one we win, and in the other we keep.

To be sure, in the establishment of parochial schools a congregation is not without its problems and difficulties. And with problems we are not limiting ourselves to finances. There are greater problems than mere dollars and cents. The establishment of every school means constant stimulation of our congregations lest they become weary and lose their interest. At times it may mean long hours of double duty for the pastor. The devil, well aware of the danger to his kingdom, tempts pastors to believe that their work as trained theologians should be beyond the teaching of the elements of reading, writing, and arithmetic. Teachers, too, are tempted to believe that there is something more important to do than to play with children all their life. These difficulties must be overcome by the prayers of faithful pastors and teachers lest by neglecting their task in the school the strength of our blessings be lost. There will be other educational problems, such as pastor and teacher relationship, community good will, and standards to be kept. But, as in other things, everything of great value has also its price. We can depend upon the devil to sow the seeds of neglect and indifference in congregations so that he might continue to effect the terrific toll which he so highly prizes. Yet the congregation that is aware of its divine responsibility and the enormous opportunities offered in the parochial school, will regard its school as its dearest possession and its crowning glory in spite of the obstacles and labors.

c. *The State.* Besides home and Church there is another divinely appointed institution interested in the welfare of our children: the State. But while the home and the Church are interested in both the spiritual and the physical welfare of its members, the

State is concerned only with the physical. Since the child is a member of the State, it has a direct interest in its temporal welfare, but only in that. By the grace of God our government is aware of its position over against the home and the Church. Concerning the home the Supreme Court stated in the *Oregon Case,* "The child is not the mere creature of the State. Those who nurture him and direct his destiny have the right, coupled with the high duty, to prepare him for additional obligations" (Atlantic, 1930, p. 22). As far as the Church is concerned, we know that the State jealously maintains a complete separation. All this, however, does not mean that the State disclaims all rights over the child. The State, for instance, is vitally interested in the education of its children, for it needs an intelligent citizenry. This is particularly true in a democratic form of government such as we have, where each individual citizen has a voice in the government. But even though we had a different form of government, the State would still be interested in education. Luther recognized this when he wrote to the mayors and the councils bidding them to exercise the greatest care over the young, "for," wrote Luther, "since the happiness, honor, and life of the city are committed to their hands, they would be held recreant before God and the world, if they did not, day and night, with all their power, seek its welfare and improvement. Now, the welfare of a city does not consist alone in great treasures, firm walls, beautiful houses, and abundant munitions of war; indeed, where these are found and reckless fools come into power, the city sustains the greatest injury. But the highest welfare, safety, and power of a city consists in able, learned, wise, upright, cultivated citizens, who can secure, preserve, and utilize every treasure and advantage" ("Letter to the Mayors and Aldermen" in F. V. N. Painter's *Luther on Education,* p. 180 f.).

But since education and religion are closely entwined, the State should omit every mandate concerning the religious aspect of education. In our country the government has been zealously trying to avoid pitfalls in its endeavor to keep the two separate. Matters become complicated when we remember that while the State is not concerned with religion, it has an interest in morality. We recognize a difference between religion and morality. The State

The Lutheran Parochial School 671

can teach us morals and say: It is wrong to steal and murder, etc., but thereby it still is not teaching religion. The State begins to teach religion only when it says God demands this or that of us. Whether the State accomplishes much thereby is another question. But for the welfare of its citizenry and specifically for its children we must expect the State to take an active interest in this matter. That such teaching does not satisfy a Christian goes without saying. But we must recognize the State's right to teach morality (Nebraska, 1906, p. 26).

Likewise the State is interested in the health and physical safety of its children, and, therefore, it has the right to prescribe certain rules of safety and health for all those who maintain schools, whether this be a public school or a church-supported school.

Concerned with the temporal welfare of the children, the State educates. It assists the home without taking away any responsibility from the parent. This was recognized by Luther, who believed that the State had the right to compel children to attend school. Luther wrote in his sermon on the "Duty of Sending Children to School": "I maintain that the civil authorities are under obligation to compel the people to send their children to school, especially such as are promising, as has elsewhere been said" (F. V. N. Painter's *Luther on Education*, p. 269).

Though the State has a right to educate and we as Christians and citizens have the duty to support such schools, we recognize them as deficient for our purposes. They are good, but not good enough for Christ's property. In the public school our children do not learn what they should know above all other things, namely, the Word of God. The secular subjects are torn out of their natural setting and are not taught in the light of Scripture.

Not only is this education deficient, but we must recognize that it is beset with dangers. Since the training ceases to be a unified whole, children meet opposing viewpoints of the materialistic and the man-glorifying over against the spiritual and the God-glorifying. A congregation which is unable to maintain a school has, therefore, a double responsibility, together with the home, in safeguarding its children against these evident dangers. It must recognize that any educational agency which it sets up as a substitute for the parochial school will fail to integrate the spiritual and the secular and can be, at best, only a makeshift arrangement. It must ever strive to keep what part-time agencies it has at the very highest level and urge parents to be all the more intent on the Christian training of its children, hoping and praying in the meanwhile that the day will soon come when it may be able to establish a school. Where there is a school, but there are children who do not attend for one reason or another, it must always be a matter of grave concern for the congregation.

On the other hand, what must be the relationship of our schools over against the State? Shall we accept State support if this assistance is offered to us? Shall we regard this as a mixing of Church and State? Synod has made an attempt to answer these questions in 1944, when it adopted the following report:

"Twofold Aspect of the State's School Program

"The modern school program of the State has two aspects:

"1. The social service program (library service, lunches, health service, transportation, etc.).

"2. The teaching program (curriculum, teaching, philosophy of education).

"A vital difference exists between these two programs. They are associated merely as a matter of convenience. The social service program is administered through the schools because schools offer the easiest access to the children.

"1. Social Service Program.

"In the social service program character-forming principles are not consciously formulated, discussed, evaluated, and implemented. Neither do these services contribute consciously and directly to the building up, the integration, and implementation of a philosophy of life.

"The social service program should in equity be available to all children of school age irrespective of their school association, just as in the case of public library service. The State can grant to children in church schools this program, since rendering this service does not promote the religious tenets of the Church. The social service program can be granted by the State to church schools, and all conditions germane to the program can be observed

The Lutheran Parochial School   673

without sacrifice of sovereignty on the part of the State or sacrifice of principle on the part of the Church. Hence the Church can accept this program as it is offered and may even be within its rights in demanding it.

"2. *Teaching Program.*

"In the teaching program character-forming precepts, motives of action, and principles of life are necessarily in the foreground, are formulated, analyzed, evaluated, and emotionalized to give them driving force in the underlying philosophy of education. Hence the Church may not subject its teaching program to the supervision, control, and direction of the State.

"The State, when authorized by law, has the right to subsidize the teaching program of church schools without prescribing the philosophy of education if all the churches are given equal privileges. When, however, the State contributes tax money, it has the right to control the expenditures, sanctioning both the purpose for which and the manner in which the money is expended. However, the Church should not ask the State for a subsidy for the teaching program of its schools, for it cannot, without becoming unfaithful to the charge and commission given it, permit its teaching program to be subjected to the supervision, direction, and control of the State, because this would inevitably open the way for demands that the teaching in the church schools accord with the philosophy of education of the State. Here we would have all the evils which follow when the divine ordinance of the separation of Church and State is violated.

"If by law the authorities of the State would be empowered to offer and actually *do* offer such subsidy, and with it relinquish the rights of supervision, direction, and control, as is done, for instance, in the granting of a subsidy to churches and schools in the form of tax exemptions, the Church might under conditions accept this subsidy without becoming guilty of wrongdoing. However, we point to the following facts which might well give pause:

"a. The State has the right at any time to exercise the control of the expenditures of tax money;

"b. The State has a right at any time to withdraw its subsidy.

"In either case disastrous results may follow. If the State should suddenly demand the right to direct, control, and supervise the expenditures of tax money, our Church will be forced to forfeit all further support for reasons stated above, and the result would be the same as if the State would have withdrawn its subsidy. Our congregations, having expanded their school system under State aid, may suddenly find themselves unable to carry on upon the withdrawal of State funds. This has in the early history of our country caused the collapse of church schools in some sections of the country.

"The argument that the State is not being asked to subsidize the religious teaching of sectarian schools, but only the teaching of the secular branches is specious and invalid, for all teaching of church schools — also the teaching of the secular branches — becomes a part of the teaching program (curriculum, teaching, and philosophy of education of the Church). Secular branches are taught in the light of the religious tenets of the Church.

"Because it is most unwise for the Church to accept such subsidy for its teaching program, even though the right to control has been waived by the State, we as citizens should not agitate for State support, but oppose the granting of State funds for sectarian use." (*Synodical Report*, Thirty-Ninth Convention, 1944, pp. 132 to 134.)

Confident of the tremendous value that our schools have for the community, we owe it to the State to erect as many parochial schools as possible. We must ever be ready to extend this blessing as far as we can. The Lutheran Church owes a special debt to this our beloved country because of the many advantages it has enjoyed throughout its history. We can show our gratitude in no better way than by the establishment of many such schools.

III. THE BLESSINGS WHICH THE LUTHERAN PAROCHIAL SCHOOL IMPARTS

Where the parochial school has been established and permitted to flourish in spite of the costs and efforts, the time and money, there God has showered His rich blessings. For He who "layeth up sound wisdom for the righteous . . . preserveth the way of His saints." For "when wisdom entereth into thine heart and knowledge is pleasant unto thy soul, discretion shall preserve thee, understanding shall keep thee, to deliver thee from the way of the evil man, from the man that speaketh froward things" (Prov. 2:7, 8, 10-12).

A. Children of God know that there is no greater blessing than a Christian home. Anything that strengthens the home heaps blessing upon blessing. Parental delinquency is the sin of our age, and it is also beginning to make its inroads into our Lutheran homes. Here the parochial school becomes a strong antidote as a unifying agency. Children guided and instructed under Christian teachers become a powerful factor in assisting parents to keep the bond and the unity of faith. Who can measure the influence that children have as they remind parents of prayer at meals and bedtime, in sickness and trouble; the childlike faith which expresses its amazement at the smallness of a parent's faith; the Bible verses and Catechism recited for the daily preparation; the simple songs in play which add cheer to a mother's heart! What blessings also in such homes that have not yet learned to know their Savior when these spiritual truths spoken by little ones become shafts of heavenly light into the corners of spiritual darkness! Here, too, only on Judgment Day shall we learn to know how many little children have led their parents and have won entire homes through the simple testimony of the truth learned in a Lutheran parochial school.

B. Similarly the blessings which come to a congregation through its school are without measure. God, who has entrusted us with these schools, has given us through them our well-indoctrinated laity. What has been the source of our strength in the past if it has not been a membership soundly grounded in the Word of God? The very form of our church government, which relies not on the resolutions of Synod, the will of its ministry or a presbytery, but upon the priesthood of believers, which gives every member a responsibility and a duty, demands that our laity be sound in doctrine and in the understanding of church polity. In addition, our schools are the training ground for future elders, officers, Sunday school teachers, and church workers who, able to withstand error, will not be tossed to and fro by every wind of false doctrine. On the other hand, where the laity lacks an understanding in sound Biblical principles, there the congregation is bound to degenerate unless a strong counteracting agency exists to strengthen the knowledge of the individuals.

Hand in hand with a thoroughly indoctrinated membership goes a faithful constituency, faithful in church attendance, in partaking of the means of grace, in submitting to the Word in Christian living, filled with the love of Christ for the Church. Much of the harmonious spirit existing between pastors, teachers, and the laity, the oneness of thinking of the past, has been due to the training which all received in our schools.

The parochial school has added value for the congregation because it is able to assist in carrying out our Missionary Commander's last orders to go into all the world. Where properly directed, the Lutheran school can become one of the most efficient missionary agencies within the church, not only in reaching out, but in firmly grounding in the Word of truth those with whom it comes into contact.

C. Any agency which strengthens the individual congregation will consequently be a blessing to the Synod as a whole. Many believe that it is here that the parochial school has been the source of greatest blessing. What was it that gave our Synod such a firm hold wherever it was established? How did it happen that our Synod has enjoyed God's blessings these one hundred years? Is it not because we have from the very beginning been so solicitous for our youth? Have we not been richly blessed in the unity of the spirit and the bond of peace because of our parochial schools? What prevented our Synod in early days from becoming another unstable sect carried hither and yon by the wind of false doctrine? Our schools were the source of strength for our Church. Wherever the Lutheran Church gave up its parochial schools, it lost in virility, for no church can be stronger than its laity. As one historian has put it: "The importance of the parochial day school as a means of keeping alive and planting a deep Lutheran consciousness in America cannot be overemphasized in the history of the Missouri Synod. Long before such men as Wyneken, Walther, and Sihler thought of gathering those of like mind with them into a synodical organization, they looked to the Christian day school as a vital part of their missionary work in the United States. One of the first tasks they performed after establishing themselves in a community was to open a Lutheran day school. No matter how arduous their pastoral duties, the school was to them a matter of vital concern.

They were convinced that through it more than through any other agency could the basic principles of confessional Lutheranism and doctrinal unity be firmly rooted in American soil" (Mauelshagen, Carl, *American Lutheranism Surrenders to Forces of Conservatism*, p. 132).

Our schools have proved a blessing to Synod in that they have been the great nursery to supply the Church with its future pastors and teachers. By far the majority of our clergy, pastors and teachers, have at all times been the product of our schools. Even today when the majority of our children are no longer in the parochial schools, they supply our seminaries and teachers' colleges with students far out of proportion to their numerical strength.

D. Lastly we are mindful of the blessings which have come upon the community and the State through our schools. We are aware of the fact that repeatedly our schools have been attacked as un-American by self-styled patriots. We can well disregard these attacks when we consider their concept of Americanism and their ideas of religion. We point with joy to the unnumbered Christian merchants, artisans, laborers, and professionals who have been sent forth into the community and who have become a solid foundation for the State. The strong American homes which our Christians have helped to establish are the best influence for good in this world.

Our Lutheran children have been taught to seek the peace and the welfare of the land according to Scriptural principles. Because they know that the fear of God is the beginning of wisdom, they have become a salt amidst the corruption of the land. When our Lutheran homes send forth their prayers in behalf of their government, are they not imploring the Help than which there is none greater? That we have not always been the power in the community which we might have been is sorely regretted. That we have frequently refrained from participating in the activities of the community in the interest of the nation's welfare when we should have been in the front ranks is not due to our schools, but it is rather the fruit of a misguided isolationism plucked from another tree. We can only hope in all sincerity that we shall exploit the blessings of our Christian citizenship to a greater extent in the second century. We owe this to our nation and to God, who would have us seek the peace of the city.

IV. IMPLICATIONS IN THE MAINTENANCE OF LUTHERAN PAROCHIAL SCHOOLS

The mere fact that we have a parochial school does not mean that we have found a solution to all our problems. In fact, it means that we have added responsibility and duties, for there are specific implications for a Church and a Synod that assumes the responsibility of conducting such schools.

A. The foremost implication is that with the help of God we keep our schools truly Christian. Not every parochial school is all that the name might imply. Just as in the past schools have permitted certain accidental matters to become their most important features, so there is also a possibility and a danger that secondary matters begin to crowd out the Christian element. Keeping our schools truly Christian implies that the chief emphasis is at all times placed on the instruction in the Word of God and Christian training. To be sure, one of the purposes of our schools is to prepare citizens of this world, but we must remember at all times that they are to be *Christian* citizens. Under no circumstances can we curtail the instruction of religion. This doesn't mean that we are unfriendly to high standards of knowledge. We indeed want our children to be equipped with the best the world has to offer, but not at the expense of their religious training. This means that we must have more than simply an hour set aside each day for the study of the Catechism or of Bible stories. For Christianity must pervade every subject every hour in order to give our children a Christian training. We fail to make our schools truly Christian if we do not integrate, for this is of primary importance. We ourselves often fail to appreciate this. What is the standard which we use in judging a school? Is this not the frequent recommendation, that in a specific school the children learn how to read well and have a firm grasp on the fundamentals of languages or mathematics, when our true gauge should be to what extent they have been instructed in the knowledge of Holy Scripture? This is the specific advantage of our schools, and this they must keep at all costs.

But even the teaching of religion and the thorough integration of the Christian viewpoint does not make a parochial school a truly Christian school. The eternal salvation of our children must be uppermost in our mind in our training. To this end the proper application of the Law and the Gospel in Christian living is of prime importance. Our schools must be training centers for Christianity establishing the right attitudes and provide a functional use of what has been learned. It may be well for us to evaluate our schools from this angle to see whether they have actually functioned as training centers for Christian life. Some of our chaplains have come back expressing their disappointment that Lutheran members of the military have not always been equipped with the proper understanding once they have left their Lutheran island home. Too many of our members were unable to give a "reason of the hope that is in them." As one chaplain has written: "Apparently their training had been emphasized from the angle of participating membership within the church and its organization and in striving to beat back the 'old Adam' within themselves. Very little emphasis had been placed upon the functions and duties of 'the new man that comes forth and arises as he daily overcomes sin and lives in true godliness,' and so the training left them ill prepared to 'function' beyond the picket fence of the Lutheran back yard." How many of these were trained in our Lutheran schools, of course, cannot be said. But it may be well for all of us to study our schools from this viewpoint.

The importance of a Christian teacher in making a school truly Christian need not be stressed. We know that as the teacher is, so is the school. While teachers need the necessary knowledge of the subjects and must have the gift of teaching, the most important requirement is that they be true children of God. We add this because in the final analysis only a Christian can instruct in a Christian way. We have sometimes misunderstood this. Sometimes it has been claimed that only a Christian can teach, because he alone has the knowledge, and they who assert this thus pass the whole responsibility on him, ignoring the power of the Word of God. This, of course, is wrong. Only a true Christian teacher can instruct in the real sense. That is based on the fact that Christian education is grounded on the proper application of the Law and the Gospel. An unconverted man might be able to teach outwardly the difference between the Law and the Gospel. He just has to memorize the particular passages in the Catechism. But applying these truths is quite impossible to an unbeliever. Only he who has experienced what sin and grace is can understand the heart of man. Even a Christian must learn throughout his whole life when and how to apply the Law and the Gospel. It is for this reason that we must demand that our teachers be true Christians. (Nebraska, 1906, p. 45.)

B. Conducting a parochial school implies also that we with the help of God maintain high standards. Since we have taken upon ourselves the task of preparing individuals for citizenship in this life, we have the obligation to offer the best possible instruction that we can give. The common school branches must be taught efficiently and effectively. We owe this to the parents, to our Church, and to the State. We need this also for an intelligent laity. We cannot be satisfied with the standards of a generation ago. While the population of the United States has tripled between 1870 to 1940, the enrollment in the high schools has increased ninety times, and in the colleges about thirty times. "And the end is not yet." (*General Education in a Free Society*, p. 7.) Our people have contributed their proportionate share in this phenomenal increase, and this throws an increasing pressure upon our schools that they keep up with these increased standards. If we neglect to do this, we give our enemies a reason to criticize us and to oppose our schools. We place an excuse into the mouths of indifferent parents who refuse to send their children.

What are some of the specific implications in improving the standards? It means that we teach such subjects as meet the child's present and future needs, and let us emphasize again, teach them from a Christian viewpoint. To this end the church at large must also co-operate in the production of suitable texts. In the past, Synod has spent only a small pittance for this work. Most of it has been done through the co-operation of Concordia Publishing House, but on a purely business basis. We take no issue with this policy, but rather we maintain that Synod as such should subsidize the production of such texts more and more. This is an expensive undertaking, and no publishing house can be expected to produce such books at a nominal cost and still operate on a sound business basis. This is, after all, one of the tasks for which Synod was founded and should not be lost sight of in the maze of its expanding work. (Original *Constitution of Synod*, Art. III, 6.)

Even more important than the subject taught and the texts used is the personal element of the teacher to achieve higher standards. To this end congregations must more and more fall in line with the practice of calling a regular teacher. While pastors will still regard it a privilege to teach school where circumstances allow it, this must, at best, be regarded as an emergency measure. It stands to reason that though a pastor be ever so diligent and capable, he cannot do the work of both pastor and teacher with the efficiency that these two callings require. The solution will be found only in calling a regular teacher as soon as conditions permit it. The use of temporary helps, as in the case of students, is an emergency measure and dare not be regarded the rule. Even the calling of a full-time teacher is no assurance that the matter has been taken care of, for he, too, must be given a teaching load that is reasonable. As his enrollment increases and grows beyond his capacity, assistance must be given him by calling additional help.

In striving to attain high standards, the matter of teacher training must receive serious consideration. This implies that we recruit students for this profession. The shortage of teachers in our Synod is well known. While partly due to the rapid expansion of our system, it is also due to our failure to exploit all possibilities in obtaining a large number of students. Though we have been reasonably successful in getting a large number of boys to study for the ministry, we have failed to take advantage of soliciting boys and girls for the teaching profession. Pastors and teachers can do the future schools no better service than by being alert to provide the Church with a good supply of students with natural endowments and, above all else, individuals in whom the fear of God and the love of Christ are dominant.

Higher standards also require that our teachers partake of an in-service training. As a matter of fact, candidates for the profession are not finished products no matter how many degrees they have obtained. Their training must be a continuous process through private study, conferences, and institutes, and especially through summer work. Here congregations can be of material assistance by offering teachers a fair salary or special subsidies to continue their education.

Present-day needs require that our schools be well equipped and that the buildings proper be adequate. We cannot hope to meet the standards required by the day where the minimum essentials are lacking. The physical appearance reflects the attitude of the congregation and, if shabby, then people will make their own evaluation and draw their own conclusions. To assist the teacher in maintaining the high standards which are implied in conducting a parochial school, it is necessary that they be visited and that there exist a close co-operation and harmony between pastor, teachers, and the congregation. To this end pastors must be faithful in their duty of visiting schools and meeting with their teachers to discuss matters pertaining to the welfare of the school. Since the pastor is responsible for the Christian training of children, teachers will not take it amiss when the pastor visits. It is taken for granted that the proper spirit is found not only with the teacher, but also with the pastor. He will not come into a schoolroom to discover faults in the manner of a dictator, but to help, encourage, and strengthen the teacher as his co-worker and brother. It is obviously a sign of tactlessness when the pastor thinks he knows everything better, especially since this is hardly true. Teachers probably know more about educational principles than the pastor does. In fact, they ought to, and the pastor will be glad to consider the viewpoint of his co-workers. Though the pastor is responsible for the task performed in the school, that does not mean that he has been placed over his teacher, for in the Christian Church there is no rank. One is the Master, and we are all brothers. (Nebraska, 1906, p. 51 f.)

But the pastor is not to be the only visitor in the school, for this is also the specific obligation of the local Board for Parish Education, which should be acquainted with the principles and policies of our schools and take a real interest in every phase of the church's educational task. In fact, the entire congregation should be conscious of its school and show its interest by visiting and thus assist the school in maintaining high standards. Where the District has a superintendent of education or his equivalent, much can be done to maintain a high level of efficiency.

More important than anything else are the prayers which Christians offer to the Throne of Grace in behalf of their teachers, pupils, and the schools, placing their temporal welfare with Him who is the great Shepherd of His flock.

C. Mindful of the fact that our parochial schools are such a boon to the work of the Church, Christians will be concerned in the extension of the parochial school system to the many congregations now without them. To accomplish this it will be necessary to indoctrinate an ever-widening circle of our membership in the proper understanding of the principles, functions, and benefits of the Lutheran parochial school. This is one of the chief duties of the synodical Board for Parish Education, to be carried out with the assistance of the several District boards. A loyal membership, however, cannot be satisfied with leaving this task to designated boards when in the final analysis it is the obligation of every member of our Synod. Therefore every pastor must ever make known to his congregation the basic principles of Christian education by sermons, by addresses before the various organizations, especially the voters' assembly, and in his pastoral calls. The founding congregations of our Synod had the firm faith in God and the necessary confidence in the school to establish it wherever possible. Their zeal may well be our model. Where congregations are too weak to establish their own schools, serious consideration should be given to the establishment of consolidated schools. Undoubtedly we will find a growing number of such schools in the coming decades as the maintenance cost mounts with higher standards.

Speaking parenthetically, District mission boards may well consider adopting a more aggressive policy in subsidizing schools as outlined by synodical resolution. Too often when application is made by a mission congregation, the cupboard is bare because it is deemed wiser to spend money to win souls than to keep them.

D. If the parochial school is the powerful influence for good that we say it is, the implication follows that we cannot limit this power to our own children. The one great purpose of our lives and the Church is to extend the Kingdom of God. Every agency of the Word must be shaped to that end. There is no room for isolationism in the Church of Christ. We are ever to spread, propagandize, and make deep inroads into the kingdom of Satan, and to this end we must use our parochial schools as the powerful mission agency which they are. Our schools have in theory always been a mission agency. The literature of our Church repeatedly calls attention to this as one of the great benefits of our schools. Yet in practice it is often incidental or an accidental appendage. We make no persistent and general effort to accomplish this purpose. Here and there congregations have been conscious of this implication and have recognized that having a school also implies using them to extend the Kingdom. But even today such effort is spotted. About 9½% of the total enrollment of our schools is among mission children. Small as this may be, it compares favorably with the Sunday school which ostensibly is our chief mission agency among the children and yet has an enrollment of only 12½% of unchurched children. But there is a growing consciousness to use our schools for mission purposes as revealed in the fact that almost 30% of the growth in the enrollment for the past five years is among unchurched children and only 35% of the increase is among our own children, while about 35% is among children of other denominations.

E. The final implication in the maintenance of a Lutheran school is that with the help of God we ward off all possible inroads. When we speak of inroads we are not only considering outside obstacles. The devil has a way of boring also from within. He sees to it that our precious jewel is not appreciated, and for this reason the Church must be constantly on the alert to safeguard our congregations in retaining the proper understanding and appreciation of our schools lest they become complacent and grow indifferent. Indifference will lead to forfeiture. The spirit of materialism which looks to the temporal advantages and greedily counts dollars and cents can also make us weary. In the past God has permitted bitter school battles to molest us. These have frequently been turned into blessings where they shook congregations out of their complacency and forced them to re-evaluate and improve their schools. We can be confident that God will permit such battles to come in the future. We know the devil will not let opportunities go by. Inroads may not be made as aggressively as in the past, but may come in a more subtle manner. Let us be on our guard lest we be tempted by present advantages at the price of future defeat and find that we have sold our educational birthright for a mess of pottage. Here in particular we must implore God to assist us, for the devil's plans are much too powerful and subtle for us to fight alone.

"My friends, it is one thing to be sentimental about our children and their education; but it is quite another thing to have good judgment and proper zeal combined with right sentiment. Surely we love our children. They are our own flesh and blood; they are the future of our Church; they are the hope of our community and nation. We would do anything for them. But we do not love them as Jesus loves them. Oh, how precious they are to Jesus! Who does not feel something of the great love in that divine heart of His when He lifts this little child in His arms, presses it to His heart, and says: 'Whoso shall receive one such little child, receiveth Me'? We do not love them as Jesus loves them. He gave His life for them; He shed His blood to redeem them from death and hell; He makes them His own and gives them His name in Holy Baptism. We cannot do for them what He can do. We cannot be their God, their Savior, their Lord. We cannot even control their hearts and cause them to grow up as His children. He must do that. And He does do it through His Word and through the Spirit, who is active in that Word. How important, therefore, that we give the Lord a chance to do this for them! How important that we teach them His Word! How important is Christian education!

"Every child placed in your care is a sacred trust. Its spiritual care is the responsibility of its parents first of all; for Christian education, like charity, begins at home. Yes, it is already the responsibility of the grandparents — for the Christian education of the child really begins many years before it is born, in the preparation of its parents for Christian parenthood. But it is also the responsibility of the Church. When Jesus told Peter: 'Feed My lambs,' He commended all children to the care of His Church. And everyone who is a member of His Church, whether a parent or not, whether preacher or layman, must be conscious of this great responsibility and will not seek to shirk or evade it. Every child is a holy treasure, which we must guide and instruct, prayerfully and conscientiously, *and so keep it for God and Christ*, that on the Last Day we may joyfully say, as Jesus once said: "Father, those that Thou gavest me I have kept, and none of them is lost!" (Southeastern, 1942, p. 12.)

Adiaphora

I. DEFINITION OF THE TERM

THE title of the topic which has been assigned for our mutual study and discussion during this convention solicits an explanation, for here we are confronted with a technical expression which generally has meaning only for the professional theologian or, at any rate, for one who has a closer acquaintance with theological phraseology.

Various English equivalents may be offered for *adiaphora*. The word itself is of Greek origin and signifies "indifferent." Some Bible students have adopted these terms: indifferent matters, matters of indifference, or non-essential matters (*Triglot*, pp. 829, 1053; Fritz, *Pastoral Theology*, p. 318), acts or matters whose observance or non-observance, whose acceptance or non-acceptance, whose practice or non-practice make no difference. Others prefer the terminology: "things lying in the middle." From this the familiar German word *Mitteldinge* is derived, which is perhaps the most descriptive and the most adequate of all the equivalents for adiaphora. Accordingly, adiaphora are, to coin a new term, "middle-things," "middle-matters," matters lying in the middle between the commands and prohibitions of the Word of God. Undoubtedly the best definition of our subject is still found in the Confessions of our Church. Although numerous references are made to matters indifferent in our confessional writings, twice do they discuss this matter specifically and at great length, in each instance relating it to "Church rites which are neither commanded nor forbidden in God's Word." (Formula of Concord, Epitome X, *Triglot*, p. 829 ff.; Thorough Declaration X, *Triglot*, p. 1053 ff.)

There are certain areas of activity and being in which there is no real middle sphere, no real neutral ground. Let us adduce a few examples from the field of ethics, science, and religion. Where, by way of example, is the middle between right and wrong? Can the solution to an arithmetical problem be anything but correct or incorrect? We are either dead or alive; half-dead and half-alive are approximations and not exact expressions. Where is the neutral ground between Kansas and Oklahoma? Where is the middle sphere between God's kingdom and the devil's kingdom? We are either Christians or non-Christians, either God's children or not God's children. Upon death our souls pass either to a blessed or to a damned existence, and in eternity we shall live eternally either in heaven or in hell. And so we could continue.

It is decidedly different, however, in this matter under discussion. There is a definite province of activity which is not specifically covered by either God's command or God's prohibition. If it were possible, we could consider every conceivable act of man and evaluate it on the basis of the revealed will of God in His Holy Word in order to establish whether or not any divine statement has any bearing on it. If not, it is quite evidently a non-essential matter, an adiaphoron. Every day of our life is literally filled with acts and decisions concerning which there is no specific Scriptural injunction. Such matters are left by God to our personal discretion and judgment.

The lives of the believers of the Old Dispensation were far more circumscribed by specific divine decree, their freedom of action far more constricted than our lives. In their economic, social, and religious existence they lived and moved by many and varied divine directions. Certain meats could not be eaten. Fields had to lie fallow at seven and forty-nine-year intervals. Slaves were periodically freed from bondage. All of the flagrant sins and most of the lesser ones were to be atoned for by prescribed sacrifices. The successive steps in offering a sacrifice were exactly detailed. Physical perfection standards were laid down for the priests. The priests were permitted to wear only certain types of official attire. Tithes were demanded. Weekly, monthly, and annual religious days and festivals were observed by direction. The various appointments of such days were outlined in great detail. The encampments, the journeys, the conquest and settlement of the Land of Promise, the building of the Tabernacle and the Temple, —

all these and many more steps of personal and official living were taken at the specific behest of God. Only a casual reading of Leviticus or Deuteronomy is required to sharpen one's recollection of the extent to which God directed the lives of His people of old by instruction, command, and prohibition. Even after more than three years of association and study with Jesus, these regulations were so deeply ingrained with the Apostle Peter that it required a special divine demonstration in order to conquer his inhibitions. (Acts 10.) Accordingly, the same Apostle significantly refers to the Old Testament regulations as a "yoke . . . which neither our fathers nor we were able to bear" (Acts 15:10). Similarly, the Apostle Paul designates the attempt to impose circumcision upon Titus as a return to bondage (Gal. 2:4: "that they might bring us into bondage"). And he exhorts the Galatian Christians: "Stand fast therefore in the liberty wherewith Christ hath made us free, and be not entangled again with the yoke of bondage" (Gal. 5:1).

Neither was this all. The scribes and Pharisees had imposed human ordinances and appendages to the divine commands, all of which Jesus characterized as follows: "They bind heavy burdens and grievous to be borne, and lay them on men's shoulders; but they themselves will not move them with one of their fingers" (Matt. 23:4). These human additions to God's laws on the part of the elders of the people are said to have exceeded four thousand in number (Nebraska, 1912, p. 28). Thank God, therefore, that under the New Covenant He Himself has lifted this yoke from our necks, that He Himself has not framed all human activity with His commands and prohibitions, that He Himself has consigned many acts to the discretion and judgment of the Christian.

How, now, can we prove this? As always in such questions, we turn to God's Word for instruction.

When St. Paul twice writes to the Corinthians: "All things are lawful unto me, but all things are not expedient" (1 Cor. 6:12; 10:23), he clearly indicates that there is a domain between the commands and prohibitions of God in which he as a Christian has liberty of action. That such liberty is not to conflict with the express terms of the Law of God is evident a) from the entire discussion, which deals with freedoms enjoyed by some Christians, and b) from the following verse, in which the Apostle shows that the body is intended for service to God and not for impurity, such as adultery.

In the fourteenth chapter of his Letter to the Romans the same Apostle writes: "Let not him that eateth despise him that eateth not; and let not him which eateth not, judge him that eateth" (14:3). Among the Roman Christians, as among others at that time, there were such as had absolutely no scruples about eating certain meats which were formerly on the forbidden list, while others, bound by inhibitions and conscience restraints, restricted themselves largely to a vegetable diet. Some felt in conscience bound to adhere to the Old Testament regulations with regard to clean and unclean animals. The Apostle here does not condemn either action, but rather accepts both with only one exhortation, namely, that neither should be the occasion for spiritual pride or arrogance on the part of one, or condemnation on the part of the other. In a word, to eat meat or not to eat meat was committed to the decision of the individual, but this eating or non-eating should in no way lead to contempt or to judgment.

In a similar vein he writes in the fifth verse: "One man esteemeth one day above another; another esteemeth every day alike." There were those who selected a certain day for their religious observance, while others deemed one day as good as another for prayer and worship. Again the Apostle finds no fault with either opinion or action. He does, however, add: "Let every man be fully persuaded in his own mind." The selection of a certain day for their worship or the selection of every day for worship was a matter entirely within their own discretion, and each followed his own persuasion in the service of God. (Rom. 14:6.)

Again, St. Paul sets the matter clearly before us when he writes to the Colossian Christians: "Let no man therefore judge you in meat, or in drink [for eating or drinking], or in respect of an holy day, or of the new moon, or of the Sabbath days, which are a shadow of things to come, but the body is of Christ" (Col. 2: 16-17). This meant nothing less to these Colossians than that there were no restrictions on their selection of their diet, their drink, or their day or days of worship. The Old Testament ceremonial prescriptions no longer applied to them. And these Apostolic words mean nothing less to us. Other things being equal, we can eat or drink what we wish. We can worship God in public assembly on any day of our choice. The fact that we do worship on Sunday is in itself an adiaphoron, something neither commanded nor forbidden in God's Word.

While it is evident from some of the verses cited above that God Himself removed some matters from the domain of divine Law to the domain of adiaphora, it should also be noted in this connection that adiaphora (*in abstracto*) may cease to be adiaphora (*in concreto*) under certain circumstances. Martha's activity in behalf of the Savior's physical welfare was in itself a praiseworthy thing, but if such interest and energy betrays a lack of interest in the one thing needful, it becomes sinful. The anointing of Jesus by Mary was in itself a matter of indifference, but her love for the Master made it a compelling act of Christian devotion. The savings account or the insurance policy of the Christian is commendable foresight, but if lack of trust in God is the basic urge, they become objectionable. To smoke is in itself neither good nor bad, but smoking may be bad for the individual if the nicotine affects the purity of the blood stream and impairs heart action and thus the health. Drinking of alcoholic beverages is not a violation of God's Law, but if such drinking is beyond moderation, or if such drinking promotes an ulcerous condition, it ceases to be an adiaphoron. The manner in which water is to be applied in the administration of the Sacrament of Holy Baptism is not designated in Holy Writ; however, those who defend immersion — in itself entirely valid and permissible — as the only correct method, have thereby moved it from the sphere of neutrality. Actually to break the bread in the celebration of the Lord's Supper, while not commanded by the Lord Jesus, would be following His example at the time of the institution of this Sacrament; but to insist that this is the only correct way violates the law of Christian liberty, and therefore we do not break the bread. (Cf. the discussion of this and related questions in the *Proceedings* of the Western District, 1856, pp. 33—34.) Moreover, when this insistence is made with the express purpose of bolstering the thesis that thereby the symbolic nature of the Lord's Supper is maintained, it vitiates the Scriptural doctrine of the Sacrament of the Altar. Cremation of the body in itself is neither right nor wrong; it may even become a

Adiaphora 691

necessity; but if cremation becomes an expression of atheistic principles, it should be studiously avoided by Christians.

There were those who denied the existence of *Mitteldinge*. The Pietistic movement and thought under the leadership of Philip Jakob Spener (1635–1705) and August Hermann Francke (1663–1727), though at first having the object of a reconsecrated Christian life, seemed to lose sight of the fact that such a Christian life must rest upon the proper foundation, namely, on pure doctrine. Purity of doctrine was apparently of lesser importance to the Pietists than purity of Christian life. By inference, and as a result of their doctrine of the rebirth (*theologia regenitorum*), they taught that as soon as one has been reborn and has arrived at the stage of full spiritual manhood, one is free of sin already in this life. (Krauss, *Lebensbilder*, p. 601; Kurtz, *Church History*, III, p. 106.) Therefore every act which flows from such a regenerated heart is necessarily good, and every act which is not the result of such rebirth is evil. Let us note, this is not merely: Only Christians can do good works in the Scriptural sense of the term, but also: Christians can do only good works. Therefore there can be no neutrality of acting. In answer, we must say that the entire argument rests on an unScriptural, therefore an incorrect, premise. There simply is no perfection in anyone; there is no perfection in the Christian, and no one is more truly aware and conscious of this than the sincere Christian himself.

Again, the Pietists asserted that the purpose of all activity on the part of the Christian must be to honor and glorify God, for St. Paul writes to the Corinthians: "Whether therefore ye eat, or drink, or whatsoever ye do, do all to the glory of God" (I Cor. 10:31), and to the Colossians: "Whatsoever ye do in word and deed, do all in the name of the Lord Jesus" (Col. 3:17). Accordingly, they say, there can be no adiaphora. It has been correctly pointed out by way of rebuttal: a. Eating and drinking in themselves are not to the glory of God, for in that event heathen would thereby also honor God; b. Paul informs us how such eating and drinking can be to the glory of God. Writing to the Romans, he states: "He that eateth, eateth to the Lord, for he giveth God thanks" (14:6). (Cf. Nebraska, 1912, p. 24.) Our eating and drinking in itself can only indirectly be to the glory and honor of God, in so far as it sustains a life consecrated to further service of God.

The Pietists also cite the Apostle's statement to the Romans: "Whatsoever is not of faith is sin" (14:23). Whatever results from faith is good, they assert; everything which does not result from faith is evil. Extreme Pietists have even placed such acts as smiling, laughing, witticisms, and playing on the forbidden list, because they felt that such activity could not be the result of faith. This entire argument, however, rests upon a misinterpretation of the passage: "Whatsoever is not of faith is sin." The faith of which the Apostle speaks here is not justifying or saving faith, but rather confidence, trust, persuasion, conviction of the rightness of one's action. (Cf. Rom. 14:2, 5, 23 a; also the discussion of this passage in Stoeckhardt, *Kommentar ueber den Brief Pauli an die Roemer*, pp. 593—594.) The Christian is to be sure that his action does not violate God's Law; "he that doubteth is damned if he eat" (v. 23). To be sure, such conviction rests upon justifying and saving faith, for only the Christian is intent on doing God's will, but such conviction is not to be identified with saving or justifying faith.

II. IMPORTANCE OF THE SUBJECT

This subject is important doctrinally. Adiaphora lie within the domain of Christian liberty. Christian liberty may be defined as consisting of the freedom of believers from the curse and coercion of the Law, from Levitical ceremonies, and from human ordinances (*Menschensatzungen*). The believer is *free from the curse of the Law*. In Galatians 3:13 we read: "Christ hath redeemed us from the curse of the Law, being made a curse for us; for it is written: Cursed is everyone that hangeth on a tree." Christ was not merely cursed for us, but He became a curse for us, the universal curse for all humanity. Thus He effected our release from the bondage into which the Law had placed us, the bondage in which all place themselves who trust in the Law for salvation. The Christian is *freed from the coercion of the Law*. St. Paul writes: "For sin shall not have dominion over you; for ye are not under the Law, but under grace" (Rom. 6:14). Christians are not coerced by the Law, they are not under the Law, they are under grace, and this grace makes them both able and willing to do good works. This does not mean that the Christian dispenses with the Law, but it does mean that the Law is necessary for the old man within him rather than for the new man. The Formula of Concord therefore says: "For although the Law is not made for the righteous man, as the Apostle testifies I Tim. 1:9, but for the unrighteous, yet this is not to be understood in the bare meaning that the justified are to live without Law. . . . But the meaning of St. Paul is that the Law cannot burden with its curse those who have been reconciled to God through Christ; nor must it vex the regenerate with its coercion, because they have pleasure in God's Law after the inner man." (Art. X, par. 5, *Triglot*, p. 963.) The believer is also *free from all human ordinances with regard to his religion.* In God's kingdom all members are brothers, not rabbis, not fathers, not masters, but brothers (Matt. 23:8-10); here the greatest shall be as the younger and the chief as those who serve (Luke 22:26); and even though the followers of the Lord Jesus are designated as priests and kings (Rev. 5:10; I Peter 2:8), let us not forget that they are all priests and kings of the same level, the same privilege, the same authority, and the same freedom.

This liberty is the direct result of justification. Justification is that act of God whereby He imputes to the believer the righteousness of Christ. St. Paul writes to Timothy: "The Law is not made for the righteous man, but for the lawless and disobedient, for the ungodly and for sinners," etc. (I Tim. 1:9) and to the Romans: "For Christ is the end of the Law for righteousness to everyone that believeth" (10:4). He who believes in Christ is righteous; the Law makes no further indicting demands on him, for all these demands have been met by and in Christ Jesus. This freedom from the demands of the Law, this Christian liberty, is the direct result of justification. In another passage the Savior Himself says to the Jews: "If the Son therefore shall make you free, ye shall be free indeed" (John 8:36). Jesus is speaking of freedom to the Jews, who prided themselves on never having been slaves (servants) of anyone, and He reminds these Jews that they are slaves of sin. Slaves, however — so runs the argument — remain slaves until they are freed by the son of the house, or the master of the house. This Son, this Master He is, and thus He can free them from the bondage of sin-enthrallment. Thus "if ye continue in My Word, then are ye My disciples indeed, and ye shall know the truth, and the truth shall make you free" (John 8:31-32). Faith in the Lord Jesus would grant them freedom from sin and bestow upon them all the wonderful liberties of the children of God. With the advent of Christ many of the ceremonies affecting the personal and religious life of the people ceased to have any specific value; they were transferred to the realm of Christian liberty, they became adiaphora. This liberty was conferred upon the Christian as a result of his faith. Adiaphora, then, are intimately related to the doctrine of justification.

It should be noted, however, that adiaphora in themselves are not a part of justifying faith. In the first place, *they are not a product of that faith.* Christian prayer, church attendance, observance of the Sacraments, our relation toward our neighbor — these and many other steps along the pathway of a Christian life are the inevitable result of a God-created and God-nurtured faith. In fact, our entire attitude toward God's Law is formed by our fear and love toward God, even as we confess in the explanation of every Commandment. Not so in the case of an adiaphoron. To smoke a cigarette, to play a game of cards, to attend a baseball game is not in any way connected with justifying faith. Again, *adiaphora do not impose guilt upon anyone.* This is not true of violations of God's commands and prohibitions; such transgressions entail sin, guilt, and punishment. In fact, the Apostle James reminds us that not only commission of sin, but also the omission of good involves sin: "To him that knoweth to do good, and doeth it not, to him it is sin" (4:17). This is not true with regard to a real adiaphoron. Where there is no violation of a law, there can be no question of sin, guilt, and punishment. The twofold verdict of the Apostle Paul, already cited above, is: "He sinneth not. He doeth well" (I Cor. 7:36-37). In the third place, *adiaphora do not effect a different relation between God and the Christian.* We have already seen that St. Paul condemns neither those who eat meat nor those who do not, neither those who observe one day nor those who observe every day for worship (Romans 14). Moreover, he states specifically: "But meat commendeth us not to God, for neither, if we eat, are we the better; neither, if we eat not, are we the worse (I Cor. 8:8). Accordingly, the Christian who refrains from eating certain meats is no better than the Christian who eats those meats; he who worships on a

Saturday is no better than he who worships on a Wednesday; he who plays horseshoe is no better in the sight of God than he who does not, and vice versa. Man is justified by faith and not by the commission or omission of an adiaphoron. Finally and above all, *adiaphora are not to be regarded as worship of God.* Our Confessions repeatedly assert this truth. In the Apology to the Augsburg Confession the admission is made that "obedience, poverty, and celibacy are as exercises adiaphora" and that some may use them in a proper and God-pleasing way, "but to hold that these observances are services (*Gottesdienste*) on account of which they are accounted just before God and through which they merit eternal life, conflicts with the Gospel concerning the righteousness of faith, which teaches that for Christ's sake righteousness and eternal life are granted us." (Apology of Augsburg Confession, Art. XXVIII, *Triglot*, p. 427.)

This question concerning indifferent matters is of great significance also from the historical standpoint. Three times in the history of the Christian Church has the problem of adiaphora been the cause of concern and deliberation, of difference of opinion and controversy, once with regard to church rites and ceremonies, once with regard to personal life, and once with regard to a combination of both.

The first of these was in the middle of the first century after Christ, the so-called Council of Jerusalem. Certain men had come from Judea to the congregation at Antioch, composed largely of uncircumcised Gentile Christians, and had insisted that the Christianity of these brethren could not be complete without the rite of circumcision and the observance of the Law of Moses. This entire matter was now proposed to the Apostles and elders in Jerusalem for decision. In the public meeting which followed, considerable divergence of opinion was evident (Acts 15:7: "when there had been much disputing"). Three portions of the deliberations are made known to us in the chapter.

The first of these was the opinion of Simon Peter. Calling the attention of his audience to the fact that God had sent him to preach to the Gentiles, he also pointed to the proof of God's grace which was bestowed upon his work in the gift of the Holy Spirit to these Gentiles. Thereupon he pleaded that the yoke of Old

Testament ordinances, which had been too heavy for the Apostles as well as for their ancestors, should not be placed upon the Gentile Christians.

Next a report was given by Barnabas and Paul which proved that their work among the heathen had been blessed by miracles and wonders. This must have been particularly impressive to those who were acquainted with the omnipotence of God among His people both in the Old and the New Testament times.

Finally James offered his opinion. He explained that activity such as that of Simon Peter, Barnabas, and Paul was merely the practical conclusion of God's promise of old that the Gospel should be proclaimed among the Gentiles. Thereupon he urged that no greater burden than necessary should be imposed upon the Gentile Christians. Circumcision and the keeping of the Law (Ceremonial Law) were not to be demanded. These had in fact become adiaphora, which truth was later forcibly underscored by the fact that Titus, who was with Paul and Barnabas at the Council of Jerusalem, was not circumcised. The advice, however, was also given to the Gentile Christians that they were to be considerate of their brethren among the Jews by abstaining from practices which would be especially obnoxious to the Hebrew Christians.

The significant results of this convention were twofold: a. The Old Testament Ceremonial Law had become a *Mittelding*. b. The practice of some indifferent matters should, for the sake of love and consideration for brethren, be temporarily held in abeyance.

A millennium and a half later, almost immediately after the death of Martin Luther, the issue of middle things became such an animated one that the so-called Adiaphoristic Controversy raged in the Church from 1548 until 1555, and there was no satisfactory conclusion until 1577, when the Formula of Concord was adopted. Dr. Bente puts the question at issue as follows: "May Lutherans under conditions such as prevailed during the Leipzig Interim, when the Romanists on pain of persecution and violence demanded the reinstitution of abandoned papal ceremonies, even if the ceremonies in question be truly indifferent in themselves, submit with a good conscience, that is to say, without denying the truth and Christian liberty, without sanctioning the errors of Romanism, and without giving offense either to the enemies or to the friends of the Lutheran Church, especially its weak members?"

(*Triglot*, Historical Introductions, p. 108.) The solution to problems growing out of this controversy is offered in Article X of the Formula of Concord, and it is as follows: a. Such things (which are) contrary to God's Word are not to be regarded as adiaphora. b. Such ceremonies should not be reckoned among the genuine free adiaphora, or matters of indifference, as make a show or feign the appearance, as though our religion and that of the Papists were not far apart, thus to avoid persecution. c. Likewise, when there are useless, foolish displays, that are profitable neither for good order nor Christian discipline nor evangelical propriety in the Church, these are not genuine adiaphora, or matters of indifference. d. In time of persecution, when a plain confession is required of us, we should not yield to the enemies with regard to such adiaphora. e. The congregation of God . . . has the power, according to its circumstances, to change such ceremonies in such manner as may be most useful and edifying. (*Triglot*, pp. 829, 1054—55.) It is interesting to note that the summarizing statement as to the purpose of the discussion offers brief but ample guides for the discussion of the entire subject: "Everyone can understand what every Christian congregation and every Christian man, especially in time of confession (when a confession of faith should be made), and, most of all, preachers, are to do or to leave undone, without injury to conscience, with respect to adiaphora, in order that God may not be angered, love may not be injured, the enemies of God's Word be not strengthened, nor the weak in faith offended" (*Triglot*, p. 1061).

The third controversy in the Church with regard to adiaphora occurred about one hundred years after the formulation of the Lutheran confession in the Formula of Concord. It is called the Pietistic Controversy, and it has been treated in essence above. Therefore little need be added here. Pietism was a child of legalistic Calvinism and an antecedent of austere Puritanism. This controversy concerned itself with the field of personal morals rather than with church rites and customs. The Pietists "maintained that whatever action does not directly serve the honor of God, or our own and our neighbor's bodily or spiritual welfare, is sin, because at best it is a waste of time; and to rejoice in anything that, while not directly sinful, is pleasant and amusing, is in conflict with Christian self-denial. . . . Not only dancing, attending theatrical plays, playing at cards, but also innocent jests and pleasantries, taking part in festive meals, taking a walk, laughing, were regarded as sinful. In A. H. Francke's orphanage the children were even forbidden to play" (Graebner, *Borderland of Right and Wrong,* Fourth Ed., Introd., pp. IX—X). A life of abstinence, almost ascetic in nature, was regarded as the distinguishing mark of the Christian.

The subject of adiaphora, however, is not only of doctrinal and historical significance. It also has tremendous practical value. This is true with regard to church life as well as personal life. Time and again, long and earnest, not to say heated and bitter, discussion has centered in such topics as: festival days to be observed, church music, chanting, the use of exorcism, the white chrisom (*Westerhemd*), questions directed to sponsors, single or threefold pouring of the baptismal water, the sign of the cross, the common or the individual cup, the use of unleavened or leavened bread, the manner in which the bread is to be given or taken, kneeling on the part of the pastor or the congregation, vestments of the pastor, appointments in the chancel, etc. Particularly in the last two decades, congregations, conferences, and individuals have indicated a renewed interest in the order and the forms of worship, in ceremonies, in church architecture; and all such and related fields literally abound in questions which must be answered, problems which must be solved (largely in the sphere of adiaphora) for the sake of good order and in the interest of Christian edification and growth. The place of organizations in the church, the vestment of choirs, the uniformity of dress for ushers, and innumerable other items address themselves to the attention of the church membership. As a matter of fact, much, if not most, of the business procedure of board and membership meetings, of conventions, centers in an area which in itself is an adiaphoron. The elections of officers and committees, official procedure, the adoption of a budget, the external mechanics of the financial and missionary program of the Church, the envelope system, the publication of reports, financial or otherwise — all of these items are per se matters of indifference. And yet, under the blessing of God, they all may and do play a weighty part in the extension of His kingdom on earth. Therefore it is of the utmost importance for the Christian to know under what circumstances they lose their indifferent character.

Similarly in the realm of personal life. There are those among you who have had cause to ask yourselves: When must I refrain from smoking, drinking of alcoholic beverages, playing of cards? There are others among you who have been plied with such inquiries: What are acceptable Christian standards and methods of labor, leisure and enjoyment, modes of dress, union affiliation, etc.? In such instances it becomes tremendously important to know the correct answers, so much so in fact that the Apostle Paul earnestly reminds us that not only he who acts against better knowledge, but also he who acts in doubt is guilty of sin. (Rom. 14:23.)

III. ABUSES OF THIS DOCTRINE

From what has been stated thus far it is obvious that anything and everything included in God's commands or prohibitions cannot be an adiaphoron. His "Thou shalt" and "Thou shalt not" specifically remove it from that sphere. But it is a tragic truth that all doctrines have at some time or another, by someone or another, been vitiated and transgressed by violation or abuse. This applies also to the subject under discussion.

It is manifestly a violation of this doctrine of Christian liberty with regard to *Mitteldinge* when it serves as a springboard at the pools of profligate or loose living. To the Galatians St. Paul writes: "Brethren, ye have been called unto liberty; only use not liberty for an occasion (Greek has a word which means as much as incentive, occasion, or the base of operations) to the flesh, but by love serve one another" (Gal. 5:13). The Apostle had been discussing the allegation of the Judaizers that the Ceremonial Law of the Old Testament was still in force for the New Testament Christians. Then he turns with emphasis to the Christians and reminds them that they, in contrast to the legalists who are aggravating them, are in a state of liberty, liberty from the Mosaic Law, sin, and fear. There must, however, have been danger in the other direction, for the admonition is added: "Only use not liberty for an occasion to the flesh," i. e., do not permit your liberty to provide an opportunity, a base of operations, for the demands of the flesh for all kinds of excesses and indulgences.

Accordingly, excesses of any kind, and in any area which in itself is clearly a matter of Christian liberty, are a violation of this doctrine of indifferent matters. The glutton, the hard drinker (not drunkard alone), the chain-smoker, the epicurean, who argues: "If and when I die, I would rather die enjoying myself" — all such may well ask themselves whether obligations to health, to family, to opportunity and duty should not prompt a re-evaluation of their concept of adiaphora. Again, he who attends the Lord's Table only once or twice a year, who has no particular qualms about regularity at church attendance, who can somehow or other disregard appeals for foreign mission work, merely because God does not specifically demand 8, 12, or 24 Communions a year, or 52, 78, or 104 church services, or on pretext that we have enough heathen in this country — such a one may well inquire if he is not feasting his Old Adam at the banquet board of Christian liberty. In short, excesses and overindulgence of almost any kind, be that in food, drink, occupation, entertainment, care of the body, scientific study, etc., may tend toward spiritual anemia and ultimate spiritual death.

Another abuse of this doctrine results from any attempt to make adiaphora a matter of conscience for others. The word of Christ applies here: "One is your Master, even Christ; and all ye are brethren" (Matt. 23:8). It is instructive for us to note in this connection that this admonition followed a discussion of the abuses of the scribes and Pharisees in burdening men's consciences with "heavy burdens and grievous to be borne" (v. 4). Therefore our Confessions also testify: "No one is to burden the Church with his own traditions, but here the rule is to be that nobody's power or authority is to avail more than the Word of God" (Formula of Concord, Thorough Declaration, X, 21, *Triglot*, p. 1061). "Matters of indifference are and remain of themselves free, and accordingly can admit of no command or prohibition" (*ibid.*, p. 1057). "We reject and condemn also as wrong when these ordinances are by coercion forced upon the congregation of God as necessary" (*ibid.*, p. 1061).

Neither will it suffice to substitute the example of Christ or His Apostles for a specific command. Celebrating the Lord's Supper in an upper room and at night is certainly no essential part of the Sacrament. Washing of the disciples' feet was intended to be a lesson in humility and loving service and not the institution of a sacrament. The selection of Sunday as the day of worship by the Apostles and early Christians was particularly appropriate and meaningful, but it obviously lies beyond the realm of divine commands and prohibitions.

With the acceptance of the maxim that only God has the right to issue such commands and prohibitions, it follows that neither pastors nor boards, neither congregations nor groups of congregations have any such right in the field of adiaphora. Neither one nor all of these can transform indifferent matters into binding precepts.

To His disciples Christ directed these words: "Ye know that the princes of the Gentiles exercise dominion over them, and they that are great exercise authority upon them. But it shall not be so among you" (Matt. 20:25-26). St. Paul refers to himself: "Who, then, is Paul, and who is Appollos but ministers by whom ye believed?" (I Cor. 3:5.) Peter speaks of himself merely as an elder among the elders of the church, and he adds pointedly: "neither as being lords over God's heritage" (I Pet. 5:3). And while it is true that Christians holding church offices, teachers, and pastors are included among those to whom we owe honor and respect according to the Fourth Commandment, it must also be borne in mind that legislative powers have not been granted to religious leaders or organizations. The Formula of Concord uses strong language with reference to this: "Just as little as we can worship the devil himself as Lord and God, can we endure his apostle, the Pope, or Antichrist, in his rule as head or lord" (Art. X, 20, *Triglot*, p. 1059). To be sure, church officials and boards and teachers and pastors can effect desirable changes in the field of *Mitteldinge*, but it should be done by instruction and advice rather than by order and command. Likewise, the Christians, as individuals and groups, will accept this advice if it is good and expedient.

This principle must be observed by congregations and groups of congregations, such as conferences or synods. Granted that the Christian congregation is one of the most exalted and most privileged assemblies on earth, granted also that God has bestowed upon it many rights, it is nonetheless true that these rights and privileges do not include the right of prescription to individuals or groups of individuals in matters indifferent. In such instances even the majority vote cannot be imposed upon the conscience of the minority by decree, though the minority should yield for the sake of love and good order. In accord with this we read in the Augsburg Confession: "It is proper that the churches should keep such ordinances for the sake of love and tranquillity, so far that one do not offend another, that all things be done in the churches in order, and without confusion, I Cor. 14:40; cp. Phil. 2:4, but so that consciences be not burdened to think that they are necessary to salvation, or to judge that they sin when they break them without offense to others" (Art. XXVIII, *Triglot*, p. 91). Luther adds: "Whenever others insist that one must do such things (nonessential things) in obedience to them as being necessary to salvation, then one should not do anything they ask, but rather the very opposite, in order to prove that all that a Christian needs is faith and love; whether anything else is to be done or not done must be left to Christian charity, as the circumstances may demand; for to do such things out of love and Christian liberty does no harm, but to do them because of necessity and obedience is damnable" (St. Louis XII:87).

Lutheran principles differ widely from those of Catholicism and many representatives of Protestantism, who claim for the Church the right to command or forbid things neither forbidden nor commanded by God. The Mass, forbidding marriage to the priests, restrictions on meat diet for certain days of the week, are a few of the many examples of this kind demanded by the Church of Rome. On the other hand, insistence on the part of many Reformed churches (Mueller, *Popular Symbolics*, Index, pp. 497, 508) that ceremonial foot washing and anointing of the sick are sacraments, the prohibition demands with regard to liquor and tobacco (*Ibid.*, pp. 497, 525), the so-called blue laws, or blue-sky laws, with their legalistic safeguards of the "Sabbath" (*ibid.*, p. 499) — all these and many more represent the erroneous claims of many Reformed churches. The violent actions of Carlstadt and his followers in breaking all images in the churches and their demand that the judicial laws of Moses be reinstated in the land are also cases in point. (Apology of the Augsburg Confession, *Triglot*, p. 331.) Luther's reaction to their demand to eliminate the "elevation of the host"

Adiaphora

was to continue it for a time, even though he himself had decided to do away with it; he deemed it an infringement of Christian liberty.

A third abuse of this doctrine of adiaphora involves the important question of offense and the weak brother. The New Testament abounds in references to those who are commonly designated as weak brethren, and the Apostle Paul deems this such an important topic that he devotes entire chapters in his Letters to the Romans and to the Corinthians to its discussion. "Him that is weak in the faith, receive ye, but not to doubtful disputations. For one believeth that he may eat all things, another, who is weak, eateth herbs" (Rom. 14:1-2). Again: "We, then, that are strong ought to bear the infirmities of the weak and not to please ourselves" (Rom. 15:1). Or: "But take heed lest by any means this liberty of yours become a stumbling block to them that are weak . . . and through thy knowledge shall the weak brother perish, for whom Christ died?" (I Cor. 8:8, 11.) Also: "To the weak became I as weak that I might gain the weak. I am made all things to all men that I might by all means save some" (I Cor. 9:22).

Who are these weak ones? we therefore ask. They are brothers (Rom. 14:15: "But if thy brother be grieved with thy meat . . .") who have been received by God (Rom. 14:6: "for God hath received him"). What he does, he does "unto the Lord" (Rom. 14:6). He is "weak in faith" (Rom. 14:1), because he does not have sufficient knowledge and understanding (I Cor. 8:7: "there is not in every man that knowledge") with regard to Christian liberty and indifferent matters. These weak Christians refrained from the eating of meat and selected a certain day for worship in order better to serve the Lord (Rom. 14:2, 5). It may actually have become a matter of grief and a stumbling block to them to see others make use of their Christian liberty (Rom. 14:15; I Cor. 8:9). If in this state of doubt he followed the example of the strong brother, the brother who exercised his Christian liberty, he actually invoked upon himself the condemnation of his own conscience and risked eternal damnation.

Theologians designate the erring or doubting conscience as the distinguishing characteristic of the weak brother. The erring conscience is one which places matters indifferent into the forbidden list; the doubting conscience is one which is simply unable to make a decision with regard to certain adiaphora. It is not within the scope of this discussion to define the term conscience, but perhaps a doubting and erring knowledge and understanding would be more exact terminology.

What now is to be the attitude of the strong toward the weak brother? He must remember that the weak brother is a *brother in the faith;* that his weakness results from the lack of knowledge (I Cor. 8:7); that the free exercise of Christian liberty may not only become a stumbling block for the weak (I Cor. 8:9), but also cause him to perish (I Cor. 8:11). Thus the strong may destroy God's own creation (Rom. 14:20), and thus he definitely sins against God (I Cor. 8:12). Consequently, the strong is not to despise the weak or cause him to stumble (Rom. 14:15, 13), but rather bear with his weakness (Rom. 15:1) while trying to instruct him and to strengthen him.

St. Paul speaks in forceful terms with regard to the duty of the strong over against the weak. "Wherefore, if meat make my brother to offend, I will eat no flesh while the world standeth, lest I make my brother to offend" (I Cor. 8:13). And again: "To the weak became I as weak, that I might gain the weak; I am made all things to all men, that I might by all means save some" (I Cor. 9:22). And on the basis of the apostolic statement that "he that doubteth is damned if he eat" (Rom. 14:23) Martin Luther advised some of the pastors for the time being not to insist on the distribution of the wine. Applicable here is the statement in the Apology of the Augsburg Confession: "We teach that in these matters [in the Article entitled Human Traditions] the use of liberty is to be so controlled that the inexperienced may not be offended, and, on account of the abuse of liberty, may not become more hostile to the true doctrine of the Gospel, or that without a reasonable cause nothing in customary rites be changed, but that, in order to cherish harmony, such old customs be observed as can be observed without sin or without great inconvenience" (*Triglot,* p. 329).

The charitable application of this doctrine of Christian liberty in this sphere of offense is particularly difficult. In the first place, it is not a simple matter to decide what actually constitutes offense in all instances. Again, it is by no means easy to bring the necessary personal sacrifice which the required forbearance demands. Then, too, in our day and age, we are quite generally likely to err in the direction of liberalism rather than in the direction of pietism.

The guiding principle here as always must be love and charity toward the weak brother. Paul puts it this way: "Love worketh no ill to his neighbor" (Rom. 13:10), and again: "Let all your things be done in charity (love)" (I Cor. 16:14). And the Apostle followed this principle in practice: though free, he freely became a servant unto all, that he might gain the more (I Cor. 9:19). For the sake of avoiding offense he even circumcised Timothy. Luther offers the following opinion: "Christ came into the world in order to tolerate, bear with, and receive the weak. If He were as impatient as we are, He would soon say to us: 'Away with you. I want nothing to do with you, for your faith is not as it should be.' Who would be helped in this way? . . . If they (i. e., the weak) are not strong today, the hour may come when they comprehend the Word better than we" (Erlanger, XIV, 236). The example of one pastor who did not touch alcoholic beverages during the life of the Prohibition Act and the restraint of another pastor who did not smoke on the streets of his community because it was predominantly of sectarian complexion demonstrate the personal practical application of this law of love.

On the one hand, therefore, one must zealously guard against offending the weak brother (and this includes also the weak brother beyond our immediate circles). On the other hand, one must equally earnestly strive not to support and bolster and build up such weakness. The plea against offense must never be used to cover malice or stubbornness. Above all, the weakness of the brother dare never be nurtured at the expense of doctrine. When the demand was made by the Judaizers that Titus be circumcised as an essential to his Christianity, Paul did not yield in the least, "that the truth of the Gospel might continue with you" (Gal. 2:5). When the request of the iconoclasts was voiced that the rite of the elevation of the host be abolished, Luther continued it for the express purpose of demonstrating freedom of action in matters indifferent (Nebraska, 1912, p. 42).

IV. PRACTICAL EXAMPLES

With the guidelines regarding adiaphora established from God's Word, there still remains a specific application of these principles in the church life and in the personal life of the individual Christian. (Such terms as 'church life' and 'personal life' are inadequate. Perhaps a better designation would be 'religious sphere' and 'secular sphere.') Other terms are: 'adiaphora in the wider sense' (all adiaphora) and 'adiaphora in the narrow sense' (domain of the church); entertainment adiaphora, political adiaphora, and church adiaphora. (Cf. Nebraska, 1912, p. 49.)

It is manifestly impossible for us to catalog every kind of adiaphoron. Such a list would be bounded only by the imagination, the observation, and the experience of the individual Christian. The field of casuistry is not only filled with adiaphora, but is largely composed of them. Their name is literally legion.

In the domain of the Church they center in the business affairs of the congregation, its church property, the order of service, church architecture, the building and its appointments, the altar, pulpit, organ, baptismal font, crucifix. Furthermore, the time and place of worship, the church year with its festival days; again, the order of service, kneeling, bowing the head, standing; in connection with Baptism, the manner of applying the water, sponsors, questions directed to them; in connection with the Lord's Supper, the kind of bread used, the manner of its distribution, the use of the common or the individual cup. Such rites as confirmation and ordination are adiaphora. Such arrangements as congregational meetings, constitutions, the officers of the church, the Sunday school, the Christian day school, the organizations within the congregation are per se adiaphora. Synod, membership in Synod, the officials and commissions of Synod, the essayist of Synod — all these, and many more, purely human arrangements and devices are, strictly speaking, adiaphora. (Nebraska, 1913, p. 11; cf. Walther, *Pastorale,* pp. 53–54.)

Without in the least attempting to discuss any or all of these individually, it is desirable to set forth some general principles:

Human ordinances are necessary for the welfare of the Church, both locally and nationally. "Let all things be done decently and in order," writes St. Paul (I Cor. 14:40). This is true in all matters of life; it is particularly applicable to all matters pertaining to church life, for therein, too, there is opportunity for growth in knowledge and appreciation. The exact records of the treasurer are not only good business procedure; they may also become an opportunity for growth in the grace of Christian stewardship. The outward manner in which we as communicants approach the Lord's Table is not an essential part of the Sacrament, but thereby good church decorum and the sanctity (in the sense of solemnity) of the occasion are furthered.

Such ordinances are properly the province of the Christian congregation and, as such, subject to change, which change should be made carefully and for a good reason, as the Formula of Concord attests (Art. X, *Triglot*, p. 829). Desirable liturgical changes would offer an illustration.

Although unanimity of opinion is not required in matters indifferent, yet it is desirable that as many members of the congregation as possible participate in any discussion and decision relating to them. Thus peace and order will be promoted. The building program which is launched on the basis of a one- or two-vote majority in a representation of one fourth of the membership is valid and binding, but certainly not ideal or commendable.

While the will of the majority cannot absolutely be imposed upon the minority, yet in the interest of harmony and prompted by love the minority should willingly yield. Thus the merits of the envelope system in church finances have been demonstrated, but the congregation will certainly not refuse the gift of an individual simply because he does not care to use envelopes.

Uniformity with sister congregations in the field of church adiaphora is desirable and, generally speaking, it is advantageous, but not essential. The order of service and the hymnal are cases in point.

Finally, if adiaphora assume a confessional character, they cease to be adiaphora. Examples of this kind have been cited above.

It is in his position as a citizen that the Christian is confronted by the most frequent changes in the nature of indifferent matters. Year after year new statutes circumscribe and curtail certain liberties or expand others for him. The global conflict served to underscore this truth. The Church is, to be sure, not interested in politics as such; the Christian, however, is most deeply concerned with the rightness or wrongness of a political and governmental action or legislation and will therefore make the fullest use possible of his privilege and duty as citizen to leaven his community and government with Christian principles.

With regard to the personal life of the individual Christian the questions to be answered are: Does God command it? Does He forbid it? Is there any statement in God's Word which applies to it? If so, it simply is no adiaphoron. Furthermore, does the law of love or the conscience of a brother make valid demands? If so, we voluntarily forego our freedom as long as no violation of the truth or selfish hypocrisy are involved. Whether it be amusement or occupation, inclination or necessity or association, whether it be the cigarette or the glass of beer, the movie or the game, the jest or the story — they can and must ultimately be evaluated by law and by love.

We cannot close without a word of gratitude to God for His revelation of our priceless freedoms as His children of grace. This is a glorious and comforting doctrine, this doctrine of Christian liberty to which this subject belongs. Christianity is a positive force. The Christian lives and grows and thrives not by command and prohibition only or chiefly; the Christian lives and grows and thrives by divine grace and love. God has not made machines out of us. He has freed us from the yoke of the Law; He has endowed us with sanctified hearts and minds; He has blessed us with liberties which are rooted in faith, motivated by love, and expressed in service. And thus Christianity becomes a fruitful life. Just think of it! Within the framework of His divine revelation, God's grace permits you and me, sinners though we be, to devise and use new and unprescribed ways and means of applying our Christianity, limited in number and variety only by a divinely enlightened understanding of His Word and a divinely inspired love toward our neighbor. That is grace, pure grace, exalted grace, divine grace.

The Papacy

THE subject before us for consideration at this session of your District is one which at first glance takes a very subordinate rank among the doctrines of Holy Writ. So it might seem as though it could have been omitted from the list of subjects submitted for discussion at the District conventions in preparation for the Centennial of our Synod. The object of this plan was to present in the form of essays the faith and confession of our fathers during these hundred years in the language of the children. Hence all the great doctrines of Scripture have been treated in these two years and now have been published in book form as a proof and testimony to the world that the old word of St. Peter is still true: "The Word of the Lord abideth forever."

But why include our subject in the list of these great truths? It does not pertain to a truth that is necessary for salvation. And yet it is of great importance. In the first place, historically it leads to the very heart of the Reformation. We customarily date the beginning of the Reformation as October 31, 1517, the day when Luther posted his Ninety-Five Theses against the indulgence traffic. That is well; the results justify it that we consider that act as the birth of the Reformation; it started Luther out on his way as Reformer. But the Theses contain little or nothing that others had not said before him. His attitude still is that the old Church is all right; it only has spots, and it must be cleansed. He is still convinced that the Holy Father in Rome does not know of all the abuses and the corruption in the Church; if he knew, he would soon change these things.

But then came blundering Eck, challenging Carlstadt to a public debate, but in his theses attacking chiefly Luther's statement in his Resolutions denying that the Roman Church at the time of

Gregory I was superior to other churches. (XVIII:174.) And Eck drew into the controversy another matter; his thesis read: "We deny the contention that the Roman Church was not superior to other churches before the time of Sylvester (fourth century), and on the contrary, we recognize that he who possessed the seat and the faith of St. Peter was always (*semper*) the successor and the Vicar-General of Christ." And so the primacy of the Pope became the subject of the Leipzig Debate in July, 1519. Luther, preparing for this debate, examined the Papacy both on Scriptural and historical grounds; and gradually, as he got one glimpse after the other of the chasm that yawned between the ancient and the medieval Church, he also realized where the real source of all the corruption in the Church lay. Dec. 11, 1518, he wrote his friend Link: "I shall send you my trifles, in order that you may see whether I rightly suspect that the true Antichrist, as Paul depicts him II Thess. 2:3 ff., is ruling at the Roman Curia." And on March 13, 1519, to Spalatin: "I am studying the decretals of the Popes, preparing for my disputation, and (I whisper it in your ear) I do not know whether the Pope is Antichrist or his apostle."

This became the turning point in Luther's career. He now consciously became the Reformer. He saw that a conflict would come which might end in death for him and a split in the Church; but he went ahead deliberately. And he knew, too, that this fiction of the primacy of the Pope had to be put out of the way first before any other reforms could be successfully carried out; the conclusions drawn from this teaching had always been the weapon with which the Pope had frustrated all previous reform efforts (the Pope's arbitrary excommunication and interdict). So in 1520 he issued his three greatest books: the *Letter to the Christian Nobility of the German Nation; On the Babylonian Captivity of the Church;* and *The Freedom of a Christian Man.* So the power of the Pope was broken; he threatened to use his old sword, to lay the interdict on Germany if Luther was not delivered up, only to discover that through Luther's service the people had learned that the Pope's sword was nothing but tin: he had not that power to close heaven to an individual or a nation arbitrarily. And the Reformation was completed successfully.

Because of the religious laxity in the world today and through all kinds of political intrigues the power of the Papacy is again growing. And the Papacy is still one of the greatest enemies of the true Gospel of Christ. And still in place is the wish and prayer of Luther with which he sent those delegates to Augsburg when he had to stay behind at the Koburg: *"Deus vos impleat odio papae!"* May God fill you with hatred of the Pope, i. e., of this institution, the Papacy.

The discussion of this topic, then, should be eminently practical. We must be on our guard against this enemy. There is a tendency to think: Rome was, of course, a vicious enemy in the days of the Reformation and the religious wars. But today we are tolerant; even Rome does not persecute any more. Rome has reformed, too, since those days. — Well, just at present, and particularly in this country, it does not pay to persecute with fire and sword. But there are other ways, more refined ways, of killing opposition — until opposition becomes weak — then it might pay again to go back to the Middle Ages. And reform? Yes, thanks to the general change in public opinion, changed by the Lutheran Reformation, a clergy of the moral type so prevalent in the days of the *Epistolae Obscurorum Virorum*, could not exist today. But in the essentials, in her doctrine, the Papacy has not changed one hair's breadth. Nor have the papal bulls, the *Unam Sanctam* of Boniface VIII and the *Syllabus Errorum* of Pius IX (1864) been changed to this day.

It will therefore be profitable to review the characteristics of the Papacy which stamp it an enemy of Protestantism, whose every success means a curbing of the pure Gospel and whose victory would mean the end of the Lutheran Church.

I. HISTORY OF THE PAPACY

To be exact, we must distinguish between the Papacy and the Roman Catholic Church. That is not always done; the two terms are used as synonyms. And the two are so closely linked together that in fact they cannot be separated today. The Roman Church is so totally dependent on the Papacy that the two stand and fall together. But theoretically the difference is there; the Papacy is not the Roman Catholic Church; it is an institution in that Church. At certain times and in certain places the Roman Church has existed without the Papacy. For the first seven or eight names on the Catholic list of bishops of Rome there is no historic evidence;

when a Roman historian admits that and says that these names are accepted on faith because the Church says so, it may surely be set down as fact. Then, the Papacy in its modern form, as it is today, exists only since July 18, 1870, and the Papal Constitution *Aeternus Pater* of Pius IX.

Not everything that we say about the Papacy, therefore, can be applied to the Roman Church. Nothing good can be said about the Papacy. It is a thoroughly unchristian institution. No one of us would say that of the Roman Church.

How old is the Papacy? Who was the first Pope? Different answers are given to these questions. Roman Catholics say, There has been a Pope ever since Christ said to Peter, "Thou art Peter, and upon this rock I will build My Church," Matt. 16:18. Every Lutheran knows that that answer is wrong; it rests on false exegesis, which we shall take up later. — Among Protestant writers there is great divergence of opinion as to who should be called the first Pope. Some say, Boniface III († 607); he was the first to take the title "Universal Bishop" from the Roman emperor Phocas. Others hold that Gregory VII († 1085) should have that distinction, because it was he who centralized power in the Church in the Roman bishop and emancipated the Papacy from the control of the secular authorities. But while Gregory evidently marks a new stage in the development of the Papacy, what he brought in was only the actual enactment of a claim already made before him. The Pseudo-Isidorian Decretals were in use for two hundred years before Gregory.

The history of these Decretals goes back to the Roman abbot Dionysius Exiguus († 556), who gathered the decrees of general councils, plus some papal decretals from 384—498, as the law for the whole Church. They were called the Isidorian Decretals after Bishop Isidore of Seville († 636), who published the most complete edition of the Decretals. But in the first half of the ninth century appeared another collection, published under the title *Collectio Isidori Mercatoris*, containing 59 letters and decretals of the 30 oldest bishops of Rome, from Clement I to Miltiades († 313), most of them fictitious or forged; the forged Donation of Constantine; 39 false decrees of later Popes; acts of several unauthentic councils, 314—731. The whole collection was attributed to Isidore of Seville. Pope Nicholas I in 860 claimed that these documents had been in Roman archives from the beginning. It is the greatest literary forgery in the history of the world. From the contents it is evident that the object was to strengthen the authority of the bishops, particularly to establish the primacy of the Pope. Here we read: Christ made Peter ruler over all others; the Roman bishop has the rule over the whole Church and the world; he is called *Mater, caput, apex, cardo omnium ecclesiarum, quasi totius orbis caput* (Mother, head, crown, hub of all churches, as it were, the head of the whole world); disobedience to the Pope is disobedience to Christ Himself; clerics and laics, people and princes, must obey him in all spiritual matters; the Pope's rules are placed alongside of God's commandments, so that the emperor, too, must obey them. Gregory VII, far from initiating these claims, based his far-reaching demands on these forgeries. Thomas Aquinas, Bellarmine, were misled by (or used?) these spurious documents. The whole fabric of the Canon Law was reared on this rotten foundation; Gratian's *Decretum* of 1151 quotes the epistles of Popes of the first four centuries 324 times; 313 of these quotations are from letters now known to be spurious. Hincmar of Rheims († 882) already expressed his doubts about the collection, called it a honeyed poison cup; nevertheless he used it when it came in handy. Later Nicholas of Cusa († 1464) and Lorenzo Valla († 1457) exposed the fraud, and Caesar Baronius († 1607) in his *Annales Ecclesiastici* spoke with indignation of it. The whole matter speaks loudly of the uncritical spirit of the age; it should have been easy to discover the fraud. The decretals were written in Frankish Latin. A letter of Bishop Victor of Rome to Bishop Theophilus of Alexandria was included — when Victor lived 200 years before Theophilus! Institutions were mentioned (fief) which did not come into existence until 200 years after the date of the document!

Hence the Papacy is older than Gregory VII. Nor does the fact that he took the title "Universal Bishop" stamp Boniface III the first Pope; one of the patriarchs of Constantinople, John Jejunator, claimed the title before.

There are three essential claims that make the Papacy what it is: That the Pope is head and foundation of Christendom; that the Pope is the infallible teacher of Christendom; that sinners can find salvation only in the Pope's Church. We must trace these claims back to their beginning to find the beginning of the Papacy;

and all three claims antedate Trent, the Vatican Council, the *Unam Sanctam* of Boniface VIII, Canossa and Gregory VII, the Pseudo-Isidore, and the title of Universal Bishop.

Basic in these claims of the Papacy is this, that the government of the Church culminates in the bishop of Rome. The idea of human rulers, of leaders with authority in the Church, is so evidently contrary to the will of Christ that we look for its origin. Christ said, "One is your Master, even Christ; and all ye are brethren," Matt. 23:8. But more than once we read of a discussion among the disciples of Christ as to the rank they would hold in the kingdom of Christ. We read of contentions among the Corinthians, party strife, setting up one or the other of the Apostles or early preachers as a party leader. Peter in his First Epistle warns the elders to feed the flock, but not to lord it over them; evidently there was a reason for this warning. St. John, in his Third Epistle, speaks of "Diotrephes, who loveth to have pre-eminence among them." These are the seeds from which the Papacy grew. St. Paul already can write to the Thessalonians (II Thess. 2:7) that "the mystery of iniquity doth already work."

The development of this power concentration in the Roman bishop is very gradual. St. Paul's prophecy indicates that there is something hindering it. Tertullian, Ambrose, and Chrysostom held that "he who now letteth" (II Thess. 2:7) was the Roman government; and that seems right. By restrictive measures placed on all illicit religions (and Christianity was that until Constantine), sometimes by persecution, the imperial government held back the systematic development of this power policy in the Church. But gradually the monarchical episcopate developed; the conception of the Church changed; the Church was that visible organization governed by the bishops. This concentration of power, once begun, fostered by the example of the imperial government, resulted in the Papacy. Alongside of this crept another error which helped to make the Papacy a success: this, that New Testament pastors are a special priesthood, similar to that of the Old Testament, ordained by God through the bishops; they form a special caste, separate from and above the people. Through the ordination they received a special faculty (*charisma*) which other Christians did not have. They were the spirituals (*Geistliche*), the people the laity.

The Papacy

The episcopate is a gradual, perhaps a natural, development. The Roman Catholic view is expressed in the Canons and Decrees of the Council of Trent: "Bishops, being the successors of the Apostles, are placed by the Holy Ghost to govern the Church of God, and to be superior to their presbyters or priests." That is all *ex post facto* argument. In the whole New Testament there is not a trace of the Apostles' appointing any man to succeed them. St. Paul identifies elders, or presbyters, and bishops, Acts 20:17 and 28; Titus 1:5-7 (also Phil. 1:1; I Tim. 3:1, 8; I Pet. 5:1). Nobody knows how and why a difference between the two was established. All the hypotheses advanced are just guesses. I think most logical is the natural development outlined in Meusel, *Kirchliches Handlexikon*, sub *Bischof*. When the Church grew and more congregations were organized in a city and vicinity, the conference of their pastors had to have a chairman. He was perhaps the senior. The others would naturally go to him for advice. When action was proposed, he was the executive officer who acted in the name of all. And in the course of time he alone was called bishop; the others were presbyters. This may go back to apostolic times. Perhaps the *angelos* of the seven churches addressed by John in his Revelation was such a bishop. By the time the Epistle of Clement was written (ca. 95) the episcopate is established. This letter was written from Rome to Corinth, to help remove the dissension and party strife in that church. As a means to accomplish that, to establish and preserve unity in the Church, Clement points to the evidently already existing episcopate. "Our Apostles also knew through our Lord Jesus Christ that there would be a strife on account of the office of the episcopate. For this reason, therefore, inasmuch as they had obtained a perfect foreknowledge of this, they appointed those ministers already mentioned and afterwards gave instructions that, when these should fall asleep, other approved men should succeed them in their ministry."

This also points to a new phase in church history which fostered the development of the episcopate. Clement of Rome holds that orderly succession of bishops will prevent division. It is easy to see why at that time it was felt that some new bond of unity was necessary. The Apostles had died. Error was creeping in, and error of the most insidious type. Gnosticism in simply countless variations attempted to establish Christianity as a world religion by making it palatable to every kind of taste; it was to offer particularly to cultivated men a universal solvent of all religious and philosophical problems on the basis of revelation. As a rule, the Gnostics did not cast aside the apostolic writings; they used them for the support of their own views by various exegetical devices; allegory lent itself well to their purpose. And not only did they support their teaching by arbitrary interpretation of apostolic writings; they also produced forgeries, unwritten teachings of the Apostles and apocryphal gospels. This led the Church, on the one hand, to establish the true apostolic sense of the apostolic writings. How did the Apostles themselves explain these controverted passages in their letters? The answer was sought in the tradition of the Apostles, transmitted by the uninterrupted succession of bishops and thus preserved inviolate in the episcopacy. Here, then, was evidently the chief factor for the preservation of unity in the Church: the episcopate.

So Clement already implies the idea of the apostolic succession. What is merely implied by Clement we find clearly stated by Ignatius of Antioch, who on his way to prison and martyrdom in Rome under the emperor Trajan wrote seven letters, six to various churches, one to Polycarp. The chief burden of all these letters is the imperative need of unity; and the episcopacy is the means whereby order and unity are to be preserved. He writes: "Be zealous to do all things in harmony with God, with the bishop presiding in the place of God and the presbyters in the place of the council of the Apostles and the deacons, who are most dear to me, entrusted with the services of Jesus Christ. Be united with the bishop and with those who preside over you as an example and lesson of immortality. As, then, the Lord Jesus was united with the Father and did nothing without Him, neither by Himself nor through the Apostles, so do you nothing without the bishop and the presbyters" (Ad Magnes., VI, VII). "Wherever the bishop appears, let the congregation be present; just as wherever Jesus Christ is, there is the catholic Church" (Ad Smyrn., VIII). To him the bishop stands in the place of Jesus, his presbyters in the place of the Apostles; and on loyalty to them depends the unity of the Church. At the same time the bishop and his presbyters are the marks of the true Church. The trail is taken up by Irenaeus († 202), who attributes to the bishops a certain gift of grace for the custody of truth; separatists, therefore, who withdraw from the "principal succession," are heretics who have broken away from the truth. The bishop is not merely the head of the local church; he has a relation to the Church Universal; he is a part of the episcopate, which is one and single. And the climax for the time is reached in Cyprian, bishop of Carthage (258), who attributes distinct sacerdotal functions to the bishops; they are priests representing Christ, the successors of the Apostles, the conservators of apostolic grace, and the authoritative interpreters of apostolic truth; without them the Church would be without that grace which it is to impart to men, and so would cease to exist.

This again points to a significant change: a different conception of the Church. In the beginning, Church meant the communion of believers in Christ. It is a spiritual house, I Pet. 2:5; Eph. 2:22. There is no external sign by which one can recognize the spiritual bond that unites them, Luke 17:20-21. But by the beginning of the third century a change is evident; the conception of the Church changes from that of an invisible communion of believers to that of a visible organization, with the bishops as representatives; and what was true of the invisible Church, that outside of it no one can be saved, was applied to the visible organization. Montanus already (156) found it necessary to testify that while the bishop alone can excommunicate and reinstate, there can be absolution and salvation without that. With Ignatius (115) the term catholic Church still signifies Christians in general, the Church of which Christ is the Center, in contrast to the local church, of which the bishop is the center. With Irenaeus (202) catholic Church has come to signify orthodox Christianity in its organized form in contrast to heretical sects. The Church is a visible organization governed by the bishops; they, by the laying on of hands, were endowed with a very special faculty for preserving the truth; they received a special *charisma* from on high that raised them above the common mass of Christians to a position of mediatorship between God and the sinner. So the clergy was separated from the laity; the clergy became a hierarchical corporation.

The next step in this desire for visible unity of the church organization is naturally centralization of power in one head. This received a powerful impetus when in the fourth century the Church and the Roman state were united. There was the ever-present example of the empire; how marvelously the monarchical system worked there! The first Christian emperors settled controversies in the Church in Roman style: *Sic volo, sic iubeo* — and whoever objected was banished or worse. That was effective. With this example before them, and — forget it not! — bishops still being men who had the same ambitious heart that the sons of Zebedee had when they made their well-known request of the Lord, Mark 10:35 ff., is it surprising that the ruling trend in the hierarchy became centralization in one head? And with that desire in mind, most eyes naturally looked toward Rome!

What accounts for the prominence of Rome? Not, in the first place, its traditional association with Peter, but the importance and location of the city. Rome was the capital of the world, politically, socially, and intellectually. Statistics are always somewhat problematical in that and the following ages; but Rome was a large city; its population is given as anywhere between 600,000 and 1,500,000. The emperor lived there, and there were the headquarters of the government that ruled practically the entire civilized world. All roads led to Rome, literally so; on the market place in Rome stood the golden milestone from which issued the great military and commercial highways that led out into all parts of the empire. Even after the Roman Empire fell, Rome remained the center of the world. Down to the discovery of America, Europe was governed by the thalassic nations, the nations around the Mediterranean Sea; and Rome lies right in the center of them all. It soon became the spiritual center of the Church. The Roman church became the largest in Christendom. Influential people joined that church. St. Paul testifies that the church in Rome was zealous and liberal, Rom. 1:8. It stands to reason that the bishops of that church were usually outstanding men, men of deep knowledge, powerful mind, great energy, and strict orthodoxy. For that reason alone men from the vicinity, and increasingly from distant parts, would seek advice in Rome. The bishops of Rome would hold chairmanship at synods.

And then tradition entered in. Irenaeus (202) and Tertullian (222) already emphasized the exalted position of Rome for the custody of apostolic doctrine; there the great Apostles Peter and Paul have taught and lived and died; the trustworthiness of traditions preserved there is pre-eminent; it is impossible that other traditions should disagree with the traditions of the church in Rome. — Cyprian (258) bases the unity of the Church on the fact that it is built on the one Peter; it is an external, visible unity ruled by the bishops, and these again have their source in Peter, to whom Jesus originally has given all power in the Church. Someone has said that Cyprian laid the egg of primacy of Peter; but the bishops of Rome hatched something out of it that Cyprian never intended. Cyprian contends that Peter had no greater power than the other Apostles; he insists on the equality of all bishops; "No one of us makes himself bishop of bishops, nor constrains his colleagues with tyrannical intimidations to necessity of obedience, since every bishop has right and power to act as he deems right and can no more be judged by another than he can judge others, but all must await the judgment of our Lord Jesus." Yet he holds that the Roman church is the "mother and root of the catholic Church, the principal church, whence sacerdotal union proceeded." Incidentally Cyprian is the first bishop who was called *Papa*.

Around 200 A. D. also appeared the *Clementine Romance* (Dallmann), the Pseudo-Clementine Letters, allegedly written by Clement, first, second, or third bishop of Rome (97), representing Peter as primate of the Apostles, appointed by Christ Himself, founder and first bishop of the church in Rome; Peter himself had then appointed Clement as his successor and the heir of the vicarage of Christ. The letters are acknowledged forgeries; but they were used by Roman bishops to prove their claims of being the successors of Peter and rulers of the Church.

We have at this time also the first attempt on the part of a Roman bishop to exercise the authority allegedly given to him. Bishop Victor of Rome (†198) excommunicated the bishop of Ephesus, Polycrates, and "all brethren thereat," bishops and churches of a whole province, because they held to a different Easter date than he, the bishop of Rome. But "it was too early in the year, Rome's lightning struck the earth and kindled no fire, only made a great deal of noise; and Christendom at that time protested even against that noise. Not only did the Asiatics persist in their former usage, as though nothing had happened, but there arose great indignation in quarters where there was agreement with Victor on the Easter date, and a sharp rebuke issued, not against the obstinate Asiatic and his companions who boldly and impertinently had dared to oppose the authority of the Vicar of Christ and successor of Peter, but against the arrogant pontifex in Rome, who had done an unheard-of thing. Chiefly did the noted Bishop of Lyon, Irenaeus, protest" (A. L. Graebner, *Lehre und Wehre*, 35, (46 f.). The whole deal is reported in Eusebius, *Church History*, V, 27 f. Victor's attempt to extend his authority even into the Orient had failed.

And yet there was a lasting meaning to this: it was a first step. It was no longer an unheard-of thing that a bishop of Rome claimed jurisdiction over the whole Church. When it would be repeated, there might not be a Polycrates and an Irenaeus to protest and oppose him. So it was understood when the very next bishop of Rome, Zephyrinus († 218), called himself *Pontifex Maximus, Episcopus Episcoporum*. This time Tertullian protested against that title, also against his citing words of his predecessors as a final decision in a matter. But patience; perhaps next time he will be successful! In Roman Catholic history we must never forget this: Rome has always known and used the force of persistence. No matter how much a claim was opposed at first, it kept on asserting it. If the objection was too strong, it kept silence for a while, but at the first opportune moment re-iterated the old claim. This everlasting hammering away at the same idea through the centuries has made Rome what it is.

So Bishop Stephan I († 257) opposed Cyprian's and the Africans' practice of baptizing heretics not with reasons but by stating that he, the successor of Peter, was of different opinion than they; he cited tradition to support his protest. But Cyprian answered with I Tim. 6:3 f.: "If any man teach otherwise and consent not to wholesome words, even the words of our Lord Jesus Christ, and to the doctrine which is according to godliness, he is proud, knowing nothing." Stephen's reference to tradition Cyprian met with: "Custom without truth is nothing but old error."

Then the emperor, though a heathen, took a hand in the matter. Paul of Samosata, bishop of Antioch, was deposed because of heresy — he denied the deity of Christ; but he refused to move and was upheld by the Jewish queen Zenobia of Palmyra. Then Emperor Aurelian defeated Zenobia, and the Christians of Antioch appealed to him to remove their old bishop. And the

The Papacy

emperor decided that the see of Antioch should go to him who was appointed by the bishop of Italy and Rome. A victory for Rome! But note that in this controversy in 270 the Christians of Antioch addressed not Bishop Felix of Rome, but Emperor Aurelian.

Under Constantine the Church became a state Church, in which the Emperor played the dominant role. He invited the bishops to come to Nicaea and practically took the chair. Bishop Sylvester of Rome was absent, was not even represented. Yet under Constantine Rome received another boost. Centralization of power marched on; the bishop in a large metropolis became metropolitan, later archbishop, with supervision over all the bishops in an exarchate. Then, on a parallel with the four praetorian prefectures, the Church was divided into four (later five) patriarchates; three (later four) in the east, one in the west. In 326 the emperor left Rome and made "New Rome," Byzantium, his capital, later called Constantinople. Rome did not like that. But the emperor gave his Lateran Palace in Rome to the bishop, and he found that in the absence of the emperor he, the bishop, was now considered the emperor's representative. Besides, Rome was the only apostolic seat in the west; and in the west, not in the east, now came the great expansion of the Church, and everybody in the west came to Rome for guidance and decision. In the east there were several patriarchs; they often disagreed. What was more natural than that appeal should be made to Rome? And what more natural than that Rome should make use of the situation? And we'll have to admit that in the various doctrinal controversies, when the smoke of battle settled down, Rome was usually found on the side of orthodoxy.

In the Vatican Council in 1870, Cardinal Strossmayer, who opposed the infallibility decree, said, "In the first four centuries there was no Pope." We are a little in doubt whether we should call the bishop of Rome Pope by this time; but this is sure: he was not acknowledged as Pope. Catholics like to point to the Council of Sardica in Illyria (343), which resolved: A condemned bishop might appeal to Julius, the bishop of Rome, to appoint judges for a new trial. But note: He evidently did not have that right before; he could act only in a certain prescribed case and only when it was voluntarily brought to him; he could only appoint the judges; and this right was given to Julius only, not to successors. In 378 the emperor again took a hand in the development of the Papacy. Asked to compel rebellious bishops in Italy and Illyricum to be tried in Rome, the nineteen-year-old Gratian with one stroke of the pen gave Pope Damasus patriarchal jurisdiction over the whole Western Empire and placed the civil power at his command. This Pope Damasus was the first to declare boldly that Peter had taught him how to steer the Church.

What position did Christians accord to the bishop of Rome at this time? In 381 the first Council of Constantinople resolved: "Let the bishop of Constantinople have the precedence of honor next to the bishop of Rome, for as much as it is New Rome." The bishop of Rome is to have first place *honoris causa*; he is *primus inter pares*; he is to have the honor to be the first among equal bishops. Ambrose (397) gave the bishop of Rome the same position in the Church that the emperor had in the empire; but he called Peter's primacy one of confession and faith, not of rank; Paul was equal to Peter. And Strossmayer said at the Vatican Council, the councils were still called by the emperor, without the knowledge, at times against the will, of the Roman bishop.

But now we come to the period when the signs of the real Papacy become plainer. Bishop Siricius (384—398) is the first to show evident marks of Antichrist. His first decretal, dated Feb. 11, 385, states that those who differ with him separate from the rock on which Christ built His Church; he, the bishop, is the head of the body, the heir of Peter's office, in whose person Peter himself bears the burden of the oppressed and who in all things stands under Peter's protection. He particularly praised celibacy, called marriage unclean, a bestial relationship, citing Rom. 8:8: "They that are in the flesh cannot please God." Clearly an Antichristian teaching, Dan. 11:37; I Tim. 4:3. His second successor, Innocent I (402—417), demanded that all churches follow the usages and obey the decisions of Rome. He was the first to make the direct connection between the alleged successors of Peter and the primacy in Christendom (Founder of Papal Monarchy — Dallmann). His successor, Zosimus (417—418), declared that no one may question the decision of the Roman See; the successors of Peter inherit from him an authority equal to that which the Lord gave to Peter.

The next bishop, Boniface I (418–422), is surely Pope in the full sense of the word. He claims the organization of the Church was begun by Peter; the Council of Nicaea did not decide anything about the Pope, because all things had already been given to him; the Roman church is the head of all churches on earth; whosoever separates from her ceases to be a member of the spiritual body and separates himself from the Christian religion. For all this he uses the full papal method of proof: distortion of Scripture, forgery of existing church orders (e. g., the Nicene canons, which, by the way, his predecessor had done before him), and invention of new canons and decretals.

And so we arrive at Leo I (440–461), whom history calls the founder of the medieval Papacy. He claimed that Christ made Peter the chief of the Apostles. At the Council of Chalcedon (451) his legates for the first time obtained the presidency. Emperor Valentinian III gave him the charter of the modern Papacy: "Then only will peace continue throughout the Church when the bishop of Rome is recognized by all as lord and master. . . . Henceforth it shall not be permitted to dispute over church matters or to oppose the orders of the primate in Rome. . . . What is ordered by the Apostolic See, by virtue of its authority, shall be law to all, so that, if a bishop refuse compliance with the judicial sentence of the Roman primate, he shall be compelled by the provincial government to appear before him." Then Hilarius (461–468) called himself "Vicar of Peter, to whom since the resurrection of Christ belong the keys of the kingdom." Gelasius I (492–496) is called "Christ's Vicar." He says, "As the morn receives her light from the sun, so the king receives his brilliancy from the Pope." He declared Matt. 16:18 the sole ground of the Roman primacy. His letters claim almost everything the Vatican Council of 1870 decreed. It is true that Gregory the Great (590–604), when the patriarch of Constantinople called himself Universal Bishop, said it was "a name of blasphemy, by which the honor of bishops is taken away, while it is madly assumed by one man for himself." "Whoever calls himself Universal Bishop, in his presumption is a forerunner of Antichrist." But soon after Boniface III (607) took the title Universal Bishop, and since his day the Popes use the formula "We will and command" in ratifying the election of bishops.

There remains only one point. Stephen II (752) crowned Pepin king of the Franks; and fifty years later Leo III (800) crowned Charlemagne emperor of the Western Empire — both used by Popes ever since to justify their claim that the Pope is superior to secular governments. Pepin in return gave Ravenna to Stephen — the nucleus of the Papal State.

Somewhere in this time, approximately 753, was manufactured the "Donation of Constantine," an alleged letter of Constantine the Great, written about 328–330, giving to "Blessed Sylvester" and his successors to the end of time, the Lateran Palace, crown, miter, escort, couriers, and horsemen, in short, all the retinue or courtly luster of an empire. It also conferred on them the city of Rome, all Italy, and the provinces, places, and cities of the western region, with jurisdiction over Antioch, Alexandria, Constantinople, and Jerusalem. As reason for the donation is given: "It is not right that the earthly emperor have power where the prince of priests and head of the Christian religion has been installed by the heavenly Emperor." — The first historic evidence of the existence of this letter is in 868. Since that time it has been used by the Popes to support chiefly their pretensions to temporal power. The suspicion therefore has always been voiced that the forgery was produced by papal instigation. There is, however, no evidence for that; it was probably made in France, perhaps under the same auspices as the Pseudo-Isidorian Decretals. But the Popes were glad to make use of it when it did appear. It was denounced as a forgery as early as Otto III's time by his chancellor Leo of Vercelli; later by Arnold of Brescia (1152). Nicolas of Cusa exposed the fraud (1432); but particularly Lorenzo Valla (1440) made it sure that it was not genuine. Ulrich von Hutten republished the *Donatio Constantini* of Valla, dedicating it to Pope Leo X; and Luther thought very highly of Valla. Since the *Annales Ecclesiastici* of Caesar Baronius (1588) most Catholic historians have admitted the fraud.

So the Papacy originated. Even after that time it was not always acknowledged without opposition. Quite often the State refused to do so. Honorius (638) was branded a heretic. Bishops spoke highly of the Pope when they agreed with him; when they disagreed, they knew how to stress Gal. 2:11 against Matt. 16:18. The Popes strengthened the simple and crude basis on which their claim rests merely by unwavering, obstinate persistence and the ability to wait. Augustine seems to have adapted himself to what tradition offered without caring to investigate further as to its right or wrong. In the case of Pelagius he says: *"Iam de hac causa duo concilia missa sunt ad sedem apostolicam; inde etiam rescripta venerunt, causa finita est"* — giving rise to the slogan *"Roma locuta, causa finita."*

As we go on, there is until the late Middle Ages little or no opposition to the Papacy. The episcopate acknowledged it because, if they denied its right, they sawed off the limb on which they were sitting; if they were the successors of the Apostles and exercising their rights, then the Pope was the successor of Peter and so their head. And the laity was content with that centralized church organization because of the resultant order and unity. And Rome, by location and historical importance, had the power.

II. ROME'S TEACHING ON THE PAPACY

A. Peter's Primacy

What is Rome's official teaching on the Papacy? This: Jesus wanted to build His Church; hence He made Peter and, in him, his successors the foundation of His Church. He wanted to preserve His Church; hence He made Peter and, in him, his successors the teachers and leaders of His Church. He wanted to make His Church invincible; hence He set Peter and, in him, his successors to strengthen the faithful in their faith. And Peter was Bishop of Rome and appointed his successors.

It is best to cite the exact text of Rome's official document, the *Constitutio Dogmatica Prima de Ecclesia Christi*, "given at Rome in Public Session solemnly held in the Vatican Basilica in the year of our Lord one thousand eight hundred and seventy, on the eighteenth day of July." It is the translation published by Cardinal Manning. The document is headed: "Pius Bishop, Servant of the Servants of God, with the Approval of the Sacred Council, for an Everlasting Remembrance." "Chapter I — of the Institution of the Apostolic Primacy in Blessed Peter. — We therefore teach and declare that, according to the testimony of the Gospel, the primacy of jurisdiction over the universal Church of God was immediately and directly promised and given to Blessed Peter the Apostle by

Christ the Lord. For it was to Simon alone, to whom He had already said: Thou shalt be called Cephas (St. John 1:42), that the Lord after the confession made by him, saying: Thou art the Christ, the Son of the living God, addressed these solemn words: Blessed art thou, Simon Bar-Jona, because flesh and blood have not revealed it to thee, but My Father who is in heaven. And I say to thee that thou art Peter, and upon this rock will I build My Church, and the gates of hell shall not prevail against it. And I will give to thee the keys of the kingdom of Heaven. And whatsoever thou shalt bind upon earth, it shall be bound also in Heaven. And whatsoever thou shalt loose on earth, it shall also be loosed in Heaven. (St. Matt. 16:16-19.) And it was upon Simon alone that Jesus after His resurrection bestowed the jurisdiction of Chief Pastor and Ruler over all His fold in the words: Feed My lambs; feed My sheep (St. John 21:15-17). At open variance with this clear doctrine of Holy Scripture as it has been ever understood by the Catholic Church are the perverse opinions of those who, while they distort the form of government established by Christ the Lord in His Church, deny that Peter in his single person, preferably to all the other Apostles, whether taken separately or together, was endowed by Christ with a true and proper primacy of jurisdiction; or of those who assert that the same primacy was not bestowed immediately and directly upon Blessed Peter himself, but upon the Church, and through the Church on Peter as her Minister. — If anyone, therefore, shall say that Blessed Peter the Apostle was not appointed the Prince of all the Apostles and the visible Head of the whole Church Militant; or that the same directly and immediately received from the same Our Lord Jesus Christ a primacy of honor only, and not of true and proper jurisdiction; let him be anathema."

This same doctrine has been repeatedly stated. Pius IX (1846 to 1878) in his invitation "To all Protestants and Non-Catholics" said: "No one can deny or doubt that Jesus Christ Himself . . . built His Church in this world on Peter." Archbishop Ireland (1908) declared: "All who are in the Church, Apostles included, are built on Peter; all who are in the Church are fed, are strengthened, by Peter. Peter rules and governs; he is the sovereign." In the Bull *Unam Sanctam* (1302) Boniface VIII says: "In this one and holy Church there is one body and one head — not two heads as if it were a monster, namely, Christ and Christ's vicar, Peter, and Peter's successor."

There are chiefly three Bible passages on which they base this assumption that Jesus Himself gave Peter the primacy in the Church. The first is John 21:15, 17: Jesus said to Peter: "Feed My sheep; feed My lambs." Boniface VIII, in *Unam Sanctam*, after the previously quoted word, draws the conclusion: "For the Lord said to Peter himself, 'Feed My sheep.' 'My sheep,' He said, using a general term and not designating these or those sheep, so that we must believe that all the sheep were committed to him. If, then, the Greeks or others shall say that they were not entrusted to Peter and his successors, they must perforce admit that they were not of Christ's sheep, as the Lord says in John, 'There is one fold, and one shepherd.'" Why did Jesus say this to Peter? Cornelius a Lapide (van der Steen), Jesuit professor in Louvain and Rome († 1637) says: To make Peter and the Popes "head and chief of the Church; and that all the faithful, even the bishops, patriarchs, and apostles, are subject to him, and ought to be fed and ruled by him." This Roman exegesis of the text is a rather late discovery; it cannot be shown that anyone before Bernard in the twelfth century proposed it. Universally held was the exposition of St. Cyril of Alexandria († 444): Peter had grievously denied the Lord three times; therefore the Lord asked him three times: "Lovest thou Me?" And then, in the words under discussion Jesus "absolves the disgrace of his sin" and reinstates him as an Apostle. Far from Peter receiving a privilege in this passage, the whole occurrence must have humbled him; it reminded him of his sin and of his Lord's unmerited grace. By no conceivable exegesis can this text be made to say that Peter was to be the teacher and master of the Apostles and supreme and divinely appointed teacher of the whole Church at all times. Jesus recharged him with the same work that was given to all the Apostles. Peter himself in his First Epistle (5:2) bids his fellow elders to "feed the flock of God"; and Paul charges all the elders of Ephesus: "Feed the Church of God," Acts 20:28. One of the Cardinals of Pius X, his Secretary of State, Merry del Val, admitted that this text did not prove much for the supremacy of Peter; he said it is only used in addition to the other texts.

The second text isn't much better for their purposes. Luke 22: 31-32 the Lord said to Peter: "Simon, Simon, behold, Satan hath desired to have you, that he may sift you as wheat; but I have prayed for thee, that thy faith fail not; and when thou art converted, strengthen thy brethren." This is to prove that Peter can never err ("I have prayed for thee that thy faith fail not") and that he is to take Christ's place ("strengthen thy brethren"). The first attempt to apply this to Peter's primacy was made by Pope Pelagius II in his first letter to the bishop of Istria (586); but the Istrians in their reply denied that teaching. Then Pope Agatho took it up (680); Thomas Aquinas put it into his *Summa*. The Roman theologian Bellarmine quoted twenty patristic citations in its favor, all from Popes; but on examination of them eighteen of the twenty are taken from the false decretals. In reality there is not one word about a primacy of Peter in the text; Jesus prays for him that he may not remain in his sin, but arise and repent. And that word "strengthen" (*sterison*), which is to prove that Jesus appointed Peter to take His place, that word is not only used with reference to Peter, but also with reference to the activity of Paul, Rom. 1:11: "For I long to see you that I may impart unto you some spiritual gift, to the end ye may be established" (*eis to sterichthenai*); Acts 15: 41: "He went through Syria and Cilicia, confirming (*episterizoon*) the churches"; Acts 18:23: "And after he had spent some time there, he departed and went over all the country of Galatia and Phrygia in order, strengthening all the disciples"; of Paul and Barnabas, Acts 14:21-22: "They returned again to Lystra and to Iconium and Antioch, confirming (*episterizontes*) the souls of the disciples; of Judas and Silas, Acts 15:32: "Judas and Silas, being prophets also themselves, exhorted the brethren with many words and confirmed them" (*epesterixan*); of Timothy, I Thess. 3:2: "And sent Timotheus, our brother and minister of God and our fellow laborer in the Gospel of Christ, to establish you" (*eis to sterixai*). That papal explanation of "strengthen" was invented by Bellarmine ca. 1621.

Chiefly, however, it is Matt. 16:18-19 on which Catholics found their teaching of Peter's primacy: "And I say unto thee . . . that thou art Peter, and upon this rock I will build My Church; and the gates of hell shall not prevail against it. And I will give unto thee the keys of the kingdom of heaven; and whatsoever thou shalt bind on earth shall be bound in heaven; and whatsoever thou shalt loose on earth shall be loosed in heaven." The Roman explanation is best given in the words of Cardinal Gibbons, *Faith of Our Fathers*, p. 99 ff. (1876): "Here we find Peter confessing the Divinity of Christ, and in reward for that confession he is honored with the promise of the Primacy. Our Savior, by the words 'Thou art Peter' clearly alludes to the new name which He Himself had conferred upon Simon, when He received him into the number of His followers (John 1:42); and He now reveals the reason for the change of name, which was to insinuate the honor He was to confer on him, by appointing him President of the Christian Republic; just as God, in the Old Law, changed Abram's name to Abraham when He chose him to be the father of a mighty nation. The word *Peter*, in the Syro-Chaldaic tongue, which our Savior spoke, means *a rock*. The sentence runs thus in that language: '*Thou art a rock, and on this rock I will build My Church.*' Indeed, all respectable Protestant commentators have now abandoned, and even ridiculed, the absurdity of applying the word *rock* to anyone but to Peter; as the sentence can bear no other construction, unless our Lord's good grammar and common sense are called in question. Jesus, our Lord, founded but one Church, which He was pleased to build on Peter. Therefore any church that does not recognize Peter as its foundation stone is not the Church of Christ, and therefore cannot stand, for it is not the work of God. This is plain."

That text is today regarded as the Magna Charta of the Papacy as it was in the days of the Reformation. Nothing that has been said in these 400 years has made the least impression on Rome. I refer you to the late Roman Catholic advertisements in the Saint Louis newspapers. Neither have Lutherans yielded one point since the Smalcald Articles have become a confession of our Church.

Again, this present Roman interpretation of the text arose rather late in the Church. It was rejected by the most important early teachers of the Church. Hilarius (368), Gregory of Nyssa (400), Ambrose (397), Chrysostom (407), interpreted the *rock* as the confession of Peter; Jerome (420), Augustine (430), as Christ Himself. From v. 19 they infer a primacy of honor for Peter, but only in so far as Christ gave to Peter alone at first what later He gave to all Apostles and, through them, to all bishops. Tertullian (222) was the first to say that the rock is Peter; but he limits it to Peter personally and does not extend it to others as Cardinal Gibbons does (p. 100): "Thou and thy successors shall be My visible representatives to the end of time" — for which there is not a shadow of authority in the text.

Now no Protestant will deny that the words of the text were addressed to Peter. "Thou art Peter," the Lord says; "I will give thee . . . thou shalt bind . . . thou shalt loose." The whole statement is addressed to Peter and could not intelligently be referred to any other person. Nor will we deny that these words of the Lord distinguish Peter above the other disciples. But we must go to the complete story to find out why Jesus so distinguishes Peter. Jesus had asked the disciples, "Whom do men say that I, the Son of Man, am?" They answered, "Some say that Thou art John the Baptist; some, Elias; and others, Jeremias, or one of the Prophets." Then Jesus asked them, all the disciples again, "But whom say ye that I am?" To the first question there were various answers, and no doubt one disciple said this, the other that, relating what each had heard. To this second question there could only be one answer; and Peter happens to be the first one to answer. Will anyone question that what he said was the faith of all, that, therefore, he answered for all? But Peter was the first to be ready with his confession; and so the Lord directs His answer to Peter, too, and so does distinguish Peter. But why? Evidently because of what Peter had said. Even the Catholic will have to admit that Christ's words to Peter require as their logical *prius* the confession of Peter; that if Peter had not spoken as he did, the Lord would not have spoken to Peter as He did. We have no right to assume that the Lord had any other reason to speak as He did; there is nothing in the text to warrant that. If anything like the primacy of Peter as conceived by the Roman Church is laid down here, other Scripture must be adduced, and history will have to be called upon for its witness to substantiate the claim.

But appealing to other Scripture does not produce this substantiation of Peter's primacy. On the contrary! In the first place, if Jesus meant to declare Peter the foundation of the Church, why did He not say, "Thou art Peter, and on thee will I build My Church"? That would have been natural. Again, why does He change the form of the word if both mean the same? Why does He say, "Thou art *Petros*, and on this *petra* will I build My Church"?

It is evident that there must be an intended difference between the two. Next, we have the same record of Peter's confession in Luke 9:18-23 and Mark 8:27-34; but in neither of the two is there a word about the Church's being built on Peter; particularly should we expect that in Mark if it were a fact, as Mark was Peter's friend and Peter, so it is generally assumed, Mark's informant when he wrote his Gospel. When St. Paul speaks of the grand temple of the Christian Church, Eph. 2:19-21, he says: "Now, therefore, ye are no more strangers and foreigners, but fellow citizens with the saints and of the household of God; and are built upon the foundation of the Apostles and Prophets, Jesus Christ Himself being the chief Cornerstone; in whom all the building, fitly framed together, groweth unto an holy temple in the Lord." When St. John in his vision, Rev. 21:10-14, sees "that great city, the holy Jerusalem, descending out of heaven from God," he says: "And the wall of the city had twelve foundations, and in them the names of the twelve Apostles of the Lamb."

Moreover, there is no evidence in Scripture that the Apostles knew that Peter was their primate. On the contrary, Matt. 18:1 we read: "At the same time came the disciples unto Jesus, saying, Who is the greatest in the kingdom of heaven?" What a fine opportunity to appoint a Pope if He wanted one! But Jesus rebukes them for such desires. He "called a little child unto Him and set him in the midst of them and said, Verily I say unto you, Except ye be converted and become as little children, ye shall not enter into the kingdom of heaven." Again, Luke 22:24: "And there was also a strife among them which of them should be accounted the greatest." This was on that Thursday evening, after the institution of the Lord's Supper, in that upper room in Jerusalem or on the road to Gethsemane; by that time the disciples should have known of the primacy of Peter had it been a fact; but they did not. Again a fine opportunity to appoint a Pope; but Christ speaks a different language. He does not point to Peter and say, There is your head and your ruler; He says, vv. 25-26: "The kings of the Gentiles exercise lordship over them, and they that exercise authority upon them are called benefactors. But ye shall not be so; but he that is greatest among you, let him be as the younger; and he that is chief, as he that doth serve." Jesus put all Apostles on the same level. Matt. 19:28 Jesus tells them: "Verily I say unto you, That ye which have followed Me, in the regeneration, when the Son of Man shall sit in the throne of His glory, ye also shall sit upon twelve thrones, judging the twelve tribes of Israel." They all equally are the branches of Him, the Vine, John 15:5; His witnesses, v. 27. All shall receive the Comforter, John 14:16, and all were filled with the Holy Ghost on Pentecost Day, Acts 2:4. All received that great commission, Matt. 28:19-20: "Go ye, therefore, and teach all nations," etc.

Neither does Peter himself know anything of such a primacy given to him. We have a sufficient number of expressions from Peter's mouth and pen to be able to tell what he held on this matter. There is his sermon on Pentecost Day, Acts 2:14-36, in which all Apostles are put on equal standing, vv. 32, 37. There is his sermon to the Jews after the healing of the lame man, Acts 3:12-26; his defense before the Sanhedrin, Acts 4:8-12; his sermon before Cornelius, Acts 10:34-43; nowhere a sign that he considers himself more than the others. Then the first council of the Apostles, Acts 15. Peter did not call it; he did not preside in the meeting; indications in Acts 15 are that James presided, and Eusebius in his *Church History*, Book 2, chap. 28, says so. Peter at this council asked for the floor and spoke at length; what a great opportunity to make his demands: "*Sic volo, sic iubeo!* By the virtue of the power given me by Christ, this is what must be done!" None of that; he simply tells his story; not a trace in the whole chapter of any prerogative of Peter. The fact is that papal writers are totally disappointed in this council; they do not directly say so, but they indicate it plainly by their desperate exertions, their evasions and subterfuges, their ridiculous exegesis of this chapter, in the attempt to prove Peter's primacy! And after this council Peter disappears from the Acts; Paul becomes the dominating personage. Finally, we have two letters of Peter, in which there is not a trace of a claim of primacy. When he speaks of himself, he says, I Pet. 5:1: "who am also an elder"; II Pet. 1:1: "a servant and an Apostle of Jesus Christ"; and he means just that; his words are not hypocritical as the Pope's are (e. g., Boniface VIII in the bull *Unam Sanctam*), when he calls himself "Servant of servants."

In the whole New Testament none of the Apostles or of the other disciples anywhere, at any time, or in any way, give even

The Papacy

the least hint of a primacy of Peter. On the contrary, Gal. 2:11 Paul writes: "When Peter was come to Antioch, I withstood him to the face, because he was to be blamed." Peter, fearing legalistic Jewish Christians, had weakened and did not dare to confess by his actions that the Ceremonial Law is abrogated in the New Testament; and Paul publicly rebuked him, v. 14: "If thou, being a Jew, livest after the manner of Gentiles and not as do the Jews, why compellest thou the Gentiles to live as do the Jews?" And Peter took the correction: II Pet. 3:15 he calls him "our beloved brother Paul." Try it on the Pope today! (Dallmann.) Again, Paul testifies to the elders of Ephesus that he has kept back nothing that was profitable to them, Acts 20:20; that he has not shunned to declare unto them all the counsel of God, v. 27; yet nowhere in his many writings does he say a single word about the supremacy of Peter or of any privilege he enjoys before the other Apostles — surely, according to Romanists, one of the most important truths! In fact, St. Paul directly claims that he, Paul, is the equal of any of the Apostles, II Cor. 11:5: "For I suppose I was not a whit behind the very chiefest Apostles"; chap. 12:11: "In nothing am I behind the very chiefest Apostles." And in I Cor. 1:11-13 and 3:3-5 Paul rebukes the Corinthians that there are parties among them, some who say, "I am of Paul; and I of Apollos; and I of Cephas; and I of Christ." John lived many years after the death of Peter; yet never does he speak of Peter as ruler or head of the Church, nor does he know of any successors of Peter. And centuries later Chrysostom writes: "When you say *Apostle*, at once all think of Paul; just as when you say *Baptist*, they think of John."

Now all of this is argument *e silentio*, argument taken not from what the holy writers say, but from the fact that they say nothing about it; but when it concerns so prominent a matter as this, and when there are so many testimonies to the contrary, surely, so total a silence is tantamount to proof.

But now, what does the Lord mean when He says to Peter, "Thou art Peter, and upon this rock I will build My Church"? He means exactly what He says; and He does not say, "On thee I will build My Church"; hence He does not mean that. He does not say, "Thou art *Petros*, and on this *Petros* I will build My Church"; and since He does not say *Petros*, but *petra*, He evidently means something else than *Petros;* why otherwise should He use a different word?

It is illuminating, in the first place, that the Lord, vv. 17 and 18, refers to the change in the Apostle's name; his former name was Simon, and he was Bar-jona, that is, the son of Jonas. The new name Peter, or Cephas, Jesus gave him when He called him to be His disciple and Apostle, John 1:42. By the old name Jesus called him whenever his old sinful nature cropped out again, e. g., when He warned him against apostasy, Luke 22:31; when He found him sleeping in Gethsemane, Mark 14:37; when in his final examination, before reinstating him in his apostleship, He reminded him of his threefold denial, John 21:15-17. Why does Jesus here in Matt. 16 call him Peter? Because of his confession, "Thou art the Christ, the Son of the living God," a confession which not flesh and blood had revealed unto him, but his Father in heaven; by this confession, by his faith in the Son of God, he had become a Peter, a rock man, who stood on the Rock Jesus Christ. It is not to the natural Peter that Jesus speaks, but to the regenerated Peter; not to the fisherman, but to the confessor; not to Simon Bar-jona, but to Peter the rock man. And on the same Rock on which Peter stood, and thus became a rock man, on Jesus Christ Himself, the Lord will build His Church.

Does that agree with other Scriptures? For the old rule that Scripture must be interpreted by Scripture applies to Matthew 16 too. We find that Scripture often speaks of Christ as the Rock, the foundation on which the Church is built. I Cor. 10:1-5 St. Paul calls to mind how wonderfully the Lord preserved Israel, His Church of the Old Testament, while they sojourned in the desert; God gave them spiritual meat and spiritual drink; "for they drank of that spiritual Rock that followed them; and that Rock was Christ." Christ was in their midst with His gracious presence, and that sustained them throughout those long years. Eph. 2:20 St. Paul says that the Christians to whom he is writing are "built upon the foundation of the Apostles and Prophets, Jesus Christ Himself being the chief Cornerstone." The Christians, St. Luke tells us in Acts 2:42, "continued steadfastly in the Apostles' doctrine"; and the basis of that doctrine was, I Cor. 3:11: "Other foundation can no man lay than that is laid, which is Jesus Christ." This doctrine

The Papacy

of the Apostles had been taught before them by the Prophets; the Psalmist proclaimed, Ps. 118:22: "The Stone which the builders refused is become the Headstone of the corner"; and Is. 28:16: "Therefore thus saith the Lord God, Behold I lay in Zion for a foundation a Stone, a tried Stone, a precious Cornerstone, a sure Foundation." And Peter tells the Jewish Sanhedrin, Acts 4:10-12, that "Jesus Christ of Nazareth," whom they crucified, whom God raised from the dead, "is the Stone which was set at naught of you builders, which is become the Head of the corner. Neither is there salvation in any other; for there is none other name under heaven given among men whereby we must be saved." That is the foundation of the Apostles and Prophets, their teaching, in which Jesus Christ is the chief Cornerstone. And the picture of the foundation on which the Church stands is carried over into eternity, for of the Church in glory St. John says, Rev. 21:14: "The wall of the city had twelve foundations, and in them the names of the twelve Apostles of the Lamb."

So it was to the Bible student of Christ's day a familiar figure to call Him on whom their salvation rested, the Messiah, the Rock. Literally in dozens of places the Psalmist calls the Lord in whom is his hope his Rock. And here suddenly, and here alone, in Matthew 16 Jesus should designate a man as the foundation of the Church? Moreover, Catholics know that the task is so hopeless that they haven't even tried to prove that Peter considered himself the supreme head or the foundation of the Church, the primate of the Apostles, or that he acted so, or that the other Apostles regarded him as such and treated him accordingly. On the contrary, here comes Peter himself and stamps this whole Roman explanation of Matthew 16 as plain fraud; he writes, I Pet. 2:3-8: ". . . if so be ye have tasted that the Lord is gracious. To whom coming, as unto a living Stone, disallowed indeed of men, but chosen of God and precious, ye also, as lively stones, are built up a spiritual house, an holy priesthood, to offer up spiritual sacrifices, acceptable to God by Jesus Christ. Wherefore also it is contained in the Scripture, Behold, I lay in Sion a chief Cornerstone, elect, precious; and he that believeth on Him shall not be confounded. Unto you, therefore, which believe He is precious; but unto them which be disobedient, the Stone which the builders disallowed, the same is made the Head of the corner, and a stone of stumbling, and a rock of offense, even to them which stumble at the Word, being disobedient; whereunto also they were appointed."

So the result of an honest search of the Scriptures for the interpretation of Matthew 16 is this: The real Foundation Rock of the Church is Christ; on Him rests the whole Church. By confessing Christ, Peter and the Apostles become a part of the larger foundation of the Church, all resting on Christ, but bearing up by their confession others who were won by them for Christ. And so all Christians can become Peters and part of the foundation, bearing up others by their confession of Christ; as Luther says, "All Christians are Peters by reason of the same profession which Peter makes. This profession is the rock on which Peter and all Peters are built up." But the real Foundation remains Christ; men enter in only as they draw others to Christ by their confession. Compare Luther's fine explanation of Matthew 16 in answer to Eck, St. Louis, XVIII:1375 ff.; also two sermons, XI:2297 ff., 2309.

Of course, the Lord in Matthew 16, and Prophets and Apostles in other adduced passages, use figurative language. We shall therefore not quarrel with those who say that the rock in Matthew 16 is Peter's confession; nor with the slightly different explanation given in an article in *Theological Quarterly*, XIII, 109 ff., entitled "A Different Explanation of Petra," which briefly is this:

"On this Rock" refers indeed to Peter, but only as he was firmly grounded upon the *fundamentum fundamenti*, the nethermost Rock that bears up Peter and all whom Peter is to evangelize and disciple, the Lord Christ Himself. Tholuck is quoted: "By his profession Peter had uttered the fundamental confession of the Church, hence laid its foundation. Upon *this confession*, accordingly, Jesus proposes to build His Church. The declaration of Peter 'Thou art the Christ,' etc., is answered by Jesus in a similar declaration to Peter, 'Thou art Peter,' etc. Hence, not the man Peter, Jonas' son, is the foundation, but Peter the confessor, Peter in or by his confession." Peter, himself being established upon the Foundation that had been laid, was now qualified by his testimony to bear up the faith of future members of the Church, was now, and whenever he would repeat his witness for Christ in the future, a part of the "foundation of the Apostles," Eph. 2:20, on which the entire Church rests, with Jesus Christ Himself the chief Cornerstone. The sole distinction of Peter is that which priority in confessing Christ before others secures. It was shared later by the other Apostles. Christ certainly is the Rock on which the Church has been built, and Peter and the Apostles and other men may become the foundation of the faith of their fellow men only in so far as they proclaim Christ and lead men to faith in Christ.

The Roman claim, then, that Jesus in Matthew 16 made Peter His vicar on earth, the supreme shepherd of the whole Church, is fraud and can be adduced from this text only by jugglery. Jesus Himself is the Foundation, the Lord and Master, the Supreme Shepherd of the flock. Whenever the disciples showed a desire to rule, He rebuked them, made them ashamed, and taught them that in His kingdom it is not to be so. Papists in this text want Jesus for a witness to their claims; but He is not only silent where they want Him to say yes, but He distinctly says no to all their claims.

It may be interesting to hear some Catholic acknowledgment of this. Archbishop Kenrick of St. Louis, at the Vatican Council in 1870, in a prepared speech but actually not delivered, yet printed at Naples, said: "If we are bound to follow the majority of the Fathers in this thing, then we are bound to hold for certain that by the 'rock' should be understood the faith professed by Peter, not Peter who professed the faith." "The primacy of the Roman Pontiff, both in honor and jurisdiction, I acknowledge; primacy, I say, not lordship." "But that it can be proved from the words of Holy Scripture I deny. It is true, I held the opposite view when writing the *Observations*, but on closer study of the subject, I judge this interpretation must be abandoned." Cardinal Strossmayer, in a speech at the Vatican Council, in the course of which he was often and violently interrupted, said: "What Augustine taught was the conviction of all Christendom of his time. — I summarize: (1) that Jesus gave His apostles the same power as Peter; (2) that the apostles never considered Peter the Vicar of Christ and the infallible teacher of the Church; (3) that Peter never thought himself a pope and never acted as a pope; (4) that the councils of the first four centuries gave the Bishop of Rome a high position in the Church because of the city of Rome, but it was only a position of honor, not of judicial dominion; (5) that the holy Fathers never interpreted the passage Matt. 16 so, that the

Church is built on Peter, but on the rock (not *super Petrum*, but *super petram*), that is, on the confession of Peter's faith." In his "Essay on Development" Newman admits very frankly that neither Scripture nor tradition will furnish any adequate proof of Roman doctrine; that the Pope's supremacy is a development; that the Fathers never allege the sentence of a universal pastor and teacher against the Gnostic heretics; that the heathen writers are quite ignorant of such a doctrine; that the state of the primitive Church did not well admit such a universal sovereignty.

To conclude this subject of Peter's primacy, we must consider another passage of Scripture: Matt. 16:19; Jesus says to Peter: "And I will give unto thee the keys of the kingdom of heaven; and whatsoever thou shalt bind on earth shall be bound in heaven; and whatsoever thou shalt loose on earth shall be loosed in heaven." Here Jesus gives to Peter the keys of the kingdom of heaven, that is, the power to forgive and to retain sins. Roman Catholics say, Does not that establish the primacy of Peter? To Peter alone Jesus gave the keys of the Kingdom. We say no. Jesus had called His disciple Peter because of his confession of faith that Jesus is the Christ, the Son of the living God; and for the same reason He confers this power on him. It follows that the same power belongs to all who share the faith of Peter. So even this verse in its context disproves Peter's primacy.

But more. No respectable Bible teacher, either Protestant or Roman Catholic, can interpret Matt. 16:19 without drawing in two other Bible passages where Jesus speaks of the same power which He here confers on Peter. One is John 20:22-23: "And when He had said this, He breathed on them and saith unto them, Receive ye the Holy Ghost; whosesoever sins ye remit, they are remitted unto them; and whosesoever sins ye retain, they are retained." To whom was Jesus speaking? To all the disciples who were assembled there on Easter Eve behind doors barred for fear of the Jews. Moreover, again Jesus distinctly defines to whom this power is conferred: to those who have received the Holy Ghost. So, then, what Romans call the primacy of Peter is shared by all those who have received the gift of the Holy Ghost, that is, all Christians.

This is stated even more plainly Matt. 18:18: "Verily I say unto you, Whatsoever ye shall bind on earth shall be bound in heaven;

and whatsoever ye shall loose on earth shall be loosed in heaven." In the same words Jesus gives the power to loose and to bind, which formerly He had given to Peter, to others. To whom? In vv. 15-17 He had given His disciples instructions how to deal with a brother who has been entrapped in sin: first alone, then in the presence of witnesses; if that fails of its purpose, Jesus says, "tell it to the church." Note, He does not say: "Tell it to Peter"; not: "Tell it to the Apostles"; but: "Tell it to the church," the congregation of believers; they shall now try to win the erring brother. If they succeed, well; then they shall forgive him. If this, too, fails, then "let him be unto thee as an heathen man and a publican"; tell him that his sin is unforgiven, retained, that he is bound on earth and in heaven. The church it is, the congregation of believers, to whom Jesus then says, "Whatsoever ye shall bind on earth," etc.

So, then, Scripture knows nothing of the primacy of Peter. Any power that was given to Peter was also given to every Apostle and to every believing Christian. How this power, the Office of the Keys, is to be administered belongs into another chapter.

B. The Pope's Primacy

So far we have spoken only of the primacy of Peter. But Roman teaching is that this primacy in the Church now belongs to the Pope. Here again is the official text, the second chapter of the *Constitutio Dogmatica Prima de Ecclesia Christi:* "That which the Prince of Shepherds and great Shepherd of the sheep, Jesus Christ our Lord, established in the person of the Blessed Apostle Peter to secure the perpetual welfare and lasting good of the Church, must, by the same institution, necessarily remain unceasingly in the Church; which, being founded upon the Rock, will stand firm to the end of the world. For none can doubt, and it is known to all ages, that the holy and Blessed Peter, the Prince and Chief of the Apostles, the pillar of the faith and foundation of the Catholic Church, received the keys of the kingdom from Our Lord Jesus Christ, the Savior and Redeemer of mankind, and lives, presides, and judges, to this day and always, in his successors, the Bishops of the Holy See of Rome, which was founded by him and consecrated by his blood. Whence, whoever succeeds to Peter in this See, does by the institution of Christ Himself obtain the Primacy of Peter over the whole Church. The disposition made by Incarnate Truth therefore remains, and Blessed Peter, abiding through the strength of the Rock in the power that he received, has not abandoned the direction of the Church. Wherefore it has at all times been necessary that every particular Church — that is to say, the faithful throughout the world — should agree with the Roman Church, on account of the greater authority of the princedom which this has received; that all being associated in the unity of that See whence the rights of communion spread to all, might grow together as members of one Head in the compact unity of the body. — If, then, any should deny that it is by the institution of Christ the Lord, or by divine right, that Blessed Peter should have a perpetual line of successors in the Primacy over the Universal Church, or that the Roman Pontiff is the successor of Blessed Peter in this primacy; let him be anathema."

How, then, do they arrive at this teaching? In this way: Peter became the first bishop of Rome; he held that position for 25 years; then he appointed the next bishop and conferred on him all the powers Jesus had given to him; and so in uninterrupted succession the primacy of the Church as descended to the present Pope. This is chiefly a historical question which must be decided on the basis of history. However, since Peter is a Biblical character and much of his life's history is recorded in Scripture, we should expect Scripture to speak if, as the Romans say, Peter spent the greater part of his apostolic life as Bishop of Rome. And as the Romans claim that it is by Christ's own institution that Peter's rights and powers came to the Popes, we demand Bible proof for that assertion.

But what do we find? In the entire New Testament there is not one single reference to any or all of these things, much less a proof. Again, the total silence of Scripture on all of these points speaks loudly against them. More: there are facts stated in the New Testament which brand these claims of the Romans as impossible and therefore untrue.

It cannot be proved that Peter ever was in Rome. Marsilius of Padua already, in his *Defensor Pacis* (1324), says: "As to Saint Peter, I say that it cannot be proved from holy Scripture that he was Bishop of Rome; nay, more, that he was ever in Rome at all.

The Papacy

Wonderful, indeed, it seems that according to some ecclesiastical legend . . . such things are to be said of Peter, and that Luke and Paul should make no mention of them." The earliest uninspired Christian writing, the Letter of Clemens Romanus, merely mentions the martyrdom of Peter and Paul. It is perhaps fair to assume that they died in Rome; but he does not say so. Not until about 170 is the place of their death mentioned; Bishop Dionysius of Corinth states they died in Italy. Irenaeus, ca. 180, writes that Peter and Paul preached in Rome and founded the church in that city. Then in 200, the Roman presbyter Caius in a dialog states that their tomb is in Rome; since that time the tradition has been accepted. It is today generally assumed that Peter died in Rome; but real proof is still lacking.

Romans have no better case when they claim that Peter was Bishop of Rome. In fact, we can definitely say, "No, he was not," for the very simple reason that there were, in the present sense of the term, no bishops in Peter's days. As we have heard before, in the New Testament bishop and presbyter, or elder, are only different names for the same office. So do the earliest Christian writers use these terms promiscuously: Clemens Romanus in his Epistle; the *Didache*, or Teaching of the Twelve Apostles, the earliest Church manual. We have the testimony of early Church Fathers that the distinction between bishops and elders was a gradual development. Jerome says: "With the ancients presbyters were the same as bishops; but gradually all the responsibility was deferred to a single person." Augustine wrote to Jerome: "Although, according to titles of honor, *which the practice of the Church has now made valid*, the episcopate is greater than the presbytery, yet in many things Augustine is less than Jerome." Irenaeus held that the bishop of Rome was but a presbyter. At his time (ca. 180) Peter's Roman bishopric was yet unknown, for he ascribes the founding of the Roman church to Paul as well as to Peter and says that both gave the office of bishop to Linus. The Roman Catholic historian Doellinger draws the conclusion: "This makes the regulation of the Roman church and the appointment of Linus a common act of both Apostles." This same historian therefore shrinks from calling Peter bishop of Rome; he says, "The office afterward called episcopal was not yet marked off."

To show how unreasonable and impossible is the assumption that Peter was bishop of Rome for 25 years (42—67), it is best to construct a timetable of Peter's life and work after Pentecost, based on information from the New Testament and early Christian writers. 33 A. D. Peter was in Jerusalem with all the other Apostles. Ca. 36 he and John undertook a visitation of Samaria, Acts 8:14 ff. That was the year of Saul's conversion, and four years later, 40 A. D., he came to visit Peter in Jerusalem, Acts 9:26; Gal. 1:18. At that time Peter "passed throughout all quarters," i. e., visited the churches; healed Aeneas at Lydda; raised Dorcas from death in Joppa, Acts 9:32-43; also visited Cornelius, Acts 10. Then Peter was imprisoned by Herod Agrippa sometime between 41 and 44, for Herod came back to Jerusalem in 41 and died in 44. But Peter was freed by an angel and "departed and went into another place," Acts 12:17. Romanists say he went to Rome to found the church there; but wouldn't it seem strange that St. Luke should call Rome, the capital of the world, simply "another place" and say nothing more about it, not one word? Besides, St. Gregory reports that Peter here went to Antioch, which report Eusebius recorded and the great Catholic church historian Baronius accepted as true. 50 A. D. Peter is back in Jerusalem for the conference of the Apostles. That is the last year we hear of Peter in the Book of Acts. But Jerome says he traveled and founded churches in Galatia, Cappadocia, Asia, Bithynia, and Pontus, and Origen adds the Parthian kingdom to this circle of Peter's activity. Ca. 65 Peter wrote his First Epistle and dated it "Babylon." The usual assumption is that he means Rome. Opponents of this view maintain that there seems to be no other reason to assume that figurative language is used in this line, when the whole letter is without any symbolical terms, than the desire of Romanists to have Peter placed in Rome at this time; that Josephus reports that some of the Jews driven out of Rome by Claudius settled in Babylon; and they ask, why should not Peter have gone down the Euphrates valley to preach to them? Against the presence of Peter in Rome at this time speak several other facts. Ca. 58 Paul wrote his Epistle to the Romans; the sixteenth chapter is a series of greetings extended to Christians in Rome; 25 are mentioned by name, besides several households; Peter is not mentioned. In 61 Paul came to Rome; the Christians met him at the harbor; but no one speaks of Peter. Paul calls on the Jews

The Papacy 743

in Rome; they know so little about Christians that they vaguely call them a sect and want Paul to tell them more about these people; and that 20 years after Peter is supposed to have founded the church there. Paul lived in Rome two years in his own hired house; during this time he wrote four of his letters; he mentions many of his companions; but not one word about Peter. One letter without a reference to this prominent Apostle could probably be explained; but four of them! The only explanation seems to be: Peter wasn't there. In 66 or 67, Paul wrote his Second Letter to Timothy; he tells his young friend (4:10): "Only Luke is with me"; where was Peter? V. 16: "At my first answer no man stood with me, but all men forsook me; I pray God that it may not be laid to their charge." Where was Peter? — One or the other points here related may be questioned; but taking everything together, we cannot escape the conclusion: The Roman assertion that Peter was bishop of Rome for 25 years is pure fiction. The only ante-Nicene writing that plainly speaks of Peter as Bishop of Rome is the apocryphal Clementine Homily, which the Roman Church, too, rejects as a forgery; Pope Gelasius condemned it in 496. Baronius, in his *Annales Ecclesiastici*, acknowledges that Scripture argues against the belief that Peter was in Rome during the time on which the New Testament throws light. The first statement that Peter came to Rome in 42 is found in Eusebius' *Chronicon*, 300 years after the event. The modern Roman historian Alzog candidly calls it "an ancient report" and lets it go at that.

A few words must be added about the latest development in the history of the Papacy — the Infallibility Decree. The fourth chapter of the above-cited *Constitutio* is headed: "Concerning the Infallible Teaching of the Roman Pontiff." It argues "that the supreme power of teaching is also included in the apostolic primacy, which the Roman Pontiff, as the successor of Peter, Prince of the Apostles, possesses over the whole Church"; that to satisfy this pastoral duty, the Popes have ever watched that the doctrine of Christ might be preserved genuine and pure; for that reason have they defined as to be held those things which with the help of God they had recognized as conformable with the Holy Scriptures and Apostolic Traditions. "For the Holy Spirit was not promised to the successors of Peter that by His revelation they might make known

new doctrine, but that by His assistance they might inviolably keep and faithfully expound the revelation or deposit of faith delivered through the Apostles. And indeed all the venerable Fathers have embraced and the holy orthodox Doctors have venerated and followed their Apostolic doctrine; knowing most fully that this See of holy Peter remains ever free from all blemish of error according to the divine promise of the Lord our Savior made to the Prince of His disciples: I have prayed for thee that thy faith fail not, and when thou art converted, confirm thy brethren (St. Luke 22:32). This gift, then, of truth and never-failing faith was conferred by heaven upon Peter and his successors in this chair."
"Therefore . . . we teach and define that it is a dogma divinely revealed: that the Roman Pontiff, when he speaks *ex cathedra*, that is, when in discharge of the office of Pastor and Doctor of all Christians, by virtue of his supreme Apostolic authority he defines a doctrine regarding faith or morals to be held by the Universal Church, by the divine assistance promised to him in blessed Peter, is possessed of that infallibility with which the divine Redeemer willed that His Church should be endowed for defining doctrine regarding faith or morals; and that therefore such definitions of the Roman Pontiff are irreformable of themselves, and not from the consent of the Church. — But if any one — which may God avert — presume to contradict this Our definition; let him be anathema." "Irreformable" is defined in a footnote: "in the words used by Pope Nicholas I and in the Synod of Quedlinburg, A. D. 1085, 'it is allowed to none to revise its judgment, and to sit in judgment upon what it has judged.'"

We need not spend many words on this latest papal fiction. Only one Bible passage is quoted by Romans to support this teaching, Luke 22:32, where Jesus says to Peter: "I have prayed for thee that thy faith fail not." And even Roman exegesis has rarely dared so fantastic a flight as this. Even Catholic writers before 1870 recognize that. "Janus" (in a book issued by J. Doellinger, professor of church history and canon law in Munich, and Joh. Huber in 1869, under the title *Der Papst und das Konzil* — Roman Catholic, but "liberal" in view) writes: "Every one knows that the one classical passage of Scripture on which the edifice of Papal Infallibility has been reared is the saying of Christ to Peter:

'I have prayed for thee, that thy faith fail not; and when thou art converted, confirm [strengthen] thy brethren.' But these words manifestly refer only to Peter personally, to his denial of Christ and his conversion. . . . It is directly against the sense of the passage, which speaks simply of faith . . . to find in it a promise of future infallibility to a succession of Popes, just because they hold the office Peter first held in the Roman church. No single writer to the end of the seventh century dreamt of such an interpretation; all without exception — and there are eighteen of them — explain it simply as a prayer of Christ that His apostle might not wholly succumb and lose his faith entirely in his approaching trial." (Third English Ed., p. 92.)

This exegesis of "Janus" is correct. The context shows that the Lord foresaw the denial of Peter; instead of keeping his bold promise "Lord, I am ready to go with Thee both into prison and to death," Peter would thrice deny that he knew Him, and the Lord assures him of His love despite this action of his, and of His prayer that his faith might not fail altogether, but that he be converted and arise from his fall. This very promise of the Lord was to be a firm rock to which Peter might hold when on that night he went out and wept bitterly.

"Janus" continues: "The first to find in it [this passage] a promise of privileges to the Church of Rome was Pope Agatho in 680, when trying to avert the threatened condemnation of his predecessor, Honorius, through whom the Roman Church had lost its boasted privilege of doctrinal purity." Honorius, 638, had sided with the Monothelites, who taught that there is only one will in Christ.

The idea of papal infallibility antedates the Vatican Council. Thomas Aquinas already holds it; but it was condemned as heresy by the faculty of the Toulouse High School, 1388, at that time the first and most influential theological corporation of the Church. In fact, Gregory VII incorporated this claim in his *Dictatus* (1076) in such statements as this: That the Pope's decree can be annulled by no one, and that he alone may annul the decrees of anyone; that he can be judged by no man; that the Roman Church has never erred, nor ever, by the testimony of Scripture, shall err, to all eternity. The Jesuits, who since their organization were always the chief promoters of the infallibility idea, made frantic efforts to have the Council of Trent adopt a resolution promulgating papal infallibility; in the end they did not dare to submit the matter to a vote for fear of splitting the Council. Papists like to say that the decree was adopted unanimously by the Vatican Council. The fact is that it was passed by a vote of 536 against 2, and the two objectors were subsequently brought around to agree with the majority. But 106 delegates had previously left the Council and later on organized the Old Roman Catholic Church, which before the late war numbered more than a million members. Their leader was the above-mentioned Doellinger, whom James Bryce called "the flower of Roman Catholic learning"; and even Cardinal Hergenroether, in his *Irrthuemer,* calls him "an ornament and pillar of the Catholic Church in Germany." Of the Vatican Council, Bishop Strossmayer wrote, Nov. 27, 1870: "The Vatican Council was wanting in that freedom which was necessary to make it a real council. . . . Everything which could resemble a guarantee for the liberty of discussion was carefully excluded. . . . There was added a public violation of the ancient Catholic principle: 'Always, everywhere, by all.' In a word, the most hideous and naked exercise of Papal infallibility was necessary before that infallibility could be elevated into a dogma. If to all this it be added that the Council was not regularly constituted, that the Italian bishops, prelates, and officials were in a monstrously predominating majority, that the Apostolic Vicars were dominated by the Propaganda in the most scandalous manner, that the whole apparatus of that political power which the Pope then exercised in Rome contributed to intimidate and repress all free utterance, you can easily conceive what sort of *liberty* — that essential attribute of all councils — was displayed at Rome." Eighty-eight bishops had objected to the decree; but in the end they submitted; it was said that each one of them *laudabiliter se subiecit,*" laudably submitted to the decree.

Books could be filled, in fact, have been filled, with examples illustrating how unreliable the decree is when you subject it to the verdict of history; how often Popes have contradicted each other; how they have excommunicated, damned, and anathematized each other. It is not necessary to go into that here. Since 1870 it is true what Doellinger said: "A Romanist must say, I believe, because the Pope, declared to be infallible, directs that it be taught and believed; but that he is infallible I believe because he asserts it of himself." — There is no other foundation for the doctrine.

III. THE PAPACY IN SCRIPTURE

The Papacy, then, is, as our Confessions say, "a human figment, which is not commanded and is unnecessary and useless" (Smalcald Articles, Part II, Art. IV, pars. 4, 5, *Triglot*, p. 473). The Papacy has no foundation in Scripture. And yet the Papacy appears in Scripture. The classic statement of our Confessions on this point is found in the Smalcald Articles, Part II, Art. IV, pars. 4, 10 (*Triglot*, p. 475): "This teaching shows forcefully that the Pope is the very Antichrist, who has exalted himself above, and opposed himself against, Christ, because he will not permit Christians to be saved without his power, which, nevertheless, is nothing, and is neither ordained nor commanded by God."

The Scriptures employ the term "antichrist" in a general and in a special sense. In I John 2:18 it is used in a general sense: "Little children, it is the last time; and as ye have heard that Antichrist shall come, even now are there many antichrists; whereby we know that it is the last time." What John means here he explains in chap. 4:3: "And every spirit that confesseth not that Jesus Christ is come in the flesh is not of God; and this is that spirit of antichrist, whereof ye have heard that it should come, and even now already is it in the world." He therefore refers to teachers who teach another doctrine than the Gospel of Jesus Christ. In its general sense, then, the term "antichrist" refers to all false teachers.

The reason for calling false teachers antichrists is plain. Scripture demands that in Christ's Church His Word alone shall be taught and shall rule. Jesus tells His disciples to teach all nations "to observe all things whatsoever I have commanded you," Matt. 28:20. Again: "If ye continue in My Word, then are ye My disciples indeed; and ye shall know the truth, and the truth shall make you free," John 8:31-32. To Timothy, Paul writes (I Tim. 6:3, 5): "If any man teach otherwise and consent not to wholesome words, even the words of our Lord Jesus Christ . . . from such withdraw thyself." Christ wants to rule alone in His Church through His Word: "One is your Master, even Christ," Matt. 23:8, 10. But all false teachers who proclaim their own instead of Christ's Word, set themselves in Christ's place and so against Him; by teaching their own doctrine they seek to establish their own authority against Christ. All false teaching, therefore, is rebellion against Christ;

and all who teach false doctrine are antichrists, opponents of Christ, rebels in His kingdom.

But when John in the above passage says, "Ye have heard that Antichrist shall come," he evidently refers to previously written prophecies. One of them without doubt is Dan. 11:36-39: "And the king shall do according to his will; and he shall exalt himself, and magnify himself above every god, and shall speak marvelous things against the God of gods, and shall prosper till the indignation be accomplished; for that that is determined shall be done. Neither shall he regard the God of his fathers nor the desire of women nor regard any god; for he shall magnify himself above all. But in his estate shall he honor the god of forces; and a god whom his fathers knew not shall he honor with gold, and silver, and with precious stones, and pleasant things. Thus shall he do in the most strongholds with a strange god, whom he shall acknowledge and increase with glory: and he shall cause them to rule over many, and shall divide the land for gain." Moreover, Paul had already written his Letters to the Thessalonians; and there, II Thess. 2:3-10, he had said: "Let no man deceive you by any means; for that day shall not come except there come a falling away first, and that man of sin be revealed, the son of perdition; who opposeth and exalteth himself above all that is called God, or that is worshiped, so that he as God sitteth in the temple of God, showing himself that he is God. Remember ye not that when I was yet with you, I told you these things? And now ye know what withholdeth that he might be revealed in his time. For the mystery of iniquity doth already work; only he who now letteth will let, until he be taken out of the way. And then shall that Wicked be revealed, whom the Lord shall consume with the spirit of His mouth, and shall destroy with the brightness of His coming; even him, whose coming is after the working of Satan with all power and signs and lying wonders, and with all deceivableness of unrighteousness in them that perish, because they received not the love of the truth that they might be saved." As St. John had said, "Now are there many antichrists," so St. Paul says, "The mystery of iniquity doth already work." John distinguishes from the "many antichrists" the "antichrist" in a special sense. In the many antichrists, which already are apparent in the false teachers, that spirit is active which will manifest itself completely in the antichrist *kat' exochen*. John

The Papacy

means to say, The opposition to Christ and the teaching of the Gospel has begun as foretold; we behold many heretics who contradict Christ; this opposition will continue and become concentrated and embodied in the one great Antichrist, of whom Daniel and Paul have spoken." And Paul describes this opponent of Christ who in himself combines all the "many antichrists," so that in him the "falling away" *kat' exochen* appears. And taking all this together it is evident that the "antichrists" of John are not Jews and heathen, but they are all in the Church, they pose as Christians who love Christ's Gospel; but actually they hate it, they either discard it altogether, or they forge, distort, and misinterpret it.

So Scripture speaks of one Antichrist in whom the abomination of false teaching reaches its consummation and who appears by special action of Satan. The chief Scripture passages speaking of the great Antichrist are the following. II Thess. 2:2 ff. has already been cited; this is universally acknowledged as a prophecy of Antichrist, though the name is not used; but it is indicated by *antikeimenos*, "he who opposeth"; the whole text speaks of the archenemy of Christ who in the Church rises against God and Christ. Then the passage Dan. 11:36 ff., already cited; also I John 2:18. I Tim. 4:1-3: "Now the Spirit speaketh expressly that in the latter times some shall depart from the faith, giving heed to seducing spirits and doctrines of devils; speaking lies in hypocrisy; having their conscience seared with a hot iron; forbidding to marry, and commanding to abstain from meats which God hath created to be received with thanksgiving of them which believe and know the truth." Finally Revelations 13 and 17, where various marks of Antichrist are designated: hypocrisy, seduction, wonders, persecution, and glamor.

Now, who is the Antichrist? We must take all the descriptions, the marks and characteristics together; that is the intention of the prophecy. There have been various opinions. The Jews already expected an Anti-Messiah; they called him Armillus, corrupter of the people; he was to be a giant 12 cubits high and wide. Some applied the title to political tyrants, Nero, Napoleon, Boulanger, the Prussian State. The prophecy does not fit them; they did not pose as church dignitaries. Nor does it fit manifest infidels and scoffers; Mohammed; in modern times atheism; they have nothing in common with the temple of God; they are outside of the Church.

The question, Who is the Antichrist? is answered in Scripture. The prophecies of Antichrist designate, not only in general, but in detail, the characteristics and works of Antichrist; the marks of antichristian times are given. For what purpose? Evidently that future generations of Christians, who would live in the time of Antichrist, might recognize this evil foe and escape him. The Church of the Reformation has recognized him. This prophecy of Antichrist is fulfilled; we have it before our eyes. The Papacy alone bears all the marks of the prophecy. A man who otherwise stands high in church history, Th. Harms, once called this opinion *"eine missourische Schrulle,"* a crotchet of Missouri. Well, it must then be called a Lutheran *Schrulle*. It would be queer if they who learned to know the Papacy so well should have been mistaken. No; the error is on the side of those who have left the ways of the fathers. The Papacy is Antichrist. Let us compare the marks.

St. Paul describes the whole movement led by Antichrist as *apostasia*, falling away; and since the whole context speaks of religious matters, it cannot be a political or social defection or secession; nor can it be a mixed movement, partly religious, partly political. I Tim. 4:1, St. Paul says: In the latter times some shall depart — apostatize — from the faith. This is also indicated by the close connection of this "falling away" with "the man of sin" and "the son of perdition." He presents "strong delusions," "a lie"; those who follow him have not received the love of the truth and will be damned; the "falling away" is characterized as iniquity. Moreover, it is not *a* falling away, but *the* falling away, a special apostasy, of which Paul had perhaps warned orally, not a falling away from single doctrines, but from the essence of all Christian doctrine, from Christ Himself.

What is the essence of Christian doctrine, the doctrine which distinguishes it from all other religions? It is the doctrine of justification by faith in Christ without works. This doctrine that man is saved without his own works, through faith in Christ, is the only doctrine by which a man can be saved. Luther says that this article "alone begets, nourishes, builds, serves, defends, the Church of God, and without it the Church of God cannot subsist for one single hour" (XIX:158); and all Christians agree with Luther.

The Papacy

This doctrine is for spiritual life what air is for natural life. Whoever attacks this faith of Christians threatens their life. Whoever threatens and attacks this faith most, harms the Church most.

This doctrine the Papacy officially condemns. Canons and Decrees of the Council of Trent; Session VI, Canon 11: "If any one saith, that men are justified, either by the sole imputation of the justice of Christ, or by the sole remission of sins, to the exclusion of the grace and the charity which is poured forth in their hearts by the Holy Ghost, and is inherent in them; or even that the grace, whereby we are justified, is only the favor of God; let him be anathema." — Canon 12: "If any one saith, that justifying faith is nothing else but confidence in the divine mercy which remits sins for Christ's sake; or that this confidence alone is that whereby we are justified; let him be anathema." — Canon 20: "If any one saith, that the man who is justified and how perfect soever, is not bound to observe the commandments of God and of the Church, but only to believe; as if indeed the Gospel were a bare and absolute promise of eternal life, without the condition of observing the commandments; let him be anathema." (Waterworth's translation.) That is the very heart of the Papacy: denial of justification by faith. The whole machinery of the Papacy is organized against this doctrine. There are a host of teachings promulgated by the Papacy which by no stretch of the imagination can ever be brought into harmony with this cardinal doctrine, e. g., indulgences, penances, fasts, prayers, alms, pilgrimages, works of supererogation, purgatory, the mass, etc. Nor do they ever pretend that they can be harmonized; they want to have nothing to do with justification by faith. The whole edifice of the Papacy falls if justification by faith is admitted. Note the latest Roman Catholic biography of Luther, by Joseph Clayton; his book is full of admissions that Catholics have slandered Luther. Yet Luther remains the archheretic, because he taught justification by faith alone. There can be no greater apostasy from the true Christian religion than that of which the Papacy is guilty. There are other false teachings in Rome. Popes have gone astray from God's Word in other respects; in that they do not differ from others. Like the Sodomites, Popes have lived in the most abominable vices; but others have done that, too. That's not the essence of the Papacy. The heart of the Papacy is denial of justification by faith alone.

Now, as surely as the Christian Church is composed of people who by the operation of the Holy Ghost believe that they have a gracious God without their own works, for Christ's sake alone, so surely the Pope under the name of Christ bans and anathematizes the whole Christian Church, and is constantly active in destroying the Christian Church, when, e. g., children who under his rule by Baptism have become members of the Christian Church are led away from the Savior and taught to put their trust in their own works. Now look around among the enemies of the Church; who is greatest among them? Nero or Decius and their ilk, who butchered thousands of Christians? Oh, no; under their persecution Christians could retain their faith, could sing praises to Christ on the pyres and in the arenas and enter heaven. But to take faith in the Savior out of the heart of Christians, that is attacking their true life, their spiritual and eternal life. And that the Papacy does. This murder of Christians the Papacy carries on not openly, as do confessed infidels, so that Christians can easily beware of them, but under the semblance of exquisite Christianity and holiness. Luring the nations into its fold by the claim of being the only saving Church, it leads all who answer the call, not to trust in Christ as the only Savior, but on the way of works, and so to perdition. Rome is the greatest foe of the Christian Church. The Papacy is the Antichrist, constantly leading untold numbers to hell under the pretense of taking them to heaven.

A part of this apostasy will be, John says (I John 2:22; 4:3), that Antichrist denies that Jesus is the Christ, that Jesus Christ is come in the flesh. Now, the Pope calls Jesus the Christ, but he robs Jesus of that which makes Him the Christ, that His merits alone have earned for us forgiveness of all sin, life, and salvation. The Pope does not deny the fact of Jesus' incarnation, but he denies the purpose for which He came in the flesh, to be the sole Mediator between God and man. The Pope nullifies the merits of Christ by teaching that we must at least in part work out our own salvation by our works; that we must cancel the punishment for our sins by fasts, prayers, alms, and other works, or that we must have the works of supererogation done by saints put to our credit; that the Mass is an ever-repeated sacrifice for sin.

We rightly apply to the Pope the titles St. Paul gives to Antichrist: The man of sin, the son of perdition; not because of his personal wickedness (though we could demonstrate that, too; but that is not essential here), but because he originates sin and makes others sin and leads them into perdition. He robs men of the Gospel; but where that is removed, there remains nothing but sin and perdition. He abrogates and changes divine laws by decrees and dispensations; what can result but sin when people follow his edicts? With his own laws and ordinances, which are legion, to which he binds consciences and threatens curse and damnation to all who transgress them, he *makes* sin where there is no real sin, disturbing and confusing consciences, leading them to idolatry in the Mass and the veneration of saints and relics and to other sins. Thus he is a murderer of souls; but a murderer of bodies of God's children as well; the Pope has shed more blood than all the Roman emperors. And by their own confession they would do it again today! And isn't it blasphemy of the worst kind to deny that Christ "by one offering hath perfected forever them that are sanctified" and to teach that in the Mass His body must daily be offered anew for the sins of the living and the dead? And is not the Pope therefore a blasphemer (Rev. 13:5-6)?

Antichrist, according to Dan. 11:36 ff., will not regard the God of his fathers; a god whom his fathers knew not shall he honor. And the Pope establishes a new worship, a new way of serving God. The Roman doctrine of good works is a false service of God, and that in two ways: (1) because people are taught to do good works to win God's favor, and (2) because things which God has not commanded are called good works. There is the veneration of saints, angels, relics, pictures, and images; there is the Mass, which since the Middle Ages occupies the center of Roman worship, and for which there is not a scintilla of foundation in Scripture; there are pilgrimages and vigils and all the host of things in Roman culture; there is the whole system of monasticism. Many even among Protestants labor under a misconception with regard to this institution; they think the self-sacrifice of monks and nuns is rather touching and praiseworthy; they think it hard that we condemn it. But who rightly ordains what is a virtue? God alone; no one else. Now show one word of Scripture for the vast institution of monasticism. Jesus says, Matt. 15:9: "In vain do they worship Me, teaching for doctrines the commandments of men."

Let us take another item in the prophecy of Antichrist: He "sitteth in the temple of God," II Thess. 2:4. The assumption made by some, that Antichrist would choose the temples of idols as his seat, does not even deserve to be called a notion (Pieper: *"Verdient kaum den Namen eines Einfalls"*). St. Paul does not call idol temples "the temple or house of God." Nor would an Antichrist sitting in pagan temples be a "mystery of iniquity," but a very evident iniquity, obvious from the very start. St. Paul writes to the Corinthians (II Cor. 6:16): "What agreement hath the temple of God with idols? For ye are the temple of the living God." And I Tim. 3:15 he speaks of "the house of God, which is the Church of the living God." Compare also I Cor. 3:16-17. The temple of God is the Christian Church, the communion of saints. Antichrist therefore cannot be a secular ruler. And since despite his apostasy Antichrist remains in the Church, establishes there his seat and throne, and rules there, his apostasy cannot be a separation from the communion of the Church, but an apostasy from the faith of the Church. Jesus refers to this when in Matt. 24:15 He says that the abomination of desolation stands in the holy place. Where Antichrist is, among baptized Christians, there is the Church. Antichrist cannot be atheism, Communism, etc. In II Peter 3 the Apostle prophesies a great apostasy in which people totally leave the Church, turn their back on the Bible, scoff at faith, etc. But that is not Antichrist. This apostasy in II Thess. 2 is of a different kind; those addicted to it remain within the Church, but they depart from the basic teaching of the Church.

The Papacy is not outside of, but within the Church. The apostasy of the Papacy is not external, but internal. Many members of the Church are under the Papacy, chiefly the baptized children; then also many adults, who by the Gospel, which is still occasionally proclaimed, are led to trust solely in the merits of Christ, despite their seducing environment (Luther, XVII:2191; Smalcald Articles, De Potestate, 39, *Triglot*, p. 515). But take all the heretics of all times and lump all their adherents together, and they will not compare in number with those whom the Pope has led astray. The apostasy of the Papacy is so great a departure from the rule of Christian faith that saving faith is lost where that teaching is followed. The Pope has taken the heart out of Christian doctrine and faith; his teaching is directly contrary to

Christ and His Gospel. (Cp. a letter of Luther to two pastors, Walch, 17, 264 ff.)

We consider next the conduct of Antichrist. II Thess. 2: "Who opposeth and exalteth himself above all that is called God or that is worshiped; so that he as God sitteth in the temple of God, showing himself that he is God." And Dan. 11: "He shall exalt himself and magnify himself above every god and shall speak marvelous things against the God of gods. . . . Neither shall he regard the God of his fathers . . . nor regard any god; for he shall magnify himself above all." He opposes, is lawless, abolishing and changing human and divine laws. He shows himself, he acts, as though he were God. He does not claim that he is of divine essence — that would place him outside of Christendom; but he claims that he is God's representative and as such has been equipped with divine powers. He exalts himself above all that is called god or that is worshiped. That does not mean the gods of the heathen; exalting oneself above them is not godless. It means persons in the world who in their nature are not God, but who are called gods because of certain functions devolving on them which are characteristically godlike (Pieper); e. g., the government, parents. This conception of the term "gods" is clearly based on Scripture; John 10:34, 35; I Cor. 8:5; Rom. 13:1 ff. The meaning is then: He exalts himself above all authorities in the world, and his arrogance reaches so far that as God he sitteth in the temple of God and exhibits himself that he is God; he claims that his commands are divine commands; he will not let Christians be saved without him; he treads all holy things under his feet. Therefore he is called Antichrist because he is the very opposite of Christ and sets himself in Christ's place.

It is evident to all the world that the Pope will not be subject to anyone, that he claims to be supreme in Church and world. How he seized the primacy in the Church was shown in the first part of this essay. Officially he calls himself the vicar and representative of God and Christ. But more; he appropriates titles which belong only to God, and accepts divine honor and veneration. In Dau, *Doctrinal Theology*, II, p. 178 f., there is a whole page of divine names and attributes given to the Pope. One Pope says: "It is shown quite clearly that the Pope can neither be bound nor loosed by secular authority; for it is a fact that the Pope was called God by the pious emperor Constantine. It is manifest that God cannot be judged by man" (Gerhard). In his charge against the Waldensians (1520) the papal spokesman Claudius Seisselius said: "In whatever guilty transactions the Pope may be implicated, he is an angel of God, yea, more, he is the successor of the Apostles and the vicar of Christ; aye, I should rather say, he is Christ." No Pope has ever rejected that statement. In a papal encyclical the power is ascribed to the Pope that he can confer authoritative value on the Word of God; for it is there declared that the Old and New Testaments must be received not because they are in their entirety found in a canonical codex but because the holy Pope Innocentius seems to have handed down a decision to this effect. Popes have appropriated power, privileges, and dignities which belong only to God. In the encyclical *Haec quippe* the Pope claims that he can change righteousness to unrighteousness and vice versa. Pope Johannes Sylva stated that though the divine Law demanded that every matter must be established by two or three witnesses, he could decree otherwise. Pope Azorius claimed the authority to absolve himself from an oath that he had sworn. Pius IX applied Christ's word "I am the Way, the Truth, and the Life" to himself.

The Pope claims that only those will be saved who are subject to the Roman Pontiff, though he condemns and abrogates the only way to salvation. In the bull *Unam Sanctam* (1302) Boniface VIII says: "We, moreover, proclaim, declare, and pronounce that it is altogether necessary to salvation for every human being to be subject to the Roman Pontiff." Under political pressure this bull was rescinded by Clement V in the bull *Rex gloriae* (1311); but it was reinstated by Leo X in his bull *Pastor Aeternus,* and this was ratified by the Fifth Lateran Council in 1517. This bull was made a part of Roman canon law, and it stands today, despite all attempts of the Paulist Fathers and others to slur over these statements in their tracts of information on the Catholic Church.

The Pope changes God's Word and command as he pleases. Christ in the words of institution says of His Holy Supper, "Drink ye all of it"; the Pope says, No, not all; only the priest. Christ said, "Search the Scriptures"; Pope Pius IX *ex cathedra* condemned

The Papacy

all Bible Societies as a pest. And that, too, has never been changed and still stands, despite all desperate propaganda efforts today in countries where they have dangerous competition to make people believe that they encourage Bible study; in the lands in which they have undisputed control they still burn Bibles. And does not the Pope practically set the Bible aside by declaring it dark and beyond the comprehension of all who are not entitled by the Church to explain it? Christ says by His Apostle, "A bishop must be blameless, the husband of one wife"; the Pope says, No, the priest must have no wife. Christ says we must confess all our sins to God, to our fellow men only when we have sinned against them; the Pope says we must confess all our sins to a man, to the priest, under pain of not being forgiven. Christ says, "Let no man judge you in meat or in drink," Col. 2:16; again, He declares it the doctrine of seducing spirits and of devils when some who depart from the faith forbid to marry and command to abstain from meats which God hath created to be received with thanksgiving, I Tim. 4:1-3; the Pope commands numerous fasts and declares the unmarried estate of monks and nuns a peculiar sign of holiness. Christ has given to the entire Church the power of the keys of heaven; the Pope says, The power to bind and to loose is given only to Peter and his successors. Christ says, "There is one God and one Mediator between God and men, the Man Christ Jesus," I Tim. 2:5; the Pope says, No, you must get the saints, particularly Mary, to mediate for you if you want to be saved. Christ says, "It is appointed unto men once to die, but after this the Judgment," Heb. 9:27; the Pope inserts purgatory between death and the Judgment. Christ in simply innumerable parts of His Word declares that the sinner is justified by faith, without the deeds of the Law; by His Apostle, just in connection with this truth, He declares, "Though we or an angel from heaven preach any other gospel unto you than that which we have preached unto you, let him be accursed. As we said before, so say I now again, If any man preach any other gospel unto you than that ye have received, let him be accursed," Gal. 1:8-9. The Pope and his councils officially and *expressis verbis* condemn that doctrine. Emperor Henry IV, in his renowned controversy with Gregory VII, wrote him: "St. Paul, who said that even an angel from heaven should be accursed who taught any other than the true doctrine, did not make an exception in your favor, to permit you to teach false doctrine." And we subscribe that.

The Pope claims supremacy over all secular governments; he demands that as secular governments they acknowledge his authority and stand ready to serve his kingdom. Again we cite the bull *Unam Sanctam* of Boniface VIII: "Both the spiritual and the material sword, therefore, are in the power of the Church, the latter indeed to be used for the Church, the former by the Church, the one by the priest, the other by the hands of kings and soldiers, but by the will and sufferance of the priest. It is fitting, moreover, that one sword should be under the other and the temporal authority subject to the spiritual power. . . . Hence it is for the spiritual power to establish the earthly power, and judge it if it be not good. . . . Therefore, if the earthly power shall err, it shall be judged by the spiritual power; if the lesser spiritual power err, it shall be judged by the higher. But if the supreme power err, it shall be judged by God alone and not by man. . . . Whoever, therefore, shall resist this power ordained by God resists the ordination of God." In support of all this, Boniface adduces Luke 22:38: "And they said, Lord, behold, here are two swords. And He said unto them, It is enough"; and John 18:11: "Then said Jesus unto Peter, Put up thy sword into the sheath"; which with little doubt furnishes the ultimate example of peculiar papal exegesis. This claim of the Papacy has been repeated over and over again. Gregory VII proposes the argument: How could it be that he who has the power to open and close heaven should not sit in judgment over all the earth? Innocent III wrote to the patriarch of Constantinople: Christ has conferred on the Popes all earthly world government to rule it; proof: Peter walked on the sea; the sea means the whole number of nations on earth. Pius IX in 1871 declared that the Popes have the right to depose kings and to absolve subjects from their oath of allegiance; and as a concrete example that the Popes mean to apply this power over secular governments wherever they can, this same Pope, in 1868, declared laws passed in Austria, abrogating an earlier concordat with the Pope, together with their application, null and forever void by virtue of his apostolic authority.

That is a portrait of the Papacy drawn by the Popes themselves; compare it with II Thessalonians 2. He sits in the temple of God, claims to be the head of the Church, and excommunicates all who do not acknowledge his supremacy. He claims divine attributes: infallibility. He claims divine prerogatives: declares he can give dispensations from God's Law, decree articles of faith, and give new revelations; establishes a new service and teaches a new, his own, doctrine, gives rules and ordinances, many and various, and binds consciences to keep them. He claims divine authority: makes salvation dependent on the keeping of his ordinances; yes, higher authority than God, because he changes Christ's Word and command as he pleases. He extends his authority beyond the grave and by the indulgences manipulates purgatory, damns, and declares saved whom he will, claims to be the supreme judge who judges all, but is judged by none. Does he not oust God and His Son, on his part, from His dominion? Is he not the one "who opposeth and exalteth himself above all that is called god or that is worshiped, so that he as God sitteth in the temple of God, showing himself that he is God"?

Nor let anyone tell you that the Pope has changed. The old word of Osiander is still true; he said: "Also the present Pope is and is called Antichrist. The reason why he is this lies not in some personal depravity or wickedness, but in the nature of his office. Now, no Pontiff as such, however upright he has been personally, has failed to declare himself the ecumenical head of the Church or has not exercised authority in secular and spiritual affairs or has not approved the condemnatory canons of the Council of Trent, though he may for political reasons abstain for the time being from slaughter and tyranny."

The prophecy speaks of the root of Antichrist: his "coming is after the working of Satan." He is not Satan himself, as some have thought; but he is produced by Satan, "with all power and signs and lying wonders," or rather, because the attribute "lying" belongs to all three: "with all lying power and signs and wonders." His kingdom is established and supported by these things which are a part of that realm of lies whose father is the devil, John 8:44.

It is evident to the world that the Papacy uses and has used all sorts of lying powers, signs, and wonders. Luther said: The power which the Papacy exerts can be explained only on the ground of diabolical action. It is not only against the Word of God, but against all reason. Nobody loves it; even its own adherents do not love it; but all fear it, deceived and captured by an illusion of piety and by lying signs and wonders. — St. Paul directly calls celibacy and fasts doctrines of the devil. And the Catholic world to this day is full of plaudits for wonders, healings at shrines, graves, images of saints, etc. That is satanic fraud — or, if supernatural things actually do occur, they are done by satanic powers.

The last item in this picture which Scripture reveals is the time or duration of Antichrist, especially his beginning and his end. II Thess. 2 St. Paul does not say, the Antichrist will come; he says, "The mystery of iniquity doth already work." Even in the days of the Apostles this power was moving, but secretly; there is something that withholdeth, that "letteth," i. e., hinders, restrains, this power; for a time it is a mystery. But it will be revealed; the time will come when Antichrist will show himself frankly, without camouflage. And then will come his end; not suddenly: "whom the Lord shall consume with the spirit of His mouth"; that may be a gradual process of uncertain duration. He will be consumed by the Word of God, not by force of arms; hence, again, Antichrist cannot be a secular power; the Word of God does not fight against secular powers. But this revelation of Antichrist is a sign of the coming day of Christ; when that man of sin has been revealed and is being consumed by the spirit of the Lord's mouth, then the day of Christ may come at any time. And on that day, not before, the Lord will destroy him with the brightness of His coming.

Again the description fits. The chief marks of Antichrist in the Papacy began to appear in the days of Christ and the Apostles: the desire to rule in the Church, and false doctrine, especially denial of justification by faith. The first beginning we note among the disciples of Jesus, who expected Him to establish a mighty empire on earth and, when the Lord was not looking, quarreled about their place in this realm. Not long after the ascension John complains about Diotrephes, "who loveth to have the pre-eminence among them," III John 9. It is interesting to note that the word St. John uses here means literally: He loves the primacy; it is so translated in the Vulgate. And the earliest false teachers, who caused Paul so much trouble, were the Judaistic teachers, who attacked the doctrine of justification by faith alone and wanted to force Christians back under the obligations of the Law. But at first this lust for power in the Church was hindered; something kept it from unfolding. What that was, Paul, no doubt, had told the Thessalonians orally, for he says: "Remember ye not that when I was yet with you, I told you these things? And now ye know what withholdeth," II Thess. 2:5-6. What that was we do not know; but probably it was the Roman Empire; as long as there was a strong, unified world government, a power like that of the Papacy had small chance of rising, especially while Christians were scattered by persecution. But when better times came for Christians, they went to sleep, and the enemy sowed his tares unhindered; the Papacy developed.

And we have the Papacy with us today; and it is the same today as in the days when it was revealed, in the days of the Reformation; but its unlimited, absolute dominion over world and Church has been thoroughly broken. Luther has unmasked the Papacy, so that today anyone may know it and guard against it. In truth, the Reformation consisted in the discovery and exposure of the Pope as the Antichrist. That was the turning point in Luther's work when, preparing for the Leipzig Debate, he came to the conviction that Antichrist sat in Rome and from that seat on the seven hills spread his tentacles over all lands. So this doctrine that the Papacy is the Antichrist is most closely connected with the Reformation; it was then and by that work that Antichrist was revealed. He is not killed, not entirely destroyed; but he is continually being consumed by the Word of our God; he has lost his power except over those who willingly submit to him. That, too, became evident in the days of the Reformation. Every reform movement before that time was killed by the Pope's ban and interdict. Why not Luther's Reformation? Why did not the Pope lay the interdict on Germany or Saxony after he had excommunicated Luther? He threatened it; but by that time Luther had written his *Letter to the Christian Nobility of the German Nation* and his book *On the Babylonian Captivity of the Church*. He had proved to Christian people that the Pope has no power to ban individuals or whole countries and close heaven to them; so he had freed them from the fear of the Pope; and Leo X and Clement VII knew that any attempt to lay the interdict on Germany would meet with contempt and derision.

So the Pope's power and tyranny is broken. The fact that this essay can be read here is proof that the Papacy has lost its power.

But the Papacy remains *semper eadem,* always the same. They boast of it. When a Pope dies, the Papacy does not die. When the doctor declares that a Pope is dead, an official in the presence of witnesses taps his head three times with a hammer, calling his name. If there is no response, he announces, "The Pope is surely dead." But a substitute has already been provided, who takes over until a new election has taken place; then the people are told: "Behold, I bring you good tidings of great joy; we again have a Pope." And so it will continue to the end of time. The power of the Papacy, its influence in the world, may at times wax, then wane again. But the Papacy will remain what it is until the Lord by the brightness of His coming makes an end of it.

Some of the objections to what has been said in this treatise have already been mentioned, e. g., that Antichrist is modern infidelity, atheism, pantheism. None of these is enthroned in the temple of God, the Church. For that same reason Antichrist cannot be a secular power; moreover, Antichrist is to be consumed by the spirit of the mouth of God, by His Word; but the Gospel does not battle against secular powers. There is, however, one objection which we have so far not touched. It is said: Antichrist must be a single person; the prophecy calls him "that man of sin," "the son of perdition," "he who opposes," "that Wicked One"; in all of these names the definite article is used. We answer: The use of the definite article need not mean a single person; it may mean a series of men, a class of people; in fact, it is Scripture usage to designate a whole class of people by the definite singular. Dan. 8:23 ff. the Prophet speaks of a king, though it is evident that a whole succession of kings is meant. Matt. 12:35: "A good man [Greek: the good man] out of the good treasure of the heart bringeth forth good things; and an evil man [Greek: the evil man] out of the evil treasure bringeth forth evil things." But evidently Jesus speaks of good and evil men in general. Mark 2:27: "The Sabbath was made for man [Greek: for the man], and not man [Greek: the man] for the Sabbath"; but Jesus is not speaking of one specific Sabbath and one specific man. Matt. 4:4: "Man [Greek: the man] shall not live by bread alone." II Tim. 3:17, a direct parallel to "the man of sin," St. Paul says: "That the man of God may be perfect."

Matt. 22:21: "Render, therefore, unto Caesar the things that are Caesar's." John 19:12: "If thou let this man go, thou art not Caesar's friend; whosoever maketh himself a king speaketh against Caesar." V. 15: "We have no king but Caesar." The reference, however, is to the office of Caesar, to all the Caesars, to the whole series of Roman emperors or rulers. We commonly follow the same usage. We say in history: The emperor always had trouble with the cities; there was a struggle of many centuries between the Pope and the emperor. Romanists follow the same usage; they speak of the infallibility of the Pope; they mean every one in the whole series; they mean the Papacy. Gerhard turns the tables completely on papistical exegesis by citing Matt. 16:18 against them; they refer the phrase "on this rock," which was spoken to Peter, to their whole line of Popes. He reminds them that in their church canons, wherever the term "Pope" occurs, the reference is not to a certain individual, but to any scoundrel who may bear that name at that time. Papists say: If the Pope is the Antichrist, there are 200 Antichrists; we answer: If the Pope is the head of the Church, there are 200 heads, 200 bridegrooms, etc. — But now we'll turn the table still a little farther. The very prophecy, II Thessalonians 2, proves that it must refer to a series of persons. Antichrist, St. Paul says, will not meet his end till Judgment Day. And yet the iniquity was already there in the days of the Apostles; compare also I John 4:3. No single person can live as long as that.

Another objection, which some think should convince particularly Lutherans who emphasize the *sola Scriptura*, is this: The teaching that the Pope is the Antichrist does not rest on a clear word of Scripture; it is only a deduction. It is not a new objection. Eighty years ago so much emphasis was given to it that *Lehre und Wehre* in 1867 referred to it at length. The Bible does not say: The Pope is the Antichrist. But the Bible does not say in so many words: Christ's body is present in the Sacrament and is received by the communicants. The Bible does not say in so many words that infants must be baptized. These doctrines are deductions. But Christ Himself makes such deductions; from the fact that God is called the God of Abraham and Isaac and Jacob He draws the conclusion that these patriarchs must be living. If a deduction is a right deduction, if it is drawn from the Word of God, it is correct, and it stands; there can be no objection to it. — Nor is it a valid objection to say: The statement that the Pope is the Antichrist rests not on Scripture alone, but on Scripture and a historical judgment; therefore it rests partly on a human opinion. Our fathers have rightly adduced the parallel in Christ's own life. That Jesus of Nazareth was the promised Christ was for the Jews of His time such a historical question; but comparing prophecy with the words and works of Christ, they could with perfect certainty draw the conclusion that Jesus was the Christ, the promised Messiah. So here, comparing prophecy with the words and works of the Papacy, we can with perfect certainty draw the conclusion that the Papacy is the Antichrist. This teaching rests on Scripture, and not on a human opinion, but on the facts of history.

Our conclusion remains: The Papacy is the Antichrist. The prophecy of St. Paul in II Thess., of Daniel, of various places in Revelation, is fulfilled in the Papacy and only in the Papacy. In this series of persons we find all the marks which Scripture ascribes to Antichrist, even though we do not find all the marks which Scripture ascribes to Antichrist in every individual of the series.

This teaching that the Papacy is the Antichrist is not a fundamental article of Christian faith. Knowledge of this article is not needed to plant and keep saving faith in the heart. A Christian may know Christ as his Savior and be saved by Him even though he does not recognize the Antichrist in the Papacy. It is not an article on which saving faith rests, with which Christianity stands or falls. Denial of it is not, therefore, in itself alone divisive of Church fellowship. But the Christian who does not recognize the truth of this teaching is in greater danger than others of being led astray by the errors of the Papacy. And a religious teacher, a pastor, who knows the Pope's teaching and practice and yet does not recognize him as the Antichrist is a poor theologian (*"schwach in der Theologie,"* Pieper). And it is very difficult to see how such pastors can rightly perform their duty of warning the souls committed to their care against the abominations and the seduction of the Papacy if they themselves have not recognized the Papacy as the Antichrist. It is greatly to be feared that they are losing the firm conviction of the contrast between faith and works, between grace and merit, between Lutheranism and Papism. The Church of the Reformation confessed this article with one consent. A pastor who does not see the mystery of iniquity in the Roman Papacy surely has little knowledge of the history of the Church, of the meaning of the Reformation, and a poor conception of Luther's doctrine.

With those who like to sneer at this confession the error lies deeper. The rule is that they themselves hold papistic teachings, papal ideas of the Church and the ministry, or even that man must do his part to be saved; therefore they do not realize the danger that threatens from Rome, nor can they warn against it. Today a great part of Protestantism has given up the article of justification, teaching more or less crassly the way of works and so deserting to the Papacy. Again, in the matter of church government much of Protestantism has deserted to the Roman camp, giving the rule in the Church to the State, to more or less political consistories, to the preachers, etc., giving up the article of Christian liberty. Or the refusal to accept this article has its reason in the unionism and indifference of our days; the idea is so prevalent: It's sufficient for salvation to lead a respectable, pious life. So when people see that the Romans, too, believe that Christ is the Son of God, the Savior, that the Bible is God's Word, that, moreover, Romans exceed others in "pious" exercises, in penances and church services, they think there is real Christianity; they do not see that there, in work-righteousness, is the true enmity against Christ and His Gospel, that there is the deceit of Antichrist, blinding people to think that by mechanical exercises they can earn salvation. Or the pomp and the power of the Papacy impresses them. Or they see that many Popes have been great men in history, superior to their contemporaries, exerting great influence on the course of history. Or, as in our days, they hear the Pope fulminating against Communism, even calling on all Protestants to unite with Rome in the fight against that evil. By the way, that is nothing new either; the Pope did that 80 years ago. Rome has always been great in drawing such red herrings across the trail, so that while people are following the false scent, it may accomplish its own purpose, which is never friendly to Protestantism.

Despite the fact, therefore, that this is not a fundamental article of faith, that we cannot and do not deny the Christianity of a person who cannot see the truth that the Pope is the Antichrist, yet it is an important article and should not be side-stepped or slighted. It is clearly revealed in the divine Word; and there is nothing needless and useless in the Bible; God wants us to know about the Antichrist. Scripture points us to that need, describing Antichrist as very dangerous, crafty, destructive, as one who will appropriate vast power and seduce great numbers of men. Scripture pronounces a curse on all who allow the Antichrist to seduce them, Rev. 14:9 ff. According to Scripture the revelation of Antichrist and the Reformation of the Church are connected; hence, he who denies that the Papacy is the Antichrist must doubt whether the Lutheran Reformation is the prophesied work of God. Antichrist must be revealed before the end of the world; if the Papacy is not the Antichrist, the end cannot yet be impending. The teaching of this article is necessary and useful because it is a needed admonition against the leaven of the Papacy which has entered so many Protestant churches. It is a powerful consolation to Christians; it helps to prove the truth of the Scriptures; and it is a great example to strengthen our confidence in the truth of the Savior's promise that the gates of hell shall never prevail against the Church. Finally, this article is clearly expressed in the Lutheran Confessions; whoever denies it does not stand in one faith with his fathers; he is not a confessional Lutheran. A Lutheran preacher should know, believe, and teach this article, or frankly confess that he no longer subscribes to the Confessions of the Lutheran Church. And we as a Lutheran Synod cannot tolerate on the part of our teachers and preachers open attacks on this article.

God has greatly blessed us, the Church of the Reformation, by revealing to us this great enemy of true Christianity who for so many centuries has worked havoc in Christ's Church on earth. At the same time He has placed a great responsibility on us. On us particularly devolves the duty to testify against this iniquity and to warn others lest they fall a prey to it. Let us not go to sleep on this job as others did and so give Antichrist another chance to gain power and slay the sheep of Jesus Christ. Let us insistently, in season and out of season, by word of mouth and by the printed word, in church, in school, privately, by radio, preach the pure Gospel of the Savior; that is the best, the only antidote against Antichrist's poison.

Bibliography

1. HOLY SCRIPTURE THE WORD OF GOD (North Wisconsin), W. Albrecht.
Arndt, W., *Does the Bible Contradict Itself?*
Arndt, W., *Bible Difficulties.*
Collett, S., *All About the Bible.*
Dallmann, Wm., *Why Do I Believe the Bible Is God's Word?*
Drewes, C. F., *Introduction to the Books of the Bible.*
Engelder, Th., *Scripture Cannot Be Broken.*
Hastings Encyclopedia, VII, "Inspiration."
Hay and Jacobs, *Doctrinal Theology.*
Hodge, Chas., *Systematic Theology*, I.
Hoenecke, Ad., *Ev.-Luth. Dogmatik*, I.
Kretzmann, P. E., *The Foundations Must Stand.*
Luther, M., St. Louis Edition, VII:1924.
Luther, M., *Galatians*, Eerdmans, 1930, p. 448.
Luther, M., Holman Edition, II, 184.
Mueller, J. T., *Christian Dogmatics.*
Neve, J. L., *Churches and Sects of Christendom.*
Pieper, F., *Christliche Dogmatik*, I.
Pieper, F., *What Is Christianity?*
Quenstedt, J. A., *Systema*, I.
Reu, M., *In the Interest of Lutheran Union.*
Reu, M., *Luther and the Scriptures.*
Strong, A. H., *Systematic Theology*, I.
Stump, Jos., *The Christian Faith.*

Synodical Reports:
    Central, 1894.
    Eastern, 1894. T. Stiemke.
    Iowa, 1891. A. D. Greif.
    Iowa, 1892. Fr. Busse.
    Minnesota, 1882.
    Northern, 1865.
    Northern Illinois, 1909.
    Southeastern, 1939.
    Synodical Conference, 1886. A. Graebner.
    Wisconsin Synod, 1883.

Lehre und Wehre, 13:280; 17:33; 21:258; 25:257; 32:77, 161; 37:193, 225, 353; 38:193; 39:325; 57:156.
Theological Quarterly, 1; 9:32, Rimbach; 17:1.
Concordia Theological Monthly, 1939.
Lutheran Teacher, Norwegian Lutheran Church, 1938.
The Lutheran, U. L. C., 1941.

Baltimore Declaration, U. L. C.
Christian Century, March 16, 1938.
The Fundamentals, III, IV, VII.

2. BIBLE INTERPRETATION (South Wisconsin), V. E. Mennicke.
    Augustinus, Aurelius, *De Civitate Dei*. Tauchnitz, 1825.
    Augustinus, Aurelius, *De Doctrina Christiana*. St. Louis, 1882.
    Baier, J. W., *Compendium Theologiae Exegeticae*.
    Baier, J. W., *Compendium Theologiae Positivae*.
    Chemnitz, M., *Examen Concilii Tridentini*. Berlin, 1861.
    Concordia Triglotta, 1920.
    Fuerbringer, L., *Theologische Hermeneutik*. St. Louis, 1912.
    Gerhard, J., Ed. by Eduard Preuss. Berlin, 1863.
    Gibbons, J., Cardinal, *Faith of Our Fathers*. Baltimore, 1894.
    Klotsche, E. H., *History of Christian Doctrine*. Burlington, 1945.
    Koenig, Ed., *Neueste Principien der alttestamentlichen Kritik*. Berlin, 1902.
    Kromayer, H., *Theologia Positiva*, Leipzig-Frankfurt, 1695.
    Lehre und Wehre, passim.
    Luther, M., *Saemtliche Schriften*. St. Louis edition.
    New Testament, The. *A Revision of the Challoner — Reims Version*, Paterson, N. J., 1941.
    Painter, F. V. N., *Luther on Education*. St. Louis, 1928.
    Paulus, Matt., *Synopsis Criticorum*. Frankfurt, 1712.
    Pfeiffer, A., *Antichiliasmus*. Luebeck, 1729.
    Pfeiffer, A., *Thesaurus Hermeneuticus*. Leipzig-Frankfurt, 1695.
    Pieper, F., *Christliche Dogmatik*. St. Louis.
    Popular Symbolics. St. Louis, 1934.
    Quenstedt, J. Andr., *Theologia Didactico-Polemica*. Leipzig, 1702.
    Rambach, J. J., *Institutiones Hermeneuticae Sacrae*. Jena, 1732.
    Richardson, A., *Preface to Bible Study*. Westminster Press, Philadelphia, 1944.
    Smith, Roy, *How Your Bible Grew Up*. Cokesbury Press, 1943.
    Smith, Roy, *It All Happened Once Before*. Cokesbury Press, 1943.
    Swedenborg, Emanuel, *True Christian Religion*. Philadelphia, 1887.
    Synodical Report: Northern District.
    Theological Quarterly, passim.
    Waterworth's Translation of *Canons and Decrees of the Council of Trent*. Chicago.

3. THE NATURE AND ATTRIBUTES OF GOD (California and Nevada; Southern California), R. R. Caemmerer.

    Synodical Reports:
    Central Illinois, 1909, W. Heyne.
    Kansas, 1919, P. Stolp.
    Nebraska, 1888, G. Stoeckhardt.
    Western, 1906, 1907, 1909, E. Pardieck.

4. THE PROVIDENCE OF GOD (Ontario), P. F. Bente.

    Synodical Reports:
    Eastern, 1883, H. Sieck.
    Michigan, 1895, E. L. Arndt.
    Nebraska, 1892, H. Frincke.

Bibliography 769

Daechsel, August, *Die Bibel . . . mit in den Text eingeschalteter Auslegung.* Leipzig, A. Deichert.
Lund, Emil, *The Psalms, Translated and Commented Upon.* Rock Island, Ill., 1908.
Pieper, F., *Christliche Dogmatik,* I. St. Louis, 1924.
Stoeckhardt, G., *Kommentar ueber den Brief Pauli an die Roemer.* St. Louis, 1907.
Life, April 15, 1946.
The Cresset, February, 1946.

5. OFFICE, OR WORK, OF CHRIST (Atlantic), Oswald C. J. Hoffmann.
Lehre und Wehre, 20:14, 75, Burfeind.

Synodical Reports:
    Brazil, 1916, J. Kunstmann.
    Canada, 1898, F. Bente.
    Central Illinois, 1912, 1913, F. W. Brockmann.
    Eastern, 1875, F. Koenig.
    Michigan, 1900, G. Bernthal; 1903, E. A. Mayer; 1906, H. Frincke.
    Northern Illinois, 1916, H. Harms; 1918, 1919, C. Abel; 1921, H. Heyse.
    Southern Illinois, 1916, F. Pieper.
Theological Quarterly, 12, 20, Theo. Graebner.

6. SIN (Northern Illinois), Theo. F. Nickel.
Concordia Cyclopedia.
Concordia Triglotta.
Encyclopedia Britannica.
Expositor's Greek Testament.
The Holy Scriptures. English, German, originals.
Luther's Small Catechism, Concordia, 1943 ed.
Pulpit Commentary.
Popular and Critical Bible Encyclopedia.
Popular Symbolics, 1934 ed.
Barnes' Notes (New Testament).
Davis, *Dictionary of the Bible.*
Fahling, A., *The Life of Christ.*
Fritz, J. H. C., *Pastoral Theology.*
Graebner, Th., *The Borderland of Right and Wrong.*
Guenther, M., *Populaere Symbolik.*
Jesse, F. W. C., *The Decalog.*
Kretzmann, P. E., *Popular Commentary.*
Mueller, J. T., *Christian Dogmatics.*
Pieper, F., *Christliche Dogmatik.*
Walther, C. F. W., *Pastorale.*
Walther, C. F. W., *The Proper Distinction Between Law and Gospel.*
Waterworth, J., Translation of *The Canons and Decrees of the Council of Trent.* The Christian Symbolic Publication Society.
Concordia Theological Monthly, 3:7.
Lehre und Wehre, 24:193, 225, 257, 321; 37:171, 203, 232.

Synodical Reports:
    Central, 1876, 1877, E. W. Kaehler.
    Central, 1882, G. Schumm.
    Central Illinois, 1910, C. A. Huxhold.
    Nebraska, 1891, H. Frincke.
    Southern, 1913, O. C. A. Boecler.
    Texas, 1918, F. W. C. Jesse.
Theological Quarterly, 8:108, F. Bente.

7. TEMPTATION (North Dakota), R. R. Caemmerer.
Concordia Triglotta. 1921, ed. by F. Bente and W. H. T. Dau.
Synodical Catechism. 1912 ed.; 1941 ed.
Pieper, F., *Christliche Dogmatik*, 1917—1924.

Synodical Reports:
    Nebraska, 1886, W. Harms.
    Southern, 1906, 1907, J. F. K. Schmidt.
    Luther quoted according to St. Louis Edition.

8. THE GRACE OF GOD (Oklahoma), Theo. Hoyer.
Lehre und Wehre, 31:7, G. Stoeckhardt; 33:117, F. Pieper.

Synodical Reports:
    Colorado, 1921, 1922, 1924, Theo. Hoyer.
    Western, 1874.

9. THE DOCTRINE OF JUSTIFICATION (Southern Nebraska), Wm. Arndt.
Concordia Triglotta (Symbolical Books of the Lutheran Church). St. Louis, 1921.
Baier, J. W., *Compendium Theologiae*, III. St. Louis ed., 1879.
Engelder, Arndt, Graebner, Mayer, *Popular Symbolics*. St. Louis, 1934.
Klotsche, E. H., *Christian Symbolics*. Burlington, Iowa, 1929.
Krauth, C. P., *Conservative Reformation*. J. B. Lippincott & Co., 1871.
    (Now sold by United Lutheran Publication House, Philadelphia, Pa.)
Pieper, F., *Christliche Dogmatik*, II. St. Louis, 1917.
Preuss, E., *Rechtfertigung des Suenders vor Gott*. Gustav Schlawitz, Berlin. 2. Aufl. 1871.

Synodical Reports:
    Canada, 1897, H. Wente.
    Central, 1909, Th. Schurdel.
    Central Illinois, 1915, E. Flach.
    Iowa, 1903, 1904, R. Pieper.
    Nebraska, 1883, C. F. W. Walther.
    Southern, 1883, F. Pieper.
    Texas, 1921, C. W. Rische.
    Western, 1859, C. F. W. Walther. 1875.
Synodical Conference, 1882.

10. REPENTANCE (Central), Karl H. Ehlers.
Lehre und Wehre, 50:28, 75; 57:537, J. Graebner.
Synodical Report, California, 1901, G. Runkel.
Theological Quarterly, 8:215, J. A. Rimbach.

11. SANCTIFICATION (English), R. L. Sommer.
    Synodical Reports:
    California, 1897, J. W. Theiss.
    California, 1900, J. H. Theiss.
    Canada, 1892, L. Dorn.
    Canada, 1907, P. Graupner.
    Central Illinois, 1919, G. P. A. Schaaf.
    Eastern, 1898, A. Senne.
    Eastern, 1900, F. Pieper.
    Illinois, 1880, 1882, 1883, H. Succop.
    Illinois, 1895, R. Pieper.
    Illinois, 1900, F. Lindemann.
    Iowa, 1888, L. W. Dornseif.
    Kansas, 1891, C. F. Graebner.
    Kansas, 1909, H. D. Wagner.
    Michigan, 1892, C. J. T. Frincke.
    Nebraska, 1900, M. Adam.
    Northern, 1868, J. A. Huegli.
    Oregon, 1903, H. Bohl.
    Oregon, 1913, O. Fedder.
    Southern, 1900, Ad. Kramer.
    Southern Illinois, 1919, F. Streckfuss.
    Texas, 1912, H. Stoeppelwerth.
    Western, 1894, 1895, C. L. Janzow.
    Wisconsin, 1895, W. J. Friedrich.
    Wisconsin, 1900, 1901, G. Loeber.

12. SYNERGISM (Northern Nebraska), Ewald M. Plass.
    Lehre und Wehre, 19:257, 330, F. Wyneken; 20:9, F. Wyneken; 26:193; 28:145, 407, 550, W. Sihler; 30:49, 104; 43:129, 161, 193, 257, 289, 327, 353, G. Stoeckhardt; 45:257, 330, F. Pieper; 46:97, F. Pieper; 48:385, F. Bente.
    Luther, Martin, *The Bondage of the Will.* Translated by Henry Cole. Grand Rapids, Wm. B. Eerdmans Publishing Co., 1931.
    Pieper, F., *Christliche Dogmatik.* 1917—1924.
    Preger, Wilhelm, *Matthias Flacius Illyricus und seine Zeit.* 2 Baende. Erlangen, Blaesing, 1859—1861.
    Realencyklopaedie fuer protestantische Theologie und Kirche. 3te Auflage von Albert Hauck, 24 Baende. Leipzig, 1896—1909.
    Schaff, Philip, *Creeds of Christendom.* Fourth edition. 3 vols. Harper, c. 1877.
    Schmauck, Theodore, and Benze, C. Theodore, *The Confessional Principle.* Philadelphia, c. 1911.
    Triglot Concordia. Concordia Publishing House, 1921.

13. THE MEANS OF GRACE (Southeastern), E. E. Pieplow.
    Engelder, Arndt, Graebner, and Mayer, *Popular Symbolics.*
    Engelder, Theo., Classroom Notes on the Means of Grace.
    Gerberding, G. H., *Lutheran Fundamentals.*
    Kepler, Thomas S., *Contemporary Religious Thought.*
    Klotsche, E. H., *Christian Symbolics.*
    Koehler, Edward W., *A Summary of Christian Doctrine.*

Krauth, J. P., *Conservative Reformation.*
Lindberg, C. E., *Christian Dogmatics.*
Little, H. C., *Disputed Doctrines.*
Mueller, J. T., *Christian Dogmatics.*
Pieper, F., *Christliche Dogmatik*, II, pp. 121—458.
Scott, C. Andrew, *Romanism and the Gospel.*
Valentine, Milton, *Christian Theology.*
Walther, C. F. W., *The Proper Distinction Between Law and Gospel.*
Luther's Large and Small Catechisms.
Concordia Triglotta and *Concordia Cyclopedia.*
Christian Century, LXIII, Nos. 9 and 19.
Church Management, XXII, No. 6.
Concordia Theological Monthly, I, No. 3, P. E. Kretzmann; II, No. 6; VI, No. 11, W. Arndt; VIII, No. 4.
Evangelical Review, VIII, pp. 436—444.
Lutheran Outlook, XI, No. 3, p. 84.
Lutheran Quarterly, VIII, pp. 413—418; XI, pp. 262—275; XXII, p. 266; XXXVII, No. 2, p. 151.
Lutheran Standard, CIV, No. 5, p. 6.

Synodical Reports:

California, 1903, J. H. Schroeder.
Canada, 1882, J. Frosch.
Central, 1865.
Colorado, 1927, 1936, Theo. Hoyer.
Michigan, 1859.
Northwestern, 1879, C. F. W. Walther.
Oregon and Washington, 1912, F. Schoknecht.
Western, 1876, C. F. W. Walther.
Lehre und Wehre, 26:281; 36:113, F. Pieper.

14. THE GOSPEL (Iowa West), S. W. Becker.

Synodical Reports:

California and Oregon, 1895, J. M. Buehler.
Michigan, 1889, A. Spiegel.
Minnesota, 1888, C. Ross.
Nebraska, 1898, A. Graebner.
Lehre und Wehre, 10:321; 11:4, 33, 65, C. F. W. Walther.

15. THE SACRAMENTS (Central Illinois), A. Neitzel.
Baier, J. W., *Compendium*, III, pp. 40—420.
Pieper, F., *Christliche Dogmatik*, II, pp. 121—458.
Walther, C. F. W., *Gesetz und Evangelium*, pp. 334, 340—348.
Lehre und Wehre, 3:4—16; 13:39—48; 53:297—313, 345—360.
Theological Quarterly, 4:406—411.

Synodical Reports:

Proceedings of Ev. Lutheran Synod, 1891, pp. 10—17.
Central, 1910, P. Eickstaedt.
Michigan, 1883, 1885, K. L. Moll.
Northern, 1879, 1880, K. L. Moll.
Saxon Free Church, 1882, pp. 39—98.

16. HOLY BAPTISM (Southern Illinois), J. T. Mueller.
    Lehre und Wehre, 2:274; 3:326; 55:63, 161, 204, 260, 299, 359, J. A. Friedrich; 56:385, 550; 57:59, 111, 213, 261, 310, Hy. Mueller.

    Synodical Reports:
    Atlantic, 1921, J. N. H. Jahn.
    Canada, 1888.
    Central, 1879, F. W. Stellhorn.
    Central, 1910, P. Eickstaedt.
    General, 1855.
    Kansas, 1894, C. F. Graebner.
    Northern, 1879, 1880, K. L. Moll.
    South Dakota, 1912, F. Streckfuss.
    Wisconsin, 1888 (p. 24 ff.), A. Rohrlack.
    Theological Quarterly, 5, A. L. Graebner.

17. THE LORD'S SUPPER (Southern), F. R. Zucker.
    Lehre und Wehre, 16:134; 21:119, 177; 50:145, 199, 252, 321, 450, 498, G. Mezger.

    Synodical Reports:
    California, 1894 (p. 42 ff.), H. A. C. Paul.
    Central, 1888, 1889, G. Goesswein.
    Illinois, 1875.
    Kansas, 1895, 1897, F. Pennekamp.
    Southern Illinois, 1915, W. H. T. Dau.
    Western, 1870, C. F. W. Walther.
    Wisconsin, 1885, H. Sprengeler.

18. THE LUTHERAN CONGREGATION (Iowa East), G. Perlich.
    Brunn, A., *The Polity of a Lutheran Congregation*. St. Louis.
    Concordia Cyclopedia. 1927.
    Dallmann, Dau, Engelder, *Walther and the Church*. St. Louis.
    Eckhardt, E. E., *Homiletisches Reallexicon*. St. Louis. Heft G, p. 93 ff.
    Graebner, Theo., *Handbook for Congregational Officers*. St. Louis.
    Kretzmann, P. E., *Topic Leader's Manual*. 1935. St. Louis.
    Kretzmann, P. E., *You and Your Congregation*. Walther League.
    Kretzschmar, K., *Mutual Obligations of the Ministry and the Congregation*. St. Louis.
    Mueller, J. T., *Christian Dogmatics*. St. Louis.
    Prange, R., *Church Membership*. St. Louis.
    Schramm, *A Loyal Lutheran*. Columbus, Ohio.
    Schuh, *Enjoying Church Work*. Columbus, Ohio.
    Walther, C. F. W., *Von der Pflicht der Christen, sich an eine rechtglaeubige Ortsgemeinde gliedlich anzuschliessen*. St. Louis.

    Synodical Reports:
    California, 1887, J. M. Buehler; 1904; 1905, J. W. Theiss.
    Central, 1898, G. Link, Jr.; 1939 (p. 31 ff.), E. S. Husmann.
    English, 1912, W. II. Dale.
    Illinois, 1876, T. V. Grosse.
    Kansas, 1897 (p. 46 ff.), J. G. Haefner.
    Lutheraner, 6:89—92; 40:18, 28, 35, 41; 44:178, 186, 195; 51:1, 2, 9, 10.
    Theological Quarterly, 1:401. Translation of Walther's *Die rechte Gestalt*.

Concordia Theological Monthly, 6:November, Wm. Arndt; 8:March, J. A. Friedrich; 10:May, J. T. Mueller; 10:October, Paul Schulz, Theo. Laetsch.
Concordia Bible Student, 28:1.

19. THE OFFICE OF THE PUBLIC MINISTRY (South Dakota), E. E. Foelber.
Luther, M., *Saemtliche Schriften.*
Pieper, F., *Christliche Dogmatik.* St. Louis.
Schaller, J., *Katalog des Theol. Seminars der Allgemeinen Ev.-Luth. Synode von Wisconsin,* 1917. Entstehung und Ausgestaltung des neutestamentlichen Predigtamts, pp. 14—38.
Stoeckhardt, G., *Roemerbrief.* 1907.
Lehre und Wehre, 1:1, 33; 7:138, 151, 293; 8:97, 135; 16:161; 22:138; 23:289, 304, 321, 353; 24:230, 264; 25:105, 137, 220, 329, 361.
Theological Quarterly, 7:1, A. L. Graebner.
Concordia Theological Monthly, 12:721.

Synodical Reports:
Central, 1880, C. C. Schmidt.
Central Illinois, 1916, R. Biedermann.
Eastern, 1862.
Iowa, 1883, G. Stoeckhardt.
Kansas, 1900, L. Fuerbringer.
Michigan, 1907, P. Andres.
Minnesota, 1916, Hy. Meyer.
Wisconsin, 1891, 1892, Fr. Lochner.
Synodical Conference, 1935, J. T. Mueller.

20. DOCTRINE, TRUE AND FALSE (Alberta and British Columbia; Manitoba and Saskatchewan), W. Baepler.

Synodical Reports:
Northwestern, 1880, Chr. H. Loeber.
Wisconsin, 1882, Chr. H. Loeber.
Lehre und Wehre, 20:1, 33, 65, 225; 43:97, 127.
Theological Quarterly, 8:237.

21. CHURCH FELLOWSHIP (Montana), A. H. Grumm.
Synodical Report, California, 1888, J. M. Buehler.
Synodical Conference, 1872, 1873, 1874, 1876, 1878, 1880, W. Sihler; 1908, F. Pieper.

22. CHURCH DISCIPLINE (Minnesota), E. J. Otto.
Concordia Triglotta.
Fritz, J. H. C., *Pastoral Theology.*
Kretzmann, P. E., *Popular Commentary, Old Testament,* Vol. I.
Luther, M., *Saemtliche Schriften.*
Walther, C. F. W., *Pastorale.*

Synodical Reports:
Central, 1904, W. H. T. Dau.
Eastern, 1879 (p. 58 ff.), C. J. H. Fick.
Minnesota, 1918, H. J. Bouman.
Wisconsin, 1886, G. Kuechle.

Bibliography

23. CHURCH AND STATE (Colorado), Theo. Hoyer.

    Synodical Reports:
    Canada, 1909, 1910, 1913, J. Sohn.
    Central, 1866; 1874, F. Wyneken.
    Iowa, 1897, Th. Buenger.
    Kansas, 1889, C. R. Kaiser.
    Minnesota, 1910, C. Abbetmeyer.
    Western, 1885, C. F. W. Walther.
    Theological Quarterly, 12:1; 13:19, Wm. Dallmann.

24. LUTHER'S CATECHISM (Michigan), L. H. Koehler.
    Graebner, Th., *Story of the Catechism.*
    Concordia Pulpit, 1936.
    Schulblatt, 12:244, 307.
    News Service, Synod's Board of Education.
    Concordia Triglotta.

    Synodical Reports:
    Eastern, 1879, H. Hanser.
    Northwestern, 1880 (p. 57 ff.), G. Kuechle.

25. CHRISTIAN TRAINING OF YOUTH (Eastern), H. E. Plehn.

    Synodical Reports:
    Canada, 1895, A. Krafft.
    Illinois, 1891, 1892, L. Hoelter.
    Kansas, 1904, 1906, R. Miessler.
    Western, 1855; 1910, R. Kretzschmar.
    Wisconsin, 1889, Fr. Lochner.

26. THE LUTHERAN PAROCHIAL SCHOOL (Western), A. C. Repp.
    Bretscher, Paul, *The Lutheran Elementary School: An Interpretation.* Third Edition, 1941. Board of Christian Education of the Northern Illinois District, Chicago, Ill.
    General Education in a Free Society. Report of the Harvard Committee with an introduction by James Bryant Conant. Harvard University Press, Cambridge, Massachusetts, 1945.
    Information Service. International Council of Religious Education, May 29, 1943.
    Mauelshagen, Carl, *American Lutheranism Surrenders to Forces of Conservatism.* The University of Georgia, Division of Publications, Athens, Georgia, 1936.
    Building the Parochial School of Tomorrow. South Wisconsin District Teachers' Conference, 1941.

    Synodical Reports:
    General, 1847, 1944.
    Atlantic, 1930, Arthur Brunn.
    California and Oregon, 1891, J. Kogler; 1898, II. Bohl.
    Central, 1913 (p. 47 ff.); 1918, 1919, A. C. Stellhorn.
    Central Illinois, 1943, Herman H. Koppelmann.
    Eastern, 1897, J. P. Beyer.
    Illinois, 1891, L. Hoelter.

Iowa, 1919, P. E. Kretzmann; 1922, G. Mezger.
Michigan, 1943, E. M. Jutzi.
Minnesota and Dakota, 1897, W. von Schenk; 1907, Martin Kirsch.
Minnesota and North Dakota, 1909, C. W. Nickels.
Nebraska, 1906, G. Mezger.
South Dakota, 1910, F. Oberheu.
South Wisconsin, 1918, C. Bartelt.
Southeastern, 1942, L. F. Frerking.
Southern, 1886 (p. 59 ff.).
Texas, 1943, E. W. A. Koehler.
Western, 1870, 1871, J. H. Fick.
Wisconsin, 1891, B. Sievers.
Synodical Conference, 1920, 1922, J. P. Meyer.

27. ADIAPHORA (Kansas), L. Wunderlich.
Concordia Cyclopedia. St. Louis, 1927.
Concordia Triglotta. St. Louis, 1921.
Fritz, J. H. C., *Pastoral Theology.* St. Louis, 1932.
Graebner, Th., *The Borderland of Right and Wrong.* St. Louis, 1945.
Krauss, E. A. W., *Lebensbilder.* St. Louis, 1915.
Kurtz, J. H., *Church History,* Vol. III. Funk & Wagnalls, New York.
Luther, M., *Saemtliche Schriften.*
Mueller, J. T., *Popular Symbolics.* St. Louis, 1934.
Nestle, E., *Novum Testamentum Graece.* Stuttgart, 1923.
Pieper, F., *Christliche Dogmatik.* St. Louis, 1920.
Thayer, *Greek-English Lexicon.* New York, 1889.
Walther, C. F. W., *Pastorale.* St. Louis, 1906.

Synodical Reports:
Central, 1859, Aug. Craemer, H. Schwan.
Eastern, 1857.
Nebraska, 1912, 1913, E. E. Eckhardt.
Northern, 1859, M. Guenther.
Western, 1856.

28. THE PAPACY (Texas), Theo. Hoyer.
Lehre und Wehre, 15:304; 23:145; 25:289, W. Sihler; 38:365, A. L. Graebner; 39:4, 45, 74, 114, 166, 273, 333, A. L. Graebner; 40:106, 172, 269, A. L. Graebner.

Synodical Reports:
California, 1913, W. H. T. Dau.
Eastern, 1870.
Minnesota, 1910, C. Abbetmeyer.
Western, 1868.
Theological Quarterly, 12:21, 65; 13:1, 65, 104, Wm. Dallmann.

Topical Index

A

ADIAPHORA, definition, 686; Old Testament granted less freedom, 687; New Testament established liberty from Ceremonial Law, 688; existence of adiaphora denied, 691

may cease to be adiaphora, 690 f.

not product of justifying faith, 694; do not impose guilt, 694; do not affect the believer's relation to God, 694 f.

controversies concerning — at Antioch, 695; Adiaphoristic Controversy, 1548—1555, 656 f.; Pietistic Controversy, 697 f.

practical value of this doctrine, 692, 698

abuses of this doctrine, 699; giving offense, 703

practial examples, 706 f.

Allegorical and Typical Interpretation, 55

Analogy of Faith, defined and applied, 41 ff.

Atonement, vain attempts by man to merit atonement, 219 f.

full atonement through Christ, our Substitute, 221

Christ's atonement folly to reason, 222

B

BAPTISM, its essence, 394; a sacred act, 395, ordained by God, 395, in which water is applied, 396, to a living person, 397, in the name of the Trinity, 396

Infant Baptism: Scriptural proof, 398; testimony of the Christian Church, 399 f.

mode of — not prescribed in Scripture, 400 f.; Baptist insistence on immersion refuted, 401 ff.

blessings of, 403; a means of grace, 403, which individualizes God's grace, 405; is a visible seal, 405; grants forgiveness of sins, regenerates, gives eternal life, 405 f., 412; no physical effects, 407 f.; Rome perverts this doctrine, 409; denied by Calvinistic churches, 409 f.; objections answered, 410 f.

difference between — and Lord's Supper, 391

relation to Christian life, 413; mortification of old Adam, strengthening of new man, 413 f.; Scriptural proof, 414 ff.

not to be repeated, 413

its admonition, 419

its comfort, 420

Bible Interpretation, principles of — must be based on Scripture, 35; though some are self-evident, 37; Scripture interprets itself, 38; this makes for certainty, 39 f., 120; neither human tradition, 40, nor reason, 41, nor the "inner light," 41, but Scripture alone, 41.

according to the analogy of faith, defined, 42; clear passages cast light upon dark, 46 ff.; purpose and context must be observed, 49 ff.; also common usage of language, 50; original text is to be studied, 52 ff.

only one Spirit-intended meaning, 54; proof for figurative sense must be apparent and sufficient, 58; allegorical and typical interpretation, 55

C

CATECHISM, LUTHER'S, need of: God's people must be taught the fundamental truth, 609 f.; spiritual darkness preceding Reformation, 611; great blessings of Luther's Catechism, 613 f.; its need in our day, 614

importance of, 615 ff.; proved by its contents, 615; its conservatism, 618; its beauty and excellence,

777

619; serves as a symbol of the Church, 621; is a book of prayer, 622; awakens and stimulates Christian life, 623; tributes to it, 628

proper use, 624; in the home, 625; in the school, 625 f.; in the church service, 627

Christ, Office, or Work, two states in — definition of Reformed Church, 112; of Scripture, 113 ff.; Augsburg Confession on, 116

Humiliation, 116–119; conception and birth, 116; suffering, 116 f.; cross, 117; death and burial, 119

Exaltation, 119–126; descent into hell, 120–124; resurrection, 124; ascension and session, 124 f.

work in the two states, 127 ff.
  as *Prophet*, 128 ff.; unique, 131; in Old Testament, 132; in State of Humiliation, 132 f.; of Exaltation, 134 f.
  as *Priest*, 135 ff.; for our atonement, 136 f.; foretold in Old Testament, 137; passive obedience, 138; active obedience, 139; Priest eternally 140
  as *King*, 140; prophesied in Old Testament, 140; in Humiliation, 141 f.; Exaltation, 142

descent into hell, 120 ff.
obedience; passive and active, 138 ff.

Church, in America, secularized, 323

Church and State, two separate realms, 562
  both divinely instituted, 562: Church directly, 562; State indirectly, 563 ff.
  differences: in their nature, 566; in memberships, 566 f.; in their object and purpose, 568; their domain, 568 f.; their principles, 569 f.; their means used in executing their business, 570
  both should exist side by side, 571; Bible proof, 572 f.; position of our Confessions, 574; this distinction disregarded in history of the Church, 575 f.; under the Christian emperors, 576 ff.; by the Papacy, 579 ff.; Luther takes correct position, 583 f.; the development of territorialism, 587 f.

violation of separation of:
  by Church: various examples, 591 ff.; Church should not be active in politics, 591 f.; not give political laws, 592 f.; not mete out temporal punishment, 593; not strive for temporal power, 594; not use earthly means in its defense, 594
  by State: seeking to enforce Moral Law, 595; meddling in church affairs, 596; commanding what God has forbidden, 597; establishing a State Church, 599; examples of applying this principle, 599; Sunday laws, 599; religious instruction for children, 600; Bible reading in public schools, 602

how State can serve Church, 602 ff.; and Church serve State, 604 ff.

Church Discipline, commanded by Christ, 538; to every Christian, 538; neglect of —, its danger, 560

persons subject to: the communicant member, 541; guilty of doctrinal error, 542; or ungodly life, 544 f.

purpose of: to gain the brother, 545; to further the glory of God, 546; to promote proper conduct, 546; to strengthen congregational life, 546

proper attitude, evangelical yet firm, 547

proper procedure, private admonition, 548; before witnesses, 549; before the congregation, 550; validity of testimony, 551 f.

excommunication, its nature and purpose, 552; must be unanimous, 555; procedure in persistent refusal to appear, 556; counsel to be sought, 554 f.; excommunicated may appeal to sister congregations, 557; attitude towards excommunicated, 558

Church Fellowship, based on personal fellowship with Christ through faith, 518
  should manifest itself in outward fellowship, 521
  Synod not a divine institution, though God-pleasing, 523
  Christian fellowship destroyed by fellowship with errorists, 524 f.
  fellowship to be based on unity in doctrine and practice, 525 f.
  uniformity in church government, rituals, etc., desirable, but not essential, 528 ff.
  tolerance of error sinful, 530; divisions caused by error, not by refusal to join errorists, 530 f.
  purpose: strengthening in faith, 531 f.; preservation of unity of faith, 533 f.; extension of God's kingdom, 534 f.
  aim of, the glory of God and welfare of men, 535 ff.
Congregation, the Lutheran, definition, 447, 477 f.
  origin, 448
  character: holy, 449
  its rights, 450; administration of the Keys, 450; given directly to congregation, 450
  its duties, 452 ff.; preach the Word, 452, 457; administer the Sacraments, 453; care for purity of doctrine and life, 453, 459; Christian charity, 454, 459; keep unity of Spirit, 454, 467 f.; promote welfare of church at large, 455, 468; do all things decently, 454; voters' meeting, 460; church officers, 465 f.; societies, 466 ff.
  relation to sister congregations, 467
  membership, 469; every believer should join a Christian congregation, 469; qualifications for, 470; privileges of, 471; duties, 472 f.

D

Doctrine, True and False
  true —, the Word of God is source of, 494; the only source, 495; God's greatest gift to man, 498 f.; only basis for union, 499; neglect brings ruin, 500
  and Christian life, Christian life not to be underrated, 496; not overemphasized, 497; produced by Christian doctrine, 497 f.
  false —, its sinfulness, 501; its power of delusion, 502; its corrupting influence, 503; opposed by Christ, 504 f.; by the Prophets, 506; by the Apostles, 506; duty of pastor and people to denounce error, 507 ff.; to avoid error and errorists, 509 ff.; both in fundamental and non-fundamental doctrines, 511
  attitude of Church toward truth and error must be that of obedience to Scripture, 512; this the attitude of our Confessions, 512; of the Missouri Synod, 514 ff.
Christian —, its importance, 299; its unity, 300

G

God, Nature and Attributes
  natural knowledge of God imperfect, 59—62; also the believer's knowledge, 61; unbelief perverts natural knowledge, 61 f.
  revealed knowledge, 61 ff.; in Christ, 63; in Scriptures, 63; through Holy Spirit, 63; unity of God, 64; life, 65; eternity, 65; Creator, 65, 66; omnipotence and omniscience, 67 f.
  holiness and justice, 68 f.
  love, 70—72
  Trinity of God, 72; one God, 73; three Persons, 73 ff.; importance of this doctrine for our salvation, 74—77
Gospel, the, definition: the glad tidings, 104; of God's grace, 104; in Christ Jesus, 104
  Gospel and the Law: preaching of Law not unnecessary, 105; Gospel does not annul the Law, but establishes it, 105; by stating that

Christ met every demand of the Law, 105
and the Ceremonial Law: Ceremonial Law foretold and foreshadowed Christ and His work, 106
as means of grace, 107; not merely preaching about grace, but offering this grace and working faith, 107; Calvin's error, 107
and faith, 107; wrought by the Gospel, 107; Reformed objections answered, 108
basis of true morality, 108; only cause of truly good works, 109
true treasure of the Church to be cherished and preached as such, 110

Grace of God, see also *Means of Grace*
is foundation of Christian faith, 200
definition of, 201, 242; not something in man, 203, 215; but God's love toward sinners, 203 ff.
active grace, 206 ff.; prompts God to save men, 206 ff.; to declare them righteous though they are sinners, 210 ff.; justifying them for Christ's sake, 212 f.; invites man, 216; converts man, 216 ff.; sanctifies man, 217; keeps man, 218
grace for Christ's sake, 219; based on His vicarious atonement, 219
universality of, 224; Scriptural proof, 224 f.; objections answered, 225 f.; faith not a condition, 226; denied by Calvin, 228; judgment of obduracy does not argue against, 233 f.
is serious, 228 ff.; efficacious, 229 ff.
revealed in the Gospel, 233; offered and sealed by the means of grace, 233; accepted by faith, 233

I

INSPIRATION, see also *Holy Scripture*, 13 ff.
no degrees of, 494; embraces only the canonical books, 494 f.

J

JUSTIFICATION, importance of this doctrine, 236; always recognized in Lutheran Church, 235, 237; by preaching this doctrine Luther became reformer of the Church, 238 ff.
presupposes total depravity of man, 240
based on God's grace, 241; procured by Christ on Calvary for all men, 242
definition of, 245
objective, or universal, justification, 243 ff.; subjective, 249 f.
offered and sealed to us in Gospel and Sacraments, 246 f.; appropriated by faith, 248
all human merit excluded, 251; takes place outside man, 253
fruits of, 254
various characteristics: occurs in a moment, 255 f.; always complete, 256; continues as long as faith continues, 256; can be lost, 256; but can be obtained anew, 256 f.

L

LORD'S SUPPER, the, a marvelous gift, 423 f.
its essence, 425
error of the Reformed Church, 426; refutation, 427 ff.
the Real Presence, 429 f.; in, with, and under the blessed bread and wine, 432 f.; to be taken by eating and drinking orally, 434; by all communicants, 434 f.
not a sacrifice, 433
its benefits, 434: grants forgiveness of sins, 435 f., strengthens us in faith, 437, in our union with Christ, 438, in our hope of resurrection, 438, in our love toward God and our fellow men, 438 f.
power of — lies in Christ's words, 439 f.
proper use of, 441 f.; to be received in faith, 441; usually in public worship, 442; private Commun-

Topical Index 781

ion, 442; to whom it should not be given, 443 f.; self-examination needed, 445

M

Mass, Roman, a perversion of Lord's Supper, 433

Means of Grace, definition: by Lutheran Church, 325 f.; by Rome, 328 f.
- which are —: Gospel, 340, 356 f.; Sacraments, 385 ff.
- which are not —, 339
- necessity of, 329; God's relation to, 327, 331, 334; divine and unchangeable, 332 f.
- power and efficacy of, 334, 342 f.; resistible, 344
- relation of faith to, 335 f.
- importance of this doctrine, 344
- Lutheran Church clings to, 322, 325; will remain true Visible Church only if it continues, 326; errors of Rome, 335 ff., of Calvinism, 338 f., of Synergism, 339

Ministry, Office of Public, definition, 475
- conferred by local congregation, 477
- its purpose, 480; duties, 481
- instituted by God, 483; congregation obligated to establish, honor, love, and obey it, 484 f.; to provide for its servants, 486
- incumbents to be properly called, 487 ff.
- subsidiary offices, 490 ff.

P

Papacy, the, not a fundamental article, 709; but important, 709
- history of, 711; who was first Pope? 712; Pseudo-Isidorian Decretals, 712; three claims of Papacy, 713; gradual development of episcopate and Apostolic Succession, 714 f.; conception of the Church as a visible organization, 717; centralization of power in Rome, 717; the Church becomes a State Church, 721; the bishop of Rome acknowledged as head of Church, 722
- Rome's teaching on Peter's primacy, 723, 725 ff.; its refutation, 730 ff.; on the Pope's primacy, 739 ff.; its refutation, 740 f.; on infallibility of the Pope, 743; refutation, 744 ff.
- prophesied in Scripture, which speaks of Antichrist, 747 ff.
- Scriptural proof that Pope is Antichrist, 749 ff.; objections refuted, 762 ff.

Parochial School, basic principles underlying, 659 ff.; need of Christian education, 661
- its place in Christian education, 664 ff.; must serve the home, 664; the Christian congregation, 667; the State, 669
- relation of State to, 669; State support, 673
- blessings of — for Christian home, 674; for congregation, 675; for Synod, 676; for community, 677; splendid mission agency, 683
- requirements of, 678 ff.; must be kept Christ-centered, 678; maintain high standards, 680; engage trained teachers, 681; be provided with proper equipment, 681 f.
- extension of parochial school system, 683
- guard against indifference, 683
- overcoming obstacles, 684

Providence of God, its nature defined, 79; testimony of reason, 79, of nature, 80; divine revelation needed to understand —, 81 ff.; testimony of Scripture, 82.
- its scope universal, 83; extending over lifeless, 83, and living creatures, 84 ff.; grants protection to greatest and smallest, 87 f.
- its principles: normally by definite laws, 91
- its mode: ordinarily by secondary causes, 93; co-operation of God and secondary causes of mystery, 95

and human freedom, 96 ff.
and sin, 99 ff.
and men's acts, 101 ff.
no fatalism, 104; length of life, 105
its goals, 106 ff.

R

REPENTANCE, need of, generally conceded, 259 f.
various definitions of, 260 f.; correct definition of, 261 f.
errors concerning, 263 f.
sorrow a part of, 263, 265 f.; therefore the preaching of Law necessary, 267—269
faith the chief part, 270; this faith created by the Gospel, 270 f.
in narrower sense, 272
fruit of, 273; godly life, 273 f.
daily contrition and repentance, 274
Rome seeks to win America, 324

S

SACRAMENTS, various usages of the term, 367 ff.
Lutheran usage: a sacred act, 369 f.; ordained of God, 370; a visible element, 371 f.; to be used in divinely prescribed manner, 374 f.; in connection with the Word, 375.
validity not affected by administrator, 376 f.; public doctrine concerning essence of Sacrament affects validity, 378; not affected by person or character of recipient, 379
benefit of: confer all Gospel blessings, 380 ff.
are means of grace, 385 ff.
require faith, 382 ff.
difference between Baptism and Lord's Supper, 391
no absolute necessity of, 392
Sanctification, definition, 276 ff.; wider sense, 276; narrower sense, 277; work of Holy Spirit, 279; carried on only in believer, 281 f.; follows justification, 282; Christians co-operate with God, 284; is purpose of Christ's redemption, 284 f.
its imperfection, 283, 286 f.; importance of this truth for comfort, 288, for admonition, 289
means of sanctification, Gospel, 290
importance of, 293; not meritorious, 293; glorifies God, 293; helps in mission work, 295
assures Christian of genuineness of his conversion, 294; will be richly rewarded, 295
perfected in heaven, 297
Scripture, Holy, human side of, 1; men wrote it, 2; in their individual style, 3; not mechanical tools, 4
divine origin: the contents often beyond the full understanding of the human writers, 5; its wonderful unity, 6; its claim to divine inspiration, 8 ff.; Old Testament, 9; Christ and Apostles, 9 ff.
inspiration: definition of, 13 ff.; Verbal Inspiration, 14 ff.; not merely divine guidance or illumination, every word God's Word, 16; therefore infallible, 19
relation of Holy Ghost to writers, 20 ff.; He compelled and commanded to write, 21; He spoke by the Prophets, 21; used their minds, 21; intellect, 22; will, 22; a miracle, 23
objections refuted, 24 ff.; arguments taken from style, 24; from research of the writers, 25; variant readings, 25 ff.; seeming contradictions, 28; alleged misquotations in New Testament, 29; so-called trivialities, 30
God's purpose in inspiration, 32 ff.; Scripture to serve as source of correct doctrine and practice, 32 f.; is to work faith, 33
denial of inspiration a serious matter, 33
its perspicuity, 46 ff.
Sin, what it is, 145; its cause, 146 f.; its seat, 148; consequences, 148

Topical Index

original: understood fully only by revelation, 150; definition, 151; hereditary guilt, 151 f.; total corruption, 153, of mind and will, 154 f.; its universality, 156; consequences: loss of free will in spiritual matters, 156, eternal death, 157

actual: definition, 158; causes, 158 f.; relation to God's providence, 159. Classification: sins of offense, 160; voluntary and involuntary, 161; against conscience, 162; of commission and omission, 163; against God and man, 163; degrees of grievousness, 163; mortal and venial, 164; dominant, 165; secret and open, 165; partaking in other men's sin, 166; hardening oneself, 167 f.; against the Holy Ghost, 168

Societies, in congregation, 466 ff.

Synergism, origin, 302; an attempt to solve the question why not all men come to faith, 302

Scripture's answer: total depravity of man, 302 ff., 312; universal grace and grace only, 303, 313 f.

various other solutions: Pelagianism, 305; Semipelagianism, 305; synergism, 306

attempts to prove —, 306; refuted, 307 ff.

vitiates doctrine of original sin, 316; of justification by grace, 316; of faith, 317; of sanctification, 318; of certainty of salvation, 318

true Lutheran Church rejects, 320

Synod, relation of congregation to, 455, 468 f.

not a divine institution, though God-pleasing, 523

T

TEMPTATION, definition, 171; Christian to apply tests to his faith and life, 174; temptation comes from outside his regenerated self, 175; Christian tested by sin, 176 f.; and its consequences, 178 to 182

for evil, 182 ff.; for good, 186 ff.

God's purpose in —, 188 ff.

use of means of grace in, 191 ff.

V

VOTERS' MEETINGS, 460 ff.

W

WOMAN SUFFRAGE, in congregation, 461 f.

Y

YOUTH, CHRISTIAN TRAINING OF, need of — because of sinful nature of youth, 630 ff.; of influences, 632

scope of, 635; knowledge of Christian truth, 636; integration of instruction into life situations, 637, 641; by parents, 638, 640; by Church, 639, 643

Christian day school, 644, 658; objections answered, 645 f.; how to start, 654, 656 f.; other agencies, 646; high schools, 647

young people's work, 648 ff.; under proper leadership, 651; the cost, 653 ff.

www.ingramcontent.com/pod-product-compliance
Lightning Source LLC
Chambersburg PA
CBHW071428300426
44114CB00013B/1348